Certificate of The Justice of The Peace

I do herby certify That Lucian H Raines, Henry Wyche, Jackson, I, Mask, William H Reynolds, were duly sworne - to performe Their duty as appraisers of The Estate of Richard Mitchell, deceased as directed in The foregoing warrant This 13th day of May 1856

John C Browning J.P.

Inventory and appraisment of The perishable property of Richard Mitchell deceased This May 17th 1856

No.		$	Cts
1	Bill a man	1000	00
2	Sambo "	400	00
3	Sam "	1200	00
4	Lemon "	1100	00
5	Jerry "	1,000	00
6	Billy "	1000	00
7	George "	1200	00
8	Jim "	1100	00
9	Mat "	12,000	00
10	Edmond "	1,000	00
11	Albert a boy	800	00
12	Yellow Bill a man	1150	00
13	Chance, a, boy	650	00
14	John " "	600	00
15	Anthony " "	600	00
16	Ishmeal, a, man	800	00
17	Phillip a Boy	800	00
18	Rheubin " "	800	00
19	Doctor " "	1000	00
20	Old Anthony	700	00
21	" Ben	600	00
22	[illegible]	[illegible]	

The end papers of this volume are reproductions from documents pertaining to the settlement of a Georgia estate. Such legal action was a daily occurrence in the slave country. Sometimes everything was sold at auction and the proceeds were divided among heirs. Sometimes, as here, a board of appraisers established the value of every item in each category, such as tools, mules, horses, slaves, wagons, and household goods, and then divided everything in each category into equal lots to the number of heirs. The value of each category in each lot (and the total value of each lot) being approximately equal to every other, drawings for lot numbers were then made and each heir took possession of his or her property. Slaves here were valued as low as five dollars. Sometimes estates had to pay someone to take certain ones. In every case, by auction or by division, the probability of separation of families was very great. In every case, also, the value of many slaves tore to shreds the argument that all slaves were well cared for because they were valuable property.

ANTISLAVERY *The Crusade for Freedom in America*

Ann Arbor: The University of Michigan Press

ANTISLAVERY

The Crusade for Freedom in America

BY DWIGHT LOWELL DUMOND

TO JACK WESLEY DUMOND AND CARYL BELL DUMOND

who live by faith in the equality of all men

Designed by George Lenox

Copyright © by The University of Michigan 1961

All rights reserved

Published in the United States of America by

The University of Michigan Press and simultaneously

in Toronto, Canada, by Ambassador Books Limited

Library of Congress Catalog Card No. 61-5937

Manufactured in the United States of America

PREFACE / THIS IS THE STORY

of the classic contest between slavery and freedom in America. It is the story of a battle that made a continent tremble. þ Slavery was the complete subjection by force of one person to the will of another, recognized and sustained by state law. Slavery was the subordination of nearly four million Negroes to the status of beasts of the field, insofar as possible, in a nation dedicated to freedom and equality for all men. Slavery was a deadly virus which twisted and distorted intellectual processes, social attitudes, and religious philosophy. It contaminated everything it touched from earliest colonial days until 1865. þ The contest between slavery and the foundation principles of democracy began in the early eighteenth century and continues to the present time. Second-class citizenship is only a modified form of slavery. Both rest upon the barbaric, unscientific concept of racialism. The battle raged in constitutional conventions, legislative halls, courtrooms, churches, schools; in the hearts of men; and finally on the battlefield. It was romantic, almost fantastic in some respects. There were fugitive slaves, insurrections, and kidnappings. There were mobs, riots, and sudden death. Great men faltered. Political parties crumbled. Churches separated along sectional lines. þ The course of the men and women who dedicated their lives to arresting the spread of slavery was marvelously direct and straightforward. They denounced it as a sin which could only be remedied by unconditional repentance and retributive justice. They denounced it as antithetical to the foundation principles of the nation, contrary to both natural law and moral law. They were a small group in the beginning, a constitutional majority in the end. They did not deviate or hesitate until victory came in the election of 1860. Every fundamental argument, vital principle, and important fact pertinent to the preservation of the Union and in defense of the freedom of man, then and now, in this country and throughout the world, was presented in this contest. þ These people were neither fanatics nor incendiaries. They appealed to the minds and consciences of men. They precipitated an intellectual and moral crusade for social reform, for the rescue of a noble people, for the redemption of democracy. In these pages, you will find the issues, the people, and the literature of this country's greatest victory for democracy.

Who that, in his day, has been conspicuous for

his defense of slavery, has acquired meritorious

distinction of any kind, other than an ephemeral renown

among those whose passions he flattered,

and whose prejudices he confirmed.

What American of celebrity in any department of

literature, has been known to dishonor his reputation,

by attempting a vindication of slavery?

No truly great and good man has ever enrolled

his name among the advocates for human bondage.

JOHN FINLEY CROWE

1822

CONTENTS

ILLUSTRATIONS

ANTISLAVERY *The Crusade for Freedom in America*

PERPETUAL SERVITUDE

Chapter 1

The English language is not adequate to describe in a single term the relationship between the white and Negro races in the United States. Slavery existed here almost from the date of the first settlements until finally abolished by the Civil War, the Emancipation Proclamation, and the Thirteenth Amendment to the Constitution; but the term slavery ordinarily denotes only the legal bondage of some 3,500,000 men, women, and children. All of the laws, customs, and extralegal restraints embraced in relations between free Negroes and whites in the several states where slavery existed, in those states where slavery had been abolished, and in all of the states since general emancipation—all of the stresses and strains in institutional life from schools to courts to armed services—everything in fact growing out of the doctrine of biological inequality and racial inferiority of the Negro to the white is inseparable one part from the other. There is no name for all of this.[1]

One cannot repeat too often that "belief in the biological inequality and racial inferiority of the Negro not only sustained slavery and colonization, but also determined the attitude of the public, the zeal of law-enforcement officials, the reasoning of judicial bodies, the efficiency of administrative functionaries, and the definition of policies by legislatures and Congress in all matters pertaining to Negroes and abolitionists. *Slavery was not the source of this philosophy*. It merely enshrined it, prevented a practical demonstration of its falsity, and filled public offices and the councils of religious, educational, and political institu-

tions with men reared in its atmosphere. So long as the temple stood, men clung to the faith."[2] One must add, and emphasize, that the faith did not entirely die when the temple was pulled down. We abolished slavery, but we left the freed Negroes to their own resources after a time. The white population of many sections, clinging tenaciously to the belief in racial inequality, soon reduced them to a second-class citizenship, which is and always has been a modified form of slavery from colonial times to the present.

The first protests against slavery in the colonies were made almost three centuries ago. Scant attention was given to them, and the institution remained to plague the Founding Fathers, not alone as a practical problem to be resolved in the Convention, but as a dreadful barrier to full acceptance of the principles of human dignity and individual freedom. Those principles have been cherished by us since men first came to America. Presumably, few people would be willing publicly to deny them as basic in our way of life; yet for many years we tolerated, indeed stoutly defended, an institution which embodied the opposing theory that some men and a whole race of people were biologically inferior to others. We formulated ingenious rationalizations of our conduct, devised legal barriers to its correction, heaped indignities upon those who spoke out in protest, challenged the divine right of free inquiry and discussion, and finally sent our young men out to kill each other when our political machinery broke down in the process of discussion, concession, and compromise. Slavery was destroyed

The slave ship
Slave ships arrived regularly on the African coast. Spanish, Dutch, or English, they brought only fear, sorrow, and death to the wives and mothers of Africa. "The terror in Africa" (p. 6) and "The march to the sea" (p. 7) indicate the barbarity which cost so many lives. The old, the very young, the feeble, the ill, and the brave died, and dying escaped a living death.

by war almost before the armies took the field. Far-seeing statesmen then threw the protective mantle of the Constitution over the 3,500,000 people set free by the war, but the vagaries of politics have long prevented complete fulfillment of emancipation, and American democracy still seeks redemption.

We do not know the origin of slavery.[3] We only know that slaves moved in commercial channels in ancient times. They were also carried about by their owners from one political jurisdiction to another, apparently without protest or prohibition. Persons became slaves in many ways: by being born of slave mothers, by selling themselves or failing to meet obligations, by authority of parents or brothers, and most often by capture in war. War and slavery were almost universal twin relics of barbarism. No one seems to have had any certain security against enslavement; at least neither race nor religion provided any.

Change came with the spread of Christianity.[4] Here was the point at which slavery in the Western world might well have disappeared. Christian peoples of Europe continued to make war upon each other, but they ceased enslaving prisoners who were Christians. In fact the theory that a Christian could not be enslaved soon gained such wide endorsement as to be considered a point of international law. Christians and Mohammedans continued to enslave each other, but each was well organized politically and powerful, and few persons were reduced to slavery as a result of their rivalries.

Traffic in slaves on a large scale began with the penetration of African waters by the Portuguese in the fifteenth century. Africans were vulnerable because they lacked political cohesion; they were acceptable because they were not Christians. Europe would never have absorbed many slaves because there was no shortage of labor. The two American continents did because those who came and explored and finally conquered succeeded in decimating the native peoples but never successfully enslaved them—and that was true of the Spanish, the French, and the British alike. Instead, they turned to the slave traders for their labor supply, which seemed inexhaustible, and the continent of Africa was ravished that the Americas might prosper. A total of 10,000,000 men and women were carried out; 100,000,000 died.[5]

Once again, rationalization modified the institution. Rationalization is always easy. In this case, it was imperative because missionaries continued to Christianize both Negroes and Indians. Acceptance of the Christian faith failed to protect them against enslavement or to free them from bondage, as it had done for Europeans, because the basis of slavery quickly shifted from religion to race. Eventually, as we shall see, the defenders of slavery claimed it was a Christian institution and a positive good because, among other things, it brought the heathens from Africa and gave them the elements of a Christian civilization.

The controversy over slavery began at this point. Could a Christian be reduced to slavery? Did acceptance of the Christian faith alter the status of a slave? International law did not then or afterward sanction the right to hold Christians as slaves. Public opinion in England did not sanction it. The question was discussed in the English courts, but was never the basis for a decision.[6] There was, however, no declaration of emancipation by conversion. The question remained unanswered in England, probably because there were never more than 15,000 slaves in the kingdom. They seem always to have been an insecure kind of property, without strong public support, and all were freed by a single court decision. There was no statute law establishing slavery there, no legal basis for it in medieval villenage. The courts, moreover, failed to find a basis for it in the common law, and by 1705 Chief Justice Holt could say: "As soon as a Negro comes into England he becomes free."[7] The King's attorney and solicitor general denied this in 1729, but Lord Mansfield settled the argument forever in 1773 in the famous *Sommersett Case*. Said he: "The state of slavery is of such a nature, that it is incapable of being introduced on any reasons, moral or political, but only by positive law, which preserves its force long after the reasons, occasion, and time itself from whence it was created, is erased from memory. It is so odious that nothing can be suffered to support it, but positive law. Whatever inconveniences, therefore, may follow from the decision, I cannot say this case is allowed or approved by the law of England; and therefore the black must be discharged."[8]

Slavery had spread to the English colonies in America in the late seventeenth century, the same as it had spread elsewhere throughout the Western world. Call it "custom and usage" with which no governmental authority interfered. Negroes were brought to America as indentured servants, and the law of indentured servitude, both common and statute, evolved into the law of slavery. Men came to the colonies with slaves, and they bought slaves from the slave traders. All of this long before slavery was declared illegal in England. Mansfield could find no law, common or statute, sustaining slavery in England. There was a substantial body of sustaining legislation in the colonies. Parliament claimed the right to legislate for the colonies, but it never passed laws either to establish or to prohibit slavery. Neither did the colonial assemblies do so, but they gradually enacted a body of legislation in reference to slavery as the number of slaves increased. Parliament did encourage the African slave trade. It recognized the existence of slavery in the colonies. It promoted the interests of the Royal African Company. It disallowed colonial legislation limiting importations.[9] Certainly, the original draft of the Declaration of Independence would not have charged George III with forcing slaves upon the colonies if there had not been substantial basis in fact.

The Sommersett decision ended slavery in England; it did not end it in the colonies. Its impact in America might have been great under normal circumstances, but revolution was already brewing when the decision was handed down. Opponents of slavery later made much of Mansfield's statement that slavery could only be established by "positive law" without being able to prove that he meant statute law. Those who defended slavery insisted slaves were property, held as other property under the common law. Whether the common law of England extended to the colonies or not is a matter of dispute. Blackstone said it did not; Justice Story insisted it did—at least that much of it as the colonists chose to adopt.[10] In any case, the common law guarantees of personal liberty were not enjoyed by all persons in the colonies. The colonial charters guaranteed the "rights of Englishmen" to English colonists. Both the common law guarantees and the charter guarantees extended to other Europeans who came to the colonies to live because Europeans enjoyed the protection of international law and the treaty agreements of their respective countries.[11] Africans did not, and Negro slavery

The terror in Africa

was not prohibited in the colonies by any authority whatsoever. In England, Parliament never recognized the existence of the institution, never passed sustaining legislation. The courts, therefore, held that it had no basis either in statute or common law and declared it illegal. The colonial assemblies recognized its existence and passed laws to regulate and sustain it. The courts, therefore, held that it was based in the common law.[12] The colonial assemblies went farther and changed the basis of slavery from religion to race. International law made no such concession, gave no such sanction. When statute law and common law in the colonies, therefore, came to recognize Negroes, Christian or otherwise, as legitimate objects of property—and they did so almost to the point of classifying all Negroes as slaves—slavery truly became the creature of municipal or internal law.

Once the right of men to enslave others was recognized, assemblies and courts were faced with a multitude of problems common to any institution which develops contrary to natural law.[13] "When I use the word *slave* or *slaves*," said David Barrow, "I would be understood to mean such *beings* of the *human race* who are (without any crime committed by them, more than is common to all men) with their offspring to perpetual generations, considered *legal property;* compelled by *superior force, unconditionally* to *obey* the *commands* of their *owners,* to be *bought* and *sold,* to be *given* and *received,* to go and *come,* to *marry* or *forbear,* to be *separated* when *married* at *pleasure,* to *eat, drink, sleep, wear, labour,* and to be beaten at their *owner's discretion;* and all *this* sanctioned by *civil authority.*"[14]

The most difficult aspects of this bloody business were the determination of a slave's exact status as person or property, the status of the children of slaves, the extent of church authority,

The march to the sea

ways and means of attaining freedom, and the status of the freed Negro. Slaves were brought into the colonies by slave traders operating under the recognized principle of international law permitting enslavement of persons not Christians. In passing from the hands of slave traders to their new colonial owners, black skins rather than lack of Christian faith became their most important attribute. It was easier that way for the slaveholder; it was a catastrophic change for the slave.[15]

It removed the one barrier to salvation for the Negro, and also the one certain road to freedom. Convenience likewise dictated adoption of the principle of Roman law that the status of the child followed that of the mother. The mother of a child could always be determined. The wisest of men would have had difficulty finding the fathers of children born to slave mothers in all cases. The vast majority no doubt were slaves, but some were slaveowners, or slaveowners' sons, or overseers of the plantations, or whoever else was in a position to take advantage of the female slaves.

So it was that the House of Burgesses of Virginia in 1662 declared that "whereas some doubts have arisen whether children got by an Englishman upon a negro woman should be slave or free. Be it, &c., that all children born in this country shall be bond or free, only according to the condition of the mother."[16] South Carolina in 1740 decreed that "All Negroes, Indians (free Indians in amity with this government, and Negroes, mulattoes, and mestizoes, who are now free, excepted), mulattoes, and mestizoes, who are or shall hereafter be in this province, and all their issue and offspring born or to be born, shall be and they are hereby declared to be and remain forever after absolute slaves, and shall follow the condition of their mother."[17] New York, alone, among the Northern colonies had this law, declaring in 1706 that "all and every, Negro, Indian, Mulatto and Mestee Bastard child and children who is, are, and shall be born of any Negro, Indian Mulatto or Mestee, shall follow ye state and condition of the mother and be esteemed reputed taken & adjudged a Slave & slaves to all intents and purposes whatsoever."[18] This was the law also of North Carolina and Georgia and the subsequent slave states of the South.[19]

Condemning the child of the slave mother to slavery insured permanency and a large element of stability to the institution. It eliminated what might have been a very complicated category of legal cases arising out of claims to freedom and ownership of property. It guaranteed to the slave owner the profits not only of the slaves' labor but of their natural increase. More compelling than all of these reasons, however, was the fact that it turned mulatto blood back into the Negro race. In this sense it belongs with those laws which placed restrictions upon the manumission of slaves, prohibited the intermarriage of free Negroes and whites, and encouraged expatriation of free Negroes. The Maryland law of 1663 is a striking example of how the principle of the Roman law was abandoned to accomplish the latter purpose. It read: "And forasmuch as divers free born English women, forgetful of their free condition and to the disgrace of our nation, do intermarry with Negro slaves, by which, also, divers suits may arise, touching the issue of such women, and a great damage befall the master of such Negroes, for preservation whereof, for deterring such free born women from such shameful matches, be it enacted, etc., that whatsoever free born woman shall intermarry with any slave, from and after the last day of the present assembly, shall serve the master of such slave during the life of her husband; and that all the issue of such free born women, so married, shall be slaves as their fathers were."[20]

Slaves were both persons and property. Slaveholders had a natural tendency to think in terms of absolute slavery and ignore the rights of the slave as a human being. Slaves had some of the attributes of legal personality, not many, to be sure, and decreasing in proportion to the density of the slave population. They enjoyed certain privileges according to the Christian benevolence and kindliness of their owners. They had few, if indeed, any rights under the law. Being property they were under the absolute authority of their owner in almost every aspect of their daily lives. The state was interested in them as taxable property. It was responsible for protecting the property rights of the owner. It was deeply concerned with the protection of society from what seems always to have been considered a dangerous element in the population. No state, however, ever seriously undertook to provide protection for the slaves.

The basic slave code of the English colonies was written in Barbados in 1688. South Carolina adopted large parts of the Barbados code in 1712, revised it in 1739, and retained it with slight modifications until slavery was abolished. Georgia copied the South Carolina code in 1770, and at a later date Florida adopted the Georgia code. Here was slavery at its worst, with slaves outnumbering the whites, and with the whites constantly apprehensive of insurrections; with a high incidence of owner absenteeism from the plantations and enormous powers for good or evil resting in the overseers; with large slaveholdings and slight contact between slaves and owners' families; and with unhealthful working conditions. There was little enough reason for the institution to develop along humane, patriarchal lines in this area. It did not do so. The laws were severe, their enforcement rigorous, and the power of the owner unlimited.[21]

Complementing this power of one man over another, which we shall shortly analyze, was the unrestrained will of a local community to deal with a despised, feared, and utterly helpless minority in its midst. The British government allowed and the colonies insisted upon more and more local autonomy. It was thought to be so great a virtue that the principle was given a degree of recognition in the framework of the new nation after the Revolution. It ultimately led to civil war, but the perpetual and surviving evil, however much can be said for it otherwise, has been the cruel and inhuman oppression of minorities. Prejudice and fear have prevailed in writing the law, in its enforcement, and in the administration of justice.[22]

The South Carolina Code of 1712 contained the provision common to all slave codes of the English colonies that baptism in the Christian faith did not alter the status of the slave.[23] It forbade him to leave his owner's property without written permission unless accompanied by a white person, and charged every white person in the community to chastise promptly any slave apprehended without such a pass. It provided the death penalty for any person enticing a slave to run away and for any slave attempting to leave the province. Any slave absconding and successfully evading capture for twenty days was to be publicly whipped for the first offense, branded with the letter "R" on the right cheek for the second offense, and lose one ear if absent thirty days on the third offense. For a fourth offense, a man slave was to be castrated, a woman whipped,

branded on the left cheek with the letter "R" and lose her left ear. Any owner who refused to inflict these punishments was to be fined and forfeit ownership of the slave. The commander of any patrol company was to be paid £4 for the return of fugitives dead or alive. All Negro houses were to be searched every fortnight for weapons and stolen goods. For theft, successive penalties were whipping, loss of one ear, branding and nose slit, and for the fourth offense, death. No penalties were imposed if a slave died under punishment, and even intentional killing of a slave cost the owner only a £50 fine. No slave was to be allowed to work for pay, to plant corn, peas, or rice, to keep hogs, cattle, or horses, to own or operate a boat, to buy or sell, or to wear clothes finer than ordinary Negro cloth. The revision of 1739 forbade teaching slaves to write, working them on Sunday or more than fifteen hours daily in summer and fourteen in winter. It increased the fines for wilfully killing a slave to £700 and for killing in the heat of passion to £350. Subsequent additions to this code imposed fines up to $1,000 and prison sentences up to one year for concealing runaway slaves, $100 and six months for employing any Negro or slave as a clerk, $1,000 fine for trading with slaves, $100 and six months for selling or giving alcoholic beverages to slaves, $100 and six months for teaching a slave to read or write, and the death penalty for circulating incendiary literature. Manumission was forbidden except by deed, and after 1820 by permission of the legislature. Georgia required legislative approval after 1801. The Georgia code of 1770 also forbade more than six slaves to assemble at any place without the presence of a white person. Offenses carrying the death penalty in Georgia were insurrection, rape, murder, poisoning, burglary, arson, and assault upon a white person.

Trial and punishment of slaves in this area was another inherent evil of the system. They were not tried in the regular courts, and they enjoyed none of the safeguards against miscarriage of justice now known as due process of law, such as jury trial, testimony of witnesses, and counsel. The courts were not open to slaves except when suing for freedom; and all Southern states debarred Negro testimony, free or slave, in cases where white persons were involved. Whenever a complaint was lodged against a slave by anyone for any offense from theft to murder, a justice of the peace issued a warrant for the slave's arrest. The justice then associated with himself in the case another justice and the two selected three freeholders of the community to sit with them in the case. These five men heard the case and imposed sentence, even of death, the nature of which and of any lesser punishment was left to their discretion. These members of the court might be, ordinarily were, slaveholders, disposed to deal leniently with valuable property of themselves and friends, but not necessarily so. On the whole it was a wretched system, with no court records, few precedents, undue haste, intimidation, insufficient evidence and other glaring faults. The South Carolina courts of two justices and three freeholders for free Negroes and slaves were identical with the Barbados system. Georgia's special courts were composed of three justices of the peace only.

The first area of legal development touching slavery, but second in terms of severity, was the Chesapeake Bay area or tobacco colonies.[24] The laws of 1682 and 1692 constituted the basic slave code of Virginia. Maryland, Delaware, and North

Slave branding

Slave branding provided a mark of identification, facilitated the recovery of fugitives, and satisfied the satanic claim that Negroes were less than human.

Carolina copied the Virginia laws. Virginia's first law was in 1667, when there were only 40,000 people in the colony including 2,000 Negro slaves and 6,000 indentured servants. In that year she ruled that baptism did not confer freedom upon the slave and then declared that killing of slaves by "extremity of correction" was not a felony "since it can not be presumed that prepense malice should induce any man to destroy his own estate."

Virginia's main concern seems to have been with fugitives, miscegenation, and insurrection. The law of 1682 prohibited slaves to have weapons in their possession, to leave their owner's plantations without written permission, or to lift a hand against a white person even in self-defense. It also declared that runaway slaves refusing to surrender might be killed without penalty. The same law was rewritten in 1692 to provide for issuance of warrants to sheriffs for the arrest of outlying slaves, said sheriff to shoot or otherwise kill them if they resisted or ran away. A new law in 1692 imposed banishment from the colony of any free white man or woman who married a Negro, mulatto, or Indian. The penalty was changed later to six months' imprisonment and £10 fine. Any white woman having mulatto children without marriage was to be fined £15 or sold for a five-year term and the child was to be sold as an indentured servant until thirty years of age. No slaves were to be set free unless they left the colony within six months at the expense of the emancipator. Slaves were forbidden to keep horses, cattle, or hogs, and any slave charged with a capital offense was to be tried without jury and convicted on oath of two witnesses. In 1705 slaves were declared to be both personal property and real estate. They were attached to the soil in the sense that the heir to a plantation was entitled to purchase the inherited interest of others in the slaves.

In 1751 Virginia gave to the church wardens of any parish the power to sell Negroes residing there one month if they had been emancipated without the consent of the governor and Council. This law was amended in 1806 to provide that freed slaves who did not leave the state within one year were to be seized and sold. The same Assembly forbade slaves to conduct religious meetings or to attend any kind of meeting at night, without written permission. The assembly in 1824 provided twelve months' imprisonment

for anyone assisting slaves to escape, $50 fine and two months' imprisonment for teaching free Negroes to read or write, and $50 fine for failure to support aged or infirm slaves with financial liability for full support payable to the overseer of the poor. Fines up to $1,000 were imposed for written encouragement of insurrection, and $50 and six months' imprisonment for purchasing anything from slaves or selling alcoholic beverages to them. By an act of 1832 any person who apprehended a Virginia fugitive in Ohio, Pennsylvania, or Indiana and returned said fugitive received $50 and twenty cents per mile traveling expenses. Returning fugitives from the New England states or New York was worth $120 and traveling expenses. Offenses punishable by death for both slaves and free Negroes in Virginia included rape of a white woman, burning wheat worth $50, beating a white person, or inciting rebellion.

New York and New Jersey wrote their basic slave codes in 1702 and 1695, respectively. Previous to this time slaves seem to have been governed by the same criminal code and the same judicial processes as the white population. The first change in New York came in 1682 with an order by the General Court in New York City forbidding slaves to leave their owners' property without written permission or to buy or sell.[25] Additional restraints in 1702 forbade more than three slaves to assemble without the consent of the owner, gave owners wide discretion in punishments, and imposed fourteen days' confinement and whipping for a slave striking a free man.[26] In 1706 slaves were denied the right to testify in civil or criminal cases involving whites, and in 1712 were denied access to the ordinary courts and judicial processes. A new system, like that of the Southern colonies and devoid of all traditional guarantees of English law, was established. Complaints of slave offenses were made to a justice of the peace who ordered arrest and held a preliminary hearing. He then associated with himself two other justices and the three summoned five freeholders to sit with them in the case. If seven of the eight men judged the slave guilty, sentence was immediately executed. The owner of the slave could request a jury in cases involving the death sentence, but only if he was willing personally to pay the cost. Capital offenses were murder, conspiracy, rape, and arson.[27]

New Jersey's laws provided a variety of court procedures. By the Act of 1695 a slave accused of

murder was to be tried before three justices of
the peace, but guilt was to be determined by a
twelve-man jury. Stealing brought the slave before two justices of the peace with whipping as a
penalty.[28] In 1713 all slaves accused of capital
offenses—murder, conspiracy, arson, rape—were
to be tried as in New York by three justices of
the peace and five freeholders. In 1768, near the
end of the colonial period, all cases of murder,
conspiracy, arson, and rape were returned to the
regular courts and procedures.[29] Death sentences
could be imposed for manslaughter and burglary
but were not mandatory, and punishment by
whipping was provided for attempted rape, striking a white person, straying five miles from home
without a permit, carrying weapons, being abroad
after nine o'clock at night, and meeting together
in groups of more than five.[30]

Pennsylvania had relatively few slaves, a large
Quaker population generally hostile to slavery,
and a very heavy immigration of lowly people
from Europe who instinctively abhorred the institution. Nevertheless, the colonial code in its
naked provisions was not too different from that
of New York. A law of 1685 exempted slaves from
attachment for satisfaction of the master's debts.[31]
All trials of slaves were by two justices of the
peace assisted by six freeholders. Death was the
original penalty for murder, burglary, and rape,
and castration for attempted rape. The latter provision was changed to whipping in 1705.[32] Whipping was the penalty also for theft, carrying weapons, assembling in groups of more than four,
being abroad after ten o'clock at night, and straying ten miles away from home without a pass.
Slaves were not permitted to testify in cases
involving white persons.

The New England slave codes were written
between 1693 and 1714, Massachusetts being first
and New Hampshire last. Rhode Island and Connecticut wrote their basic laws in 1703. These
colonies had a much smaller proportion of slaves
in their population than those to the South. In
1715 New Hampshire had only 150 slaves and
9,500 whites, Massachusetts had 2,000 and 94,000,
Rhode Island had 500 and 8,500, and Connecticut
had 1,500 and 46,000. These colonies had some
provisions which were common to all slave codes.
For example, they required slaves to have written
passes when away from their owner's property.[33]
They forbade the harboring of runaways, trading
with slaves, and selling alcoholic beverages to

them.[34] All of them penalized the slave who
struck a white person. Beyond those things, however, there was a very real difference between
slavery in these four colonies and elsewhere.
There were no distinctions between slaves and
free white persons in cases involving the death
penalty. Courts and court procedures were the
same for slaves as for whites except in Rhode
Island.[35] They were indicted by a grand jury,
tried by a petit jury; they testified in cases involving free whites; they enjoyed the right of
appeal; and their punishment was the same.[36]
Rhode Island, by law of 1743, assigned cases of
attempted rape to the Court of Assize and General Goal Delivery, and provided a penalty of
branding, whipping, and sale out of the colony.[37]
Theft brought the slave before two justices of the
peace and was punished by whipping or banishment. Massachusetts and Connecticut imposed
the whipping penalty for striking white persons,
for profanity, and for stealing. Any person killing
a slave was punished in the same manner as for
killing a white person. New Hampshire imposed
the death penalty. Masters were liable to grand
jury investigation of cruel treatment. Massachusetts in 1705 forbade all marriages between whites
and Negroes, placed marriage rights and relationships of slaves on the same basis as free white
people, punished illegitimacy, and forbade any
master to deny the right of marriage to a slave.[38]
That colony also recognized the right of the slave
to own property and to sue his master if it were
taken away.[39]

No New England colony denied the right of
manumission, but all had some restrictions except
New Hampshire. Massachusetts in 1703 required
the master who manumitted a slave to post security of £50 that the slave would not become a
public charge.[40] Rhode Island fixed the amount
at £100 in 1728, but raised it to £1000 in 1755.[41]
New York in 1712 required the owner to pay £20
annually to a manumitted slave, the same condition to apply if the manumission was by will,
but changed it in 1717 to require only security
against the freed person becoming a public
charge.[42] New Jersey allowed manumission by
will or otherwise beginning in 1769, but required
a surety of £200. Pennsylvania in 1726 fixed the
amount at £30.[43]

It must be remembered always in dealing with
slavery that the municipal law of the colonies
did three basic things: Slaves who had been

# Negroes for Sale.

A Cargo of very fine stout Men and Women, in good order and fit for immediate service, just imported from the Windward Coast of Africa, in the Ship Two Brothers.— Conditions are one half Cash or Produce, the other half payable the first of January next, giving Bond and Security if required.

The Sale to be opened at 10 o'Clock each Day, in Mr. Bourdeaux's Yard, at No. 48, on the Bay. May 19, 1784.　　　　JOHN MITCHELL.

Thirty Seasoned Negroes

To be Sold for Credit, at Private Sale.

AMONGST which is a Carpenter, none of whom are known to be dishonest.

Also, to be sold for Cash, a regular bred young Negroe Man-Cook, born in this Country, who served several Years under an exceeding good French Cook abroad, and his Wife a middle aged Washer-Woman, (both very honest) and their two Children. *Likewise.* a young Man a Carpenter.

For Terms apply to the Printer.

The commercial slave trade, both foreign and domestic, was flourishing in 1784 in the southern states.

BRANDING SLAVES.

"TWENTY DOLLARS REWARD. Ranaway from the subscriber, a negro woman and two children; the woman is tall and black, and *a few days before she went off, I BURNT HER WITH A HOT IRON ON THE LEFT SIDE OF HER FACE; I TRIED TO MAKE THE LETTER M, and she kept a cloth over her head and face, and a fly bonnet over her head, so as to cover the burn;* her children are both boys, the oldest is in his seventh year; he is a *mulatto* and has blue eyes; the youngest is a black and is in his fifth year. [N. C. Standard, July 18, 1838.] MICAJAH RICKS, Nash County.

One hundred dollars reward for Pompey, 40 years old, he is *branded on the left jaw.*—Mr. R. P. Carney, in the Mobile Register, Dec. 22, 1838.

"Ranaway a negro girl called Mary, has the letter A *branded on her cheek and forehead.*"—Mr. J. P. Ashford, Natchez Courier, August 24, 1838.

"Ranaway, Bill, has a *burn on his buttock, from a piece of hot iron in shape of a T.*"—Mr. J. N. Dillahunty, Woodville, N. O. Com. Bulletin, July 21, 1837.

"TWENTY DOLLARS REWARD.—Ranaway from the subscriber a negro girl named Molly. The said girl was sold by Messrs. Wm. Payne & Sons, and purchased by a Mr. Moses, and sold by him to Thos. Frisley, of Edgefield District, of whom I bought her. She is 16 or 17 years of age, LATELY BRANDED ON THE LEFT CHEEK, THUS, R, AND A PIECE TAKEN OFF HER EAR ON THE SAME SIDE; THE SAME LETTER ON THE INSIDE OF BOTH HER LEGS. [Charleston, S. C. Courier, 1825.] "ABNER ROSS, Fairfield District."

"Was committed to jail a negro man, says his name is Josiah, *branded on the thigh and hips in three or four places,* thus (J. M.)—J. L. Jolley. Sheriff of Clinton, Co. M., in the Clinton Gazette, July 23, 1836.

About a year since I knew a slave, who had deserted his master, to be caught, and fastened to the stocks. On the next morning he was *chained in an immovable posture, and* BRANDED IN BOTH CHEEKS WITH RED HOT STAMPS OF IRON.—Letter from a clergyman written in Natchez, (Mi.) in 1833.

"Fifty dollars reward for my fellow Edward, he has the *letter E on his arm.*"—Mr. Thos. Ledwith, Jacksonville, East Florida, in the Charleston, S. C. Courier, Sept. 1, 1838.

"Ranaway a negro boy Harper, *has a scar* on one of his hips in the form of a G."—Mr. W. Stansell, Picksville, Ala., in the Huntsville Dem. Aug. 29, 1837.

The masters seldom, if ever, try to govern their slaves by moral influence, but by whipping, kicking, beating, starving, *branding, cat-hauling,* loading with irons, imprisoning, or by some other cruel mode of torture. They often boast of having invented some new mode of torture, by which they have "tamed the rascals."—Rev. Horace Moulton, of the M. E. Church, Marlborough, Mass., who spent five years in Georgia, between 1817 and 1824.

seized by force, reduced to slavery by force, and sold in America, were held by force. The law approved this, first because the slaves were heathens; then, to avoid loss of the slaves by Christian baptism, because they were Negroes. The law condemned the child to the status of the slave mother and the race to an infinitude of bondage. The law denied to the slave positive rights, simultaneously gave to his owner absolute control over him, and thus reduced him from the status of a person to that of an animal. Here is the category of variance from colony to colony, from plantation to plantation, and from decade to decade during the existence of slavery. Slaves were slaves because someone had hunted them, or their grandmothers, like wild beasts and had stolen them out of Africa, and had sold them like horses and cattle to someone else, who held them in subjection by brute force in a state where the law sanctioned it.

Let us examine this lack of legal personality, of positive rights, on the part of the slave. The law denied him the right to think, to know, to learn, to improve his mind by reading, by communication with his fellows, by assembly; the right to receive religious instruction or to worship in a church of his own choice; the right to move about beyond the limits of his master's property; the right to marriage, including the ordinary family relationships, parental authority, and protection of the home; the right to own, accumulate, inherit, or bequeath property; the right to choose his own occupation or to improve his natural talents and skills; the right to enjoy the fruits of his own labor; and many others. Above all else it denied him the enjoyment of the institutional safeguards devised to prevent miscarriage of justice and cruel punishments. This was an area of public authority in which the owner had no freedom of action.

The slave enjoyed no security of his person. Society gave the slaveowner the power of punishment even to the extent of killing the slave. There were laws, of course, to punish undue cruelty by fines, but the victim could not testify, no other slave or free Negro could testify, such offenses were seldom committed in the presence of white persons, and the occasional witness was rare indeed who would be willing to incur the wrath of the owner by informing and testifying against him. Moreover, society provided no test of character or intelligence for slave ownership. Anyone with the money could purchase a slave. Society also gave to any person apprehending a slave abroad without a permit authority to chastise him; it punished the slave severely, sometimes with death, for striking a white person even in self-defense; it defined rape of the female slave as trespass on the owner's property; and it ignored forced concubinage and prostitution. The slave could be punished in anger, for vengeance, and out of pure sadism. No one ever knew the why, or cared, or paid any attention to what went on even at the public whipping posts.

Perhaps the most cruel of all aspects of slavery was the fact that slaves were denied the right of self-direction, were not expected to have a will of their own, but were held responsible for their conduct. They were expected to breed like animals, remain ignorant and unprotected by the law, yet to obey the law. They ran away and were hunted down by bloodhounds, wantonly shot, publicly whipped, and mutilated by branding or otherwise so that they could be easily recovered another time. The law countenanced these things.

Manumission was made next to impossible in some colonies, restrained in all except one. This was done on humanitarian grounds to prevent owners from setting slaves free after they had passed the age of profitable labor, to protect the public interest against having to support them, to force all Negro blood back into the Negro race and prevent amalgamation, and to prevent the growth of a free Negro population to the disquiet and unhappiness of the slaves. It crushed all hope of redemption on the part of the individual slave and delayed any action toward abolishing the institution.

Finally, there was the authority of the slaveowner. He might exercise it himself or delegate it to someone else. He determined the kind, quality, and amount of food, and the time of meals, the hours of labor, the kind of tasks, and the length of rest periods, the kind of clothing, the nature of the dwelling or slave quarters, the nature and permanence of family relationships, the regularity or lack of medical care, the care of the slave children, religious services if any, the rules of conduct, infractions of the rules, and nature of punishment. He could sell, transfer, or mortgage the slave. In all things pertaining to the daily life of the slave, the owner was the law.

1840.]   *Anti-Slavery Almanac.*   13

HUNTING SLAVES WITH DOGS AND GUNS.

The St. Francisville (La.) Chronicle, of Feb. 1, 1839, gives the following account of a 'negro hunt,' in that Parish.

"Two or three days since, a gentleman of this parish, in *hunting runaway negroes*, came upon a camp of them in the swamp, arrested two of them, but the third made fight ; and upon *being shot in the shoulder*, fled to a sluice, where the *dogs succeeded* in drowning him."

The Rev. Francis Hawley, pastor of the Baptist Church in Colebrook, Ct, lived fourteen years in N. and S. Carolina. He says: " Runaway slaves are frequently hunted with guns and dogs. *I was once out on such an excursion, with my rifle and two dogs.* I trust the Lord has forgiven me !"

"HUNTING MEN WITH DOGS.—A negro who had absconded from his master, has been apprehended and committed to prison in Savannah. The editor who states the fact, adds, that he did not surrender till *he was considerably* MAIMED BY THE DOGS."—New York Com Advertiser, June 8, 1827

It is common to keep dogs on the plantations, to pursue and catch runaway slaves.—Nehemiah Caulkins, Waterford, Ct., who lived in North Carolina.

There was a man living in Savannah when I was there, who kept a large number of dogs for no other purpose than to hunt runaway negroes. And he always had enough of this work to do.—Rev. H.Moulton, Marlboro' Mass.

ADVERTISEMENTS OF RUNAWAYS.—" Ranaway Mary, has a *scar* on her back and right arm, *caused by a rifle ball*."—Natchez Courier, June 15, 1838.

" Ranaway Caleb, is *shot in the thigh*."—Macon Messenger, May 25, 1837.

" Ranaway Hambleton, *limps* where he was *shot* a few weeks ago, while runaway."—Vicksburg Register, Sept. 5, 1838.

" Sam, *several shots in his left arm and side*."—Helena Journal, June 1, '33·

" Mose, has a *wound* by a *rifle shot*."—Southern Sun, August 7, 1838.

" Allen, has *two buck shots in his arm*."—Vicksburg Register, July 18, 1838.

" Fountain, *shot in the hind parts of his legs*."—Geo. Messen., July 27, 1837.

" Isaac, has a scar made by *a pistol shot* ."—Geo. Journal, March 27, 1837.

" Jim, marked with *shot* in his right thigh."—Macon Messenger, July 27, 1839·

" Stolen, a negro named Winter—the mark of *four or five buck shot* on his legs."—Natchitoches Herald, July 8, 1837.

ADVERTISEMENTS OF SLAVES IN JAIL.—" Committed a negro man, *very badly shot in the right side* and hand."—Milledgeville Journal, May 29, 1838.

" Cuffee, is lame, occasioned *by a shot*."—Camden, (S. C.) Courier, July 8, 1837.

" Simon, *badly shot* in his back and arm."—Petersburg Intel. May 22, 1838.

" Denis, *shot* in the arm."—R. W. Sizer, in the Grand Gulf Advert., July 8, 1837.

" Elijah, has a scar occasioned by *a shot*."—Annapolis Repub. April 18, 1837.

Slaves had no protection from the brutalities revealed in these extracts from newspapers of the slave states. Note the dates 1836-39 when slavery was reputed to have become a humane and Christian institution.

FOUNDATIONS OF FREEDOM

Chapter 2

There were no antislavery societies and no anti-slavery newspapers or magazines before the Revolution. There was little of any sort of printed antislavery material, except occasional expositions, sermons, or remonstrances, published and privately distributed to small and select numbers of people, until the very eve of the Revolution. Neither were there established systems of recording and reporting court decisions or debates in colonial assemblies, so that taken in its entirety the period offers little to the historian in the way of documentary information. It offered less to the average citizen of that time in the way of enlightenment, intellectual stimulation, or persuasion. The man who opposed slavery did so, not because he had read a book, or newspaper, or otherwise digested an argument, but because he instinctively rejected a system of human relationships so utterly foreign to common decency. Roger Williams obviously was one of these people and so was Chief Justice Samuel Sewall, whose *The Selling of Joseph* (1700) was long thought to have been the first published argument against slavery in America. Nobody seems to have taken either one of them very seriously, but Sewall did state the first major indictment of slavery, one that was to be repeated a thousand times in every conceivable type of literature—the separation of men and women from their homeland, of husbands from wives, and of parents from children—and he touched lightly upon the evil effects of slavery upon the character of slaveholders.[1]

Sewall was a Puritan, and the Puritans were not the pioneers in the antislavery movement. That honor belongs to the Quakers, for the Quakers were gentle people, living by the precept of the golden rule, believing in the inherent dignity of man, the freedom of human will, and the equality of all men. They owned slaves in the seventeenth century and a part of the eighteenth, but George Fox sounded a warning against it in 1657. Thomas Drake says: "In this, his first discussion of slavery, he made only a beginning: he did not condemn slaveholding as such. But he did expound the idea of the equality of men in the eyes of God; and this idea—touchstone to the Truth—finally, more than a century later, freed the Quakers' slaves."[2]

The Quakers experienced great difficulties from the beginning, for the defense of slavery by the suppression of freedom of inquiry and discussion and other civil rights, and by the use of charges of incendiarism and of foul invective to discredit the friend of the slave, did not originate in the American South, though it reached optimum heights there; nor did it develop in response to the violent language of abolitionists as has been claimed. It came out of the practice of slaveholding, the relationship between master and slave, the intoxication of unrestrained power, and the *habit* of destroying all opposition to the master's will. Furthermore, these early Quakers were not an obnoxious group of meddlers, talking of things they knew not of, any more than were the later antislavery leaders of the nineteenth century, as was charged and commonly believed then and now. They were slaveholders, rich and powerful slaveholders, in every part of British Colonial America, just as were many of the later antislavery leaders.

These Quakers abhorred all violence. They never spoke in harsh language. They opposed slavery from first to last on moral and religious grounds—as a sin. They made tremendous financial sacrifices to rid themselves of the contamination. They never asked anything for themselves by way of profit—political, social, or economic—from their friendship for the oppressed. Nevertheless, they were violently denounced, charged with inciting rebellion, suppressed, and finally driven out of Barbados because they sought to Christianize and educate their slaves. They were denied the poor privilege of freeing their slaves in the Southern states, and in the early congresses of the United States were accused of treason and incendiarism because they petitioned for the suppression of the African slave trade.

All of this came, of course, after they had steeled themselves for the ordeal through a century of soul-searching and consultation. The second Quaker protest was a letter of advice to Friends in America by William Edmundson, at Newport, Rhode Island, in 1676, and the third a "Remonstrance Against Slavery and the Slave-trade" by the Germantown (Pa.) Friends; but it is doubtful if more than a handful of people outside Quaker circles knew anything about them. The first printed protest was George Kieth's *An Exhortation and Caution to Friends Concerning Buying or Keeping of Negroes* (1693), seven years before Samuel Sewall's *The Selling of Joseph*.[3] It insisted upon the principle of brotherhood of all men and requested Friends to seek freedom for the slaves, to free their own slaves, and to lend assistance to fugitives. Whether it had any influence outside Quaker circles there is no way of knowing, but soul-searching had begun, and as early as 1698 Quakers were discussing their responsibility as slaveholders for the carnage in Africa and their responsibility to compensate slaves at the time of manumission both for labor while in bondage and as an aid to economic independence. This was not an easy road they chose nor a journey to be undertaken lightly. They hesitated and drew back, and looked askance at those among them who became impatient with delay. In fact they disowned William Southeby

and John Farmer, and then Ralph Sandiford and Benjamin Lay. Sandiford, who published *A Brief Examination of the Practice of the Times* (1729), was probably driven to his grave (he died in 1733 at age forty) by ostracism,[4] and Benjamin Lay, who published *All Slave Keepers That Keep the Innocent in Bondage, Apostates* (1737), found no peace or comfort in even his most intimate human relationships.[5]

Then came the two great leaders of pre-Revolutionary abolitionism—John Woolman, tailor, of New Jersey, and Anthony Benezet, schoolteacher, of Philadelphia. Woolman, whom Drake calls "the greatest Quaker of the eighteenth century and perhaps the most Christ-like individual that Quakerism has ever produced,"[6] traveled widely through Virginia and northward through Maryland, his own state of New Jersey, Pennsylvania, and New England. No other antislavery leader ever traveled as much, except Theodore Weld in the 1820's and 1830's, nearly a century later, and the two men were remarkably alike in their methods. Both labored mightily with individuals, though the later Presbyterian preached valiantly, and the earlier Quaker gently persuaded. What was the secret of Woolman's power? What gave Weld his tremendous influence over other men? We only know that Woolman was forever moving about. He wrote *Some Considerations on the Keeping of Negroes: Recommended to the Professors of Christianity of Every Denomination* in 1754, and a second part to the original in 1762.[7] It was meant for the general public, not Friends alone, and it was the most widely distributed antislavery work before the Revolution. It still occupies an honored place upon the shelves of scholars. But it was this close, personal contact between Woolman and hundreds of slaveholders that was important, for the presence of the saint touches the souls of men more than a thousand printed pages influence their minds. It is one thing to listen to a sermon or read a book, and it is quite another thing to have a saintly person ask a man a question about personal conduct and then sit down with him in quiet meditation to think it over.

Woolman was a humanitarian in the finest sense of that term. He knew the truth, he spoke the truth, and men believed because they had no other choice. Wealth, war, and slavery were to him the three greatest enemies of the souls of men. He insisted that Christian doctrine em-

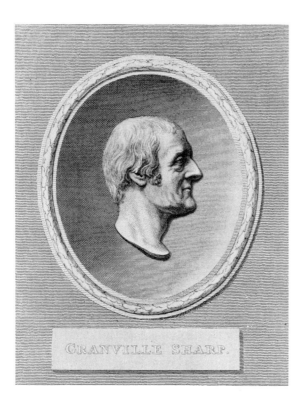

GRANVILLE SHARP.

CLARKSON.

braced all men and that all men were entitled to freedom, but, above all, that no man was mentally or morally competent to rule others independent of restraints. Slavery was unchristian, it was unjust, it was cruel, and its effect upon owners and slaves alike was evil. Merely calling persons slaves created a false notion of natural inferiority, and "where slavekeeping prevails, pure religion and sobriety decline, as it evidently tends to harden the heart and render the soul less susceptible of that holy spirit of love, meakness, and charity, which is the peculiar character of a true Christian."

Benezet did not write as much as Woolman, and he wrote mostly about the slave trade, but he made perfectly clear that there was precious little difference between enslaving a man and holding him in slavery. His most important works were *A Caution and Warning to Great Britain and Her Colonies, in a Short Representation of the Calamitous State of the Enslaved Negroes in the British Dominions* (1766), and *Some Historical Account of Guinea, Its Situation, Produce, and the General Disposition of Its Inhabitants, with an Enquiry into the Rise and Progress of the Slave-Trade, Its Nature and Lamentable Effects*

(1771).[8] It was the latter pamphlet that inspired young Thomas Clarkson's interest in the cause. Much of his other printing was compilation, but he sent his pamphlets everywhere in America, England, and the continent of Europe, particularly to France, where he had been born in 1713, of Huguenot parentage. He corresponded widely with British leaders, particularly with Granville Sharp, who represented Sommersett before Lord Mansfield, and with Thomas Clarkson whose works on the slave trade were reprinted and circulated in America. He was a friend of John Wesley, who copied his *Thoughts upon Slavery* almost verbatim from Benezet.[9] Finally, he was a magnificent organizer, who channeled Quaker doctrine on slavery to the larger audience.

Whether Benezet was more important in the movement than Woolman is of little consequence. The works of both, along with the Bible, were the most precious possessions of every antislavery leader of the nineteenth century. They lived at the same time. The work of one complemented that of the other. They were friends and colleagues. Both exerted powerful influence in the movement. One was born in 1713, the other in 1720. Woolman, the mystic, died in England of small-

Granville Sharp

Sharp, in England, was a contemporary of Benezet in America. His argument before Lord Mansfield in the Sommersett case freed the slaves in England, but not in the British empire.

Thomas Clarkson

Clarkson's antislavery writings were the most widely distributed in the United States of any British leader.

pox in 1772. Benezet, the propagandist, died in 1784. One can only speculate on the terrible loss to the country at this critical period, for the real greatness of Benezet and Woolman, it seems to me, lies far beyond their emphasis upon the brotherhood of man and the inconsistency between slavery and Christianity—even beyond their persuasive power with slaveholders and their lifelong devotion to the cause.

These men grasped four truths which were so basic in man's struggle for freedom as to be almost overpowering in their simplicity. Whether they came by way of revelation, or by agonizing mental concentration, the important thing is that they came to men who lived, and whose people lived, by the truth.

All men were equal in the sight of God. Slavery was a violation of the Christian principle of human brotherhood and the golden rule. There was no sanction for holding anyone in slavery in the Christian faith, and those who bought slaves and those who owned slaves were as guilty of the murderous warfare in Africa as if they were active participants.

This was a generation before the Revolution. Early Quaker literature was religious literature,

and these men were working largely within the framework of a religious society. This ceased to be true when the Quakers had rid *themselves* of slavery, and at the time of the Revolution they contributed to the general emphasis upon the natural rights of man. When James Otis said in *The Rights of the British Colonies Asserted and Proved:* "The Colonists are by the law of nature free born, as indeed all men are, white or black,"[10] he was speaking the same language as Benezet. And Thomas Paine merely summed up the whole business in the concise fashion of an indictment in his *Slavery in America* (1775), when he said: "But to go to nations with whom there is no war, who have no way provoked, without farther design of conquest, purely to catch inoffensive people, like wild beasts, for slaves, is an height of outrage against Humanity and Justice, that seems left by Heathen nations to be practiced by pretended Christians . . . As these people are not convicted of forfeiting freedom, they have still a natural, perfect right to it; and the Governments, whenever they come, should in justice set them free, and punish those who hold them in slavery . . . Certainly one may, with as much reason and decency, plead for murder, robbery, lewdness, and barbarity as for this practice."

The Quakers first abolished the practice of buying and selling of slaves. Buying a slave created a demand for another to be imported, thus stimulating the foreign slave trade, and directly implicating the purchaser in the African business. Buying was necessary to successful slaveholding operations because natural increase did not supply the losses, and abolishing the trade would ultimately abolish slavery. Probably, too, it was necessary to approach the final decision by degrees. In any case, buying and selling among them ceased in Philadelphia in 1758, London, England, in 1761, Maryland in 1768, New England in 1770, and New York in 1774. The abolition among them of slavery itself came more slowly, for various reasons, but it came, in the New England and Middle states before the close of the Revolution, and in Maryland and Virginia by 1788.

There was no basis whatever for doubting the mental and moral capacity of the Negroes to support themselves in a status of freedom as useful and creative members of society. Why there should have been any doubt about it when they had been taking care of themselves and the whites, too, for a long time, remains a mystery. Some people argued the point as a collateral issue to draw attention from the main idea of emancipation. With some it was a rationalization, but men of intelligence and honesty of purpose stumbled over it—Jefferson,[11] for instance, Washington, and probably Lincoln. Thousands joined in a movement to colonize the free Negroes in Africa or somewhere on this continent. The idea of biological inequality crystallized to the point where in my own time scholars have argued that Negroes who achieved greatly were of mixed blood, and literature of the most diabolical character depicting Negroes as apes is allowed to circulate freely.

The Quakers rejected all such nonsense. They set about educating their slaves for freedom. They established day schools for Negro children, Sabbath schools and evening schools (first and fifth day) for adults. They appointed committees of inspection to plan and advise the Negroes, committees of guardians to protect the orphans, committees on education, and committees for employment.

Whatever difficulties, problems, or necessary sacrifices might be connected with emancipation should be borne by those who were responsible for the outrage of slavery, not by the victims. There is record of a revealing letter from Patrick Henry to Robert Pleasants (1773) in which he said: "I am drawn along by the general inconvenience of living without them. I will not, I can not justify it. However culpable my conduct, I will so far pay my devoir to virtue, as to own the excellence and rectitude of her precepts, and to lament my own want of conformity to them."[12] No Quaker was allowed such latitude of conduct. He freed his slaves. He was not allowed to take the easy way of selling them to someone else, or of freeing the children after a certain age as was later done by law. Financial ruin, abandonment of plantations, scorn and persecution by one's neighbors, migration to a city, a new state beyond the mountains—all of this, and more for many—such was the way of righteousness for those who had erred. None among them puts it quite as forcefully as Hugh H. Brackenridge in his brilliant satire, *Modern Chivalry* (1792): "It would greatly inconvenience thieves and cutthroats, who have run risks in acquiring skill in their profession, to be obliged all at once to desist from this and apply themselves to industry in

other ways for a livelihood," but all understood the principle.[13] They never countenanced economic arguments, either against slavery, or in defense of gradual emancipation. Some of them, like the families of Warner Mifflin of Delaware and Robert Pleasants of Virginia, gave freedom to nearly one hundred slaves; and most of them left Virginia and the Carolinas for the new west.

Slaves were entitled to retributive justice. They must be compensated for work done while deprived of their freedom. Failure to educate and train them for responsible citizenship must be corrected. They must be assisted to economic independence. All of this by the man who owned them and must set them free. So well did they fulfill this obligation that in a reasonably short time there were two Negro schools in New York, seven in Philadelphia, one even in Alexandria, Virginia; and Negroes were building their own economy, establishing churches, and setting themselves up as tradesmen and skilled mechanics.

The Quakers had written a brilliant chapter in the moral progression of man. Other religious groups had failed at an earlier date to contest the political decision that Christians could be held as slaves *providing they were Negroes,* and they had failed fatally. They now agreed *in the slave country* that the whole question of slavery was a political question. They did not then, or later, do anything about it. In fact they threw the social teachings of Jesus out on the scrap heap and went along with the claim that slavery was a Christian institution.

Benezet was still active in Philadelphia when the first Presbyterian of distinction entered the movement and published a summation of arguments against slavery.[14] Benjamin Rush's *An Address to the Inhabitants of the British Settlements in America, upon Slavekeeping* was published in Philadelphia in 1773. Rush was a distinguished Philadelphia physician, sometime professor of chemistry at the College of Pennsylvania, and an original member of the Philadelphia College of Physicians. He was a member of the American Philosophical Society and published an early treatise on the subject of psychoanalysis. He was one of the first presidents of the first great antislavery society and remained active in the movement until the end of the century.

Rush approached the subject as a physician, psychologist, and philosopher might have been expected to do, and he cited evidence to prove his logic. Negroes are not inferior intellectually or morally, there is too much proof to the contrary, and even the absence of proof would not justify the conclusion because: "Slavery is so foreign to the human mind, that the moral faculties, as well as those of the understanding are debased, and rendered torpid by it. All of the vices which are charged upon the negroes in the southern colonies and West Indies . . . are the genuine offspring of slavery, and serve as an argument to prove they [Negroes] were not intended by Providence for it."[15] To say their black skin is the mark of Cain is too absurd to need refutation. Actually, it fits them for life in a hot climate, and as a physician he had seen less of the ravages of "heat, disease, and time" in their faces than in those of white people.

He met the argument that the slaves were necessary to the economic development of the South —specifically, to the cultivation of sugar, rice, and indigo—with evidence that sugar was produced in Cochin China by free labor and at half the cost. Not only was no industry of enough importance to justify a violation of the "laws of justice and humanity," but: "Liberty and property form the basis of abundance, and good agriculture: I never observed it to flourish where those rights of mankind were not firmly established."[16]

The argument that slavery was a Christian institution, not condemned by the Bible, and that importing slaves to America gave them an opportunity to become acquainted with the principles of Christianity, he met on advanced ground. It required courage and independent thinking of a high order to say in 1773: "If it could be proved that no testimony was to be found in the Bible against a practice so pregnant with evils of the most destructive tendency to society, it would be sufficient to overthrow its divine Original."[17] Why? Because "Every prohibition of Covetousness—Intemperance—Pride—Uncleanness—Theft—and Murder, which he delivered—every lesson of meekness, humility, forbearance, charity, self-denial, and brotherly love, which he taught, are levelled against this evil;—for slavery, while it includes all the former vices, necessarily excludes the practice of all the latter virtues both from the Master and the Slave."[18] Still Rush was not finished, for he said: "Christianity will never be propagated by any other methods than those employed by Christ and his Apostles. Slavery is an engine as little fitted for that purpose as Fire or

the Sword. A Christian slave is a contradiction in terms."[19] He spoke of the terrible atrocities in Africa occasioned by our demand for slaves, of the unbearable suffering of separations from homeland, friends, and loved ones, of the cruel loss of life in the crossing, of brandings and whippings and maimings, without law and without justice. This was a diagnosis—clear, concise, complete.

What should be done about it? How should we go about getting rid of slavery? Stop importing slaves. Petition the British government to dissolve the African Company, "an incorporated band of robbers." Retain under our personal care all aged and infirm slaves. Educate the youngsters, train them in some business, put a limit on their period of service, then free them and give them all the privileges of free-born British subjects. This was gradual emancipation—a little more than Pennsylvania shortly did, a little less than the Quakers had done before on a personal basis. Rush was not alone in prophecy, for Americans have always

Benjamin Rush

Benjamin Rush, physician, writer, and renowned humanitarian, was a close associate of Paine, Adams, and Jefferson.

Samuel Hopkins

been prone to say that evil will befall the unrepentant, but his words might still be dwelt upon with profit: "National crimes require national punishments, and without declaring what punishment awaits this evil, you may assure them, that it cannot pass with impunity, unless God shall cease to be just or merciful."[20]

Then came the first important contribution of the Congregationalists. Samuel Hopkins, close associate of Jonathan Edwards, and pastor of the First Congregational Church of Newport, Rhode Island, who had many slaveholders in his congregation, published *A Dialogue, Concerning the Slavery of Africans*. Hopkins painted a picture of the African slave trade with bold strokes as a background for his discussion and called it a "scene of inhumanity, oppression, and cruelty, exceeding everything of the kind that has ever been perpetrated by the sons of men."[21] He dwelt on the scenes of war, death, and destruction in the heart of Africa, on the purchases at the seaports, the brandings, the terrors of the passage across, the 30,000 deaths each year from the process of acclimatization, the brutal whippings, the atrocious punishment—from all of which the slave had no appeal save to merciful death. There was no essential difference between what went on in Africa, on the high seas, and in America—

all of it was a flagrant violation of the laws of God, and there was "a palpable inconsistency in resolving to import and buy no more slaves; and yet refusing to let those go out free, which we have already enslaved, unless there be some insuperable impediment in the way."[22]

The argument that we were bringing the slaves from a heathen land to places of gospel light was ridiculous. First, because the slave country was far from qualifying, and second, because the slaves were denied both mental and moral instruction, were deprived of their freedom by Christians, and were brutally treated by Christians. They could hardly be expected, therefore, to be receptive to the religion of their oppressors. Then Hopkins got to a discussion of what had been only hinted at by others. We talked of not knowing how to go about freeing the slaves. If they were our own children, we would quickly enough find a way. We simply were not concerned about the slaves: "The reason is obvious. Tis because they are Negroes, and fit for nothing but slaves; and we have been used to look on them in a mean, contemptible light; and our education has filled us with strong prejudices against them, and led us to consider them, not as our brethren, or any degree on a level with us; but as quite another species of animals, made only to serve us and our children; and as happy in bondage, as in any other state."[23]

Slaveholders were so conditioned to the ordinary restraints and harshness toward slaves that they were utterly incapable of judging their own treatment. What to them appeared kindness would, to the disinterested observer, be cruelty. As for the slave: "A state of slavery has a mighty tendency to sink and contract the minds of men, and prevent their making improvements in useful knowledge of every kind . . . And shall we because we have reduced them to this abject, helpless, miserable state, by our oppression of them, make this an argument for continuing them and their children in this wretched condition?"[24]

Woolman had breathed the spirit of the New Testament; Hopkins spoke of the Old Testament. His references were to Isaiah, and Jeremiah, and Ezekiel: "Wash you, make you clean; put away the evil of your doings from before mine eyes; seek judgment, relieve the oppressed, judge the fatherless, plead for the widow.[25]

"For if ye thoroughly amend your ways and your doings; if ye thoroughly execute judgment

THE AMERICAN DECLARATION OF INDEPENDENCE ILLUSTRATED.

between a man and his neighbor; if ye oppress not the stranger, the fatherless, and the widow, and shed not innocent blood in this place, neither walk after other gods to your hurt; Then will I cause you to dwell in this place, in the land that I gave to your fathers, for ever and ever."[26]

"The people of the land have used oppression, and exercised robbery, and have vexed the poor and needy; yea, they have oppressed the stranger wrongfully. Therefore have I poured out mine indignation upon them; I have consumed them with the fire of my wrath; their own way have I recompensed upon their heads, saith the Lord God."[27]

Hopkins' *Dialogue* was published in 1776. This was the year of declared independence. Everyone was familiar with George Mason's Declaration of Rights and Thomas Jefferson's Declaration of Independence. It would have been strange indeed if Hopkins had received much of a hearing amid such distinguished competitors for attention. Later, his book was circulated widely. At the moment, the struggle for political rights of Americans versus the British government was reaching a critical stage. Political leaders had taken a position beyond the point of no return. Many of them were as much opposed to slavery as they were to British tyranny. They were conscious, too, of the inconsistency of the American position in fighting for their own rights while retaining hundreds of thousands of people in abject slavery, and of the need for doing something about it.

The Continental Congress, October 20, 1774, adopted "The Association" which included the clause: "We will neither import nor purchase, any slave imported after the first day of December next; after which time, we will wholly discontinue the slave trade, and we will neither be concerned in it ourselves, nor will we hire our vessels, nor sell our commodities or manufactures to those who are concerned in it." Phillips called

this "mainly a political stroke against the British government," but it was more than that. Too much had been said about the trade, and too many colonies had tried to abolish importations, to disregard the widespread opposition to slavery embodied in the declaration.

More important over the long view, however, were the classic statements of natural rights of the period, and the various charges made against the British by the Congress. Natural rights of man, as we shall see, meant to people of the revolutionary and postrevolutionary periods what divine law had meant in the earlier period. The merger of the two is clearly revealed in the statement of a great preacher before a constitutional convention in 1792: "Human legislatures should remember that they act in subordination to the great Ruler of the universe, have no right to . . . enact laws contrary to his . . . cannot make that right which he has made wrong . . . and thereby set free the people from their obligations to obey the laws of nature."[28]

The more immediate development, however, was the formulation by political leaders of many public statements which were turned against them by the opponents of slavery. In 1783 David Cooper, a friend of Benezet from Woodbury, New Jersey, published the next important antislavery pamphlet after that of Hopkins. He used the pseudonym "A Farmer," and *A Serious Address to the Rulers of America, on the Inconsistency of Their Conduct Respecting Slavery* was long thought to have been written by John Dickinson.[29]

Cooper quoted the opening statement of the Declaration of the Causes and Necessity of Taking Up Arms, July 6, 1775: "If it was possible for men, who exercise their reason to believe that the divine Author of our existence intended a part of the human race to hold an absolute property in, and an unbounded power over others . . . the inhabitants of these colonies might at least require from the parliament of Great Britain some evidence that this dreadful authority over them has been granted to that body."[30] He quoted the same document in which, speaking of Howe's conduct in Boston, the Congress said: "By this perfidity, wives are separated from their husbands, children from their parents, the aged and sick from their relations and friends, who wish to attend and comfort them."[31] He quoted the statements regarding natural rights in the Declaration of Independence, in the Pennsylvania Declaration of Rights (July 15, 1776), and in the Massachusetts Declaration of Rights (Sept. 1, 1779), and other documents of the Congress. He compared these statements by which we justified our cause to the rest of the world, and ended with this terrible indictment:

"If neither the voice of *justice,* the dictates of *humanity,* the rights of human nature, and establishment of impartial liberty now in your power, the good of your country, nor the fear of an avenging God, can restrain your hand from this impious practice of holding your fellow men in slavery . . . then let justice, humanity, advocates for liberty, and the sacred name of Christians, cease to be the boast of American rulers."[32]

It is a singular fact that a great many learned men in England thought that slavery had been abolished in America by the Declaration of Independence. William Agutter of St. Mary Magdalen College said before the Corporation of the City of Oxford, in 1788: "The Western Empire is gone from us, never to return; it is given to another more righteous than we; who consecrated the sword of resistance by declaring for the universal abolition of slavery"; and he specifically called attention to the words of the Declaration "we hold these truths to be self evident. That all men are created equal and endowed by their Creator with certain inalienable rights. That among these are life, liberty, and the pursuit of happiness."[33]

H Stands for **Harvest.** We reap as we sow:
    If thistles you plant, do you know what will grow?
Enlarge your plantations, and multiply slaves,
Till luxury gets what it wrongfully craves,—
Yet woe be to *him* who the inquiry scorns,
Do grapes grow on brambles or figs upon thorns?
Consider it well, ere the summer be past,
And the harvest be ended, with gloom at the last·
And ever this adage in memory keep,
Who sows to the wind, of the whirlwind shall reap.

The evils of Slavery to the *white* race, in a material sense, are clearly shown by statistics; but no one can reckon the low estate of education, religion, and morals, especially in the country-districts of the South. The larger the plantations are, the wider is the space between the white families; and an increase of the number of slaves, is no increase of exalting social intercourse. The mansion cannot escape the malaria of the hovels, nor can any one escape the just judgment of the Almighty.

A page from Gray's *Gospel of Slavery*.

IMPACT OF THE REVOLUTION

Chapter 3

The American Revolution is one of the great events in man's long struggle to be free. It has many facets. For instance, one may look at the developing system of liberal ideas in England and America in the eighteenth century with their concepts of a fundamental law, the social compact, and the natural rights of man, or at the manner in which the English colonies in the same period became a haven of refuge for all who sought freedom—English Puritans, Dutch Reformers, Scotch Presbyterians, German Lutherans, French Huguenots, Quakers, Anglicans, Jews—or at the leveling processes of frontier life which made these divers groups one people, strongly individualistic but strongly democratic in the broadest sense of the term, or at the principles immortalized in those two incomparable charters of Western liberalism —the Declaration of Independence, and the Virginia Declaration of Rights—or at the manner in which the Revolution here implemented and inspired the revolutions in France and in Latin America.

Everyone is familiar with the far-reaching domestic reforms initiated by the Revolution: breaking up landed estates and abolition of quitrents, revision of cruel criminal codes, separation of state and church, abolition of primogeniture and entail and of imprisonment for debt, ultimate adoption of universal manhood suffrage, equal division of estates, bankruptcy laws, and free public schools. In fact, most of the inequalities, class distinctions, and injustices based upon the idea of biological inequality were abolished out-

right before the Revolution had run its course. How, then, did slavery, most monstrous of all evil institutions, survive? The melancholy answer is, exactly the way it survived the impact of Christianity! Local communities made a mockery of the natural rights philosophy just as they had of the social teachings of Jesus.

The Declaration of Independence was a statement of principles upon which this nation was established. It states the case for freedom with the utmost clarity. We glean from it and from the many other documents and speeches and writings of the founding fathers, certain basic ideas. Among them are four which are singularly pertinent to the question of slavery: Natural law is unchangeable and everlasting, and the natural rights of man are above the power of government to destroy or deny. All men are equal in their natural endowment of rights. Governments derive their authority from the people, and their primary purpose is to make these natural rights of men more secure, and to protect the individual in their enjoyment. All citizens, therefore, are entitled to equality under the law and in the administration of justice. A great jurist could have started with these principles and abolished slavery. John Marshall started with less in some of his greatest decisions, but John Marshall was more interested in property rights than in human rights, and, instead of building a case for freedom based on the natural rights of man, in his declining years he prevented the adoption of universal manhood suffrage and emancipation of the slaves in Virginia. Such was not true of another renowned magistrate who was both wise and just—Chief Justice William Cushing of Massachusetts.

The number of slaves and free Negroes in the population of the colonies had increased markedly between 1715 and 1776, but no where did it approach equality with the white population except in the tobacco and cotton-rice growing areas of Virginia, South Carolina, and Georgia.[1] It has been said many times that the New England states abolished slavery because it was not profitable in that area. That is a most superficial interpretation. At no time in the long struggle for emancipation was the economic motive dominant, and more times than not men acted directly contrary to their economic interests. It is not even correct to say the Southern states did not abolish slavery because slavery was profitable with them. It is correct to say Negroes were a very much smaller part of the population in the northern area than in the southern area: 1.4 per cent in Massachusetts, 6.3 per cent in Rhode Island, 7.6 per cent in New York, as compared with 43 per cent in South Carolina in 1790. Comparative statistics would indicate that an all free Negro population might well have been thought to be of manageable proportions in the one area and to present insurmountable difficulties in the other. Actually, however, it is very clear that there never was a remote possibility of slavery surviving anywhere north of Maryland and Virginia, that this would have been true had the slave population been much larger than it actually was, that there was strong antislavery sentiment in Virginia, but very little in South Carolina, and there was not that much difference in the percentage of Negroes in the populations of the two states at the close of the Revolution.

Five of the original thirteen states—New Hampshire, Massachusetts, Connecticut, Rhode Island, Pennsylvania—initiated programs of complete emancipation before the federal Constitutional Convention met in 1787. The independent state of Vermont did likewise, and New York and New Jersey followed very soon. These states abolished the foreign and domestic slave trade. The Congress of the Confederation prohibited the introduction of slaves into the Northwest Territory. Very definite progress was made in improving the status of free Negroes. Power was given to Congress in the Constitution of 1787 to abolish the foreign slave trade, the domestic slave trade, and

George Mason, constitutionalist of first rank, was a Virginia slaveholder who opposed slavery. He wrote the Virginia Declaration of Rights, refused to sign the Constitution because it compromised on slavery, and remained a consistent champion of human rights throughout his life.

slavery in all the territories. To say there was an economic motive back of all of this is sheer nonsense.

Thomas Jefferson said: "The abolition of domestic slavery is the great object of desire in those colonies where it was, unhappily, introduced in their infant state. But previous to the enfranchisement of the slaves we have, it is necessary to exclude all further importations from Africa."[2] In his original draft of the Declaration of Independence, he condemned George III for having "waged cruel war against human nature itself, violating its most sacred rights of life and liberty in the persons of a distant people . . ." He spoke of the slave trade as "piratical warfare" and "execrable commerce"[3] and gave a classic condemnation of slavery itself in his notes on Virginia. Said he, "The whole commerce between master and slave is a perpetual exercise of the most boisterous passions, the most unremitting despotism on the one part, and degrading submissions on the other. Our children see this, and learn to imitate it; for man is an imitative animal . . . The parent storms, the child looks on, catches the lineaments of wrath, puts on the same airs in the circle of smaller slaves, gives a loose to the worst of passions, and thus nursed, educated, and daily exercised in tyranny, cannot but be stamped by it with odious peculiarities."[4] This charge here made by Jefferson that slavery degraded the manners and morals of the slaveholding whites later aroused the most violent rejoinders when made by antislavery people. Jefferson went even farther, and with obvious reference to insurrections said: "Indeed I tremble for my country when I reflect that God is just; that his justice cannot sleep forever . . . The Almighty has no attributes which can take sides with us in such a contest."[5]

Turning to the author of the other foremost charter of Western liberalism, George Mason, we encounter the same attitude toward slavery. Mason, says his biographer, "more than perhaps any other American statesman of the period . . . represented the rationalist spirit, the Enlightenment in its American manifestation."[6] In the Constitutional Convention, he said: "Slavery discourages arts and manufactures. The poor despise labor when performed by slaves. They [slaves] prevent the immigration of whites, who really enrich and strengthen a country. They produce a pernicious effect on manners. Every master of slaves is born a petty tyrant. They bring the judgment of heaven on a country."[7] He refused to sign the Constitution because it compromised on the slave trade, and in the Virginia ratifying convention, speaking of the clause allowing importations for twenty years, he said: "Under the royal government, this evil was looked upon as a great oppression, and many attempts were made to prevent it . . . It was one of the great causes of our separation from Great Britain. Its exclusion has been a principal object of this state and most of the states in the Union. The augmentation of slaves weakens the states; and such a trade is diabolical in itself and disgraceful to mankind . . . As much as I value a union of all the states, I would not admit the Southern States into the Union unless they agree to the discontinuance of this disgraceful trade, because it would bring weakness, and not strength, to the Union."[8]

Jefferson's and Mason's positions on the question were not different from those of lesser men of distinction. Gouverneur Morris of Pennsylvania, in the Constitutional Convention, called slavery a "nefarious institution . . . the curse of Heaven on the state where it prevailed", and he spoke of the slave trade as "a defiance of the most sacred laws of humanity."[9] Luther Martin, of Maryland, declared the constitutional provision allowing

continued importation of slaves "inconsistent with the principles of the Revolution and dishonorable to the American character."[10] James Madison found prevailing opinion so abhorrent to an admission in the Constitution that there could be property in man that he had no difficulty in keeping the words "slave" and "slavery" out of it.

One cannot place too much emphasis upon the attitudes of these men toward slavery. Jefferson, Mason, and Madison made the finest contributions to political literature ever produced in this country. Their writings cannot be said ever to have been surpassed, nor their influence in developing constitutionalism, nor their actual services in public office. They did not come from New England where slaves were few. They represented Virginia, where slaves at this particular time constituted about as large a proportion of the population as they did in South Carolina and Georgia. Morris, actually a New Yorker, his colleague John Jay, and Luther Martin, all represented large slaveholding constituencies. All of them, too, and the trio of Virginians, represented the widespread desire to rid the country of slavery, a desire admirably expressed by Judge St. George Tucker of Williamsburg, who said: "The introduction of slavery into this country is at this day considered among its greatest misfortunes by a very great majority of those who are reproached for an evil which the present generation could no more have avoided than an hereditary gout or leprosy."[11]

One of the earliest manifestations of antislavery sentiment was the opposition to the African slave trade. Not everyone opposed to importations was hostile to slavery. Some were afraid the slave population was becoming too large; some feared introductions of uncivilized Negroes from Africa; and some wanted to protect the value of their slave property against depreciation by oversupply. Several colonies had attempted to prohibit further importations by commercial traders by law, or to accomplish the same objective by prohibitory duties. All such legislation had been vetoed by the royal governors on specific instructions from England or had been disallowed by the Privy Council.[12] Just as soon as English authority was denied, there was a revival of this type of legislation. Virginia stopped all importations in 1778 with 1000-pound fines and freedom for all slaves brought illegally into the state. Maryland stopped them in 1783. North Carolina imposed prohibitive duties in 1786. South Carolina forbade importations between 1787 and 1803.

One may well ask, how much of the impulse for this legislation came from the belief that the trade must be stopped as the first step in a program of emancipation? To what degree was it part and parcel of an emancipation movement? Opposition to slavery was the dominant motive in the northern states, and it certainly was a very powerful factor in Virginia and Maryland. Even recognizing that those states stood to gain by supplanting Africa as the source of supply for the cotton states, they could not have anticipated the invention of the cotton gin, nor have expected much of a market in view of existing economic conditions. Nevertheless, these states only prohibited importation of slaves from Africa and not export of slaves for sale—not then, or ever—and there is a vast difference between prohibiting commercial imports and prohibiting exports or, more important, prohibiting citizens from engaging in buying or selling in any manner whatsoever.

The manner in which states abolished slavery during the Revolutionary period is of major importance because of later political and legal contests over the status of slavery under the Constitution. Anyone with more than a superficial knowledge of American history knows the Southern claim that slaves were property based in the common law; that the definition of property is an exercise of sovereign power; that the most sovereign body in our governmental system is a state constitutional convention; therefore, that slavery could be abolished only by a state constitutional convention and was lawful wherever it had not been so prohibited. Slaveholders insisted that, wherever slavery had been abolished in the original states, it had been done by constitutional provision or by judicial interpretation of constitutions. This was only partially true as to procedure, and ignores completely the principles embraced within these expositions of fundamental law.

The first state to abolish slavery was Vermont. Its action was simple and direct. New Hampshire Grants, in 1777, held a revolutionary convention, established the Republic of Vermont, and embarked upon an independent career. The other states, fearful of offending New Hampshire and New York, excluded her from the Confederation and then from the Union until 1791; but none attempted to interfere with her freedom of action. The Constitution of this new state contained the

general proposition: "No male person, born in this country, or brought from over sea, ought to be holden by law, to serve any person, as a servant, slave, or apprentice, after he arrives at the age of twenty-one years, nor female in like manner, after she arrives to the age of eighteen years, unless they are bound by their own consent, after they arrive at such age, or bound by law, for the payment of debts, damages, fines, costs, and the like."[13] This clause in the Bill of Rights was accepted by the people generally as inaugurating gradual emancipation and was held by the Supreme Court of the state in 1802 to have abolished slavery.[14] In 1786, to prevent former owners from carrying off their former slaves and disposing of them outside the state, the legislature passed a kidnapping law imposing a fine of one hundred pounds upon anyone convicted of interfering with a legally free Negro.[15] This was included later among the rigid personal liberty laws of the state.

It is now necessary to quote from the Declaration of Rights of Virginia, written by George Mason, because it was drawn upon by Jefferson in the Declaration of Independence, and is strongly reflected in the Bill of Rights of Massachusetts and New Hampshire. It was rewritten, in a very practical way into the Bill of Rights of the Federal Constitution, and strongly influenced the French Revolution. Mason said in the Virginia Bill of Rights, June 12, 1776: "That all men are by nature equally free and independent, and have certain inherent rights, of which, when they enter into a state of society, they cannot by any compact deprive or divest their posterity; namely, the enjoyment of life and liberty, with the means of acquiring and possessing property, and pursuing and obtaining happiness and safety." Jefferson said in the Declaration of Independence, July 4, 1776: "We hold these truths to be self-evident, that all men are created equal, that they are endowed by their Creator, with certain inalienable Rights, that among these are Life, Liberty, and the pursuit of Happiness."

The Bill of Rights of the Constitution of Massachusetts, adopted by popular vote in 1780, contained the following clause: "All men are born free and equal, and have certain natural, essential, and inalienable rights; among which may be reckoned the right of enjoying and defending their lives and liberties; that of acquiring, possessing, and protecting property; in fine that of seeking and obtaining their safety and happiness."[16] Finally, the New Hampshire Constitution of 1784 contained a Bill of Rights which said: "All men are born equally free and independent; therefore, all government of right originates from the people, is founded in consent and instituted for the general good. All men have certain natural, essential, and inherent rights; among which are—the enjoying and defending life and liberty—acquiring, possessing and protecting property—and in a word, of seeking and obtaining happiness."[17]

Defense of slavery in any manner, shape, or form was a contemptuous defiance of all of these historic documents, three of which provided the bases and foundations of governments of great states, the other the basic principles on which all government in the United States rested, and one of the four the basis for the Bill of Rights of the federal Constitution. What the courts did with the clause in the Massachusetts Constitution, the courts of Virginia could have done with the clause in that state's Declaration of Rights, and the Supreme Court of the United States could have done with the clause in the Declaration of Independence and the Bill of Rights. What the courts did in Massachusetts was to abolish slavery. There is no court case of record involving slavery in New Hampshire after her constitution was adopted, but there may have been a case because printed reports in that state did not begin until 1816. The United States Census shows 157 slaves in 1790, and only eight in 1800. This would indicate a general acceptance of the Constitution as abolishing slavery, or complete agreement with the principles of the Constitution and manumission of all slaves by voluntary action.[18]

The state of Massachusetts followed a pattern of emancipation that could have been and should have been used to abolish slavery completely in the country. There were court cases in the colony as early as 1766 certainly, and perhaps many years before that date, in which Negroes successfully brought suits for freedom (actions of trespass) against their masters.[19] The presumption is strong, however, that the legality of slavery was not the issue in any of these cases, but rather the status of the *particular person* claimed as a slave. No decision of the courts undertook to decide the question of the legality of slavery; and, it is quite possible, in some if not in all such cases, the owners were as anxious to rid themselves of aged,

infirm, or incompetent slaves as the slaves were to attain freedom. Successful suit by the slave was less likely to entail financial responsibility for maintenance on the part of the former owner than was voluntary manumission.[20]

The Assembly of the state undertook to write a constitution itself in 1778, without calling a convention, and submitted the results of its work to the voters for approval. It contained no Bill of Rights, and it recognized slavery and excluded Negroes from the franchise. The voters rejected it. A Constitutional Convention then was called, and the second constitution with a Bill of Rights containing the clause patterned after Mason's Declaration of Rights was adopted by popular vote.[21]

Three years after the adoption of the constitution an interesting case came before the Supreme Court of the state. A man named Quaco Walker, held as a slave by Nathaniel Jennison, was severely beaten by his owner. He ran away, sought refuge with a neighbor of Jennison's, and was hired to work by his protector. Jennison sued the new employer for enticing his slave and lost his case. Criminal action finally was brought for assault and battery and false imprisonment against Jennison, who insisted Walker was his slave and subject to correction at the discretion of his owner.

William Cushing, former member of the Constitutional Convention of Massachusetts, was chief justice of the state Supreme Court. There is no question of his stature as a jurist. He was the first associate justice appointed by President Washington to the United States Supreme Court. He acted as chief justice of the United States when John Jay was absent in England (1794). He was appointed chief justice of the United States as Jay's successor but declined the post for reasons of health. In this case, *Commonwealth v. Jennison* (1783), Chief Justice Cushing, speaking for the Supreme Court of Massachusetts, declared slavery contrary to the fundamental law of the state. Said Cushing: "As to the doctrine of slavery and the right of Christians to hold Africans in perpetual servitude, and sell and treat them as we do our horses and cattle, that . . . has been hertofore countenanced by the Province Laws . . . a different idea has taken place with the people of America more favorable to the natural rights of mankind, and to that natural, innate desire of Liberty, with which Heaven . . . has inspired all the human race. And upon this ground our Constitution of Government, by which the people of this Commonwealth have solemnly bound themselves, sets out with declaring that all men are born free and equal—and that every subject is entitled to liberty, and to have it guarded by the laws, as well as life and property—in short is totally repugnant to the idea of being born slaves . . . the idea of slavery is inconsistent with our own conduct and Constitution; and there can be no such thing as perpetual servitude of a rational creature, unless his liberty is forfeited by some criminal conduct or given up by personal consent or contract."[22] This decision was accepted by the people of the state as abolishing slavery. No slaves were reported in the first federal Census of 1790.

The historic case of *Commonwealth* v. *Jennison* (1783) would not be complete without reference to *Commonwealth* v. *Aves* (1836). The system of reporting court decisions had not been perfected at the time of the earlier case, so Chief Justice Shaw in 1836 did not have it as a precedent, which makes his own conclusions far more revealing of the power of natural rights philosophy. Shaw's reputation, based upon his thirty-year service as chief justice of the state, places him high in the ranks of able magistrates. His biographer says: "Probably no other state judge has so deeply influenced commercial and Constitutional law throughout the nation." Shaw's statement was as follows: "How, or by what act particularly, slavery was abolished in Massachusetts, whether by the adoption of the opinion in Sommersett's case, as a declaration and modification of the common law, or by the Declaration of Independence, or by the Constitution of 1780, it is not now very easy to determine, and it is rather a matter of curiosity than utility; being agreed on all hands, that if not abolished before, it was so by the declaration of rights."[23]

There is not much question but that Shaw believed slavery in Massachusetts could have been abolished by the Declaration of Independence, or by court acceptance of the principles of the Sommersett case. It is unfortunate that we do not have some exposition of his views along those lines. Like Chief Justice Cushing, he accepted fully the thesis that a constitution is a fundamental law and can be enforced by the courts without sustaining legislation, and acted upon it. The Court took this position again in 1856, in the case of *Parsons* v. *Trask,* when it said the first article of the Declaration of Rights not only abolished slavery "but rendered every form of it thereafter legally impossible. That article has always been regarded not simply as the declaration of an abstract principle, but as having the active force and conclusive authority of law."[24]

The colonial assembly of Massachusetts had passed an act in 1774 to prevent the importation of slaves into the province, but both Governor Hutchinson and his successor, Governor Gage, refused to sign such measures as contrary to their instructions. Finally, in 1788, having abolished slavery, the Assembly forbade all citizens of Mas-

Always a slave! Never a man!

sachusetts to engage in buying, selling, or transporting slaves, declared insurance void on all ships used in violation of the law, and imposed heavy fines upon anyone convicted of kidnapping free Negroes.[25]

Rhode Island, having almost as high a percentage of slaves in the population as New York and New Jersey, though far less in actual numbers, and more deeply involved in the African slave trade than any other state, took the first feeble action against slavery in 1774. The Act of that year was an amiable recognition of revolutionary philosophy, if little more. It stated in the preamble that since "the inhabitants of America are generally engaged in the preservation of their own rights and liberties, among which, that of personal freedom must be considered as the greatest; as those who are desirous of enjoying all the advantages of liberty themselves should be willing to extend personal liberty to others."[26] It was intended to prevent slaves from being brought into Rhode Island for sale. Any such were to be free and the

person responsible to be subject to one hundred pounds fine for each violation. Persons coming into the colony, either as visitors or as permanent residents, might bring their slaves, but must take them away with them. Even ship owners engaged in the African trade, if unable to dispose of a cargo of slaves in the West Indies, might bring them to the colony under bond to remove them within one year.[27] The same year (1774) Connecticut forbade anyone to bring slaves into the Colony "to be disposed of, left, or sold," under penalty of one hundred pounds fine.[28]

Five years later (1779) Rhode Island enacted what must be recognized as antislavery legislation. The law of that year forbade persons not residents of the state to purchase slaves for removal from the state. Any attempt to take a slave from the state without a certificate attesting the slave's consent and signed by two justices of the peace entitled the slave to freedom.[29] Taking slaves away, without their consent, said the law, "to perpetuate their slavery in foreign Parts re-

The crime against motherhood

mote from their Friends and Acquaintances, is against the rights of human nature, and tends greatly to aggravate the Condition of Slavery, which this General Assembly is disposed rather to alleviate, till some favorable Occasion may offer for its total Abolition."

Emancipation came after another five-year interval (1784), and once more the law leaves no doubts of the legislators' sentiments: "All men are entitled to Life, Liberty, and the Pursuit of Happiness, and the holding of Mankind in a state of Slavery, as private Property, which has gradually obtained by unrestrained Custom and Permission of the Laws, is repugnant to the Principle, and subversive of the Happiness of Mankind, and the great End of all civil Government." All children born of slave mothers after March 1, 1784, were to be held as apprentices, males until twenty-one, females until eighteen, then to become free. The children were to go free with the mother should she be manumitted before they reached the specified age.[30]

Connecticut, keeping pace with Rhode Island, also provided for gradual emancipation in 1784. Actually, Connecticut had enacted a law in 1777 which is unique in the history of emancipation and deserved universal attention. When a slaveowner desired to manumit a slave, the selectmen of the town were charged with the responsibility of passing judgment in the case. If they decided, after considering the circumstances, the age and abilities, and the character of the slave, that said slave would be able to make a living and would benefit by manumission, they were to give the owner a certificate freeing the slave and relieving him of further responsibility for the slave's care. A later provision limited such cases to slaves under forty-five years of age.[31] The Act of 1784 gave all children born of slave mothers after May 1, 1784, freedom at age twenty-five. Birth certificates had to be filed by the owners before the child reached six months of age.[32]

Finally, in 1787 Rhode Island forbade citizens of the state to participate in any way in the African slave trade. The penalty for violation was fixed at 100 pounds per slave and 1,000 pounds per ship. The following year (1788) Connecticut forbade all inhabitants of that state to engage directly or indirectly in the African slave trade and imposed a fine of 100 pounds for kidnapping any Negro covered by the provisions of the emancipation act. In 1792 all commercial transactions involving slaves and all movement of slaves, except by slaveowners leaving the state permanently, were forbidden.[33]

The legislature of Pennsylvania, under strong pressure from the Quaker population, passed a gradual emancipation act in 1780. All children born of slave mothers after passage of the act were to have the status of indentured servants. They were to be free if the owner of the mother failed to make public record of their birth. Otherwise, they were to serve until twenty-eight years of age. No Negro over twenty-one could be apprenticed for a longer period than seven years. The law applied to any Negroes brought into the state.[34] The law placed the trials, offenses, and punishments of slaves, servants, and free men, whites and Negroes alike, on the same basis, but forbade the testimony of slaves against free men.[35] All special courts and penalties were abolished, and the law forbidding marriages of Negroes and whites was repealed. Fugitives coming into the state were not protected by the provision of the law. War refugees from other states were allowed by law of 1781 to bring their slaves with them, but they were required to register them, forbidden to sell them, and were required to remove from the state within six months after the cessation of hostilities.[36]

Finally, in 1788 an act was placed on the statute books forbidding citizens of the state to engage either in the foreign slave trade or the coastal slave trade under penalty of loss of ship and 1000 pounds fine. No one coming into the state for permanent residence could bring slaves. No Negro servants or slaves could be taken out of the state without their consent, certified by two justices of the peace, and the consent of parents in case of children. Husbands and wives, either servants or slaves, were not to be separated more than ten miles, and children under four years of age were not to be separated from their mothers. The penalty for kidnapping was fixed at 100 pounds fine and six months at hard labor.[37]

New York did not emancipate until 1799, New Jersey until 1804. As early as 1773 New York declared void fictitious sales of slaves to improvident persons, a device used to escape from the burden of supporting aged or infirm slaves.[38] In 1785 the legislature of the state passed an act for gradual emancipation, which was vetoed by the Council of Revision. The Senate passed it over the veto, but the House failed to do so. However, there was written into law some important legislation respecting slave trading. No slaves could be brought into the state under penalty of 100 pounds fine and freedom for the slaves, and three years later (1788) buying for export from the state was forbidden under the same penalties.[39] Owners wishing to free slaves could do so without giving bond for their care if the overseer of the poor certified the slave to be under fifty years of age and capable of self-support. Slaves were given jury trials in all cases involving the death penalty.[40]

New Jersey in 1786, declaring "the Principles of Justice and Humanity require that the barbarous custom of bringing the unoffending Africans from their native country and Connections into a State of Slavery ought to be discountenanced, and as soon as possible prevented," forbade importations of any slaves from Africa under penalty of 50 pounds. This law permitted persons removing from the state permanently to take their slaves with them, and it also allowed slaveholders to travel through the state with their slaves, but movement of slaves in commerce into and out of the state was forbidden.[41] Two years later (1788) a new law provided for confiscation of ships intended for the slave trade, required permission from a justice of the peace to remove slaves over twenty-one years of age from the state, and required permission of the parents of slaves under twenty-one years of age.[42] The law of 1786 also provided that all criminal offenses by Negroes, slave or free, were to be "enquired of, adjudged, corrected, and punished," in the same manner as if committed by free whites, and provided grand jury investigations and indictments in cases of inhumane treatment or abuse of slaves. The law of 1788 required slaveowners to teach them to read if under twenty-one years of age and provided fines for failure to do so.

Further evidence of the general desire for ultimate abolition of slavery is contained in the action of the Congress of the Confederation with reference to the Northwest Territory. The French had introduced slavery into the Illinois country, and the British had not interfered with it when they took possession in 1764.[43] The region passed under the control of Virginia in 1778, as a result of George Rogers Clark's expedition, and was organized as the County of Illinois, with all religions and civil institutions and property rights then existing in the Illinois country guaranteed to the inhabitants.[44] The British surrendered all claim to the region by the peace treaty of 1783, and Virginia ceded her claims to the United States as the first step in creating a national domain and orderly program of expansion.[45] The Congress then passed the Ordinance of 1785, regulating the survey and sale of public lands, and in 1787 the Northwest Ordinance.

The Northwest Territory was the region north of the Ohio and east of the Mississippi, which eventually became the states of Ohio, Indiana, Illinois, Michigan, Wisconsin, and a part of Minnesota. The Northwest Ordinance was the basic plan for the government of territories and admission of states. It was as much a part of the fundamental law of the land as the Declaration of Independence and the Constitution. The fourth part of the ordinance stated fundamental principles for governing the territory. Freedom of religion was guaranteed and inhabitants were assured of ordinary civil rights, such as jury trial. Education was encouraged, and slavery was prohibited. The major principle established by the ordinance was the equality of the new states with the original thirteen. This principle now seems just and reasonable, but was not the common practice among nations. This ordinance was a bold stroke along new lines; men were building for the future—a future of freedom for all men.

Inspection and sale of a Negro

SLAVERY AND THE CONSTITUTION

Chapter 4

Did the Fathers of the Constitution look to the ultimate abolition of slavery? That question has been asked many times. The only reasonable answer is that they could not have done otherwise. They were men of great intellectual power, of courage, and above all, of integrity. It is unthinkable that they could have forgotten so soon the freedom for which they themselves struggled as to have fastened perpetual slavery on others and their descendants. They had gone too far in endorsing the principles of the Declaration of Rights and Declaration of Independence, too far along the road of emancipation in the several states, to have framed consciously a document incompatible with those principles. They knew that there was an irreconcilable repugnance between the principles under which they had secured independence and the practice of slavery. They sought permanence and stability as a nation in the family of nations. That alone would have impelled them to avoid charges of inconsistency in their conduct. Certainly, old hands at framing constitutions, as these men were, would not have hesitated to use the words slave and slavery in the new instrument of government if they had intended that slavery was to be protected forever by the government they were creating. They did not do so, obviously being restrained by some very strong motive.

Evidence of the strong desire to avoid endorsement, or even recognition, of the right of property in man, is overwhelming. James Iredell, of North Carolina, later Associate Justice of the Supreme Court of the United States and a lead-

ing architect of state rights philosophy, said in the North Carolina ratifying convention: "The northern delegates, owing to their particular scruples on the subject of slavery did not choose the word slave to be mentioned."[1] Roger Sherman, of Connecticut, the only man to sign the Articles of Association, the Declaration of Independence, the Articles of Confederation, and the Constitution, opposed a tax on slaves imported because a tax would imply that they were property.[2] So too did Madison, who thought that allowing twenty years of the slave trade would "be more dishonorable to the American character than to say nothing about it in the Constitution."[3] It is a singular fact that the giants among the members were opposed, as we shall see, to slavery, to the slave trade, to slave representation, and to slavery expansion.

There were three provisions written into the Constitution dealing directly with the subject of slavery, and two others which were of considerable collateral importance. These were: Article I, Section 2, "Representatives and direct taxes shall be apportioned among the several States which may be included within this Union, according to their respective Numbers, which shall be determined by adding to the whole Number of free Persons, including those bound to Service for a term of Years, and excluding Indians not taxed, three fifths of all other Persons"; Article IV, Section 2, "No Person held to service or Labour in one State, under the Laws thereof, escaping into another, shall, in Consequence of any Law or Regulation therein, be discharged from such

Roger Sherman

Service or Labour, but shall be delivered up on Claim of the Party to whom such Service or Labour may be due"; and Article I, Section 9, "The Migration or Importation of such Persons as any of the States now existing shall think proper to admit, shall not be prohibited by the Congress prior to the Year one thousand eight-hundred and eight; but a tax or duty may be imposed on such importation, not exceeding ten dollars for each Person." Two other clauses, indirectly touching slavery, were vitally important: Article I, Section 8, "The Congress shall have power . . . to regulate Commerce with foreign nations, and among the several States, and with the Indian Tribes"; and Article IV, Section 3, "The Congress shall have power to dispose of and make all needful Rules and Regulations respecting the Territory or other Property belonging to the United States."

The fatal error so far as the opponents of slavery were concerned was in adopting, early in the Convention, the three-fifths rule. This clause, ap-

portioning direct taxes and representation on the basis of population, to be determined by adding three-fifths of the slaves to the total number of free persons, was just about as confusing to some members of the conventions as it is to us today. No other provision comparable to it in its evil consequences has ever been proposed, let alone written into our governmental system. Actually, it had a historical basis. By resolution of September 6, 1774, the Congress of the Confederation had adopted a method of voting by states, each state having one vote. It knew the method to be improper, inequitable, and unjust, according to the testimony of James Wilson: but, as Congress said in its own defense, it was not "possessed of, or at present able to procure, materials for ascertaining the importance of each colony."[4] Population data, for example, were almost totally absent. The difficulties of Congress did not end there because, among other things, the Articles of Confederation provided that contributions of the several states to the general treasury should be in proportion to land values and other enumerated property, and there were no data pertaining to assessed valuations. The system proved unworkable, and Congress (1783) recommended "in conformity with the powers they possessed under the Articles of Confederation, that the quota (of each state) should be according to the number of free people, including those bound to servitude, and excluding Indians not taxed." Eleven of the thirteen states approved the recommendation, and the Convention adopted it into the Constitution.

Taxation and representation were tied together, therefore, by the Constitutional Convention for a very obvious reason. Men who were consciously trying to avoid the slightest recognition of property in man, and insisting on every occasion that slaves were persons, could present little argument against all of them being counted in apportioning representation. Slaveholders argued for that, but they, in turn, were in a difficult position in the matter of taxation on the basis of population. The three-fifths rule in each case was thought to be an equitable compromise. Not everyone agreed by any means. Gouverneur Morris, in a slashing, bitter attack on slavery, asked some pertinent questions: "Upon what principle is it that the slaves shall be computed in the representation? Are they men? Then make them citizens, and let them vote. Are they property? Why, then, is no other property included?" Then he went to the heart of the matter with an observation which proved to be correct, but the correctness of which few men were prepared to admit at that time: "Let it not be said that direct taxation is to be proportioned to representation. It is idle to suppose that the general government can stretch its hand directly into the pockets of the people scattered over so vast a country. They can only do it through the medium of exports, imports, and excises."[5]

Endless strife was to flow from this compromise. Morris was correct. Direct taxes were not levied, and the three-fifths rule in representation gave to the slave states through the years a voting power in the House of Representatives and in the Electoral College far beyond that to which their free population entitled them. It was a moral question, as well as a practical political one, because, as Morris said, "the inhabitant of Georgia and South Carolina, who goes to the coast of Africa, and, in defiance of the most sacred laws of humanity, tears away his fellow creatures from the dearest connections, and damns them to the most cruel bondage, shall have more votes, in a government instituted for the protection of the rights of mankind, than the citizen of Pennsylvania or New Jersey, who views, with a laudable horror, so nefarious a practice."[6]

The real significance of what happened here, however, goes far beyond the evil of representation of persons—even great numbers of persons—who had no will of their own. This clause was adopted early in the proceedings of the Convention. It had a direct bearing upon the settlement of other matters of first magnitude, touching upon slavery still to be considered.

The Convention wanted to abolish slavery, but it could not risk, or thought it could not risk, losing ratification by the cotton states of Georgia and South Carolina by outright emancipation of the slaves. Exclusion of slavery from the territories, however, coupled with prohibition of the foreign slave trade and the internal slave trade, would prevent the spread of slavery and the admission of any more slave states. Slavery was promptly excluded from all of the territory under control of the federal government, while the Convention was still in session. The clause in the Northwest Ordinance excluding it was written by a member of the Convention, Rufus King of Massachusetts, and was presented in Congress by King's colleague in Congress while King was in the conven-

James Wilson

tion at Philadelphia. All that was then needed was to cut off the importation of slaves from Africa, but the three-fifths rule destroyed all possibility of ending the foreign slave trade at once.

Slavery, horrible everywhere, was unspeakably cruel in the most southern area. The loss of life was terrific and foreign importations were regarded the only effectual means of replacing the losses. There were some hard-headed, very able, but very practical men in the Convention from these states. They were aristocrats, firmly convinced that only persons of African descent could safely cultivate their crops, either blind to the truths of the Declaration, or quite willing to explain them away, and more interested in protecting the interests of their area than in promoting the national interest. Charles Cotesworth Pinckney said in the South Carolina Convention: "While there remained one acre of swampland uncleared in South Carolina, I would raise my voice against restricting the importation of negroes. I am as thoroughly convinced as that gentleman is, that the nature of our climate, and the flat, swampy situation of our country, obliges us to cultivate our lands with negroes, and that with-

Stowing the cargo on a slaver at night

Cruelty at its worst was the dominant note when slave ships rode the waves. Thousands died in the holds of ships. All were expendable.

out them South Carolina would soon be a desert waste."[7] Here was one point in the emerging, historic positive-good argument in defense of slavery. The American South must have slave labor.

What of the principle involved? John Dickinson of Delaware "considered it as inadmissible on every principle of honor and safety, that the importation of slaves should be authorized to the states by the Constitution. The true question was whether the national happiness would be promoted or impeded by the importation; and the question ought to be left to the national government, not to the states particularly interested."[8] Time after time in the long struggle here begun and extending over nearly two centuries, the principle stated was to be trampled underfoot. The idea that freedom could be preserved only by reverent maintenance of decentralization, respect for state rights, and local control of all matters intimately touching the lives of the people showed remarkable longevity. It was, and is, a delusion of first magnitude, growing out of the lack of communication between the colonies and a remote central government in England, but due to the lack of equitable representation in that government. Actually, decentralization has meant oppression for minorities, and the appeal to state rights has always been contrary to the national interest and more often than not for an evil purpose.

John Rutledge of South Carolina said: "Religion and humanity had nothing at all to do with this question. Interest alone is the governing principle with nations. The true question at present is, whether the southern states shall or shall not be parties to the Union."[9] He then went on to say: "If the Convention thinks that North Carolina, South Carolina, and Georgia, will ever agree to the plan [of union], unless their right to import slaves be untouched, the expectation is vain. The people of those states will never be such fools as to give up so important an interest."[10]

The interest he was talking about may have been economic, and it may have been, certainly was to a large extent, political. Gouverneur Morris was keenly aware of this and openly charged that the Southern states would increase their slave imports, encouraged to do so *by an assurance of having their votes in the national government increased in proportion.*[11] Luther Martin and Rufus King both dwelt on this point, and Edmund Randolph of Virginia said he would rather "risk the Constitution" than agree to it.[12] The men

from the lower South were not disposed to debate the issue on the basis of representation, preferring to keep the discussion on economic grounds, but they added a second point to the emerging positive-good argument. Said Charles Pinckney: "If slavery be wrong, it is justified by the example of the world . . . In all ages, one half of mankind have been slaves. If the Southern States were let alone, they will probably of themselves stop importations . . . An attempt to take away the right, as now proposed, will produce serious objections to the Constitution, which he wished to see adopted."[13] Charles Cotesworth Pinckney "thought himself bound to declare candidly, that he did not think South Carolina would stop her importations of slaves in any short time; but only stop them occasionally, as she now does."[14] James Wilson, undeceived by Pinckney's argument, insisted that "if South Carolina and Georgia were themselves disposed to get rid of the importation of slaves in a short time, as had been suggested, they would never refuse to unite because the importation might be prohibited."[15]

George Mason, constantly pressing his fight against slavery, insisted that the entire western country would fill with slaves if they could be secured from Africa through South Carolina and Georgia, that importation and migration of slaves would prevent the emigration of white settlers, that an increase of slaves in the southern area would constitute a dangerous national weakness, an ever-present invitation to invasion, and that slavery produced a pernicious effect on manners.[16] Gouverneur Morris concurred in the dangerous character of slavery with regard to possible insurrections and invasions. "Compare," he said, "the free regions of the Middle States, where a rich and noble cultivation marks the prosperity and happiness of the people, with the misery and poverty which overspread the barren wastes of Virginia, Maryland, and the other states having slaves. Travel through the whole Continent, and you behold the prospect continually varying with the appearance and disappearance of slavery."[17]

Why, then, did a Convention in which the opponents of slavery and the slave trade included Rufus King, Roger Sherman, Gouverneur Morris, Luther Martin, James Wilson, John Dickinson, Edmund Randolph, George Mason, Benjamin Franklin, and James Madison fail to abolish the foreign slave trade immediately? It was fairly certain that South Carolina and Georgia, perhaps

North Carolina, would not join in the Union unless they could have their own way in the matter; but, even now, we cannot say with absolute certainty that they would not have done so. Moreover, the Convention had power to decide how many states must ratify to put the Constitution into effect, and it probably could have denied to any state freedom of choice with regard to joining or not joining. In short, failure to ratify might not have allowed a state to remain out of the Union. These are all matters on which the historian can make only casual observations.

There are, however, some singular facts. Charles Cotesworth Pinckney gave us a delightful bit of testimony that fits perfectly into Convention records. In the South Carolina ratifying convention, January 17, 1788, he said: "Show us some period, said the members from the Eastern States, when it may be in our power to put a stop, if we please, to the importation of this weakness, and we shall endeavor, for your convenience, to restrain the religious and political prejudices of our people on this subject. The Middle States and Virginia made us no such proposition; they were for an immediate and total prohibition. We endeavored to obviate the objections that were made in the best manner we could . . . A committee of the states was appointed to accommodate this matter, and after a great deal of difficulty, it was settled on the footing recited in the Constitution."[18] Even then a politician could explain a "deal" in a disarming sort of way, and this was a "deal" any way it is viewed, between the New England states and the Southern states—meaning, of course, South Carolina and Georgia.

The draft of the Constitution then being considered contained two clauses of vital concern to the two areas: Article 7, Section 6, "No navigation act shall be passed without the assent of two thirds of the members present in each House"; and Article 7, Section 4, "No tax or duty shall be laid by the legislature on articles exported from any state; nor on the migration or importation of such persons as the several states shall think proper to admit; nor shall such migration or importation be prohibited." South Carolina and Georgia, therefore, were in a strong position. They could refuse to join the Union unless their right to import slaves was granted; they could grow, by slave labor, a great deal more produce for the carrying trade; and they were willing to agree to a grant of ordinary power to control

commerce to the general government in return for the right to import slaves. Debate on these questions of slave imports and navigation acts came to a crisis on Wednesday, August 22, and both were referred to a committee consisting of John Langdon, Rufus King, William S. Johnson, William Livingston, George Clymer, John Dickinson, Luther Martin, James Madison, Hugh Williamson, Charles Cotesworth Pinckney, and Abraham Baldwin.

It was largely due to the slashing attacks of George Mason and Edmund Randolph that the clause allowing unlimited importations of slaves was modified. Judging from the behavior of the men from the Eastern states, it is perfectly clear that they had entered into a bargain. Sherman, Ellsworth, Gerry, and Gouverneur Morris abandoned their strong attacks on slavery. The committee reported out a new provision in the following words, "The migration or importation of such persons as the several states now existing, shall think proper to admit, shall not be prohibited by the legislature prior to the year 1800, but a tax or duty may be imposed on such migration or importation, at a rate not exceeding the average of the duties laid on imports." The following day the date was changed to 1808, and Madison made his famous remark, "So long a term will be more dishonorable to the American character than to say nothing about it in the Constitution." This clause was passed by the affirmative votes of New Hampshire, Massachusetts, Connecticut, Maryland, North Carolina, South Carolina, and Georgia. New Jersey, Pennsylvania, Delaware, and Virginia voted no. Said Charles Cotesworth Pinckney, utterly frank to the end: "It was the true interest of the Southern States to have no regulation of commerce; but, considering the loss brought on the commerce of the Eastern States by the Revolution, their liberal conduct toward the views of South Carolina [he meant the permission to import slaves], and the interest the weak Southern States had in being united with the strong Eastern States, he thought it proper that no fetters should be imposed on the power of making commercial regulations, and that his constituents, though prejudiced against the Eastern States, would be reconciled to their liberality."[19] Having made it perfectly clear to everyone that South Carolina and Georgia were granting a favor, a pure concession, and after a great deal of flattery, the clause, Article 7, Section 6,

"No navigation act shall be passed without the assent of two thirds of the members present in each House" was stricken out. Pierce Butler, of South Carolina, immediately moved to insert the clause providing for rendition of fugitive slaves and it was agreed to without debate.[20]

The clause relative to the slave trade requires analysis. It embraces far more than the foreign slave trade. The Convention would have allowed the trade, both foreign and domestic, to remain untouched if slavery had been thought beneficial. The New England states and Pennsylvania had emancipated their slaves, and all of the states except the Carolinas and Georgia had prohibited the importation of slaves, before the Convention met. Faced with a proposal denying to the gen-

eral government the power to prohibit the importation of slaves, opponents of the institution of slavery threatened to strike out that denial of power and leave the general government free to legislate against it. There is no reason to suppose they would have failed, had the eastern states remained as firm as the middle states on the subject. Even so, in face of a remarkable resort to bargaining and loss of support from those eastern states, the convention acted vigorously against slavery.

They started with these words: "No tax or duty shall be laid by the legislature on articles exported from any state; nor on the migration or importation of such persons as the several states shall think proper to admit; nor shall such migration or which might be created, not the territories, not anywhere *after* twenty years. The very wording of the clause indicates its purpose. Congress was to have power to admit new states. Congress was to have power to govern the territories. Congress was to have power to control interstate commerce. Its power to keep slavery out of the territories, to prevent new slave states, to prohibit the internal slave trade was here doubly reinforced.

Testimony of members of the Convention on this point is indisputable. James Wilson, soul of honor, and unsurpassed even by Madison in thorough understanding of everything done in the Convention, said in the Pennsylvania ratifying convention that since Congress was to have the right of admitting new states into the Union, there would never be another slave state. Speaking of the clause on the foreign trade, he said: "I consider this as laying the foundation for banishing slavery out of this country . . . I am sorry it was not more; but from this I think there is reason to hope, that yet a few years, and it will be prohibited altogether; and in the meantime, the new states which are formed will be under the control of Congress in this particular, and slaves will never be introduced amongst them."[21] General William Heath was even more emphatic in the Massachusetts Convention, saying: "The migration or importation, is confined to the states now *existing only;* new states can not claim it. Congress, by their ordinance for erecting new states, some time since, declared that the new states shall be republican, and that there shall be no slavery in them."[22] Judge Dawes of Massachusetts said, "We may say, that, although slavery is not smitten by an apoplexy, yet it has received a mortal wound and will die of consumption."[23] These remarks show what opinions were entertained by those who helped to frame and ratify the Constitution—men who must be presumed to have had accurate information.[24]

Among the first petitions presented to Congress after the new government got started was one headed by Benjamin Franklin admonishing the members of that body to go to the limits of their authority to give the same freedom to the slaves which they enjoyed. Franklin, next to Washington perhaps, had been the most distinguished member of the Convention and knew Congress had power under the Constitution to end slavery —power, that is, in conjunction with the courts to undermine slavery and destroy it.

Capture of a slaver off the coast of Cuba
The African slave trade never ceased until the Civil War in the United States. It was piracy under the law, but profits were very great.

importation be prohibited." They ended with this peculiar wording, and the changes were made deliberately and for an obvious reason: "The migration or importation of such persons as *any of the states now existing* shall think proper to admit; shall not be prohibited by the Congress *prior to* the year one thousand eight-hundred and eight, but a tax or duty may be imposed on such importation, not exceeding ten dollars for each person." There is not any doubt about the meaning of migration as the word is used in the Constitution. It meant the selling or carrying of slaves to any part of the country where slavery existed. Congress was prohibited to interfere with migrations and importations among the *then existing states* for twenty years, but not any new states

Slavery had been a legal institution in all of the colonies. It had been customary for the owner of a fugitive to recover him without great difficulty. This situation was drastically changed by the Declaration of Independence and events which followed. States at the North moved rapidly in the direction of emancipation, and enacted laws to prevent kidnapping and protect free Negroes. Madison said, in the Virginia Convention called to ratify or reject the Constitution of the Union: "At present, if any slave elopes to any of those states where slaves are free, he becomes emancipated by their laws; for the laws of the states are uncharitable to one another in this respect."[25] He then went on to say of the fugitive slave clause: "This clause was expressly inserted, to enable owners of slaves to reclaim them. This is better security than any that now exists." Charles Cotesworth Pinckney said in the South Carolina Convention: "We have obtained a right to recover our slaves in whatever part of America they may take refuge, which is a right we had not before."[26]

There is no evidence of any controversies over recovery of slaves in colonial times or during the period of the Confederation. The war certainly had greatly disturbed the security of slave property. Large numbers of slaves had been carried away by the British. A considerable number had been freed by the several states in return for military service. War, and revolution, and all the talk about natural rights and freedom were not conducive to stability. There was a general feeling that slavery was coming to its end, and a situation was developing rapidly which demanded rigid precautions against free Negroes being carried off into slavery. But no legal obstacles seem to have been thrown in the way of recovering fugitives. If there had been any such, the debates in the federal Convention and the state conventions would have taken notice of them. The subject, in fact the clause in question, was not mentioned in the papers of the Federalist; nor is it discussed in Madison's voluminous correspondence; nor in any of the plans drawn up previous to the meeting of the Convention. It was not offered in the Convention until August 29, very late in its proceedings, immediately after acceptance of the compromise about importation and migration of slaves and the passing of laws regulating commerce. No remarks were made in relation to it in the Convention before or after it was offered.

It was passed without debate. All of this proves rather conclusively that the matter was regarded as of little importance.

By no stretch of the imagination, then, can it be presumed that the clause gave the power and the responsibility to the general government. The states agreed by this clause to pass no laws by which fugitive slaves coming within their borders would be free. They did not do more than that. On proper application, the slave was to be delivered up to the person authorized to demand him. There was no grant of power to the general government to surrender slaves, and the whole tenor of the proceedings indicates that any effort to put the general government in the slave-catching business would have been summarily and indignantly rejected. There was no agreement that slaves were to be considered property on a par with horses and cattle, and in like manner recovered, because the greatest care had been exercised to refrain from any recognition of property in man. It is absurd to suppose the members would have agreed to the surrender of an alleged fugitive immediately on demand, or without examining testimony as to ownership, or on the simple statement of one person. It is not likely they would knowingly have agreed to the right of the claimant to seize an alleged fugitive without application to law enforcement officials, or to greater haste in procedures than is ordinarily observed in the courts, or to a breach of the peace in the process of recovery. All of this is made clear, as we shall see, by the early court cases.

Adoption of the Constitution automatically broadened the scope of the slavery controversy. Congress, under the Articles of Confederation, had excluded slavery from all the territory under its control. Its powers in this respect had been greatly reinforced by authority to make all needful rules and regulations for the territories, to control interstate commerce, and to regulate the migration of slaves except for twenty years into the existing states. The old Congress had not controlled the lands west of the Alleghenies and south of the Ohio over which the states of Virginia, North Carolina, South Carolina, and Georgia claimed jurisdiction. If and when those states lived up to their agreement to cede whatever claims they possessed to this area and the question of establishing territorial governments or creating states arose, Congress would have to decide for or against slavery expansion.

The general expectation was, in 1787, that there would be no expansion of slavery and little increase in the number of slaves. That is what makes the three-fifths rule stand out as the most fateful blunder of the Convention. Exclusion of slavery from the territories and abolition of the foreign and domestic slave trade were made doubly difficult. Whatever tendency there was for South Carolina and Georgia to stop importations was now reversed. Slavery had suddenly become more than an economic and social system, more than a system of racial adjustment—it was the foundation of political power. Twenty thousand slaveowners of 50,000 slaves would have a political power equivalent to 50,000 free persons. When the importation of slaves was stopped finally in 1808, the South already had fifteen representatives and electoral votes by reason of its slaveholdings. The warning of Thomas Branagan, in 1805, takes on new meaning in the light of history: "The tyrants of the South, gain an ascendancy over the citizens of the North, and enhance their paramount rights of suffrage and sovereignty accordingly as they enslave and subjugate the inoffensive sons of Africa . . . I am astonished at the stupidity of our citizens, in suffering such palpable villainy to be rewarded by political, as well as pecuniary gratifications . . . Unless this villainous inequality is in time remedied, the rights and liberties of our citizens will be eventually swallowed up."

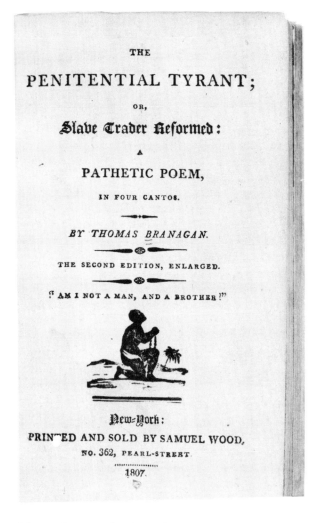

Thomas Branagan had been a slave trader, overseer, and owner of slaves in the West Indies before coming to the United States. His books were powerful indictments of the institution.

GRADUAL EMANCIPATION

Chapter 5

Formal opposition to slavery, through societies organized for that purpose, began in 1787, but on a very limited scale. Slavery had been abolished completely in Vermont (1777), Massachusetts (1780), and New Hampshire (1784) by constitutional provisions. Those three states, therefore, experienced none of the complex problems of gradual emancipation. They had relatively few Negroes, and their remoteness from the slave states relieved them of the associated complications of fugitives and kidnapping. There was no need for antislavery societies, and very little for organized effort to aid free Negroes. The assistance of those three nonslaveholding states, consequently, was denied to the over-all antislavery movement at this critical period by lack of interest and organization.

There were no new nonslaveholding states for a long time. Pennsylvania had adopted *gradual emancipation* in 1780, Connecticut and Rhode Island in 1784. New York and New Jersey did not adopt gradual emancipation until 1799 and 1804. Maryland and Delaware never quite reached the point of emancipation. They remained slave states in theory until the Civil War, but the number of free Negroes increased very rapidly. Of these states Connecticut and Rhode Island were deeply involved in the foreign slave trade. Maryland and Delaware were overrun by kidnappers. Pennsylvania, New York, and New Jersey encountered all of the problems connected with gradual emancipation. Organized effort was essential in all of these states to deal with the problems of Negroes illegally held in bondage, of child indentures, of

kidnapping, of violations of state laws against importations, of economic assistance to free Negroes, and of fugitive slaves; and to promote emancipation in the four states which had not acted, printing and distributing literature, and sending memorials to congress and to legislatures of the slave states on matters of broad national policy.

State organizations were formed for these purposes, and then were brought together in a loose federation. The great handicap, however, was the countless distractions presented by the meetings of the Constitutional Convention of 1787, the several state conventions called to ratify or reject the Constitution, and the first Congress, charged with the responsibility of creating governmental agencies and defining public policy. There were many men of influence, courage, and real ability, who were bitterly opposed to slavery, but who were unable to do much for its abolition because their energies and attention were completely absorbed by political affairs.

The first of the state organizations was a Quaker society in Pennsylvania. It met for the first time in 1775, suspended operations during the war, and became active again in 1784. A new constitution was adopted by the Society in April, 1787, just prior to the meeting of the federal Constitutional Convention, and people other than Quakers were brought into membership. Finally, it was incorporated by the state legislature in 1789 as the Pennsylvania Society for Promoting the Abolition of Slavery, the Relief of Free Negroes Unlawfully Held in Bondage, and for Improving the Condition of the African Race.[1] Benjamin Franklin was its first president.

The work of this pioneer society was typical of organized antislavery effort thereafter except in one very important respect: the agency system. That method of operation was not devised until the 1830's; and lack of communication of ideas remained the tragic weakness of the antislavery movement throughout this early period. The Pennsylvania society encouraged the organization of other societies; sent memorials (later called petitions) to Congress; publicized state laws relative to slavery and free Negroes; printed and distributed antislavery literature, both foreign and domestic; corresponded with prominent antislavery leaders in England and France; and initiated a policy of assistance to free Negroes and to those illegally held in bondage. The latter work was so important and time consuming that one would not be too far wrong in calling the early organizations antikidnapping societies. They helped free Negroes to find employment, educated them, registered deeds of manumission, and discouraged the use of slave products. Connecticut and Rhode Island, like Pennsylvania, had adopted gradual emancipation. They were the only states in New England where societies were organized. The Rhode Island Society for Abolishing the Slave Trade was organized in 1785;[2] and the Connecticut Society for the Promotion of Freedom, and for the Relief of Persons Holden in Bondage was organized in 1790.[3] The president of the Connecticut Society was president Ezra Stiles of Yale College, and the secretary was Judge Simeon Baldwin. Its most immediate contribution probably was the sponsorship of lectures or orations, some of which are choice items among late eighteenth-century antislavery literature, though none belongs among the top twenty-five of the entire movement. It was important, however, that men like Zephaniah Swift,[4] Jonathan Edwards,[5] James Dana,[6] Noah Webster,[7] and Theodore Dwight[8] should have spoken boldly against the slave trade and slavery, at this time.

The only one of the men who added anything new to the argument was Noah Webster. "That freedom," he said, "is the sacred right of every man whatever be his color, who has not forfeited it by some violation of municipal law, is a truth established by God himself in the very creation of human beings. No time, no circumstances, no human power or policy can change the nature of this truth, nor repeal the fundamental laws of society by which every man's right to liberty is guaranteed."[9] He then listed various reasons why slavery was repugnant to private interest and public happiness, including dwelling among the evil results of an exercise of uncontrolled power by slaveholders. Webster rejected immediate emancipation of large numbers of slaves as likely to bring ruin to society. He also rejected colonization for three reasons which are proof that it was being widely discussed by this time: because of the terrific expense involved, because the slaves would not be willing to go, and because of the inability to replace such a large labor force. His remedy was to raise the slaves to a status of free tenantry, a subject soon to be dwelt upon by others.

The first of the antislavery societies to be organized on a *public* basis had been in New York state. New York and New Jersey were the only two Northern states in which steps had not been taken to bring about complete emancipation. More than two years before the federal Constitutional Convention met, in January 1785, there was formed the New York Society for Promoting the Manumission of Slaves.[10] John Jay, first chief justice of the United States and diplomat extraordinary, was its first president and Alexander Hamilton the second. No one, probably, would give either of them a minor rating among early American statesmen. John Jay, himself, was strongly opposed to slavery, but he could not actively participate in the organized movement nor speak publicly on that or any other question after 1789, because of his position as chief justice of the United States. This incapacity, however, was compensated for by the work of his two sons, Peter A. Jay (1776–1843) and William Jay (1789–1858), and of his grandson and namesake, John Jay (1817–94). The New York Society rivaled that of Pennsylvania in its distinguished membership and was responsible for the wide distribution of Samuel Hopkins' *Dialogue Concerning the Slavery of Africans.*

The Delaware Society for Promoting the Abolition of Slavery and for the Relief and Protection of Free Blacks and People of Colour Unlawfully Held in Bondage was organized in 1788, one year after the federal Constitutional Convention met.[11] The following year the Maryland Society for Promoting the Abolition of Slavery, and the Relief of Free Negroes and Others Unlawfully Held in Bondage was organized.[12] The New Jersey Society for Promoting the Abolition of Slavery was not organized until 1793.[13]

In January 1794 an assembly of delegates from various societies met at Philadelphia. The New York, Pennsylvania, New Jersey, Delaware, and Maryland societies were represented, and these states constituted the important area of activity during the latter years of the eighteenth century. Connecticut was represented in the organizational meeting, as was a society in Virginia. There was formed at this meeting the first "national" organization devoted to the racial question: The American Convention for Promoting the Abolition of Slavery and Improving the Condition of the African Race.[14]

The American Convention was an association of delegates from, or a loosely organized federation of, the several state societies. It held its last regular meeting in that fateful year, 1832, and was formally dissolved in 1837. There were twenty-six meetings; annual to 1806, triennial until 1815, and biennial after that date.[15] Attendance at the meetings was not large, and in some years not all of the state societies sent delegates, Pennsylvania and New York being the only ones represented at every meeting. The convention had limited funds with which to operate. It did not develop a system of publications. It maintained no agents. It had no permanent secretariat. It always remained moderate—one might say on the defensive—yet it did provide some cohesion, and it established the broad outlines of the organized antislavery movement. Meanwhile, most of the practical problems were handled by the state organizations.

What was done in the several states to promote emancipation, and to consolidate the gains already made? One important task was the prosecution of suits for freedom in the courts. Pennsylvania had provided for gradual emancipation in 1780, by which time the Quakers had disassociated themselves completely from slaveholding. The law designated as indentured servants until age twenty-eight all children thereafter born of slave mothers. It compelled slaveowners to register all slaves owned by them, and to register all children of slaves born thereafter within six months of birth with the clerk of courts, by name, age, and sex, and to identify themselves properly as owners. It gave the Negro equality before the

Ezra Stiles
Stiles, an early opponent of slavery, was president of Yale College and president of the Connecticut Society for the Promotion of Freedom.

law and in the courts and provided security against kidnapping and against transfer outside the state to evade provisions of the law.[16]

There were three principal reasons for adopting gradual emancipation: deference to property rights and unwillingness to become involved in all the legal complications that might ensue from emancipation without compensation, desire to protect aged and infirm Negroes and those unqualified to provide an independent livelihood for themselves, and unwillingness to assume public guardianship, involving education, sustenance, and moral supervision for a large number of persons. Gradual emancipation, however, gave rise to a multitude of problems. People opposed to slavery became impatient and welcomed every failure of owners to comply with technicalities of the laws as an opportunity to press for the freedom of individual slaves. Unscrupulous persons sought every opportunity to realize some profit by disposing of slaves outside the state in violation of the law. Criminals took advantage of the proximity to slave states to engage in kidnapping.

The presence of three classifications of Negroes —those who were free, those who were slaves, and those who were indentured servants—not to mention those in the state as fugitives from other states provided fertile ground for the operations of the kidnapper. The profits were enormous, the risks not great. No one ever could hope to reconstruct the history of kidnapping in this period, but there is enough evidence to show that it was as prevalent as horse stealing or cattle rustling at later dates and a thousand times more terrible because human beings were being carried away into servitude and the kidnapper was not loathe to commit murder to avoid detection and identification.

The High Court of Errors and Appeals refused by unanimous decision (1798) to declare slavery contrary to the provisions of the state constitution.[17] There can be no doubt, however, that the courts decided every possible case from the legal and common sense view in favor of freedom and against slavery. Slaves born before the emancipation act was passed and not registered in compliance with the law were freed.[18] Slaves brought into the state for permanent residence were freed.[19] They were freed because their sex was not stated in the registration,[20] because they were not registered within six months after birth,[21] because someone other than the owner or his legal representative filed the registration,[22] and because the registration did not show the occupation of the owner.[23] Owners who sought to take advantage of the technicalities of the law in order to provide a basis for automatic freedom and thus evade responsibility for a slave's support were stopped from doing so. The diabolical character of human bondage, where there were no restrictions on slave ownership, is revealed in some of these cases. The utmost vigilance of men, even where slaves were few and the courts favorably disposed to freedom, was not sufficient to prevent unashamed barbarism. One slave, born in 1774, and entitled to freedom because not properly registered, was fraudulently held in bondage until 1818 by his owner and his owner's heirs. The latter then refused to support him on the grounds he had always been free and pleaded the statute of limitations to avoid payment. They were overruled by the courts. This is one of the last of the slave cases on record in the Pennsylvania Courts, not being decided until 1849.[24]

Under the law children of slaves were to be indentured servants until age twenty-eight, and no Negro could be held beyond that age to the terms of a personal contract for service. No one, except members of Congress and foreign ministers, could bring slaves into the state for more than six months, and no one could bring them at all who intended to reside permanently in the state. The courts freed slaves held for longer than six months even though they had been taken out of the state at intervals.[25] They allowed former slaves to be brought into the state as indentured servants for a period of seven years or until age twenty-eight, but they refused to permit persons who had come for permanent residence to bring slaves and then sell them as indentured servants.[26]

The law and the courts did not give freedom to fugitive slaves in violation of the federal fugitive slave act, but they did not permit slave owners to *bring in slaves* under the provisions of the act. Pierce Butler of South Carolina, father of the fugitive slave clause in the Constitution, was a member of Congress from 1789 to 1796 and from 1802 to 1805, but he maintained a permanent residence, staffed by slaves during the whole of the period. Since he was not a member of Congress for two years, the Court of Common Pleas in Philadelphia gave freedom to one of his slaves. The case was carried to the United States Circuit Court where, in another of the famous decisions of this early period, the right of a state to declare free any slaves brought in by their owners was upheld.[27] The state emancipation act had abolished slavery for children born of slave mothers; and a child, born in Pennsylvania of a female fugitive from Maryland, was declared free.[28] Immediate freedom was given to the children born of those Negroes being held as indentured servants until age twenty-eight in spite of the financial burden thus placed upon the owner.[29]

The amount of litigation in the courts of Connecticut and Rhode Island was much less than in Pennsylvania. Connecticut had fixed the age of freedom for children of slaves at twenty-five. This was changed in 1797 to age twenty-one. All of the colonial legislation touching upon control of slaves was repealed at this time. The number of slaves dwindled rapidly through the years. In 1790 there were 2,648 slaves and 2,771 free Negroes; in 1800 the numbers were 951 and 5,330; and in 1810 they were 310 and 6,453. Probably all or nearly all of the slaves held after 1800 were incapable of looking after themselves or were devoted household servants. Connecticut adopted a new constitution in 1818, and efforts were made to secure a court decision declaring slavery abolished by its Bill of Rights, but without success.[30] The decision did, however, declare free any slaves brought into the state. The legislature finally abolished the last vestiges of the institution in 1848 and made former masters or their heirs responsible for the care of needy ex-slaves.[31]

Rhode Island had provided for the freedom of children of slaves when they reached the ages of twenty-one (males) and eighteen (females). Her principal concern and her biggest problem from the beginning had been the slave trade. Most of her slaves were freed before the first federal census in 1790. There were 958 slaves and 3,484 free Negroes at that time. Ten years later, there were 380 slaves and 3,304 free Negroes. In 1810 there were 108 slaves and 3,609 free Negroes. Slavery was formally abolished by legislative action in 1844, and former slave owners were made financially responsible for the care of the Negroes they held at that time.[32]

New York did not pass an emancipation act until 1799, but private manumissions and an influx of free Negroes from elsewhere began long before that date. The first census (1790) showed 21,193 slaves and 4,682 free Negroes; that of 1800, before the emancipation act could take effect, showed 20,903 slaves and 10,417 free Negroes. In 1810 there were 15,017 slaves and 25,333 free Negroes. By 1830 there were only 75 slaves and 44,870 free Negroes. The emancipation act of 1799 was very similar to the Pennsylvania law, providing freedom for all children born of slave mothers after July 4, 1799, at age twenty-eight for males and twenty-five for females. These children, meanwhile, were indented servants and had to be registered within nine months after birth, but the owner could surrender all claim to them at any time during the first year, in which case they were indentured by the overseers of the poor.[33] In 1804 the ages were lowered to twenty-one and eighteen.[34]

Extreme precautions were taken to protect the Negroes against fraud. No slave could be brought into the state or taken out of the state for purposes of sale. After 1801 no slave could be brought into the state unless the owner swore under oath that he had owned the slave for at least one year and intended to reside permanently in the state.[35] No one could leave the state with slaves purchased less than one year previously. Finally, after 1807 no persons could take slaves out of the state unless they had owned them ten years, and after 1810 no one coming into the state for permanent residence could bring any slaves. The courts, as in Pennsylvania, leaned strongly toward freedom in all cases. They freed fugitives whose owners recovered them and then sold them as servants;[36] they freed slaves manumitted in other states and indentured to citizens of New York; they freed slaves given promises of freedom and subsequently sold,[37] even though the promise was verbal and had been given twenty years previous.[38]

The state legalized slave marriages in 1809, making the law retroactive to give legitimacy to all children of slaves, and extended jury trial to all slaves in 1813.[39] Finally, in 1817 every slave born before passage of the emancipation act (1799) was given freedom as of July 4, 1827. This emancipated practically every one of the 10,088 slaves listed in the 1820 census who were still living in 1827, without compensation to their owners, and the courts upheld the law.[40]

Emancipation in New Jersey came very slowly,[41] in spite of a large Quaker population. The state legislature was unwilling to pass a general emancipation act, but the courts were liberal in their interpretation of manumission laws. They welcomed suits for freedom and were disposed to grant freedom to individual slaves whenever possible.[42] They freed slaves who had been promised freedom by their owners even where no formal act of manumission had been executed,[43] and they freed slaves where no security had been given despite the requirements of the law.[44] The legislature put a stop to the liberality of the courts in 1798 by requiring juries in all suits for freedom, and to uncertainties about manumission by requiring them to be executed in writing with two witnesses.[45]

Gradual emancipation was adopted in 1804, with children born of slave mothers after July 4, 1804, becoming indentured servants until the ages of twenty-five for males and twenty-one for females. Owners could renounce claim to their services within one year of birth. They were indentured as pauper children in such cases.[46] Indentures of children could be sold without sale of the slave mother, and mothers could be sold without affecting the indenture of the child. No slave or servant could be taken out of the state

Kidnapping of free Negroes was a grave problem in states which had adopted gradual emancipation. Children disappeared with sickening regularity in the cities.

without his or her consent under penalty of $500 fine. After 1818 owners moving from the state permanently could take only slaves they had owned for five years, and only those who consented to go. Violations were punishable by fines of $2,000 and imprisonment at hard labor for two years.[47]

Slavery died out very slowly in the state under the law of 1804. There were 12,422 slaves in 1800 and 4,402 free Negroes, 10,851 slaves in 1810 and 7,843 free Negroes, 7,557 slaves in 1820 and 12,460 free Negroes. The number of slaves declined to 2,254 in 1830, and to 674 in 1840. A state constitutional convention in 1844 failed to abolish slavery, and the courts refused to abolish it by judicial interpretation of the Constitution.[48] The state legislature passed an act in 1846 declaring "that slavery in this state be and it is hereby abolished," but there were eighteen slaves listed in the state by the census of 1860.

It must be assumed that antislavery societies or individuals initiated, provided the legal counsel for, and financed all cases involving the freedom of Negroes. How many cases there were involving kidnapping and recovery of fugitives by their owners or agents, either before or after the Fugitive Slave Act of 1793 was passed, is pure guesswork. So few records were kept that the societies themselves had difficulty in making reports to the American Convention. The convention requested lists of persons liberated by the societies, and accounts of trials and decisions, neither of which could be furnished. The New York society, from January 1796 to May 1797, a period of about eighteen months, received ninety complaints. Twenty-nine of these persons were freed under provisions of the law prohibiting importations, seven were freed because they were born free and were paid heavy damages, nineteen cases were still in progress. The New Jersey society reported (1797) "many manumissions," which may have meant exactly that, or because of the loose use of the term, freedom from illegal detention of one sort or another. Pennsylvania said the number of cases in this same period numbered in the hundreds. The Wilmington, Delaware, society between 1788 and 1795 secured release for eighty persons. The society at Choptauk, over a seven-year period, freed fifty and failed in only one case. The Baltimore society reported "many" freed. Alexandria, Virginia, had twenty-six complaints, six releases under the importation law, five probable, and fourteen cases pending.[49] Allowing fifteen years as a conservative length of time for this confusion to have continued (and kidnapping became more prevalent and more skilfully organized with each passing year), the persons rescued and restored to freedom and happiness must have numbered many thousands.

The second most important field of activity directly touching the lives of the free Negroes was education, religious instruction, and training in the mechanical arts (and notice the wording of Benjamin Rush's report to the 1794 convention) "to prepare them for becoming good citizens of the United States."[50] The Convention, from time to time, published addresses to the people of the United States, urging upon them the obligations of justice, humanity, and benevolence toward slaves and free Negroes. It also published frequent addresses to the "Free People of Color." They urged them in the first address to attend public worship regularly; learn reading, writing, and arithmetic, educate their children, and read the Bible; have their children taught useful trades; practice the virtues of diligence, faithfulness, justice, simplicity, and frugality; avoid spiritous liquors; avoid "frolicking," variously designated as expensive amusements and dissipation and vice; contract legal marriages and register all births and deaths; save some money; be civil and respectful in relations with others.[51] The convention of 1797 further urged them to avoid gaming,

by which probably was meant gambling of one sort or another.[52] This was not just a resolution or published statement without meaning. The state and local organizations had committees of men who worked diligently with the free Negroes, visited them in their homes, advised them, and protected them and helped them in many ways. The advice to Negroes was actually a summary of the work being done by societies like those of New York and Philadelphia on an individual basis.

The work of education was handled by state and local societies and centered largely in Philadelphia and New York City. Benezet had established a school for Negroes in Philadelphia as early as 1750. They had two schools in operation by 1771, and by 1797 they had accumulated enough endowment, including some funds from England and a legacy from Benezet, to provide 200 pounds annual income. They had one school of thirty pupils taught by a Negro woman teacher, an evening school for adults after 1788 with fifty persons in attendance, a Sunday school to teach reading and writing to men, a school for Negro women, after 1795 sustained and taught by young women, with thirty in attendance, and after 1796 a Sunday school for all ages of Negroes with a regular attendance of sixty to ninety persons.[53] The New York society by 1797 owned a building for which they had paid 1400 pounds and were spending $1,000 a year to maintain the school in which 112 students (53 males and 59 females) were taught reading, writing, arithmetic, grammar, geography, and needlework. They also had forty-four persons in an evening school for adults.[54] The society at Alexandria, Virginia, had Sunday schools by 1796, with 108 pupils receiving regular instruction in reading, writing, and arithmetic. The New York society reported in 1797 that there were 2,000 Negroes in the city working as servants, laborers, sailors, mechanics, and traders, that they had established a church, and that many owned hundreds of dollars worth of property.

NATIONAL POLICY

Chapter 6

The first Congress under the Constitution met during the summer of 1789. The American Convention for Promoting the Abolition of Slavery and Improving the Condition of the African Race met for the first time on January 1, 1794. The four years between were years of retrogression for the cause of human freedom—about as black as any similar period in history. Benjamin Rush was not far from the truth when he said in the Address of the Convention to the Citizens of the United States: "Freedom and slavery can not long exist together. An unlimited power over the time, labor, and posterity of our fellow-creatures, necessarily unfits man for discharging the public and private duties of citizens of a republic."[1]

The ink was hardly dry on the Constitution when the powers of Congress relative to slavery were called into question, the right of petition was challenged, and the first talk of civil war was heard—all in Congress and by congressmen from South Carolina and Georgia. The Quakers, meeting in annual assembly in September 1789, and representing Pennsylvania, New Jersey, Delaware, Maryland, and Virginia, had prepared a petition to Congress relative to the slave trade. The Quakers of New York had prepared another petition. These were introduced in the House of Representatives February 11, 1790. They spoke of the "licentious wickedness" of the trade, and of the "inhuman tyranny and blood guiltiness inseparable from it." They said that the "debasing influence" of the trade "tends to lay waste to virtue, and, of course, the happiness of the people," and requested Congress to abolish it.

Bitter debate followed the reading of the petitions on the question of reference to a committee. The question carried over until the following day, when another petition more general in character was presented. This was the antislavery petition of the Pennsylvania Society which Benjamin Franklin signed as president. It said in part: "From a persuasion that equal liberty was originally the portion, and is still the birthright of all men; and influenced by the strong ties of humanity, and the principles of their institution, your memorialists conceive themselves bound to use all justifiable endeavors to loosen the bonds of slavery, and promote a general enjoyment of the blessings of freedom. Under these impressions, they earnestly entreat your serious attention to the subject of slavery; that you will be pleased to countenance the restoration of liberty to those unhappy men, who alone, in this land of freedom are degraded into perpetual bondage, and who, amidst the general joy of surrounding freemen, are groaning in servile subjection; that you will devise means for removing this inconsistency from the character of the American people; that you will promote mercy and justice towards this distressed race, and that you will step to the very verge of the power vested in you for discouraging every species of traffic in the persons of our fellow-men."[2]

These petitions were finally referred to a committee by a vote of 43 to 14, all of the opposition votes coming from South Carolina and Georgia with two exceptions: Isaac Coles of Virginia and Michael Stone of Maryland.[3] The leaders of the opposition were William Smith and Thomas Tucker of South Carolina and James Jackson of Georgia. They insisted that Congress was specifically restrained by the Constitution from interfering with the slave trade for a period of years, and any petition asking Congress to commit an unconstitutional act should be summarily rejected. They denounced the Quakers. They denounced Franklin as a "man who ought to have known the Constitution better." They opposed discussion of the slave trade as likely to raise false hopes among the slaves, induce them to rash conduct, and result in severe repressive measures; as indicating to the Southern people a disposition towards complete emancipation; and as an improper interference with the rights of the South. They defended slavery as necessary to the economic prosperity of their area; as a Christian institution; and as the basis of all past cultures. Jackson admonished the Quakers to consult the Bible and "find that slavery is not only allowed but commended," and declared: "There never was a Government on the face of the earth, but what permitted slavery." Said Smith: "When we entered into this confederacy, we did it from political, not from moral

Elias Boudinot

motives, and I do not think my constituents want to learn morals from the petitioners; I do not believe they want improvement in their moral system; if they do, they can get it at home." Said Tucker: "Do these men expect a general emancipation of slaves by law? This would never be submitted to by the Southern States without a Civil War." Said Jackson: "The other parts of the Continent may bear them [Southern people] down by force of arms, but they will never suffer themselves to be divested of their property without a struggle."[4]

These gentlemen from the slave country were no match for the talent arrayed against them. Elias Boudinot of New Jersey, brilliant lawyer and statesman, trustee of Princeton, former president of the Congress of the Confederation, and secretary of foreign affairs, expressed surprise that anyone should question the right of the Quakers to petition Congress on the subject of slavery "after it has been so lately contended and settled, that the people have a right to assemble and petition for redress of grievances." He supported the commitment of the petition "because it comes from citizens of the United States who are equally concerned in the happiness and welfare of their country with others."[5] Elbridge Gerry of Massachusetts said "that it was the right of the citizens to apply for redress, in every case in which they considered themselves aggrieved; and it was the duty of Congress to afford redress as far as in their power."[6]

Josiah Parker, of Virginia, thought it his duty "as a citizen of the Union" to support the petition, and that it was incumbent upon every member "to sift the subject well, and ascertain what can be done to restrain a practice so nefarious."[7] John Lawrence of New York called the trade a "disgrace to human nature."[8] Thomas Scott spoke of it as "one of the most abominable things on earth." Said he, "if there was neither God nor devil, I should oppose it upon the principles of humanity, and the law of nature." Pledging himself to "support every constitutional measure likely to bring about its total abolition," he said: "Perhaps, in our Legislative capacity, we can go no further than to impose a duty of ten dollars, but I do not know how far I might go, if I was one of the Judges of the United States, and those people were to come before me and claim their emancipation; but I am sure I would go as far as I could."[9] Jackson of Georgia replied that "his judgment would be of short duration in Georgia, perhaps even the existence of such a Judge might be in danger."[10] Coming from a man who had killed the lieutenant-governor of his state in a duel, this remark may be regarded as approaching the limits of congressional decorum.

The limits of congressional power were stated broadly by James Madison and Elbridge Gerry, and both revealed a clear understanding of the scope of the slave-trade clause. We must constantly bear in mind that it covered the foreign and domestic slave trade and expansion of slavery to the territories and was so interpreted at the time. Madison "admitted that Congress is restricted by the Constitution from taking measures to abolish the slave trade; yet there are a variety of ways by which it could countenance the abolition, and regulations might be made in relation to the introduction of them [slaves] into the new States to be formed out of the Western Territory."[11] Gerry thought the interference of Congress fully compatible with the Constitution. He insisted that Congress had power to control abuses in the trade, and to regulate it; and that they might purchase all the slaves for freedom and use the resources of the western lands to do it.[12]

The committee to which the petitions were referred undertook to define the limits of congressional authority with respect to slavery. Its report was a remarkable document in some ways, stating that the "general government was restrained from prohibiting importations of such persons as any of the states now existing shall think proper to admit," until 1808, and that Congress "by a fair construction of the Constitution are equally restrained from interfering in the emancipation of slaves, who already are, or who may, within the period mentioned, be imported into, or born within any of the said states." This implied a rather wide latitude of congressional power after 1807 and the clause was later stricken out.[13]

The third clause was the interesting one—somewhat nauseating to be sure, but important. "Congress has no authority to interfere in the internal regulations of particular States, relative to the instruction of slaves in the principles of morality and religion, to their comfortable clothing, accommodation and subsistence; to the regulation of their marriages, and the prevention of the violation of the rights thereof, or to the separation of children from their parents; to a comfortable provision in the case of sickness, age, or infirmity, or

to the seizure, transportation, or sale of free negroes; but have the fullest confidence in the wisdom and humanity of the Legislatures of the several States, that they revise their laws, from time to time, when necessary, and promote the objects mentioned in the memorials, and every other measure that may tend to the happiness of slaves."[14] This self-denial of particularized powers apparently was too much for some members to approve, though we have no way of knowing who they were, and a substitute written in more general terms was adopted, as follows: "That Congress have no authority to interfere in the emancipation of slaves, or in the treatment of them within any of the States; it remaining with the several states alone to provide any regulations therein, which humanity and true policy may require."[15]

Writing in the New York *Evening Post*, August 29, 1835, William Leggett said of this resolution: "It is a great mistake to say that the power of the southern states over slavery *and all its incidents* was in no degree diminished by the adoption of the federal constitution . . . The Constitution, no matter what were the previous laws of the state, became, on its adoption, the supreme fundamental law of the confederacy. So far from the incidents of slavery being in no wise impaired, many of the sagest men in the Virginia Convention, among them Governor Randolph, Mason, and Patrick Henry, were decidedly of opinion that the Constitution gave the general Government the power of abolishing slavery altogether, in various ways, either by the operation of inordinate taxes, or by requiring the slaves to do military service, and emancipating them as a reward. One of the first things, it is true, which the Congress did under the existing Constitution, was to disavow any right on the part of the General Government to interfere with the subject of slavery. But a resolution of Congress has not the force of Constitutional law. It can be rescinded or expunged."

That part of the declaration most clearly associated with the object of the Quaker petition dealt with the power of Congress over the slave trade before 1808. It stated that Congress did have authority to prevent "citizens of the United States" from engaging in the trade to foreign countries, to prevent foreigners engaged in the trade from fitting out their vessels in ports of the United States, and to require humane treatment on the high seas of slaves being imported into the United States.[16]

It is a singular fact that these petitions precipitated a full-scale debate in the second session of the first Congress. We do not have complete records of what was said, but the *Annals of Congress* contain enough to leave no doubts about the scope of the argument or its intensity. Burke and Smith of South Carolina displayed a viciousness, a callousness, and a surprising ignorance in their studied insults of Quakers generally, and of particular individuals. Burke was once called to order for his remarks. Elias Boudinot made a brilliant defense of Benezet and others, and of the Quaker war record, near the close of the debate. Reading the speeches, one almost comes to believe that the Quakers rather than slavery were under indictment. In fact Smith at one point said that, in

Driven to the fields without respite, knowing not the father of the child she suckled.

The driver's whip unfolds its torturing coil.
"She only Sulks —— go lash her to her toil."

the Constitutional Convention, the North knew the South had slaves and the South knew Quaker doctrines had taken root in the North. So, said he, we "made a compromise on both sides—we took each other, with our mutual bad habits and respective evils, for better, for worse; the Northern States adopted us with our slaves, and we adopted them with their Quakers."[17]

Even more remarkable than the attack upon the Quakers, was Smith's exhaustive defense of slavery. He argued against any power in Congress to emancipate the slaves. He argued at length against any program of colonization. He quoted Jefferson's *Notes on Virginia* as proof that Negroes were by nature an inferior race of beings. He talked of slavery in Greece and Rome and of its approval by the early Christians. He denied that the South was vulnerable to attack because of slavery. He insisted that South Carolina required slaves for cultivation of her crops because "the climate, the nature of the soil, ancient habits, forbid the whites from performing the labor." He warned that social chaos would follow any attempt at emancipation because "either a mixture of the races would degenerate the whites, without improving the blacks, or . . . it would create two separate classes of people in the community, involved in inveterate hostility, which would terminate in the massacre and extirpation of one or the other."[18]

The most significant fact about the entire debate, however, was that despite its completeness, no denial was made of the power of Congress to exclude slavery from the territories, or to stop the slave trade completely, both foreign and domestic, after 1808, or to deny admission to new slave states. Either the power of Congress to do these things was so evident to everyone as to be universally acknowledged, or the issue was thought too remote for present consideration.

As Congress failed to act upon its acknowledged powers to regulate the slave trade, the various abolition societies in Rhode Island, Connecticut, New York, Pennsylvania, Maryland, and Virginia sent in a series of memorials which were presented in the House of Representatives on December 8, 1791. All of these petitions were simple requests for the implementation of the House Resolution of March, 1790. The petition of the Providence Society, signed by David Howell, brilliant professor of jurisprudence and acting president of Brown University, expressed the hope

that "our commercial system, yet in embryo, will be strongly impressed with those great principles of natural and political law, which gave birth to the late Revolution and form and consistency to this great empire."[19] The petition of the Connecticut society was signed by Ezra Stiles, president of Yale; that of the New York society by Matthew Clarkson, regent of the State University of New York.

The Baltimore society protested strongly that a "traffic so degrading to the rights of man, and so repugnant to reason and religion as that in human flesh, is carried on by the free citizens of these free governments, for the supply of foreigners,—thus exhibiting to the world the curious and horrid spectacles of liberty supporting slavery, and the successful assertor of his own rights, the unprovoked and cruel invader of the rights of others." They reminded Congress that "to correct practices so dishonorable and inconsistent with the principles which freemen profess,—practices, which immediately tend to the corruption of morals, the annihilation of religion, and total debasement of the human character, must be worthy of legislative wisdom and attention"; and that "the rights of man can never be seriously venerated, or long supported, by a people familiar in the abuse of those rights."[20] The petition of the Virginia Society, signed by Robert Pleasants, with equal frankness, called slavery "not only an odious degradation, but an outrageous violation of one of the most essential rights of human nature, and utterly repugnant to the precepts of the gospel."[21]

The prayers of these learned gentlemen received less consideration than those of Benjamin Franklin and his associates at an earlier date. Consigned to a committee of which William Smith of South Carolina was a member, the petitions were promptly buried. They were not printed, neither were they debated, and nothing was done about slavery or the slave trade. So the matter stood when the American Convention was formed at Philadelphia in January 1794. The Convention sent memorials to the legislatures of South Carolina and Georgia, denouncing slavery as "a dishonorable stain upon the country," and "an evil of great magnitude," and urging those states to prohibit the foreign slave trade. These memorials were entrusted to carefully selected agents, but there is no evidence that they were ever read or discussed in the legislatures. They also sent a

58 ANTISLAVERY

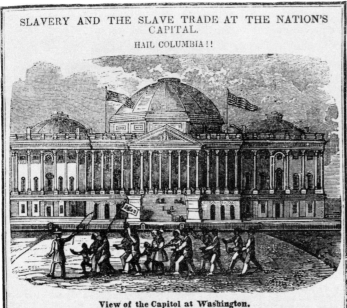

SLAVERY AND THE SLAVE TRADE AT THE NATION'S CAPITAL.

HAIL COLUMBIA!!

View of the Capitol at Washington.

One would think that slavery and the slave trade were the last things to have a legal and protected existence in the capital of a boasted free nation. But there they are—unpaid toil, whips, chains, dungeons, separations, murders, and all That slave coffle marching by the capitol is not fancy, but a fact not unfrequently occurring. Dr. Torrey (Portraiture of Domestic Slavery, p. 64), states, on the authority of Mr. Aldgate, a member of the House of Representatives, that " during the last session of Congress (1815-16), as several members were standing in the street near the new capitol, a drove of manacled colored people were passing by, and when just opposite, one of them elevating his manacles as high as he could reach, commenced singing the favorite national song, " Hail Columbia ! happy land," &c.

So late as the session of 1838-9, a similar scene was enacted. The House, in base subserviency to the slaveholders, had passed resolutions declaring that Congress had no constitutional power to abolish slavery in the District of Columbia, and excluding all petitions on the subject of slavery from being read or referred. " Nine days after the adoption of these resolutions," says Hon. J. R. Giddings (Rights of the Free States subverted, p. 13) " a coffle of thirty slaves chained together, and followed by about the same number of females, who were permitted to travel unchained, were driven past the capitol, on their way to a southern market."

Slavery and the Slave Trade no Right at the Nation's Capital.

When the people of this country rose in resistance to British oppression, they declared to the world (Dec. Am. Ind.)—" We hold these truths to be self-evident : That all men are created equal : that they are endowed by their Creator with certain inalienable rights: that among these are life, liberty and the pursuit of happiness."

When the same people adopted the present Constitution of Government, they also declared, in the preamble, that its object was " to form a more perfect union, establish justice, insure domestic tranquility, provide for the common defence, promote the general welfare, and secure the blessings of liberty to ourselves and

Slavery and the slave trade in the District of Columbia provided one of the most bitter facets of the slavery controversy.

strongly worded memorial to Congress, and Congress finally responded with the Act of March 22, 1794. This Act forbade any person in the United States, citizen or foreigner, to engage in the carrying of slaves from Africa to countries other than the United States. Any ships fitted out for that purpose were subject to seizure. Any person building, equipping, or sailing such ships was liable to a $2,000 fine. The law also placed ships clearing for African waters under bond for nine months to make certain they would not engage in the trade and imposed fines of $200 for each person carried in violation of the law.[22] This was the beginning of a long struggle to control effectively a trade which France, Great Britain, and, after 1807, the United States totally prohibited. Men opposed to slavery were to discover that no law is any more effective than those charged with enforcement want it to be. In this case, there seems to have been widespread evasion.

Meanwhile, Congress had passed the Fugitive Slave Act of 1793—a law which unquestionably stands alone as the most flagrantly unconstitutional act of Congress ever enforced by the courts, or as the most misunderstood and incorrectly interpreted law ever passed by Congress. There is no mystery about the origin of the Act. It began with a clear case of murder of Delaware Indians, and later kidnapping of a Negro, by citizens of Virginia in the state of Pennsylvania; a demand by Governor Thomas Mifflin of Pennsylvania for the surrender of those guilty; a refusal by the governor of Virginia to comply; and reference of the dispute to the attorney general and the President of the United States. All of this happened in 1791.[23] President Washington laid the matter before Congress. A committee reported out a bill, substantially the Act of 1793. It lay on the table for two sessions and finally became a law February 12, 1793.[24]

The first part of the act provided that the governor of a state should deliver any person charged with crime to the governor of the state from which said person had fled, upon demand. The second part of the Act said: "That when a person held to labor in any of the United States or in either of the Territories on the Northwest or South of the river Ohio, under the laws thereof, shall escape into any other of the said States or Territory, the person to whom such labor or service may be due, his agent or attorney, is hereby empowered to seize or arrest such fugitive from labor, and to take him or her before any Judge of the Circuit or District Courts of the United States, residing or being within the State, or before any magistrate of a county, city, or town corporate, wherein such seizure or arrest shall be made, and upon proof to the satisfaction of such Judge or magistrate, either by oral testimony or affidavit taken before and certified by a magistrate of any such State or Territory, that the person so seized or arrested, doth, under the laws of the State or Territory from which he or she fled, owe service or labor to the person claiming him or her, it shall be the duty of such Judge or magistrate to give a certificate thereof to such claimant, his agent, or attorney, which shall be sufficient warrant for removing the said fugitive from labor to the State or Territory from which he or she fled." The Act then provided that any one obstructing the seizure, rescuing the prisoner, or harboring an alleged fugitive should be subject to $500 fine and possible suit for damages.

Why fugitives from justice and fugitives from labor were tied together by this legislation is not clear. There is not the remotest connection, the one having sole reference to crimes perpetrated against the public peace and safety, the other to the reclamation of private property. Southerners had tried in the Constitutional Convention to provide for the rendition of fugitive slaves in the same manner as criminals and the idea had been summarily rejected. Now the two were put together by Congress in the same law. Fugitives from labor were not to be arrested and surrendered by the governors of the states upon demand of another governor. Alleged fugitives were to be seized anywhere by anyone who was willing to go before any magistrate from lowly justice of the peace to circuit judge of the United States and swear that the alleged fugitive was his property.

The law was clearly unconstitutional and should have been so declared by the courts at the earliest opportunity. In the first place, the Constitution did not confer upon Congress the power to act in the matter, and it is difficult to see how such power could be derived from the "necessary and proper" clause. The Act, by conferring powers upon state magistrates, was an expression of consolidation doctrine few men would have endorsed at that time. In the second place, it violated the well-known and acknowledged principles of law and reason, erecting courts to examine only one side of the testimony, a power conferred

only in regard to the Negro, and a superlatively mean and oppressive contradiction of justice. In the third place, the Constitution of the United States did not recognize *property* in man. The proceedings of the Constitutional Convention clearly show that they were very careful not to use the words slave or slavery for that very reason. Even in this Act Congress carefully refrained from doing so. The words "persons held to service or labor" were not adopted for the sake of convenience. They were adopted because men were not willing to agree that some persons could be owned as property by others. To have done so would have been to deny that freedom was an inalienable right of every person. Slaves in this country were slaves from the very beginning by force of local statute law. The Constitution recognized that fact. Let us state it another way. *A slave in Virginia was a slave because someone had reduced him to slavery by force and his owner held him in slavery by force, and state law enabled him to do so. Children of slave mothers were slaves because state law said so and for no other reason. But the public power of Virginia did not extend beyond the limits of Virginia, and any slave crossing the boundaries of Virginia into Pennsylvania became instantly free, not because Pennsylvania said he was free but because Virginia law could no longer say he was a slave.* Nothing in the Constitution of the United States said otherwise. On the contrary, by the use of the term "persons held to service or labor," and by counting three-fifths of the slaves as persons for purposes of apportioning representation and direct taxes, the Constitution clearly recognized the slaves as persons, not as property, and to have denied the inalienable right of freedom to any slave escaping from the jurisdiction of a slave state would have been a repudiation of the basic political philosophy of the nation too shameful to be accepted. In the fourth place, conferring power upon private persons to seize another person without legal processes was clearly contrary to due process; and allowing a person to be carried away to servitude for life, without benefit of habeas corpus, jury trial, counsel, witnesses, or the opportunity to testify in his own behalf—all of which placed every Negro, be he fugitive, slave, indentured servant, citizen, or otherwise, in constant jeopardy—and imposing a fine of $500 upon anyone attempting to insure justice in a particular case was a monstrous perversion of justice. It

Victims of kidnapping

Another picture from Torrey's *Portraiture* showing chains and leg irons on victims of kidnappers. Victims were often killed to seal their lips.

opened the door wide to kidnapping. It placed the lives of men at the mercy of criminals. It set aside all presumption that men are by nature free.

There is no use in saying that the law was intended to apply only to indentured servants and not to fugitive slaves. The circumstances of its origin disprove any such interpretation. There is no use in saying the Congress expected the states to supply the deficiencies of the law for the protection of their citizens. The Constitution clearly left the states free to do so; but this law provided for federal processes. There is no use in trying to explain it away as a simple attempt to implement the power of *recaption*. If it was so, then it was unconstitutional in its basic premises, because slaves were persons primarily and property only in a peculiar sense and within a limited jurisdiction. The men who passed the Act were not stupid, and not all of them were reactionaries. Certainly, men like Elias Boudinot and Elbridge Gerry, who voted for it, were not in sympathy with slavery. A good many members of Congress were well trained in the law. Some of them must have been aware of the problem being encountered in controlling kidnapping.

Why then was the Act passed? A partial answer may lie in two other questions. Why was it allowed to lie on the table for two sessions? Why was it passed with no debate of record? The only explanation that seems to make any sense whatever in the light of all ascertainable facts is that the matter seemed to be of such relative unimportance in comparison with other things that the bill passed as a routine procedure. Men were not thinking of political rights. The Revolution was over; even the first ten Amendments had been passed and ratified. We can only speculate on why seven members of the House voted against passage. Samuel Livermore, member of Congress as representative and senator from 1785 to 1801, and chief justice of the state of New Hampshire, was one. Others were John Francis Mercer of Maryland, Nathaniel Niles of Vermont, Josiah Parker of Virginia, Jonathan Sturges of Connecticut, George Thatcher of Massachusetts, and Thomas Tredwell of New York.[25] Perhaps these men were wiser than their colleagues. But all of this fails to explain why the law was allowed to stand by the courts.

The third defeat for freedom in these fateful years was the admission of Kentucky as a slave state, and the seating of its senators and representatives without protest in November 1792. The area embraced in Kentucky had never been under control of Congress; but it was the first state west of the Alleghanies and the first slave state to be admitted into the Union. The vote in the Kentucky convention in favor of slavery was 26 to 16; and the only encouraging circumstance was the speech of Reverend David Rice of the Presbyterian Church of Danville, the most comprehensive indictment of slavery to that time, one of the finest of all time.

Rice was a Virginian by birth, who had come to be known as the "father of Presbyterianism in Kentucky"—a humanitarian and an educator, cofounder of Hampden-Sydney College and Transylvania University. He represented the antislavery sentiment of his adopted state and his speech, "Slavery Inconsistent with Justice and Good Policy," was a masterpiece of sustained argument. His definition of slavery equals that of Salmon P. Chase, later chief justice of the United States. Rice said: "A slave is a human creature made by law the property of another human creature, and reduced by mere power to an absolute, unconditional subjection to his will."[26] Chase later said:

"A slave is a person held, as property, by legalized force, against natural right."[27]

Expanding upon his definition of slavery, Rice said: "A slave claims his freedom; he pleads that he is a man, that he was by nature free, that he has not forfeited his freedom, nor relinquished it . . . His being long deprived of this right, by force or fraud, does not annihilate it; it remains; it is still his right . . . If my definition of a slave is true, he is a rational creature reduced by the power of legislation to the state of a brute, and thereby deprived of every privilege of humanity . . . that he may minister to the ease, luxury, lust, pride, or avarice of another, no better than himself . . . a free moral agent, legally deprived of free agency, and obliged to act according to the will of another free agent of the same species; and yet he is accountable to his Creator for the use he makes of his own free agency."[28]

Rice went on to say that thus reducing men to slavery constituted a "degradation of our own nature" and was possible only because we had "lost a true sense of its dignity and worth," that "either the laws of nature or the laws of man are wrong," and that a state of constant and open warfare between master and slave is inherent in the system as a result. On this point, Rice's analysis was never surpassed: "A slave is a member of civil society, bound to obey the laws of the land; to which laws he never consented; which partially and feebly protect his person; which allow him no property; from which he can receive no advantage; and which chiefly, as they relate to him, were made to punish him. He is therefore bound to submit to a government, to which he owes no allegiance; from which he receives great injury; and to which he is under no obligation; and to perform services to a society, to which he owes nothing, and in whose property he has no interest . . . He is then, a member of society, who is, properly speaking, in a state of war with his master, his civil rulers, and every free member of society. They are all his declared enemies, having, in him, made war upon almost everything dear to a human creature."[29]

Rice then reproached men in public office for their duplicity and fraud. "In America," said he, "a slave is a standing monument of the tyranny and inconsistency of human governments." One can only reflect, at this point, how much misery and suffering we would have been spared, and how much brighter the past history of the country would have been, had a few men like David Rice, Richard Rush, and George Mason sat in the early Congress under the Constitution. Rice would have been a congenial colleague also of the judges like Cushing who were true magistrates, for he said "I never can trust to the integrity of that judge, who can sit upon the seat of justice, and pass an unrighteous judgment, because it is agreeable to law; when that law itself is contrary to the light and law of nature."[30] Passionate defense of natural rights may have subsided in the East, but the new West gave promise of its revival. Those who made the laws were as culpable as those who interpreted them in Rice's judgment, when they declared their constituents free men and passed laws to make them slaves.

Turning to that aspect of slavery so much emphasized by Luther Martin in the federal Constitutional Convention—its effect upon the general economy—Rice said: "Idleness will produce poverty; and when slavery becomes common, industry sinks into disgrace. To labour, is to *slave;* to work, is to *work like a Negro;* and that is disgraceful."[31] This effect of slavery upon poor white men was to be emphasized over and over again in the great struggle to keep the territories free, as a haven for poor people. Rice saw, in 1792—what was plain to everyone not blinded by prejudice fifty years later—that slave labor and free labor could not exist side by side. Man could not long retain his self respect and live in a community where honest toil was looked upon with contempt. "When he sees an open way to remove from this situation," said Rice, "and finds it may be done consistent with his interests, he will not long abide in it."[32]

Probably no group of people ever sat down to discuss the question of slavery in the days of slavery, or segregation in the days since slavery was abolished, without some one raising the question of amalgamation. Everyone knew that miscegena-tion was prevalent wherever slavery existed. Slaveholders refused to discuss it or blamed it upon overseers, and they stood ready to do violence upon anyone who intimated that they or their friends might be involved. Whenever other arguments failed, they reverted to the charge the antislavery people favored amalgamation of the races. Stephen A. Douglas made the charge in the Lincoln-Douglas debates, and a thousand men in public life had done it at other times. One thing is certain. The amount of mixed blood was so great, even by the time of the Revolution, that the desire to force it back into the Negro race was a major reason for laws against manumission and against intermarriage of free Negroes and whites.

Rice met the issue squarely by saying that amalgamation could not be prevented and that it was proceeding more rapidly in slavery than it ever could otherwise. It took courage and intellectual independence of a high order to stand before slaveholders in Danville, Kentucky, in 1792 and say: "My own pride remonstrates against it; but it does not influence my judgment, nor affect my conscience . . . it is too late to prevent this great imaginary evil; the matter is already gone beyond recovery . . . future inhabitants of America will inevitably be Mulattoes . . . this evil is coming upon us in a way much more disgraceful, and unnatural, than intermarriages. Fathers will have their own children for slaves, and leave them as an inheritance to their children. Men will possess their brothers and sisters as their property, leave them to their heirs, or sell them to strangers. Youth will have their grey-headed uncles and aunts for slaves, call them their property, and transfer them to others. Men will humble their own sisters, or even their aunts, to gratify their lust. An hard-hearted master will not know whether he has a blood relation, a brother or a sister, an uncle or an aunt, or a stranger from Africa, under his scourging hand."[33]

SLAVERY AND POLITICAL POWER

Chapter 7

Year by year, slavery in the United States became more sinister. It contaminated the body politic. It exerted an evil influence in all institutional life. It was inherently aggressive. It was a veritable colossus of greed and arbitrary power by 1793. The steps by which it had reached its exalted position are very clear:

1. The denial of emancipation by conversion to Christianity had shifted the basis of slavery from heathenism to race. The consequences were frightful. It unloosed on Africa for generations a terror unequaled in human history—a terror that did not cease until 100 million human beings perished. It introduced race prejudice into America. Race prejudice was hostile to democratic institutions, and it was a hundred times more difficult to destroy than was slavery. It caused the churches of the lower South to become bulwarks of slavery.

2. The consignment to slavery of every child born of a slave mother made slavery perpetual and ever-increasing in volume. One's pen falters in any attempt to describe adequately its crushing impact upon motherhood, family relationships, and the awakening spirit of youth. It exposed every female slave to abuse by members of the white race and consigned tens of thousands of the children of white men to slavery. Miscegenation and separation of families were among its evil consequences.

3. The gift to men, in a nation dedicated to political democracy, of extra political power as a reward for owning slaves, with power increasing in direct proportion to the number they owned, created an almost unbelievably rotten political

system that perpetuated slavery, lived on after slavery was abolished, and exists today in a nation which claims to be a classic land of liberalism.

4. The gift of complete freedom of action to all states for twenty years, to import slaves from Africa in order to buy their support for a new Constitution was a public admission of national weakness of great magnitude. It sacrificed the national interest to sectional greed. It gave to the proslavery extremists an undue sense of power and readiness to make further extreme demands.

5. The public confession by Congress that it had no power over slavery in the states was not binding upon future congresses, but it influenced the determination of public policy for a long time. As a constitutional interpretation it was neither in accord with all the facts nor worthy of men engaged in implementing the fundamental law.

6. The grant of power to slaveholders to roam the country seizing Negroes to carry home as alleged fugitives was an open invitation to kidnapping. There was precious little difference between the pursuit of fleeing men in Africa and in the United States—none whatever between the fox hunt and the slave hunt, and none between the enslavement of a free person in Africa and in a free state of the United States.

7. The admission of Kentucky as a slave state was both a betrayal and a precedent. If there ever had been an intention to admit any more slave states into the Union, it was not made clear to the opponents of slavery in the Convention and was not so understood by the ratifying conventions of states then in process of emancipation. Ad-

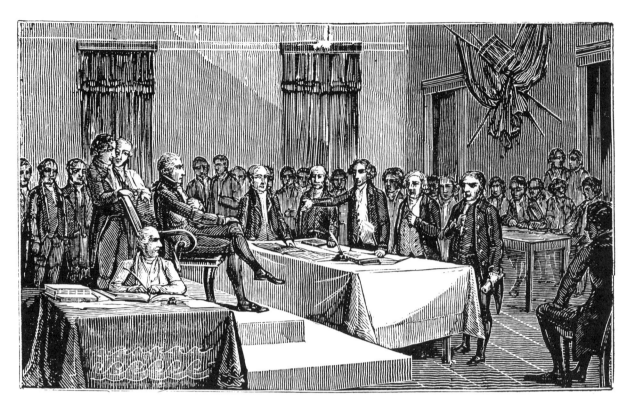

The land of the free

mission of a slave state was a betrayal of the free states which ratified. States which had claimed the right to import slaves now claimed the right to demand the continuation of slavery in the states to be formed from lands to which they surrendered claims, however ephemeral their claims may have been.

This was not the end; it was only the beginning. These things had been done when men were opening a new continent and were desperately in need of labor, when the government in England was strongly supporting the slave trade, when the Founding Fathers were hard pressed to frame and secure the adoption of a stronger instrument of government in the face of external dangers, when emancipation was in progress, and when economic conditions were unfavorable to slavery and there was every reason to suppose it would quickly disappear. The Constitution, however, gave Congress power to confine slavery to the original slave states; power it failed to use. Instead, it passed the Fugitive Slave Act and admitted a new slave state. Congress did these things at the very time drastic action against slav-

ery was most needed. It did them before an increase in the profits from slave labor built up added pressure for the protection and expansion of slavery. Once that had happened the golden opportunity to put an end to slavery by peaceful means was gone.

In 1793, six years after the Constitution was written, the cotton gin was invented. Whatever the economic benefits of this invention, it must stand high on the list of the instruments for exploitation of human life. Without conceding at this point that slavery was in course of ultimate extinction before the invention of the gin, we must admit that *to have been the general understanding.* Some of the Founding Fathers may have been guilty of rationalizing. Lacking courage to meet the issue squarely, they may have found it easier to believe in economic determinism than facts warranted. But the tobacco country had passed its peak of prosperity, and the rice-indigo country was encountering difficulties because of the loss of British bounty on indigo. Cotton was introduced in 1786, but long-staple cotton could not be grown inland and short-staple cotton could

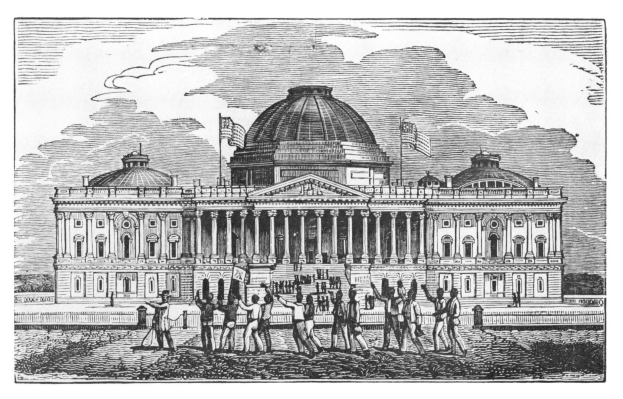

The home of the oppressed

not be grown commercially because of the cost of separating by hand the fiber from the seed. The cotton gin completely altered this situation and opened up a vast area, stretching westward from South Carolina and Georgia, to potential production of green-seed cotton.

Much has been written about the economy of slave labor. No one has proved that it was as profitable as free labor, but it was available, at a price, and the children of the slaves grew into money. Virginia, Maryland, and Delaware, and, after a time, all of the original slave states, could not supply the demand for slaves in the Black Belt, particularly in Alabama, Mississippi, Louisiana, and Texas. Slavery became profitable again in the older states because of this added profit from breeding. Everywhere, slave prices increased through the years; the supply never fully met the demand. Men could become wealthy by bringing land and slaves together for the production of cotton, and the profit motive again reinforced other motives for a continuation of slavery.

Two other motives were fairly obvious from early *colonial* times. Men wanted slaves to clear the land and drain the swamps, but they wanted them and their families wanted them, too, as servants. Slavery not only relieved *men* of all necessity to work with their hands, it relieved women of the drudgery of household tasks. It enabled families to enjoy gracious living, to be hospitable, to travel. It was a social system; one which gave feet of clay to Patrick Henry of "give me liberty, or give me death" fame, and I suspect to Washington and Jefferson as well. It would have spread everywhere, regardless of whether it was profitable in agriculture, or industry, or mining, if it had been allowed to do so—that is, it would have gone wherever people could have afforded the luxury and could have lived with themselves as owners of other men.

Slavery automatically became a system of racial adjustment from the first day of its introduction into America.

Far from being the humane institution ofttimes claimed for it, slavery was diabolically cruel and debasing in the sense that it robbed the individual slave of man's four most precious possessions: namely, the sense of dignity and self esteem, the right of ownership, the aspiration to achieve, and the satisfaction of learning. Life, here or hereafter, held no promise to the slave. He was caught in a system that reduced him to the status of an animal. There was no opportunity for him to develop his intellectual and moral powers, and no incentive for him to give full expression to his talents. His mind was depressed by ignorance. The white population was responsible, but it blamed nature for what it had done. It argued a natural from an artificial inferiority of its own producing. It enslaved the Negro by force, then argued he was naturally inferior. The logic was that a subject race was an inferior race.

Whether they were willing to admit it or not, men feared the slaves in the aggregate. Critics of the institution were correct in saying that slavery was perpetual war between the slaves on the one hand, their masters and society on the other. The elaborate system of control measures, private and public, the vicious opposition to a discussion of the question of slavery, the rejection of any and all programs of gradual emancipation, all of these things signify fear. The white race took the position that there must be no loosening of the bonds of slavery.

Finally, in addition to being an economic system, a social system, and a system of racial adjustment, slavery was political power, in the state and in the nation. That power was derived from the three-fifths rule which gave slave areas excessive representation, and from the technique of pressure politics in parties and legislative bodies. So it was that aggression was inherent in the slave system. Slaveholders could never admit its evils; they could never anticipate its extinction; they could never accept its limitation or circumscription. To have done so would have been to dissemble a way of life and the psychological basis upon which it rested. Short of congressional action to limit slavery to the original states, by prohibiting migration of slaves to the territories or to new states, and by refusing to admit states into the Union unless their constitutions prohibited slavery, it certainly would have spread westward in any case. The cotton gin, however, caused the institution to expand with an explosive force beyond all control.

One could paint a glorious word picture of how this simple contraption of cylinders and spikes transformed the virgin lands of the old Southwest into a cotton producing empire of great wealth, fed the machines of a vast new cotton textile industry in New England and old England, and gave to the world an abundance of cheap cloth. It would have been better for the lands to have remained in the hands of the hardy pioneers and for the world to have gone naked, for the cotton gin created the Black Belt and the Black Belt became and remained the curse of the nation—birthplace of state rights, secession, and Civil War, stronghold of slavery and race prejudice, center of exploitation of the soil and of human life.

There were 60,000 Negroes in the Colonies in 1715, about 500,000 when the Revolution began, 697,000 at the time of the first census, and 1,000,-000 when the foreign slave trade was abolished in 1807. More than one-half of the slaves in 1783 were in Virginia, nearly two-thirds of them in Virginia and Maryland. South Carolina and Georgia together had less than one-half as many as Virginia, and the area of commercial agriculture in those states was severely limited to the tidewater region. Even sea-island cotton (1786), althought it brought great wealth to a few planters, could not be grown more than forty miles away from the coast. The Revolution was followed by depression everywhere in the slave country. Tobacco production remained stationary; tobacco prices remained low. Plantations operated on a small margin of profit—sometimes at a substantial loss. In the more southern states, indigo production ceased, except for domestic use. This all added up to a stagnant economy, without much prospect of recovery. Then the cotton gin was invented.

Production of upland cotton immediately assumed commanding and steadily increasing importance. Everything else gave way before it, and with every mile it moved westward the chains of slavery were riveted more securely upon one million human beings. The immediate effect, however, was a new prosperity for the seaboard states. Cotton production in South Carolina reached twenty million pounds annually by 1800, and forty million pounds by 1810. In Georgia the figures were ten million and twenty million; in North Carolina, four million and seven million; and in Virginia, five million and eight million. Enough was grown west of the mountains to give Tennessee a recognized production of one million pounds in 1800 and three million pounds in 1810. Louisiana was producing two million pounds by 1810, two years before admission into the Union.

This was only a token of what was about to happen in the next thirty years. Cotton moved westward with the same ease and adaptability as the pioneers. It could be grown on any kind of soil and in any amount. Yeoman farmers could have grown it—in fact they did do so in the days of slavery—and they continued to do so either as independent farmers or as share-croppers after the Civil War. Cotton, however, was peculiarly suited to plantation operations rather than farming. The entire operation from preparing the soil to shipping to market lasted a full year. The work was not too heavy for women and children, but it was continuous. The greatest amount of labor was required in the picking season, which allowed a surplus for cultivation. Cultivation by hand, therefore, lingered on through the years. Small farmers simply could not compete in the system against large-scale operations. For that reason,

and others, men interested in developing plantations found little difficulty in buying land from the original settlers, the latter moving on to newer frontiers.

It was at this point that the marriage of slavery and cotton production occurred. Ambitious men purchased a slave, or a family of slaves. The owner, his family, and the slave or slaves worked together in the fields. They planted some cotton in addition to foodstuffs. The family prospered and bought more land and more slaves, and the cycle continued until the size of the operation reached the point of diminishing returns. Cotton grew best in the lower South, from the South Carolina and Georgia coast westward through Alabama, Mississippi, and Louisiana to Texas. This was the area of developing cotton plantations through the first half of the nineteenth century. The demand for slaves was insatiable, and

SLAVE HOUSE OF J. W. NEAL & CO.

This establishment was owned by W. Robey, who is also engaged in the trade. In May 1834, a gentleman visited it and fell into conversation with the overseer of the pen. He heard the clanking of chains within the pen. "O," said the Overseer—himself a Slave, "I have seen *fifty* or *seventy* Slaves taken out of the pen, and the males chained together in pairs, and drove off to the South—and how they would cry, and groan, and take on, and wring their hands but the driver would put on the whip and tell them to shut up—so they would go off and bear it as well as they could.'

The standing advertisement of this house is as follows:

"CASH FOR 200 NEGROES."

"We will give cash for two hundred likely young negroes, of both sexes, families included. Persons wishing to dispose of their slaves, will do well to give us a call, as we will give higher prices in cash than any other purchasers who are now, or may hereafter come into this market. All communications will meet attention. We can at all times be found at our residence on 7th street, immediately South of the Centre Market House, Washington, D. C."   "JOSEPH W. NEAL & CO."

the price rose steadily because there were never enough slaves. That, and that alone, kept slavery from further expansion.

Georgia had imported slaves after the Revolution and did not prohibit the trade until 1798. South Carolina imported until 1787, prohibited the trade from that date until 1803, then brought another 40,000 from abroad in the four years before congressional prohibition. By that time (1807) there were a million slaves, and cotton production was more than fifty million pounds. Thirty years later, there were more than two million slaves, and cotton production was approaching 500 million pounds. There were 12,000 slaves in Kentucky in 1790, and 165,000 in 1830; 3,500 slaves in the area to become Alabama and Mississippi in 1800, and 183,000 in the two states in 1830; 35,000 slaves in Louisiana in 1810, and 110,000 in 1830. By 1835 Alabama and Mississippi were the two leading states in cotton production with 85 million pounds each—a combined total greater than that of the four eastern states of Virginia, North Carolina, South Carolina, and Georgia.

The above statistics are sufficient to show the tremendous migration of slaves to the south and west. Some of them were taken by migrating slaveowners, some of them by men who traveled north and east to buy slaves for their own use, and the majority by commercial slave traders. Some of them walked the long road, some were carried by boat in the coastal trade. There was an inevitable tendency to sell unruly slaves, which meant those with spirit enough to resist abuse or to run away. Those found guilty of crimes were sold, if possible. Slaves of all ages and both sexes went on the auction block when estates were settled; but the bulk of those sold, regardless of who carried them away, were young men and women and children. Thus was added to the evils of slavery one of its worst features. The older states, and the border slave states particularly, took the place of Africa as the source of supply. They raised slaves to sell. That was the slaveholder's one certain profit.[1]

The breeding of slaves was denied in the days of slavery and has been denied consistently since that time. Those who deny it simply evade the issue. Breeding consists of herding male and female live stock together in order to get an abundance of young pigs, lambs, colts, calves, or what you have for sale. That is exactly what slave owners did with the slaves, and there were no excep-

tions. No one knew who the father of a slave child was, and no one cared. They were sold with their mothers and without their mothers. The number of slaves exported from Virginia to the lower South was estimated by Governor Thomas Mann Randolph in 1832 at 8,500 yearly over a twenty-year period. He fixed the total number between 1790 and 1832 at 260,000 and said: "It is a practice and an increasing practice, in parts of Virginia, to rear slaves for market. How can an honorable mind, a patriot and a lover of his country, bear to see this ancient dominion converted into one grand menagerie where men are to be reared for market, like oxen for the shambles."[2] Robert Finley, of the American Colonization Society, said in 1833: "In Virginia and other grain growing states, the blacks do not support themselves, and the only profit these markets derive from them is, repulsive as the idea may justly seem, breeding them, like other live stock for the more southern states." Henry Clay said, in 1829, before the Colonization Society: "It is believed that nowhere in the farming portion of the United States, would slave labor be generally employed, if the proprietor were not tempted to raise slaves by the high price of the southern market, which keeps it up in his own"; and the New Orleans *Courier*, 1839, said: "The United States law may, and probably does put millions into the pockets of the people living between Roanoke and Mason and Dixon's line; still we think it would require some casuistry to show that the present slave-trade from that quarter is a whit better than the one from Africa."[3] The Wheeling *Virginia Times* estimated the value of slaves sold out of Virginia at $24,-000,000, the total taken out at $72,000,000. The Natchez *Courier* said 250,000 slaves were brought into Louisiana, Mississippi, Alabama, and Arkansas during 1836. Some of this, of course, was to replace losses. The annual decrease—losses over births—on Louisiana sugar plantations was estimated by the Agricultural Society of Baton Rouge and by Congressman Josiah S. Johnson at 2.5 per cent.

Plantation owners wanted strong young men and women for their field hands. They wanted young women who were good breeders, and one or two children by a woman's side was proof positive. They wanted children, because they were unspoiled, and not likely to be ill or injured or filled with hatred. Everywhere, from Baltimore, Washington, Richmond, south to Charleston and west to Louisville, there were buyers—permanent residents who combed the surrounding area for slaves, and held them in detention pens for auction to buyers who came north and east. These buyers were sometimes commercial traders. They were often planters, because the laws of many states forbade the bringing in of slaves for sale; but none, except Kentucky, forbade owners to bring them in for their own use. These laws, therefore, in no way lessened the number of slaves carried to the southwest, and the breeding, and selling, and transporting went on without interruption.

The rise of the cotton kingdom soon gave to the larger slave states an undue weight in the nation's councils of startling proportions. Let us call this the political power of slavery. It operated in three ways: three-fifths of the slaves were added to the whole number of whites to arrive at the apportionment population; the combined effect of slavery and cotton kept the Southern states producers of staple crops, without industries or cities, and, compared to the nonslave states, low in population, so that a relatively few people had exceedingly great power in the Senate; and the political parties gave to each state delegation in their national conventions a vote equal to that state's vote in the electoral college.

The first census was taken in 1790, and the first apportionment act was passed in 1792. This provided for a ratio of one member of the House for each 33,000 persons in the apportionment population. The ratio was not changed after the 1800 census, the increased population providing an increase in the House membership from 105 to 141. The ratio was changed to 35,000 in 1811, to 40,000 in 1822, to 47,700 in 1832, and to 76,680 in 1842. There were changes in membership in these years to 181, to 213, to 240, and to 223. After the 1850 census, the total membership of the House was fixed at 233 and the population was divided by this number to find the ratio.[4] The system worked in this manner: Virginia had, by the 1800 census, 514,280 free whites, and 365,920 slaves. Three-fifths of the slaves, or 219,552, added to the 514,280 free persons gave an apportionment population of 733,832 and a representation of twenty-two members. Slaves, under this apportionment, were represented by seventeen of the 141 members of the House; New York, for example, with a population of 557,000 having seventeen representatives, and Virginia with a free population of 514,000 having twenty-two representa-

1840.]   *Anti-Slavery Almanac.*   15

SELLING A MOTHER FROM HER CHILD.

" 'Do you *often* buy the wife without the husband ?'   'Yes, *very often*; and *frequently*, too, they sell me the mother while they keep her children. I have often known them take away the infant from its mother's breast, and keep it, while they sold her.' "—*Prof. Andrews, late of the University of N. C., in his recent work on Slavery and the Slave-Trade, p.* 147, *relates the foregoing conversation with a slave-trader on the Potomac.*

Hon. James K. Paulding, the Secretary of the Navy of the U. States, in his " Letters from the South," published in 1817, says he heard a slave-trader say—" Many is the time I have separated wives from husbands, and husbands from wives, and parents from children; but then I made them amends by marrying them again as soon as I had a chance; that is to say, I made them call each other man and wife, and sleep together, which is quite enough for negroes. I made one bad purchase, though,' continued he. 'I bought a young mulatto girl, a lively creature, a great bargain. She had been the favorite of her master, who had lately married. The difficulty was to get her to go, for the poor creature loved her master. However, I swore most bitterly I was only going to take her to her mother's at——, and she went with me, though she seemed to doubt me very much. But when she discovered, at last, that we were out of the state, I thought she would go mad; and, in fact, the next night she drowned herself in the river close by. I lost a good five hundred dollars by this foolish trick.' "—*Vol.* I. p. 121.

" One of my neighbors sold to a speculator a negro boy, about 14 years old. It was more than his poor mother could bear. Her reason fled, and she became a perfect *maniac*, and had to be kept in close confinement. She would occasionally get out and run off to the neighbors. On one of these occasions she came to my house. With tears rolling down her cheeks, and her frame shaking with agony, she would cry out, ' *don't you hear him—they are whipping him now, and he is calling for me !*' This neighbor of mine, who tore the boy away from his poor mother, and thus broke her heart, was a *member of the Presbyterian church.*"—*Rev. Francis Hawley, Baptist Minister, Colebrook, Ct.*

" Absconded from the subscriber, a negro man, by the name of Wilson. He was born in the county of New Kent, and raised by a gentleman named Ratliffe, and by him sold to a gentleman named Taylor, on whose farm he had a *wife* and *several children*. Taylor sold him to Mr. Slater, who, in consequence of removing to Alabama, Wilson left; and when retaken was sold, and afterwards purchased, by his present owner, from T. McCargo & Co., of Richmond."--*Richmond Whig, July* 25, 1837.

Separation of families was one of the worst features of slavery. It was universal despite all protests, past and present.

tives. Virginia, the great breeding ground for slaves, continued to have seven extra members of the House of Representatives for her slaves until after the census of 1840. By the census of 1820 New York and Pennsylvania, with combined populations of 2,352,000, had sixty members in the House, and Maryland, Virginia, North Carolina, South Carolina, Georgia, Kentucky, Tennessee, and Louisiana, with combined free populations of 2,554,000, had eighty-four members. Moreover, New York and Pennsylvania had four United States senators, and the eight slave states had sixteen. In short, 2,352,000 citizens of the United States living in two states without slaves had sixty-four members in the Congress and 2,554,000 citizens of the United States living in eight slave states had 100 members of Congress.

This situation grew worse, year by year, until the Civil War. The Census of 1850 gave Ohio and Indiana a combined population of 2,932,204. They had thirty-two members in the House, four in the Senate. The six largest slave states—Virginia, North Carolina, South Carolina, Georgia, Alabama, and Mississippi—had combined populations of 2,966,195. They had forty-seven members in the House, twelve in the Senate. The Census of 1860 gave the seven largest slave states—Virginia, North Carolina, South Carolina, Georgia, Alabama, Mississippi, and Louisiana—a total of 3,298,000 free whites. Their slave populations were: Virginia, 712,080; North Carolina, 361,522; South Carolina, 412,320; Georgia, 465,698; Alabama, 437,770; Mississippi, 437,404; and Louisiana, 350,373. Three-fifths of these slaves numbered 1,906,299, which number added to the whole number of free persons to arrive at the apportionment population, gave these states a total of forty-five members in the House. Their fourteen senators raised their membership in the Congress to fifty-nine. New York, with 3,831,590, had only thirty-one members in the House, and two senators for a total of 33 votes in Congress.[5]

What of the twentieth century, after the slaves had been freed and then abandoned to the tender mercies of those who hated and feared them? What of 1910, when few, if any, Negroes voted in these seven southern states? The seven listed above then had a combined white population of 6,357,312, and a representation in the Congress of sixty-five members of the House and fourteen senators, for a total of seventy-nine. New York and Ohio had 13,880,735 people, sixty-five mem-

Separation of a mother from her last child

bers of the House and four senators. California, Michigan, and Connecticut, with a combined population of 6,302,478, approximately the same as the seven southern states, had twenty-nine representatives as compared to their sixty-five, and six senators compare to their fourteen. It must be remembered that this excessive political power was wielded by the white men of the slave states in Congress, in Whig party conventions and caucuses, in Democratic party conventions and caucuses, and in the Electoral College. It nominated presidents. It confirmed appointments to the courts and to diplomatic posts. It defined public policy. It *controlled* the nation.

There is, then, no mystery about the political power of these states, but the story has only been half told. The contest between the financial, commercial, and industrial interests on the one hand, and the agrarian interests on the other, has continued throughout our entire history; but overshadowing and severely modifying it with increasing importance each year after 1789 was the contest over slavery. Virginians spoke for the agrarians, and provided the intellectual leadership for their party, through the administrations of Jefferson, Madison, and Monroe; then the leadership of the party, and the center of political power, shifted to the South and West. Slavehold-

Sale of estates, pictures, and slaves
The great slave mart at New Orleans was the focus of the harshest system of labor in the world. Barbarous slave auctions were held here day after day.

Can a mother forget her suckling child?

Pictorial portrayal of one of the harshest features of the slave trade, from one of the best of slave narratives.

Pictorial portrayals of slave auctions were numerous and diverse because sales were so frequent, especially in settlement of estates.

SALES BY AUCTION OF MEN, WOMEN, AND CHILDREN,

WITH HOUSES, LANDS, AND CATTLE, &c.

Husbands, Wives, and Families sold indiscriminately to different purchasers, are violently separated—probably never to meet again.

ers provided the intellectual leadership for the agrarians. There was, however, a real basis for a vigorous two-party system in every Southern state; and, the southerners, therefore, were either Whigs or Democrats as the case might be. Their power was so great in Congress and in the Electoral College that they were not only tolerated, they were patronized, and pampered, and allowed to dictate. If they had not enjoyed the representation provided by the three-fifths rule, or if they had all been in one political party, they would never have gained control of the government.

Finally, if slavery had not meant political power for the owners, and political power of enormous proportions to slaveholders in the aggregate, there never would have been such a continuing struggle for expansion of slavery. Once Kentucky and Tennessee were admitted as slave states in 1792 and 1796, it was inevitable that Alabama and Mississippi should be slave states. Slavery existed in Louisiana when it was purchased by the United States, and it had to be acquired for other reasons. But the long agitation for Cuba, the bitter argument and chicanery for Texas, the effort to make Illinois a slave state, the Missouri contest, and the ensuing struggle over slavery in the territories, culminating in the election of 1860 and secession, were manifestations of a tremendous, internal pressure, of a fear amounting to claustrophobia on a sectional scale, and of a colossal conceit born of uncontrolled power over the slaves and over the rest of the nation.

When we speak of the representation of slaves in the House of Representatives and the Electoral College, we must remember that the one and only excuse for it was this: the slaves occupied the place and ate the food of what would otherwise have been a free laboring class. But we must never forget that the slaves had no will, therefore could not be represented by any one. They were held in subjection by force. They exercised no judgment. They had no rights, only occasional privileges. They were in the eyes of the law not human beings but chattels, not persons but things. Anyone can argue about the treatment of slaves but never whether there was any expression of opinion, of desires, of personal interest, nor whether these votes represented the interest of the congressman's constituents: *the slaves.* They did not, and to pretend otherwise would be an insult to intelligence. The simple, inescapable fact is that slaveholders possessed enormously excessive political power because they owned slaves; and, after the Civil War, those states possessed even more power because they were allowed to deny the franchise to free Negroes. They used their votes to strengthen and expand slavery.

The scope of this study does not permit an exhaustive analysis of the use to which this excessive power was put, but the facts pertaining to the presidential election of 1800, the foreign slave trade act of 1807, the organization of Arkansas Territory, the admission of Missouri, and the Kansas-Nebraska Act are very revealing.

Thomas Jefferson defeated John Adams for the presidency in 1800 by an electoral vote of seventy-three to sixty-five. This election enabled Jefferson to lay solidly the foundations of the party of agrarianism, slavery, and decentralization. Despite some support for Adams in Delaware, Maryland, and North Carolina, the full weight of the slave power went to Jefferson. Whatever antislavery leanings the Jeffersonians had were tarnished by their strong endorsement of racial inequality. They were anti-Negro and procolonization. They always voted for anti-Negro black laws in the states of the Old Northwest. Slavery was not a prominent issue in this election of 1800, neither was it a dead issue. Adams received every electoral vote from the free states except twelve from New York and eight from Pennsylvania.[6] Jefferson received every vote from the slave states except three from Delaware, five from Maryland, and four from North Carolina. Delaware had only one member in the House of Representatives, so the slave population did not count in apportionment. Maryland had eight representatives and two senators for a total of ten electoral votes, two of which derived from the slave population, but her vote was evenly divided and does not count in this analysis. North Carolina had twelve votes, two representing the slave population; but she gave eight to Jefferson and four to Adams. Jefferson, however, received all of the votes from Virginia, South Carolina, Georgia, and Kentucky, a total of thirty-seven, and ten of them derived from the slave population. Those ten constituted the margin of victory because he defeated Adams by a vote of seventy-three to sixty-five. Neither he nor his successors in the presidency from the Jeffersonian and Democratic parties ever spoke against slavery after that election.

Effective legislation to stop the importation of slaves from abroad had to include penalties of such severity that no ship captain would risk conviction. It also had to provide freedom for the persons being brought in as slaves in violation of the law. Legislation was presented in Congress to prohibit the trade after January 1, 1808, and the important area of debate centered around penalties, and what should be done with the illegal cargoes. Should the government sell them, free them, or send them back to Africa?[7] The first important decision in the House of Representatives was on the question of the death penalty for violation of the law. It was defeated by a vote of sixty-three to fifty-three.[8] The second decision was on a proviso, offered by Bidwell of Massachusetts, that no person being imported illegally should be sold as a slave. It was defeated by a vote of sixty-one to sixty. The sixty-one votes included all but five of the votes from the slave states. They included, also, every one of the fifteen votes derived from the slave population. Even then, the Speaker of the House, Nathaniel Macon, a slaveholder from North Carolina, cast the deciding vote.[9]

The theory supported by the above vote was that the United States government owned the slaves by virtue of seizure and was bound by the laws of the slave states to sell them in the state where seized.[10] The penalty for violation was fixed at a maximum of ten years imprisonment and $10,000 fine, and the federal government was required to dispose of cargoes according to state law, which meant to sell them into slavery.

The next great debate in Congress on slavery occurred in the years 1819–21. It involved the question of the power of Congress to exclude slavery from the territories and to refuse admission of a new state which tolerated slavery. The territorial question arose in connection with the organization of Arkansas Territory, and the slave state which sought admission was Missouri. The bill to create the territory of Arkansas was presented in the House of Representatives, February 17, 1819.[11] An amendment was offered to prohibit further introduction of slaves into the territory and to free all children born of slaves in the future at the age of twenty-five years. The amendment was bitterly contested, along sectional lines, and was defeated by a vote of 68 to 80. Separate amendments, to prevent further introduction of slaves, and to free children at age twenty-five were then submitted. The first was defeated by a vote of seventy to seventy-one, and the second

The first of Branagan's several confessions and revelations concerning the barbarous slave trade and equally cruel system of slavery.

And lo ! he darts his piercing eye profound,
And looks majestically stern around !

The husband and wife, after being sold to different pur-chasers, violently separated....never to see each other more.

A

Preliminary Essay,

ON THE

OPPRESSION OF THE

EXILED SONS OF AFRICA.

CONSISTING OF

ANIMADVERSIONS ON THE IMPOLICY AND BARBA-RITY OF THE DELETERIOUS COMMERCE AND SUBSEQUENT SLAVERY OF THE

HUMAN SPECIES ;

TO WHICH IS ADDED,

A DESULTORY LETTER WRITTEN TO

NAPOLEON BONAPARTE,

ANNO DOMINI, 1801.

BY THOMAS BRANAGAN,

Late Slave-trader from Africa, and Planter from Antigua ; who, from conscientious motives, relinquished a lucrative situation in that island ; and now from a deep sense of duty, publishes to the world the tragical scenes, of which he was a daily spec-tator, and in which he was unhappily concerned.

PHILADELPHIA :

PRINTED FOR THE AUTHOR, BY JOHN W. SCOTT, NO. 27, BANK-STREET.

1804.

was approved by a vote of seventy-five to seventy-three. A final vote to recommit the bill, with instructions, removed the amendments, and Arkansas Territory was organized without restriction on slavery by a vote of eighty-nine to eighty-seven, February 19, 1819.[12] Every vote from the slave states, including the seventeen derived from the slave population, was cast against restrictions.

The theoretical question of the right of Congress to place restrictions on new states and the very practical question of prohibiting further introduction of slavery into Missouri were involved in the debates on the bill to permit that territory to frame a constitution. The House of Representatives first voted to exclude slavery from Missouri, but in the face of Senate resistance it gave up its slavery restriction in a decisive vote, March 2, 1820. This vote to admit Missouri as a slave state was ninety to eighty-seven, the alignment being almost exactly the same as the vote on Arkansas, with every vote from the slave states, including the seventeen representing slaves, being for admission and every vote against admission being from the free states.[13]

The Missouri Act embraced the first real victory for antislavery forces after the Northwest Ordinance. It excluded slavery from the area of the Louisiana Purchase north of 36° 30′, except for Missouri. This restriction was repealed and slavery was admitted into the territory by the Kansas-Nebraska Act of 1854. The sanctity of the Missouri Compromise was scorned, the power of Congress to exclude slavery from the territories was denied, and actual hostilities culminating in the Civil War were commenced by this Act. It was passed in the House of Representatives by a vote of 113 to 100.[14] There were eight votes from the slave states against repeal, ninety-two from the nonslaveholding states. There were sixty-three votes from the slave states for repeal, including the twenty-one representing slaves, and fifty from the free states representing Democrats who were still seeking to accommodate principles to party harmony.

The three-fifths rule allowed one slaveholder after another to be president of the United States. It prevented suppression of the African slave trade. It allowed slavery to spread to the territories, and it brought new slave states into the Union. Except for the concept of racial adjustment, it was the most powerful factor in support of slavery.

Slave suicide

Death was the only escape for millions of people held in perpetual slavery. It was a blessed release for many.

FOREIGN SLAVE TRADE

Chapter 8

The organizational meeting of the Convention of Abolition Societies in Philadelphia, January 1, 1794, issued an address to the citizens of the United States in which it emphasized the obligations of justice, humanity, and benevolence toward slaves and free Negroes; and urged the states to "refrain immediately from that species of rapine and murder which has improperly been softened by the name of African trade." This address was prepared by Benjamin Rush, Warner Mifflin, and Isaac H. Starr.[1] Its memorial to Congress, as we have seen, resulted in the Act of 1794, which was a feeble attempt to assist Britain and France in suppressing the trade to their colonies. It did not attempt to regulate and control the trade to the United States, probably because men shrank from exposing anything so repulsive, or because its depravity was so complete as to defy reform.

It was appropriate that Warner Mifflin should have been associated with Benjamin Rush in the preparation of the address to the people. He had been raised a slaveholder on the eastern shore of Virginia. He had freed his wife's slaves in 1774, and his own the following year. Through his influence the Mifflin families gave freedom to nearly one hundred slaves, and in the Quaker tradition they assisted them in every possible way to become established in independent status. His influence was not as great as that of Woolman or Benezet, but he traveled widely in the cause of freedom, appeared before many legislatures, and was instrumental in securing legislative sanction to private manumissions in Virginia. He had sent a memorial to Congress under date of November 22, 1792, protesting against the foreign and domestic slave trade. The House of Representatives had engaged in the bitter debate over petitions in February 1790; it had received and buried in committee the petitions from the various abolition societies in December 1791; and it now did what Southerners had wanted to do in the first instance —refused to accept it and returned it to Mifflin. Sharp things were said about Mifflin's opposition to the war. His petition was denounced as unconstitutional, mischievous, disturbing to the harmony of the Union, and likely to precipitate insurrections among the slaves. Stung by this insult from Congress, Mifflin promptly published *A Serious Expostulation with the Members of the House of Representatives of the United States.*[2]

This remonstrance followed the pattern of David Cooper's *A Serious Address to the Rulers of America*, published ten years earlier. It quoted from the Articles of Association (October 20, 1774), the Address to the Inhabitants of Canada (May 29, 1775), the Declaration of the Causes and Necessity of Taking up Arms (July 6, 1775), the Address to People of England (July 8, 1775), the Address to Ireland (July 28, 1775), the Declaration of Independence (July 4, 1776), and the Observations on the American Revolution (1779). Criticism of his antislavery activities and his advocacy of peace principles continued to such a degree that in 1796 he published *The Defense of Warner Mifflin Against Aspersions Cast on Him on Account of His Endeavors to Promote Righteousness, Mercy, and Peace Among Mankind.*[3]

His death two years later deprived the antislavery cause of one of its most able leaders.

One year after Mifflin published his *Serious Expostulation,* and the year of the organization of the Convention (1794), Timothy Dwight published his *Greenfield Hill.*[4] Dwight was pastor of the Congregational Church at Greenfield Hill and was to become president of Yale the following year (1795). In this poetical description of social conditions Dwight included a bitter denunciation of the cruelties of slavery, particularly the conditioning of slaves to the level of brutes by whippings, brandings, compulsory submission to the wills of others, and by the complete lack of praise, ownership, kind esteem, and equality with other men. Dwight was for more than a quarter of a century thereafter a great educator and a dominant intellectual of New England. His denunciation of slavery must have carried great weight; it was vivid and devastating:

"O thou chief curse, since curses here began;
  First guilt, first woe, first infamy of man;
Thou spot of hell, deep smirch'd on human kind,
The uncur'd gangrene of the reasoning mind;
Alike in church, in state, and house hold all,
Supreme memorial of the world's dread fall;
O slavery! laurel of the Infernal mind,
Proud Satan's triumph over lost mankind!"[5]

"Yon mother, loaded with her suckling child,
  Her rags with frequent spots of blood defiled,
Drags slowly fainting on; the fiend is nigh;
Rings the shrill cowskin; roars the tyger-cry;
In pangs th' unfriended suppliant crawls along,
And shrieks the prayer of agonizing wrong."

"Why shrinks yon slave, with horror, from his meat?
Heavens! 'tis his flesh, the wretch is whipped to eat.
Why streams the life-blood from that female's throat?
She sprinkled gravy on a guest's new coat!"[6]

Poetic license? Exaggeration? Fantasy? *Only half the truth, if a thousand witnesses are to be believed.*

Meanwhile, in Williamsburg, Virginia, the distinguished St. George Tucker was writing to many people for information on the progress of emancipation in the middle states and preparing for publication *A Dissertation on Slavery with A Proposal for the Gradual Abolition of It, in the State of Virginia* (1796). It was and is important because of Tucker's prominence and influence. It was important because of its sharp indictment of slavery by a Virginian and its plan of gradual emancipation. Its real significance, however, lies

in its epilogue, for here was the key of colonization. Tucker lined up squarely with the critics of the Founding Fathers: "Whilst we were offering up vows at the shrine of Liberty, and sacrificing hecatombs upon her altars; whilst we swore irreconcilable hostility to her enemies, and hurled defiance in their faces; whilst we adjured the God of Hosts to witness our resolution to live free or die, and imprecated curses on their heads who refused to unite with us in establishing the empire of freedom; we were imposing upon our fellow men, who differ in complexion from us, *a slavery* ten thousand times more cruel than the utmost extremity of those grievances and oppressions, of which we complained. Such are the inconsistencies of human nature . . . such that partial system of morality which confines rights and injuries, to particular complexions."[7]

Tucker made one of the earliest references to slavery as a sin of our fathers visited upon succeeding generations. He dwelt upon the evil of profits from the natural increase of slaves, upon the crime against Africa, and upon the conflict between slavery and our expressed national ideals. Speaking of the slave trade, he said: "That such horrid practices have been sanctioned by a civilized nation; that a nation ardent in the cause of liberty, and enjoying its blessings in the fullest extent can continue to vindicate a right established on such a foundation; that a people who have declared 'That *all men* are by nature *equally free* and *independent'; and have made this declaration the first article in the foundation of their government,* should in defiance of so sacred a truth, recognized by themselves in so solemn a manner, and on so important an occasion, tolerate a practice incompatible therewith, is such an evidence of the weakness and inconsistency of human nature, as every man who hath a spark of patriotic fire in his bosom must wish to see removed from his own country."[8]

Tucker condemned in strong terms the act of 1669 in Virginia that a slaveowner could kill a slave in process of correction without serious consequences—a law re-enacted in 1705, 1723, and 1748 and not repealed until 1788—as a "cruel and tyrannical" act which "disgraced our code." Like all writers of his day, he listed the essential civil rights of the individual as personal security, personal liberty, and private ownership of property. Like all other opponents of slavery, also, he strongly emphasized that "all men are by nature equally free and independent, and have certain rights of which they cannot deprive or divest their posterity—namely, the enjoyment of life and liberty, with the means of acquiring and possessing property." This, he said, was only a recognition of the first principle of the law of nature, and it would be impossible to reconcile reducing Negroes to slavery with those principles unless we first degraded them below the level of human beings. So legislatures called them goods and chattels. Consciously or not, Tucker was here stating one of the strongest arguments that slavery was based, not in the common law, but upon statute or municipal law.

Thus far Tucker's thesis was historically and logically sound, and it was in harmony with current liberalism. Then came the mental block, confusion, and defeat. Property rights cannot be disregarded. Public security must not be neglected.

Colonization is too expensive to be considered. Support and protection of colonists is too difficult. So, Tucker said, we should retain all males in slavery but free every female born after passage of an act for gradual emancipation. That would give freedom to all their children. They should serve their former owners until twenty-eight years of age and then go completely free with twenty dollars, two suits of clothes, a hat, a pair of shoes, and two blankets. All Negro children should be registered within one month after birth. Then, said Tucker, there should be imposed upon the free Negroes and mulattoes, the most severe restraints. They should be denied the franchise and the privilege of officeholding. They should not be permitted to possess arms of any sort, or to own land, or to serve on juries, or as witnesses except against Negroes, or administer estates, or devise wills, or inherit property. "By

A front and profile view of an African's head, with the mouth-piece and necklace, the hooks round which are placed to prevent an escape when pursued in the woods, and to hinder them from laying down the head to procure rest.—At A is a flat iron which goes into the mouth, and so effectually keeps down the tongue, that nothing can be swallowed, not even the saliva, a passage for which is made through holes in the mouth-plate.

An enlarged view of the mouth-piece, which, when long worn, becomes so heated, as frequently to bring off the skin along with it.

A view of the leg-bolts or shackles, as put upon the legs of the slaves on shipboard, in the middle passage.

An enlarged view of the boots and spurs, as used at some plantations in Antigua.

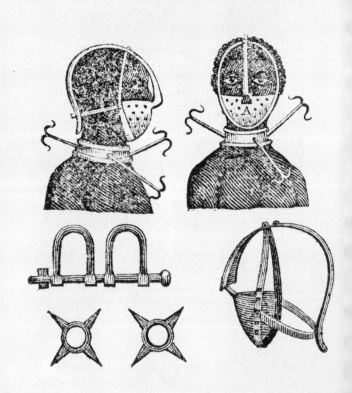

denying them the most valuable privileges which civil government affords," said Tucker, "I wished to render it their inclination and their interest to seek those privileges in some other climate."

Was this an antislavery document? The answer is a qualified no! Tucker could not deny or excuse the evils of the foreign slave trade; they were too well known. He could not repudiate the natural rights of man; they were too universally endorsed. He could not contemplate slavery in perpetuity; it stood condemned. He could not bring himself to suggest the slaves be killed off, or public funds be used to rehabilitate them in Africa; but he could and did present a system of oppression and diabolical cruelty worse than slavery—worse because designed deliberately to drive them out of the land. Greater men than he were soon to do the same.

Head frames and log necklace
Methods of control common in the West Indies and not unknown on the continent. Many devices, particularly leg irons, were used to prevent flight.

parties, from the river Gambia to Bambarra; each party having from one hundred to one hundred and fifty slaves.

The Log-Yokes are made of the roots of trees, so heavy as to make it extremely difficult for the persons who wear them to walk, much more to escape or run away.

Where the roads lie through woods, the captives are made to travel several hundred miles with logs hung from their necks, as described in the plate.

A representation of a slave at work cruelly accoutred, with a Head-frame and Mouth-piece to prevent his eating—with Boots and Spurs round his legs, and half a hundred weight chained to his body to prevent his absconding.

In 1802 another distinguished *Presbyterian* preacher, Alexander McLeod, publicly joined the antislavery forces with his *Negro Slavery Unjustifiable*.[9] McLeod had been licensed to preach in the Reformed Presbyterian Church in 1799 and had been assigned a dual pastorate at Coldenham, New York, and the First Reformed Presbyterian Church in New York City. He refused to accept the Coldenham assignment so long as there were slaveholders among its communicant membership. The Reformed Presbytery thereupon judicially condemned the practice of slaveholding and warned all members against it. Two years later, McLeod could say: "There is not a slaveholder now in the communion of the Reformed Presbytery." McLeod was at this time only twenty-six years of age. He went on to become one of the leading preachers of the country, a powerful champion of individual freedom. His work in the antislavery movement was confined to colonization at a later date, but this one sermon was published in eleven separate editions, the last in 1863. He denounced slavery as immoral, contrary to the rights of man, and destructive of intellectual powers and finer sensibilities. Punishment of the nation, said McLeod, would be inevitable. The most important part of his argument, however, was his emphasis upon the way in which the inferiority of the Negroes to the whites had been so grossly exaggerated. This, said he, was the essence of tyranny. It was important because it went beyond slavery itself to the more fundamental and lasting doctrine of racial inferiority. It is interesting because the colonization movement, as we shall see, inevitably tended to strengthen rather than to destroy acceptance of that doctrine.

The most prolific writer of this period was Thomas Branagan. Born in Dublin in 1774, he had engaged in the slave trade and then settled in Antigua as an overseer on a plantation and as a slaveholder. He came to Philadelphia in a spirit of humble repentance and actively engaged in the antislavery movement. In 1804 he published *A Preliminary Essay*[10] announcing the forthcoming publication of a poem on slavery. This was published under the title *Avenia*[11] the following year, and by the poem *The Penitential Tyrant*,[12] and by another argument in prose, *Serious Remonstrances, Addressed to the Citizens of the Northern States*.[13] These works of Branagan had a tremendous influence. They were published shortly after South Carolina reopened the slave trade. Public opinion was being marshaled to secure the earliest possible action by Congress to stop the trade completely. Speaking as a former slave trader, from his own experience and observations, Branagan received widespread attention.

"The wretched Africans are not merely enslaved," said he, "they are in instances innumerable, oppressed, and starved, and tormented, and murdered."[14] His descriptions of the slaughter attendant upon the capture of Negroes in Africa, both in *A Preliminary Essay* and in *Avenia*, while restrained, are very vivid: "Children," he said, "are torn from their distracted parents; parents from their screaming children; wives from their frantic husbands; husbands from their violated wives; brothers from their loving sisters; sisters from their affectionate brothers. See them collected in flocks, and, like a herd of swine, driven to the ships. They cry, they struggle, they resist; but all in vain. No eye pities; no hand helps."[15] His estimate of those who died in transport on the high seas each year was 30,000; in seasoning, which implies more accurately than acclimatization the process of adjustment to slave status in a new country, many thousand more. It was one of the more conservative estimates by competent observers.[16]

Branagan addressed a series of devastating remarks to the legislature of South Carolina. "Your conduct, I can assure you," he said, "has excited astonishment and consternation from one end of the Federal Union to the other . . . Is it possible an individual villain, or a government of them, could sanction such a law?"[17] Then turning to the problem of what to do about the slaves already here, he asked for the enactment of rigid laws requiring owners to provide sufficient food, shelter, and clothing, to allow relief from work as a minimum on Saturday afternoon and Sunday, to forbid, by heavy penalties, miscegenation and separation of families by sales, to require instruction of the slaves in the Christian faith, to allow slaves to own property, to place slave marriages on a legal basis, to provide for properly conducted trials and humane punishments, and to set up adequate safeguards for the care of slaves in old age. This was the sort of program originally discussed in Congress. It indicates the degree to which all of these evils of slavery were recognized and talked about at this early date.

Speaking of slavery, Branagan said "it is to the body politic what a galloping consumption is to an individual body." "Slave holders and slave dealers," said he, "are not only literally murderers but barbarous robbers too . . . The fact is, slavery is an indelible disgrace to the American Constitution, as well as an eternal reproach to the whole nation . . . It is inhuman, it is diabolically wicked, for any government or nation to suffer thousands of human beings to be consigned to unutterable wretchedness, to support an individual villain, or a family of them in their idleness, luxury, and dissipation."[18]

Speaking of the natural tendency of slavery to create an aristocracy, Branagan insisted that slaveholders were unfit to be legislators in a republic because "their ideas of distributive justice are corrupted in the very source. Their juvenile employment is to trample on the rights of their fellow men, and look with contempt on their poor neighbors . . . With what idea of justice can such persons enter a house of legislation, or take the reigns of government in their hands, who rob their African brethren of their lives and liberties because forsooth they are black, and despise their fellow citizens, because they are poor. Can a government consisting of such characters long continue free . . . The idea of a slaveholder being a good legislator or governor, is as inconceivable as to suppose a wolf would be a good shepherd, and defend, not devour the sheep; or a fox would protect, not destroy, the poultry."[19]

Speaking of slavery and the standing of the United States in the family of nations, Branagan said that European despots were carefully watching to see if our actions corresponded with our pretensions, in order to find evidence which would "render our professions suspected, and our republicanism a farce." Americans, he said, are professional devotees of liberty and equality, "butchers of their brethren, destroyers of liberty and the rights of man, promoters and supporters of legal barbarity."[20]

John Parrish, in his *Remarks on the Slavery of the Black People* (1806), dwelt long and earnestly on the conflict between slavery and the foundation principles of the nation: "I am no politician," he said, "but it is clear that the fundamentals of all good governments, being equal liberty and impartial justice, the constitution and laws ought to be expressed in such unequivocal terms as not to be misunderstood, or admit of double meaning."[21] "*A house divided against itself cannot stand*," said Parrish, "neither can a government

or constitution."[22] National sins bring punishments upon nations in the form of wars, pestilence, and famines. We tolerate the domestic slave trade with the herding of droves of slaves like cattle through the country. Congress draws back from interfering with slavery through purported respect for constitutional tolerance, but does not hesitate to enact a nefarious fugitive slave law which permits persons to be reduced to slavery on testimony of one man before a single magistrate who may be an interested party. We sustain a system of slavery so cruel that innumerable slaves commit suicide, are hunted with dogs and killed, are burned and sometimes decapitated so their heads may be presented for rewards, or are whipped to death. We permit 600 persons to be kidnapped in six months from the Eastern shore of Maryland alone because people want to get rid of the free Negroes. "What will posterity think of such abuse of power entrusted to rulers for the benefit, protection, and general good of the people?"

He urged that a date be set for the freedom of the slaves, and that all Negro families willing to go to the western domain be given one to two hundred acres of land. In the appendix of his pamphlet he gave a fully documented account of the free Negroes sold back into slavery by the government of North Carolina after they had been freed by the Quakers, with names, dates, and copies of the public records.

It was against this background of antislavery publications that the second great debate in Congress occurred. Congress, in May 1800, had placed additional restrictions upon the foreign slave trade. No citizen of the United States, or person residing in the United States, could legally have any financial interest in any vessel engaged in carrying slaves from one foreign place to another, under penalty of confiscation of such financial interest and fine equal to double the amount. No person could serve on such a vessel under penalty of a $2,000 fine and two years in prison, nor serve on any foreign-owned vessel engaged in the trade. Naval vessels were authorized to seize as prizes any ships violating the Act, and the officers and crews of such ships were to be turned over to the civil authorities of the United States for prosecution.[23]

There was no further discussion of the subject in Congress until South Carolina reopened the trade in 1803. The whole question was then

The manner in which slaves are placed to be flogged.

Another method of fixing the poor victims on a ladder to be flogged, which is also occasionally laid flat on the ground for severer punishment.

opened up for discussion by a resolution of David Bard, representative from Pennsylvania, February 14, 1804: "Resolved, That a tax of ten dollars be imposed on every slave imported into any part of the United States."[24] Thomas Lowndes of South Carolina immediately protested. He insisted that his state had repealed the prohibition because it could not be enforced and slaves had been brought into the state as freely as if there had been no law. The ten-dollar tax would not restrict the trade, and it would provide little revenue. On the contrary, it would be in the nature of a sanction of the trade by the general government.

Bard clarified the issue by frankly stating that the resolution would "show to the world that the General Government are opposed to slavery, and willing to improve their power, as far as it will go, for preventing it . . . for we owe it indispensably to ourselves and to the world, whose eyes are on our Government, to maintain its republican character." Bard then addressed himself to the question of constitutional powers, which was rapidly assuming major importance in all slavery

debates. He pointed out that all of the states had prohibited the importation of slaves and that Congress had aided them by imposing fines and forfeitures upon anyone engaging in the trade. Then South Carolina had repealed her prohibition. Said Bard: "South Carolina is a sovereign state, and has a right to consult and pursue her own interest, *so far as the general good will permit;* for hitherto she may come, and no further. Every state has a right to import slaves if it so chooses, and Congress has a right to tax all the slaves imported; *but when the powers of a State, though Constitutional, operate against the general interest, then the exercise of those powers are politically wrong, because it is contrary to the fundamental principles of society, the public good, which is paramount to law and the Constitution itself.*"[25] Here, though imperfectly stated, was the first expression in Congress of the higher law doctrine.

Thomas Moore of South Carolina was not satisfied with an expression of disapproval by taxation, but proposed "that this House receive with painful sensibility information that one of the

Whipping slaves
Thirty-nine strokes with the lash was the usual punishment inflicted by owners, overseers, or at the public jail. Methods of torture were as numerous as sadism could spawn, and arbitrary power nourished the art.

Southern States, by repeal of certain prohibitory laws, have permitted a traffic unjust in its nature, and highly impolitic in free Governments."[26] Benjamin Huger of South Carolina, on the other hand, although opposed to the reopening of the trade by his state, defended her constitutional right to do so, and then pronounced a theory contrary to that of Bard, which ultimately evolved into the philosophy of Calhoun's Resolutions of 1837: "Each State, so long as she confines herself within the limits of her Constitutional powers, must be the exclusive judge of her own conduct; and it becomes not one State, influenced by different feelings, habits, and interests, to pronounce upon the conduct of another. All, so far as regards themselves, are judges of right and wrong."[27] John B. C. Lucas of Pennsylvania recognized the transitory character of the institution and supported the tax to diminish the trade, saying that the action of South Carolina was the same as admitting slaves into every state "for once introduced into one State, and they will soon find their way into the others where slavery is allowed." "Wherever they go," said Lucas, "the poor white

man need not fix himself; for his labor and relative importance in society will be as nothing."[28]

It is a singular fact that in this debate there was no defense of slavery whatever, and no defense of the slave trade. Several members of the House, notably Andrew Gregg of Pennsylvania, remarked about the unanimity with which every member of the House opposed the slave trade. Members from South Carolina defended the right of their state to make its own decisions in the matter, but they did not defend the trade on moral grounds, and they expressed confidence that the law would be repealed. There was honest disagreement as to how a tax would be interpreted, whether it would be considered as a sanction or as a condemnation. Gregg expressed the feelings of many when he said: "Sanction the trade by imposing the tax, and soon the traders will demand your protection."[29] Those who feared that failure to take some action would convey the idea that Congress did not consider the traffic an evil, who were concerned about insurrections, who wished to increase the revenues, who wished soundly to reprimand South Carolina for action contrary to the general interest joined in passing by a vote of 71 to 45 a resolution to impose a tax of ten dollars on each slave imported into any part of the country.[30] The Committee on Ways and Means was ordered to prepare the bill.

Consideration of the bill itself, however, resulted in some moderation of the demand for immediate action. Caesar A. Rodney of Delaware, later attorney general of the United States under both Jefferson and Madison, and staunch opponent of the extension of slavery to the territories, was in large measure responsible for the reversal. He was unwilling to derive revenue from a tax on slaves, but would have supported a tax if Congress had possessed the power to make it large enough to be prohibitory. Rodney expressed a hope that he might live to see complete emancipation, saying: "When we shall proclaim to every stranger and sojourner, the moment he sets his foot on American earth, the ground on which he stands is holy and consecrated by the genius of universal emancipation. No matter in what language his doom may have been pronounced; no matter what complexion, incompatible with freedom, an Indian or an African sun may have burnt upon him; no matter in what disastrous battle his liberty may have been cloven down; no matter with what solemnities he may have been devoted on the altar of slavery; the first moment he touches the sacred soil of America, the altar and the god shall sink together in the dust; his soul shall walk abroad in her own majesty; his body shall swell beyond the measure of his chains, which burst from around him, and he shall stand redeemed, regenerated, and disenthralled by the great genius of universal emancipation."[31] The final vote to postpone action was fifty-six to fifty with a considerable number of members absent or not voting; and with a notation in the *Annals of Congress* to the effect that many who voted for postponement did so with the expectation that South Carolina would reverse her action on importations.[32] The state did not do so and, in January, 1806, Thomas Moore explained that the House of Representatives of South Carolina had acted twice to repeal the law, but the State Senate had failed to concur by a single vote. Men had not been guilty of duplicity, he said, they had been justified in their optimistic expectations.[33]

Massachusetts, New Hampshire, Vermont, Maryland, and Ohio presented resolutions to Congress in 1806 requesting a constitutional amendment giving Congress immediate power to prohibit the trade.[34] This initiated the final struggle which ended in the prohibition of importations after January 1, 1808. At the very beginning of the debates two significant statements were made. Barnabas Bidwell of Massachusetts clearly indicated that some representatives feared a tax of ten dollars upon slaves currently imported would establish an important source of revenue and thus restrain Congress from prohibiting the trade in 1808. The debate indicates that some proslavery men might well have had that in mind when they refrained from speaking out against the proposed tax at an earlier date.[35] Bidwell also spoke to the question of national interest. He said: "A new doctrine has been broached and held by some gentlemen . . . that the importation of slaves cannot be prohibited by Congress, even after the year 1808. The sum of the reasoning, in which this novel doctrine is attempted to be supported, is, that the clause in the Constitution providing that the importation of such persons as any of the existing States might think proper to admit shall not be prohibited prior to 1808, is a mere negative provision, without any positive words of grant, and does not consequently give Congress a power to lay such a prohibition after that time; and all powers not delegated are reserved."[36]

Bidwell, of course, gave the correct and fairly obvious answer that there would have been no point to restraining until a certain time the exercise of a nonexistent power, and stated, also correctly, that slaves were bought and sold and therefore came under the power of Congress to regulate (and to prohibit) foreign and interstate commerce. He said further: "The Constitutional restriction applies only to the importation, not the exportation, of slaves; and it extends only to the States existing at the date of the Constitution, and not to the Territories of the United States. Accordingly, Congress have already, by law, prohibited the importation of slaves into the Territories."[37]

Nothing was accomplished in the closing days of the first session of the ninth Congress (Spring, 1806) and the subject was taken up again in December 1806. Thomas Jefferson in his sixth annual message (December 2, 1806) congratulated Congress on its approaching opportunity "to withdraw the citizens of the United States from all further participation in those violations of human rights which have been so long continued on the unoffending inhabitants of Africa, and which the morality, the reputation, and the best interests of our country, have long been eager to proscribe."[38] Bills to prevent the trade after December 31, 1807, were presented in both the House and the Senate. A meeting of minds on the terms of the prohibition proved most difficult; and some things said in the debate were as shameful as any ever uttered in Congress.

Short of an armed squadron to patrol the coast of the United States, there was no way of preventing some landing of slaves by men willing to risk drastic fines and forfeiture of ships. The United States government, in such cases, must depend upon informers; it must then proceed in the courts against those charged with violations. *What was to be done in such cases with the slaves being illegally imported?* Sell them to private owners! Men opposed to slavery refused to countenance such procedure, not alone on moral grounds, but because it would encourage violations. Set them free! The laws of the slave states forbade it, and the victims were utterly helpless to support themselves in a country where they knew nothing of the language, customs, and economy. Send them to Africa! How could they be returned from the coast to their homelands and protected against recapture? This was not a simple problem. It called for a complete subordination of private interests, local prejudices, and legal technicalities. It got nothing of the sort.

The House Bill was written by Peter Early of Georgia. It provided, in substance, for forfeiture and sale of slaves seized by the government. Speaking against freedom for these people, he said: "Suppose the power of the General Government able for a while to enforce such a provision, and to turn loose a few, or even a single cargo of persons of color, what do gentlemen suppose would become of them? Do they suppose the people of those States would permit them to live among them? They are mistaken. We are told it is cruel and disgraceful to keep them in slavery. There is no doubt of it. But would it not be more cruel to place them in a situation where we must in self-defense—gentlemen will understand me— get rid of them in some way. We must either get rid of them, or they of us; there is no alternative, and I leave it to gentlemen to determine which course would be pursued. There can be no doubt on this head. I will speak out; it is not my practice to be mealy-mouthed on a subject of importance. *Not one of them would be left alive in a year.*"[39] In short, men and women seized and dragged to America in violation of the laws of the United States, if set free by the courts of the United States, must die. The people of Georgia could not have it otherwise.

Faced with the choice of no prohibition, or one which could only be enforced by confiscation and sale of the persons being imported illegally—a dilemma which seemed to give some members of the House ill-concealed satisfaction—John Smilie of Pennsylvania moved that anyone importing slaves into any place within the jurisdiction of the United States "be considered as guilty of felony, and on being convicted, suffer death."[40] Southerners fought to defeat the proposal. It was intended to prevent violations. It was regarded by its sponsors as a justifiable and equitable punishment for the offense. It was also, and was intended to be, a stigma, a constant reminder of the shame of slaveholding.

The debate on the question of penalty—whether forfeiture of cargo or death—now became bitter, because back of the immediate issue, in men's minds, was the question of slavery. This was to be true at all times, and on all issues, until the Civil War. In this current dispute antislavery men were opposing the principle of forfeiture. Slave traders, they said, would continue to go to Africa

and seize or buy a cargo of Negroes. In either case, these persons would be, forcibly and without their consent, carried out of Africa. Those who did not die of disease or commit suicide would be brought to the United States, where they would be met by the law under discussion. Said they: "It finds them by the laws of God and man, entitled to their freedom as clearly and absolutely as we are. They are not, by any law, human or divine, the slaves of any master. They are not the lawful property of any owner . . . Their detention is a wrongful, false imprisonment. In this very bill we declare it to be a high crime. By the same law we condemn the man-stealer and become the receiver of his stolen goods. We punish the criminal, and then step into his place, and complete the crime which he has only begun . . . We sell his victims as slaves, receive the price of their slavery and put it into the public treasury; and the vendee holds them and their children, from generation to generation, in perpetual slavery, by a title derived from our law."[41]

The death penalty was opposed by some members as too harsh for the offense, but largely on the grounds that it would be ineffective: people would not inform, juries would not convict, slaves would be landed in the Spanish colonies of Florida and the carriers would be beyond reach. The only possible solution, said the men from the lower South, was forfeiture of all slaves brought in violation of the law. No one would buy a slave likely to be seized by the government. These arguments were all valid from the practical point of view. It was when they turned to the question of why people would not inform or vote to convict that we reach a meeting of minds on the level of moral principles.

Peter Early of Georgia once more said exactly what the people of Georgia thought; and, since he was afterward elected governor of the state, we may rightly assume he spoke correctly. Foreign slave traders, he said, would bring their slaves to the slave states "where there is no such abhorrence of the crime of importing them, and where no man dare inform . . . It would cost him more than his life is worth . . . A large majority of the people in the Southern States do not consider slavery as a crime. They do not believe it immoral to hold human flesh in bondage . . . If they considered the holding of men in slavery as a crime, they would necessarily accuse themselves, a thing which human nature revolts at.

I will tell the truth. A large majority of people in the Southern States do not consider slavery even an evil."[42]

Proof of Early's statement was not long in coming. The death penalty was stricken out and imprisonment of five to ten years substituted by a vote of sixty-three to fifty-three. Antislavery men then sought to add the provision "that no person shall be sold as a slave by virtue of this act." This would have saved from slavery every Negro brought in illegally and seized by the government. Some other method of disposing of them would have had to be devised. This was the acid test of proslavery and antislavery strength in the House. Previously, Peter Early had said that if the government seized them and set them free the people of Georgia would kill them. Now, the government must sell them into slavery. That was considered essential, "without it, no person would be found to give information of the infraction of the act." Finally, as a sort of omen of things to come, Early offered a specious argument, one might almost say falsification, of constitutional

interpretation. Congress, he said, did not have the right to prevent the sale of these persons, because the laws of the Southern states required that persons of color who came into or were brought into those states should be sold as slaves.[43]

The vote on prohibiting the sale of these persons was a tie, sixty to sixty, and the Speaker of the House, Nathaniel Macon of North Carolina, who was a staunch defender of slavery, cast the deciding vote against the prohibition.[44] So, slave traders who brought Negroes from Africa to the United States were not to be punished by death, and their victims were to be sold into an eternity of slavery, and these decisions were made by the slave power. In both cases, it was the votes of men representing slaves, who had no wills, no judgments, no powers, that were the deciding votes. The antislavery men made a final effort to secure freedom for the Negroes illegally brought into the country by providing that the government should remove them after seizure to any state where slavery was illegal. Peter Early then made his final threat: "We want no civil wars, no rebellions, no insurrections, no resistance to any authority of the government. Give effect then to this wish, and do not pass this bill as it now stands."[45] The first threat of rebellion and war had now been made in Congress by the slaveholders. Whether beaten down by threats or weary of argument, the House submitted to his demands, and the Congress passed what appeared to be and has always been represented as a humane and liberal piece of legislation. Illuminated by the debates of the House of Representatives, it was a victory for the slave power, little less disgraceful than the Fugitive Slave Act of 1793.[46] The men who bought persons or seized persons in Africa and brought them to the United States contrary to law were to lose their ships and cargo, perhaps to be fined and imprisoned for not more than ten years. The poor victims were to be turned over immediately to the state authorities to be disposed of as the laws of the state might direct, which meant be sold into slavery.

TREAD-MILL SCENE IN JAMAICA.

"As I have made mention of the Tread-Mill, I shall endeavour to describe what it is, for I believe the people of this country have no idea of it. Almost every one of these instruments of punishment is of a different construction. This was a cylinder about ten feet in diameter, with broad steps. The hand-rail above it has eight pair of straps fastened to it, with which the hands of the prisoners are secured. The board under the hand-rail descends perpendicularly towards the wheel, and does not therefore afford the slightest protection to the prisoners in case of their hanging. The steps of the wheel project about twelve or fifteen inches beyond the board, and are bevelled at the edge, so that the keen side revolves much against the bodies, knees, and legs of the prisoners with torturous effects. We asked the jailor whether the driver was allowed to use a cat, and asked to see the instrument. It was a whip composed of nine lashes of small cords knotted. He said it was absolutely necessary to "touch them up," women as well as men. They struck the latter on the back, but the women on the feet. Not only all the steps, but the very drum of the mill were stained with old and recent blood, the latter being that of a poor old woman, which had been shed so profusely, that even the sand on the floor underneath was thickly sprinkled with it. I saw the blood, and put the question myself to the jailor respecting the cause of it, who informed me that the poor old woman had been put on the Mill that morning, and being unable to keep the step, hung for the whole fifteen minutes, suspended by the wrists, with the revolving steps beating against, and bruising her body the whole time."—*Joseph Sturge, Esq. Birmingham.*

THE Women of Great Britain are earnestly appealed to on behalf of upwards of 700,000 of their Fellow-subjects suffering many of the worst incidents of Slavery, under the delusive name of Apprenticeship. The condition of the Women and Children of the Colonies specially demands sympathy and succour. Evidence, the most abundant and authentic, has shown the present state of things to be unjust and oppressive, and an effort is being made to bring it to a speedy and perpetual end. Pecuniary aid is imperatively required. Will not British females answer the call, and remember them that are in bonds as bound with them?

Subscriptions will be thankfully received by the Treasurer to the Glasgow Ladies' Emancipation Society, Mrs Nelson, Port-Dundas; or by Miss Smeal, one of the Secretaries, 161, Gallowgate.

Treadmills in Charleston and New Orleans were of the type pictured here.

MIGRATIONS TO THE FREE STATES

Chapter 9

One of the strangest aspects of the slavery controversy was the way in which the spokesmen of the slave power vehemently defended the institution of slavery as a positive good, denounced all programs for the amelioration of its harsher features, and at the same time, sometimes in the same breath, cast the blame on someone else. The slave was a slave because he had a black skin. He could not have an education or religious instruction because it would increase his desire for freedom. He could not be set free because someone in the North insisted he should be freed; it was the fault of the abolitionists that he was kept in slavery. People who spoke out against slavery and were mobbed, or hanged, or shot had only themselves to blame; they should have remained silent.

The idea that the South was turned away from emancipation, and toward a defense of slavery by the abolition movement of the North is a monstrous fiction. There was no recognizable North and South on the slavery question until the Black Belt was developed. We have seen that the leading opponents of slavery in the Constitutional Convention of 1787 were from Virginia, Maryland, and New York, all of them slave states, and that slavery was in process of gradual extinction in Connecticut, Rhode Island, New York, and Pennsylvania until well past the turn of the century. There were men within the limits of slave states in the early years of the republic who were opposed to slavery and said so. Woolman, Benezet, Franklin, Mason, Rush, Hopkins, Webster, Jay,

Dwight, Rice, Cooper, and McLeod all lived in slave states and helped to make them free.

No one of the people we have been talking about, however, came from Georgia or South Carolina. Men from those states spoke, if at all, in defense of slavery and in defiance of every critic. There never was tolerance of dissent or freedom of expression on the subject in *proslavery circles,* or where slaveholders dominated a community and controlled public opinion. Later on, they, and some historians, tried to blame their severity and uncompromising attitude on William Lloyd Garrison. Actually, of course, they did not become severe and uncompromising, they always had been that way. William Lloyd Garrison was a Johnny-come-lately in the business of abolishing slavery, and no one in the slave country ever defended slavery more violently than the spokesmen from the lower South *before* 1830.

Richard Furman, leader of the Southern Baptists, wrote a strong defense of slavery as a Christian institution in 1822. He insisted that discovery of the Charleston insurrection in 1822 was evidence of God's approval and protection of slaveholders, and he urged religious instruction for the slaves that they might be taught respect for their masters.[1] Frederick Dalche, an Episcopal minister of Charleston, in 1823 urged religious instruction that the slaves might be indoctrinated with the place in society assigned to them by their Creator.[2] William Barlow, rector of the Claremont Protestant Episcopal Church in Charleston, in 1826 urged the church to preach the acceptability of slavery to divine law. He proposed a constitution for an "American Society for Promoting Christian Knowledge" to promote proslavery doctrine with the senior bishop of the Episcopal Church as its president.[3] When Stephen Grellet visited North Carolina in 1824 to influence officials of the state and slaveowners to take steps toward "amelioration of the condition of slaves in that state, and to prevent the arbitrary cruelty exercised by many of their masters" Governor Holmes insisted that educating the slaves would render them unhappy and religious instruction would increase their family attachments and add to their sorrow at separation by sale.[4]

Antislavery sentiment was expressed in the early years only by men who lived in states where the slave power was too weak to prevent it, or by men powerful enough—most of them slaveholders from Virginia—to defy the slave power, or by men who lived in the *nonslaveholding communities* of the South. Just as soon as, and wherever, the slave power became consolidated, antislavery utterances were silenced. It was consolidated, it was militant, it was on the march, by the 1830's; and *far from reconstructing its defenses from a feeling of desperation and exasperation, it was reaching out to silence its critics everywhere and to expand its power to the whole of the continent. It moved from strength and a sense of power, not from fear and weakness.*

One reason, indeed the primary reason, for this unwarranted sense of power—and, of course, it was unwarranted—was the fact that the South had lost its balance and sense of proportion. As the Black Belt developed and slavery and the power of the slaveholders began to dominate the lower South, liberals moved out. They went to the free states. They became the most outspoken critics of slavery, and they knew whereof they spoke. Most of them were slaveholders previous to their migration, or came from slaveholding families. They were exiles in a very real sense, for some of them, certainly, would have been killed had they ventured back to the South.

The migration of these people was not a part of the westward movement. People moved west from the Carolinas, and Georgia, and Virginia, just as they moved west from New York, Pennsylvania, and New England. They moved southwest and northwest. We can identify many such. They moved for diverse reasons: to get away from the restraints and conventions of old, established com-

munities, to find more elbow room, to get land or cheaper land. There is a voluminous literature on the subject, familiar to everyone. Some of these people were honest, hard-working people of all sorts from homestead farmers to carpenters and woodcutters who found intolerable the stigma on honest toil in the slave country. Some farmers moved because the entire economy was geared to the needs of slaveholding planters, and marketing and shipping became increasingly difficult as plantations developed. Some were paid high prices for their lands. Some were bitter because legislatures dominated by slaveholders, who could afford private instruction for their children, refused to build public schools.

Let us dwell a moment on this point of non-slaveholders' grievances. The legislature of North Carolina, for example, refused until 1840 to provide in any way for a system of public education. In consequence, the Census of 1850 showed 80,000 illiterate free persons in the state.[5] One writer puts the figure at 71,150 persons over twenty-one years of age.[6] The argument over schools and roads became so serious that it finally led to threats of violence.[7] Benjamin Sherwood Hedrick, professor of chemistry at the University of North Carolina, said of migration from that state: "Of my neighbors, friends and kindred, nearly one-half have left the State since I was old enough to remember. Many is the time I have stood by the loaded emigrant wagon and given the parting hand to those whose faces I was never to look upon again. They were going to seek homes in the free West, knowing, as they did, that free and slave labor could not both exist and prosper in the same community."[8] Still more to the point was the statement of Henry Ruffner, president of Washington College (Lexington, Va.), in 1847. Saying that Virginia had lost by emigration 300,-000 more persons than all of the old free states, he continued: "She has sent—or we should rather say, she has driven from her soil—at least one third of all the emigrants, who have gone from the old States to the new. More than another third have gone from the other old slave states . . . These were generally industrious and enterprising white men, who found by sad experience, that a country of slaves was not the country for them. It is a truth, a certain truth, that slavery drives free laborers,—farmers, mechanics, and all, and some of the best of them too—out of the country, and fills their places with negroes."[9]

The African slave trade

These slaves, taken from a slaver by the British ship "Undine," show a preponderance of the young men and boys so greatly desired by buyers in America.

All of this was part of the westward movement —very important in the slavery controversy as we shall see—but not in this particular aspect of it. The movement we are talking about was a distinct, easily recognizable, and clearly defined migration of people away from the slave power. These were men and women who simply refused to live in the *atmosphere* of slavery. They were cultivated men and women in the finest tradition of those who had preceded them in the contest: of Franklin, Rush, and Rice, for example. Fortunately, life loses meaning for our choicest souls unless they can help the underprivileged and oppressed. The mere sight of the victims of prejudice and greed, in slavery, was unbearable to these people. Honorable men and women, given to honest thinking, simply could not breathe in an atmosphere where they not only could do nothing about it, and say nothing about it, but were expected to condone and publicly approve it. The rapid rise of the slave power bore them down and drove them out.

Once out of the reach of the slave power, these people were free to speak and to write, which they did with telling effect. Some men who have written about the South and slavery have refused to recognize what they said as valid source materials. Others have looked casually at a few items and professed to have seen it all. Actually, it is our finest evidence as to what slavery really was, because these people had been slaveholders, had been reared in slave communities, had gone into exile rather than be silent about it, and were free to tell what they knew. They were relatively free from violence, they could find publishers and establish printing presses, and the public was willing to read and listen. Naturally, they became leaders in the antislavery movement. They would have been, had they been allowed to remain in the slave states. Among them were James Gillespie Birney, foremost exponent of constitutional theory and champion of civil rights; Edward Coles, governor of Illinois and staunch opponent of slavery expansion; Levi Coffin, "president" of the underground railroad; John Rankin, defender of the faith in one General Assembly of the Presbyterian Church after another; Angelina Grimké, champion of women's rights and coauthor of the greatest indictment of slavery ever written; and a host of others of equal stature.

Preachers were among the first to feel the pressure for conformity, because there never was a more pronounced moral issue, and the slave power insisted it was and must remain a political question. Eventually, the Southern churches accepted that point of view, officially at least, but not until a good many incidents occurred. The Baptist David Barrow was one of these men. He was born in 1753 and preached in southern Virginia and northern North Carolina. In 1795 he founded the Portsmouth-Norfolk church and installed Jacob Bishop, a Negro, as pastor, with a mixed Negro-white congregation. He was subjected to much criticism and some violence, and moved in 1798, under strong pressure, to Kentucky. In Kentucky in 1805 he was expelled from the North District Association of Baptists because of his views on slavery, wrote his pamphlet *Involuntary, Unlimited, Perpetual, Absolute, Hereditary Slavery Examined on the Principles of Nature, Reason, Justice, Policy, and Scripture,* and served as president of the Kentucky Abolition Society for many years. He died in 1819.

David Rice was a Virginia Presbyterian and a graduate of Princeton. He was much older than Barrow, having been born in 1733, and having begun his ministry in 1767. He left Virginia in 1783 because of opposition to his antislavery principles and went to Kentucky, where he established the first grammar school in the West, helped to found Transylvania, and served as chairman of its board of trustees for many years. We are already familiar with his remarkable speech in the Kentucky Constitutional Convention. He afterward was active in the Kentucky Abolition Society, which failed to survive.[10]

We are more familiar with the work of Barrow and Rice because they left us written records of their antislavery views, but there were others in this area. William Hickman, born in Virginia in 1747, settled near Lexington, Kentucky, in 1784 and became pastor of the Baptist Church at Forks of the Elkhorn. The Elkhorn Association censured him in 1805 saying "this Association judges it improper for ministers, churches, or associations, to meddle with emancipation from slavery or any other political subject, and as such, we advise ministers and churches to have nothing to do therewith in their religious capacities."[11] Hickman threw the slaveholders out of his church, but was forced to resign. He returned later, obviously with an understanding to avoid the subject.

George Smith, born in Virginia in 1747 of Episcopalian parents, went to Kentucky as a Baptist preacher in 1804. His strong antislavery views made him exceedingly unpopular, but he preached until his death in 1820. Carter Tarrant, one of the earliest settlers in Logan County, Kentucky, came from Virginia and preached at the Hillsboro and Clear Creek churches. He and a member of his church, John Sutton, founded the first antislavery church in Woodford County. He died while serving as a chaplain in the Army in the War of 1812. Another antislavery church was founded at Bardstown by Joshua Carman, in 1796, but failed to survive.

Here was the record of honest, sincere frontier preachers who failed to gain more than a momentary hearing in their struggle against slavery, just as Rice had failed in the constitutional convention of the state. There was no central governing body of the Baptist churches to which they could carry an appeal. But over the long view, they did not fail, because other men were coming from the deep South to build on the foundations they had laid and this was soon to become a very important area of antislavery activity.

James Gilliland was born (1761) and reared in South Carolina. He was opposed to slavery, and, after graduating from Dickinson College, Pennsylvania, returned to South Carolina to preach in 1796. He was charged by twelve members of his congregation with political treason for preaching against slavery, and the Presbyterian Synod of the Carolinas, meeting at Morganton, November 3, 1796, decreed that he could not speak publicly for emancipation.[12] He obeyed for a time, but moved to the greatest single mecca for emancipated slaves and ex-slave holders, Brown County, Ohio, in 1805. Here, he served as pastor of the Red Oak church for thirty-nine years, to a congregation of ex-slaveholders and other emigrants from the South. He was an uncompromising advocate of immediate emancipation and was second on the list of vice-presidents of the American Anti-Slavery Society when it was organized in 1833. He was affectionately known as Father Gilliland and founded churches at Ripley, Russellville, Decatur, and Georgetown.

There was born in Virginia in 1749 a most remarkable man, Samuel Doak, who graduated from Princeton in 1775 and was licensed to preach by the Presbytery of Hanover, Virginia. He married, moved to Fork Church, North Carolina (later Tennessee), and founded (1783) at Little Limestone, near Jonesboro, Martin Academy, with

a charter from the state. He founded Washington College in 1795 and served as its president until 1818, at which time he founded, at New Bethel, Tusculum Academy. He was opposed to slavery; freed his slaves and sent them to Brown County, Ohio; and trained a host of young preachers, nearly all of whom went to the Old Northwest. Among them were Gideon Blackburn, John Rankin, and David Nelson. Sometime in the 1820's, Doak moved to Ohio, where he died in 1830.

Doak's son-in-law was John Rankin, born in Tennessee, in 1793. He studied under Doak, later married his daughter, and was licensed to preach in 1817. He was a staunch opponent of slavery and active in the Kentucky Abolition Society while preaching at Carlisle in 1817–21. He then moved to Ripley, Ohio, where he served as pastor of the Presbyterian Church for forty-four years. He converted his home into a haven of refuge for fugitives crossing the river and was mobbed many times by irate Kentuckians. A series of his letters first published in 1823 and reprinted in book form as *Letters on American Slavery, Addressed to Mr. Thomas Rankin, Merchant at Middlebrook, Augusta County, Virginia* remains one of the twenty-five most important antislavery publications.[13] He later served as a lecturer for the American Anti-slavery Society, but his most important contribution was in the Presbyterian General Assemblies, where year after year he led the fight against slavery until the schism of 1837.

There came also to the Chillicothe Presbytery in early years, James H. Dickey, born in Virginia in 1780, and William Dickey, a native of South Carolina. James began his ministerial career as a missionary in Tennessee, but freed the slaves inherited by himself and his wife, and went to South Salem, Ohio, in 1810, where he became widely known for his antislavery work. William Dickey moved with his family from South Carolina to Kentucky where he preached for seventeen years. He went to Ohio, organized a church at Bloomingsburg in 1818, and served as its pastor for forty years. Finally, there came from Pennsylvania by way of Kentucky, Samuel Crothers. He had intended to make Winchester, Kentucky, his home, but moved to Ross County, Ohio, where he preached from 1810 to 1820 and then went to Greenfield, where he organized the Paint Valley Abolition Society. Gilliland, Rankin, the two Dickeys, and Samuel Crothers made the Chillicothe Presbytery of Ohio an antislavery stronghold before 1820. Rankin quickly emerged as a national figure in the movement.[14]

Another of the giants in the movement was Levi Coffin, born in North Carolina in 1789. He was of a family of Quakers, by instinct and tradition opposed to slavery. Opposition to his religious instruction of the slaves in the New Garden area led to his migration to Newport, Indiana, in 1826. Here he devoted as much time to aiding the fugitives as to business, helped three thousand slaves on their way to freedom, and ultimately became the most important figure in that exciting phase of antislavery work. He was in Cincinnati during the riotous forties and continued his aid to freedmen until long after the Civil War.

From the schools of Samuel Doak in Tennessee came a number of men. Gideon Blackburn was born in Virginia, in 1772. His family moved to Tennessee, where he attended Martin Academy. He was licensed to preach at twenty, founded a church at New Providence in 1792, and conducted a school for Cherokee children from 1804 to 1810. He became pastor of the Presbyterian church at Louisville in 1823, and president of Centre College at Danville in 1827. He went to Illinois in 1833, assisted Elijah P. Lovejoy in organizing the Illinois Antislavery Society, and founded Blackburn College at Carlinville.

David Nelson, born in Tennessee in 1793, studied under Doak, served as a surgeon in the War of 1812, became pastor of the Presbyterian church in Danville in 1828, rose to national prominence as director of education for the church, freed his slaves in Kentucky and went to Palmyra, Missouri, as president of Marion College. He was driven from his pulpit and from the state for advocating compensated emancipation, and barely escaped with his life into Illinois.

Thomas Morris was born in Virginia in 1776. He was bitterly opposed to slavery and moved to Ohio in 1795, where he studied law at night while making a living, as a brickmaker, for a family of eleven children. He served in the Ohio legislature from 1806 to 1830, as chief justice of the state from 1830 to 1833, and as United States senator from 1833 to 1839. In the Senate he led the fight for the right of petition, fought Calhoun's resolutions of 1837, and delivered a masterful defense of civil rights in debate with Henry Clay. He was read out of his party and promptly joined in the political movement to abolish slavery.

Two Virginians of equal stature went to Illinois to escape slavery, and their combined efforts probably kept that state free. James Lemen settled at New Design in 1786, organized the first eight Baptist churches, all on an antislavery basis, diligently counteracted the many proslavery petitions sent to Congress while William Henry Harrison was governor of Indiana Territory, and organized "The Baptized Church of Christ, Friends of Humanity, on Cantine Creek," with a constitution "denying union and communion with all persons holding the doctrine of perpetual, involuntary, hereditary slavery." This close-knit organization gave tremendous weight to Lemen's work as a member of the first Constitutional Convention. "The church," it was said, "properly speaking, never entered politics, but presently, when it became strong, the members all formed what they called the 'Illinois Anti-Slavery League,' and it was this body that conducted the anti-slavery contest. It always kept one of its members and several of its friends in the territorial legislature, and five years before the constitutional election in 1818 it had fifty resident agents—men of like sympathies—in the several settlements throughout the territory quietly at work."[15]

Edward Coles was born in Virginia in 1786, of wealthy, slaveholding parents. He was educated at Hampden-Sidney College and William and Mary College, served as private secretary to President Madison from 1809 to 1815, and went to Russia on a diplomatic mission in 1816. Coles made plans to free his slaves as early as 1815. In the spring of 1819 he took his slaves by boat to the West and gave them freedom and land upon which to start a new life. He immediately made common cause with the antislavery forces of Lemen's association, was elected governor in 1822 by a narrow margin, and was a tower of strength in preventing adoption of a new proslavery constitution.

Finally, there came into this area two stalwarts of the later movement: William T. Allan and James A. Thome. Allan was the son of the Presbyterian minister at Huntsville, Alabama, and Thome the son of a wealthy slaveholding planter of Augusta, Kentucky. Both came to Lane Seminary, Cincinnati, in 1833, under the influence of Theodore Weld. Both took part in the great debate there, and in the contest over academic freedom, with which we shall deal at length. Both joined the exodus to Oberlin, became antislavery lecturers and ministers, and remained active in the movement until slavery was abolished. Thome went to the British West Indies for the American Anti-Slavery Society in 1836; Allan was undoubtedly the most powerful force in Illinois for freedom after Governor Coles removed to Philadelphia in the early 1830's.

George Bourne was born in Westbury, England, in 1780. He came to America and became pastor of the Presbyterian church at South River, Virginia, in 1814. Two years of contact with slavery so shocked him that he published, in 1816, *The Book and Slavery Irreconcilable*. He was immediately charged with heresy and condemned by the Presbyterian Council. He went to Germantown, Pennsylvania, ultimately joined the Dutch Reformed Church, and wrote some bitter denunciations of slavery: *An Address to the Presbyterian Church, Enforcing the Duty of Excluding All Slaveholders from the "Communion of Saints"; Man Stealing and Slavery Denounced by the Presbyterian and Methodist Churches; Picture of Slavery in the United States of America;* and *Slavery Illustrated in Its Effects upon Women and Domestic Society*. Bourne's attack upon slavery was bold. Some would say that it was extreme, but no one knew better than he the relentless fashion in which the slave power was silencing its critics, and he retaliated in kind.

The list of exiles grows long; but there were others: Andrew Bankson of Tennessee who came to Illinois in 1808, became a state senator, and worked actively in the antislavery cause; William Brisbane of South Carolina who freed his slaves, moved to Cincinnati in 1835 and ultimately to Wisconsin, where he was pastor of the Baptist Church in Madison and chief clerk of the state senate; Alexander Campbell of Virginia, who went to Kentucky in 1796 and to Ripley, Ohio, in 1803, where he freed his slaves, served in the Ohio legislature and in the United States Senate, and became the first vice-president of the Ohio Anti-Slavery Society in 1835; Peter Cartwright, of Virginia, who moved to Kentucky in 1790, and from fear that his daughters would marry slaveholders, to Illinois in 1824, where he served in the state legislature and ran against Lincoln for Congress in 1846; Obed Denham of Virginia, who went to Ohio in 1797, founded the town of Bethel, and endowed a Baptist church for those "who do

not hold slaves, nor commune at the Lord's Table with those that do practice such tyranny over their fellow creatures."

Others were William Dunlop who went from Kentucky to Ohio in 1796, freed his slaves and settled them on land near Ripley, and further proved his steadfastness in the cause by paying $1600 for the release of John B. Mahan when he was kidnapped and taken to Kentucky for trial on a charge of abducting slaves; Samuel Grist of Virginia, who bought land in Brown County, Ohio, for one thousand slaves to whom he gave not only farms but livestock and tools; and Risdon Moore, who lived from 1760 until 1812 in his native state of Delaware, then in North Carolina, and then in Georgia, moved to Illinois in the latter year, freed his slaves, served as speaker in the territorial legislature, and as a member of the state legislature, was burned in effigy by proslavery men because of his activities in behalf of the Negroes and against slavery.

This does not by any means exhaust the list. There were hundreds who came North to escape slavery and worked quietly for emancipation in local antislavery societies and at the ballot box. There were the two—James G. Birney and Angelina Grimké—whose lives are woven inextricably into every phase of the struggle. Finally, there were the thousands of fugitives who settled in Northern communities and by their industry and good citizenship bore mute testimony of the falsity of the proslavery doctrines, and thousands, too, who bore the indestructible marks of cruelty.

The people who have been here mentioned, with very few exceptions left the South about 1800, shortly before or shortly after the turn of the century, when the Revolutionary impulse for emancipation was checked and the South was dedicated to perpetual slavery. They left because so-called security regulations impinged upon their freedom to discuss slavery, to educate or preach to the slaves, and to ease their distress and set them free; or because they feared the baneful influence of slavery upon their children, or because they lost faith in the future of the slave country. Almost all of them were slaveholders who freed their slaves at tremendous financial sacrifice. There was no quibbling on their part about gradual emancipation, or compensated emancipation, and they did not participate in that refined form of brigandage known as "allowing the slaves to

Whipping of Amos Dresser
Mob violence against an inoffensive theological student who ventured into a slave state with antislavery literature in his luggage.

purchase their freedom." They emancipated them, and in most cases brought them North and gave them a start as free men.

These people, also, were not lowly people seeking to improve their economic status. All of them were men of assured positions and security in their communities. If there is one thing crystal clear about the antislavery movement up to this point—and it continued to be true to the end—it is this: *it was an intellectual and moral crusade for social reform and common decency in human relationships, initiated and carried through at great personal sacrifice by men of property and high position in religious and educational institutions, in public life, and in the professions.* These exiles from the South were that kind of people. Those who became active in the agitation against slavery were devoted to the cause and effective in their contributions. One does not ask, *Could slavery have been abolished* without Rankin, Coles, Birney, and Angelina Grimké? One shudders at the possible consequences to the Presbyterian church, to the state of Illinois, to the Constitution, to women's rights, had these great intellects and courageous souls become hostages to the slave power.

There were champions of the right to discuss emancipation who remained in the South for a time, but they fought a losing battle.[16] An immense institution, grounded in force and recognized by law, supported by financial interest, political power, fear and prejudices, spread out over all parts of the South. What chance did a few men whose only recourse was an appeal to the reason and consciences of men have to survive? There was only one newspaper editor in North Carolina—William Swain of the Greensborough *Patriot*—who managed to defy the restraints of the law and the threats of violence until his death in 1834, and only because he lived in the center of the Quaker population. There was no discussion of slavery in Virginia after the Revolution until the great debates of 1832, and in this case the slaves themselves, by their threat of mass uprising, momentarily accomplished what liberals had not been able to do. Almost at the same time James G. Birney, one of the greatest intellects in the South and a man of tremendous courage, was forced out of Alabama for the mildest sort of antislavery statements, and then out of his native state of Kentucky. There is not the slightest shred of evidence of any tolerance of emancipation debate in South Carolina, Georgia, or Mississippi at any time.

In Kentucky, David Barrow and others organized the Kentucky Abolition Society in 1808. The Society never succeeded in increasing its membership above two hundred, and it passed out of existence sometime in the early 1820's. Meanwhile, however, it established a monthly magazine in 1822, the *Abolition Intelligencer and Missionary Magazine*. The society and the magazine were denounced as seditious by the newspapers and the churches, threats of violence against the editor John Finley Crow were frequent, and financial support was so meager that only twelve numbers were issued.[17]

Charles Osborn and John Rankin had organized the Manumission Society of Tennessee in 1815. Elihu Embree, former slaveholder, was a member. Rankin went to Kentucky and then to Ripley, Ohio. Osborn went to Mt. Pleasant, Ohio, and began publication of *The Philanthropist* in

1817. Embree began publishing the weekly *Manumission Intelligencer* at Jonesboro in 1819 and changed it to the monthly *Emancipator* in 1820. He died in that year and there was no one to take his place. Osborn ceased publication of his paper at Mt. Pleasant in 1818. In the publications of these three men—Embree's *Intelligencer* and *Emancipator*, March, 1819–December, 1820, Osborn's *Philanthropist*, August, 1817–October, 1818, and Rankin's *Letters* in the *Castigator* (Ripley), 1824—we have as strong a defense of the inalienable right to freedom and of racial equality and as complete denunciation of slavery as was ever published. Their philosophy was the sound, traditional, and unchangeable doctrine of the long line of pioneer antislavery men who had preceded them—immediate and unconditional emancipation. It cannot be emphasized too often, nor too emphatically, that colonization was a disrupting influence in a well-established and progressive trend for emancipation. These men were not deceived by it.

Benjamin Lundy, another Quaker who had come to Ohio from New Jersey, by way of Virginia, moved into Mt. Pleasant when Osborn left and began publication of his *The Genius of Universal Emancipation* in 1821. He moved the paper almost immediately to Greenville, Tennessee, where it was published for three years, before transfer to Baltimore. Lundy was a colonizationist. Rankin, Coffin, Osborn, and Embree were courageous and outspoken antislavery men. All were gone by 1826, and East Tennessee, last stronghold of emancipation in the South, was conquered. The last antislavery publication from that area, and one of the very few ever, was by the Manumission Society of North Carolina, four years before William Swain's death in 1834. Swain was secretary and probably wrote *An Address to the People of North Carolina, on the Evils of Slavery, By the Friends of Liberty and Equality*.

One must remember that slavery was a system, not an individual relationship. No matter how Christian, benevolent, and kind a slaveholder might be, he himself was a captive of the system, and it was the system which gave the spirit of despotism so much power. The failure of the antislavery movement to survive in northern Kentucky is evidence of its strength and vindictiveness. David Rice failed to overcome it; so did David Barrow. John Finley Crow was its victim, and James G. Birney was going to be.

THE OLD NORTHWEST

Chapter 10

We discussed earlier the powers given to Congress to prevent the spread of slavery and the forces creating an almost irresistible pressure for its expansion. The first contest over expansion came between 1787 and 1821 and involved the Northwest Territory and the Missouri Valley. The two areas were inseparable in the political and judicial contest. It involved the power of Congress to exclude slavery from the Northwest Territory by the Ordinance of 1787; the power of Congress to impose binding provisions on states at the time of admission; the constitutional right of a state to disregard such provisions by changing its constitution after admission; and the force of conditions stated in the surrender of Virginia's claims and in Jay's Treaty. The Congress, the President, the territorial governors and councils, the territorial legislatures, the constitutional conventions, and the judges of the several courts were all involved in the contest. It was, however, largely a *political question.*

Some settlers in the Old Northwest were willing to own slaves in order to profit from the labor and natural increase. Some wanted servants and the social prestige of slave ownership. But the drive to introduce slavery here, as was true in regard to the trans-Mississippi region at a later date, came from the aggressive character of the slave power. It was psychological in origin, and it had all the attributes of power politics. Slavery in Ohio, Indiana, and Illinois would mean slavery in Missouri and the Missouri Valley, and a political alliance of great strength.

The Ordinance of 1787, as we have seen, prohibited slavery in the existing national domain; and the Constitution, drafted at the same time, forbade Congress to use its authority for twenty years to prevent "the migration or importation of such persons as any of the states now existing shall think proper to admit." No where else do we find the terms "states now existing" and "original states." They were coined for the specific purpose of confining slavery to its then existing limits. The Northern states, slave and free, had abandoned their claims to western lands that new states might be created from a national domain. There were to be no slaves in this Northwest Territory, which was all the territory under federal jurisdiction *free of state* claims, but that prohibition was not to be construed to free fugitives from the existing slave states. Nothing was said about new slave states—there were not to be any. Virginia, North Carolina, South Carolina, and Georgia, however, never lived up to their agreement. They delayed a surrender of their claims to the region south of the Ohio until slavery had invaded it and then qualified their action with a condition that the new states be slave states.

Said a Committee of the Delaware Society for Promoting the Abolition of Slavery: "If it had been suggested, that one object of the union, was not only to perpetuate the odious state of slavery, but to extend it beyond its present limits; that so far from a right being reserved to the federal government to restrict the evil, they might be compelled to aid its extension; the accusation would have been repelled with indignation, and considered a libel upon the American character." And again, speaking of the nonimportation prohibition of April 6, 1776, and the Northwest Ordinance of July 13, 1787, it said: "They show . . . that previous to the adoption of the Constitution, Congress, deriving its powers from the Articles of Confederation, which, as far as it regards this subject, gave less jurisdiction than they now possess under the present Constitution; did possess the power, and exercise the right, of legislation on the subject of slavery, to the fullest extent, so far as it did not affect those who were then within the actual limits of the States composing the Confederation. The existence of this power was not then denied; against its exercise there were no objections. These Acts, exhibiting a contemporaneous exposition of the powers of Congress . . . afford the best rule of construction that can be given."[1]

Congress prohibited *importations* as of January 1, 1808, but not *migrations*. It regulated the coastwise trade by law of March 1, 1807, but not the overland trade. The yearly meeting of Quakers of Philadelphia petitioned Congress in January, 1805, to prevent the introduction of slavery into all of the territories.[2] The petition was referred to the Committee on Government for Louisiana Territory. The American Convention sent a memorial to Congress in January 1804 praying for a prohibition on importation of slaves into Louisiana Territory as had been done with the Northwest Territory.[3] Divers other petitions and memorials went to Congress from time to time, but Kentucky and Tennessee had been admitted as slave states and there was no possibility of getting restrictive legislation from Congress at that time. Congress, however, did not renounce its control over slavery in the territories as it did its control over slavery in the states. Instead, the first Congress reaffirmed the binding force of the Ordinance of 1787.

The Ordinance included six articles dealing with civil and religious liberty, education, slavery, and division into states. These were to be the principles "which form the basis whereon these republics, their laws and constitutions are erected; to fix and establish those principles as the basis of all laws, constitutions, and governments, which forever hereafter shall be formed in the said territory," and these articles were to be "considered as articles of compact between the original States

and the people and States in the said territory and forever remain unalterable, unless by common consent."[4]

One would suppose the language of the Ordinance to be a clear, unequivocal, and incontestable prohibition of slavery. It was not so interpreted because of two rather ephemeral guarantees of property rights. The first of these was in the Ordinance itself, which guaranteed to settlers "who have heretofore professed themselves citizens of Virginia, their laws and customs now in force among them, relative to the descent and conveyance, of property."[5] The second guarantee was made in Jay's Treaty seven years later to the effect that "all Settlers and Traders, within the Precincts or Jurisdiction of the said Posts shall continue to enjoy, unmolested, all their property of every kind, and shall be protected therein."[6]

It would require a far stretch of imagination to regard the first as a guarantee of slave ownership, especially in view of the effort of the federal Constitutional Convention to avoid any statement in the Constitution which could be interpreted as a recognition of property rights in man; and one certainly may present a strong argument that the British were in these military posts contrary to treaty agreements and did not in any way exercise jurisdiction over the whole of the territory or more than fleeting authority over the inhabitants.

Whatever one may say about that aspect of it now is of little consequence. The people of the Territory were not at all certain about the security of their property in slaves—slaves which they held from the days of the French regime. They were so certain, in fact, that the Ordinance *did abolish slavery* that they petitioned Congress to repeal the clause insofar as it operated as an *ex post facto* law.[7] A committee of Congress, to whom the matter was referred, reported that it had been the intention of Congress "merely to restrain the Settlers in future from carrying persons under Servitude into the Western Territory," and that the Ordinance should not be construed to deprive the inhabitants of their "right and property in Negro and other Slaves which they were possessed of at the time of passing the said Ordinance." This committee report was made in the winter of 1788–89, near the close of the Continental Congress, and no action of any sort was taken on it by the Congress.[8]

Governor Arthur St. Clair, however, gave the same interpretation, and so reported to President

George Washington.[9] St. Clair had been president of the Continental Congress, 1785 to 1787, and was governor of the Northwest Territory from 1787 to 1802. Neither St. Clair nor any one of the judges who together constituted the Council of the Territory had any interest in slavery or apparent sympathy with it,[10] and the laws selected for the territory did not violate the conditions of the Ordinance. Subsequently, Congress authorized a constitutional convention to frame a constitution for a new state of Ohio and prescribed the condition that the constitution should not be repugnant to the Ordinance of 1787. That same condition was imposed by Congress on the people of Indiana and Illinois. No one questioned the exercise of this power by Congress; all three states complied and framed constitutions excluding slavery.

Only one petition went to the territorial legislature asking permission to bring slaves into the territory (1799) and that body refused to violate the provisions of the Ordinance.[11] The constitution of Ohio, 1802, contained a clause which read: "Nor shall any indenture of any negro or mulatto, hereafter made and executed out of the State, or, if made in the State, where the term of service exceeds one year, be of the least validity except those given in the case of apprenticeships." An attempt was made in the convention to eliminate this clause and open the way to introduction of slavery under the circumvention of indentures. It was defeated by a vote of twenty-one to twelve.[12] The constitution also contained a clause saying "no alteration of this constitution shall ever take place so as to introduce slavery or involuntary servitude into this state."[13]

Pursuing the history of the restriction still further, we find that in 1796 and again in 1800 petitions went to Congress from the Illinois regions of the territory seeking amendments (1) to allow children of slaves born after 1787 to be held as slaves, and (2) to allow the introduction of slaves, whose children should be free at ages thirty-one and twenty-eight, respectively. Congress took no action, and a third petition, in 1802, requested suspension of the prohibition for ten years.[14] A congressional committee, in this case, declared it would be "highly dangerous and inexpedient to impair a provision wisely calculated to promote the happiness and prosperity of the northwestern country, and to give strength and security to that extensive frontier."[15]

Could Ohio or any one of the other states later created from the Northwest Territory have amended its constitution after admission into the Union to legalize slavery? Probably, in later years, when the slave power controlled the government, they would have been permitted thus to violate the terms of their admission. Congress had the power, of course, to force compliance quickly and effectively, as it later demonstrated, by denying seats to senators and representatives. It has other powers if it cares to use them, but the question is a political one and hardly worthy of discussion on a constitutional level. Exclusion of slavery from a territory almost certainly guaranteed free states. In this case slavery in the region was an inheritance from the French regime, and the number of slaves was not large. It would seem that this circumstance should have resulted in immediate, complete emancipation. Actually, because there were so few, nothing was done. No laws were enacted admitting others, however, and the territorial period was of short duration. There were in Ohio some slaves owned by people in Kentucky. They were there illegally; all were entitled to freedom by decision of the courts. Some of them were paying for their freedom; some, probably, were working for their owners. There were also many free Negroes working to buy their wives and children. Who was interested enough to sort out the slaves and plead their cases? In Philadelphia, where this phase of the antislavery movement was of long duration, many people; in Ohio, before 1830, no one.

Separation of Ohio from the remainder of the territory in 1800 and its admission as a state in 1803 removed the more compact communities and antislavery areas from territorial status. Indiana Territory then wrote a chapter into the history of the region little short of disgraceful. The governor and judges should have selected laws for the territory from the free states, because the region was solemnly dedicated to freedom. That would have been the normal procedure. They selected laws, instead, from the Virginia code, and laws utterly contrary to the spirit if not, indeed, to the very letter of the Northwest Ordinance. These laws permitted slaves to be brought into the territory as indentured servants. They provided punishment by whipping. They placed them on the rolls of taxable property as livestock. The territorial legislature after 1805 permitted any slave over fifteen years of age to be brought in and then sent out again into slavery for refusal to sign a contract of public record for service. It subjected children of such indentured servants to be held in servitude until ages thirty (males) and twenty-eight (females). It permitted children under fifteen to be brought in and held to ages thirty-five (males) and thirty (females).[16] Governor Harrison, himself, owned slaves and was guilty of violating the laws of Congress and his oath of office. His successor, Thomas Posey, was a slaveholder as long as he lived. Both were Virginians.

This was the point at which Congress should have acted. It was the point at which the President should have acted. Congress had the power to abolish territories even as it created them. It had the power to set aside territorial laws. It had the power to deny Indiana permission to frame a state constitution. Neither President Jefferson nor Congress took any action, nor did President Madison. The Virginia presidents were building a political party which depended heavily on the slave power for its strength. They would not deny their own. In the Congress the slave power was too great as yet to be successfully challenged on a matter requiring positive action.

The result of opening the door to slavery was immediately apparent. The same thing happened that always happened in gradual emancipation and caused antislavery men eventually to reject it completely as a method of operation. Slaveholders simply would not accept it as final. The only way to abolish slavery was to do it immediately and completely. Anything else led to interminable strife and renewed efforts to perpetuate it.

Once the slave interests had been allowed to execute indentures as a screen for slavery, they turned to Congress, their greed forever insatiable, with renewed petitions for the emasculation of the Ordinance of 1787. They presented the old argument that slaves were needed for the economic prosperity of the region. They presented a new argument that was to be heard many times in the years ahead. Great numbers of slaves in the South, they said, rendered the peace and tranquility of that section problematical and emancipation impossible; the solution lay in dispersion to the North and West. Later, they were to say that restrictions were most severe where slave concentrations were greatest and dispersal would

lead to more humane treatment. It was sophistry of the first magnitude, but a committee of the House of Representatives accepted the argument and recommended a ten-year dispensation. The slave power was strong enough to have prevented disciplinary action but not to carry this sort of proposal and nothing was done.

Undaunted, the slave interests in the territory sent another petition, supported by the specious argument that the abstract question of slavery versus freedom would not be involved in a ten-year suspension of Article 6 of the Ordinance since the slaves brought to Indiana would come from the slave states, not from abroad, and the total number of slaves in the country would not be increased. Again, a committee of the House reported favorably to the request, and again the House took no action. Then, in 1807 the territorial legislature and council combined their support of a final petition to Congress, without success.[17]

The nadir of disgraceful legislation was reached by the territorial legislature in the winter of 1806–7, when it gave any persons who found slaves or servants loitering on their property the right to inflict ten lashes upon them and provided public whippings for these people if guilty of any one of numerous offenses, including trespass and unlawful assembly. This was the type of legislation which inaugurated and maintained perpetual war between the races and sustained belief in racial inferiority of the Negro.[18]

Division of the Territory in 1809 left Indiana Territory predominantly antislavery and Illinois Territory temporarily proslavery. This is what had happened when Ohio was separated from the more western region. The steady movement westward of yeoman farmers and urban artisans settled the question of slavery, and by 1810 the Illinois region alone of the original Northwest Territory was debatable ground. The Indiana territorial legislature repealed the indenture law in 1810. Slaves of the old regime and slaves vaguely camouflaged by the indenture law were not rescued from slavery nor from the rigid control laws, but their number was not increased.

Permission was granted by Congress April 19, 1816, for a constitutional convention in Indiana, with the provision that the new instrument of government was to conform to the principles of the Ordinance of 1787.[19] Antislavery sentiment in the Territory was so strong by this date that the constitution contained the clause "as the holding of any part of the human Creation in slavery, or involuntary servitude, can only originate in usurpation and tyranny, no alteration of this Constitution shall ever take place so as to introduce slavery or involuntary servitude in this State, otherwise than for the punishment of crimes, whereof the party shall have been duly convicted."[20] The Constitution also said there should be neither slavery nor involuntary servitude in the state, and the court held this to be final and decisive with respect to any rights based upon the French regime or the Virginia cession.[21] In both Ohio *and* Indiana, therefore, slavery was abolished completely by the original state constitutions; and, it should be remarked, *regardless* of the degree to which those constitutions represented freedom of choice or compliance with the dictates of Congress and the Ordinance of 1787. The constitution of Indiana did not abrogate existing indentures as in Ohio, but it prohibited the execution of any more.

In Michigan Territory, separated from Indiana Territory in 1805, there were few slaves and little proslavery sentiment. The British controlled the area until 1796, and in 1793 a law of Upper Canada forbade the introduction of any more slaves and gave freedom at age twenty-five to future children of slave mothers. The Supreme Court of Michigan, Judge Augustus Woodward presiding, decided in 1807 that laws of the United States applied to the region only after 1796. All persons who were slaves in 1793 remained slaves. Children born of slave mothers between 1793 and 1796 remained slaves until age twenty-five by the law of Upper Canada. All children born after 1796 were free by provision of the Ordinance of 1787.[22] The court also, 1807, decreed that slaves escaping from Canada to Michigan were free, but fugitives from any part of the United States were still slaves by force of the Fugitive Slave Law of 1793.[23] Fortunately for the historian, there were few slaves in Wisconsin, because the region was a part of the Northwest Territory (1787), then of Indiana Territory (1800), then of Illinois Territory (1818) and finally was given independent territorial status in 1836.

When Illinois Territory was created (1809), President Madison appointed Ninian Edwards to the governorship. Edwards was from Kentucky. He was a staunch champion of slavery and had worked diligently to keep Kentucky a slave state.

He took his slaves with him to Illinois and did everything possible to make Illinois a slave state. His character may best be judged by his claim that slavery was not morally wrong, but that failure of the government to protect slave property was morally wrong. He insisted that Negroes were biologically inferior and incapable of making advancement and that emancipation would lead to submergence of the white race by racial war or by amalgamation. In Illinois he quickly identified himself with the proslavery forces in the legislature. The indenture law and all special police regulations affecting Negroes were kept in force. Free Negroes were forbidden to come into the territory; slaves could be brought as contract labor.[24]

The movements for statehood for Illinois and Missouri are scarcely separable as far as slavery *vs.* freedom is concerned. The one bulwark against Illinois becoming a slave state was the Ordinance of 1787. Edwards, as governor, was as proslavery as William Henry Harrison, and, as the first senator from Illinois, worked for the admission of Missouri as a slave state. The proslavery forces, however, had to weigh the possibility of Congress rejecting the new constitution for Illinois if it went too far in violating the principles of the Ordinance. Illinois undoubtedly would have been a slave state if these men could have had some assurances on that point, because antislavery sentiment in Illinois at that time was not strong enough to have prevented it. Governor Edwards vetoed a legislative repeal of the indenture law previous to the meeting of the constitutional convention. This was the first step in keeping the state slave in all but name.

Congress passed an enabling act April 18, 1818, providing, as in the cases of Ohio and Indiana, that the constitution must not be repugnant to the principles of the Ordinance of 1787.[25] In the end the Illinois constitution was an insolent defiance of those principles. Slavery dominated the election of delegates and it dominated the proceedings of the convention. Instead of abolishing slavery the constitution said: "Neither slavery nor involuntary servitude shall *hereafter* be introduced." It permitted slaves to be sent in to work the salt mines. It held all slaves serving under indentures to fulfillment of their contracts. It held their children to service until ages twenty-one (males) and eighteen (females). It retained the slaves of the old French regime in servitude.[26] It freed no one. It did not prohibit future amendment to admit slavery. The proslavery forces intended to wait for admission, then ask for a new constitutional convention, and write a new *proslavery* constitution.

James Tallmadge of New York challenged the right of Illinois to come into the Union with the constitution as framed because (1) it completely recognized existing slavery, and (2) it seemed to provide for its further introduction by allowing the hiring of slaves of nonresidents. He compared it unfavorably to the Indiana Constitution which had scrupulously guarded against slavery in every form and had prohibited future amendment to introduce slavery.[27] This precipitated a debate which indicated to some degree what was coming in the days ahead with reference to Missouri. George Poindexter of Mississippi, expressing the hope that Ohio, Indiana, and Illinois would remain free, said, nevertheless: "As to a constitution like that of Indiana, prohibiting the introduction of an amendment to it, of whatever nature, if the people were to form a convention tomorrow, that provision would be of no force: the whole power would be with the people, whom, in their sovereign capacity, no provision of that nature can control."[28]

In reply, Tallmadge said: "With respect to the power of a State to change its constitution, he was not prepared to say that a State was, in that respect, under no restraint." He then asked whether Congress would permit a state, admitted under a republican form of government, to change to a monarchy, and gave as his opinion that violating its terms of admission with regard to slavery was in the same class. He said further that "the interest, honor, and faith of the nation, required it scrupulously to guard against slavery's passing into a territory where they [Congress] have power to prevent its entrance."[29]

William Henry Harrison, presently a representative from Ohio, revealed what anyone cognizant of the record would have long suspected, that he had "always considered it [the Ordinance of 1787] a dead letter," and "wished to see that State [Illinois], and all that Territory, disenthralled from the effects of articles to which they never gave their assent, and to which they were not properly subject."[30]

The vote in the House to admit Illinois was 117 to 34. This was probably not a true measure of antislavery strength because Illinois was officially a free state and certain to remain free because of the steady flow of settlers westward. Its laws for a time, however, would have justified some doubts about its status. Its Black Code required registration of free Negroes and the carrying of registration certificates, prohibited assemblies, forbade any slaves to be brought in for emancipation, allowed the sale of indentures, classified slaves and indentured servants as live stock, and taxed them as chattel property.

In accordance with their previous intentions, and perhaps encouraged by the debate in the House of Representatives, the slavery interests in the state undertook to call a convention to amend the constitution. The question of calling a convention was the principal issue in the gubernatorial contest of 1822 in which the staunch antislavery candidate, Edward Coles, was elected. Coles immediately took the offensive against the proslavery interests which controlled the legislature. He insisted that slavery was contrary to the Ordinance of 1787 and should be abolished, urged the repeal of the Black Laws, and asked legal protection for free Negroes against kidnapping. The legislature insisted that it could not constitutionally do these things and that a convention must be called for the purpose. The expectation was that a convention could be persuaded to legalize slavery. The question was submitted to the voters at the next general election and nearly two years of intensive antislavery campaigning defeated the proposal by a popular vote of 6,640 to 4,972. The margin of victory was not large, but organized antislavery effort on a national scale was approaching, and this contest provided a solid foundation for it in Illinois. An effort to call a convention for the same purpose in Indiana in 1823 was likewise defeated 11,991 to 2,601.

THE MISSOURI CONTEST

Chapter 11

In November, 1818, Missouri requested permission of Congress to frame a constitution for admission into the Union as a state.[1] The request was taken under consideration by the House of Representatives on February 13, 1819, at which time James Tallmadge of New York moved to add to the enabling act: "That the further introduction of slavery or involuntary servitude be prohibited except for the punishment of crimes, whereof the party shall be duly convicted; and that all children born within the said State, after the admission thereof into the Union, shall be free at the age of twenty-five years."[2]

Tallmadge was a man of broad humanitarian principles, strongly opposed to slavery, and his action was in the liberal tradition of those who had abolished slavery in New York state and had labored diligently to assist and protect the free Negroes in New York City, and of those who had enacted and sustained the Ordinance of 1787.[3] Much of the debate which now ensued centered around that historic document and the basic questions of (1) whether Congress had the constitutional power to exclude slavery from the territories, (2) whether Congress had the constitutional power to impose binding restrictions upon a new state other than that its government be republican, and (3) whether a state, once admitted under an antislavery restriction, could alter its constitution to legalize slavery.

The second debate—which ensued after Missouri had framed her constitution—embraced the questions of (1) what were the attributes of citizenship, (2) were free Negroes citizens, and (3)

what were the privileges and immunities of citizens of the United States.

Other issues emerged in the course of the debate which were important. For example, certain representatives from the South continued the threats of violence begun in the early Congresses, this time in a manner calculated to arouse the people of Missouri to unlawful procedures, and they condemned public discussion of the question in a manner prophetic of Calhoun's resolutions of 1837. Southern intolerance had not only driven out many liberals—the migration was almost complete by 1830—but was condemning free enquiry and discussion of slavery anywhere in the country and was denying the right of petition with renewed vigor, *by 1819*. Thomas W. Cobb, of Georgia, with direct reference to Tallmadge, said: "We have kindled a fire which all the waters of the ocean cannot put out; which seas of blood can only extinguish," a remark which he repeated a second time.[4] John Scott, delegate from the Territory of Missouri, was particularly ferocious in praising the prowess and courage and willingness to resist oppression of the sturdy inhabitants of Missouri and warned supporters of the Tallmadge Amendment to "beware the fate of Caesar and of Rome." Edward Colston of Virginia told Arthur Livermore of New Hampshire that he was no better than Arbuthnot or Armbrister, two British subjects hanged by Jackson in Florida, and that he deserved the same fate. Elliott of Georgia insisted that slavery was not an issue and that Congress should disregard all public agitation.[5]

William Smith of South Carolina said the "excitement" began in the city of New York, at a meeting called by Peter Jay on November 17, 1819.[6] This meeting, he said, requested the speeches of Rufus King, which were furnished November 22, and printed. "It is certainly worthy of remark," said Smith, "that it is a little unusual for a dignified Senator of this body to publish his speeches for the purpose of popular excitement. These speeches, and a letter containing not more than twenty lines, wrote by the Honorable John Jay, who was now in his dotage, furnished the textbook, which, in the hands of this self-created assembly, commenced the excitement.[7] These textbooks were published in every newspaper throughout the Northern and Eastern states. They were accompanied by the most violent resolves against slavery and slaveholders, until the people became inflamed as far as that part of the project could be carried on."

"Then, sir, comes your cross-road meetings and your tavern meetings—your town meetings and your city meetings . . . Add to these the pamphlets of Marcus, Raymond, and fifty other scribblers, sending forth their venom. The whole of this group poured forth their abuse, and left the constitutionality on the authority of the two speeches and the little letter."[8]

"The feelings of humanity and benevolence have taken such complete possession of certain sections of our country," said Freeman Walker, of Georgia, "that every other consideration is made to bend to the irresistible inclination to ameliorate the condition of the slaves."[9] What would be the consequence? Said Walker: "I behold the father armed against the son, and the son against the father. I perceive a brother's sword crimsoned with a brother's blood. I perceive our houses wrapt in flames, and our wives and infant children driven from their homes, forced to submit to the pelting of the pitiless storm, with no other shelter but the canopy of heaven; with nothing to sustain them but the cold charity of an unfeeling world."[10] All of this, and more, because people wanted to arrest the spread of slavery.

Tallmadge promptly replied to threats in a manner indicative of new firmness on the part of antislavery men and of full realization of the importance of the issue. "Sir, has it already come to this," he asked, "that, in Congress of the United States—that, in the legislative councils of republican America, the subject of slavery has become a subject of so much feeling—of such delicacy—of such danger, that it cannot safely be discussed? Are members who venture to express their sentiments on this subject to be accused of talking to the galleries, with intent to excite a servile war; and of meriting the fate of Arbuthnot and Armbrister? Are we to be told of the dissolution of the Union? of civil war, and of seas of blood? And yet, with such awful threatenings before us, do gentlemen, in the same breath, insist upon the encouragement of this evil; upon the extension of this monstrous scourge of the human race? . . . Its present threatening aspect, and the violence of its supporters, so far from inducing me to yield to its progress, prompts me to resist its march. *Now is the time. It must now be met, and the extension of the evil must now be prevented, or the occasion is irrecoverably lost, and the evil can never be contracted.*"[11] Said John Sergeant, of Pennsylvania, one of the brilliant minds of the country, in reply to the threats of force in Missouri, "Such intimations can have no other effect than to create a very reasonable doubt whether Missouri is yet fit to be admitted."[12]

In some ways, this was the most important aspect of the entire discussion. Illinois and Missouri had applied for admission into the Union, the first nominally free but mildly slave, the other frankly so. They lay athwart the path of westward expansion. They were the key to a vast river valley. Suddenly, without previous notice, without political planning, and without anything to gain, a representative of one of the two early centers of antislavery activity stood up in the House of Representatives, said slavery should be excluded from this area and restrained, and received the support of the representatives of the vast majority of free inhabitants of the country. There followed a lot of political chicanery on the part of Clay and others, but there was no compromise as in the Constitutional Convention.

Henry Clay, speaker of the House of Representatives, who was so prominent at the moment in the colonization movement, threw his weight against the amendment and argued that dispersal of slavery would greatly improve the lot of the slaves. Elliott of Georgia stated the principle very cogently by saying: "The comforts and privileges of this people being generally in an inverse ratio to the numbers placed on any one plantation, the wider their dispersion, the greater will be their comforts and the less burdensome their servitude."[13] One after another of the Southerners argued that it could make no difference, from the standpoint of humanity, whether slaves were held in Missouri or in Kentucky, or elsewhere, so long as they came from the existing slave states and not from abroad.[14] They insisted that *if* slavery were an evil—and they were divided on that point —the correct procedure was dispersal.[15] They argued that dispersal was necessary to save the white population from insurrections—again without complete unanimity—and that exclusion of slaves would shut out slaveholders.[16]

They were told by Tallmadge and others that the opening of a vast new area to slavery would greatly increase the demand for slaves and the pressure for removing the restrictions on importations; and that it would lead to increased violation of the laws against importations, stimulate kidnapping of free Negroes, reduce the number of manumissions, and retard the colonization program. In one way or another, slave labor would be found and the political power of slaves greatly enhanced by expansion. They were told, also, that exclusion of slavery would not exclude any person. Any citizen of any state could go to the territories on a basis of equality with all the rest, but not take slaves. Said Arthur Livermore, of New Hampshire: "In the present slaveholding States let slavery continue, for our boasted Constitution connives at it; but do not, for the sake of cotton and tobacco, let it be told to future ages, that while pretending to love liberty, we have purchased an extensive country to disgrace it with the foulest reproach of nations."[17] "Our votes this day," said John W. Taylor of New York, "will determine whether the high destinies of this region, of these generations, shall be fulfilled, or whether we shall defeat them by permitting slavery, with all its baleful consequences, to inherit the land."[18]

Southerners were almost as sensitive on this point as upon the morality of slavery because they had no answer. How could men answer this plea of Taylor's without confessing insincerity? "How often, and how eloquently," said Taylor, "have they deplored its [slavery's] existence among them? What willingness, nay, what solicitude have they not manifested to be relieved from this burden? How have they wept over the unfortunate policy that first introduced slaves into this country! How have they disclaimed the guilt and shame of that original sin, and thrown it back upon their ancestors . . . let not our children,

looking back to the proceedings of this day, say of them, as they have been constrained to speak of their fathers: we wish their decision had been different; we regret the existence of this unfortunate population among us; but we found them here; we know not what to do with them; it is our misfortune, we must bear it in patience."[19] Finally, cognizant of world opinion, as were men like Cooper, Branagan, and Mifflin at an earlier date, Timothy Fuller of Massachusetts said: "All Europe, the whole civilized world, are spectators of the scene. Our Declaration of Independence, our Revolution, our State institutions, and, above all, the great principles of our Federal Constitution, are arrayed on one side, and our legislative acts and national measures, the practical specification of our real principles and character, on the other."[20]

Interspersed throughout this general discussion was a debate on constitutional principles which antedated the Webster-Hayne debate by more than a decade, and in many ways surpassed it for cogency and sustained argument. "The time has arrived," said Philip P. Barbour of Virginia, later speaker of the House, "which brings to the test the theory of the Constitution."[21] "The great and cardinal principle of the Constitution," replied Henry R. Storrs of New York, "created a National Government of the people of the United States. Its powers were derived from, and delegated by, the people, in their conventions, not as citizens of distinct sovereignties, but in their collective capacity, as citizens of one great Republic."

Once in a great while there appears in the annals of Congress for a moment, as it were, a brilliant intellect, who speaks and then moves on to other fields of activity. Such an one was Walter Lowrie, school teacher and store keeper from Butler in western Pennsylvania. Lowrie served one term in the Senate, then served as secretary of the Senate from 1825 to 1836, and thereafter was corresponding secretary of the Board of Foreign Missions of the Presbyterian Church from 1836 to 1868. He stepped into the argument in the Senate with as much confidence as he ever walked into a classroom and gave the senators a lesson in American history the like of which is seldom heard in Congress.

"The Government of the Union," said he, "flows as directly from the people as does the government of any of the States. The circumstance that the delegates who formed the present Constitution, were appointed by the State Legislatures does not detract from this idea; because the instrument was afterward submitted to the people, and had it not been approved by them, it would have had no more authority than the sweeping of your floor. The Government of the United States, though limited in its powers, is supreme within the proper sphere of its action. The respective Governments of the United States and of the several States are sovereign within their proper spheres, and no farther. Hence it follows that the States are limited sovereignties. It follows, also, that the right to admit new States, being within the sphere of the General Government is a right which, to that Government, is perfect . . . the power to dispose of and make all needful rules and regulations for the territories, and the power to admit new States into the Union, have been given, by the people of the United States, to Congress. They are powers of the General Government, within the proper sphere of its action, and of course sovereign and supreme."[22]

"I am not, sir, for annihilating the States," said Joshua Cushman, Congregational minister from Massachusetts. "They ought to possess full power to enact municipal laws and to administer municipal justice—to regulate their internal police—to conduct their local concerns. But I deny the right of the proudest among them to interfere with the high prerogatives of the National Government."[23] Going one step farther, John Sergeant of Pennsylvania said: "It is to no purpose, to say that the question of slavery is a question of state concern. It affects the Union, in its interests, its resources, and character, permanently; perhaps forever. One single State, to gratify the desire of a moment, may do what all the Union cannot undo; may produce an everlasting evil, shame and reproach. And why? Because it is a State right." Here, of course, Sergeant pinpointed the fatal weakness of the doctrine of state rights. And then Sergeant continued: "Sir, you may turn this matter as you will; Missouri, when she becomes a State, grows out of the Constitution; she is formed under the care of Congress, and admitted by Congress; and *if she has a right to establish slavery*, it is a right derived directly from the Constitution, and conferred upon her through the instrumentality of Congress."[24]

Could Congress exclude slavery from the region west of the Mississippi—constitutionally speaking, from the territories? Could Congress compel Mis-

souri, as a condition of admission as a state, to abolish slavery by constitutional provision? Could Congress prevent migration of slaves? Could Missouri, or any other state, even one of the original slave states, once free, re-establish slavery? Those were the main issues.

Whence came the power to exclude slavery from the territories? From the clause in the Constitution (Article I, Section 9) which said: "The Migration or Importation of such Persons as any of the States now existing shall think proper to admit, shall not be prohibited by the Congress prior to the year one thousand eight hundred and eight; but a tax or duty may be imposed on such importation, not exceeding ten dollars for each Person"; and from the Clause (Article IV, Section 3) "The Congress shall have Power to dispose of and make all needful Rules and Regulations respecting the Territory or other Property belonging to the United States."

Elliott of Georgia denied that migration could apply to slaves. "Migration," he said, "implies volition, choice, self direction—but these belong not to a slave. He may be carried or imported, or he may abscond, but he can never migrate."[25] This argument, if dwelt upon, would have provided a field day for the opponents of slave representation, and the indenture laws of Indiana and Illinois, and all those court decisions, including the later *Dred Scott* decision which placed so much emphasis upon a slave's voluntary return to a slave state. Actually, migration was a voluntary change of residence. No slave ever went anywhere by his own decision. The will of a master was the will of the slave, and a master's orders made a slave's acts voluntary. The laws and the courts held them to be so.

David L. Morril of New Hampshire stated again the antislavery position. "The states now existing which have thought proper to admit slavery, may retain their slaves as long as they please; but, after the commencement of 1808, Congress may by law prohibit the importation of any more, and restrain those who are then in servitude to the territory or States where they may be found."[26] This clause, he said, was carefully phrased and inserted as a suspension, a restraint, of pre-existing and unlimited powers. Congress could not apply its power to the existing states before 1808. It could apply its power elsewhere, and did in the Ordinance of 1787, which the ensuing Congress, under the Constitution, ratified. The clause, therefore, did not grant power; it limited the action of an existing power for a specified time.

Some Southerners denied the validity of the Ordinance of 1787 completely; others denied that it could have any binding force in Ohio, Indiana, or Illinois now that they had been admitted into the Union. Congress, they claimed, had no right to specify details of state government as a condition of admission, except that it should be republican, and any state, once admitted, was on a basis of complete equality with the other states and could alter its constitution to permit slavery. Pinkney of Maryland conceded that Congress was not obliged to admit a new state, a position quite different from that of most Southerners, but he declared that it could not "make it less in sovereign power than the original parties to the Union."[27]

Antislavery spokesmen insisted that Congress did have the constitutional power to stipulate conditions for admission, and that slavery was incompatible with republican institutions. They emphasized the broad discretion possessed by Congress in the exercise of its powers to govern the territories and admit new states.

On this point they took advanced ground: Congress had imposed a great many restrictions upon new states which placed them in a very different position from that of the original states. They required Louisiana, in her Constitution, to recognize trial by jury and habeas corpus, civil and religious liberty, and official use of the English language. They retained ownership and control of all public lands, and forbade the new states to tax any lands sold by the federal government until five years after the sale. They imposed restrictions as to highways and navigable streams. They imposed every single restriction of the Northwest Ordinance upon Alabama and Mississippi except slavery, and made that single exception in deference to the terms of cession from the original states.

The United States had full power to contract with a state, and a state with the United States. Ohio, Indiana, and Illinois had entered into such a contract, making the Ordinance of 1787 a fundamental law, and the contract was irrevocable except by mutual agreement. Congress had broad powers to insist upon terms compatible to the general welfare, before bestowing upon the people of any territory the privileges and benefits of statehood in the Union.

Congress possessed the power to stop the migration of slaves from one state to another, and from states to territories not only by the specific clause under discussion, but by their power to control interstate commerce.

No state in the Union, once free of slavery, could restore it without the consent of Congress. The words "slave" and "slavery" were so hateful and offensive as to have been held unfit for inclusion in the Constitution. Nowhere in that instrument, or in the principles on which the nation was founded, or in law, was there any right given to reduce a free man to slavery. Congress would not permit slaves to be imported; Congress would not permit them to migrate. How then could a state, either new or old, establish slavery or reestablish slavery?

If any state were admitted under an antislavery agreement and should then authorize slavery, the courts would be obliged to free any individual suing for his freedom, and Congress would be obliged to take punitive action.

Said Tallmadge: "If the western country cannot be settled without slaves, gladly would I prevent its settlement till time shall be no more."[28] Said Sergeant: "If Missouri be permitted to establish slavery, we shall bring upon ourselves the charges of hypocrisy and insincerity, and upon the Constitution a deep stain, which must impair its lustre, and weaken its title to the public esteem."[29] Neither of these men was to have his way. The House of Representatives passed the Tallmadge Amendment, the Senate refused to do so, and the House by a vote of seventy-eight to seventy-six refused to abandon its position.[30] The Fifteenth Congress adjourned on March 3, 1819, with no decision having been reached. Meanwhile, in February, a bill creating Arkansas Territory was passed, and an attempt to exclude slavery was beaten down by votes of eighty-nine to eighty-seven in the House of Representatives and nineteen to fourteen in the Senate. Every vote from the slave states both in the House and in the Senate was for slavery in Arkansas. Sixteen northern votes in the House and four in the Senate were for slavery. The four Senate votes were from Ohio, Indiana, and Illinois (2). The Sixteenth Congress convened December 6, 1819. Maine applied for admission December 8, and the Senate Judiciary Committee tied the Maine and Missouri bills together. Smith of South Carolina was chairman of the committee. Henry Clay was party to the transaction. James Barbour, of Virginia, said quite frankly it was done so that those who wanted Maine in the Union would have to take Missouri also.[31] The action was approved in the Senate by a vote of twenty-three to twenty-one.

On February 18, 1820, the Senate passed an amendment offered by Thomas of Illinois forever prohibiting slavery in the Louisiana Purchase north of 36° 30', except in Missouri. The Senate passed this amendment on February 18, but it was rejected by the House of Representatives. Ultimately, the House voted ninety to eighty-seven to remove the restrictions from Missouri and the Thomas Amendment excluding slavery north of 36° 30' except for Missouri was passed 134 to 42. In the end, then, there was no compromise. The territorial restriction was an antislavery victory with thirty-nine Southerners voting for it and thirty-seven against it. The Tallmadge Amendment was defeated in the House only because fourteen Northerners voted with the South. All of them were Democrats, and frankly and admittedly frightened by threats of disunion. In the Senate the margin of victory for the South was provided first, last, and always by Edwards and Thomas of Illinois, Taylor of Indiana and, later, Hunter of Rhode Island and Parrott of New Hampshire. Never, in all the annals of the slavery controversy, were the awful consequences of the three-fifths rule more fully revealed than in these votes.

Here is where the history of the so-called Missouri Compromise normally ends. Actually, here is where the most important phase of the controversy began, because the Missouri Constitution, when presented to Congress, contained a clause making it mandatory for the legislature to pass a law "to prevent free negroes and mulattoes from coming to and settling in this State, under any pretext whatsoever."[32] Few debates, if any, in Congress, have ever equaled in importance the one which followed. The Constitution of the United States says that "the citizens of each State shall be entitled to all privileges and immunities of citizens in the several states." The debate on this matter of citizenship and privileges and immunities led straight to the Fourteenth Amendment of 1867. Southerners said Negroes were not citizens of a state, therefore not citizens of the United States, and regardless of any rights they might have in any states, they had no federal rights and could not be considered citizens of the United States.

What did the Constitution do in this respect? Said Sergeant: "The powers vested in the Government now operated directly on the people. Its legislature and judiciary are the legislature and judiciary of the nation. The public will no longer applies for aid to the Legislatures of the States, but extends its authority as the universal law of the nation to every citizen. The citizens of the respective States are no longer alien to each other as subjects of different sovereignties. In relation to the powers vested in the General Government, we have become emphatically one people, under one National Government—allied to each other as *citizens of one country*—responsible to one supreme authority—controlled by the same laws—enjoying equally the blessings it dispenses, and truly brethren of the same family."[33] "Is it possible, then," said Sergeant, "that we can mistake the intention of the framers of this Constitution, or our own rights, so far as to hesitate on the true construction of that clause which secures to the citizens of each State the privileges and immunities of citizens in the several States? The foundation of this article of the Constitution is laid deep in the structure of the Government. It is capable of no construction which does not plainly denote the universality of its operation and its uniform application to *individual right* throughout every portion of the nation." Refine this statement for simplicity, and every person, unless otherwise specified, is a citizen of the United States, and privileges and immunities are the natural rights of man. What were these privileges and immunities? Sergeant listed the right of a citizen of one state to inherit lands in another, the right of every citizen to enter the courts of justice of any state, the right to purchase lands, to enter private contracts, to settle in other states, and an infinite variety of civil rights.

Joseph Hemphill of Pennsylvania carried the concept of citizenship to its logical conclusion, when he said: "If being a native, and free born, and of parents belonging to no other nation or tribe, does not constitute a citizen in this country, I am at a loss to know in what manner citizenship is acquired by birth . . . when a foreigner is naturalized, he is only put in the place of a native freeman. This is the genuine idea of naturalization . . . *But citizenship is rather in the nature of a compact, expressly or tacitly made; it is a political tie, and the mutual obligations are contribution and protection.*"[34]

"To this relationship of a free citizen to his State, *protection* and *allegiance* were the necessary incidents," said Otis of Massachusetts, "and these imply, of necessity a right to reside within the jurisdiction, and to be secure of life, liberty, and property, under the guardianship of the laws."[35] "If there was any way to which a citizen of one State can enjoy all the privileges and immunities of a citizen of another State, and yet not be permitted to set his foot in it, Mr. S[ergeant] said he should be glad to be informed of it."[36]

In the arguments establishing proof of Negro citizenship are the clearest statements of the attributes of citizenship, all of them, of course possessed by Negroes and whites without distinction under the laws of the states as claimed:

Birth. With few exceptions, they were born in this country. This is their native land. Thousands of them were free born, and were a part of the people when the state and federal constitutions were formed. The Articles of Confederation had said: "The free inhabitants of each of these States shall be entitled to all the privileges and immunities of free citizens in the several States; and the people of each State shall have free ingress and regress to and from any other State," thus using the terms inhabitants, citizens, and people synonymously and interchangeably. All free inhabitants at the time of adoption of the Constitution were citizens of the United States and all persons born free thereafter were citizens of the United States. Story of New York insisted that slaves restored to their liberty were citizens of the United States because they were born in this country and did not owe allegiance to any other.

Contribution. They were identified with the nation, in the sense that their labor had contributed mightily to its wealth; they had fought in the Revolutionary armies; they had participated in the elective franchise; they were taxed.

Rights and privileges. The Constitution did not contain any sort of expression that could be construed as depriving them of rights enjoyed by others. Said Joseph Hemphill of Pennsylvania: "They have a right to pursue their own happiness, in as high degree as any other class of people. Their situation is similar to others in relation to the acquirement of property, and the various pursuits of industry. They are entitled to the same rights of religion and protection, and are subjected to the same punishments. They are enu-

merated in the census. They can be taxed, and made liable to militia duty; they are denied none of the privileges contained in the bill of rights . . . When they enjoy all these rights, civil and religious, equally with the white people; and when they all flow from the same Constitutions and laws, without any special designation or reference to them, I have a curiosity to learn upon what principle any right can be singled out as one of which they are to be deprived."[37]

Protection. In Vermont, said Mallary: "All the security which the Constitution gives to the most distinguished citizen for the protection of his life and reputation, is afforded to every freeman, whatever may be his circumstances or color. The spirit of the Constitution watches with equal eye over the rights and privileges, civil and political, of the negro and mulatto, and would chastize the least attempt to offer violation."[38] Speaking for Massachusetts, Eustis said that even if it could be shown that they were restricted in some degree, they nevertheless owned real and personal property, owned and conveyed land, had the right of trial by jury and habeas corpus and the elective franchise; and by the laws and constitutions of the state were citizens equally with the whites. He said, furthermore, that in Massachusetts they were "an elementary part of the Federal Compact. They were as directly represented as the whites, in the initiatory process; and, from their votes, in common with those of the whites, emanated the convention of Massachusetts by whom the Federal Constitution was received and ratified." He emphatically declared that every member of the House from Massachusetts was elected by some votes of Negro citizens and in one district, at least, their votes controlled elections.[39]

It was also demonstrated that the United States government had made no distinctions with regard to Negroes in all actions protecting them from impressment by Great Britain and from enslavement by the Mediterranean powers. It was repeated many times that so long as a man enjoyed the right of protection in life, liberty, and property, and of residence where he would, and of inheritance, and of equality in the courts of justice, and in administration of criminal law, so long was he a citizen.

What then were they asking in the case of Missouri and free Negroes? As Sergeant put it, only "the humble, simple privilege of locomotion."

INSURRECTIONS

Chapter 12

On 14 February 1804, David Bard said in the House of Representatives: "Gentlemen tell us, though I can hardly think them serious, that the people of this description can never systematize a rebellion . . . experience speaks a different language—the rigor of the laws, and the impatience of the slaves, will mutually increase each other, until the artifices of the one are exhausted, and until, on the other hand, human nature sinks under its wrongs, or obtains the restoration of its rights. . . . To be convinced of this, we have only to look at St. Domingo. There the negroes felt their wrongs, and have avenged them; they learned the rights of man, and asserted them; they have wrested the power from their oppressors, and have become masters of the island."[1]

Bard's statement of fact has the clarity and completeness of a geometrical theorem. No man was ever born to be a slave. The will to be free and the imperious longing for something better in life are universal among men. Persons who were deprived of their freedom, and then denied all the attributes of rational human beings, and then reduced, insofar as was possible, to the status of animals, were likely to assert their inalienable rights at any time—by flight or by physical force, individually or in groups. It has always been so, always will be so, while man survives. People who lived in the slave states knew it, and one cannot dig very deep into the history of slavery without encountering sundry evidences of a great fear which pervaded the region at all times. The slaveholders sought safety in repression, but as Bard said, every act of repression drove more slaves to

resistance, and every act of resistance led to more repression, so there was no end to the vicious circle. We shall have occasion to deal with many aspects of slavery which are indisputable proof of constant apprehension:

The rigor, amounting to fanaticism, with which all discussion of the evils of slavery and programs of emancipation was suppressed. This ultimately reached the point of excluding antislavery literature from the mails, forbidding all discussion of the subject in Congress, and attempting to outlaw antislavery societies in the free states. Fear that the discussion would be introduced into the slave states under a Republican administration was a major cause of secession.

The harsh and arbitrary manner of enforcing submission to the master race. Fear is the mother of cruelty, and cruelty was the rule, not the exception. Proof of a constant warfare was everywhere. There were the laws subjecting every slave away from his master's property without a pass to chastisement by anyone who might apprehend him, the barbarous mutilations of those who ran away and were not killed in the hunt, the brutal whippings, and the murders without penalty committed in course of corrections. The newspapers of the South are filled with advertisements for runaway slaves, listing scars from the whip, brandings, gunshot wounds, eyes and teeth missing, cropped ears, mutilations by dogs, and sundry other marks of violence. Every driver carried his whip. Every jail had its whipping post, and every community its bloodhounds. Yet, in spite of all this, slaves ran away in such numbers that an esti-

A slave caught without a pass

mated 1000 each year succeeded in reaching the free states and recovery of fugitives became a major political issue.

The inhuman punishments meted out to those suspected of conspiracy. When slaves banded together in armed revolt, it often happened that reason was abandoned and unrestrained sadism prevailed. They were hunted down and shot without mercy. They were given the semblance of a trial, and hanged, burned at the stake, or beheaded. Rewards of money and freedom were offered for information. Testimony of other slaves was accepted without reservations. Torture was applied to obtain confessions. Even those seeking to escape without injury to anyone were shot unless they surrendered, the general principle prevailing that it was better to kill them than to allow them to go free.

The persistent efforts by some states to exclude slaves suspected of criminal tendencies, including those indoctrinated with ideas of freedom or contaminated by insurrections. Georgia permitted the importation of slaves from Africa until 1798, but she forbade importations from the West In-

dies, the Bahamas, and Florida after 1793. South Carolina excluded slaves from the West Indies and required certification of good character for slaves from other states. All of the slave states, in one way or another, sought to get rid of recalcitrant slaves, and to keep others out—the latter not too successfully. One of the strange attitudes in this respect was the vehemence with which fugitives were hunted down and returned if possible, when they were certain to be firebrands, and when the constant draining away of these courageous souls, in all probability, prevented mass revolt.

The effort to reduce the number of free Negroes. The mere presence of free Negroes in a community was regarded as a disquieting influence upon the slaves. There were laws to prevent manumission, and there were laws requiring freed Negroes to leave the state. Virginia, in 1795, imposed a $100 fine on anyone who supported a slave's claim to freedom if it failed, and in 1798 forbade any member of an antislavery society to serve as a juror in such cases.[2] In 1806 she required all Negroes given their freedom to remove from the state within one year.[3] South Carolina, Georgia, Alabama, and Mississippi forbade manumission by the owner, except by action of the legislature. North Carolina required removal within ninety days. Only in Kentucky, Missouri, Maryland, and Arkansas was the slaveowner reasonably free to act.[4] There was, also, as we shall see, strong support for colonization of free Negroes in Haiti or Liberia.

There were other manifestations of fear, such as the suspicion with which any communication between slaves and strangers, particularly Northerners, was viewed by everyone. The point is that fear led to stern and unrelenting cruelty to the slaves, reluctance to meliorate their condition, and petulance toward anyone who showed an interest in the matter.

There were a score of recorded insurrections of some magnitude in colonial days: in New York, in Charleston, in New Orleans, and in various rural communities from Maryland to Georgia. In New York City in 1712 nine white persons were killed, six slaves committed suicide, and nineteen were hanged or burned. More Negroes died than were involved in the uprising. In the same city in 1741 four whites died and twenty-nine Negroes were hanged and burned, some on flimsy evidence of a witness later discredited. In South Carolina in 1739 twenty-one whites and forty-four Negroes lost their lives in the largest uprising up to that time. Serious trouble began, however, with the period of the Revolution.

War is an unsettling affair at best, and slavery was exceedingly dependent upon quiet for stability. Negroes fought in the Revolutionary armies, with the approval of the Continental Congress.[5] Rhode Island inducted two battalions of slaves, paid their owners up to 120 pounds each for their freedom, and in 1785 provided for the survivors' maintenance at public expense.[6] Slaves who enlisted in New Hampshire, in Connecticut, and in Virginia[7] were given their freedom, and in New York slave owners were given a grant of land for each slave who served in the army, and the slaves were given their freedom.[8] Probably as many as 4,000 Negroes served in the Continental armies.[9] The British made sporadic efforts to encourage fugitives to join their armies and probably toyed with the idea of inciting insurrections. They carried away some slaves. Others were freed when Tory estates were confiscated. Still more were given their freedom by their owners. None of

[1840.]   *Anti-Slavery Almanac.*   7

HOW SLAVERY IMPROVES THE CONDITION OF WOMEN.

"John Ruffner, a slaveholder, had one slave named Piney, whom he, as well as Mrs. Ruffner, would often flog very severely. I frequently saw Mrs. Ruffner flog her with the broom, shovel, or anything she could seize in her rage. She would knock her down and then kick and stamp her most unmercifully, until she would be apparently so lifeless, that I more than once thought she would never recover. The cause of Piney's flogging was not working enough, or making some mistake in baking, &c. &c."—Mrs. N. Lowry, a native of Ky., now member of a Church, in Osnaburg, Stark co. Ohio.

"My uncle used to tie his "house wench" to a peach tree in the yard, and whip her till there was no sound place to lay another stroke, and repeat it so often that her back was continually sore. Whipping the females around the legs, was a favorite mode of punishment with him. They must stand and hold up their clothes while he plied his hickory."—Wm. Leftwich, a native of Virginia, and son of a slaveholder, now member of the Presbyterian Church, Delhi, Ohio.

"In the winter of 1828-29, I put up for a night at Frost Town, on the national road. Soon after there came in a slaver with a drove of slaves. I left the room, and shortly afterwards heard a *scream*, and when the landlady inquired the cause, the slaver coolly told her not to trouble herself, he was only chastising one of his women.—It appeared that three days previously her child had died on the road, and been thrown into a crevice in the mountain, and a few stones thrown over it; and the mother weeping for her child was chastised by her master, and told by him, she 'should have something to cry for.'"—Colonel T. Rogers, a native of Kentucky, a Presbyterian elder at New Petersburg, Highland co. Ohio.

"Benjamin Lewis, an elder in the Presbyterian church, engaged a carpenter to repair his house. Kyle, the builder, was awakened very early in the morning by a most piteous moaning and shrieking. He arose, and following the sound, discovered a colored woman, nearly naked, tied to a fence, while Lewis was lacerating her. A second and a third scene of the same kind occurred, and on the third occasion the altercation almost produced a battle between the elder and the carpenter."—Rev. George Bourne, of New York, who was a preacher seven years in Virginia.

James T. De Jarnett, Vernon, Autauga co. Alabama, thus advertises a woman in the Pensacola Gazette, July 14, 1838. "Celia is a *bright* copper-colored negress, *fine figure* and *very smart. On examining her back, you will find marks caused by the whip.*"

P. Abdie, advertises a woman in the N. O. Bee, of Jan. 29, 1838, "having marks of the whip behind her neck, and *several others on her rump.*"

O'er me, weighed down by care,
    Pierced through by sorrow's stings,
O'er me from day to day the same,
    The slave-whip ceaseless swings.

Whipping slaves
One barbarity, often talked about, and apparently practiced, was pulling a cat by the tail across the bare back of
the slave. This is one of the few pictorial representations.

these things, certainly, made happy any slave
retained in slavery, and there must have been
many thousands bitterly disappointed.

The most disturbing event of the revolutionary
period was the revolt in Santo Domingo. This
subsidiary revolution against tyranny was a night-
mare to slaveholders, an inspiration to slaves.
Nothing new can be added to the history of the
event. Santo Domingo was the richest of the
French West Indian colonies, with 28,000 whites,
22,000 free Negroes, and 405,000 slaves. Its industry centered in 800 sugar plantations, where the
slaves were heavily burdened and harshly treated.
General knowledge of the French Declaration of
the Rights of Man is said to have caused some
uprisings in 1791, and severe repressive measures
precipitated a general revolt. There was a massacre of the white population, survivors migrating,
many to the United States. The slaves under the
leadership of Toussaint L'Ouverture repelled a
British attempt at invasion. Toussaint was crowned
monarch only to be betrayed by the French to an
ignoble death in France. His successor, Dessa-
lines, renamed the colony Haiti, and it became
the first all-Negro state in the New World. It was
shunned like the plague by American diplomats.
Slaveholders would have remembered what had
happened there without any of the constant
reminders by antislavery people.

Slavery in the French and British colonies of
the West Indies was terribly cruel. There was a direct connection between slavery there and in the
United States, because the colonies on the continent had copied the slave codes of the islands,
slaves were brought by their owners to the United
States, and slaves were remarkably well informed
at all times of what was transpiring by a communication system of their own. They knew about
the Santo Domingo affair from the first.

This was the period, also, of many exposés by
British authors, who wrote of the terrors in Africa,
on the middle passage, and in the colonies. Their
works were reprinted in the United States along
with those of Benezet, Branagan, and others. The
most notable of these publications were Clarkson's
Essays,[10] Sharpe's *Essays*,[11] Benezet's *Serious
Address*,[12] Newton's *Thoughts*,[13] Day's *Tracts*,[14]
Stanfield's *Guinea Voyage*,[15] and Belsham's *Essays*.[16] These and many more published in the late
1780's were enough to have converted the most
hardened soul to complete abolition; and, when
the House of Commons finally got around to ex-

amining conditions in the Islands, England was shocked into an early abolition of slavery in her Empire.[17] The trouble was, in the United States at least, so few people read or had access to this literature, particularly the slaveholders.

Then, in late summer, 1800, came Gabriel's revolt in Henrico County, Virginia. Gabriel was a slave of uncommon attainments owned by a planter near Richmond. Associated with him were a number of equally able men, natural leaders and educated to some degree. The plans for a general uprising along the lines of the Santa Domingo revolt were so elaborate as to indicate probable success had they not been revealed by two slaves who were later purchased by the state and liberated. Gabriel claimed to have had a following of 10,000 men. Allowing for some exaggeration on his part, the situation was ominous enough for Governor Monroe to have given it his personal attention and to have arranged such elaborate defense measures as required the services of three personal aides-de-camp. Ninety-one slaves were convicted before the affair ended, of whom twenty-five were executed and ten deported. Slaves in the area continued restless for a time, and fourteen more were executed in 1802.[18]

This was what Bard had been talking about in 1804 in the House of Representatives: the inherent longing for freedom, stimulated by the language of the revolution and nourished by the successful revolt in Santo Domingo—rebellion, savage repression, disaster for everyone. When would it come? How could it be prevented? What would be done on the day of retribution? Every antislavery pronouncement of any importance in this period warned of impending disaster unless steps were taken to abolish slavery.[19] Some emphasized the certainty of God's judgments. Some reminded the slaveholders of Santo Domingo. Some talked of foreign invasions. All, either directly or by implication, correctly analyzed the situation as critical and of national import.[20] Southerners insisted it was nobody's business but their own. They called slavery *a domestic institution*, one they alone were qualified to judge, one they were perfectly capable of controlling.

Jefferson warned that God would not help the master race in case of insurrection, but what was more to the point, antislavery men assured them that Northerners would not either. Theodore Dwight, as early as 1794, had said: "The same law, which justifies the enormities, committed by

Toussaint L'Ouverture

civilized nations, when engaged in war, will justify slaves for every necessary act of defense, against the wicked, and unprovoked outrages, committed against their peace, freedom, and existence."[21] Then he warned: "Surely, no friend to freedom and justice will dare to lend them [slaveholders] his aid."[22] The American Convention, following the Gabriel plot in Virginia, said in an address to the citizens of the United States: "While we all revolt with horror from the anticipation of an organization on the part of the slaves, we conceive there is a certain state of degradation and misery to which they may be reduced, a certain point of desperation to which the human mind may be brought, and beyond which it cannot be driven." The society urged an entirely new approach to the problem from that currently practiced in the slave states, with a program of gradual emancipation, including cessation of severe punishments, intellectual and religious instruction, and freedom for good behavior.[23]

The excitement occasioned by the Gabriel plot in Virginia never really subsided. In fact that event seemed to usher in a long period of turbulence. South Carolina reopened the African slave trade, and the contest began in Congress for a Federal prohibition. The Act of March 2, 1807, dealt only with importations, not with migrations, and the bitter debate which preceded passage of this Act continued and culminated in the Missouri controversy. Meanwhile, an entirely new contest began over colonization—not new in the sense of not having been mentioned before, but new in the sense of dealing with free Negroes and not slaves. All of this occurred while the War of 1812 was being fought. It was not a period of tranquility to say the least, and the Missouri debates may well have influenced the followers of Denmark Vesey in South Carolina, as the French Declaration of the Rights of Man influenced the followers of Toussaint L'Ouverture in Santo Domingo.

Denmark Vesey was a brilliant man. Twenty some years the slave of a slave trader, he purchased his freedom in 1800 and became an independent artisan in Charleston. Thereafter, he became an employer, acquired considerable property, and fathered many children by slave mothers. The children, like their mothers, were doomed to a lifetime of servitude. Vesey had traveled widely. He spoke several languages. He was thoroughly familiar with the Bible. He was respected and obeyed by the Negroes, slave and free alike. He knew the history of the Santo Domingo affair and the philosophy of the American Revolution. He followed the debates in Congress. In short, few men were better informed than he in the history of race relations. Associated with him were a group of lesser, but withal, remarkable men; artisans for the most part, but including two slaves of Governor Thomas Bennett. No women were admitted to the conspiracy, and in the end, all but one of the men went to their executions without revealing anything, so that the full extent of their plans are not known. Certainly, they included the complete destruction of the white population of Charleston as a first step, on July 14, 1822. The hope was for the total destruction of slavery, possibly with aid from Great Britain and Santo Domingo. That such elaborate plans could have been devised without the assistance of any white persons and in spite of the difficulty of communication among the slaves was remarkable. Only by accident was the plan prematurely revealed and only from lack of arms, probably, did it fail.

The trial court, by law in South Carolina, was composed of two justices and five freeholders. Conviction was to be assessed, according to precedent, upon testimony by two witnesses. In the end, thirty-five persons were hanged, thirty-four were exiled, and sixty-one were acquitted. The trials were conducted with as much secrecy as possible. Torture was used to wring confessions from some, and those who were acquitted were nevertheless mercilessly whipped before being released. Because Vesey had been a free Negro, there was increased agitation to drive all of them out of the state; and to enact new restrictions against the education of Negroes, slave or free, and upon their opportunity to own property or to operate independently in the crafts and services. The immediate result was a law requiring every free Negro to have a respectable white guardian, and another providing imprisonment for teaching a Negro to read or write. In an informal way, slaves were more carefully supervised, were allowed fewer privileges, and were punished more severely than before the revelations. It was the usual, perhaps inevitable, sequence of events.[24]

Not all of the natural leaders of the Negroes who kept emerging in spite of the impediments were disposed to violence. Each served the cause of his people in his own way, and who can judge the gain. There is something rather pitiful, however, about the effort to find security by driving out of the South men of courage and ability. Pitiful, because, as we have seen, once it began with Negroes, it continued with whites. Pitiful, too, because in exile they could speak freely, and the anger of the slaveholders at their inability to seize and destroy them knew no bounds.

Such an one was David Walker, born in Wilmington, North Carolina, in 1785. His mother was free, his father a slave, and this reversal of ordinary relationships gave him freedom to roam the South, to read, to go eventually to Boston, bearing in his heart a terrible hatred of the oppression. Walker set himself up as a clothing merchant in Boston. He was a Methodist, and he gave generously of his time and money to assist the Negroes of the city. In 1829 he published his appeal to the colored citizens of the world: a clarion call for achievement and for war.[25] Said Walker, "We colored people of these United States are the most degraded, wretched, and abject set of beings that ever lived since the world began." This he explained was the result of slavery, and not of racial inferiority. Jefferson had said the opposite, and Walker quoted from Jefferson's *Notes on Virginia* the statement: "It is not their condition then, but nature, which has produced the distinction." "Do you believe that the assertions of such a man will pass away into oblivion by this people and the world?" asked Walker. "If you do, you are much mistaken." [26] His answer to this charge of inferiority was simple and direct. "It is indeed surprising that a man of such great learning, combined with such excellent natural parts, should speak so of a set of men in chains. I do not know what to compare it to, unless, like putting one wild deer in an iron cage, where it will be secured, and hold another by the side of the same, then let it go, and expect the one in the cage to run as fast as the one at liberty." [27]

"The whites," said Walker, "have always been an unjust, jealous, unmerciful, avaricious and blood thirsty set of beings, always seeking after power and authority." [28] And, again: "The whites want slaves, and want us for their slaves, but some of them will curse the day they ever saw us. As true as the sun ever shone in its meridian splendor, my Colour will root some of them out of the very face of the earth. They shall have enough of making slaves of, and butchering, and murdering us in the manner which they have." [29] Finally, he said, "The whites shall have enough of the blacks, yet, as true as God sits on his throne in heaven." [30]

Walker, of course, was not allowed to live in peace; in fact, there is strong reason to believe that he was not *allowed* to live at all. The governor of Georgia requested Mayor Harrison Gray Otis of Boston to suppress the *Appeal*. Otis, a strong advocate of freedom of speech and of the press, refused to do so. A group of men in Georgia then offered $1,000 for Walker's head and $10,000 for him alive. This business of offering large sums for antislavery leaders was soon to become a sort of hobby in the South, but in this case it may have resulted in Walker's death. He died very suddenly in 1830. He may have been poisoned. A son, born shortly after Walker's death, served in the Massachusetts legislature after the Civil War. Walker's *Appeal* was published again in 1848 by Henry Highland Garnet, together with Garnet's own appeal for every slave to cease work

increase the torture; that they are often stripped naked, their backs and limbs cut with knives, bruised and mangled by scores and hundreds of blows with the paddle, and terribly torn by the claws of cats drawn over them by their tormentors;

BARBAROUS MODE OF PUNISHING A SLAVE WITH THE PADDLE.

that they are often hunted with bloodhounds, and shot down like beasts, or torn in pieces by dogs; that they are often suspended by the arms, and whipped and beaten till they faint, and, when revived by restoratives, beaten again till they faint, and sometimes till they die; that their ears are often cut off, their eyes knocked out, their bones broken, their flesh branded with red hot irons; that they are maimed, mutilated, and burned to death over slow fires; are undeniable facts.

The enormities inflicted by slaveholders upon their slaves will never be discredited, except by those who overlook the simple fact, that he who holds human beings as his *bona fide* property, regards them as property, and not as *persons;* this is his permanent state of mind toward them. He does not contemplate slaves as human beings, consequently does not treat them as such; and, with entire indifference, sees them suffer privations, and writhe under blows, which, if inflicted upon whites, would fill him with horror and indignation. He regards

A page from *Leeds Anti-Slavery Series* containing an often used picture, and text from Weld's *American Slavery as It Is.*

Leeds Anti-slavery Series. No. 7.

SLAVERY A SYSTEM OF INHERENT CRUELTY.

FLOGGING A SLAVE FASTENED TO THE GROUND.

THIRTY HUNDRED THOUSAND PERSONS in the United States of America, men, women, and children, are in SLAVERY. Is slavery, as a condition for human beings, good, bad, or indifferent? We submit the question without argument. You have common sense, and conscience, and a human heart—pronounce upon it. You have a wife, or a husband, a child, a father, a mother, a brother, or a sister—make the case your own, make it theirs, and bring in your verdict. The case of human rights against slavery has been adjudicated in the court

Sold by W. and F. G. CASH, 5, Bishopsgate Street, London; and by JANE JOWETT, Friends' Meeting Yard, Leeds, at 3s. 6d. per 100; or 6d. per doz.

Tied to the rafters
One of the most cruel and most common forms of punishment.

and walk away, a most intriguing, perhaps sensible, solution of the problem.[31]

Shortly after David Walker's death in Boston, Nat Turner, known as the Prophet among the slaves, began the work of destruction in Southampton County, Virginia. Nat's father and mother were both native Africans. The father simply refused to live in bondage. He fled to the North and later went to Liberia. Nat was given some education as a boy by the sons of his master. He was sold and resold, but gradually developed an intense religious fervor and was allowed to move about rather freely preaching to the Negroes on the plantations. He believed, and the slaves believed, that he was chosen of God to lead them out of bondage. August 13, 1831, was finally selected as the day of destiny.

Nat, with an initial band of seven men, began the bloody work by murdering his master and family, then moved from plantation to plantation,

gathering followers as he went until there were probably sixty or seventy in his band, and fifty-one white persons had been killed. Once the alarm was sounded and armed resistance began, the revolt collapsed. Turner himself was not apprehended for six weeks. Fifty-three Negroes were arrested and tried. Twenty of these were hanged, twenty-one were acquitted, twelve were transported out of the state. That was the official record. No count was ever made of those slaves who were shot down by the self-appointed and irresponsible posses who roamed the countryside compiling a record of brutality and bloodshed exceeding anything the Negroes had done. Their victims numbered in the hundreds.

This was not unusual. Whipping, hanging, burning, shooting Negroes, or otherwise torturing and killing them by whatever gang might have an inclination for it, did not begin in Reconstruction after the Civil War. That notion is a part of Southern mythology. It began in slavery and was as prevalent before the war as afterward. The law paid little attention ever. The master, in the days of slavery, tried to protect his property, but that was impossible at times of public frenzy. Thirty-nine lashes with a cowhide whip was moderate punishment, and the moaning of the slaves moved with the sun from one end of the South to the other. Night brought out the patrols, who began where the overseers left off, and masters who advertised for runaway slaves, dead or alive, had little recourse if their slaves were slaughtered when the mobs took over.

The greater importance of these uprisings lay in the reaction which followed. Free Negroes and preaching Negroes, and Negroes who could read and write were blamed; whites who were strangers in the community were suspected. There was an immediate demand for the removal of free Negroes from the slave country and for enforcement of the several laws restricting the activities of slaves. There was also a demand for the abolition of slavery, and one of the great debates on the question of emancipation followed in the General Assembly of Virginia of 1831–32. The period 1829–33 was one of crisis, of new direction, of resolute and distressing decision. The slave power won again and went on to new heights of arrogance in its attempts to beat down the spirit of revolt among the slaves and the humanity of those who befriended them. Our immediate interest is in the repressive legislation.

The staking out and flogging of the girl Patsey

The fundamental principle of all relationship between the slave and society was that the slave was subject to control but was *not entitled to protection*. There was nothing to protect. His body, intellect, labor, belonged to his owner. He could make no contracts, had no wife and no children in the eyes of the law. He had no rights, could not testify in court except against another Negro. He had no civil rights—to learn, to speak, to possess, to defend himself. There was no place to which he could flee and no person to whom he could appeal for protection. The point is that in whatever respects the slave, any slave, all slaves, lived above the level of cattle, there was an element of intervention by some white person. There were slaves who were fortunate enough always to have had adequate food, shelter, and clothing, and never to have been beaten, branded, or tortured.

Some among them were fortunate enough to have enjoyed privileges beyond that: to have been taught to read and write, to have been cared for when ill, to have been allowed to attend religious services, to own some trifling possessions, to maintain a family relationship. Some were given their freedom. But, in times of agitation and apprehension, legislatures wrote new laws, patrols rode at night, masters ruled more sternly. Then, the law sought to make sure that slaves lived without knowledge; to emphasize the fact that they were not people, that they never could speak for themselves, that they possessed none of the attributes of human beings.

Said John Finley Crow, editor of the *Abolition Intelligencer and Missionary Magazine* of Shelbyville, Kentucky, in 1822: "The rigor of oppression has broken the proud spirit of the man and transformed him into the obsequious slave." However good the condition of the slaves might have been at times, it depended not on the spirit of the law or wisdom of institutions but upon the humanity of particular masters, and that was precarious tenure indeed.

Discovery of Nat Turner

FREE NEGROES

Chapter 13

There was once a disastrous fire in Savannah, and donations for relief poured in including $100 from Elihu Embree, editor of the *Emancipator* at Jonesboro, Tennesee. When he discovered that a $10,000 donation from New York City had been returned because the donors requested that Negroes share in the relief funds, he expressed amazement that a righteous God had not "destroyed its [Savannah's] proud inhabitants with fire unquenchable!" Said he: "I am truly ashamed that they are human beings, as this act of theirs disgraces human nature . . . we can not suppose that having given to all men rational and immortal minds God intended the difference of color in our species, either as the brand of slavery or the title to oppression; we rather view it as a providential trial to our hearts; to prove what is in us."[1] Embree was talking about race prejudice, which is an outward expression of inherent meanness and stupidity. It was a great obstacle to emancipation.

Some people, as we shall see, sought to escape the presence of a permanent Negro minority in the United States by persuading them to move out of the country, but the organized effort known as colonization came too late to succeed. Too many free Negroes already had proved their ability to live creatively and usefully as free and independent citizens. They had done it under the most adverse circumstances, so that only the blind could fail to realize their vast potential capacity for achievement. Moreover, the movement to abolish slavery and to give equal justice and opportunity to the Negro had gone too far by 1817

to be halted by prejudice. Few persons who favored colonization were honestly opposed to slavery. Holding a person in slavery because of his color and driving him out of the country because of his color were both oppression based on a belief in racial inequality. Antislavery people rejected the philosophy and opposed the oppression.

The entire group of Pennsylvanians—Franklin, Woolman, Benezet, and others—spent more time, money and energy helping the free Negroes than in trying to persuade other people to free their slaves. The American Convention was composed of state organizations that did little more than assist slaves legally entitled to freedom and educate, train, and protect free Negroes. Franklin wanted a national program of that sort. Time after time slaveholders were urged to modify the system of slavery by some program of education, religious instruction, agricultural peonage, and so forth, and there can be no question but the full resources of the country could have been thrown into such a program at any time after the Revolution. Organized antislavery men and individuals always sought to ameliorate the condition of slaves, to protect the free Negro before the law, to raise his standard of living, to provide social justice.

There is, of course, a vast distinction, as we shall see, between political privileges, civil rights, and social justice. Avoiding all entanglement in a lengthy discussion of citizenship—British, Colonial, and United States—we can still make several statements of fact not open to successful refutation. Free Negroes, born in the colonies, were

British subjects. All British subjects residing in a colony were citizens of the state after independence unless disqualified from citizenship by state constitutional provisions. The Constitution of the United States spoke of "the people of the United States," "persons," "citizens of the United States," and "citizens of each state." There was no need to define citizenship. People who were citizens of the several states at the time, people born thereafter in the United States and subject to its authority, and people naturalized by the authority of the United States government were universally regarded as citizens. Certainly a Constitutional Convention, which authorized the new United States government to exercise the wholly new and revolutionary principle of naturalization, would have stated some qualifications if there had been objection to endowing with United States citizenship the citizens of the states and persons born thereafter in the United States. Negroes, therefore, were citizens.

No one among the great liberals of the Revolutionary period would have questioned the endowment of all men with equal and inalienable rights. No one among the great liberals fifty years later would have done so, but we have to remember that not every one in this country supported the Revolution or subscribed to the principles on which the new nation was founded. We have to remember, furthermore, that slavery was antithetical to natural rights, equality, and justice and that the slave power not only controlled the slave states, it wielded tremendous power in Congress, the courts, the churches, the educational institutions, and the political parties. It was a moot question for a long time as to whether the basic principles on which the nation was founded would survive. In fact, the day came when the question no longer was equality for the Negroes, or freedom for the slaves, but freedom for white men as well. We shall shortly discuss this struggle. The point presently is that a good many people, including even legislators, judges, and other public officials, in their behavior and in their pronouncements, and in their public conduct, did violence to our declared principles and constitutional guarantees.

On another occasion I have stated those principles as follows: Natural law is unchangeable and everlasting and the natural rights of man are above the power of government to destroy or deny. All men are equal in their natural endowment of rights. Governments derive their author-ity from the people, and their primary purpose is to make these natural rights of men more secure and to protect the individual in their enjoyment. All citizens, therefore, are entitled to equality under the law and in the administration of justice.[2]

All of the original states which abolished slavery did so on the basis of the revolutionary impulse and officially lived up to these principles to a remarkable degree in their treatment of the emancipated slaves. They were citizens of their respective states the same as were Negroes who were free at the time of independence. They voted in every one of these states for many years after the Revolution. There never were any legal distinctions of race or color in Vermont or New Hampshire, only a trace of such in Maine and Massachusetts, and few of consequence in the other states of the East or in Michigan or Wisconsin when these states came into the Union at a later date. Citizenship and the right of suffrage are not synonymous. Nevertheless, bestowal of the franchise upon Negroes; or, stating it another way, failure to deny them the franchise, is very strong presumptive evidence of citizenship; and, when reinforced by complete or nearly complete equality in the enjoyment of civil rights and enforcement of the criminal laws, is proof positive.

Vermont made no distinction in her constitution or laws between persons on the basis of color. There is no such term as free person of color to be found anywhere in her statutes. Her constitution of 1777 gave the franchise to all males of mature age, and specifically extended jury trial and habeas corpus to fugitives. New Hampshire, like Vermont, had no distinctions between individuals on the basis of race or color. After the tissue of inconsistencies and denials of historical facts embraced in the *Dred Scott* decision were published, both states were quick to reaffirm citizenship of Negroes. In words copied almost verbatim by Vermont, New Hampshire said: "Neither descent, near or remote, from a person of African blood, whether such a person is or may have been a slave, nor color of skin, shall disqualify any person from becoming a citizen of this State, or deprive such person of the full rights and privileges of a citizen thereof."[3] The legislature of New Hampshire then went on to say: "Section first, of Chapter twenty-five of the compiled statutes shall not be construed as in any case to deprive any person of color or of African descent, born within the limits of the United States and having the other requisite qualifications, from voting at any election; but such person shall have and exercise the right of suffrage as fully and lawfully as persons of the white race."[4]

It should be stated at this point that New Hampshire, by law of 1792, prohibited Negro enlistments in the state militia and that the law was repealed in 1857.[5] This does not represent discrimination by the state. General George Washington had opposed the enrollment of Negroes in the Continental armies, but a great many did serve, and several of the states went so far as to enroll *slaves* and afterward reward them with freedom and public support. Congress, however, in May, 1792, in that reactionary period of congressional legislation including the Fugitive Slave Act, passed a law limiting enrollment in state militia to white men. Thereafter, all states passed laws in conformity with this act of Congress and exclusion of Negroes from military service cannot be considered evidence of prevailing sentiment in a particular state. As has been stated, Vermont repealed the exclusion in 1857 despite the federal law, and Massachusetts would have done so in 1859 had not her Supreme Court advised that such an act in contravention of federal law would be unconstitutional.[6]

Massachusetts, like New Hampshire and Vermont, made no distinctions as to color in voting qualifications. She, too, has given us clear evidence of her intent. The franchise was limited to white persons in the proposed constitution of 1778 and the voters rejected it. The constitution of 1780 did not limit the franchise to white persons and the voters approved it.[7] This grant of the franchise to Negroes was never retracted.[8] There is, moreover, abundant evidence of Negro participation in elections to be found in the bitterly fought contests between Federalists and Democrats in 1800 and again in 1813. Intermarriages between Negroes and whites had been prohibited by colonial law in Massachusetts. This was reenacted into state law in 1786 and was not repealed until 1843.[9]

Another law which lingered on the statute books of the state, as outmoded state laws ordinarily do, was one which prohibited Negroes from coming into the state and remaining longer than two months, unless they were citizens of another state and could prove it by a certificate from the secretaries of the states of which they were citizens. This law is important not as evidence of prejudice because it was not, but as evidence of fulfillment of obligations under the fugitive slave provisions of the Constitution.[10] Massachusetts established schools for Negro children in 1820; and, in 1855, ended segregated schools by decreeing that no distinction should be made "on account of race, color, or religious opinions of the applicant or scholar." Maine, under the jurisdiction of Massachusetts until 1821, prohibited intermarriages but gave full citizenship and the franchise to Negroes.[11]

In Connecticut Negroes were citizens of the state, and the legislature reaffirmed the fact after the Dred Scott decision, by stating that all persons born in the state or coming into the state for permanent residence were citizens of the state, excepting only aliens, and fugitives.[12] They were given the franchise in 1784, but a law of 1814, although it did not disqualify those already listed as freemen of the towns, provided that thereafter only free white males should be admitted as freemen. This provision was written into the constitution of 1818.[13] In 1833 a law specifically enacted for a particular case forbade schools for any Negroes not citizens of the state. This law, which we shall consider later, was repealed in 1838.

Rhode Island had some slaves in the state until 1842. Nevertheless, Negroes were citizens of the state, without any distinctions as to civil rights, and enjoyed the franchise until 1822. The legislature at that time denied them the right to become freemen of the towns, but did not deprive those already listed of the franchise. The restriction lasted only twenty years. The constitutional convention of 1842 not only abolished the last vestiges of slavery in the state, but corrected the injustice of 1822 by deliberately removing the word white from the franchise provision and giving the right to vote to "every male citizen of the United States" who qualified under the residence and property holding qualifications of the state.[14]

New York had some slaves until 1827, Pennsylvania until 1840, and New Jersey until 1846. They had much larger numbers of free Negroes, and Pennsylvania at least was a refuge for fugitives and a happy hunting ground for kidnappers. The New York constitution of 1777 gave "every male inhabitant of full age" the right to vote, except that Negroes had to secure certificates of freedom certified by the judge. This was a legitimate requirement in view of the large numbers of slaves and fugitives. The clear intention to give them the franchise was shown not only by this requirement but by the fact that a bill of the legislature (1785) for the abolition of slavery was vetoed because it disfranchised free Negroes.[15] The constitutional convention of 1821 provided that "no man of color unless he shall have been for three years a citizen of this state" and have a freehold estate of $250 could vote. Other than that there were no legal distinctions. Negroes were never excluded from the schools by law, although provision was made for separate schools, and they were never prohibited from voting in school elections.[16]

In New Jersey the constitution of 1776 gave the franchise to "all inhabitants of this colony of full age" who could meet the residence requirements. Under this broad provision, everyone voted: white men and women, Negro men and women, married and single, and apparently at least some slaves; and they continued to do so until 1807. Slaves were excluded by law from voting (perhaps it would be more correct to say from being voted) in 1790. The Federalists were accused in New Jersey, as they were in New York and Massachusetts, of using Negro votes to defeat the Democrats. In 1807 the franchise was restricted to free white male citizens of twenty-one years of age.[17]

Nearly all of the restrictions upon free Negroes in Pennsylvania were removed in November, 1780. The constitution of 1790 said that every eligible freeman should enjoy the franchise. Negroes voted under the provisions of this constitution until 1837. At that time the Pennsylvania Supreme Court decided that Negroes were not freemen and not eligible to vote. There was a constitutional convention in session at the time, and after extensive debate the franchise was limited to white freemen. Negroes had enjoyed full civil rights, however, and these were not disturbed. In 1854 provision was made for separate schools for Negroes if there were twenty or more pupils.[18]

Passing to the states of the Old Northwest which had not gone through the experience of the Revolution, nor of slavery and emancipation, we find a less liberal attitude toward free Negroes. There was a very close economic tie between these states and the lower Mississippi Valley, which was not materially lessened until completion of the Erie Canal in the 1820's. There was a preponderance of Southern immigrants in the populations. Ohio particularly received a great influx of emancipated slaves. The three states were separated from slavery only by the Ohio River. They had the misfortune of having some incompetent territorial governors, for example, William Henry Harrison. Finally, they became states and framed constitutions after the revolutionary period and before the reform period, when liberalism seemed about to perish.

Ohio framed her first constitution in 1802. She limited the franchise to white inhabitants who paid a state or county tax.[19] Every other state carved from the Northwest Territory followed her example, and no one of them admitted Negroes to the franchise before the Civil War.[20] Ohio also enacted a law in 1803 limiting jury service to those persons enjoying the franchise.[21] This provision, which effectively excluded Negroes, was written into the territorial laws and then the state laws of Michigan and of Wisconsin.[22] Illinois limited jury service to white citizens of the United States.[23]

The first governor of Indiana Territory was William Henry Harrison. He was a thoroughgoing anti-Federalist which meant being allied to Southern politics. He had gone to Philadelphia to study medicine under Benjamin Rush, but unfortunately did not remain long enough to be influenced by Rush's humanitarian, antislavery principles. He would have been perfectly willing to open the Northwest to slavery; he went along with St. Clair's view that the Ordinance of 1787 only prohibited the introduction of new slaves; and he and the judges of Indiana Territory adopted laws from the code of Virginia. One such law (1803) barred Negroes and Indians from testifying in court in cases involving white persons.[24] There never were any such laws in New England, New York, Pennsylvania, or New Jersey. It was a clear case of borrowing from the slave codes for the basic laws of territory forever dedicated to freedom and was thoroughly reprehensible. This same principle was written into the laws of the state of Indiana[25] and of Illinois.[26] Ohio adopted it in 1807,[27] and Indiana extended it to anyone possessing one-eighth Negro blood in 1853.[28] There is no reason for thinking that these states ever would have passed such laws if they had started in the territorial stage with laws borrowed from the New England states.

One of the most difficult restrictions to interpret is the prohibition of intermarriages between members of the two races. There was a great deal of miscegenation involving both sexes of both races in slave states and in free. An effort was made to force the issue of these unions back into slavery, which was obviously impossible in the case of free mothers. Antislavery people insisted that slavery increased miscegenation enormously. They condemned it. In the free states some effort was made to prevent it by making it illegal, but the right of the individual to choose his or her own mate is difficult to dispute and even more difficult to control. None of the states which abolished slavery had inherited such laws from colonial days except Pennsylvania and Massachusetts. Pennsylvania repealed her colonial law.[29] Massachusetts re-enacted her prohibition and retained it until 1843. Rhode Island enacted a prohibition in 1798.[30] In the original states of the East, therefore, Negroes and whites were free to intermarry everywhere except in Massachusetts before 1843 and in Rhode Island.

Indiana, still looking to the South rather than the East, forbade intermarriages in 1818 and clung steadfastly to her decision through a series of laws until, by 1840, the penalty for the offending parties was $1,000 to $5,000 fine and ten to twenty years' imprisonment.[31] Ohio did not enact a prohibition on intermarriages, Michigan did in 1837, when she became a state.[32] Illinois did so in 1829 with a barbaric penalty of fine, imprisonment, and whipping not to exceed thirty-nine lashes for both parties.[33]

Not content with legislation drastically curtailing the freedom of Negroes, these states passed exclusion laws. There was no precedent for this type of legislation in the eastern states. Ohio enacted the first of these laws in 1804, strengthened it in 1807, and kept it on the statute books until 1849.[34] The original law forbade a Negro to settle in the state unless he could furnish a certificate of freedom from some court. All Negroes already residing in the state were required to register and were required to present a certificate of registration to prospective employers. The revised law of 1807 required bond of $500 from immigrant Negroes as a guarantee of good behavior and ability to maintain themselves. Illinois passed her exclusion law in 1819. The incoming Negro had to produce to the county clerk a certificate of freedom bearing a description of himself and family. Anyone bringing a Negro into the state to emancipate him was required to post a bond of $1,000 as a guarantee against his be-

coming a public charge. Negroes found without certificates of freedom were to be taken into custody as fugitives. All Negroes resident in the state in 1841 were allowed to register and receive certificates of freedom, but in 1853 all Negroes were forbidden to enter the state, they and anyone aiding them being subject to arrest, and the latter to $500 fine and one year in prison.[35] Indiana waited until 1831 to pass an exclusion law similar to that of Illinois, then in 1851 wrote into her constitution the provision that "no Negro or mulatto shall come into, or settle in the state, after the adoption of this Constitution." Anyone employing such Negroes was subject to a fine.[36] None of the three states made provision for public education of Negro children.

Viewing the over-all legal status of Negroes in the free states around 1830, we can state certain incontestable facts:

There were no restrictions prior to 1800 upon Negroes voting in any state which had abolished slavery. They were voting at that time and continued to vote without interruption in New Hampshire, Vermont, Rhode Island, and in the two slave states of New York and New Jersey. Restrictions were imposed at a later date in Connecticut (1814) and Pennsylvania (1837). There is some evidence of voting by slaves in New Jersey.

The slave codes of New York, New Jersey, and Pennsylvania had forbidden slaves to testify in court in cases involving white persons. These laws never applied to free Negroes, and there were no such laws in New England. Nor were there any distinctions whatever in criminal law, judicial procedure, and punishments.

Negroes were free to marry whites except in Massachusetts before 1843, and in Rhode Island. They could go and come as they pleased, wherever they pleased, and there were no distinctions as to ownership of property or taxation.

Negroes were citizens in all of these states. They were citizens by enjoyment of full political equality, by lack of any statements to the contrary in any constitution or law, by complete absence of legal distinctions based on color, and by specific legal and constitutional declaration, and any statements to the contrary by courts, federal or state, were contrary to historical fact and are worthless as historical evidence.

In the three states of Ohio, Indiana, and Illinois, Negroes were not given the franchise, were not admitted to jury service, could not testify in cases involving white persons, could not inter-marry with white persons, and were required to have certificates of freedom and post bonds for good behavior and economic competence. They were annoyed by many minor restrictions in their efforts to live decently in freedom.

Restrictions upon free Negroes in Ohio, Indiana, and particularly Illinois were in harmony with the laws of the slave states. The legislatures of slave states tried to prevent manumissions, and placed all possible obstacles in the way, until it became almost impossible for a slaveholder to free a slave except for some meritorious service to the owner or to the state, and then only by special permission of the legislature.[37] Free Negroes were liable to seizure and sale to satisfy claims against their *former* owner.[38] They could not travel without certificates of freedom.[39] They could not own dogs or grocery stores.[40] Their homes were liable to search by slave patrols to prevent unlawful assemblies.[41] They could be whipped for associating with slaves or free whites under many diverse circumstances and for being disrespectful to whites.[42] They could not own fire-arms.[43] They could not testify in cases involving white persons.[44] Trials and punishments in civil and criminal cases were controlled by the judicial processes of slavery.[45] They could not trade with slaves. They could not own or rent houses. They were forbidden to assemble for purposes of religious or mental instruction. They were barred from employment in printing establishments and apothecary shops.[46]

In the area of punishments, free Negroes were in a separate category from whites: whipping, not to exceed thirty-nine lashes for giving illegal passes to slaves; ten years in the penitentiary for assisting slaves to escape; sale into slavery for life for enticing slaves away; imprisonment and fines for insulting white persons; death for assaulting with a weapon; death for arson, for poisoning, and for insurrections; and ten years in the penitentiary for distributing "incendiary" literature.[47] The settled purpose of all such legislation was to discourage manumissions, to force free Negroes back into slavery or out of the area, to discipline those who remained to the point of submissiveness and abasement. They seldom entered the public consciousness, because there were only approximately 30,000 in South Carolina, Georgia, Alabama, Mississippi and Louisiana combined in

1830; but misconduct brought swift retribution and drastic restrictions.

By 1830 the states of the lower South, and other slave states to a degree, were striving to eliminate free Negroes from their populations completely. Georgia in 1818 prohibited manumissions, irrespective of reasons, circumstances, or methods. Private or public administrators of estates who attempted to comply with manumission provisions of wills were subject to $1,000 fine.[48] Mississippi was equally severe.[49] Alabama permitted emancipation only under posted security for quick and definite removal from the state.[50] South Carolina in 1800 forbade free Negroes to enter the state, and in 1820 imposed fines of $500 on masters of ships who brought any nonemployed Negroes into the state.[51] Other states copied this legislation, and free Negroes who violated the prohibition were sold into slavery.

What was the relationship between these conditions and the treatment of free Negroes in states like Pennsylvania, Ohio, Indiana, and Illinois? Four types of Negroes were coming into those states: fugitive slaves, to the estimated number of one thousand each year; slaves freed by their owners and brought or sent to the free states to circumvent the laws against manumission; slaves who were allowed to cross over into a free state and work for wages to pay for their freedom, numbering about one-third of the seventy-five hundred in Ohio in 1830; free Negroes of spirit leaving the slave states to escape harsh restrictions or severe punishment. A very high percentage of the populations of the three western states in the early years came from the slave states. The tendency to follow the legislative pattern and social customs of states from which they came was universal with the early settlers. The people of these states did not relish an influx of these low-ly people, and there no doubt was considerable feeling that since the South had insisted slavery was its own problem it ought to care for its own derelicts.

The legal restraints upon free Negroes everywhere reveal elements of anger and fear, of self-ishness and of downright meanness. They reveal a halting uncertainty about political and social equality, a conflict between convictions and prejudices, and, unfortunately, a too ready acceptance of the idea of racial inequality. The important fact about all of these laws is that after all they were laws, not attitudes. They do not speak too well for the people because laws cannot live unless they find lodgment in the hearts of the people. These did in the early years, less as time passed and the antislavery movement progressed. Its emphasis upon equality for the Negro made the states where public opinion was hostile to the Negro the battle grounds for civil rights. Finally, we have said nothing about legislation protecting the Negro in his person and property and everyday activities against discrimination and persecution by his white neighbors. There was no such legislation. It would have been class legislation and would have been resisted by both Negroes and antislavery men. They were entitled to the same protection as any other person under the law.

This represents one of the efforts by antislavery people of Cincinnati to promote the relief and improvement of the Negro population of that city.

TO THE FRIENDS
OF THE
POOR COLORED ORPHANS.

"Blessed is he that considereth the poor, the Lord will deliver him in the time of trouble." In 1844 an Asylum was started at Cincinnati for the poor colored Orphans of Ohio, by Mrs. Mott, Mrs. Judge McLean, and others. They purchased a large building for $1000, which is paid, except $100. The house needs repairing to the amount of $400 to make it comfortable and convenient for the reception of one hundred children, who will be received if the means of support, for them, can be obtained.

The Asylum was chartered in 1845. It has nine faithful Trustees and other *necessary* Directors *only*. Some of whom, Judge Bellamy Storer says, "I am personally acquainted with and they have my *perfect* confidence, and from the mode in which the Institution is managed, I have no doubt, that any contributions the agent may receive from the friends of the colored people will be faithfully and judiciously applied. And S. P. Chase, Esq., says, "I KNOW THE INSTITUTION TO BE EVERY WAY WORTHY OF AID."

There are only fifteen children in the Asylum at present, and the reason for this small number is, the want of means to take care of a greater. The Institution has never received any foreign help but $100 from Philadelphia. It is for you, friends of God and his poor, to say whether the Trustees shall have what is needed to carry on this great and good work. The Trustees ask you. " *Shall we have one spot of earth —one house, where* OUR *poor and destitute may find relief, and shelter from the storm?*"— Who will say, yes? Hear what the True Democrat of the 2d of Oct. says, " We trust that those who are called upon to give, will remember that our beautiful republican laws do not extend the same blessing to *colored* children that they do to *white :* hence if they are educated at all, it has to be accomplished by their own perseverance against deep rooted prejudice, and with what little they may obtain f─── ──nevolent fri─── ───rlin Evangelist of the 12th ─f O──

COLONIZATION

Chapter 14

"Under the Federal Government which is now established, we have reason to believe that all slaves in the United States, will in time be emancipated, in a manner most consistent with their own happiness, and the true interest of their proprietors. Whether this will be effected by transporting them back to Africa; or by colonizing them in some part of our own territory, and extending to them our alliance and protection until they shall have acquired strength sufficient for their own defense; or by incorporation with the whites; or in some other way, remains to be determined. All these methods are attended with difficulties. The first would be cruel; the second dangerous; and the latter disagreeable and unnatural. Deep-rooted prejudices entertained by the whites; ten thousand recollections, by the blacks, of the injuries they have sustained; new provocations; the real distinction which nature has made; besides many other circumstances which would tend to divide them into parties, and produce convulsions, are objections against retaining and incorporating the blacks with the citizens of the several states. But justice and humanity demand that these difficulties should be surmounted."[1] So wrote Jedediah Morse in his *American Geography* in 1789.

Morse saw clearly the evil of slavery, but his approach to the problem of emancipation was that of Madison and Washington and Jefferson and Patrick Henry. Those men were perfectly willing to spread carnage over the face of the earth to establish their own claim to freedom, but lacked the courage to live by their assertions of the natural rights of men. Twenty years later emancipation had run its course; Virginia had become the breeding ground of slaves for the emerging cotton kingdom, and slavery was so deeply rooted in the Black Belt as to be indestructible. The Southern position was made crystal clear in the debates over prohibiting the foreign slave trade. It was to be perpetual slavery or civil war. Three powerful pillars supported the superstructure: slaves constituted the labor force; slaves gave the white people tremendous political power; and slaves were the living proof of racial superiority.

In no respect was this determination to strengthen and perpetuate the institution more clearly demonstrated than in the movement to colonize the free Negroes. Morse was correct when he said to transport the Negroes to Africa would be cruel; it was all of that—as cruel as death. Everyone who studies the documents on this subject should start with Benjamin Franklin. In the "Address to the Public from the Pennsylvania Society for Promoting the Abolition of Slavery, and the Relief of Free Negroes Unlawfully Held in Bondage," Franklin said:

"The unhappy man, who has long been treated as a brute animal, too frequently sinks beneath the common standard of the human species. The galling chains that bind his body do also fetter his intellectual faculties, and impair the social affections of his heart. Accustomed to move like a mere machine, by the will of a master, reflection is suspended; he has not the power of choice; and reason and conscience have but little influence over his conduct, because he is chiefly governed by the passion of fear. He is poor and friendless; perhaps worn out by extreme labor, age, and disease.

"Attention to emancipated blacks, it is therefore to be hoped, will become a branch of our national policy; but, as far as we contribute to promote this emancipation, so far that attention is evidently a serious duty incumbent on us, and which we mean to discharge to the best of our judgment and abilities.

"To instruct, to advise, to qualify those who have been restored to freedom, for the exercise and enjoyment of civil liberty; to promote in them habits of industry; to furnish them with employments suited to their age, sex, talents, and other circumstances; and to procure their children an education calculated for their future situation in life,—these are the great outlines of our annexed plan, which we have adopted, and which we conceive will essentially promote the public good, and the happiness of these our hitherto too much neglected fellow creatures."[2]

This statement of Franklin was in the finest tradition of Woolman and Benezet and of the Quakers generally. It was the program of the several state societies affiliated in the American Convention. It constituted an important part, in some respects the most important part, of the work of antislavery societies down to the Civil War. Franklin said this program should be a part of national policy. This was precisely what was being argued in the House of Representatives in February 1790, when petitions from the several societies were introduced. It will be recalled that the House undertook to discuss the limits of congressional power in regard to slavery in great detail and finally adopted a self-denying resolution leaving treatment of slaves within the purview of state governments.

The mere existence, North or South, of free Negroes was a constant torment to slaveholders. Their presence in a slave community increased the individual slaveholder's problem. Marriages between slaves and free Negroes, though not recognized by law or by the churches, created all sorts of difficulties, particularly absences and running away. The mere presence of Negroes who were free increased the slaves' desire for freedom. They constituted a potential source of conspiracy and insurrection. They were proof of the Negroes' ability to progress, a denial of his animal status. The slave states simply refused to countenance any program of assistance to these people. They

tried to discourage manumissions. They tried to force free Negroes to move out. They finally tried to get them back into slavery. The objective always was to strengthen slavery, not to aid the Negro.

Against this background of antislavery efforts to educate and train free Negroes for individual competence and intelligent citizenship on the one hand, and proslavery efforts to prevent emancipation, stands the organization of the American Colonization Society in 1817. President Thomas Jefferson and Governor James Monroe of Virginia tried to inaugurate colonization in 1800 and failed. The scheme lay dormant until 1816 when Henry Clay revived it.

Virginia wanted to get rid of her free Negroes. The legislature requested the governor, December 23, 1816, to make representations to the President of the United States for a territory in Africa or elsewhere outside this country to which they might go or be sent. The resolution did not clearly indicate whether this was to be voluntary or compulsory. It is of little consequence, since direct action by Congress was never obtained. Some days later a private meeting of some prominent men in Washington, D. C., was held to discuss the matter, and out of this meeting came the American Society for Colonizing the Free People of Color of the United States, commonly called the American Colonization Society. Its constitution declared its purpose "to promote and execute a plan for colonizing (with their consent) the free people of color, residing in our country, in Africa, or such other place as Congress shall deem most expedient. And the Society shall act to effect this object in Cooperation with the general government, and such of the states as may adopt regulations upon the subject."[3]

The organization was nourished and kept alive, not by pride in its achievements, but by blind devotion to the doctrine of racial inferiority. The arguments of its sponsors were always subtle, always specious, and always bad in their effects upon race prejudice. President Monroe was so completely captivated by them as to say that the manumission of slaves in Virginia at the time of the Revolution (these are the words of John Quincy Adams, Secretary of State) "had introduced a class of very dangerous people, the free blacks, who lived by pilfering, and corrupted the slaves, and produced such pernicious consequences that the Legislature were obliged to prohibit further emancipation by law. The important object now was to remove these free blacks, and provide a place to which the emancipated slaves might go; the legal obstacles to emancipation might then be withdrawn, and the black population in time be drawn off entirely from Virginia."[4] Adams refused, as secretary of state, to have anything to do with putting the United States into the business of supporting colonies, Negro or otherwise, and he was too shrewd an observer of domestic affairs to credit the founders of the society with the charity and sagacity of long-range emancipation objectives. Among those supporting the organization, he said, were "some exceedingly humane, weak-minded men, who have really no other than the professed objects in view, and who honestly believe them both useful and attainable; some, speculators in official profits and honors, which a colonial establishment would of course produce; some, speculators in political popularity, who think to please the abolitionists by their zeal for emancipation, and the slaveholders by the flattering hope of ridding them of the free colored people at the public expense; lastly, some cunning slave-holders, who see that the plan may be carried far enough to produce the effect of raising the market price of the slaves."[5]

Most of the support for colonization, through the years, actually came from the politicians and from people who, like politicians, were in positions where it was profitable to maintain an appearance of antislavery feeling without supporting the cause. Antislavery people would have no part of it.

It was just as cruel, just as inhuman, just as much an invasion of man's natural rights as the rape of Africa had been in the first place. It was rooting people out of their homeland, tearing them away from their families and friends, transporting them across the sea to a strange, new environment. It was robbing them of whatever property they had accumulated, depriving them of an opportunity for an education and economic advancement, snatching away from them the opportunity to live a free life in the country their unrewarded labor had helped so largely to build.

The very idea of sending the free Negroes out of the country was, on the face of it, an endorsement of biological inequality and racial inferiority. It was either an attempt to remove from society an element in the population believed to be incapable of progress, or an attempt to avoid the

expense and effort of compensating, by special devotion to the task, for the years of soul-destroying oppression. Antislavery people denied the rationalization and scorned the evasion.

Free Negroes could not be persuaded to go to Africa or anywhere else of their own free will. They had been born in the United States. This was their home, and however underprivileged they might be, there was nothing at the other end of the migration pulling them. Africa was a continent, strange and far away. Nobody knew what conditions existed there, what the climate was like, what opportunities there were for making a living. Actually, the Negroes showed no interest whatever in migrating. Some few went, largely slaves who were offered freedom if they would go, but there never were enough volunteers to justify the effort.

Antislavery people quickly realized three developments. Slaveholders, to the degree they were supporting the organization, were interested only in removing an element from the population thought to be dangerous and known to create by its presence alone a restlessness among the slaves. Their purpose was to strengthen slavery and make it more secure. Antislavery men realized, also, that the cost of removing the free Negroes was beyond the limits of private resources and that no appreciable number of slaves would ever be emancipated and sent out of the country. Finally, they knew the free Negroes were needed here for leadership of their people when emancipation came.

There were three powerful reasons why slaveholders would never go along with the program of colonization. Even granting they could have been persuaded to forego the ease, and luxury, and wealth derived from slave ownership, they could never have sent their labor supply out of the country. They would not have agreed, and never did, to any expenditure of public funds for colonization, because it would have opened the way to a full-scale program of emancipation. They would have demanded compensation for their slaves, something antislavery people would never have supported.

The combination of antislavery opposition to colonization and proslavery opposition to government participation prevented Congress from taking any action. Congress, however, amended the act prohibiting the foreign slave trade (March 3, 1819), thus disposing of the old problem of what to do with Negro captives of intercepted slave traders. Whether the provision for their sale as slaves in the Act of 1807 had served as an incentive to violations, as antislavery people had claimed, or not, there had been violations, and there was as much reason to oppose sale in 1819 as there had been at an earlier time. The revised law authorized naval patrol of African and American waters; equal division of all prize money between the United States government and the officers and crew of the ship making a seizure; payment of twenty-five dollars to the officers and crew for safe delivery of each Negro rescued to United States officials; return of such Negroes to Africa; appointment of a resident agent there to receive them; prosecution of any person holding Negroes unlawfully imported; payment of fifty dollars to the informer for each such Negro so determined by a jury; and expenditure up to $100,000 for enforcement of the Act.[6] President Monroe interpreted the act broadly and appointed a member of the Colonization Society as agent of the government in Africa, thus giving to the society semiofficial recognition. This did not provide financial assistance, but it did provide prestige at home and abroad.

The society encountered much the same difficulties establishing a permanent settlement in Africa that the London Company had experienced in Virginia. A much higher percentage of Negroes taken to Africa died during the period of acclimatization than of slaves brought to America. The first settlement, on Sherbo Island (1820), was a total failure, and it was not until 1822 that the region later known as Liberia was secured. Another decade passed before the colony reached the point of assured permanence. In 1830 there were 2,000,000 slaves in the United States, and 319,000 free Negroes. The Colonization Society sent out only 2,228 before 1831, fewer than four thousand in twenty years. In 1832 the society had 228 auxiliary societies throughout the country, but its income was only $43,000, and the number of emigrants sent to Liberia was only 796. Ohio had thirty-seven auxiliary societies by 1832, but sent out only fifty-five emigrants by 1860. Kentucky, a slave state, had thirty-two auxiliary societies, but sent out less than six hundred emigrants by 1860; and from the entire country only twelve thousand went by the end of the Civil War. In short, few, if any, national organizations ever failed so miserably. It had no money to send emigrants, and Negroes refused to go. It never made provision for the care of emigrants after they reached Africa. Its importance lies in its effect upon the progress of emancipation, upon the status of the free Negro, and upon the growth of race prejudice.

The American Convention reported in 1818 that it had not "been able to discern, in the constitution and proceedings of the American Colonization Society, or in the avowed sentiments of its members, anything friendly to the abolition of slavery in the United States."[7] Three years later (1821) it said "a colony, either in Africa, or in our own country, would be incompatible with the principles of our government, and with the temporal and spiritual interests of the blacks."[8] Instead of colonization, it urged, as preliminary steps in a general plan of emancipation, that all migration, transportation, and sale of slaves be prohibited; that they be attached to the soil, paid wages, and allowed to work some land as renters; that the children be given an education; and that all arbitrary punishments cease, and a system of humane laws for control be enacted.[9]

The Colonization Society received strong support from humanitarians for a few years. The interval between the close of the War of 1812 and the late 1820's embraced the early years of the Colonization Society and the late years of the American Convention. The antislavery people won their first real victories in these years. They had suffered only defeats since the Ordinance of 1787, until the act for the control of the foreign slave trade was amended in 1819 and the Missouri Compromise line was established in 1820. The era of benevolent enterprises and moral reform began. It was not to end until slavery was abolished; in fact, that reform was long overdue and quickly took precedence in absorbing the interests and efforts of humanitarians. It was perfectly natural, therefore, that colonization should have appeared to a great many people to be the simple, quick, and complete solution of the racial problem.

The colonizationists presented their program to the country as a benevolent enterprise, designed to accomplish four primary objectives: to remove the free Negro population from an atmosphere of prejudice and oppression to one of wholesome freedom, equality, and opportunity; to pave the way for thousands of slaveholders voluntarily to free their slaves, which state laws presently forbade; to provide in Africa the nucleus of an intelligent, Christian civilization for redemption of the continent; and to remove from society an element which was, in the free states, idle and vicious, and in the slave states a corrupting influence upon the slaves. Said Henry Clay: "Can there be anything, to a reflecting freeman, more humiliating, more dark and cheerless, than to see himself, and to trace in imagination his posterity, through all succeeding time, degraded and debased, aliens to the Society of which they are members, and cut off from all its higher blessings."[10]

In this statement of Clay's we have the key to the history of the organization, in fact to the entire history of race relations: *acceptance of the immutability of Negro inferiority*. The first annual report of the society devoted nearly one half its space to a letter from Robert G. Harper, United States senator, Federalist candidate for the vice-presidency in 1816, and a founder of the organization. Said Harper: "These persons are condemned to a state of hopeless inferiority and degradation, by their colour; which is an indelible mark of their origin and former condition, and establishes an impossible barrier between them and the whites. This barrier is closed forever . . . you may manumit the slave, but you cannot make him a white man. He still remains a negro or a mulatto. The mark and the recollection of his origin and former state still adhere to him; the feelings produced by that condition, in his own mind and in the minds of the whites, still exist; he is associated by his colour, and by these recollections and feelings, with the class of slaves; and a barrier is thus raised between him and the whites, *that is* between him and the free class, which he can never hope to transcend."[11] The publications and the speeches of the colonizationists contain enough repulsive stimulants to race prejudice, many of them so vicious as to be almost unprintable, to fill an encyclopedia.[12] This was the first reason for the importance of the society. Men talked of the inherent incapacity and depravity of Negroes until they came to believe it themselves and inflexibly opposed emancipation. They converted thousands to the same belief, thus creating an unreasoned proscription of Negroes and antislavery leaders in hundreds of communities and precipitating a major contest over civil rights. The task of attaining equal protection of the laws for Negroes became more difficult, and emancipation of the slaves was long delayed.

The second reason for the importance of the colonization movement was that it provided anchorage for men who sought escape from the responsibility or penalty of taking a forthright stand for or against slavery. Thomas Jefferson, James Madison, John Marshall, John Randolph, John Taylor of Caroline, Bushrod Washington, and Henry Clay are typical of prominent men who favored colonization and either gave active support to the organization or allowed their names to be used. These men were but mildly opposed to slavery if at all. They were slaveholders; and they were politicians. Marshall voted against the abolition of slavery in Virginia. Bushrod Washington, first president of the Colonization Society, sold his fifty slaves to the commercial traders when they became restless. Charles Carroll, second president, owned 1,000 slaves and never freed any. James Madison, third president, left 100 slaves to his heirs. Henry Clay, fourth president, was always firm in his defense of slavery. Thomas Jefferson appears to have favored compulsory emigration, and always subscribed to the doctrine of racial inferiority. John Randolph and Henry Clay both emphasized the fact that colonization of the free Negroes would strengthen slavery. It is a moot question whether the men to whom the American Colonization Society was "bread and butter" sought out persons prominent in political and religious life to lend dignity and prestige to the activities of the society, or whether these persons attached themselves to the society for security reasons.

Equally important is the fact that neither the parent society, nor the auxiliary societies, nor any of the great variety of persons speaking before and for the societies ever gave more than casual lip service to the improvement of the status of Negroes in society. They did not recognize that the deficiencies of the Negro resulted from the debasing effects of slavery, from the black laws of the free states, and from all kinds of prejudice and denials. They did a great deal of talking about the wretched status of the Negro, but they did nothing to secure the repeal of oppressive legislation, nor to accelerate emancipation, nor to educate or train free Negroes, nor to protect them against violence and abuse. Negroes were not underprivileged people in the eyes of colonizationists; they were undesirable people. Colonizationists sought relief, not for the Negro, but for society from the Negro's presence. Their objective was not to assist the Negro but to put him away from sight. Neither did the colonizationists move against slavery. They did nothing to prevent kidnapping, or to repeal the laws by which free Negroes could be reduced again to slavery; or to repeal the laws of the slave states circumscribing the activities of the slaves and forbidding their education. The parent society itself formally disclaimed any intention of doing these things, saying: "The moral, intellectual, and political improvement of people of color within the United States, are objects foreign to the powers of this Society."[13]

The third reason for the importance of the colonization movement was the violent reaction of the lower South, under the leadership, as it had been since 1787, of South Carolina and Georgia. Colonization, debated by Congress and financed by the federal government, would open the way to emancipation of the slaves. Colonization, also, to whatever degree it succeeded either with or without government assistance, would deprive the slave states of political power; they would lose votes in Congress and in the Electoral College. They would also lose their labor supply, but that seems to have been of secondary importance to them at this time. The first great debate directly involving the question of slavery in the states had occurred over the foreign slave trade. The second, as we shall see, was over the question of using the public lands to finance colonization. The subject was brought up during the debates in 1820 and emerged as a major issue in 1825.

The legislature of Ohio passed resolutions (January 17, 1824), recommending gradual emancipation. The plan called for all children of slaves to be given freedom at age twenty-one, providing they agreed to colonization. The resolution said: "It is expedient that such a system should be predicated upon the principle that the evil of slavery is a national one, and that the people and the States of this Union ought mutually to participate in the duties and burthens of removing it." These resolutions were sent to the other state governments and to Congress.[14] Vermont, Massachusetts, Connecticut, Pennsylvania, New Jersey, Delaware, Indiana, and Illinois approved the plan. The states of the Black Belt—South Carolina, Georgia, Alabama, Mississippi, and Louisiana—disapproved most emphatically.

One year later (February 18, 1825) Rufus King of New York, whose unceasing war upon slavery

dated back to the Ordinance of 1787, offered a resolution in the United States Senate to pledge all future proceeds of the public land sales "to aid the emancipation of such slaves, within any of the United States, and to aid the removal of such slaves, and the removal of such free persons of color, in any of the said States, as by the laws of the States, respectively, may be allowed to be emancipated, or removed to any territory or country without the limits of the United States of America."[15] Jefferson had favored this method of financing emancipation, either under a broad definition of federal power or by constitutional grant of power through amendment.[16] Madison also favored it, by amendment, if necessary.[17] John Marshall, a vice-president of the American Colonization Society and chief justice of the United States, frankly said Congress had the power and should use it.

Finally, the American Colonization Society petitioned Congress, January 29, 1827, for assistance. The petition embraced a short history of the movement, described the colony in Africa, and carefully defined its objectives in the narrow terms of removing from this country only the free Negroes willing to go. It said the Colonization Society lacked the authority and power to govern a distant colony, and lacked sufficient funds to finance the undertaking. It requested assistance, without being specific, relying upon the wisdom of Congress to act effectively and expressing confidence in its constitutional power to act "to provide for the common defense, and promote the general welfare."[18] In this connection, it is a singular fact, worthy of careful attention, that the two men who had written the Virginia and Kentucky Resolutions, Jefferson and Madison, and John Marshall, chief justice of the United States, slaveholders all, and all opposed to emancipation without deportation, and Rufus King whose public career extended back into the Congress of the Confederation—all of these venerable statesmen—should have believed the powers of Congress adequate to take direct action in expending federal funds to encourage and accelerate emancipation. It is important because Robert Y. Hayne who had not been born when Franklin, Jefferson, Madison, and King were founding the nation, and John C. Calhoun and George Troup, who were babies at the time, presently undertook to lecture them and the country on the nature and constitutional powers of the government.

It all began with the Ohio resolutions of January 1824. The Senate of South Carolina termed them "a very strange and ill-advised communication." It protested against any interference with "that part of her property which forms the colored population of the state," and refused to permit that property "to be meddled with, or tampered with, or in any manner ordered, regulated, or controlled by any other power, foreign and domestic, than this legislature."[19] Other states in the Black Belt supported this position.[20] While state after state was passing resolutions for or against the Ohio proposal, Rufus King offered his resolution in the Senate (February 18, 1825). King had avoided all debate on his resolution by having it read, printed, and laid on the table. This prevented debate, and Robert Y. Hayne of South Carolina took the unusual course of laying on the table a counterresolution which said that Congress possessed no power to appropriate public lands to aid in the emancipation and removal from the country of slaves, and that such action "would be a departure from the conditions and spirit of the compact between the several States; and that such measures would be dangerous to the safety of the States holding slaves, and be calculated to disturb the peace and harmony of the Union."[21] Once more, then, here was the threat of war—delivered with a little more finesse than the threats of Jackson and Early but of the same character.

Governor Troup of Georgia, who never seemed to tire of setting up straw men and of tearing them down and who spent many waking hours snarling at the government of the United States, warned the legislature of his state: "Soon, very soon, therefore, the United States Government, discarding the mask, will openly lend itself to a combination of fanatics for the destruction of every thing valuable in the Southern country; one movement of the Congress unresisted by you, and all is lost. Temporize no longer—make known your resolution that this subject shall not be touched by them, but at their peril . . . If this matter be an evil, it is our own—if it to be a sin, we can implore the forgiveness of it—to remove it we ask not even their sympathy or assistance; it may be our physical weakness—it is our moral strength . . . I entreat you, therefore, most earnestly, now that it is not too late, to step forth, and having exhausted the argument, to stand by your arms."[22]

The memorial of the Colonization Society to Congress was promptly challenged by Hayne (Feb. 7, 1827), who said "he denied the Constitutional power of the Government so to act; and if they had the power, he should still deny the policy, justice and humanity of such proceeding."[23] He argued against the government's embarking upon a colonial policy, and that was his strongest argument against the proposal. He insisted that the government would become a purchaser of slaves to be sent to Africa, that resolutions and speeches in state legislatures would soon force down the price of slaves, and that general emancipation would inevitably follow, all of which was logical and probably correct. Then he followed the usual pattern of defense: "The only safety of the Southern States is to be found in the want of power on the part of the Federal Government to touch the subject at all. Thank God, the Constitution gives them no power to engage in the work of colonization, or to interfere with our institutions, either for good or for evil. This is the very 'Ark of the Covenant' in which alone we will find safety."[24]

VOICES FROM THE WEST

Chapter 15

It was in the year 1808 that Kentucky gave to the country its second great indictment of slavery. David Rice had been a Presbyterian; David Barrow was a Baptist. Both were renowned preachers, but their everlasting fame rests, for each, upon a single antislavery pamphlet. Barrow was the leader of the antislavery Baptists of Kentucky until his death in 1819. He was the most distinguished and able of their preachers, a highly esteemed citizen, and a gifted writer. He worked indefatigably for the improvement of the free Negroes and inspired a petition to Congress requesting a haven for them in the public domain and the expenditure of unlimited public funds to assist them. This was something quite different from colonization, and the true test of the antislavery man.[1]

In 1807 Barrow wrote his *Involuntary, Unmerited, Perpetual, Absolute, Hereditary Slavery, Examined; on the Principles of Nature, Reason, Justice, Policy, and Scripture.* It was published the following year at Lexington. We are already familiar with his definition of a slave. His thesis was that perpetual and hereditary slavery could not be supported on the principles of nature, reason, justice, good policy, or the Scriptures.

Barrow, as Rice had done, was exploring the field of natural law. The West was slowly moving toward the clarification and full acceptance of the higher law doctrine. If man would obey the laws of nature, then peace, love, and harmony would prevail, and slavery, being an unnatural usurpation, simply would not be able to exist. Man's mental faculties alone set him apart from beasts and lead him to nobility or to tyranny depending on whether they were dedicated to reason, justice, and mercy, or prostituted to passion, ease, and selfish interest![2] Reason and justice clearly demonstrate that anyone claiming property must have acquired it lawfully, and it must be a lawful kind of property. Slaves were obtained by fraud and violence, and neither the laws of England nor of America could operate contrary to reason, justice, and "the grand *Charter* given to the human race by the God of the Universe." "That innocent, unoffending persons and their posterity," said Barrow, "should suffer the most degrading kind of slavery to perpetual generations, only because some of their fellow creatures, through covetousness, imprudence, or ignorance, had paid inconsiderable sums of money for their parents several generations past, has no foundation in reason and justice . . . shall their misfortunes deprive others of unalienable and invaluable rights forever? Reason and justice must answer in the negative; any human law to the contrary notwithstanding."[3] This was Rice's unjust law thesis, the basis of the higher law doctrine, the simple, but unassailable answer to property rights in slaves and to the demand for compensated emancipation.

What is the function of government, asked Barrow? Certainly something more than the protection of property rights. Government policy which fails to "secure the lives, limbs, characters, liberty, property, equality, peace, harmony, happiness, and safety of the whole, and every virtuous rational creature within its dominions, is tyrannic,

John Rankin, New York philanthropist

or in other terms, is wicked policy."[4] Slavery not only constituted a constant threat to the safety of the whole of the people, but it deprived at least one-sixth of them of these enumerated blessings, placed their lives and limbs in constant jeopardy, and exposed them to unending cruelties. It deprived them of their liberty, of their right to own and enjoy property, of that equality in the enjoyment of natural rights so essential to peace and harmony in society. "The love, or desire of happiness, is coeval with human nature," said Barrow, "and is the pursuit of all mankind. And that kind of slavery I am examining, appears to operate against it in every point of view."[5] Specifically, it destroyed all family relationships, particularly marriage, which "ought to be held sacred by every civil government which contemplates the good of the community."

Barrow then examined the terrifying subject of eternal discord as he called it—warfare as Rice had called it—between masters and slaves, and between slaves and society. It was a foolish policy, said Barrow, to keep a minimum of 100,000 able-bodied men in the country, whose bonds of affection for their fellow men and for the government had been destroyed, when they could be made everlasting friends so easily. "Civil or foreign war will come, and they will constitute an awful peril," said Barrow. Why? Because the slaves still possessed their natural endowments. Deprived of their birthright: freedom, they still could see, hear and feel; they could think, reason, reflect, and "draw conclusions, *independent* of all the tyrants on earth." They had been greatly influenced by the philosophy of the revolution and by the ideas expressed in the subsequent political campaigns; and they could be expected to turn that philosophy against their masters in a stroke for their own freedom.[6]

Barrow had been a victim of the slaveholders' efforts to purge the churches of antislavery discussion. He saw clearly the inevitable tendency of slavery to suppress civil rights and insisted that, regardless of a man's *professions of loyalty* to the philosophy of the Revolution, if he defended his right to hold in absolute subjection a half dozen men, he would do the same for that many thousands or a million men, given the power. "Fellow citizens open your eyes," said Barrow, "and do not rest your invaluable *liberties* on the sandy foundation of the colour of your skins, or on the fanatical declarations of our noisy patriots . . . he who will enslave a black man, or his own, or his son's, nephew's, or fellow-citizen's children begotten on a black woman, or slave, even if she were seven-eighths white . . . would not spare you, if he had you legally in his power."[7] It was a shocking public policy, explained Barrow, which permitted men to commit adultery and then enslave their own children, and it was a strange doctrine of a Christian church that forbade ministers to condemn sin simply because it was authorized by the government.[8] That was the doctrine of passive obedience, whereas no law was binding on any rational creature if it infringed the rights of conscience, or violated the laws of God.

Barrow, like Rice, remained in Kentucky until his death in 1819. Rice had died in 1816. Their work had laid the foundations of the antislavery movement in the second and most important area. They were to the Ohio Valley what Benezet and Woolman had been to the Philadelphia area. Two years before Barrow wrote his powerful treatise, Father Gilliland crossed the river to begin his two score years of work at the Red Oak Church, above Ripley. Two years before Barrow died, John Rankin came to preach at Carlisle, Kentucky, and to assist in the work of the Kentucky Abolition Society. Two years after Barrow's death, Rankin followed Gilliland across the river to serve the Presbyterian Church at Ripley and to labor unceasingly for forty-four years for the slaves and free Negroes. One year before Barrow's death William Dickey, formerly of South Carolina, moved across the river to Bloomingsburg, to serve for forty years. Samuel Crothers had come from Lexington to Chillicothe, Jesse Lockhart to Russellville. Soon other men of powerful stature came to continue the work of Rice and Barrow in Kentucky: James G. Birney, David Nelson, Gideon Blackburn, and many others. They, too, were driven out eventually, but not until the entire area of the state north from Danville, and southeastern Indiana, and southern Ohio had made a major contribution for freedom. It is worthy of note that there was brought to Georgetown, Brown County, in 1823, at the age of one, Ulysses S. Grant, who grew up within a few miles of Father Gilliland, John Rankin, Jesse Lockhart, and Thomas Morris.

John Rankin wrote his thirteen letters to his brother in 1823, publishing them in the local newspaper of Ripley, Ohio, the *Castigator*. They were a remonstrance against his brother's purchase of slaves, but they were, and were intended to be, a public analysis of slavery and a condemnation of the system in its entirety. Said Rankin, by way of introduction: "I consider involuntary slavery a never-failing fountain of the grossest immorality, and one of the deepest sources of human misery; it hangs like the mantle of night over our republic, and shrouds its rising glories. I sincerely pity the man who tinges his hand in the unhallowed thing that is fraught with the tears, and sweat, and groans, and blood of hapless millions of innocent, unoffending people."[9] Rankin then proceeded with the analysis and indictment, developing eight principal theses:

The color of the Negro was not proof of divine punishment—the so-called curse of Noah and mark of Cain—but the effect of climate.

Lack of knowledge, and energy, and mental alertness were not proof of racial inferiority, but of cruel oppression, denial of opportunity and incentive, and the crushing prospect of perpetual bondage. "What people," asked Rankin, "have ever given stronger marks of genius than are exhibited by the enslaved Africans in the United States?"[10]

The love of gain, source of all misery and evil, introduced slavery into the world, and continued to spawn and sustain all the arguments against emancipation. It perverted the judgment and blunted the finer sensibilities of men in every walk of life; contaminated the legislative halls, the courts, and the churches; and, operating silently and unseen, bound the chains of perpetual servitude more securely upon the slaves.

Negroes were not born for servitude. They were rational beings, possessing the attributes common to all people. Chief among these was an instinctive urge to be free, to know, to possess, to love and cherish, to participate in the affairs of society. The law of slavery said this could not be. "It is considered a crime for him [the slave] to aspire above the rank of the grovelling beast," said Rankin, "he must content himself with being bought and sold, and driven in chains from State to State, as a capricious avarice may dictate."[11]

Slaves were denied knowledge because of the expense involved in educating them, and because of the fear of insurrections, and they were almost everywhere denied religious instruction. "I am no Kentuckian," said Rankin, "yet I must say that if any slaveholding people can be generous, the Kentuckians are such. But the mildest form of slavery is like 'the tender mercies of the wicked,' very cruel. Though there is no law in Kentucky designed to prohibit the teaching of slaves, yet such is the opposition made against it by the populace, that but few Sabbath schools for the instruction of the Africans are permitted to exist in the State."[12]

A great wealth of talent and ability was submerged beneath the tyranny of servitude. If released and improved, it would add tremendously to the strength, wealth, and intelligence of the nation.[13]

There were many evils inherent in the system: among them were inadequate provisions for the common requirements of food and clothing, miscegenation, separation of families, and cruel punishments. Slavery created a contempt for honest labor, promoted idleness, intemperance, and vice, and encouraged denial of the basic principles upon which the nation was founded.[14]

The right to freedom was original in all human beings. Slaves were originally deprived of their freedom by violence, theft, or fraud, and neither they nor their descendants were or ever could constitute a lawful kind of property.[15]

Rankin later was commissioned an agent by the American Anti-Slavery Society and lectured widely throughout Ohio. He was one of the first to realize the need for force to abolish slavery, and his sons, like those of Birney, served nobly in the Union armies during the Civil War. His house was the first haven of refuge for hundreds of fugitive slaves through the years. It was on a high bluff above the town of Ripley, and a guiding light was always shining from the window. He was the leader of antislavery forces in the Presbyterian General Assemblies, was present at the Lane Seminary debate, and was beloved by all who knew him.[16]

The man who had organized the Tennessee Society for Promoting the Manumission of Slaves in 1814 was Charles Osborn.[17] This society had been reorganized as the Manumission Society of Tennessee in 1815 and had included among its active members the two students of Samuel Doak, John Rankin and Jesse Lockhart, who had come by way of Kentucky to Ripley and Russellville in Brown County, Ohio. Osborn had come to Ohio also in 1816 and had later settled at Mt. Pleasant, not far from the Ohio River, near Martin's Ferry. There had been a large migration of Quakers from the South into this general area of Jefferson and Belmont counties. Here also, besides the Quakers, were the grandfathers of Woodrow Wilson, of William Dean Howells and of Mark Hanna, and the grandmother of Edwin M. Stanton, and her children. Here also was Benjamin Lundy.[18]

Lundy had come from New Jersey by way of Pennsylvania to Wheeling, and later to St. Clairsville, Ohio, not far from Mt. Pleasant. Here in 1815, this mild mannered and self-educated Quaker organized the Union Humane Society, and it, like the Tennessee Society of Osborn, affiliated with the sixteenth American Convention for Promoting the Abolition of Slavery, in Philadelphia, in 1819.[19] The constitution of the society displayed a marked clarity of perception on the part of its sponsors. It began by quoting the golden rule and the immortal lines from the Declaration of Independence asserting the inalienable rights of man, thus bringing together the two unbroken lines of thought from Woolman and Benezet on the one hand and David Cooper and David Rice on the other. It also stated the objective of destroying race prejudice (which was about to become a major issue in its own right), of removing legal restrictions (the black laws), of

helping Negroes illegally held in bondage, of protecting and aiding free Negroes, and of working for the abolition of slavery. Finally, this organization, like Osborn's Tennessee society, had the specific, unique, and highly important provision that members were not to vote for any persons except opponents of slavery.[20]

Osborn settled down at Mt. Pleasant long enough to publish *The Philanthropist* from August 1817 to October 1818. Lundy was invited to assist him and did so. The paper discussed all aspects of the slavery controversy, but the one real contribution of Osborn was his immediate and forceful rejection of colonization when the American Colonization Society was organized in 1817. He saw clearly that it would strengthen slavery rather than expedite emancipation. He was very skeptical of the possibility of Christianizing Africans in this way. He knew the inevitable tendency of colonization would be contrary to the best interests of the free Negroes, and confusing to the cause of emancipation. Osborn was a minister in the Society of Friends, who traveled widely through the years, in the United States, Canada, and Great Britain. He sold his paper in 1818 to Elisha Bates and moved to Wayne County, Indiana, but continued his antislavery work among the Quakers until his death in 1850.

Lundy was a restless soul. In 1830 he said he had traveled 5000 miles on foot and 20,000 miles otherwise. He visited nineteen states, went twice to Haiti, once to Canada, and three times to Mexico. When Osborn sold his *Philanthropist* and moved from Mt. Pleasant, Lundy was in Missouri, ostensibly on business, but actually arguing the slavery question while the debates raged in Congress. During his absence, Embree had died at Jonesboro, Tennessee, and the *Emancipator* was no longer being published. Lundy did not regard the *Philanthropist* as an adequate antislavery organ under Elisha Bates' editorship, although he never explained his reasons. He was convinced that the West should have a strong antislavery paper. He began publication of *The Genius of Universal Emancipation* in October 1821. Seven issues were published at Mt. Pleasant, the first being printed by Bates, the next six by James Wilson at Steubenville. Lundy then started for Greenville, Tennessee, where Elihu Embree had published the *Emancipator*. He stopped at Zanesville, Ohio, to publish the eighth number of the *Genius.* It was then published at Greenville, center of the antislavery Quaker settlements of North Carolina and Tennessee, until 1825 when Lundy moved to Baltimore, Maryland.

In the first issue of his *Genius* at Mt. Pleasant he condemned slavery as a great evil and insisted that it must be abolished. He never departed from this basic principle. He urged congressional action to abolish slavery in the District of Columbia, in the territories, and wherever else the jurisdiction of Congress extended. He believed that Congress possessed the constitutional power to bind a new state to remain free of slavery. He insisted that Congress possessed the power, and should use it, to abolish the domestic slave trade and effectively to prevent kidnapping. Free Negroes should possess the right to move about freely in the United States, from state to state at their own pleasure. Negroes desiring to emigrate should be given financial assistance by private and public agencies. Gradual emancipation should be renewed and adopted by all of the slave states. Restrictions upon free Negroes in the slave states should be removed. The three-fifths rule should be abolished. Finally, Lundy urged the same sort of national program for emancipation and aid to free Negroes that the Pennsylvanians, through Franklin's memorial, had proposed many years before. His own plan was for an annual convention of delegates, one from each state, responsible to their respective legislatures, meeting to plan and operate a system of emancipation and improvement of free Negroes. He definitely advocated enlisting as many people as possible in the program and then defeating the obdurate defenders of slavery by political action.

Lundy never broke away from the idea of colonization. He was opposed to slavery; and he definitely was devoted to the improvement of the Negroes, which most colonizationists were not, but never seemed to appreciate the damage colonizationists were doing to both causes. In September 1829, at Baltimore, Lundy began the tenth volume of his *Genius* with William Lloyd Garrison as "Co-editor." He personally had interested Garrison in the cause. The association of the two men did not last long, however, for many reasons. They differed on political action, on colonization, and on the use of harsh and intemperate language. Garrison returned to Boston to lead the organization of the movement in another important area.

Meanwhile, in Ohio, Benjamin Ladd, Elisha

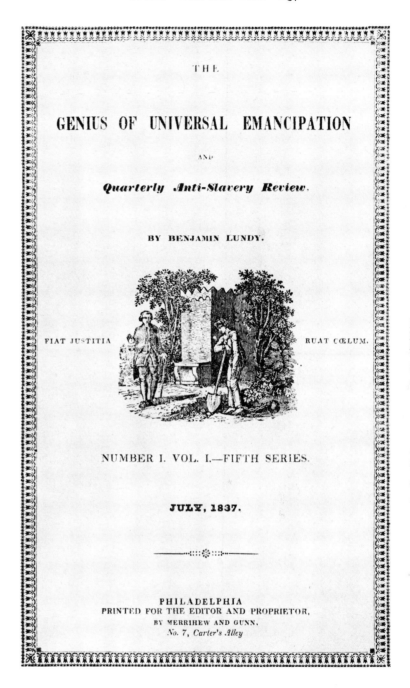

THE

GENIUS OF UNIVERSAL EMANCIPATION

AND

Quarterly Anti-Slavery Review.

BY BENJAMIN LUNDY.

FIAT JUSTITIA   RUAT CŒLUM.

NUMBER I. VOL. I.—FIFTH SERIES.

JULY, 1837.

PHILADELPHIA
PRINTED FOR THE EDITOR AND PROPRIETOR,
BY MERRIHEW AND GUNN,
No. 7, Carter's Alley

The Genius, by Lundy, was probably the earliest anti-slavery publication.

Bates, and Benjamin Hanna had taken the lead in putting aid to the Negroes on an organized basis after the manner of their Philadelphia and New York predecessors. In 1820, the Ohio yearly Meeting of Friends set up a committee of eighty-

138 ANTISLAVERY

one persons to protect Negroes against kidnapping, advise them and assist them in financial matters, provide schools, represent them in legal problems, and help them to find employment. They operated on a wide scale to bring manumitted slaves from the South to Ohio. They solicited and received financial aid from Europe. The Indiana yearly meeting of Friends did likewise. All of them assisted fugitives. The result was that fugitive slaves were funneled through Ohio, with the Presbyterian preachers—the Dickeys, Gilliland, Rankin, Lockhart, Crothers and others —the Quakers, and the free Negroes, of whom there were 4,723 in 1820, making recapture almost impossible once the fugitive crossed the river. An estimated 1,000 had passed through the Chillicothe Presbytery by 1817, and 50,000 by 1860.

There were published in 1824 two antislavery treatises which rank among the best twenty-five in analysis and erudition and the influence of which were immeasurable. The first was by an English lady, a resident of Leicester, England, Elizabeth Heyrich, who wrote *Immediate, Not Gradual Abolition; or, An Inquiry into the Shortest, Safest, and Most Effective Means of Getting Rid of West Indian Slavery.* There is some evidence that this pamphlet was circulated in Indiana before publication in England, and in Philadelphia, in 1824. Its influence in the West was very great in any case. It was reprinted again in New York in 1825, in Philadelphia in 1836, by the Antislavery Society of Philadelphia in 1837, and by Garrison's publishers in Boston in 1838. It was so persuasive that it converted Wilberforce and his colleagues in England to immediate emancipation and is given a large share of credit for the early abolition of slavery in the West Indies by act of Parliament.

Mrs. Heyrich pointed out the futility of Britain's efforts to stop the slave trade so long as she permitted slavery in her colonies, and the equal guilt of the British people with the slaveholders so long as they used the products of slave labor, particularly sugar; the deception of the planters in saying their slaves were well treated and happy; and the error of weighing the interests of the planters against the rights of the slaves.[21] "The cause of emancipation has been long and ably advocated," said she. "Reason and eloquence, persuasion and argument have been powerfully exerted; experiments have been fairly made,—

facts broadly stated in proof of the impolicy as well as iniquity of slavery,—to little purpose; even the *hope* of its extinction, with the concurrence of the planter, or by any enactment of the Colonial, or British legislature, is still seen in very remote perspective—so remote that the heart sickens at the cheerless prospect."[22] Why was the prospect so depressing? Because everything that could be presented in the way of evidence and argument had been presented in vain. There had been too much talking, too much time lost. Something more decisive and effective must be tried. Everyone must unite to stop purchasing the products of slavery.

There was no reason to fear emancipation, said Mrs. Heyrich. Careful investigation had disclosed no idleness or bad behavior in Santo Domingo, and all of the violence had occurred before, not after, the emancipation. There was no sense in talking about improving the lot of the slaves or giving them religious instruction. There was nothing but deception and defeat in talk of gradual emancipation. Why was this so? Because gradual emancipation would beget gradual indifference.[23] Then she gave the classic indictment of gradual emancipation: not the only argument against it to be sure, but an unanswerable one and one which had powerful effect in the United States as well as in Britain: "He [the slaveholder] saw, very clearly, that the time for the extermination of slavery was precisely when its horrid impiety and enormity were *first distinctly* known and *strongly felt.* He knew that every moment's unnecessary delay, between the discovery of an imperious duty and the setting earnestly about its accomplishment was dangerous, if not fatal to success. He knew that strong excitement was necessary to strong effort; that intense feeling was necessary to stimulate intense exertion; that, as strong excitement, and intense feeling are generally transient, in proportion to their strength and intensity, the most effectual way of crushing a great and virtuous enterprise, was to gain time, to defer it to a more convenient season, when the zeal and ardour of the first convictions of duty had subsided; when our sympathies had become languid; when consideration of the difficulties and hazards of the enterprise, the solicitations of ease and indulgence should have chilled the warm glow of humanity, quenched the fervid heroism of virtue; when familiarity with relations of violence and outrage, crimes and miseries, should have abated the horror of their first impression, and at length induced indifference."[24]

Mrs. Heyrich then considered the charge that emancipation would be injurious to the slave, and the demand that it should apply only to children born after a certain date. Not only did common equity and common decency require that those who had borne the yoke of oppression and suffered interminably should enjoy the blessings of freedom during the remainder of their lives, but common sense required it also, because here again it was difficult to generate and sustain enthusiasm for the freedom of persons yet unborn.[25] She ridiculed the talk of incapacity of slaves for freedom, of violence, and idleness, and pillage. Emancipation from lawless tyranny did not mean release from law and responsibility and moral restraints. It was ridiculous to suppose that lifting oppression from people would precipitate revenge. Continued slavery might end in terrible vengeance, but freedom would not.

There was no point, Mrs. Heyrich said, in arguing, reasoning, or pleading with slaveholders. Slavery had a more debasing effect upon them than upon the slaves, perverting their moral and rational perceptions. "The gains of unrighteousness," said she, "familiarity with injustice and cruelty, have rendered the slaveholder, more obstinately, more incurably blind and inaccessible to reason, than the slave. And what justice or retribution would there be in the world, were un-

AN AMERICAN WOMAN.

There are tens of thousands of such scenes witnessed in this country every year. The picture represents a mother, whose children have been sold on the auction-table, and who are about to be torn from her for ever—so far as this world is concerned—pleading with her master not to separate her from her loved ones. She appeals to him as a husband and a father; and beseeches him, for God's sake, not to put asunder the mother and her darling little ones. He is inexorable. With horrid imprecations, and perhaps a lash upon the back of the poor pleading woman, he turns away from her entreaties. What can she do? She can only direct her weeping eye to the God of the oppressed, and cry, "*How long wilt thou forget me, O Lord? forever?*"

POPULATION STATISTICS.

These statistics furnish strong evidence that slavery must cease, in consequence of natural causes, in several States that are now resisting the discussion of principles that lead to voluntary emancipation, and abusing those who advocate them. The following table shows the population of the two sections of the Union in 1850, compared with that of 1840:—

FREE STATES.

Free population in 1850,	13,574,797
Do. do. 1840,	9,728,972
Increase,	3,845,825

Rate of increase, 39½ per cent.

SLAVE STATES.

Free population in 1850,	6,409,938
Do. do. 1840,	4,848,150
Increase,	1,561,788

Rate of increase, 32¼ per cent.

Slave population in 1850,	3,175,783
Do. do. 1840,	2,486,231
Increase,	689,552

Rate of increase, 23.6 per cent.

The law, economic necessity, and hardness of heart were not influenced by the pleas of a heartbroken woman.

lawful possessions never to be reclaimed till there was a disposition in the possessor *voluntarily* to relinquish them,—till he was convinced that it was his *interest* to part with them."[26] Pursuing this point of property in slaves, she said it made no difference how, where, or when a slaveholder acquired his slaves, whether by purchase, violence, or inheritance, his claim to them was contrary to nature, reason, and religion and was an illegal claim insofar as legality had "any foundation of justice, divine or human, to rest upon."[27]

James Duncan, minister of Indiana, and father of Alexander Duncan, United States representative from Cincinnati, published at Vevay, Indiana, a river town below Cincinnati, in 1824, the second of the powerful treatises of that year: *A Treatise on Slavery. In Which Is Shown Forth the Evil of Slaveholding. Both from the Light of Nature and Divine Revelations.* A real slaveholder, said Duncan, was one who fully intended to bequeath his slaves to his heirs—in short, real slavery was perpetual slavery. Slavery prevented the slave from performing the duties every person owed to God, to his family, and to his neighbors. Three things were essential to its permanent existence. Slaves must be kept in ignorance to prevent them from pleading their case for freedom or escaping. They must be barred from the courts of law in all cases involving white persons. The master's will must always be superior to relative obligations, rights, and privileges.[28] Moral law, said Duncan, is a "transcript of divine character," and is called natural law because nature reveals the relationship between persons and between persons and God. The freedom of individuals to perform all of the obligations arising out of their relationships to God and to each other is what we call natural rights. They could not be surrendered or transferred, and it was the duty of the slave to run away if he had an opportunity.[29]

The slaveholder, said Duncan, had power to interfere with the private relative duties of the slave at his own discretion, and "without being controlled by the laws of government." This was a usurpation of power, and was the great sin, evil, or whatever one wishes to call it. The slaveholder used this power, unrestrained by government, in a cruel and brutal fashion, but cruelty and brutality were only aggravations: "The grand radical point in which the most deadly criminality lies, is the usurped office or station which he occupies."[30] Pursuing this point still further—and

this is important because men were moving rapidly toward clarification of the ideas ultimately enshrined in the Fourteenth Amendment—Duncan said: "All men have a natural right to be citizens, and to enjoy civil protection in that nation or government where they have a permanent residence, except some legal cause shall prevent it." If they did not enjoy that protection, he said, they had a right to move. Slaves had not protection; they could not move; they could not testify in court. Forbidding them to improve their intellects and natural talents was a further violation of natural rights: "A contradiction of God's great end in giving mankind those faculties, by reducing them down to the level of brute creatures, which is a crime so directly at war with the very light of nature and conscience, that it appears almost an insult to the human understanding to attempt its further demonstration."[31]

Duncan then took the Ten Commandments and one by one demonstrated the way in which slavery was a violation.[32] In connection with the sixth commandment, he not only called the attention of the reader to the fact that the very roots of slavery were deep in the violence and death of millions in Africa, but that the "sin of murder" was something more than depriving a person of his life, it was depriving him of the enjoyments of life and of the opportunity for religious and scientific knowledge which would increase his own happiness and make him a more useful member of society. With regard to theft, slavery robbed a man of his freedom, of his labor, of whatever possession might come to him, often of his wife and of his children, the latter, "the greatest outrage upon moral justice that is possible to be committed in either earth or hell."[33]

What should be done about slavery? Requirements of the moral law forbade individuals to do certain things. No person should have Christian fellowships with slaveholders; nor vote for any man not dedicated to the cause of freedom; nor, if an officer of the law, apprehend fugitives or assist in the capture and return of fugitives; nor have any part in advertising for the return of fugitives; nor hire the labor of slaves; nor assist in suppressing any insurrection; nor countenance the assistance of any state government or the federal government to any state beset by insurrection; nor refrain from speaking against slavery, particularly if a minister of the gospel, because it was the duty of ministers to point out the whole duty of man and to denounce everything which was "dishonoring to God and ruining to the souls of men."[34]

Slavery, said Duncan, was absolutely contrary to the Constitution of the United States, and all state laws legalizing and sustaining slavery were unconstitutional. This was the constitutional theory advanced by Alvan Stewart of New York fifteen years later. Duncan here was using the term constitution in the sense of a fundamental law and was approaching closely the final clarification of the higher law doctrine, when he said that the Declaration of Independence was the foundation and groundwork of the Constitution, that it condemned slavery in clear and explicit terms, and that it could be used to justify a slave insurrection. "The Declaration of Independence," said Duncan, "exhibited the moral ground on which

the nation could justify herself in acting as a political body, independent of Great Britain . . . The equal rights which the nation, by her representatives, had then bound herself to maintain and defend, being secured, was an encouragement to the people not only to prosecute the war with firmness, but to expect that any future form of Constitution which might be adopted, would correspond with the principles of equal rights established in the declaration of independence."

All of this, in itself, would have given Duncan's treatise a leading place among antislavery pronouncements; but he incorporated "The Slaveholders Prayer," which was later extracted and published by the American Antislavery Society as a four-page leaflet and was distributed by the thousands. The treatise itself was republished both in New York and in Cincinnati in 1840.

The friends of humanity
This lithograph by J. Valentine of England compares slavery to the Upas tree of Java, the milk of which provides a deadly arrow poison.

PULPIT AND COURTROOM: AN ANTHOLOGY

Chapter 16

Now and then in this long struggle for human rights a masterpiece of argument and erudition makes its appearance. How many have been lost through the years for want of printing, of course, we shall never know. The period of the Missouri debates was especially rich in argumentation, and two splendid treatises that deserved a better fate have been all but lost to us.

A Methodist camp meeting, one of America's most colorful institutions, was in progress in Washington County, Maryland, on August 16, 1818. The preacher appointed to conduct the services on that Sunday evening was indisposed, and the presiding elder of the district, Jacob Gruber, unsuccessful in finding a substitute, reluctantly preached to the three to five thousand whites and three to five hundred assembled Negroes. The text of his sermon was Proverbs 14:34, *Righteousness exalteth a nation, but sin is a reproach to any people.* In substance, he said that the sort of righteousness here indicated embraced right principles, right spirit, and right conduct. Sin or transgression of the Law was a reproach to any person be he rich or poor, parent or child, ruler or ordinary citizen, old or young. There were also national sins, that is, generally prevalent sins. He specified infidelity, intemperance, profaneness, and slavery and oppression.

Gruber's remarks about slavery caused trouble, to some degree, perhaps, because he was from the nonslaveholding state of Pennsylvania. He spoke of the inconsistency in supporting Bible and missionary societies while holding slaves. He spoke of the sale of human beings as livestock, of sep-

aration of loved ones by sale, and of rewards for the return of fugitives. He spoke of the uncertainty of the future, and especially of the danger of race warfare plunging everyone, white and black, into eternal damnation in a riot of bloodshed. Then he urged the slaves, sitting back of the platform, to be devout Christians and faithful and obedient servants.

The grand jury of Washington County afterward was prevailed upon by slaveholders to issue an indictment charging Gruber with being a person of evil, seditious, and turbulent disposition, who encouraged divers Negro slaves to resist the lawful authority of their masters, with intent to instigate and incite mutiny and rebellion. Roger B. Taney and associates were engaged for the defense. Knowing that fair and impartial trial in Washington County would be difficult to obtain, Taney had the case transferred to his own town of Frederick. Taney was opposed to slavery. He freed his slaves, bought others to give freedom, and treated all with kindness. Somehow, nearly forty years later, as chief justice of the United States, he handed down the no less than tragic *Dred Scott* Decision. This, however, was in 1819, and even though we do not have Taney's summation, we do have enough of the argument of Taney and his supporting attorneys to constitute a valuable antislavery document.[1]

One witness at the trial said that Gruber spoke "of the tyranny of masters, and gave a dialogue of what was to pass in hell between masters and slaves on hot grid-irons." Another said that he declared Negroes were born free and quoted the

Declaration of Independence to the effect that all men were equal and entitled to life, liberty, and the pursuit of happiness. A third said that he called slavery a national sin and spoke of the inconsistency of holding the Declaration of Independence in one hand and a slave whip in the other. A fourth said that he belabored the cruelty of some masters to the point of amazement that slaves did not come into their bedrooms at night and cut their throats and said it so passionately as to be heard a half mile away. A fifth said he insisted that slavery was a violation of moral and natural law, contrary to Christian precepts and the foundation principles of the nation. Another said he condemned slavery as contrary to natural law, national policy, and human rights. Apparently, the good reverend gave a sharp antislavery sermon, and, whether or not he convinced anyone of the necessity of saving his soul, he frightened a good many into the necessity of saving their necks. He afterward said that he had often heard the words 'Republican slaveholder,' but that they meant no more to him than the term 'sober drunkard.'

Taney, in presenting the basis of defense, said there was no precedent for such a trial in Maryland since the Revolution. He said also, since the Constitution fully protected freedom of speech, "subjects of national policy may, at all times, be freely and full discussed in the pulpit or elsewhere, without limitation or restraint." However much Gruber might have alarmed or offended some people, unless his doctrines were immoral or calculated to disturb the peace, he had a perfect right to "preach them and to clothe them by such facts and arguments as to him seemed proper . . . Their feelings, or their fears, would not alter the character of his doctrine, or take from him a right secured to him by the Constitution and laws of the state."[2]

It must be proved that he preached the sermon and said what he did say with the intent of inciting insubordination and insurrection among the slaves. "For, when it is alleged, on the part of the prosecution, that a clergyman of a Christian society, while professing to be engaged in the high and solemn duties of religion, was, in truth, seeking to produce insubordination and insurrection among the slaves . . . the party accused, has a right to refer you, in proof of his innocence, to the general scope and object of his sermon; to the other topics introduced and discussed; to the

Roger B. Taney

occasion on which it was preached; to the character of the congregation to whom it was addressed; to the opinions known to be held by the society to which he belongs; and above all, to the history of his own life, which, in this instance, would, of itself, be abundantly sufficient to repel such a charge, bottomed on such evidence."[3]

"It is well known, that the gradual and peaceable abolition of slavery in these states, is one of the objects which the Methodist society have steadily in view. No slaveholder is allowed to be a minister of that church. Their preachers are accustomed, in their sermons, to speak of the injustice and oppressions of slavery. The opinion of Mr. Gruber on this subject, nobody could doubt. And if any slave-holder believed it dangerous to himself, his family, or the community, to suffer his slaves to learn, that all slavery is unjust and oppressive; and persuade himself, that they would not of themselves be able to make the discovery; it was in his power to prevent them from attending the assemblies where such doctrines were likely to be preached. Mr. Gruber did not go to the slaves; they came to him. They could not have come, if their masters had chosen to prevent them

Slave coffle crossing the Rapidan

. . . Many of the most respectable gentlemen of Washington County, and many of the principal slave-holders were there, when the sermon in question was delivered . . . His appeal to his hearers, on this subject, was directed exclusively to the whites. The impression was intended to be made on them . . . he could not have designed, in that part of his discourse, to influence the conduct of the slaves, but was obviously, and clearly, seeking to reform the hearts of the masters."[4]

"The learned District Attorney has said that the language of Mr. Gruber was injudicious; that it was not calculated to do good; that it would necessarily irritate and offend the masters, and make the slaves more dissatisfied with their unhappy condition . . . And if the learned attorney for the state shall be able to satisfy you that the opinions of Mr. Gruber on slavery, and the treatment of the slaves, are unsound; that his arguments were injudicious and impolitic; that his language was inflammatory, and calculated to produce evil; still he will not have advanced one step toward the accomplishment of his object, until he can prove to you, that these opinions were uttered, these arguments were used, and this language employed, with the criminal intention, and for the wicked purpose laid in this indictment. I might, therefore safely rest the defense on this ground . . . But the Reverend gentleman merits a defense on very different principles . . . *We cannot consent to buy his safety by yielding to passion, prejudice, and avarice, the control of future discussions on this great and important question. He must not surrender up the civil and religious rights secured to him in common with others, by the Constitution of this most favored nation* . . . There is no law that forbids us to speak of slavery as we think of it. Any man has a right to publish his opinions on that subject whenever he pleases. It is a subject of national concern, and may at all times be freely discussed. Mr. Gruber did quote the language of our great act of national independence, and insisted on the principles contained in that venerated instrument. He did rebuke those masters, who, in the exercise of power, are deaf to the calls of humanity; and he warned them of the evils they might bring upon themselves. He did speak with abhorrence of those reptiles, who live by trading in human flesh, and enrich themselves by tearing the husband from the wife—the infant from the bosom of the mother; and this I am instructed was the head and front of his offending. Shall I content myself with saying he had a right to say this? that there is no law to punish him? So far is he from being the object of punishment in any form of proceeding, that we are prepared to maintain the same principles, and to use, if necessary, the same language here in the temple of justice, and in the presence of those who are the ministers of the law. A hard necessity, indeed, compels us to endure the evil of slavery for a time. It was imposed upon us by another nation, while we were yet in a state of colonial vassalage. It cannot be easily, or suddenly removed. Yet while it continues, it is a blot on our national character, and every real lover of freedom, confidently hopes that it will be effectually, though it must be gradually, wiped away; and earnestly looks for the means, by which this necessary object may be best attained. And until it shall be accomplished; until the time shall come when we can point without a blush, to the language held in the Declaration of Independence, every friend of humanity will seek to lighten the galling chain of slavery, and better, to the utmost of his power, the wretched condition of the slave."[5]

What must have been the feelings of Taney about conditions fifteen years later, when the distinguished William Leggett felt impelled to write the following editorial comment, we can only guess:

"Nothing, in these days of startling doctrines and outrageous conduct, has occurred to occasion us more surprise than the sentiments openly expressed by the southern newspapers, that slavery is not an evil, and that to indulge a hope that the poor bondman may be eventually enfranchised is no less heinous than to desire his immediate emancipation. We could have hardly believed, if we had not seen these sentiments expressed in the southern newspapers that such opinions are entertained by any class of people in this country . . . we could not have believed that the madness of the south had reached such a climax. Not only are we told that slavery is no evil, but that it is criminal toward the south, and a violation of the spirit of the federal compact, to indulge even a hope that the chains of the captive may some day or other, no matter how remote the time, be broken."

New York *Evening Post*,
September 9, 1835.

Returning to the Gruber trial, Mr. Martin then spoke for the defense, and inquired whether a minister of the gospel could be brought from his church to the prison box for preaching to his own congregation on a subject of general conversation.

"The right of slavery is a question of abstract morals, of natural law, and human policy; a subject upon which the judgment ponders and the intellect suspends; discussed in the councils of the nation, it has called forth the efforts of the benevolent and the learned; and the matter of that memorable sermon, which now arraigns this reverend gentleman, has been long since proclaimed by elevated statesmen . . . Men high in office, eminent in science, fair in character, and exalted in the confidence of their fellow citizens, have arrayed themselves the champions of emancipation, and condemned a system they conceived unwise and unnatural, dangerous to the morals and strength of the people, poisoning the springs of social felicity, and repugnant to the principles of free constitution."[6]

"As an American citizen, he was authorized to discuss the policy of a *system* interwoven with the well-being of his government; as a man, moved by the feelings of benevolence, and glowing with enthusiasm of philanthropy, he was privileged in condemning a practice he thought inconsistent with both; as a minister of the gospel, directed by the laws of his church, and instigated by conscience and belief, he was bound to tender his advice.[7]

"The internal slave trade of this country formed a consideration of part of his discourse; and he displayed in the severest terms the sin and wickedness of such atrocious commerce . . . Is there a man on this jury, or in this court, who would not raise his voice and power in suppressing a traffic opposite to the laws of God, and repugnant to the rights of man . . . No motive can authorize a trade that separates the husband from the wife, the parent from the child, and the relation from the friend; that tears asunder all the ties of social connection and breaks apart all the ligaments of natural union; steeping yet deeper in misery this unfortunate population, and forcing from their embrace the last relic of human happiness."[8]

"The African slave trade has engaged the attention, and attracted the notice of almost every part of Christendom . . . And is that more to be deprecated than this? The same cruelties are practiced, the same ties are broken, the same agents employed. Traffickers in blood and panders of avarice, are engaged in both; and the Vultures who hover over the coast of Africa, and the Vultures that crowd from the sugar farms of America, are equally destructive; alike, they feed upon

"HAIL COLUMBIA! HAPPY LAND!!!"

AUTHENTIC ACCOUNTS OF UNITED STATES' SLAVERY.

" A good tree cannot bring forth evil fruit, neither can a corrupt tree bring orth good fruit. Wherefore by their fruits ye shall know them."

Coffle of slaves
Pictorial satire at its best.

the vitals and fatten upon the miseries of an unfortunate and degraded people."[9]

"Gentlemen of the jury, this trial is new in America; it is novel in the jurisprudence of our country. You must, for example, unfold the blood-stained page of the fifteenth century. Go back to that season of religious fury; recur to that black and disgraceful period of intemperate opinion, when bigoted belief was supported by the jibbet and the stake, and the very temples of justice 'smoked with bloody execution.'"[10]

Mr. Beene Pigman, speaking for the defense, said:

"Negro slavery, as it exists in this country, is evidently a violation of the natural law, and is contrary to the principles of the Christian religion. When we speak undisguised truth from an honest heart, we pronounce it an absolute despotism, at which we should all shrink with horror if it was fixed upon our white population, and to prevent it from involving the whites . . . even in a much milder form, we would readily consent to rise en masse, and pledge the last drop of our blood, and the last cent of our treasure."[11]

"It is evident that the traverser in this part of his sermon, was discussing a principle of natural law, which he found in the declaration of independence, admitted in all parts of the Union, as the sound and proper basis of republican government. Finding that the colonies, in their struggle for liberty, had, in the declaration of independence, avowed the sentiment without reserve, that all men have equal rights; he argued as a corollary, that if *all men* have *equal* rights, it was at once destroying the very principles of *free* government, to exclude men from the enjoyment of liberty and the pursuit of happiness, on account of the darkness of their skin, or fleecy locks; and that it would no more comport with the principles of republicanism to do so, than it would to exclude all men from the enjoyment of liberty who had not attained a certain position of wealth, or stature of body . . . who would have supposed, that principles so fraught with truth, and which cost this nation so many years of blood, carnage, peril, and anxiety to maintain, would so early in the history of the republick, lay the foundation of a prosecution against a preacher, because he maintained them in the pulpit."[12]

"In all probability, this case will make a part of the future history of this nation, both in the civil and ecclesiastical department, and how astonished will the republican reader be, that truths proclaimed to the world and left upon record by Jefferson, Adams, Hancock, and other worthy sages, and which deserve to be written in letters of gold, should be brought against the preacher as evidence of a crime . . . Wretched indeed, would be the liberty of the citizen, if he could not discuss plain, or even doubtful questions in metaphysics, philosophy, natural law or in theology, without danger of being condemned. It would be introducing in miniature at least, some of the horrors of the inquisition . . . If the possibility of negroes getting to know what may be written or spoken upon the subject constitutes a crime, no man could write or speak on it without making himself liable to a prosecution."13

"The only credible account extant, of the origin of mankind is that which we have in scripture. And if we acquiesce in it we must believe that God hath made of one blood all nations of men, for to dwell on all the face of the earth, and hath determined the times before appointed, and the bounds of their habitation, Acts xvii, 26 . . . We must argue, therefore, from the nature of the thing, if we argue at all on the subject; and I think there is nothing in the nature of the negro, in his soul or in his body, which may not easily be accounted for, on the supposition that he and the whites are of the same family . . . What a scene do we behold, one part of a family enslaved by another part, entailing upon innocent children a thraldom for no offence, which can only end with life, and at which the whites would shrink with horror, if it was inflicted upon them or their children, even for a crime."14

"The traverser, like his Master once was, is now humbled in the furnace of affliction, to rise presently in a splendid glory and triumph he little anticipated . . . this prosecution will bring him before the world as a distinguished philanthropist, declaring no other thing on this subject, than eminent philosophers have declared before him, whose declarations . . . I will read to you; beginning first with the sentiments of Dr. Beatty."15

"[After this account, which I believe is not exaggerated, it must be unnecessary to add, that] slavery is inconsistent with the dearest and most essential rights of man's nature; [that] it is detrimental to virtue and industry; [that] it hardens the heart to those tender sympathies which form the most lovely part of the human character; [that] it involves the innocent in hopeless misery,

in order to procure wealth, and pleasure for the authors of that misery; that it seeks to degrade into brute beings whom the Lord of heaven and earth endowed with rational souls; and created for immortality—; It is impossible for a considerate and unprejudiced mind to think of slavery without horror: that a man, a rational and immortal being, should be treated on the same footing with a beast, or piece of wood, and bought and sold, and entirely subjected to the will of another man whose equal he is by nature, and whose superior he may be in virtue and understanding, and all for no crime, but merely because he differs from us in the shape of his nose, the color of his skin, or the size of his lips; if this be equitable, or excusable, or pardonable, it is vain to talk any longer of the eternal distinctions of right and wrong, truth and falsehood, good and evil."

One year after the trial of the Reverend Jacob Gruber at Frederick, Maryland, Josephus Wheaton, pastor of the church in Holliston, Massachusetts, preached a remarkable sermon which might well have been a part of the defense in the Maryland courtroom. His remarks were so pertinent to the long controversy then beginning that they must, in part, be here retrieved from oblivion also. His thesis was the equality of mankind.16

"Most of the peculiarities which distinguish them from each other, may be traced to the operation of natural causes. Climate, education, and habits of life, will produce a surprising effect upon the constitution, character and appearance of man. Many have regarded these as amply sufficient to account even for the difference of complexion between the European and the African."17

"God hath made of one blood all nations of men to dwell on all the face of the earth . . . This passage not only teaches us that mankind have a common origin and are united by a common nature, but suggests that they are originally and naturally equal . . . When we speak of the equality of mankind, we do not mean an equality which denies or which has a tendency to level all the distinctions, which prevail in society . . . The equality which we have in view, is consistent with any distinction which is either naturally or lawfully made, and operates against those which are unnatural, unlawful and morally wrong."18

It may be observed:

"That mankind are equal in respect to the nature of their faculties. Their minds are similarly constituted. Thought, memory, reason and imagination, volition, affections and passions, are common to men in all nations, whether civilized or savage, whether Christian or barbarian. They are as conspicuous in the Indian and the African as in the European; in the ignorant as in the learned; in the most depraved as in the most virtuous. No nation or tribe of men has ever been discovered in which these faculties are not perfectly obvious. In all they appear the same, in all they are exhibited by articulate language . . . It may here likewise be noticed, that there is a much nearer equality in the *capacities* of men than is generally imagined. It is education principally which gives to the character of one individual, or one nation, its superiority over that of another. This was regarded by Sir William Jones, one of the most distinguished scholars of the last century, and has been regarded by numerous others, as alone sufficient to account for all the diversity which is observable in the capacities of different persons. Without fully subscribing to the correctness of this opinion, it is evident that education does much. It produces astonishing effects upon the intellectual powers."[19]

Had Newton been a West Indian slave:

"Who would have discovered the strength and comprehensiveness of his mind? And who will say, that some African boy, blessed with all the education of a Newton, enjoying like him the smiles of fortune and of science, would not in an age less enlightened than the present, have enriched mankind with his philosophical discoveries? Admitting that the highest attainments in knowledge are not equally within the reach of *every* person; admitting that among individuals some are inferior to others in their native capacities; yet, that such an inferiority pervades a whole nation, there is no evidence . . . and were the means of education equally diffused and equally improved through the world, it would appear that the original difference in the capacities of mankind in general is not great."[20]

"Mankind are equal in respect to their moral agency. Moral agency is that which renders a man accountable to God for his conduct. It implies not only intelligence, but a power of distinguishing right from wrong, and of acting voluntarily in view of motives. It is accompanied with a perception of duty and a consciousness of moral obligation. In these features of character one man has no superiority to another. They are

essential properties of human nature, and are conspicuous in every human being whose mind is in a state of sanity. All men are conscious that they are accountable creatures. There is universally implanted within them a principle, which we denominate conscience, by which they distinguish, or are capable of distinguishing, right from wrong, and which excites a conviction in their minds, that they are bound to love and practice the former, and to shun the latter."[21]

"Mankind are naturally equal in respect to their moral characters. They enter the world with similar propensities, and no sooner become moral agents than they become sinners . . . Wherever we turn our eyes we see indications of depravity. Under whatever modifications the human character presents itself, this feature is ever prominent . . . It is no less obvious in civilized than in savage nations. In the former it is restrained by the influence of religion, government, and laws; and in the hearts of individuals it is partially removed by divine grace, but there is no nation, and there are few individuals in whom it is not sufficiently exhibited, to demonstrate that in reference to this, there is no original difference in the characters of men. Though some doubtless become better, and others worse, as they pass through life, under the various disciplines with which divine Providence is pleased to visit them, the moral characters of all are naturally the same."[22]

"Mankind are equal in respect to their immortality. Their bodies alike frail and perishable, are destined to decay and to sleep in the dust, and their souls are all equally destined to survive their bodies and to live forever. Whatever proves that one man has a soul proves the same of another; and all the evidence which the light of nature affords that the soul of any individual is immortal, is equally conclusive in proving that the souls of all mankind are so . . . In regard to immortality, therefore, one nation or one individual has no preeminence over another. A perfect equality prevails through the world. The veriest savage that roams the forest, has commenced an existence as interminable as that of the Christian and the philosopher. The most abject slave . . . has a soul as deathless as his haughty master."[23]

"Mankind are equal in respect to their native rights. As they are united by a common nature, and are all members of the same great family; each individual possesses certain rights which others are bound to respect. In reference to these, superiority is unknown. Every person has a perfect right to his life, to his liberty, to the property which he lawfully acquires, and to whatever happiness he may enjoy without injuring himself and others. There is no one who is not conscious that these rights belong to himself, and we instinctively perceive that they belong to all mankind. They do not depend for their existence on any civil institutions, but are natural. Men are born with them. Government can neither create nor destroy them. It is her legitimate province to watch over and protect them. Such is the depravity of human nature, that the weak are exposed to injuries from the strong; the simple and ignorant, from the artful and intriguing. The rights of some are liable to be disregarded and trampled on by others. For this reason, governments are instituted and laws are enacted, that what an individual could not do to secure his rights, might be done by a more powerful arm. But the rights which have been mentioned and others which might be noticed, *exist* independently of governments and of laws. They prevail throughout the world and are common to all mankind in every age and in every nation. In this respect all men are equal. The God of nature has made them so, and it cannot be otherwise. It is one of those self-evident truths which, though it may be illustrated, neither needs nor admits of proof. Whatever be a man's complexion, nation or language, however remote from the blessings of civilized society may be his residence, however deeply his mind may be depressed by ignorance or superstition, he possesses the same native rights with his fellow men in all parts of the earth. Of these nothing can de-

prive him. And this equality of rights is unalterable. One may acquire a superiority to others in wealth, in power, in knowledge, in virtue; but in reference to those rights which have been mentioned, they will always remain equal with himself."[24]

"In thus illustrating the equality of mankind, it has been my object to invite your attention to the atrocious criminality of trading in slaves and holding them in a state of bondage . . . This inhuman traffic is still carried on. The negroes are not yet safe in their native land. Thousands of those ill-fated creatures are annually torn from their country, from the endearments of home and of kindred, and hurried across the Atlantic to drag out their lives in miserable servitude . . . He has no prospect of liberation or reward. He is a slave for life. He must spend each day in labouring to enrich another, without the smallest recompense. He is shut out from the consolations of religion . . . he is studiously kept in ignorance of everything which might meliorate his condition . . . he is treated with severity and often with wanton cruelty . . . Worse than a humane man would treat his cattle."[25]

"Is it not a first principle of republicanism, that the native rights of men are equal and should be inviolable. The phrase republican slave holder is a solecism . . . Nero, who once expressed a wish that all the people of Rome had but one neck, that he might cut off their heads at one blow, in my opinion had as good a claim to be called a republican, as any man who traffics in slaves or unnecessarily holds them in bondage."[26]

Selecting the breeders
Women brought the highest prices, particularly when ac-
companying children gave proof of fertility.

IMPULSES FOR REFORM

Chapter 17

When John Rankin, James Duncan, and Elizabeth Heyrich were writing their pamphlets and Charles Osborn and Benjamin Lundy were printing their newspapers at Mt. Pleasant, the country was in the midst of a momentous freshening of the wells of liberalism. It was on the verge of a great reform movement. The period was one of intellectual ferment, and of devotion to progress. Had the impulses for reform been uniformly felt in all parts of the country, slavery must quickly have disappeared. They scarcely touched the slave states, however, and that section soon passed from a state of conservatism to one of reaction.

The first of these impulses derived from westward migration. History does not reveal another migration of people equal to that which poured *no less* than six million souls across the Alleghenies in three decades after 1810; nor a habitation so congenial to the development of great wealth and political power as was the transmontane area; nor so fortuitous a convergence of intellectual and religious impulses for reform on the one hand, and black reaction, born of fear, greed, political power, and ignorance, on the other.

A deep depression settled down upon the Eastern states, particularly the cities, when the government sought to defend neutral rights by nonintercourse, and then embargo in 1807. The West was truly a land of promise and opportunity to older people who had fallen upon adversity and to young people unable to find a place for themselves in the stagnant economy of the Eastern cities. They crossed the mountains in a steady stream year after year. The government sold

13,000,000 acres of land between 1814 and 1820, and in the West five new states were added to the Union: Indiana (1816), Mississippi (1817), Illinois (1818), Alabama (1819), and Missouri (1821).

The process of state-making was ever a rich experience in the nation's cultural development. It could only happen when men and women of many divers religious and national and cultural origins came together to build new homes for themselves and new schools for their children, and to form new church congregations, and to create new governments, local and state. Whatever it was they were building, be it log cabin, or roads, or schools, or churches, or governments, there had to be co-operative effort, exchange of ideas, recourse to past experience, assessment of current requirements, discussion, concession, agreement, contract, experimentation, and, out of it all, one universal hope, one prayer, one common objective: a new and better life for themselves and their children. America was built by co-operative effort and by faith. Within a period of thirty years these people transformed a virgin wilderness into homestead farms, towns, and cities, with roads and churches, and schools and governments. So much of the culture of these people was indigenous, and the sense of power which came from their achievement was so overwhelming that they sometimes forgot the source of their strength and security—forgot, that is, that every essential element of their institutional life flowed from basic principles of the fundamental law.

EXTRACT FROM AN AMERICAN GAZETTE,

ENTITLED

Freedom's Journal.

EDITED BY A MAN OF COLOUR.

MOTTO—"RIGHTEOUSNESS EXALTETH A NATION."

———oooo———

SERIOUS ADDRESS TO THE MISSIONARY SOCIETIES.

YOU send Bibles and Missionaries to the uttermost ends of the earth—you compassionate the wanderers of the house of Israel—you use your utmost endeavours to enlighten the idolatrous Heathen, and to teach them the knowledge of the only true God :—nor is the rude Barbarian, or the lawless Savage forgotten.—Wherever human footsteps mark the earth, the knowledge of God is proclaimed, the Gospel preached. Your ministers daily implore the Almighty, to bless the efforts of the wandering Missionary, that through his means the Heathen might be enlightened, the Barbarian softened, the Savage tamed. The objects of your solicitude are afar off ! And are their none in this happy land, who have a claim upon your bounty, upon your compassion ? I blush for my country ! Must I tell it ? Yes : In the United States, a land blessed with a free government, salutary laws, and a delightful climate, are thousands, and tens of thousands of our fellow-creatures groaning in darkness, in bondage, and in despair.

The Bramins, Hindoos, Heathen, perish in Ganges sacred stream ; are crushed beneath the iron car of Juggernaut ; or are consumed upon the funeral pyre. *They* live *free*, and die voluntarily. Yet you think their situation deplorable, and leave no means untried to remedy it. Look in our Southern States ; you will there see a class of degraded beings, abject, miserable beyond description, who have been cruelly torn from kindred and Country, inhumanely yoked with brutes, and fettered to the soil ! These poor slaves are too low and degraded to excite compassion in the breasts of Christians ; they are not remembered in the prayers of the righteous—the light of truth breaks not upon *them ;*—to *them* the Bible is not sent ;—to their benighted souls no kind Missionary whispers words of comfort. Notwithstanding they are kept in a situation by their cruel tyrants, in which they can learn nothing but to till the soil, or to bear heavy burdens ; yet, even in this degraded state, the feelings of nature triumph over bondage ; the Slave (yes, a *Slave)* dares to love ; his barbarous master suffers him to live with the woman of his choice :—for what ? To augment the number of human wretches, and when it is for his interest, he inhumanly tears the wife from her husband—the children from their parents : ties, that to the *free*, constitute the dear felicities of life, serve but to agravate *their* woes. The generous parent's heart is broken, when he contemplates his wretched offspring doomed to slavery from their birth ; all the ties of love, of kindred, disregarded by the lawless tyrants. I ask you, I appeal to your feelings, as men, as Christians, if these are not more objects of compassion than those to whom you send Missionaries ? The sufferings of the slaves cry loudly for vengeance ! The means are in your power to alleviate those sufferings ; will you neglect to improve those means ? Shall it be said that the Americans are less humane than the English ? Shall it be said, that you traverse the seas and the farthest corners of the earth to find objects of charity ; while the most abject, miserable race on earth, remained unpitied, unsuccoured in the bosom of your own country ? Forbid it righteous Heaven !

Freedom's Journal was the first paper published by Negroes in the United States. Samuel E. Cornish and J. B. Russwurm were the editors.

In 1825, one year after Duncan's pamphlet was published, the Erie Canal was completed, providing rapid transportation between New York, New England, and the Great Lakes. By that time also, the national road was a great highway into the West, and steamboats were simplifying travel on the Ohio and Mississippi from Pittsburgh to New Orleans. Eventually, New England, New York, and Pennsylvania were tied to the Old Northwest and then to the upper Mississippi Valley by powerful economic and cultural bonds. Eventually, also, the region would be tied to the Atlantic seaboard by railroads and relieved of its dependence upon river traffic.

The depression in the East, in addition to implementing the westward migration, produced a startling increase in crime, intemperance, and poverty in the cities, and excessive demands by charitable agencies for relief funds led to organized studies of divers subjects such as unemployment, intemperance, imprisonment for debt, prostitution, education, and many others. One-seventh of the people in New York City were supported by charity. There were 1,800 grog shops and 10,000 prostitutes in a population of slightly more than 100,000 people, and in 1816 a total of 1,984 people were in prison for debt, nearly 1,000 for amounts under $25. Conditions were equally bad in Philadelphia, Boston, and Baltimore. In the country at large the annual per capita consumption of distilled spirits was seven gallons.

Intelligent men were deeply concerned about these conditions, and out of the initial discussions, not alone of organized committees but of a meeting of minds of many sorts, came numerous benevolent and reform societies. The American Bible Society (1816), the American Tract Society (1825), the American Sunday School Union (1825), the American Home Missionary Society (1826), the Society for the Promotion of Temperance (1826), and the American Peace Society (1828) are among the more important and permanent agencies formed at this time. The Tract Society distributed 65,000,000 tracts within six years, the Sunday School Union had 60,000 teachers and 400,000 children under instruction within two years, and the Home Missionary Society had 201 missionaries operating in eighteen states within two years. Fifty thousand churches were built between 1815 and 1860, and the number of church members increased from 365,000 to 4,000,000.

Much of this cultural effort was directed toward the new West, and a host of great men went westward personally to devote their lives to the effort. I have said previously, and see no reason to change that interpretation, that even as a century before the Valley of the Mississippi had been the focal point of imperial rivalry, so now it became the battleground of ideas. Men of vision, to whom life holds no greater meaning than service to humanity, were drawn here by an irresistible force. Said one: "The destinies of this Republic and perhaps of the world, depend upon the intelligence and moral character of the mighty West." Whatever else the movement represented, it was an effort on the part of the intelligent and enlightened few to give right direction to the cultural development of the new region.[1]

Churches and new public schools needed preachers and teachers, and the children of the West needed higher education. The several church denominations established colleges to supply the need. The Presbyterian Church, which furnished 75 per cent of the ministers and laymen interested in the early stages of the benevolent movement, founded fifteen colleges between 1812 and 1840, eleven of them in the Old Northwest. The Methodists, who had no institutions of higher learning before 1830, founded thirty-four before 1860, eighteen of them in the Old Northwest. The Baptists founded twenty-five colleges between 1820 and 1860, the Congregationalists twenty, the Catholics fourteen, the Episcopalians eleven, and the Lutherans six; the overwhelming majority of these were in the Mississippi Valley. These Western colleges represented the culture and religion of the East in the frontier regions, and they relied heavily upon the East for financial support. The Tappan brothers and others who came to be known as the Association of Gentlemen in New York considered themselves trustees of their wealth for use in Christian benevolence. In their philosophy and their philanthropy they antedated Carnegie's generation by half a century.

Easterners not only sent their wealth and their representative agents to the West, they came themselves. From a multitude of such people, one invariably thinks of Lyman Beecher and his son, Edward Beecher. The father was rated the greatest of New England divines, but he came West in 1832 to be president of a new theological seminary at Cincinnati. Edward had come west in

1830 to be president of Illinois College, an even more humble institution housed in a small brick building at Jacksonville. These two men left positions of ease and luxury and highly cultivated parishioners in Boston. The father wanted to establish in the West a more liberal Calvinism than that of the New England Orthodox Congregationalists. His son, speaking of the morning of Elijah Lovejoy's death, said: "Who that has stood on the banks of the mighty stream that then rolled before me can forget the emotions of sublimity that filled his heart, as in imagination he has traced those channels of intercourse opened by it and its branches through the illimitable regions of this Western world."[2]

A young home missionary in the west wrote from Lexington: "You are well aware of the fact that this Western country is soon to be a mighty giant that shall wield not only the destinies of our own country but of the world. Tis yet a babe. Why not then come and take it in the freshness of its infancy and give a right direction to its powers that when it grows up to its full stature we may bless God that it has such an influence?"[3] The students at Lane Seminary said: "We were connected with an institution freighted with the spiritual interests of the West . . . The Valley was our expected field; and we assembled here, that we might the more accurately learn its character, catch the spirit of its gigantic enterprise, grow up in its genius, appreciate its peculiar wants, and be thus qualified by practical skill, no less than by theological erudition, to wield the weapons of truth."[4] Such recorded statements could be multiplied tenfold. Men knew the strategic importance —the potential power—of the Mississippi Valley. Politicians knew it, financiers and industrialists knew it, and religious leaders knew it. And sooner or later every one of them came to realize that here would be fought to conclusion the battle between slavery and freedom.

In 1825, also, there began in western New York, the great revival of Charles Grandison Finney.[5] His evangelism did more than spread the Gospel of Christ, it lighted a new path to salvation: confession and forgiveness of sin, right conduct, and good works. Man was now not only the architect of his physical and political environment, he was the master of his own soul. His religion was a religion of achievement in a most peculiar sense. No man, however, could live by Christian ethics and be at peace unless he strove mightily to give

new purpose and new direction to the lives of erring neighbors, something which had seemed to be quite futile under the discarded doctrines of predestination and original sin. No man could feel his task complete who set his neighbors' feet upon the road to salvation, yet failed to do all within his power to remove obstructions and restraints. The Presbyterian Church, already democratic, suddenly vibrated with new life and purpose. It became the institutionalized agency for social betterment. The new religious doctrines harmonized perfectly with the political philosophy and the material achievements of the New West. An intellectual and religious crusade for social reform, heavily flavored with Christian benevolence, was inevitable, one might almost say mandatory.

The basic elements in responsible, individual freedom had been established by 1825. Not the least of these was manhood suffrage, and in adopting manhood suffrage a severe blow was dealt the inequitable prestige of property rights. Vermont had manhood suffrage when admitted to the Union in 1791. Every other state had property holding qualifications or religious tests for the franchise. On the theory that the more property a man owned the more responsible he was, there were higher qualifications for officeholding than for voting and still higher requirements for eligibility to the highest offices. Beginning with Kentucky in 1792, the Western states came into the Union without these restrictions, and by 1825 both Massachusetts and New York had universal manhood suffrage. The older states had property-holding qualifications for the franchise; some limited public service to Christians, or Protestants, and even in the West, Tennessee and Mississippi excluded atheists from civil offices. Tennessee had also the following provision: "Whereas ministers of the gospel are, by their profession, dedicated to God and the care of souls, and ought not to be diverted from the great duties of their functions, therefore, no minister of the gospel, or priest, of any denomination whatever, shall be eligible to a seat in either House of the Legislature." These restrictions had been swept away by 1825.

Imprisonment for debt was also abolished. The colonies of Virginia and Massachusetts had passed such laws before the Revolution only to have them disallowed. The several states continued for a time without legislation in the matter, and the courts made no distinction between persons who were *not willing* to meet their honest obligations and those who were *not able* to do so. Failure to pay a debt, however small, was cause for imprisonment. Prisoners of all sorts were herded together in the vilest sort of quarters and were dependent on charity for blankets and fuel. Many of them were women, some with nursing babies or dependent children at home. No one could pay a debt while in prison; many resorted to crime and prostitution to avoid conviction. Changes in the laws began about 1815. Pennsylvania, New York, and Vermont drastically limited the cause for imprisonment. Indiana, Illinois, Alabama, and Mississippi forbade imprisonment for debt provided the debtor was willing to surrender any property he possessed to be used for the benefit of his creditors, and, gradually, the Eastern states added a provision which permitted a debtor to retain his homestead.

Society also took over from the family responsibility for education and established public schools. So long as education was regarded as a private affair, the children of wealthy parents enjoyed a tremendous advantage in politics and in the professions, and in the control of the courts, the churches, and the colleges. There were public schools in the Northern states, but they were scattered, poorly staffed, and without supervision. Little improvement was made from colonial days until about 1815. Organized labor demanded universal, free, and equal education for all children. The Northwest Ordinance had set aside certain lands in each township for school purposes. The regular system of land survey and public roads made possible the bringing of sufficient children together under one roof in that area to establish district schools. These schools soon became the intellectual and social centers of rural areas. Then it was that school laws were passed in Indiana (1816), New Jersey (1817), Pennsylvania (1818), New York (1821), Ohio (1824), Illinois (1825), Maryland (1825), Massachusetts (1826), and Delaware (1829). These laws laid the legal basis for a new educational system in the nonslaveholding states. In the slave states there were no public schools.

So it was that man's fierce passion for individual freedom and equality of opportunity brought about a great social revolution at the North, in orderly fashion and by democratic processes, by the end of the 1820's. Class distinctions, artificial badges of superiority, injustices based upon belief in biological inequalities were not completely destroyed, but they were under severe indictment and fast disappearing. The situation of women is a case in point. Men insisted they lacked those sound qualities, mental and physical, which capacitate men for suffrage and officeholding. That honorable men should have thrust wives, mothers, sisters, daughters into that legal limbo of disfranchised citizenship, with fools, maniacs, and felons, balks all rational belief. It indicates the impregnability of prejudice to reason and common sense. Yet, so strong were the reform impulses that a multitude of men *and women* rose up against such nonsense and secured substantial gains in the emancipation of women during these years, and women made a tremendous contribution to the emancipation of the slaves and elevation of the free Negroes.

In many ways the most important development was in communication of ideas. People had lived in cultural isolation for a long time. It is difficult to get a proper perspective of life in the early years of the Republic because the cultural isolation in which people lived is so foreign to our own experiences. There were no radios, motion pictures, telephones, or telegraph lines and no mail delivery. Days of difficult travel were required to reach the nearest city from most little towns or rural communities. There were few newspapers, and news from distant places was months old when received. Few people traveled; there was not much exchange of ideas over long distances, and there was a dearth of reading material even for those who could read.

Sometime before 1825 the term lyceum began to be used in the Western area. Visitors to a community known to be distinguished men, or who claimed to be important persons, or sometimes just because they were visitors from the outside world, posted notices and gave public lectures on some subject of their choice. Churches and schoolhouses were the forums whenever governing boards were convinced of the *quality* and *propriety* of the performance. Warehouses, barns, storerooms often were used. Sometimes the meetings were held out-of-doors, weather permitting. Frequently the visitor was challenged to debate by some local person. Always there was some discussion and intellectual stimulation. The custom was perfectly suited to the work of the benevolent and reform societies when they were organized.

It was the tract societies which charted the way for reform operations. The Religious Tract Society of London was organized in 1799 to distribute religious literature.[6] The Massachusetts Society for Promoting Christian Knowledge was organized in 1803,[7] the New England Tract Society in 1814. The New England Society became a national organization, with 250 auxiliary societies by 1823 and an annual publication list of 770,000 tracts, a magazine, and children's books. The guiding genius of the New England Society was William Allen Hallock.[8] In New York a society sponsored by Arthur Tappan had been organized in 1812. It was a local society, but contributed to the movement the important principle of unified effort of the several church denominations. Representatives of tract societies throughout the country met in New York in 1825 and organized the American Tract Society. This represented national consolidation.[9]

The society was controlled by an executive committee, including the corresponding secretary. Hallock came to New York and occupied that post for forty-five years. By 1829 the society had receipts of $60,000 and was publishing 6,000,000 tracts annually.[10] Twenty years later its annual budget was $258,000; it was still publishing 5,000,000 tracts, of which 600,000 were in foreign languages, and its publishing list included 800,000 volumes of library books.[11] All of these publications were furnished to local societies at cost. The society was nondenominational, the executive committee being composed of preachers from six denominations: Episcopal, Presbyterian, Reformed Dutch, Congregational, Baptist, and Methodist. No tract was ever published without unanimous approval of the committee.

"Much of what they published," said a leading authority, "could hardly be considered as great literature, but it furnished reading matter of some merit to many intellectually famished communities."[12] Some of the tracts were written anonymously. Their source is a mystery. They may have been written by direction of the publishing committee or by members of the committee. Some were premium tracts (prize essays). Some were sermons of renowned preachers of an earlier day. Some were little stories of converted sinners. Some were serious discourses on religious doctrine. All the simpler and more beautiful passages of the Bible were woven into these discourses. Many dealt with sins and vices: drinking, danc-

ing, gambling, profanity, slander. They were directed to people who were sick or afflicted, to children, to mothers, to the aged. All were designed to carry the message of salvation. They were published in many languages, including Arabic, Burmese, and Chinese, for distribution by foreign missionaries. They were distributed in the cities, in the mountains, and on the frontier. This was world evangelism at its best.

The society selected New York as its headquarters because one-third of all foreign goods entered there and merchants came there to buy. It was the gateway to the interior, also the shipping point for raw materials brought by coastwise traffic. The other reform societies located there also, and for the same reason. Let me repeat that the reform movement was an intellectual and religious crusade for social progress. Preachers, professional men (doctors, lawyers, teachers), and wealthy merchants and landowners comprised the vast majority of the active participants. Henry B. Stanton said 98 per cent of the antislavery people were Whigs and they were the professional men, merchants, financiers, and property-holders.[13] The largest donors of funds by far were Arthur and Lewis Tappan of New York, wealthy merchants and importers. Add all of this together and what does it mean? That reform activity was the beneficiary of business activity and business expansion. Business communications of all kinds from men like the Tappans to clients in the West carried postscripts *in re* such subjects as moral reform, temperance, and slavery. Business men went to New York to buy and stayed on to attend the annual conventions of reform societies. Young attorneys in every community of the West, who acted as credit advisers and collectors for the New York merchants, caught the spirit of reform.

The tract society also set a pattern for distribution of literature.[14] It began with what we may call miscellaneous distribution, with interested persons and members of the society carrying a supply of tracts and handing them to people or scattering them around railroad stations and other public places. In 1828 it introduced systematic monthly distribution. New tracts were delivered every month to the same families in the Eastern cities. The cities were divided into wards, and into districts of not more than sixty families to each distributor.[15] Orman Eastman was sent west to direct the work of five agents in the Mississippi

Valley. Then, in 1831 tract visitation began, with the representatives of the society visiting homes, distributing tracts, praying with the family, and encouraging church attendance. By 1838 there were eight general agents, one each for the large cities of New York; western New York; southern New York; Virginia, Ohio, Indiana, and Kentucky; Missouri and Illinois; northern Ohio and Michigan; the Western states.[16]

The agents raised funds for the society, organized auxiliary societies, distributed literature, set up depositories, served as visiting preachers in the churches, conducted revivals and prayer meetings. They were itinerant preachers, traveling salesmen, and publicity agents, and some traveled as much as 16,000 miles annually. Finally, the society introduced colportage. The colporteurs were laymen, sometimes seminary students. They were paid $150 a year, and they were forbidden to discuss religious controversies and politics. They visited destitute families, conversed and prayed with individuals, gave tracts away, sold them, organized Sunday schools, promoted temperance and church attendance, ofttimes taught children to read, and worked particularly among families of immigrants.[17] The Bible has ever been the greatest single stimulus to the desire to read, but it was expensive and bulky to distribute and difficult to understand. These tract publications, in a very real sense, took its place in that respect.

Equally important with social reform was the emergence of political democracy. Universal manhood suffrage made politics important to the common man. Soon after Monroe's election to a second term in 1820, a realignment of political parties began. It was completed by 1830, with popular government a reality, including nomination of candidates by representative conventions and active participation in politics by the people. By that date the parties had developed to much like

their present form. Parties could not prosper on a diet of internal dissension, and politicians resisted all efforts to introduce such subjects as slavery into politics, but the people would have none of it. The reform movements gave politicians and political parties a terrific jolt. Candidates were questioned by opposing newspapers and by public letters and were expected to answer.

The benevolent and reform societies and the political parties all established newspapers. Among the denominational journals and reform publications was William Ellery Channing's *Christian Examiner* in Boston, Lyman Beecher's *Spirit of the Pilgrims* in Boston, John Greenleaf Whittier's *Pennsylvania Freeman* in Philadelphia, William Goodell's *Friend of Man* at Utica, and William H. Burleigh's *Christian Witness* at Pittsburgh. Other important papers were the New York *Evangelist*, the *Genius of Temperance*, and the *Ohio Observer*. Daily newspapers that were to play an important part in the next three decades were Benjamin H. Day's New York *Sun* (1833), James Gordon Bennett's New York *Globe* (1832), and George D. Prentice's Louisville *Journal* (1830). These are only examples. Actually, hundreds of newspapers came into existence to advance the fortunes of the reform societies and the political parties, beginning in the 1820's; and by 1860 there were more than 400 dailies and 2,500 weeklies and monthlies.

Need one look beyond these impulses for the intellectual ferment of the three decades before the Civil War? Need one wonder why an institution at war with the natural rights of man, the cardinal principles of the Christian faith, and the ideals of individual freedom and social progress was swept away? Is it necessary to labor over the source of opposition to the extension of slavery beyond the Mississippi and to colonization? The answer, of course, is an emphatic no!

LANE SEMINARY

Chapter 18

The crucial battle between slavery and freedom lasted about a decade, ending in 1839. The decade began with strong centers of antislavery organization and Negro culture in New York and Philadelphia, which had been well established and active from the days of Franklin and Benezet. These two urban centers constituted the main support of the American Convention which held its last important meeting in 1829. It began with Benjamin Lundy and his *Genius of Universal Emancipation* in Baltimore, next to New York and Philadelphia the most active center of antislavery activity in the East. It began with the publication of David Walker's *Appeal* and his probable murder in Boston; and to the South with the Nat Turner insurrection in Virginia. It began with a very powerful group of antislavery Presbyterian preachers entrenched in the Chillicothe Presbytery of southern Ohio and a well-organized system of aid to fugitives and free Negroes throughout the state. It began with Christian benevolence and reform radiating north and west from New York City, which was headquarters of the societies, of organizational genius, and of financial support; and to the South with Hayne and Calhoun devising an ingenious philosophy by which the moral standards of the lowest cultural areas could determine the public policy of the nation.

Everyone who had attempted to emphasize the social teachings of Jesus in reference to the racial problem had been summarily rejected by the slave areas. That was true of the Quakers who were driven out of Barbadoes and so persecuted and restrained in the states like North Carolina that they moved out in large numbers. It was true of Presbyterian preachers like Gilliland, Rankin, and Lockhart. It was true of the home missionaries, many of whom asked to be transferred from the slave states to other areas. The cold, hard fact is that the slave states retained their religious fundamentalism, representing eighteenth-century dogma, and rejected *in toto* the social welfare aspects of the evangelistic crusade and the doctrine of Christian benevolence and good works of the Finney revival. Evangelism and the antislavery movement were inseparable. This was so because slavery and Christianity were absolutely antithetical to such a degree that from the days of Woolman and Benezet greater emphasis was placed upon the sin of slavery—its denial of the equality of all men in the sight of God—than upon any other indictment. Even slavery's violation of the natural rights of man took second place.

The evangelistic movement, particularly Finney's revival, provided a host of young men dedicated to preaching the Gospel. They inevitably gave support, and many of them undivided attention for a time, to one or another of the reform movements. Antislavery attracted more than any other because slavery was the greatest existing social evil—war excepted. Antislavery appealed to the intellectuals, and for the same reason: slavery crucified intelligence. The combination gave to the antislavery movement the greatest concentration of moral and intellectual power ever assembled in support of any cause before or since.

Finney resisted defection of young evangelists to specific reforms, particularly to the antislavery movement.[1] There were two reasons: his faith in the power of evangelism to cleanse the hearts of men, and his fear that a direct attack upon slavery would end in civil war. The conflict raged in his own heart and caused much anguish to his students. It led to a test of strength between two intellectual giants: himself and Theodore Weld. Eventually, it contributed heavily to a split in the association of Congregational ministers in New England and in the American Anti-Slavery Society.

The Great Revival, then, gave the antislavery movement, already one hundred years old, an unprecedented number of devoted apostles. The Presbyterian and Congregational churches provided the forums for these men, and bread and butter sustenance for most. Their power derived from numbers and from organization. They had the Bible. They had the great charters of Western liberalism. They had the writings of Woolman, Benezet, Rush, Hopkins, Cooper, Rice, Branagan, Barrow, Duncan, Rankin, and a host of British liberals such as Sharp, Clarkson, and Wilberforce. They needed all of this and more to beat down and destroy the doctrine of racial inequality, enshrined in slavery, and upheld by the courts, the churches, and the political parties.

The first group came into the movement by way of Lane Seminary in Cincinnati. Charles Grandison Finney's Great Revival in western New York had brought together four persons of superior ability and of the utmost importance to the movement: Finney himself, who went to New York to be the pastor of the Chatham Street Chapel, built by the Tappan brothers, and later to Oberlin to direct the theological department; Charles Stuart, leading British antislavery leader who wrote the most cogent argument against colonization, financed Weld's education, and provided valuable connection with the British liberals; Theodore Weld, son of a conservative Presbyterian minister in Cazenovia; and Lewis Tappan. When Finney went to New York, Weld gathered about him the finest of the young men converted in the revival and went to Oneida Institute to prepare for the ministry. Oneida had been founded by George Washington Gale in 1827. Gale had converted Finney and founded Oneida to prepare Finney's converts for the ministry. He remained at Oneida until replaced by Beriah Green in 1834

Lewis Tappan

and then went farther west to found Knox College.

Weld, although a relatively young man, was a well-known lecturer on temperance, moral reform, and the science of memory. The Society for Promoting Manual Labor in Literary Institutions was formed in 1831 by a group of distinguished men, including among others George W. Gale, William Jay, Joshua Leavitt, and Lewis Tappan. It appointed Weld to be general agent and sent him on an extensive tour of the North and West.[2] He traveled through Ohio, Indiana, Illinois, Missouri, Kentucky, Tennessee, and Alabama, lecturing on temperance and manual laborism, and holding long and earnest conversations about slavery and colonization with leading men. Some of the men upon whom he exerted great influence were Beriah Green, professor of sacred literature in Western Reserve College, whose later writings Birney said were the "most forceful and convincing" of all antislavery literature, and who became president of Oneida Institute in 1833;[3] James G. Birney, distinguished attorney and planter of Huntsville, Alabama, who was about to become a general

Lane Seminary in 1841

agent for the American Colonization Society; and Reverend William Allan and son of Huntsville, of whom we shall shortly say more. In Cleveland, also, he discussed the subject earnestly with his old friend, John Keep, and with Elizur Wright and President George Storrs. In Nashville, he won Marius Robinson to the cause.

Weld had a special commission from the Tappans to explore the area for a suitable location for a theological seminary. Rochester was considered, but Cincinnati was chosen. Extensive negotiations, largely by the Tappan brothers, since they were providing the bulk of the money, ended in founding Lane Seminary with Lyman Beecher as president. Weld and most of the other students at Oneida transferred to Lane, and the school opened under favorable circumstances in the autumn of 1833. There were several aspects of this educational enterprise which give it a lasting place in history: This was a major venture by Eastern men to give right direction to the cultural development of the Mississippi Valley, fully understood and concurred in by the students. Lyman Beecher and everyone initially connected with the enterprise endorsed the principle of full

academic freedom—free enquiry and discussion of all subjects. Cincinnati was the most flourishing urban and industrial center in the West with close commercial ties to the slave states; Cincinnati also contained more than one-third of the 7,500 Negroes in the state of Ohio, three-fourths of the adults being emancipated slaves who had paid or were then paying for themselves, their friends, or relatives still in bondage; and Cincinnati was close to a strong antislavery area and a strong proslavery area, and Weld, Tappan, and Stuart at least knew the students intended to undertake antislavery activity.

Let me say once again that improvement of the free Negroes was coequal with freedom for the slaves with every antislavery man. There were many humanitarians, especially Quakers, who honestly believed colonization was best for the future of the race, but they were always vigorous and alert and even generous in their efforts to protect and aid the free Negro. A man could be a colonizationist and be a strong antislavery man, but the proof lay in his attitude toward free Negroes; and nearly all humanitarians who were opposed to slavery drifted out of the colonization movement during the late 1820's. No place in the country offered a better opportunity to test the ability of the Negro to make advancement if given an opportunity than did Cincinnati. The students undertook this missionary or social service work without restraint, as an essential part of pastoral training. They established Sunday schools, day and evening schools, a circulating library, and a lyceum where they lectured four evenings a week on grammar, geography, arithmetic, and natural philosophy. They mingled freely with the Negro population, relieving distress and cultivating intellectual and moral progress. Two of the students, Augustus Wattles and Marius R. Robinson, withdrew from the seminary in order to conduct a school for the Negroes.[4]

Thirty members of this theological class were over twenty-six years of age, fourteen were over twenty-eight, and nine were between thirty and thirty-five. All were college graduates, most of them having received degrees from eight to seventeen years previously. Six were married men. One was a practicing physician, and twelve had been public lecturers of prominence. Many of them were from the slave states, fourteen of them representing an aggregate residence of twenty-nine years in Virginia, twenty-three years in South Carolina, twenty-four years in Alabama, twenty-two years in Tennessee, twenty-three years in Missouri, and sixty-four years in Kentucky.

The student body was divided on the question of colonization, probably representing a variety of attitudes toward the question of race relations, though we have no way of knowing how many, or who, were for immediate emancipation. Practically all of the twenty-five trustees were colonizationists. Beecher himself never took a positive stand in favor of emancipation. He was not forthright in defense of academic freedom. There is some substantial evidence that he agreed to initiate at Lane Seminary an administrative policy of enforcing silence on the slavery question upon student bodies. In any case the students discussed freely such questions as temperance and then undertook to do the same with slavery and colonization.[5]

The time first chosen for opening the discussion at Lane was the first week of December 1833, but it was afterward postponed to about the middle of January 1834. Some news, at least, of what was going on, seems to have been widely disseminated, because John Rankin wrote to Weld and asked permission for himself and others of the Chillicothe Presbytery to attend. Gilliland, Rankin, and Lockhart we know were there, and, since Weld later said some of them came as much as sixty-five miles on horseback and that all of them were born, educated, and became preachers in the slave states, probably the Dickey brothers and Samuel Crothers. Weld, himself, later said that when he began lecturing in southern Ohio the region where these men preached was so thoroughly abolitionized that it was the only place where his meetings were never mobbed. Certainly, the area was thoroughly leavened with antislavery lore because Weld lectured in these churches for several weeks to quiet audiences.

The discussion was in the nature of a public lyceum, popular at that time. It began on the question: "Is it the duty of the people of the slaveholding states to abolish slavery immediately?" Weld led off the discussion, speaking three hours on each of the first four evenings.[6] Weld was unquestionably one of the most effective public speakers this country has ever produced. In this case his presentation of the subject was so convincing that those previously selected to defend slavery surrendered their allotted time and let their case go by default. He covered every aspect of the institution as was his custom, from the points of history, philosophy, scriptures, fundamental law, morality, justice, and common sense.[7] Weld was followed by Henry B. Stanton who spoke for two evenings. If anyone in the whole movement could match Weld in masterly speech, logic, wit, sarcasm, pathos, and glowing appeal, it was Stanton. Later, when he got involved in politics as the leader of the Democratic Party in New York, he lost much of his spontaneous appeal, but in his antislavery prime he was a master. Both Weld and Stanton dwelt upon principles, the laws of mind, its structure, and nature; the nature of slavery, its fundamental principles; and the way in which despotic power victimizes those who wield it. They then called upon the men from the South to speak from personal knowledge of the nature of slavery and its destructive powers over all concerned with it.

There were about twenty students who had been born and had always lived in the midst of slavery, not including the visiting preachers, so that this was fact—no one could question the truth of what was said. These young men were the sons of slaveholders and heirs of slave property. The first to speak was William T. Allan, son of a distinguished Presbyterian preacher of Huntsville, Alabama. Allan was twenty-three years old, a graduate of Centre College at Danville, Kentucky. He stood more than six feet tall, was utterly frank and courageous in stating his convictions, and was a man of commanding presence. He spoke for two hours in great detail of what he had seen, known, and experienced of the slave system, and of the effects upon the slaves, the slaveholders, and their families of the exercise of arbitrary power. He avowed his complete conversion to antislavery principles with emphasis and fervor. He afterward was elected president of the students' antislavery society.

Allan was followed by James A. Thome of Augusta, Kentucky, whose father was a slaveholder and a visiting elder of the Presbyterian church and whose family was of high social position. Thome was twenty-two years old, but seemed much younger. He was a man of fine literary taste and culture. His dark hair and eyes and high brow, and his winning smile, combined with graceful movements and a very kindly disposition, won instant friendship from strangers. After Thome had spoken, the debate lost its formal character and devolved into a general roundtable discussion in which all participated. It ended with an almost unanimous vote by the participants and spectators that slavery should be abolished immediately and that Christians could not support the colonization movement.

The Lane debate probably did not add very much that was new to the antislavery indictment, although it systematized it and brought it to the attention of many thousands of people who had never read an antislavery pamphlet. It did, however, bring to a sharp focus the developing cleavage between anti-Negro colonizationists and antislavery humanitarians. The latter organized the American Antislavery Society just previous to the Lane Debate, and militant antislavery activity thereafter steadily gained support. The colonizationists struck back with viciousness, intensifying their anti-Negro propaganda, inciting more violence against both Negroes and antislavery whites, and striving to suppress antislavery activity by every possible means, legal and otherwise. The result was a decade of violence. It involved almost all of the natural rights of men and the basic principles of democracy. We shall deal with it separately in another chapter.

Cincinnati seethed with excitement and strong pressure was brought by public sentiment to suppress all discussion of slavery. Representatives of the several colleges in the country met in New York and agreed upon a policy of silence.[8] Students were forbidden to organize antislavery societies or to discuss the question at schools such as Harvard, Yale, Princeton, Amherst, and Andover, and apparently there was no further student activity, at least for a time, except at Centre College, Kentucky. The trustees of Lane Seminary undertook to impose drastic restrictions upon the students and Beecher remained in the East for several months during the crisis.

The trustees commanded the students to discontinue their antislavery society and forbade public discussions with one another at table or elsewhere without permission. A committee of the trustees was vested with discretionary power to dismiss any student without statement of cause to faculty, students, or the public. Steps were taken to dismiss both Theodore Weld and William Allan, and Professor John Morgan was relieved of his duties. They meant business.[9] Later, after the students were gone, Beecher tried to disclaim responsibility, but Gilbert Barnes, who made an exhaustive study of the case, places full blame upon his vaccilation and cowardice. Beecher succeeded in having authority transferred from the trustees to the faculty, but no discussion of slavery was allowed, and Beecher remained as president. The action of the college administration was thoroughly reprehensible and indicative of the awful consequences of race prejudice. Here was a new theological seminary with as fine a body of young men as any school in the country, as proved by their later accomplishments, and with assured financial support sufficient to make it the center of the cultural and intellectual life of the entire Mississippi Valley. All of this was sacrificed on the altar of prejudice and oppression. Worse still, every possible obstacle was thrown in the way of the students, and extreme measures were taken to discredit them in the eyes of the public.

Fifty-one of the students signed a public statement of their case and withdrew from the seminary in the autumn of 1834.[10] They rested their case for academic freedom upon the inalienable right of free enquiry and discussion, thus adding to the evolution of the higher law doctrine so ably begun by Rice and Barrow. "Proscription of free discussion," said they "is sacrilege! It is boring out the eyes of the soul! It is robbery of mind. It is the burial of truth. If institutions cannot stand upon this broad footing, let them fall. Better, infinitely better, that a mob demolish every building or the incendiary wrap them in flames . . . than that our seminaries should become Bastiles, our theological students thinkers by permission, and the right of full discussion tamed down into a soulless thing of gracious, condescending sufferance."

The right cannot be abridged by allowing investigation and proscribing discussion, because, said they, "discussion is the standard test for the detection of fallacies and the revelation of truth. It is the furnace where gold and alloy separate. It is the fan which drives the chaff and wheat asunder. It is the court of errors where the decisions of individual tribunals are reversed or confirmed."

How can an institution lay claim to the function of training the powers of intellect, if it commands its students to surrender the right to the exercise of their reason in specific cases? "All the giant sins," said they, "which have ever made havoc in society, have been tolerated and sanctioned by public sentiment . . . Are our theological seminaries to be awed into silence upon the great questions of human duty? Are they to be bribed over to the interests of an unholy sentiment, by promises of patronage or threats of its withdrawal . . . In selecting topics for discussion, are the students to avoid those which are of great public concernment, whose issues involve all human interests, and whose claims are as wide and deep as right and wrong and weal and woe can make them? . . . Whom does it behoove to keep his heart in contact with the woes and guilt of a perishing world if not the students . . . Is anything better adapted to quicken sympathy and enlarge benevolence, than deep pondering of the miseries and wrongs of oppressed humanity, and thorough discussion of the best means of alleviation and redress? It is false both in fact and philosophy, that anything is lost to the student by engaging in such exercise. Instead of his progress being retarded in the appropriate studies of a theological course, it will be *accelerated*. Whenever intellect moves in the sublimity of power, the heart generates its momentum. It is when the deep tides of emotion well out from full fountains—that intellect is buoyed upward, and borne onward in majesty and might. A subject so deeply freighted with human interests as that of slavery,

cannot be investigated and discussed intelligently and thoroughly, without amplifying and expanding the intellect and increasing the power of its action upon all subjects . . . He who would preach in the nineteenth century, must *know* the nineteenth century. No matter how deeply read in the history of the past, 'if not versed in the records of his own day, he is not fit to preach the gospel.'"[11]

The students were given the use of a large home belonging to the brother-in-law of Salmon P. Chase. Huntington Lyman said, fifty years later, they found a "deserted brick tavern," five miles from the seminary. In any case, they set up classes of their own with two of their number, George Whipple and William T. Allan, and a young physician of Cincinnati of whom we shall hear a great deal, Gamaliel Bailey, perhaps others, serving as instructors. Then came John J. Shipherd who had founded a college at Oberlin the previous year. It was a college in name only, and Shipherd's description and promises were extravagant, but the former Lane students literally took possession of the embryo institution. Asa Mahan was made president. John Morgan was made a professor. Negroes were admitted. The Tappans gave thousands for endowment. Charles Grandison Finney came to head theology, and what was to become one of the most renowned and influential colleges in the world began its first actual work in the spring of 1835.[12]

What of the Lane Seminary students after they left Lane or Oberlin as the case might be? Weld had been on a lecture tour for a year and came back in the autumn of 1835 to train twelve of them to abolitionize Ohio.[13] We shall come back to that story. William T. Allan (1810–82) became an agent of the American Antislavery Society in 1835. During a two-year period he lectured throughout northern Ohio, western Pennsylvania, and in Monroe, Orleans, and Niagara counties, New York.[14] He then spent most of his life preaching in Illinois, where he helped to organize the Illinois Antislavery Society and served as its agent in the proslavery area between Alton and Jacksonville.[15] During the Civil War, Owen Lovejoy told Theodore Weld in Boston that he owed his seat in Congress to Allan. Said he: "I had heard of him as an abolitionist whom mobs could not scare, but had never seen him, until one day a tall man laid his hand on my shoulder with the grip of a giant as he said: 'Mr. Lovejoy you ought to be in Congress, you are just the man to lock

John Morgan

horns with those bellowing slaveholding animals.' Well, I said nothing short of a miracle could compel my congressional district to send an abolitionist to Washington. Said Allan: 'I am going to stump your district. I'll lecture wherever I can get a church, a hall, a schoolhouse, a private home, or a barn. If I can get none of them, I'll call meetings and talk abolition in God's open air, and I'll keep it up 'til the thing is done.' That man did just that thing. He actually abolitionized my congressional district and sent me to Washington."

John Watson Alvord (1807–80)[16] became an antislavery agent with Allan in 1835, covering the area around Euclid, Willoughby, Rutland, and Mentor. He served as a pastor at Maumee, Ohio, then at Barkhamstead, at Stamford, Connecticut, and at Boston. He served as secretary of the Boston Tract Society for fourteen years, and then as chaplain in Sheridan's army. One of the great services of the chaplains in the Union armies was the care and education of the refugee slaves, a phase of the war almost totally neglected by historians. Alvord's work in this respect led to his appointment as superintendent of schools in the Freedman's Bureau in 1866. He afterward was treasurer of the Freedman's Bank and Trust Company.

Henry B. Stanton (1805–87) probably the most effective agent next to Weld, and one of the three top men in the movement—Weld, Birney, and Stan-

ton—became financial secretary of the American Antislavery Society. He lectured widely in Great Britain, Ireland, and the United States on slavery, wrote a great deal for the antislavery newspapers and journals, and led the battle to prevent hostile state legislation for suppression of antislavery societies. He was always close to Birney and approved his political action movement, but did not fully participate until the point of reorganization into the Free Soil Party. He remained a Republican until after the Civil War, then became a Democrat and edited the New York *Sun* until his death.

Augustus Wattles (1807–83) devoted his entire life to teaching free Negroes to become economically self-sufficient. He was in that respect the Benezet of the later movement.[17] He and Marius Robinson left Lane Seminary before the exodus to establish the school for Negroes in which the students taught in rotation. He then became an agent of the American Antislavery Society in charge of the welfare of free Negroes and formulated the plans for getting them located as mechanics and farmers. He used his entire inheritance to establish schools for them in Ohio and Indiana and thousands of dollars solicited for that purpose from friends. Finally, he went to Lawrence, Kansas, with the crusaders of the Emigrant Aid Society, where he edited the *Herald of Freedom*. Marius Robinson (1806–76), who had taught in a Cherokee Indian Mission School before going to Lane Seminary, was a partner with Wattles in the education of the Cincinnati Negroes. He afterward assisted James G. Birney in editing the *Philanthropist* and served as an antislavery agent. He was so severely beaten by a mob at Berlin, in Mahoning County, that he never fully recovered his health. He later edited the *Antislavery Bugle* at Salem, Ohio, and served as president of the Ohio Mutual Fire Insurance Company.[18] Hiram Wilson went to Canada to do for the fugitives there what Wattles was doing in Ohio and Indiana, serving for a time, as did Wattles, as an agent of the American Anti-Slavery Society.[19] He first visited the settlements of the Negroes, studied their condition, and made plans for relief, education, and religious instruction. He founded the British-American Manual Labor Institute of the Colored Settlements of Upper Canada and was aided at one time by fourteen teachers from Oberlin. He was aided in the Institute work by Josiah Henson, an ex-slave. The school—a teacher-training school—was at Dawn, and had about sixty students. There were other missionaries in Canada, but as a relief agent, a friend of the refugee, as preacher, and teacher, Wilson had no peer.

Many other students served for a time as agents for the antislavery societies. George Whipple, who was one of the teachers of the Lane students after their withdrawal, lectured for a time, then became principal of Oberlin's preparatory department and professor of mathematics. When the Antislavery American Missionary Association was organized, he served as its corresponding secretary. He participated in the work of the Freedman's Bureau, and was president-elect of Howard University at the time of his death in 1876. James A. Thome first lectured in and around Akron, Tallmadge, Canton, New Lisbon, and Cadiz, Ohio, then went to the West Indies to prepare a report on the results of emancipation for the American Antislavery Society. In 1838 he became professor of rhetoric and belles-lettres at Oberlin and later pastor of a church in Cleveland.[20]

Philemon Bliss practiced law in Elyria, helped to organize the Free Soil Party, was elected to Congress in 1854, accepted an appointment as chief justice of Dakota Territory in 1861, was elected to the Supreme Court of Missouri in 1868, and was appointed dean of the Law School of the University of Missouri in 1872.[21] He held this post until his death in 1889. Asa Mahan, who came with the students to Oberlin, served as president of that institution, and then as president of Cleveland University and of Adrian College.

Most of the other students held prominent pastorates in the West, some of them serving also as antislavery agents until the agency phase of the movement was supplanted by political action. All of them, without any known exception, were courageous and outspoken opponents of slavery.

Christopher Rush

WILLIAM LLOYD GARRISON

Chapter 19

Benjamin Lundy,[1] lonely, wandering saddlemaker, who had dedicated his life to emancipation of the slaves and had begun publication of his *Genius of Universal Emancipation* at Mount Pleasant, Ohio, in 1821, arrived in Baltimore, Maryland, in the autumn of 1824. He had published forty-four monthly issues before coming to Baltimore. He resumed publication there in October 1824, changed the paper to a weekly in September 1825, and continued it as such until January 1829.

Lundy, it will be recalled, had gone to Greenville, Tennessee, from Ohio, and had published there for nearly three years. East Tennessee probably was the only place in the slave states, aside from Baltimore, where he would have been tolerated. He was relatively secure *there* because of the large Quaker population, the Tennessee Manumission Society, and the previous defense of freedom of the press by Elihu Embree and William Swain. He had attended the eighteenth session of the American Convention in Philadelphia in October 1823, meeting many antislavery men from the East for the first time. He walked to Baltimore in the summer of 1824, saving his meager funds to establish a press. William Swain came to assist with the editing.

Lundy prospered for three years, then lost subscriptions so rapidly that his press was taken over by his creditors and publication was suspended after the January 3, 1829, issue. Swain returned to North Carolina, Lundy went to Haiti in the interest of colonization. Colonization was the key both to his success and to his failure. In 1821 he had favored congressional exclusion of slavery from the District of Columbia, from the territories, and from new states, prohibition of the domestic slave trade, equal civil rights for free Negroes, and abolition of the three-fifths rule. These were standard antislavery principles at that time and remained so. Lundy, however, unlike Osborn, had favored colonization and remained a colonizationist. In 1825 he endorsed Frances Wright's scheme of permitting slaves to purchase their freedom by co-operative labor on the land, followed by compulsory colonization.[2] His search for a suitable colony took him to Haiti in 1825 and 1829, to Canada in 1832, and to Texas in 1830, 1833, and 1834. A great deal of space in the *Genius of Universal Emancipation* was devoted to colonization, and if Lundy ever lost faith in colonization it was near the end of his career.

Lundy also favored gradual emancipation. In Baltimore he was in an area friendly to both ideas. Maryland alone of all the states was willing to appropriate large sums of money to remove the Negroes to Africa, and in a manner closely approaching compulsory emigration.[3] Neither gradual emancipation nor colonization, however, had ever been approved by all antislavery men. By 1829 gradual emancipation was recognized as imperfect, inequitable, and indecisive, and colonization was known to be a complete failure. Men lined up for or against the *Negro* between 1828 and 1833; freedom, equality, justice on the one side—slavery and/or colonization on the other. Men like James G. Birney, Gerrit Smith, and Beriah Green thought clearly and acted vigorously for freedom. They publicly rejected colonization and joined antislavery societies. Southerners moved with equal resolution to defend slavery and to silence all antislavery arguments even though coupled with colonization. Lundy was trapped by his inability to face reality. Southerners dropped their subscriptions because he was opposed to slavery and Northern antislavery men did not come to his support because he supported colonization, although they always recognized his heroic devotion to the cause.

Lundy had gone to Philadelphia, Providence, New York, and Boston in March 1828, in search of subscribers to his paper. He met the Tappan brothers, long-time members of the New York Society for Promoting the Manumission of Slaves and foremost patrons of the reform and benevolent societies. He also met William Goodell, prominent lecturer and editor, whose chief interests were temperance and antislavery, and who was to become editor of the *Genius of Temperance* and then the *Friend of Man*.[4] In Boston he assembled eight preachers of various denominations at his rooming house for a discussion of slavery. William Lloyd Garrison, also a roomer in the house, was present at the meeting. Lundy failed to enlist the support of the clergymen, but he did arouse the interest of Garrison.

Garrison was twenty-two years of age at the time. He had learned the printer's trade on the Newburyport *Herald,* then had edited and published the *Free Press.* He published here the first writings of young John Greenleaf Whittier. In January 1828 he became editor of the *Boston National Philanthropist,* a temperance paper. Three months later he listened to Lundy's discussion of slavery. Lundy was back in Boston again in August 1828, and Garrison heard him speak again, this time at the Federal Street Baptist Church. Shortly afterward, Garrison assumed the editorship of the Bennington (Vt.) *Journal of the Times* on condition he might discuss antislavery, temperance, peace, and moral reform as well as politics. This was the beginning of his career as a reformer and Christian anarchist. He was at this point, with reference to slavery, a Lundy colonizationist, urging the formation of antislavery societies, the petitioning of Congress for abolition of slavery in the District of Columbia, and transportation elsewhere of liberated slaves and free Negroes willing to go. He circulated and sent to Congress a petition for abolition in the District signed by 2,352 citizens of Vermont. This peti-

William Lloyd Garrison

tion, written by himself, reveals one of his great weaknesses, about which we shall say much later: ignorance of American history, constitutional law, and previous antislavery tradition and literature. Speaking of slavery in the District of Columbia, he said: "The proposed abolition will interfere with no State rights. Beyond this District, Congress has no power to legislate—so far, at least, as slavery is concerned; but it can, by one act, efface this foul stain from our national reputation." Quite obviously he was not familiar with the long history of the territorial question.[5]

Garrison then gave a fourth of July address in Boston in 1829 which showed him to be at the age of twenty-four strongly opposed to slavery, but still a colonizationist and in favor of gradual emancipation by action of the slave states. He argued that the free states were "constitutionally involved in the guilt of slavery, by adhering to a national compact that sanctions it"; that Negroes could be elevated to intelligent citizenship by freedom and education; that the churches were neglecting their responsibility to the slaves; that the vast majority of the Negroes, slave and free, were born in the United States and were entitled to all the privileges of citizenship; that the variance between our professed devotion to liberty and equality and our oppression of the Negroes was shameful; that the free states might rightfully demand gradual emancipation; and that all citizens should assist in systematically promoting colonization through societies, private contributions, and congressional action.[6]

Benjamin Lundy had asked Garrison to join him in resuming publication of the *Genius of Universal Emancipation*. Garrison finally accepted the invitation and went to Baltimore in August 1829. He had by this time recognized the logic of immediate emancipation, although he probably was not acquainted with the tremendous problems involved in the administration of gradual emancipation or the way in which it prolonged resistance in defense of slavery. He had not yet read Elizabeth Heyrich's pamphlet or become familiar with the British movement. This difference in regard to gradual emancipation *versus* immediate emancipation between the two men was composed by agreement for each to express his own views and sign his own articles.

Whatever chance Lundy might have had to revive the weekly *Genius* was destroyed by Garrison's inexperience and youthful exuberance. Intolerance toward antislavery speeches and publications had been increasing everywhere since the Missouri debates, and as more and more antislavery people had withdrawn their support from the colonization societies those organizations had assumed a strongly *anti-Negro bias*. Antislavery pronouncements almost disappeared from the colonization journals. Garrison's articles in the *Genius* were strongly antislavery. They frankly urged immediate emancipation, and, admitting the failure of colonization, insisted upon education, religious instruction, and useful employment of the Negroes for intelligent citizenship. It was at this time that Garrison became acquainted with the pamphlets of Elizabeth Heyrich and James Duncan and the letters of John Rankin, and at this time, also, that he fully understood, from the Baltimore Negroes themselves, how bitterly they were opposed to colonization.[7] Certainly, for the first time he realized the degree to which the antislavery crusade embraced comprehensive welfare activities among free Negroes, and opposition to race prejudice as well as to slavery.

Lundy was a man of vast experience in the slave country. He knew first hand what he was talking about. He was truthful, he was moderate, he was a man of peace. Yet, even he had been assaulted and nearly killed by a slave trader in Baltimore the previous year.[8] Garrison was a different type of man. He knew nothing of slavery first hand, he was far from tolerant even in his religious views, and he was given to saying things in a way that hurt men—needlessly and sometimes cruelly. He lost subscribers for the *Genius* faster than Lundy could find new ones. Finally, in November 1829 he published a castigation of Francis Todd of Newburyport, Massachusetts, openly accusing him of amassing great wealth by surreptitiously engaging in the slave trade. Todd's ship had carried a cargo of slaves from Baltimore to New Orleans, but there was no evidence that Todd or the ship's captain were involved in any way other than as carriers. Garrison said: "It is no worse to fit out piratical cruisers, or to engage in the foreign slave trade, than to pursue a similar trade along our coasts; and the men who have the wickedness to participate therein, for the purpose of heaping up wealth should be *sentenced to solitary confinement for life; they are the enemies of their own species—highway robbers and murderers;* and their final doom will be, unless they speedily repent, *to occupy the lowest depths of perdition.*"[9]

The Baltimore grand jury indicted Garrison for libel. He was brought to trial, convicted, and fined the sum of $50. Unable to pay the fine and costs, he was sent to jail April 17, 1830. He was released on June 5, 1830, after payment of fine and costs by Arthur Tappan of New York. Lundy was unable to resume publication in Baltimore and returned to publishing a monthly, this time in Washington, D. C. Garrison went once more to Massachusetts where he lectured on slavery and began publication of the *Liberator* on January 1, 1831.

Lundy was well known to the antislavery men of Great Britain. He carried on an extensive correspondence with them and received their literature. Garrison learned his antislavery lessons from this literature, and in the Baltimore jail he wrote three lectures on slavery and colonization. The British government had long urged their West Indian colonies to develop programs of gradual emancipation. They had failed to do so. The result was a demand for immediate emancipation by act of Parliament. Elizabeth Heyrich's pamphlet had been one of the most powerful of the early arguments. The crusade for emancipation throughout the Empire came to a climax in the great parliamentary debates of 1830, with Thomas Clarkson, William Wilberforce, Zachary Macaulay, Thomas F. Buxton, and Henry Brougham leading the attack. They won their victory, finally, in 1833.

The British contest was of tremendous importance to the United States. Liberals in the United States did not need British denials of the right of property in man to inspire them; they had their own literature on the subject. In fact it was Anthony Benezet who had first inspired Sharp and Clarkson. But Charles Stuart, who had been responsible for Theodore Weld becoming an antislavery crusader, and had financed his education, had gone to England in the summer of 1829 to press for immediate emancipation. He contributed mightily to the cause in Great Britain, wrote his persuasive pamphlets on colonization from which Garrison borrowed heavily at a later date, and sent voluminous literature to Theodore Weld. The result was that Weld became the master authority in the field. He dominated the Lane Seminary debates, he trained the antislavery agents, he wrote the greatest of the antislavery pamphlets. The great newspapers of the United States could not ignore the debates in Parliament nor the act of emancipation. They were news. Nor could they refrain from comparing British performances with our own inaction. The parliamentary act was a milestone in the history of man's long struggle for freedom. Champions of slavery were dismayed, both by the widespread discussion and by the commencement of emancipation in the nearby islands. Nat Turner's insurrection and Walker's *Appeal* had revived all the fears of a Southern Santo Domingo. Freedom for the Negroes in the British West Indies would increase unrest among slaves in the United States. The slaves must be restrained at all costs. All agitation for emancipation in the United States must cease.

When Garrison left Baltimore in June 1830, he spoke in Philadelphia and New York to the members and friends of the societies for the abolition of slavery and improvement of free colored people, and in New Haven to the Negro parishioners of Simeon S. Jocelyn, a white home missionary. He then spoke in his home town of Newburyport in September 1830 and in Boston. Even those who recognized his talents and complete devotion to the cause were disturbed by his strong language, and particularly by his denunciation of the churches. On the other hand, some men who did not fully agree with him, but recognized his ability,

gave him support, among them Samuel J. May.[10]

The first issue of the *Liberator* contained the words, many times repeated, "I will be as harsh as truth, and as uncompromising as justice. On this subject, I do not wish to think, or speak, or write, with moderation." Far more important, however, was the following repudiation of gradual emancipation: "In Park Street Church, on the Fourth of July, 1829, in an address on slavery, I unreflectingly assented to the popular but pernicious doctrine of *gradual* abolition. I seize this opportunity to make a full and unequivocal recantation, and thus publickly [*sic*] to ask pardon of my God, of my country, and of my brethren the poor slaves, for having uttered a sentiment so full of timidity, injustice, and absurdity."

Garrison's complete repudiation of colonization came more slowly, but with equal finality. Speaking before the Negroes of New York and Philadelphia in June 1831, he quite frankly condemned colonizationists for their harsh treatment of Negroes, particularly their refusal to provide employment and education in order to drive them out of the country, for intensifying prejudice by repeatedly asserting that Negroes were incapable of elevation to equality with the whites, and for their apologies for slavery. Two years before he had urged Negroes to go to Liberia; now he said: "Every intelligent man of color, whom the Colonization Society induces to go to Liberia, ought to be considered as a traitor to your cause." This was the sort of free and easy imperiousness which caused men to hate him. On the other hand, there was a large element of truth in his sweeping indictment that followed: "Now," said he, "what a spectacle is presented to the world! . . . The story is proclaimed in our pulpits, in our state and national assemblies, in courts of law, in religious and secular periodicals,—among all parties, and in all quarters of the country,—that there is a *moral incapacity* in the people to do justly, to love mercy, and to walk uprightly—that they must always be the enemies and oppressors of the colored people—that no love of liberty, no dictate of duty, no precept of republicanism, no dread of retribution, no claim of right, no injunction of gospel, can possibly persuade them to do unto their colored countrymen, as they would that they should do unto them in a reversal of circumstances."[11]

That phase of the antislavery movement which dealt with the improvement of the free Negro was of major importance in the long contest for freedom. Benezet and others had made it the basis of all their activities in Philadelphia and New York, and by 1830 their work was bringing rich returns. One of the men educated in the Philadelphia schools was Samuel Cornish, a free-born man from Delaware. Cornish organized the first Negro Presbyterian congregation in New York in 1822. In 1827 he began publication of *Freedom's Journal*, the first Negro newspaper in the United States. In the prospectus, Cornish said: "As education is what renders civilized man superior to the savage; as the dissemination of knowledge is continually progressing among all other classes in the community; we deem it expedient to establish a paper and bring into operation all the means with which our benevolent Creator has endowed us, for the moral, religious, civil and literary improvement of our injured race . . . In our discussion of political subjects we shall ever regard the Constitution of the United States as our political star."[12] Cornish was the leader in the drive for Negro education and was one of the first to approach the race problem from an economic point of view. He served on the board of the American Anti-Slavery Society and the later American and Foreign Anti-Slavery Society.

Also in Philadelphia was Bishop Richard Allen,[13] associate of Bishop Asbury and founder of the African Methodist Episcopal Church; James Forten,[14] wealthy sailmaker, advocate of tem-

Bishops of the A. M. E. church

perance, peace, and woman's rights; Abraham Jones, founder of the African Protestant Episcopal Church; and many others. Forten called a convention of these men and others at Allen's church in January 1817 to combat the slanderous assertions of the newly organized American Colonization Society that Negroes were inherently inferior to the whites and their status unchangeable.[15] The convention opposed colonization and appointed a committee of correspondence. Large protest meetings and demonstrations soon followed in such cities as Boston, New York, Albany, and Hartford.[16] They failed to gain much of a hearing during the 1820's, but they gave solidarity to the free Negroes' refusal to migrate to Africa.

Anti-Negro riots in Cincinnati in 1829,[17] of which we shall speak later, forced many Negroes to flee into Canada, Michigan, western Pennsylvania, and New York. Negro leaders, fearful that colonization propaganda would precipitate mob action elsewhere, decided upon national organization to curb the repression. Cornish, Allen, and others called a convention at Philadelphia on September 15, 1830. There were delegates present from state organizations in Pennsylvania, New York, Rhode Island, Connecticut, Delaware, Maryland, and Virginia.[18] This convention approved migration to Canada for relief from persecution, but strongly opposed African colonization. A permanent organization was formed under the title American Society of Free Persons of Colour, for Improving Their Condition in the United States, for Purchasing Lands, and for the Establishment of a Settlement in the Province of Upper Canada. This organization, known as the Negro National Convention, met annually for five years.[19]

Samuel Cornish in 1827 had urged that a manual-labor college be established to train young men, in a practical demonstration of the error of colonization doctrine.[20] Simeon S. Jocelyn, the home missionary minister of a Negro congregation in New Haven, gave vigorous support to the idea between 1829 and 1831. His plan was for a part of the teaching to be done by members of the Yale faculty. Arthur and Lewis Tappan intended to give the school financial support. Benjamin Lundy presented the plan to the legislature of Connecticut, and apparently it was favorably received. Jocelyn, Lundy, Arthur Tappan, and Garrison were present at the First Annual Negro Convention in Philadelphia, June 6–11, 1831. The plan for the school was discussed and was ap-

Simeon S. Jocelyn

proved.[21] Steps were taken by Jocelyn and Tappan to push the project to early conclusion. The people of New Haven, however, where colonization received strong support, purported to believe that the city soon would receive an influx of Negroes from all over the world, to be trained as incendiaries and sent into the slave states to incite rebellion. The mayor called a public meeting, September 8, 1831, which resolved to "resist the establishment of the proposed college . . . by every lawful means." David Daggett was the leader of the colonizationist forces which opposed the school. He was professor of law at Yale. He had been elected mayor in 1828. He was soon to be chief justice of the state and to preside in the trial of Prudence Crandall, Quaker school teacher. He was a proud and prominent figure in his day, but in retrospect a tragic figure, nevertheless, because his dictum that Negroes were not citizens of the United States was totally wrong and grievously hurt an oppressed people. Roger S. Baldwin, later governor of the state and United States senator, spoke in vain against the action.[22]

The idea of establishing a Negro manual-labor college was not immediately abandoned by the

Negroes. The second annual convention in Philadelphia, June 4–13, 1832, concerned itself mainly with colonization in Canada and Africa. A debate was arranged between Garrison and R. R. Gurley, secretary of the American Colonization Society, and the convention reaffirmed its opposition.[23] The third annual convention, however, in Philadelphia, June 3–13, 1833, approved a trip by Garrison to England for funds for a college.[24] Garrison, who unquestionably had used his presence at the 1831 meeting to secure subscriptions to the *Liberator*, was not as much interested in securing funds in England for a school as he was in securing funds from the Negroes for passage to England. He went to England with aid from the Negroes but brought no money back for education. We shall come back to the Connecticut story in the case of Prudence Crandall.

Failure to establish the school in Connecticut or elsewhere was not as serious as it might seem. There had been opposition to it from the beginning by the Negroes and whites of the antislavery, humanitarian group. In a sense the colonizationists of New Haven did them a favor. There was a Negro among the students at Lane Seminary, and the Lane Rebels went to Oberlin only on condition Negroes would be admitted. They were admitted to Oneida Institute and to Hudson College. A group of influential and far-seeing Philadelphia Negroes, led by Richard Purvis, William Whipper, and James Forten, refused to recognize the need for special, separate organizations. They were very wise men who saw that unless Negroes remained part and parcel of the general community, without distinctive services, race prejudice would continue. The first annual report of the American Anti-Slavery Society said: "There is no way to destroy the prejudice which lies at the foundation of slavery, but to invite our colored brethren to a participation with us in all those happy and elevating institutions which are open to others. No efforts, however powerful or well-intended, which aim only to build up separate institutions for their special benefit, under the denomination so odious to them, of 'colored' or 'African' can heal the wound. They will end only in conferring upon their objects a keener sensibility to insult, and in establishing between the races an animosity, settled and remediless. Providence seems most kindly to have opened before us the path of safety and success, in creating so strong an anti-slavery sentiment in many

of our most hopeful seminaries."[25] The Fifth Annual Convention in Philadelphia, June 1–5, 1835, recommended that as far as possible the word "colored" be abandoned and the title "African" be dropped from institutions, such as churches, lodges, and societies. This group also was opposed to migration to Canada. Later, they favored political action to abolish slavery. It was never easy to make a choice between unfair treatment in mixed institutions on the one hand and segregation in all Negro schools and churches on the other.[26]

Out of this general background William Lloyd Garrison emerged as one of the most controversial figures of the antislavery movement. Opposition to publication of the *Liberator* was not slow to develop during the summer of 1831. It was neither more nor less than that which Birney and Lovejoy were to experience in Ohio and Illinois. Considering the rather more incisive language of Garrison, the publication of Walker's *Appeal* in Boston, and the Nat Turner insurrection, both at about the same time that the *Liberator* was founded, it was less than might have been expected; and it unquestionably was softened by Garrison's strong emphasis upon temperance, peace, and women's rights. So far as slavery was concerned he favored immediate emancipation and opposed colonization. He favored emancipation in the District of Columbia and abolition of the three-fifths rule in apportionment. He vigorously denied that there could be such a thing as property rights in man or that men could be denied natural rights because of race or color. He was opposed to violence and insurrection.

There was nothing new in any of the above. Garrison was sustained in his tenacious adherence to the principles by Rankin's *Letters* which he republished in the *Liberator* and by George Bourne's *The Book and Slavery Irreconcilable*. Fifteen persons assembled in Boston on November 13, 1831, about a year after the *Liberator* was launched, for the purpose of organizing an antislavery society. The basis of discussion was Elizabeth Heyrich's principle of immediate emancipation. Six persons refused to endorse it. Another meeting of ten persons assembled on December 16, and out of this meeting developed the New England Anti-Slavery Society. It was a fancy name for a feeble organization, because the Constitution, published in the *Liberator*, February 18, 1832, was signed by only a dozen men.[27] Membership increased very slowly, and after three years the name was changed to the Massachusetts Anti-Slavery Society.

Garrison's third contribution to the cause was publication in the *Liberator*, following the organization of the New England Society, of a portion of Charles Stuart's works on colonization, and publication of his own *Thoughts on African Colonization*. He brought together in this volume a veritable anthology of colonization diatribe, extracted for the most part from the *African Repository*.[28] The anti-Negro character of the organization was clearly demonstrated by the eloquent assertions of its corresponding secretary, its public speakers, and its resolutions and declarations of sentiments:

1) that the free Negroes were "notoriously ignorant," "degraded," "miserable," "mentally diseased," "broken spirited," "debased," "indolent," "abject," "sorrowful," "vicious," "corrupt," and "depraved";

2) that the public safety required rigorous treatment of the slaves and restraints upon the free Negroes;

3) that all Negroes must be removed from the country and their condition here be made so uncomfortable as to force them to want to go;

4) that any effort for the moral, intellectual, and political improvement of the Negroes within the United States was foreign to the organization's objectives and powers;

5) that the society had no intention of interfering with slavery and quite properly remained aloof from the question.

The result of its activities was a general deterioration of public support for employment, education, and equality of the Negroes, encouragement of mob violence, and strengthening of slavery.

Garrison sailed for England on May 1, 1833. He went as the agent of the American Convention to collect funds for a Negro college, and as agent of the New England Anti-Slavery Society to counteract the activities and influence in that country of the American Colonization Society. He certainly was proceeding on the basis of a lack of information, and, perhaps, as one very reliable scholar implies, on the basis of a desire for notoriety.

It can be demonstrated that the Reverend Nathanial Paul, Negro leader in opposition to colonization, had been in England for a considerable length of time collecting money for education, that Garrison went to England on funds solicited from the Negroes for the purpose of duplicating

Paul's efforts, that he collected no money, and that he returned to the United States on funds advanced by Paul in response to incomplete representations of Garrison. It can also be demonstrated that Charles Stuart's indefatigable labors over a three-year period, his brilliant exposé of colonization, and his enviable reputation among British statesmen had destroyed all possibility of British support for the American Colonization Society before Garrison's arrival in England. Garrison became acquainted with the British leaders. He obtained a wealth of information, a large collection of British antislavery literature, and the inspiration of association with other great humanitarians—all invaluable to one who had dedicated his life to freedom for the slaves and was editing an antislavery newspaper. Garrison returned to the United States in the late summer of 1833. It was four years since he had gone to Baltimore to assist Benjamin Lundy. Long and careful study of his writings, speeches, and relationships in comparison with other men in the movement leads one to certain inescapable conclusions.

He had an ability to write. In fact, at times he wrote brilliantly. There was a certain positiveness, even a doctrinaire quality about his ideas, and a harshness, sometimes a fury, in his language. Slaveholders hated him because of it, but that was of little consequence. They hated anyone who spoke against slavery. What was its effect upon the progress of emancipation? The answer must be paradoxical. Nothing short of intense, uncompromising, even violent denunciation of slavery and of slaveholders would have aroused the country, but it alienated the support of some moderate men. It did not retard emancipation because there was nothing to retard. It did not evoke a violent defense of slavery because slaveholders had always been vehement in its defense. However, Garrison gloried in opposition, magnified it beyond reality, thought of himself as a potential martyr, and became insufferably arrogant at times in his treatment of other men, to the detriment of the cause.

He did not aid slaves to escape in the manner of Levi Coffin or a hundred other men. He did not establish schools and teach Negroes in the tradition of Benezet, as did Marius Robinson, Hiram Wilson, and others. He did not aid them in mastery of mechanical arts and agriculture as did Augustus Wattles. He did not brave the fury of countless mobs as did Theodore Weld, Henry

B. Stanton, and Elijah Lovejoy. He did not write
the solid treatises of antislavery literature. He did
not aid the Negroes financially, rather he relied
heavily upon *them* for support of his paper and
purchase of his books. He did not provide legal assistance in cases of Negroes who were kidnapped
or white men who were prosecuted for assisting
fugitives. He did not engage in the furious contests in political campaigns and legislative halls
as did Thomas Morris, James G. Birney, and
Joshua Giddings. In fact, *he was a man of distinctly narrow limitations among the giants of the
antislavery movement.* But he provided, in the
Liberator, an opportunity for the Negro leaders
to express their views and encourage their people. His strong, relentless championship of human
rights; his refusal to recognize distinctions of color
or race with respect to ability, achievement, and
rights; his condemnation of every sort of injustice
were an encouragement and a blessing to an
oppressed people which can not be measured but
was very great.

Finally, Garrison denounced the Constitution
as a proslavery document. It was not—and was
not intended to be—a proslavery document. In
fact it provided ample scope for antislavery legislation by Congress. Garrison's intemperate language regarding the Constitution and government
of the United States, and his ultimate refusal to
vote because government rested upon force hurt
the cause of emancipation. It was ill-considered
and without justification. It played into the hands
of the proslavery men. It was an obstacle to political action against slavery. It split the American
Anti-Slavery Society, and ultimately the church
associations of New England. It need not have
done so had the colossal conceit of the man not
led him to claim credit for almost everything that
was done in the movement before 1840. He made
a contribution. It was neither a large nor an overpowering one, and sometimes it was a negative
one.

THE AMERICAN ANTI-SLAVERY SOCIETY

Chapter 20

The antislavery movement did not begin with the organization of the American Anti-Slavery Society in December 1833. That would seem to be a simple truism at this point in our discussion, but it needs re-emphasis. The movement began with the Quakers and continued with the Presbyterians and Baptists. In pre-Revolutionary days, it was largely denominational with the Quakers, less so with the Presbyterians and Baptists. It ceased to be strictly denominational with the organization of the Eastern abolition societies in the post-Revolutionary period. It broadened out in the evangelism of the 1820's, but remained largely Presbyterian and Congregational even during the 1830's. *The movement, however, was as much political as it was religious, even more so.* We have traced it in the political treatises of the Revolutionary period; in the legislative acts and court decisions of those states which abolished slavery; in the debates of the Constitutional Convention, the Congresses of the United States both before and after 1789, and the conventions of new states; and in the climactic public discussion of the Missouri question. The movement, then, was both religious and political, and it did not suddenly change with the organization of the American Anti-Slavery Society in 1833, nor with the schism in the society in 1840.

Early in 1831 in New York City a small group of men began to pull together for the first time the widely scattered threads of moral democracy reaching back to pre-Revolutionary days. They were Lewis Tappan, George Bourne, Joshua Leavitt, Simeon Jocelyn, William Goodell, and Theodore Weld.[1] What a combination of intellect, courage, and Christian faith! What a solid foundation of antislavery tradition, evangelistic fervor, and equalitarianism! Tappan represented the Eastern liberal tradition of opposition to slavery and aid to the Negroes extending back to Woolman and Benezet, and including in its long history men like Benjamin Franklin, Benjamin Rush, William Rawle, John Jay, Rufus King, Theodore Dwight, and Elias Boudinot. Tappan spoke always for his brother Arthur also, and for the numerous wealthy patrons of Christian benevolence in New York City.

George Bourne, who had said that "every man who holds Slaves and who pretends to be a Christian or a Republican, is either an incurable Idiot who cannot distinguish good from evil, or an obdurate sinner who resolutely defies every social, moral, and divine requisition," represented the Presbyterian preachers from the South whose opposition to slavery had led to exile, including men like Gilliland and Rankin.[2]

Joshua Leavitt was a stolid New England lawyer and preacher, trained at Yale by the liberal Nathaniel Taylor. He edited the New York *Evangelist*, the paper founded by the Tappans to expound and popularize in New York City the new theology of Charles Grandison Finney. He had been writing against slavery since 1825 and was destined to be, as editor of the *Independent* after 1848, one of the most respected journalists in the country.[3]

Simeon S. Jocelyn was a home missionary serving the Negroes of New Haven. He was busily engaged in trying to establish the Negro manual-labor school in that city for the free Negroes of the United States and West Indies. William Goodell was the editor of the *Genius of Temperance*. Theodore Weld represented liaison with England through Charles Stuart, with the Finney converts at Oneida Institute, and with the Presbyterian preachers of southern Ohio. He also provided the most profound knowledge of the literature on slavery and the greatest experience in public address.[4]

These were able men, and out of this original meeting came plans for a new antislavery society of national proportions. The American Convention had done significant work in the period of gradual emancipation, but it was a loose confederation of state societies designed to deal with a practical problem of assistance to free Negroes. It did not have the funds, the press, or the agents needed to conduct a campaign of education, and it was definitely local in character. The new society was two years in the making. The final step was the formal organization of the American Anti-Slavery Society, with a constitution and Declaration of Sentiments by a convention in Philadelphia, December 4, 1833. The foundations of the society were laid during the two intervening years. Its formal organization could have come at one time as well as another, either earlier or later than that date, for the society did not initiate the movement, *the leaders of the movement organized the society for a purpose.* Before we expand upon that statement, let us explore the development of these two important years.

Theodore Weld went west after the New York meeting, on that all-important survey for the Society for Promoting Manual Labor in Literary Institutions. He conferred with Beriah Green and Elizur Wright at Hudson College in the Western Reserve, with Birney and the Allans at Huntsville, Alabama, and with Marius Robinson at Nashville, Tennessee. He was active in founding Lane Seminary at Cincinnati, in bringing the students from Oneida Institute, and in making preparations for the Lane debate which took place in January 1834, directly following the organization of the American Anti-Slavery Society. This action channeled into the antislavery movement the main stream of Christian evangelism, drew together the most able of Finney's converts under Weld's antislavery tutelage, and marshaled the antislavery forces precisely where the political

leaders of the next three decades were presently serving their apprenticeship.

The British during these two years moved relentlessly forward to emancipation in the West Indies by Act of Parliament. Some men said this was Britain's finest hour. All men agreed, though for different reasons, that her decision was a momentous one. The United States could not possibly have avoided its impact. It was news of first magnitude and received coverage by the public press to a degree the antislavery cause could never have had under other circumstances. More important was the fact that the American Colonization Society was in trouble and was seeking endorsement of the colonization principle by the British liberals. The Negroes were consolidating their opposition to the society, and humanitarians were withdrawing their support in ever-increasing numbers. The society sent Elliot Cresson to Britain to gain the support of men like Wilberforce. It is not likely that British men of so much stature could have been persuaded to give unqualified endorsement to expatriation of the Negroes. Charles Stuart's work in Britain, and especially his pamphlets against colonization, which gave to the antislavery movement in the United States the prestige of British support, was of paramount importance.

During these two years James G. Birney, slaveholding planter and distinguished lawyer of Huntsville, Alabama, traveled the lonely road previously taken by Rankin, Gilliland, and others from the lower South to Kentucky and eventual exile. He was a slaveholder when Weld talked to him in the spring of 1832. He was an agent of the American Colonization Society for a year beginning in September 1832. He then organized a society to promote gradual emancipation in Kentucky. After the Lane Debate in January 1834, he supported immediate emancipation and became an agent of the American Anti-Slavery Society. The articles which Birney wrote in support of colonization and published in the Alabama newspapers were more profoundly critical of slavery than any others ever published in the states of the Black Belt. They were as free of anti-Negro bias as any ever published in support of colonization. He never believed in biological inequality and racial inferiority, and he moved instinctively out of the slave country, out of the colonization movement, and away from gradual emancipation. He moved more slowly during these two years, perhaps, than some other men, but he moved with dignity and conviction and power, and above all, with a devotion to human rights seldom equaled, never surpassed.[5]

Meanwhile, Elizur Wright, professor of mathematics and natural philosophy at Western Reserve College, was brought to New York. He served as corresponding secretary of the committee during the two years of preparatory work. He then continued in that post after formal organization in December 1833, without any change in his official duties. He was in charge of all publications, all correspondence, and all field agents, without much assistance until 1837. He wrote and published in two separate editions in 1833 *The Sin of Slavery, and Its Remedy; Containing Some Reflections on the Moral Influence of African Colonization.* He also supervised the republication and distribution of earlier antislavery pamphlets, both British and American. These were not previously available, except to a select few. He supervised the launching of the *Emancipator* as the official antislavery newspaper of the national organization under the editorship of Charles W. Dennison, then of William Goodell, and finally of Joshua Leavitt. He corresponded with a great many men in all parts of the free states who could be counted on to join in forming the national organization.[6]

Finally, during these two years, William Lloyd Garrison established the *Liberator* in Boston, in January 1831. He organized the New England Anti-Slavery Society in Boston in January 1832. He wrote his *Thoughts on African Colonization* and established a firm relationship with the free Negroes of the East. He journeyed to England in 1833 in time to witness the excitement of final victory in Parliament. He had, by December 1833, gained wide notoriety. He was regarded as a fanatic by many, in the South as an incendiary.

Little more remains to be said about the years 1831–33. The most significant development had been the exodus from the colonization society by the antislavery men, the consolidation of Negro opposition to colonization, failure of the colonizationists to gain approval of the British antislavery leaders, and publication of the powerful anticolonization arguments of Charles Stuart, William Lloyd Garrison, and Elizur Wright.[7] These were to be followed by Birney's *Letter on Colonization* in 1834 and by William Jay's *Inquiry* in 1835.[8] Together, they constituted a solid and unanswerable indictment of the principle of expatriation

and an exposé of the anti-Negro bias of the organization. The society was never again able to bring liberals to its support. The way was open for a militant antislavery crusade.

There was lingering opposition from some of the leaders of the old abolition societies in the East, but the last regular session of the American Convention was held in Philadelphia in 1829.[9] There was hesitation and some confusion for a time over endorsement of immediate emancipation. There was too much initial reliance upon British precedent. There was some thought of continuing the fatal loose association of local and state societies of the convention period. Somehow, wise counsels prevailed, and the American Anti-Slavery Society quickly became the most powerful of all the benevolent and reform organizations.

The society was formally organized in Philadelphia on December 4, 1833. The meeting was called on very short notice, and the fifty-six persons who came and were allowed membership did not represent the strength of the movement. Nor were the statements of objectives and declaration of sentiment adequate. The first anniversary meeting, which was held in New York, May 6–8, 1834, was far more representative, not being so exclusively Eastern, and antislavery principles and objectives were shortly defined more clearly by the instructions to agents and otherwise than by the organizational meeting.[10]

Every person who subscribed to the principles of the society and made a contribution (paid dues) was a member and was entitled to vote at the business meetings. Theoretically, this requirement excluded slaveholders and colonizationists, but there is no record of slaveholders having applied nor of colonizationists having been rejected. The principles of individual membership made this a national organization rather than a federation of local societies whose delegates met in the annual conventions. It was important for a number of reasons. Men in all parts of the free states were members of the American Anti-Slavery Society. They were also members of state societies and of local societies. Membership in one was not dependent upon membership in the others, some people belonging only to the national organization, and a great many more belonging only to the local societies. Cultural isolation was not as great in 1830 as it had been twenty years previously, but a trip to the nearest city for most people required days of difficult travel. There were

few communities in which more than a half dozen men had made such a trip, and those who had were regarded as quite out of the ordinary. Thus it was that the annual meetings of the society were dominated by men from the East, and the state societies soon came to be larger, financially stronger, and more important than the parent organization, which exercised no direct supervision or control over them.

The objectives of the society were stated in the constitution as follows:

"The object of this Society is the entire abolition of slavery in the United States. While it admits that each State in which slavery exists, has, by the Constitution of the United States, the exclusive right to *legislate* in regard to its abolition in said State, it shall aim to convince all our fellow-citizens, by arguments addressed to their understandings and consciences, that slaveholding is a heinous crime in the sight of God, and that the duty, safety, and best interests of all concerned, require its *immediate abandonment,* without expatriation. The Society will also endeavor, in a constitutional way, to influence Congress to put an end to the domestic slave trade, and to abolish slavery in all those portions of our common country which come under its control, especially in the District of Columbia—and likewise to prevent the extension of it to any State that may be hereafter admitted to the Union.

"This Society shall aim to elevate the character and condition of the people of color, by encouraging their intellectual, moral, and religious improvement, and by removing public prejudice, that thus they may, according to their intellectual and moral worth, share an equality with the whites, of civil and religious privileges; but this Society will never, in any way, countenance the oppressed in vindicating their rights by resorting to physical force."

The Declaration of Sentiments—Garrison's one contribution—was a journalistic triumph but little else. It added to the antislavery program a strong denial of the right of the slaveowner to compensation, and it stated certain reasons why slavery was a national problem. Once more, however, Garrison curtsied to the doctrine of state rights by saying: "We fully and unanimously recognize the sovereignty of each State, to legislate exclusively on the subject of slavery which is tolerated within its limits; we concede that Congress, under the present national compact, has no right to interfere with any of the slave States in relation to this momentous subject."

Despite an elaborate hierarchy, the affairs of the American Anti-Slavery Society were controlled by the original committee members and a few others they brought into the select circle. Arthur Tappan was elected president and held that office until 1840. His brother and business partner, Lewis Tappan, was a member of the executive committee and was in the office to attend to details some part of every day. John Rankin, New York merchant and trustee of Auburn Theological Seminary, was a member of the executive committee until 1838, and William Green, Jr., another New

Convention of the Anti-Slavery Society, London, 1840

York merchant, served as treasurer until the same date. Elizur Wright was the only corresponding secretary, in charge of publications as well, until 1837. Then James G. Birney was brought in to supervise the agency system, and Henry B. Stanton to supervise public relations and finance. These men, together with Joshua Leavitt, editor of the New York *Evangelist* and later of the *Emancipator*, Amos A. Phelps, the first successful agent of the society, and John Greenleaf Whittier, gentle Quaker poet, were the New York axis of the organization. Theodore D. Weld, Henry B. Stanton, and James G. Birney were the great triumvirate, dominating the agency system, finance, and public affairs.

We come back now to our earlier statement that the American Anti-Slavery Society did not initiate a movement, but that the leaders of the movement organized the society for a purpose. The antislavery movement which these men directed after 1830 and to which they dedicated their lives and fortunes was not encompassed within the stated objectives and activities of the American Anti-Slavery Society. There was nothing new in the statement of objectives or in the declaration of sentiments. In fact, except for the preamble of the constitution, it was a weak statement of an inadequate program. It was a retrogression because it ignored the Fugitive Slave Act, kidnapping, and the entire field of citizenship and civil rights of Negroes so thoroughly discussed in the Missouri debates. Worst of all were its near fatal concession to state rights with re-

spect to slavery and the way in which it shied away from an endorsement of direct political action. We must not, then, take these original documents too seriously. We must go beyond them for the full understanding of what was happening.

The leaders of the movement were devout Christians and men of exemplary character. The evidence on that point is overwhelming. The antislavery movement reached maturity by way of Christian benevolence. Evangelism provided the antislavery lecturers, churches served as their forums, and the sin of slavery was the central theme of the indictment during the early 1830's. But, just as the antislavery indictment was broader than the creed of any one denomination and profited greatly from the interdenominational co-operation of the evangelistic movement, so too was the antislavery indictment broader than the *sin of slavery*. Slavery was established by law and sustained by law, and it had to be overthrown by political action. The civil rights of Negroes had to be protected by the law, and unconstitutional laws had to be repealed. In fact, the full scope of antislavery action from colonial days had lain more completely within the political arena than within the church. It continued to be so. These men used the full strength of the church in the early 1830's, but they moved from the beginning along the lines of political action as well, and they sacrificed church support to whatever degree, and whenever, it was necessary to do so.

The men who constituted the power and directive force of the American Anti-Slavery Society—Lewis Tappan, Elizur Wright, Joshua Leavitt, James G. Birney, Theodore Weld, Henry B. Stanton, William Goodell—combined the two between 1829 and 1839 in a giant religious and intellectual crusade. Their appeal was to professional men—men of property, position, and influence in their communities. These men were offended and repulsed by Garrison's vagaries and vehemence and above all by his cheap cynicism toward political institutions. He had no office in the society, but succeeded in gaining control in 1840 by the simple process of swamping the convention with votes from Boston.

The New York group organized the American and Foreign Anti-Slavery Society after Garrison took the parent society off to Boston. Neither of the two societies was thereafter of much importance. The movement had become primarily political in 1839. It was scarcely touched by the schism in 1840, but, under the hard core of leadership established in 1829, moved forward through the agency of the Liberty Party, then the Free Soil Party, and finally the Republican Party, expanding with each reorganization. How did it gain enough support in ten years to permit successful launching of a new political party? The answer lies in publications, agents, auxiliary societies, and a bitter contest over civil rights.

The official organ of the American Anti-Slavery Society (every reform society had an official organ) was the *Emancipator*. The paper was established before the society was formally organized. It was edited first by Charles W. Dennison, then by William Goodell, and finally by Joshua Leavitt. Dennison and Goodell were both able men, though not brilliant, but the mediocrity of the paper under their editorships may well have been due to lack of perspective in the front office. Leavitt, who edited the New York *Evangelist* before taking over the *Emancipator* in 1837, was an excellent editor. He had been a powerful member of the central organization from the first. He wrote vigorously; he was alert to political implications of the movement; and he pressed relentlessly for greater emphasis upon direct political action. The *Emancipator* in the first three years, however, was not of sufficient quality to gain converts or to divert attention from the *Liberator*, and the two newspapers combined, or a half dozen such could never have carried the antislavery message convincingly enough, or to enough people, to have promoted organized effort. Only lecturing agents were able to do that, and they had to be devout, courageous, dedicated men and women. They had to have access to church congregations, and they had to be able speakers. The society developed an elaborate publications program which we shall consider presently, but publications did not make converts. The converts bought publications.

The second initial effort of the general management was the appointment of agents. Elizur Wright wrote to Weld on December 31, 1833: "We want a number of faithful mighty agents, in whose persons the Society shall live and breathe and wax strong before the public. We must have men who will electrify the mass wherever they move,—and they must move on no small scale."[11] Wright was urging Weld to accept an agency. He did not know that Weld was presently arranging the Lane Seminary debate. Weld and Stanton, who towered above everyone then enlisted in the

cause, were about to systematize the entire antislavery argument in a brilliant indictment for the training of agents, to chart the way for them by spectacular campaigns, Stanton in Rhode Island and Weld in Ohio, New York, and Pennsylvania, and to find and train the men the society needed. Meanwhile, the executive committee had appointed William Lloyd Garrison, Amos Phelps, and Samuel J. May as traveling agents.[12] These appointments were followed by those of Calvin Pepper, Ray Potter, Thomas Williams, John Greenleaf Whittier, Charles W. Dennison, William Goodell, Beriah Green, Charles Stuart, and George Thompson. Theodore Weld refused to go out until the autumn of 1834, and James G. Birney was given a special agency to establish a newspaper in Kentucky.

Each agent was given a commission and was paid the salary of eight dollars a week and expenses usually paid to agents of the Tract Society. The commissions stated the purpose of the society to be "awakening the attention of our whole community to the character of American Slavery, and presenting the claims and urging the rights of the colored people of the United States; so as to promote, in the most efficient manner, the immediate abolition of slavery, and the restoration of our colored brethren to their equal rights as citizens."[13] The particular instructions clearly indicated a campaign of education and persuasion to "produce a just public sentiment, which shall appeal both to the conscience and love of character of our slave-holding fellow-citizens, and convince them that both their duty and their welfare require the immediate abolition of slavery."[14] Agents were to emphasize the "*Sin of Slavery*, because our main hope is in the consciences of men, and it requires little logic to prove that it is always safe to do right." They were to oppose compensated emancipation. They were to oppose all colonization programs. They were to emphasize the right of the slaves to freedom and to equal rights as citizens, and they were to refrain from all discussion of plans of emancipation, as designed and calculated to detract from the main question and create confusion and dissension. On this point the instructions contained one of the most relevant statements of the entire movement: "What ought to be done can be done. If the *great* question were decided, and if half the ingenuity now employed to defend slavery were employed to abolish it, it would impeach the wisdom of American

Anti-Slavery Meeting, Exeter Hall, 1841

statesmen to say they could not, with the Divine blessing, steer the ship through."

Agents were instructed to become familiar with certain antislavery literature which had been printed or reprinted by the society, including Thomas Clarkson's *Thoughts,* Charles Stuart's *West India Question,* Lydia Maria Child's *Appeal,* George Stroud's *Laws Relating to Slavery,* John Paxton's *Letters,* John Rankin's *Letters,* David Lee Child's *Despotism of Freedom,* and William Lloyd Garrison's *Thoughts on Colonization.* They were to approach every community through a church and minister of the gospel if possible. They were to form auxiliary societies. They were to solicit funds but not by collections in public meetings.[15]

The first agents appointed by the society were not qualified to promote even this abbreviated program. Charles Stuart and George Thompson encountered the usual public antipathy for British men and measures. Stuart remained in the United States and rendered additional great service to the cause, but not as a public speaker. Thompson was literally driven out of the country by mob violence.[16] Garrison, being a timid soul except when safely behind the editorial desk, hastened back to Boston at the first sign of violence. Whittier, too, was such a kind and gentle soul as

Amos A. Phelps

to be utterly unfitted for the rigorous job of publicly advocating unpopular causes. William Goodell was an extremely able lecturer. He was a kindly man, and he believed thoroughly in the Union and the constitutional power to abolish slavery. Later, he was to edit the *Friend of Man* at Utica and to emerge as a stalwart in the political action phase of the movement, but he was too dull, factual, perhaps one might say scholarly, to be a successful lecturer at this stage. Beriah Green was handicapped by too much responsibility. He had become president of Oneida Institute only to lose his students to Lane Seminary. Nevertheless, he made Oneida an important center of antislavery philosophy and training, lectured widely in western New York against strong opposition, and wrote some very powerful monographs. Calvin Pepper was primarily interested in the temperance movements and lectured for the American Anti-Slavery Society only for a short time in western New York.[17] Ray Potter was a Baptist minister in Pawtucket, Rhode Island, and his work in the antislavery cause was limited largely to that state. He paved the way for Stanton's agency in 1835 and was active in the organization of the Rhode Island Anti-Slavery Society.[18] Charles W. Dennison began his agency in Connecticut and then moved to eastern New York. Apparently, the executive committee doubted his ability as a public speaker. He later helped found the Delaware State Anti-Slavery Society and became its corresponding secretary.[19] Samuel J. May, Unitarian minister at Brooklyn, Connecticut, who had helped Garrison organize the New England Anti-Slavery Society and served as general agent for the Massachusetts Anti-Slavery Society for eighteen years, was an agent for the American Anti-Slavery Society in 1834 and again in 1835. He lectured first in Vermont, where he encountered some opposition. He was interested in a multitude of reform and benevolent activities; and, later, was active in the underground railroad. Amos A. Phelps was given a permanent appointment in January 1834 at a salary of $1,000 a year plus traveling expenses. He worked in Maine and New Hampshire principally, later publishing his lectures. He was the only successful New England antislavery lecturer before Wendell Phillips, though not the only one to work in that area. Except for Beriah Green, these first agents operated in the East on limited appointments, largely on a local basis, and without too much success.

THEODORE WELD:
THE AGENCY SYSTEM

Chapter 21

The Lane Seminary students withdrew from that institution on October 21, 1834, and intensified their welfare work among the Negroes of Cincinnati. Theodore Weld and Henry B. Stanton left Cincinnati about the same time to begin work as agents of the American Anti-Slavery Society. Weld stayed in Ohio, Stanton went to Rhode Island. These two men were the masters of argumentation and antislavery philosophy. They had great physical stamina, courage, and devotion to the cause. No other person ever remotely approached the achievements of either in the movement except Birney, and his talents lay elsewhere than in public address.

This was the crucial test. It was clear by this time that antislavery literature would not arouse the nation. Newspapers, periodicals, and pamphlets were invaluable sources of inspiration and education, and they provided a cohesive element to the movement, but at least a few people in any given community had to be aroused and enlisted in the cause before this literature could come into the community and through these few people be passed on to others. Agents, more specifically, lecturers, whether local men or from outside, had to awaken the community and do it effectively enough to establish a local antislavery society. No one among the earlier agents of the society had been even moderately successful. It was Weld and Stanton who proved the efficacy of the agency system and thereby saved the movement.

Weld began his work at Ripley, in the church of his old friend, John Rankin. He spoke elsewhere in the churches of the antislavery preach-ers from the South, below Chillicothe, then moved north through Frankfort and Bloomingsburg to Circleville.[1] This area, embracing several counties, was already organized as the Paint Valley Anti-Slavery Society. When Weld finished his work here, the society had 4,000 members and was the largest in the nation. In fact, at the end of Weld's lecture tour in Ohio that state had one-third of all the antislavery societies in the country. Weld went from Circleville to Putnam and paved the way for organization there, in April 1835, of the Ohio State Anti-Slavery Society. The students from Lane Seminary had gone to Oberlin meanwhile and were just beginning their work in the spring term of 1835.

Weld went from Putnam to Pittsburgh, Pennsylvania, to the General Assembly of the Presbyterian Church. His work among the delegates was remarkably successful, owing no doubt in part to the long-continued activities of John Rankin in the church. In his report to Elizur Wright, Weld said: "I find that *forty-eight* Commissioners in the assembly are decidedly with us on the subject of slavery—believing slavery a *sin* and *immediate emancipation a duty. Twenty-seven* of this number are ministers in *slave states.* Last year, it is not known that there were more than *two decided immediate abolitionists* in the Assembly . . . This year immediate abolitionists constitute nearly *one-fourth part* of the Assembly."[2]

Weld returned to Ohio by way of Washington, Pennsylvania, and took a number of former Lane Seminary rebels from Oberlin to Cleveland. He trained them during August and September 1835 as agents in the law office of John W. Sterling, who had been present at the organization of the American Anti-Slavery Society and in later years served as trustee of Oberlin College. Six of these—Samuel L. Gould, James A. Thome, Huntington Lyman, John W. Alvord, William T. Allan, and Sereno W. Streeter—were then appointed agents by the society and assigned to Ohio.[3] Weld went on to Oberlin where, in November 1835, he lectured for three weeks, thoroughly indoctrinating the college and the community, continuing the training of the six agents, and recruiting others for the cause. He then went to Pittsburgh in December, to Utica, New York, in January and February 1836, to Rochester in March and April, and to Troy in May and June.

The young men Weld had trained at Cleveland and Oberlin lectured throughout Ohio during the winter of 1835–36, then returned to Oberlin. These, as we shall see, were the awful years of mob violence, and Weld was breaking under the strain, but he and Stanton, who almost single-handed had converted Rhode Island, and Weld's trainees, had won a tremendous victory. They not only had resisted intimidation and carried their message to hundreds of thousands, they had, in doing so, established a multitude of state and local societies and had brought to their support the men of influence, position, and power in every local community they visited. The agency system was proved to be the key to a successful anti-slavery crusade.

Weld made his last antislavery address on July 4, 1836. The executive committee had decided to commission a total of seventy agents to complete the work in the Northern states, and the responsibility of finding these agents fell principally to Weld and Stanton with some assistance, though very little, from Whittier. Weld went first to Utica, from which place he canvassed the Lane Seminary-Oberlin men. He then toured Ohio, New York, and New England. Stanton and Whittier went to Pennsylvania, and Stanton then joined Weld in western New York. Finney was causing trouble, and Weld took time to go once more to Oberlin to wage with him again the battle over evangelism *versus* direct antislavery action. Weld had defended Finney against criticism by the New York committee as vigorously as he now argued with. Finney's theological students that they should battle for the Lord first by attacking the giant sin of slavery.

Weld won on all accounts as usual. He could say in one letter, with reference to Finney: "I have no doubt but that he has thought, felt, said and done less on the subject than he should have done. I have no doubt but he ought to have given it more prominence in his public prayers and preaching. He should have encouraged the monthly concert for the abolition of slavery more heartily. This I have told him in full." Then Weld made his defense of Finney: "The truth is Finney has always been in revivals of religion. It is his great business, aim, and *absorbing passion* to promote them . . . Finney feels about revivals of religion and the promotion of the church and ministry in doctrines and measures, just as you and I do about anti-slavery . . . He never prays you know for Temperance, Moral Reform, or any other moral enterprise in public except at a meeting held expressly to promote that object . . . Here I am persuaded he misconceives duty, for the sin of slavery in this country is *Omnipresent*. At the present crisis it not only *overshadows* all others, but it involves all others, and *absorbs* them into itself; and it is my deliberate conviction that re-

Theodore Weld at ninety years of age

vivals, moral reforms, etc., must and [will] remain stationary, until the Temple is Cleansed."[4] This conviction Weld pressed upon the students with such force that all but one returned to the ranks of antislavery agents.[5]

All of the Lane-Oberlin men were sent directly into the field to work. Most of the others from all parts of the country were taken to New York where, between November 8 and November 27, 1836, they were put through an intensive training. Weld organized the program and followed the same general outline embraced within the Lane Seminary debates, the training program at Cleveland, and on his own agency. Other men were brought in to assist in the meetings, which were held regularly three times each day. Beriah Green was there, and Henry B. Stanton, Charles Stuart, Simeon Jocelyn, and William Lloyd Garrison.

The agents were trained to meet mob violence as well as the devious arguments of hostile audiences. They were made familiar with every aspect of the broad, general indictment of slavery, including the terrible effects of perpetual servitude and debasement of the intellect, denial of personal rights, cruelties, and effects upon the slaveholders of the exercise of unlimited powers; the necessity for immediate rather than gradual emancipation; the national, rather than limited sectional, interest and responsibility in slavery and emancipation; the broad problems of race prejudice and the treatment of free Negroes; the evils of colonization; the constitutional arguments and legal aspects of the problem of emancipation; the positive-good argument in defense of slavery; and the responsibility of Christian men and women to act against slavery. All imaginable objections to emancipation, based upon the experiences of men like Weld and Green, were brought up and refuted.

The theoretical number of seventy agents never became a reality. Five of those originally chosen did not go out to lecture because of illness, death, or changed circumstances. Twenty of the original ones were dropped in June 1837 because they were not successful and, in at least one case, not responsible. This was a year of economic distress in the country and both a shortage of funds and rapidly increasing costs forced the society to discontinue all but the most efficient and successful agencies. The number of agents, therefore, steadily declined, and, as state and local societies increased in number and importance, more and more reliance was placed upon local rather than traveling agents. Meanwhile, however, the "seventy" performed a miracle of organization at the local level and revolutionized public sentiment at the North.

Who were the men and women selected by Weld and Stanton to carry on the work they themselves had begun? First of all, there were the Lane Seminary-Oberlin men. We are already acquainted with the work of eight of these men, not including Weld and Stanton, who had been agents of the society in Ohio and New York. They were William T. Allan, John W. Alvord, Augustus Wattles, Marius Robinson, Hiram Wilson, James A. Thome, Huntington Lyman, and Samuel Gould. Six others, original Lane Seminary rebels, were now appointed. Hiram Foote (1808–89) lectured at Hartford, Brookfield, Hubbard, Youngstown, and Poland, in Ohio, returned to Oberlin Theological Seminary in 1838, and filled pastorates, 1839 to 1875, at Joliet, Illinois, and Racine, Waukesha, and Broadhead, Wisconsin.[6] Edward Weed lectured in Adams, Brown, Clermont, Pike, and Highland counties, Ohio.[7] George Whipple was principal of Oberlin's preparatory department and professor of mathematics, secretary of the American Missionary Association, and at the time of his death in 1876 president-elect of Howard University.[8] He lectured for the society only during vacations. In addition, there was Calvin Waterbury, who lectured in Ohio and New York, and Courtland Avery.

Weld, who went into the New York office as general supervisor and consultant, insisted upon expansion of the work among free Negroes. Two other Lane Seminary rebels were commissioned to work along the same lines as Augustus Wattles and Hiram Wilson. John Miter worked in the schools of Newark, New Jersey, and William Yates at Flushing, Long Island. The total number of Lane Seminary-Oberlin men working actively in the movement in these critical years was twenty, nearly one-third of all the agents of the parent society.

Amos Phelps, who had been the only successful agent in 1833, and later had edited the *Emancipator,* was one of the "seventy." So, too, was John Rankin of Ripley, Ohio. James G. Birney and Angelina Grimké, with whom we shall deal separately in the next two chapters, were commissioned. Beyond these, there were about twenty more distinguished persons commissioned as agents.

Jonathan Blanchard (1811–92), a native of Vermont, educated at Middlebury College, Andover, and Lane Theological Seminary, became pastor of the Sixth Presbyterian Church in Cincinnati in 1838. He became president of Knox College in 1845 and president of Wheaton College in 1860. Weld met him at Lane Seminary in 1834, either before or just after he became a strong antislavery convert, and appointed him one of the "seventy." Blanchard went to the agents' convention, then lectured in Adams County, Pennsylvania, and in Maryland. His most important convert was Thaddeus Stevens. He continued his antislavery work in Cincinnati, engaging in a four-day debate with N. L. Rice, on the "Sin of Slavery," in 1845, which attracted nationwide attention.[9]

The two Burleigh brothers, Charles Calistus and William Henry, of Connecticut, also were commissioned. Both came into the movement in defense of Prudence Crandall and her Negro school. Charles, one of the most conscientious and accurate workers in the antislavery movement, was a close associate of Samuel J. May and William Lloyd Garrison. He lectured widely and edited the *Pennsylvania Freeman* for the Eastern Pennsylvania Anti-Slavery Society after 1844. William was editor of the *Christian Freeman* for the Connecticut Anti-Slavery Society after 1843. Both men were thoroughly Garrisonian in the sense of being journalists and reformers. They were as deeply involved in the temperance, peace, and women's rights movements as in the antislavery movement.[10] Charles lectured in Pennsylvania and Delaware, and William in Chaplin, Windham, Hampton, and Mansfield, Connecticut, during their agencies.[11]

Wendell Phillips, like the Burleigh brothers, entered vigorously into the movement because of proslavery brutality. He was a young, handsome, brilliant lawyer of Boston when he was appointed a local agent to serve in Massachusetts, September 2, 1837. Three months later (December 8, 1837) he replied to a eulogy of the men who murdered Elijah P. Lovejoy, presented by Attorney General James T. Austin at Faneuil Hall, December 8, 1837. His eloquence and his weighty condemnation of the outrage gave him immediate recognition and prominence in the movement. He was more of a Garrisonian than the Burleighs, supporting Garrison's denunciation of the Constitution as a proslavery document and demanding a separation of the free from the slave states.[12]

Two powerful agents, less well known than some, who began work in the East and eventually went to Illinois, were Ichabod Codding and John Cross. Codding was recommended by Stanton, Cross by Weld. Codding was a student at Middlebury College when commissioned in August 1836. He lectured first in Vermont, then at Bedford, Round Ridge, South Salem, Somers, Yorktown, Peekskill, and Sing Sing, New York. He was sent in 1838 to Maine, where he laid the solid foundations of the state society. He preached from 1840 to 1842 in Connecticut, then moved to Illinois. He devoted more than half of his time to antislavery work with Owen Lovejoy, William Allan, and others in Illinois and Wisconsin.[13] Cross was a Congregational minister of Geneva and Oriskany Falls, New York, who had received his training for the ministry and his interest in the antislavery movement at Oneida Institute. He lectured at Wilkes Barre, Copenhagen, Collinsville, Constableville, and Talcottville, and in New York City. He then went to Illinois, where he served a prison sentence for assisting a fugitive slave. He lived at Wheaton and served as agent for the Methodist Collegiate Institute.[14]

Amos Dresser, one of the Lane Seminary rebels, who had been active in the teaching program in Cincinnati, set out to visit an uncle in Mississippi, but was seized by a mob in Nashville, and accused of peddling antislavery literature and of being a member of the students' antislavery society at Lane. The mob whipped him in the public square, tarred and feathered him, and drove him from the city. This episode gave him wide notoriety and added zeal in the cause. He went to Oberlin for a time, then accepted an agency as one of the "seventy." He worked with Stanton in Worcester County, Massachusetts, lecturing at Athol, Ashburn, and Slatersville, Rhode Island. He then went to Berkshire County, Massachusetts, and in 1839 to Jamaica to assist another Lane rebel, David Ingraham, in missionary work among the Negroes. Both men broke under the strain. The devoted Ingraham died shortly after his return. Dresser survived and went to Olivet College, Michigan, to teach.[15]

Two very distinguished local agents who did not agree with the Garrison-Phillips antipolitical philosophy were Ellis Gray Loring of Boston and Francis J. Lemoyne of Washington, Pennsylvania. Loring was a lawyer, a very distinguished lawyer in fact, in Boston. He had helped organize the

New England Anti-Slavery Society, but was in favor of gradual emancipation and refused to sign the constitution of the society. Later, he gave heavy financial support to the *Liberator* and counsel to Garrison, served ably as a member of the committee appointed to represent the antislavery societies in the battle over repressive legislation in Massachusetts, and represented the antislavery cause in the famous case of the slave girl "Med." Loring strongly supported petitions, questioning of candidates, and voting against proslavery candidates, but opposed the third party movement.[16]

Lemoyne was a physician and strong opponent of slavery, probably one of Weld's converts. He was very active in the underground railroad and was interested in scientific farming. Later, in 1870, he gave $20,000 to found Lemoyne College at Memphis, Tennessee, and established professorships at Washington and Jefferson. Lemoyne lectured one day each week for the antislavery cause in the region about Washington. He was nominated as the first candidate of the Liberty Party for the vice-presidency, but refused to serve because he felt political action to be as much a distracting issue as the Garrisonian vagaries of women's rights, peace, and no human government.[17]

Orange Scott, a young Methodist minister of Springfield, Massachusetts, was brought into the antislavery movement by Stanton in 1834. He began lecturing immediately in the cities of New England, and for years battled against the bishops of the church who sought to silence all discussion of the subject. As an agent of the society, he lectured first at Springfield, Natick, and Middleburg, Massachusetts. He then attended annual conferences in Maine, New Hampshire, and New York. In 1839 he began publication of the *American Wesleyan Observer* as an antislavery magazine. Opposition within the church became so strong that he, Jotham Horton, and LaRoy Sunderland directed the withdrawal of antislavery Methodists from the church and formed the Wesleyan Methodist Church in 1843.[18]

Another Methodist clergyman, Guy Beckley of Northfield, Vermont, was commissioned as one of the "seventy" and attended the agents' convention in New York City. The Methodist churches in the city were closed to him because of his antislavery connections. He lectured in Vermont and New Hampshire, then moved to Ann Arbor, Michigan, in 1839, where he served as pastor of the First Methodist Church and edited with Theodore Fos-

Wendell Phillips

ter the *Signal of Liberty* from 1841 to 1846. James G. Birney, twice candidate of the Liberty Party for the presidency, was living at Bay City, Michigan, and the *Signal* was the official organ of the Michigan Anti-Slavery Society and of Birney.

A third Methodist preacher, who had no end of trouble with both church and civil authorities, was George Storrs. He was a member of the New Hampshire Conference, which organized an antislavery society in 1835. The General Conference of the church formally censured him in 1836 for his antislavery activities. He was arrested while praying in church, December 14, 1835, by virtue of a warrant issued by Nathan Wells, as "an idle and disorderly person . . . a common railer and brawler . . . going about the town and country and disturbing the public peace." He was arrested again in March 1836, after lecturing at Pittsfield, New Hampshire. His agency, as one of the "seventy," took him to Hampton and Andover and then to New York state.[19]

Other agents among the "seventy," besides Stanton, Birney, David Nelson, and Angelina Grimké, whom we shall treat elsewhere, were the Congregationalist minister George Allen of Worcester, Massachusetts, who lectured in Ohio, at Fitchville, Wellington, Jeromesville, Wooster, Mt. Vernon, and Mt. Gilead, traveling 170 miles on foot in the course of his lecture tour,[20] J. M. Blakesley, who organized fifteen societies in Chatauqua and Erie counties, New York,[21] Nathaniel Colver, Baptist minister, who lectured in New York state for two years, then founded Tremont Temple, and after the Civil War, Colver Institute for the training of Negro ministers,[22] Edward H. Fairchild, who lectured in Erie and Crawford counties, Ohio, and later became the first president of Berea College,[23] Cyrus P. Grosvenor, Baptist minister of Salem, Massachusetts, whose lecture tour took him 200 miles through Franklin, Hampshire, and Berkshire Counties, and then from Pittsfield to Sunderland,[24] Horace Kimball, first editor of the *Herald of Freedom,* official organ of the New Hampshire Anti-Slavery Society, who was sent to the British West Indies with James A. Thome to observe and report on the results of emancipation there,[25] James M. McKim, member of the organizational meeting in Philadelphia, 1833, who lectured in Newton, Falsington, Lower Wakefield, Morristown, Plymouth, and Gulf Mills, Pennsylvania, then became publishing agent of the Pennsylvania Anti-Slavery Society and succeeded Whittier as editor of the *Pennsylvania Freeman.*[26]

Weld never recovered from the physical exhaustion of his lecture tour and agents' convention. His voice was gone forever. Only he and Stanton could have paved the way for the abolitionizing of Indiana and Illinois after the manner of Ohio, or of the border slave states. Neither was physically able to repeat his earlier performance; both were needed elsewhere; and it was probably better so in the end. Local agents were selected and traveling agents were assigned in such manner as to cover new territory between the existing societies, to strengthen the rapidly growing state organizations, and to energize the movement at the local level. This was wise and fruitful procedure. It consolidated the movement and gave it such power and permanence that it once more flowed into its earlier, normal channels of political action.

Weld and Stanton moved into the New York office to direct this vast antislavery empire they had so largely created, and they brought with them James G. Birney. The time had come, with the rapid multiplication of local societies, to execute a special publications program, and thus make available to the reading public the complete anthology of antislavery indictments. Weld's contribution to publications was as remarkable as his agency system. Birney supervised the agents and undertook to maintain harmonious relations in the expanding family of antislavery societies. Stanton supervised the financial agents and somehow found the money for this extensive campaign for three years. His more immediate task was to organize a vast petition campaign. Whether men realized it or not, and a good many did not, this was the channel by which the stream of antislavery sentiment found its way back to direct political action. Finally, Stanton defended before legislative committees the right of free enquiry and discussion of the slavery question. Elizur Wright gave full time to editing the periodicals and to foreign correspondence. Joshua Leavitt continued to edit the *Emancipator.* John Greenleaf Whittier was indispensable to the petition campaign and to the distribution of publications. All of these men had complete mastery of the subject and had done nothing else for nearly a decade. They were men of fine physique and winning personality. Birney was a former slaveholding aristocrat, with a fine legal training and judicial mind. Stanton was charming, persuasive, brilliant alike in the drawing room, the legislative hall, or on the public platform. Weld, for all his rugged and severe exterior, was a kind and gentle soul, thoroughly democratic, efficient, and meticulously accurate.

There already were some powerful state societies before the parent organization entered upon its expanded program. The New England Anti-Slavery Society, which Garrison's little group had formed at Boston in late December 1831, had been formally changed after three years to what it actually had been from the beginning: the Massachusetts Anti-Slavery Society.[27] This was Garrison's organization, and its official organ was the *Liberator.* Later, when the American Anti-Slavery Society split, there was organized at the Marlboro Hotel in Boston, May 27, 1839, the Massachusetts Abolition Society, by the anti-Garrisonians.[28] The Providence Anti-Slavery Society had been organized June 7, 1833, six months before the organization of the American Anti-Slavery Society. Henry B. Stanton went to Rhode Island on his first agency in 1834–35 and organized the Rhode Island Anti-Slavery Society at Providence, February 2–4, 1836.[29] The Vermont State Anti-Slavery Society had been formed at Middlebury, May 1, 1834, and the New Hampshire State Anti-Slavery Society at Concord, November 11–12, 1834.[30]

Weld, working in Ohio while Stanton was in Rhode Island, organized the Ohio State Anti-Slavery Society at Putnam, April 22–24, 1835.[31] The New York City Anti-Slavery Society was formed in October 1833, and the New York State Anti-Slavery Society at Utica and Peterboro, October 21–22, 1835.[32]

Most of the state societies, and the three most powerful and important ones, from any standpoint—Massachusetts, New York, and Ohio—were organized before the "seventy" were appointed in the autumn of 1836. In Pennsylvania, where the old Society for Promoting the Abolition of Slavery and the Relief of Free Negroes Unlawfully Held in Bondage continued to function in Philadelphia, the Pennsylvania State Anti-Slavery Society was organized at Harrisburg, January 31–February 3, 1837.[33] The first antislavery Convention of American Women was held in New York City, May 9–12, 1837.[34] In the West, the Michigan State Anti-Slavery Society was organized at Ann Arbor, November 10–11, 1836, the Illinois State Anti-Slavery Society at Upper Alton, October 26–28, 1837, and the Indiana State Anti-Slavery Society at Milton, September 13, 1838.[35]

Each of the state societies had a newspaper which was regarded as its official organ.[36] The larger ones maintained agents and depositories for the distribution of literature and published a considerable number of titles. There were a good many local societies before the American Anti-Slavery Society was organized. There were more than five hundred when the appointment of the "seventy" began, more than twice that many one year later, and probably fifteen hundred by 1840.[37] Most of these societies were auxiliaries of both their state societies and the national society—auxiliaries, that is, in the sense of making a financial contribution, and reports, and receiving literature. They were never controlled or supervised by either, yet they were the working organizations, spreading the antislavery gospel, distributing literature, circulating petitions, collecting money, holding prayer meetings, bazaars, Fourth of July celebrations; and, above all, putting a relentless and ever-increasing pressure upon local and state officials in both political parties, assisting fugitives, and waging the seemingly endless battle for civil rights. There were hundreds of communities, however, where there were no societies, and membership in societies is no indication of antislavery strength.

The agents were the antislavery evangelists. Weld counted the conversion of a distinguished lawyer, or physician, or educator more important than forming a society. He and Stanton labored mightily with the intellectuals and men of standing in every community. Other agents followed their example. They stayed out of the cities for the most part, and they kept the agents out of the cities as far as possible because this was an agricultural society, and cities were growing by migration from the rural areas. Moreover, the cities were strongholds of colonization, they seemed to nurture mob violence, and the large newspapers were political and therefore vicious in their attacks upon antislavery people. As it was, Weld and Stanton and Rankin and many others were so close to death from mob violence so many times it seemed to be a part of their daily routine. Agents met violence, almost without exception, with dignity and Christian charity. They were men of peace. They were selected with great care, and those who faltered in any respect were not long retained. Some money was collected by the general agents, much more by the financial agents, though never at public meetings. The movement, at all levels from local to national, was financed largely by small individual donations, though the money might find its way into the treasuries of the state or national societies by way of pledges from the local organizations.

Agents were selected with great care also, because this was an intellectual and religious crusade for social reform. The appeal was to cultivated men and women. Demagoguery would not have succeeded. From first to last many people in the country wrote for money or cheap notoriety. The men who were directing the movement could not do any more about it than scholars can do about such things today. All the publications of the American Anti-Slavery Society, however, while headquarters were in New York, were supervised with the utmost care. Weld was more meticulous about accuracy than are most scholars, and agents were warned over and over to stick to facts, never to exaggerate, and not to get into the habit of emphasizing cruelties, because such accounts lose their effectiveness by repetition unless constantly enlarged upon. The steady diet of antislavery argument, therefore, was of high order, and attempts to suppress it by mob violence or by legislation, as we shall see, brought many an able man to the support of the cause.

ANGELINA GRIMKÉ: WOMEN'S RIGHTS

Chapter 22

The men who were making the decisions in this gigantic enterprise—and that meant Weld, Stanton, Birney, Wright, Lewis Tappan—always were able to reconcile their differences and to make whatever accommodations of personal interest were necessary to achieve a maximum effort against slavery. Speaking of these officers of the society, Catherine Birney, who knew the antislavery movement as well as anyone, said in 1885: "Their moderation, good judgment, and piety had been seen and known of all men. Faithful in the exposure of unfaithfulness to freedom on the part of politicians and clergymen, they denounced neither the Constitution nor the Bible. Their devotion to the cause of abolition was pure; for its sake they suppressed the vanity of personal notoriety and of oratorical display . . . Such was their honest aversion to personal publicity, it is now almost impossible to trace the work each did. Some of their noblest arguments for Freedom were published anonymously. They made no vainglorious claims to the original authorship of ideas. But never in the history of reform was work better done than the old American Anti-Slavery Society did from its formation in 1833 to its disruption in 1840."[1]

These men were constantly distressed, however, by Garrison's conduct of the *Liberator*. He used intemperate language. He departed from a discussion of issues to deal in personalities. He confused the issue of slavery by excessive championing of women's rights. He was a pacifist and an anarchist. The women's rights issue was a deviation which dissipated the strength of the antislavery movement. The rejection of governmental authority, denunciation of the Constitution as a proslavery document, and refusal to exercise the franchise or to countenance coercion by the government in enforcement of law constituted a misconception of the duties and responsibilities of citizenship and a totally unsound interpretation of the Constitution.

Garrison did not represent the antislavery men of New England, or Massachusetts, or all of Boston. The idea that all of new England was Garrisonian is at odds with the facts. He had the support of some wealthy patrons in Boston and of some very able women, but others who recognized his contribution to the antislavery cause—and that included the New York group—deplored his aberrations. Internal pressures finally split the national society asunder in 1839. Meanwhile, the women made a rather remarkable contribution in Boston. The most important of these women by all odds was Angelina Grimké of Charleston, South Carolina.

Angelina, and her elder sister Sarah, were daughters of the aristocratic, Oxford-trained Judge John F. Grimké of the South Carolina Supreme Court. They came from a combination of French Huguenot, English Puritan, and Irish stock. One brother, Thomas Smith Grimké, was a leader of the law-abiding elements in the state during the Nullification controversy. He was an orator, a man of letters, a bold advocate of reforms. He and the two girls were born humanitarians. Another brother, Frederick Grimké, was a member of the Supreme Court of Ohio and author of *Nature and Tendency of Free Institutions.*[2] The girls revolted against the formalism of the Episcopal Church, the shallowness of social life, and the restraints upon education and useful activity for women. They hated the barbarism of slavery and the laws which forbade the education of the slaves. Finally, they fled from the stifling environment of the deep South and went to Philadelphia, where both became Quakers. Here, among the Friends, they found at least partial release from restraints upon free discussion.

There was no need for conversion to antislavery because they were natural enemies of oppression, and they eventually took slaves as their share of the family estate in order to give them freedom. In the summer of 1829 Angelina had written in her diary: "Yesterday was a day of suffering. My soul was exceedingly sorrowful, and out of the depths of it, I cried unto the Lord that he would make a way for me to escape from the land of slavery." Again, she wrote: "Sometimes I think that the children of Israel could not have looked towards the land of Canaan with keener longing than I do to the North . . . it looks like a promised land, a pleasant land, because it is a land of freedom; and it seems to me that I would rather bear much deeper spiritual exercises than, day after day, month after month, to endure the countless evils which increasingly flow from slavery."[3] Angelina, shocked by violent opposition to Garrison and his British protégé, George Thompson, wrote Garrison a letter which he published in the *Liberator.*[4] Destiny hovered over her when she wrote that letter. It was the most important event in an exciting and noble life. It brought her to the attention of her future husband, Theodore D. Weld. Neither Weld nor Stanton subscribed to the current subordination of women in all but family life. Weld had created a sensation by urging women to participate in Finney's revival meetings. He and Stanton enrolled Angelina as one of the "Seventy," and later Weld encouraged Abby Kelly and others to take to the lecture platform. Both men married feminists: Angelina Grimké and Elizabeth Cady. Angelina's first timid entry into the antislavery movement raised a storm of protest and insults no end, especially from the Quakers, of whose society the two sisters were members and ministers. Her resolute adherence to her convictions gave the women's rights movement two members of a nationally known South Carolina family, and a brilliant lecturer and pamphleteer.

Elizur Wright wrote to her in the name of the executive committee of the American Anti-Slavery Society, requesting that she come to New York to speak on slavery at women's private gatherings. She rejected this invitation to complete her *Appeal to the Christian Women of the South.* Sarah published in the same year an *Epistle to the Clergy of the Southern States.*[5] Angelina's *Appeal* was published by the American Anti-Slavery Society and distributed widely throughout the country. The Quakers threatened to disown her for having published. The pamphlet was publicly burned by postmasters in the South. The Charleston authorities instructed the police, if she returned to that city, to prevent her landing while the steamer remained in port and to see to it that she should not communicate by letter or otherwise with any person in the city, and, further, that if she should elude their vigilance and go on shore she should be arrested and imprisoned until the return of the vessel. She also was threatened with mob violence should she visit her home in Charleston.[6]

Angelina's prominence as the sister of Thomas S. Grimké; her birth and long residence in the slave country; the unholy row kicked up in the South over a public pronouncement about slavery by this blue-eyed aristocratic daughter of a slaveholder; the ensuing wrangle at the North over the propriety of women participating in discussions of public affairs; and the cogency of her appeal to Southern women; all give the pamphlet a high place on the list of antislavery literature.

Since the Bible argument was so much a part of the South's defense of slavery, Angelina dissected American slavery to show that there never had been anything like it in Jewish servitude or elsewhere. Slavery here was *hereditary* and *perpetual.* Slave labor was compulsory and uncompensated. Slaves could be sold or leased. Slave families could be ruthlessly separated. They could make no contracts and own no property. They could not testify in court against a white man. They could be punished at the discretion and direction of their owner and could offer no resistance. There was no way by which they could redeem themselves from slavery. The law placed almost prohibitory restrictions upon manumission. They were unprotected in their domestic relations. They were kept in ignorance by the requirements of the law. They could not claim religious instruction. Oppression of free Negroes was little short of that imposed upon slaves. Actually, said Angelina, the South denies that Negroes are human beings.

Slave-trading was a sore point with apologists for slavery in the 1830's, and has been ever since. Angelina made short shrift of that business: "There is no difference in *principle*, in Christian ethics, between the despised slave dealer (who makes his fortune by trading in the bodies and souls of men, women and children) and the Christian who buys slaves from, or sells slaves to him; indeed, if slaves were not wanted by the respectable, the wealthy, and the religious in a community, there would be no slaves in that community and of course no slave-dealers. It is then the Christian and the honorable men and women of the South, who are the main pillars of this grand temple built to Mammon and to Moloch."[7] Slavery, she said, was contrary to the first charter of human rights given to Adam, contrary to the example and precept of Jesus and the Apostles, and contrary to the Declaration of Independence. It reduced man to a thing, robbed him of all his rights as a human being, fettered his mind and body, protected the master in unnatural power, and denied to the slave the protection of the law.[8]

"It is manifest to every reflecting mind," said Angelina, "that slavery must be abolished; the era in which we live, and the light which is overspreading the whole world on this subject, clearly show that the time cannot be far distant when it will be done. Now, there are only two ways in which it can be effected, by moral power or physical force, and it is for you to choose which of these you prefer. Slavery always has, and always will produce insurrections wherever it exists, because it is a violation of the natural order of things, and no human power can much longer perpetuate it."[9]

Having recited at length examples of female leadership from the days of Moses to the present —and it was a most impressive record—she described the activities of British women in keeping the public informed on the slavery question, particularly the petitioning of Parliament. She asked the women of the slave states to read the Bible in a spirit of inquiry and see for themselves that it did not sanction slavery; to pray for understanding for the slave and for his master; to speak out on the subject to relatives and friends; to set their own slaves free or educate them and pay them wages; to join in societies and send petitions to legislatures; and to entreat husbands, fathers, brothers, and sons "to abolish the institution of slavery; no longer to subject woman to the scourge and the chain, to mental darkness and moral degradation; no longer to tear husbands from their wives, and children from their parents; no longer to make men, women, and children work without wages; no longer to make their lives bitter in hard bondage; no longer to reduce *American Citizens* to the abject condition of slaves, of chattels personal; no longer to barter the *image of God* in human shambles for corruptible things such as silver and gold . . . Is it right, is it generous, to refuse the colored people in this country the advantages of education and the privilege, or rather the right, to follow honest trades and callings merely because they are colored."[10]

Catherine Beecher, who had listened to the Lane Seminary debates, but had remained as temporizing as her father on the subject, attempted to belittle Angelina and to correct her at almost every point. In *An Essay on Slavery and Abolitionism, with Reference to the Duty of American Females*,[11] she presented a specious argument to show that slavery was a domestic concern of the South; that antislavery men and women were neither peaceful nor Christian in their methods; that they were incorrect in their approach to colonization, race prejudice, and Negro education; and that public discussion by women was undignified and vulgar. It gave Angelina a rare opportunity to drive home once more her main points, which she did in *Letters to Catherine E. Beecher*.[12] A few cogent statements reveal her forthright position:

"The great fundamental principle of abolitionists is, that man cannot rightfully hold his fellow man as property. Therefore, we affirm, that every slaveholder is a man-stealer."[13]

"We assert that it is a national sin."[14]

"Our principle is, that no circumstances can ever justify a man in holding his fellow man as property; it matters not what motives he may give for such a monstrous violation of the laws of God."[15]

"We say that all the laws which sustain the system of slavery are unjust and oppressive—contrary to the fundamental principles of morality—and, therefore, null and void."[16]

"We hold that all the slaveholding laws violate the fundamental principles of the Constitution of the United States."[17]

"If our fundamental principle is right, that no man can rightfully hold his fellow man as property, then it follows, of course, that he is bound immediately to cease holding him as such."[18]

"Our main principle of action is embodied in God's holy command: 'Wash you, make you clean, put away the evil of your doings from before mine eyes, cease to do evil, learn to do well; seek judgment, relieve the oppressed, judge the fatherless, plead for the widow.'"[19]

"That the Colonization Society is a benevolent institution, we deny ... And it is a perfect mystery to me how men and women can conscientiously persevere in upholding a society, which the very objects of its professed benevolence have repeatedly, solemnly, constantly and universally condemned."[20]

"What man or woman of common sense now doubts the intellectual capacity of the colored people? Who does not know, that with all our efforts as a nation to crush and annihilate the minds of this portion of our race, we have never yet been able to do it?"[21]

Meanwhile, Weld and Stanton had recommended Angelina for a commission as one of the "seventy." The executive committee gave the agency committee power in the matter and the appointment was made, July 13, 1836. From then until Angelina's marriage to Weld in May 1838, she blazed a trail of oratory from New York to Boston and Providence which Wendell Phillips said doubled the hold of the antislavery cause in Massachusetts.[22] She knew the South and its institutions better than anyone in the movement except James G. Birney. Weld had trained her in public speaking. She was passionately devoted to the cause of freedom and determined to discredit her detractors.

Neither Angelina nor Weld, nor even Stanton, left much in the way of lecture notes. The newspapers, of course, are of little help in the matter. They had no peers in platform oratory, but most papers were unfriendly, and a *friendly* reporter once said in reference to Stanton "that he could not attempt to report a whirlwind or a thunderstorm." Weld and Angelina, after their marriage, compiled and wrote the great classic of antislavery literature, so, all in all, it is not easy to separate the work of one from the other. We do have enough of her notes, however, to reconstruct some of the ideas she emphasized.

Time and again the charge was hurled at those engaged in the antislavery movement, and it has been repeated by many pseudohistorians since, that the antislavery movement rolled back and long delayed the cause of emancipation. Henry Clay said fifty years, Robert J. Breckinridge said one hundred years, and Lyman Beecher said two hundred years. It was an assertion without proof; and, of course, disputed by events. The idea sought to be conveyed was that slavery was a local institution and responsibility of the Southern states, and that the South was so embittered by Northern interference that a strong movement for emancipation was reversed. This has since become a part of Southern mythology.

Angelina paid particular attention to the question, What has the North to do with slavery? First, the Congress of the United States, representing a far greater population and wealth in the free states than in the slave states, had complete control over the District of Columbia, where slavery existed and slave traders plied their trade; and over interstate commerce, of which the domestic slave trade constituted a considerable part; and over the territories like Florida where slavery existed; and over foreign affairs, including recognition of the independence of Texas; and over the admission of states, seven of which had been slave states. Second, Congress had enacted the Fugitive Slave Law, providing for the return of alleged fugitives in complete violation of all constitutional guarantees of individual rights, and had struck down the right of petition in 1836 and again in 1837. Third, persons working for the overthrow of slavery were outlawed at the South and numerous rewards had been offered for their delivery dead or alive to Southern mobs or to state authorities. Fourth, Southern states had demanded, and had sent delegates to the North to secure, laws which would make illegal all antislavery associations and all antislavery pronouncements. Northern churches and pulpits were closed to antislavery lecturers. Fifth, the deep, underlying evil was race prejudice, sustained by slavery at the South and by the colonizationists at the North. Sixth, Northern merchants, manufacturers, and consumers had close economic ties with the South. Seventh, slavery was making fearful encroachments on the liberties of Northern citizens, while it branded her honorable working men with the epithet of white slaves. Eighth, slavery always had been, and was, and ever would be dangerous to the harmony of the nation in times of

Emancipation

Before and after freedom came to a noble people, as conceived by Thomas Nast.

peace and to its safety in time of war. Ninth, slaveholders and others reared in the atmosphere of slavery held high positions in the churches, educational institutions, and the government.

Northerners should make a vigorous effort to convince slaveholders of the sin of slavery. They should refuse to recognize them as Christians or ministers and should reject their contributions to all benevolent societies. They should give a faithful exhibition of the real condition of the slaves, make a fervent appeal to the world in their be-

half, and constantly petition for their relief. They should assist fugitives from slavery, heeding the language of Jehovah in Edom: "Neither shouldst thou have stood in the crossway, to cut off those that did escape; neither shouldst thou have delivered up those in the day of distress." They should make unceasing efforts to elevate the moral and intellectual character of the free Negroes, treat them as equals, comfort them in their trials, visit them in their homes, assist them in their schools, and at the day of emancipation go into the South, supply them with books, and in every way aid their transition to freedom. They should throw open to Negroes seminaries of learning instead of building separate academies for them, and let them, according to their merits, share equally with their fellow citizens in the privileges of professions, trades, and civil offices. They should repeal all laws which permitted slaveholders to bring their slaves into free states and remove from office all who had voted to strike down the right of petition.

Angelina covered fully the Bible argument regarding slavery, dwelling at length upon the New Testament, in which the crime of oppression is more often reproved than any other. The announcement of the birth of Christ—Peace on earth and good will to man—was utterly incompatible with slavery; and His whole character and ministry, all His commandments, and all His precepts were at variance with the spirit of slaveholding. His Sermon on the Mount, if nothing else were left on record, killed slavery root and branch. Slavery was oppression in its worst form. Search the catalogue of human wrongs, trace the history of those who had suffered most from oppression, follow them through every scene of bodily and mental anguish, and then compare their tale of woe with that of slaves in America and ask yourself, What should we do to be saved? Why? Because the terrible judgments of the Almighty had made oppression always dangerous to the lives of tyrants. Man as a moral being could be governed safely only by moral power. His high-born spirit never could be entirely subdued by the naked power of despotism. It would resist physical oppression whenever it felt strong enough to do so. Shame, disgrace, infamy, the blighting of all hopes, the withering of all joys, a lifetime of woe and a forgotten grave—all, and more, were in the words *he is a slave*. It was a ferocious tyranny, at war with every law of nature and with reason itself, which doomed to slavery the children of slaves. Man had an inalienable right to liberty, and any denial of that right was an outrage against justice and common decency.

Angelina made her contribution to the higher law doctrine, then in rapid process of clarification. Slavery involved crime and suffering, therefore every human being was bound to investigate it, bound to search out the cause. Every moral being had an unquestionable right to examine the crimes of his fellow beings and to endeavor by moral means to bring them to repentance and

amendment. They were only doing for the slaveholders what the missionaries were doing for the heathen. Slavery in its *best* form was grievous oppression, high-handed sin against God and men. It annihilated the sacred distinction between a person and a thing. The creative act of God gave to man the attributes of intelligence, morality, accountability, and immortality. Slavery trampled them underfoot. That was its vital principle. That made it a sin in itself, under all circumstances. Slaves were deprived of the means and opportunity of moral and intellectual cultivation: the more ignorance the more safety. Laws in slaveholding states adjudged slaves to be chattels personal in the hands of their masters. Slavery was hereditary and perpetual. The law said all their issue should be and remain forever absolute slaves and follow the condition of the mother. Reduced to the state of animals, their lives were unprotected. They could be killed when outlawed, by moderate chastisement, in a sudden heat of passion, and if they resisted. This gross violation of the laws of nature, which transformed men into chattels and infringed upon the prerogatives of God by tearing immortal man from the sphere he was designed to fill and casting him down with the brutes, created a mighty energy of evil that seared the soul of the South. Christianity simply could not coexist with slavery, for where the spirit of Christ is, there is liberty. In three centuries after the Christian era began, scarcely a vestige of slavery remained in the Roman Empire, and as the Christian religion spread northward slavery was abolished in all of Europe.

There had been considerable support during the 1820's for some plan of compensated emancipation and for the use of the proceeds of the public lands for that purpose. Georgia and South Carolina, it will be recalled, had denounced most vigorously the mildest sort of proposal to use funds from the sale of public lands for colonization. Antislavery leaders rejected the principle of compensation in its entirety. Most of them would not even discuss it. Angelina gave a thorough explanation of why compensation could not be given to the slaveholder. Slavery was a sin, she said, which must be repented of just like every other sin and not disposed of for a monetary consideration. There might well be some financial loss and suffering on the part of the slaveholders; there always was for those who expected permanence in institutions which violated fundamental morality. Suffering was inevitable and inseparable from great revolutions. The slave, however, was entitled to compensation, if any were given, for his lifetime of unrequited toil. The real reason, however, why compensation could not be countenanced was that compensation would be an acknowledgment of the right of the master to the slave as property, and such an acknowledgment would counteract all appeals to his conscience, and soften his sense of guilt and need for retributive justice. Nothing could possibly do the work effectively in the heart of the slaveholder but preaching the truth and nothing but the truth to him. This was not a matter of sentiment. A sense of guilt and repentance on the part of the slaveholder was absolutely essential because emancipation could not take the Negroes out of the power of the slaveholders. The attitude of the present slaveholders after emancipation would be of the greatest importance. Mere redemption of the Negroes from slavery would not safeguard them from exploitation.

The quarrel within the ranks of the antislavery societies over women's rights was a sore affliction to Angelina, not because she intended to let it interfere with her public appearances, but because she saw with remarkable clarity how it was playing into the hands of the proslavery forces. Every church denomination in the South was shirking its responsibility in the matter of slavery by insisting it was a political question. Angelina, therefore, in emphasizing its moral aspects and the deep concern of women with such questions of public morality, was striking hammer blows at the proslavery and procolonization arguments.

Why was there such confusion with regard to women's duty on this great subject, asked Angelina? Every enemy of freedom in the country dreaded the influence of women, reprobated their interference in the slavery argument, and tried to blind them to their duty. Some who pretended to be very zealous for the honor of the female sex and very anxious that they should scrupulously maintain the dignity and delicacy of female propriety insisted that slavery was a political subject and women ought not to meddle with it. Grant that it was a political subject and show how that exonerated women from their duty as human beings. Women had interfered wisely and laudably

many times in political affairs, and they had a right to do so in the country in which they lived, because the honor and happiness and well-being of women and their children and their homes were bound up in the politics and government and laws of the country. Slavery, however, was as much a moral as it was a political subject. It exerted a desolating influence not only on the region where it actually existed, but far beyond its own boundary, and was utterly incompatible with fundamental morality.

Stanton and Weld steadfastly encouraged Angelina during the first trying months of her agency. The executive committee of the American Anti-Slavery Society could not exercise any control over her because she was paying her own expenses and drawing no salary. Weld and Stanton, of course, exercised a great deal of influence over her; and Weld gently persuaded Sarah after a time to recognize her deficiencies as a speaker and desist. Stanton offered to work out a joint itinerary with Angelina under the firm conviction that it would strengthen the movement in Massachusetts. His reputation would also take a little of the pressure of criticism off Angelina. She was afraid such an arrangement would have the opposite effect and demurred. He then insisted that she should appear before the legislative committee on petitions and other antislavery activities, and she did so in spite of the opposition of the Boston group.

Garrison, who had beyond all question compromised the antislavery movement by a vicious attack on the churches and by his antigovernment vagaries, now sought notoriety from the women's rights controversy by posing as the patron of Angelina and persuading her to prepare a series of lectures on women's rights to be given in Boston. It was at this point that Weld intervened and scolded her in no uncertain terms. She had been advancing the cause of freedom, a great moral enterprise, in a brilliant manner, and in doing so had advanced the cause of women's rights by practical demonstration on the lecture platform. Now, to abandon the former and enter into an argument over the latter was sheer madness. Angelina did not give the series of lectures, but it was only after her engagement to Weld that she admitted her previous error.

JAMES GILLESPIE BIRNEY

Chapter 23

Last of the Southern exiles from point of time, but first in service to the antislavery cause, was James Gillespie Birney.[1] His father and his mother's father had come to America from Ireland only a few years before James was born in Danville, Kentucky, in 1792. James was only a few weeks old when David Rice, pastor of the Presbyterian church in Danville, delivered his philippic against slavery in the first constitutional convention of the state.[2] He died three years before another of Kentucky's sons, Abraham Lincoln, was elected to the presidency of the Republic. His years of accountability, therefore, covered the rise of the cotton kingdom, the slave power's bid for supremacy in the nation, and the rise of that political party which guided the nation through secession and war.

Birney was a cultivated man of the world, trained in the law and experienced in public affairs, when he discussed slavery with Theodore Weld and the Reverend John Allan at Huntsville, Alabama, in June, 1832.[3] He had studied law under Alexander J. Dallas of Philadelphia; was the son-in-law of William McDowell, United States district judge for Kentucky; and was the law partner of Arthur F. Hopkins, later United States senator from Alabama. He had served in the legislature of Kentucky and in the first general assembly of Alabama, and had taken a leading part in establishing the University of Alabama. He had been a slaveholding planter, a trustee of Centre College, mayor of Huntsville, and one of the most courageous prosecuting attorneys in the South-

west. He was opposed to slavery, determined to move North in order to rear and educate his sons in the free states, and deeply shocked at the studied defense of slavery in the South.

The summer of 1832 was the time of decision for Birney. Ralph R. Gurley of the American Colonization Society offered him the permanent agency for the fifth district, comprising Tennessee, Alabama, Mississippi, Louisiana, and Arkansas. Theodore Weld, on his western trip for the newly organized Society for Promoting Manual Labor in Literary Institutions, urged him to accept the appointment. He gave up his legal practice, made a study of the colonization society's operations, and entered upon his agency in September, 1832.[4] No man ever knew the deep South better, nor the evils of slavery, and the colonization movement never had a more able solicitor. There was something almost tragic about his experience—a man of fine legal mind and warm humanity lecturing to small church groups, collecting piddling amounts for the cause, working diligently to send to Africa about as many free Negroes as there were slaves on one large plantation, and in the end receiving only abuse from his own people.

Birney wrote a series of articles for the newspapers. He tried to convince the people, perhaps even himself, that colonization was a benevolent enterprise and that the standard arguments in its behalf were valid. Removal to Africa would greatly enhance the opportunities of the free Negroes, promote the redemption of Africa for Christianity, and remove from the South a disturbing element in the population. Colonization was not an antislavery measure, as shown by the fact that abolitionists were opposed to it.[5]

So great was Birney's desire to secure a hearing in the deep South that he erred grievously on some points. He argued that Northern antislavery men were ill-informed about slavery and that their activities were retarding emancipation. He denied there was a guarantee of individual rights in the Declaration of Independence. He would have choked to death on such assertions two years later. He did not, however, endorse the doctrine of biological inequality, he admitted that slavery drove yeoman farmers and white laborers away, and he spoke with approval of the trend toward emancipation by the border slave states. This was the mildest sort of antislavery argument, but it was rank heresy in the slave country. On August 10, 1833, he wrote the last of his series of fifteen articles for the papers. His law partner and others advised against its publication. He had written that by 1850 the Negroes would outnumber the whites in the slave states by two and one-half to one. He then asked: "Can the lower South maintain its present condition—Can things be kept stable—can the blacks be retained in subjection when an inequality in numbers so great shall be found to exist? It is believed, they *cannot*—that it will be utterly impracticable, and that if we wait, supinely—or indeed without putting forth the most vigorous efforts for our relief—until this period shall arrive, there will be no alternative but an utter abandonment by us of one of the fairest and most delightful sections of our country." Slaveholders might have dismissed this as visionary, but not his statement that "Rome, it is thought, fell at last by the corruption and effeminacy introduced by her system of slavery—and there were in all these republics [Athens, Sparta, Rome] instances of cruelty in the treatment of them against which humanity revolts and the whole soul of modern civilization rebels . . . Is it prudent, whilst there exists in our country such an *instrument* as the slave population constitutes, with the mind and intelligence of half a million free people of color—at heart hating our institutions, to influence and direct it—I say, is it the part of wisdom to act as if no danger were to be apprehended when they shall have tripled our numbers?"[6]

This was incendiary literature in the accepted usage of that term in the lower South; and Birney discovered what many men had discovered be-

fore him—that when anyone spoke of slavery in *that* region, even a slaveholder, he spoke in defense of it, and that to violate the code was to incur the displeasure of one's associates, social ostracism, even economic ruin. Birney was not a man to sacrifice principles for expediency, and bitter days were upon him. He had experienced firsthand, also, a demonstration of the sheer inhumanity of colonization under the cloak of Christian benevolence. Many of the Negroes he sent out to Africa as agent were slaves who had been freed on condition they go; some of them were old men and women, some were children. Their going scarcely could be called freedom of choice, their future anything but promising.

Birney went home to Kentucky, recoiling from the very thought of remaining in the deep South as a professional man or planter. He was convinced that unless Virginia, Maryland, and Kentucky could be persuaded to emancipate their slaves, the Union would be dissolved. He expected the lower Mississippi Valley ultimately to be abandoned by the whites. He was depressed by the whole-hearted support of slavery by religious people. Seven years later he was the candidate for the presidency of a party determined to challenge the aggressions of the slave power, and those seven years were replete with as choice a repertoire of human drama as this country has ever produced.

Birney returned to Kentucky in November 1833. He was once more within the orbit of the antislavery movement. Danville, Louisville, Indianapolis, and Chillicothe were on the outer fringes of the most fertile area of antislavery sentiment in the nation. Intellectual giants throve here like the tall corn of the Pickaway plains. Four powerful antislavery pamphlets had been produced, written by David Rice, David Barrow, James Duncan, and John Rankin. Five preachers reared in the slave country had their roots down as deep as the rugged oaks of Brown County—James Gilliland, John Rankin, Jesse Lockhart, and the brothers James and William Dickey. Over at Newport, Indiana, was Levi Coffin, already deeply engrossed in the rescue of fugitive slaves. Thomas Morris of Bethel, late chief justice of Ohio, was newly elected to the United States Senate, where he would lead the fight for the right of petition.

In and around Danville itself were Gideon Blackburn, until recently president of Centre College, and the new president, John C. Young. The former had been a student of Samuel Doak and was strongly antislavery. He was soon to assist Lovejoy in Illinois. Young was mildly antislavery, particularly because education for Negroes was prohibited and for whites neglected in the slave country. Here, too, were David Nelson, pastor of the Danville Presbyterian church and traveling agent for the American Education Society; Luke Munsell, superintendent of the Deaf and Dumb Asylum, and Judge John Green. Across the river at Lane Seminary the debate on slavery and colonization and the struggle for academic freedom were about to begin, from which were to come the stalwarts among the antislavery agents and eventually *Uncle Tom's Cabin*.

The "Kentucky Society for the Gradual Relief of the State from Slavery" was organized at Lexington, December 6, 1833.[7] This was two days after the organization of the American Anti-Slavery Society at Philadelphia, and about one month before the Lane Seminary debates. All white citizens of Kentucky willing to set free at age twenty-five children born thereafter to any slaves they might own were invited to become members. Birney wrote an "Address" to the public for the society in which he used far stronger language than he had used in Alabama and with about the same result. Slavery was a "foul blot" on the character of Kentucky. It was a great moral and political evil. "The sentence of condemnation has been passed upon it by the *civilized world*," he said, "and we venture the opinion that no respectable person will be found in our State, to arraign the decision." Reducing men to slavery and continuing to hold men in slavery were "both violations of the law of nature; for the God of nature creates no slaves . . . The one consisted of a few acts of heartrending oppression—kidnapping in Africa; transporting to America; and selling to the Colonists. The other consists of innumerable wrongs inflicted on the slave and his posterity for a period of time already amounting to two hundred years, and extending an unknown length along the dark vista of futurity."

Having challenged the sin-of-our-fathers argument, Birney then took a firm stand on emancipation. A decision must first be made *that slavery shall cease to exist—absolutely, unconditionally, and irrevocably. When that is settled, then, and not until then, the whole community will feel a common interest in making the best possible preparation for the event.* But so long as *perpetual*

slavery remains engrafted on our constitution, there will be found a powerful and influential class of the community interested in opposing all attempts to bring the system to a termination." Pursuing the point, Birney said that all of those people who were opposed to emancipation, being unwilling to argue in *defense of slavery*, raised incidental issues. They were accustomed to say that Negroes could not be emancipated and allowed to remain in Kentucky because "they are too ignorant and degraded to appreciate the blessings of civil liberty and be governed by the laws of a free people." They must not be educated in preparation for freedom or they "will soon become our equals and aspire to equal rights and honors with ourselves." The state could not afford to colonize them in Africa and the federal government had no right to interfere in any way with slave property.[8]

Every antislavery man eventually came to this realization of the futility and fundamental error of discussing anything but the yes or no of emancipation, and, almost without exception, *immediate* rather than gradual emancipation. That had been Elizabeth Heyrich's great contribution.[9] The few men who organized this society in Kentucky had been colonizationists. They did not now attack colonization, they only asked that it not be made a condition of emancipation. Their position in December 1833—and it was essentially the position of the students at Lane Seminary on this eve of their lengthy debate—graphically illustrates the accuracy of Ralph Gurley's statement of December 17, 1833. No man in the country was in a better position to know whereof he spoke, because he was in a very real sense the heart and soul of the colonization movement. He said in a letter to Birney: "I deeply regret that there should exist so much apathy, indeed may I not say error of opinion, on the subject of slavery at the South . . . My own opinion is, that the South must, if its own dearest interests are to be preserved, if the Union is to last, act with vastly more zeal and energy on this subject than has yet been manifested . . . If it be once understood that the South designs to *perpetuate* Slavery, the whole North will be speedily organized into Anti-Slavery Societies, and the whole land will be flooded with antislavery publications."[10]

This was the day of understanding, as Gurley well knew. Charles Stuart had published his condemnation of colonization in England and Garrison his two volumes in the United States. The American Anti-Slavery Society already had been organized when Gurley wrote his letter, and the Lane Seminary boys were about to reject the principles of colonization for those of immediate emancipation. Birney followed the debate at Lane very closely. He visited the seminary for long talks with the students, and from that time forward the triumvirate of Weld-Stanton-Birney was a reality. We are familiar with the Lane debate and the emergence of Weld and Stanton as the two foremost authorities and lecturers. Birney went back to Danville, resigned from the colonization society and the Kentucky Society for the Gradual Relief of the State from Slavery, and publicly freed his slaves. He then wrote his *Letter on Colonization,* in which he exposed its utter failure to accomplish anything over a period of seventeen years and its tendency to oppression rather than Christian benevolence.[11]

The colonization principle and the complete failure of the movement had now been thoroughly discussed. The arguments presented were unanswerable and unanswered. Scores of prominent men throughout the North abandoned the movement and threw their support to antislavery societies, as Gurley had predicted they would do. Birney's shift to emancipation was a terrific blow to the Colonization Society. Gerrit Smith of New York criticized him severely, and Birney won him to the cause. His letter to Smith was written early in November 1834. In it, he made three very significant statements:

"It is the total failure of *gradualism* to lay hold of men's consciences, that must ever render it ineffectual for the extermination of slavery in our country."

"Truly, it seems to me, that Colonization has done more to rock the conscience of the Slaveholder into slumber, and to make his slumber soft and peaceful, than all other causes united."

"Do you not think it probable, that very gentle and calm measures would not have been sufficient to rouse up from its torpor the public sentiment of this nation, and make it, in spite of itself, look steadfastly at the sin and injustice of Slavery?"

Birney said to Smith that, by supporting colonization, he was doing more than any other living person to perpetuate slavery. "Against all efforts for the extirpation of slavery here," he said, "your name, your character, your arguments, your benefactions, are unceasingly arrayed."[12] Smith fol-

Gerrit Smith

lowed Birney into the movement for emancipation almost immediately and became one of the leaders in organizing the New York State Anti-Slavery Society the following year.

Meanwhile, Birney had written his *Letter to the Ministers and Elders of the Presbyterian Church in Kentucky.*[13] Slavery, he said, was born of violence and sustained by violence. It was an organized system of theft, by which the returns from the labor of some men were seized to provide ease and luxury for others. It was a system which brutalized master and slave alike, stimulating the most evil passions and impairing both mind and conscience. He discussed the Bible argument in support of slavery and challenged the ministers to lead a movement for complete emancipation by freeing their own slaves. The letter was, in some degree, a prelude to his later indictment of the churches as the bulwark of slavery. It was also an exposé of the deceptive excuse that the slaves were not prepared for freedom when nothing ever had been done, and nothing was presently permitted to be done, to qualify them for freedom by education. Both of Birney's letters were mailed by the hundreds to ministers and other professional men in the Mississippi Valley by the Lane Seminary students. The first had been published in the Lexington *Intelligencer,* the second in the Cincinnati *Journal.* They were reprinted in the New York *Evangelist* and *Emancipator* and as pamphlets by the American Anti-Slavery Society.

Birney now had gone farther than any other man or woman had ever been permitted to go in criticism of slavery and remain in the South. His friends urged him to "do nothing, say nothing, get along quietly—make money." Henry Clay warned him that opposition to slavery inevitably disqualified a man for public service.[14] He could not find a single member of the state legislature who favored emancipation. He was denied a professorship at Centre College, and he would have been denied support for any other public post or in any professional capacity. He was charged with mental illness by his old friends in Alabama, but his family connections and his record and reputation in public service had saved him from violence. Such dispensation by a people long accustomed to the exercise of arbitrary power would not long continue. The price of remaining in the South was silence. He was determined not to pay that price.

Weld and Elizur Wright secured Birney's appointment as a permanent agent of the American Anti-Slavery Society in October 1834.[15] He and Weld had been in constant communication, and before Weld began his agency in Ohio and Stanton went to Rhode Island, both in October, it was understood that Birney would remain in Kentucky to organize an antislavery society and publish an antislavery newspaper.

The Kentucky Anti-Slavery Society was organized at Danville, March 18, 1835.[16] It was little more than a formal association of Birney's friends who had courage enough to endorse publicly his antislavery activity. Birney then announced plans for the publication of an antislavery newspaper. Finally, he went to Putnam, Ohio, for the organization of the Ohio State Anti-Slavery Society, April 22, 1835. He went from there to New York for the annual meeting of the American Anti-Slavery Society, the second week in May, and then to the annual meeting of the Massachusetts Anti-Slavery Society in Boston.[17]

Birney's exile from Kentucky now was inevitable. He, himself, probably did not know, and much less can anyone say today, which of four actions was most offensive to the slave power.

He had tipped the scales against colonization in Kentucky, if not indeed in the nation. The de-

fections of Birney and Gerrit Smith were a terrific blow to the American Colonization Society. It had been particularly strong in Kentucky. Now, fewer people were interested in the subject, and contributions were harder to come by. Few Negroes ever had been expatriated, now there were almost no volunteers. Birney said in New York: "The Kentucky Colonization Society has now 1500 dollars on hand, and it is the general impression, that when this money is expended, nothing further will be done on the subject . . . The subject of colonization does not come into discussion."[18]

He had associated himself with a group of nationally known humanitarians and reformers: Theodore Weld and the Lane rebels, Arthur and Lewis Tappan, William Jay, William Lloyd Garrison, George Bourne, James Forten, and George Thompson from England, among others. Some of them were Negroes. All of them had been slandered and branded as incendiaries through the length and breadth of the slave country.

He had organized an antislavery society in the heart of Kentucky, and had announced his intention of publishing an antislavery newspaper. Since the Kentucky Society was auxiliary to the American Anti-Slavery Society, it was assumed that the paper would be supported by the latter organization, and at a time when the publications of the organization were being banned by the slave states and from the United States mails.

He was both informer and prosecutor. He knew the darker shadows of the slave system, and he exposed them mercilessly. He knew the foundation principles of the Republic, the Constitution, and the law, and he was no more deceived by the devious arguments of Calhoun than by the vagaries of Garrison. His indictment of slavery, made in his two published letters, in the constitution of the Kentucky Anti-Slavery Society, and in his speeches in Kentucky, New York, and Boston contained several points which always infuriated slaveholders.

Slaveholders always talked about Southern rights and Southern interests as if slavery was beneficial to everyone in that section. They talked Southern solidarity, they turned viciously upon any Southerner who deviated, and they greatly feared anything which might turn nonslaveholders against them. Birney simply said that these people who had any direct connection with slavery constituted less than one-third of the white population of the slave states, yet slavery was a menace to the peace and safety of all. It cast a stigma upon the honest toil of white men. It forced nonslaveholding farmers to move out of the slave country.

Slavery, he said, was a sin sustained by the churches and defended by the ministry. It was contrary to the principles on which the nation was founded, yet was sustained by the political press. It was condemned by the civilized world. It survived as an institution peculiarly American, and only because of the great power of the nation. Any idea that the slave states could strike out on an independent course and survive was pure nonsense. They had survived so far only because the slaves knew powerful forces were at work for their freedom.

Birney made very clear at New York why he had come to the North and affiliated with the American Anti-Slavery Society. Slavery was a national problem, and "the whole moral power of the free states should be concentrated, and brought into action for the extermination of slavery." Constant pressure must be brought to bear. Northern people were deeply involved, not only because education, religion, and politics brought slaveholders and nonslaveholders together in determination of policies, but because nonslaveholders sustained by their votes slavery in the District of Columbia, surrendered fugitive slaves, and oppressed free Negroes. "Look at your treatment of the free colored population," said Birney. "What have you done for them? You have persecuted them, you have taken no care of them, but have trampled them down, and kept them down, and then wondered that they did not rise up to the heavens, and have been astonished that they betray no brilliancy of talent, no splendor of intellectual attainment."

Then, turning upon the South once more, he ridiculed the idea that slavery was any better in Kentucky than in Mississippi, or any better in Virginia than in Louisiana, or any better than it had been two hundred years before. "Slavery," he said, "is substantially the same everywhere. Does not its essence lie in the counteraction of the human will?" The number of slaves in the market place had not declined; it had increased. It had become a system which "will not be shaken but by shaking this government." The slaveholders' power over the slaves had not been curtailed in the slightest degree, because "slavery" was an unnatural state, and it required an unnatural power

to uphold it. Just as many children were now separated from their parents, and just as many wives from husbands as ever, and the churches had been reduced to a state of moral paralysis. "Slavery never can be better," he said. "Power ever leads to its own abuse. After two hundred years, there is still no change for the better." Unless the operations of the American Anti-Slavery Society could succeed, slavery would end in "tremendous and desolating violence."[19]

Birney returned to Danville, Kentucky, to battle once more for the constitutional right to publish. Thirty-three prominent citizens presented to him a remonstrance of most remarkable character. Many of them were colonizationists; all professed to believe slavery a moral and political evil. They did not threaten Birney with violence if he insisted upon publishing his antislavery paper; they said they were seeking to protect him from violence that would materialize in some mysterious fashion by prevailing upon him not to publish. Would he refrain from attempting to do what "no *American Slaveholding Community* has found itself able to bear" until legislation could be secured which would prevent publication of an antislavery paper.[20]

Birney's reply was a denial of legislative power to interfere with freedom of the press. No one could stop the discussion of a question so vital to the interests of all the people. It was well started, and would continue, and any effort to force it underground would be very dangerous. The discussion must continue in the slave states else it would be intensified in the free states.[21]

The slaveholders then called a public meeting at the Baptist Church in Danville, July 25, 1835. Birney had said in his reply to their first remonstrance "that the *slaveholding spirit produces the aristocratic spirit*—and the *slaveholding practice*, especially in the *planting South*, the *aristocratic practice*—with as lofty a spirit in each large slaveholder, as if he had his patent of nobility in his pocket." The meeting, of some five hundred persons, was of the aristocracy. Money, education, and religion were represented. James Barbour, president of the Branch Bank of Kentucky and treasurer and trustee of Centre College, presided. The Reverend J. K. Birch, moderator of the Presbyterian Synod of Kentucky, spoke at the meeting. Three important resolutions were passed. One denounced the attempt of Birney to publish a paper supported by distant strangers "as a direct

attack upon, and a wanton disregard of our domestic relations." A second one asserted that less
than one-tenth of the people in the area supported
Birney. A third denounced his project as "wild,
visionary, impracticable, impolitical, and contrary
to the spirit of our laws, and at war with the
spirit of our Constitution."[22] "The Devil," wrote
Weld, "will not give up his hold without a death
struggle."[23]

The organized antislavery movement in Kentucky ended at this point. A mob gathered on the
morning of July 29 to destroy the press of the
Olive Branch which was to publish Birney's *Philanthropist,* perhaps to do violence to the man
himself. There were some courageous men prepared to defend him and his right to publish, but
violence was avoided by the transfer of the property back to its original owner, J. J. Polk, who, by
his own testimony, had a legal claim to it. Polk
said, after the Civil War, that at the time of this
incident, it "was as much as a man's life was
worth to say [in Danville] he was in favor of
emancipation." Birney stated publicly at the time
that Polk was one of the instigators of the mob.[24]

Birney now had no place to publish. An ignorant
postmaster refused to deliver antislavery publications sent to him from the Northern states. His
former law partner, Arthur F. Hopkins, warned
him not to come to Alabama. He could not collect moneys due him there because no attorney
would handle his business. He was slandered
from one end of the South to the other as a victim
of mental hallucinations and a madman bent on
inciting a slave insurrection. One meeting spoke
of Arthur Tappan as a fanatic and amalgamation-
ist, another said Birney was worse than Tappan.
There was nothing for him to do but to leave the
South, or to remain there in silence and lifelong
disgrace. There was nothing else for his close
associates to do. Birney settled his business affairs
and moved to Cincinnati, and his father later
warned him not to come back across the river
even for a visit.

James G. Birney

CIVIL RIGHTS

Chapter 24

James G. Birney, writing to Gerrit Smith on September 13, 1835, said that it was time for Christians to leave the slave states because there was no longer hope for redemption of that section, then went on to say: "It is as much as all the patriotism in our country can do, to keep alive the spirit of liberty in the *free states*. The contest is becoming—has become—one, not alone of freedom for the *black*, but of freedom for the *white*. It has now become absolutely necessary, that Slavery should cease in order that freedom may be preserved to any portion of our land. The antagonist principles of liberty and slavery have been roused into action and one or the other must be victorious. There will be no cessation of the strife until Slavery shall be exterminated, or liberty destroyed."[1]

The contest over civil rights was far advanced when Birney made this observation. He himself had experienced the loneliness of a man condemned by his former friends and neighbors: unable to publish, denied his mail, shunned by professional men as though a carrier of the plague. He was one of many. Free enquiry and discussion can not be said to have existed anywhere in the country in 1835.

The slave power threatened everyone with mob violence who spoke against slavery; imposed extreme legal penalties of life imprisonment and death upon anyone circulating antislavery literature in the slave states; invaded post offices and censured the mails; denied the right of petition and for a time suppressed all discussion of slavery in Congress; devised an ingenious philosophy of

silence which it sought to engraft upon the fundamental law of the nation; demanded suppression by the federal and northern state governments of all antislavery activities; sought to restrain churches and schools from their normal processes of mental and moral improvement of society; incited mob violence against free Negroes and antislavery men; and dug down deep into the relics of barbarism for three ideas: charging the guilt of mob violence upon the victim of the mob; subordinating individual rights to social interests as determined at any time by public sentiment; and allowing law enforcement officials to protect persons and property at their own discretion.

No part of this arbitrary and proscriptive action can be separated out from the rest. Slaveholders and colonizationists were back of the whole of it. Slaveholders were defending a system of racial adjustment, a large capital investment, and the basis of excessive political power. Colonizationists, who believed implicitly in the doctrine of biological inequality and racial inferiority of the Negro, were the right arm in the North of the slave system.[2] They controlled in the North the newspapers, the general church associations, the political parties and the professions, as the slaveholders did in the South. They were not interested in emancipation of the slaves, nor in the elevation of the free Negroes, but in ridding their communities of what was regarded as an undesirable and permanently degraded element. They hated the Negroes and their white friends because all of these opposed expatriation. They encouraged outrages against them to force them out. The mass of the people had nothing to do with all of this. Even the persecution of free Negroes and mob violence against antislavery men were not sudden outbursts of popular fury. Men of every social class, religion, and station in life were involved, but the social aristocracy was responsible, and where it did not actively participate it contributed mightily by winking at any action the ruffians might take. No evidence exists of mob action except where it was incited by newspapers, preachers, politicians, or large property holders. They accepted uncritically the idea of Negro inferiority, or they knew better and were unwilling to make the effort to help a people suffering from generations of oppression.

Henry B. Stanton said: "The criminal public sentiment that grinds down with an unrelenting prejudice the colored people, is the same public sentiment that supports the Colonization Society and is wielded by it."[3] Stanton and Weld were the two greatest antislavery lecturers and the two most mobbed men in America. They knew almost every crossroads in the country, all classes of people, and the currents and crosscurrents of public opinion. Weld was in Washington, D. C., during the antibank riots in Cincinnati, in 1842. Writing to his wife, Angelina Grimké Weld, he said: "A Cincinnati paper has just come to hand informing that a mob has been raging there for six hours. Failure of the banks to pay specie was the occasion. Three banks were destroyed, their books were scattered to the winds, and their vaults forced. The city authorities, military and all, were beaten off the field. They that sow the wind shall reap the whirlwind. The city authorities themselves, the bankers and brokers, were the leaders of the mob against the abolitionists. Now the cup of trembling is pressed to their own lips. They raised the storm whose fury now spends itself on them."[4] A catalogue of events and a categorical analysis of those events throws much new light on the subject.

We know that Angelina Grimké was warned by the public authorities of Charleston not to visit her home after she espoused the antislavery cause. We know that James G. Birney was warned by no less a person than his own father that his life would be forfeit if he returned to Kentucky. We have the long list of prominent men who left the South because they were commanded by church and civil authorities to remain silent on the slavery question. We have the well-documented story

of Amos Dresser, the inoffensive college student who went to Nashville to sell Bibles, was seized by a mob on July 11, 1835, publicly whipped, and expelled from the community.[5] We have the equally well-documented story of Aaron W. Kitchell, a young man from Princeton Theological Seminary. He was seized by a mob at Hillsborough, Georgia, June 8, 1836, on suspicion of talking with slaves, and was whipped, tarred and feathered, and expelled from the state.[6] We know that a committee of vigilance of Feliciana Parish, Louisiana, offered $50,000 for the delivery to them of Arthur Tappan of New York and that such offers for the Tappans, William Lloyd Garrison, and others were common throughout the South. Any one of them, had he gone to Charleston, New Orleans, Vicksburg, perhaps even St. Louis, would have been summarily hanged, perhaps worse, instantly upon recognition. This public attitude was condoned, aided and abetted by the newspapers.[7]

South Carolina in 1820 made it a high misdemeanor to introduce into the state any written or printed matter subversive to slavery. On the evening of July 29, 1835, a mob at Charleston, South Carolina, broke into the United States Post Office, removed a bag of mail containing antislavery publications addressed to prominent citizens of the state, and burned them in the public square. The City Council then called a general meeting of citizens, which appointed a vigilance committee of twenty-one persons, under the direction of Robert Y. Hayne, of national reputation from the Webster-Hayne debates. This committee made arrangements with the postmaster for members of the committee to meet the mail boats, escort the mail to the post office, and remove and destroy all offensive publications. This was not an isolated incident, and the matter did not end in Charleston, any more than mob action against Birney's press ended in Danville.

Two weeks after the Charleston invasion of the United States mails, the legislatures of that state and of North Carolina passed resolutions variously restating the doctrine of delegated and restricted powers and making certain demands upon the free states. Resolution No. 4 of North Carolina, December 19, 1835, read as follows: "Resolved that our sister states are respectfully requested to enact penal laws, prohibiting the printing within their respective limits, all such publications as may have a tendency to make our slaves discontented with their present condition, or incite them to insurrection." South Carolina, December 20, 1835, went much farther. Resolution No. 3 of that state read: "Resolved, That the legislature of South Carolina, having every confidence in the justice and friendship of the non-slaveholding states, announces to her co-states her confident expectation, and she earnestly requests that the governments of these states will promptly and effectually suppress all those associations within their respective limits, purporting to be abolition societies, and that they will make it highly penal to print, publish and distribute newspapers, pamphlets, tracts and pictorial representations, calculated and having an obvious tendency to excite the slaves of the southern states to insurrection and revolt."

Georgia, Alabama, and Virginia followed with resolutions of their own in January, February, and March, 1836. Resolution No. 3 of Georgia said: "Resolved, That the perpetuity of this glorious Union, which has shed such blessings on us as a people, is only to be ensured by a strict adherence to the letter of the Constitution, which has guaranteed to us certain rights with which we will suffer no power on earth to interfere—that it is deeply incumbent on the people of the north to crush the traitorous designs of the abolitionists, and that we look with confidence to such movements on their part as will effectually put an end to impertinent, fanatical and disloyal interference with matters settled by the Constitution." Alabama, in Resolution No. 1, said: "That it is the decided sense of this general assembly, that we call upon our sister states, and respectfully request them to enact such penal laws, as will finally put an end to the malignant deeds of the abolitionists, calculated to destroy our peace, and sever the Union."

Resolutions No. 2 and 3 of Virginia were elaborate:

2. "Resolved, that the State of Virginia has a right to claim prompt and efficient legislation by her co-states to restrain as far as may be, and to punish, those of their citizens, who, in defiance of the obligations of social duty and those of the Constitution, assail her safety and tranquility, by forming associations for the abolition of slavery, or printing, publishing, or circulating through the mail or otherwise, seditious and incendiary publications, designed, calculated, or having a tendency to operate on her population, and that this right, founded as it is on the principles of inter-

national law, is peculiarly fortified by a just consideration of the intimate and sacred relations that exist between the States of this Union."

3. "Resolved, That the non-slave-holding states of the Union are respectfully, but earnestly requested, promptly to adopt penal enactments, or such other measures as will effectually suppress all associations within their respective limits, purporting to be, or having the character of, abolition societies; and that they will make it highly penal to print, publish, or distribute, newspapers, pamphlets, or other publications calculated or having a tendency to excite the slaves of the southern states to insurrection and revolt."[8]

The next step in this unfolding drama involved the post-office department because the postmaster in New York City, following the Charleston obstruction of the mails, detained all publications of the American Anti-Slavery Society addressed to persons in the slave states. Postmaster General Amos Kendall, of Kentucky, then issued a most remarkable statement, saying: "After mature consideration of the subject, and seeking the best advice within my reach, I am confirmed in the opinion, that the Postmaster-General has no legal authority, by any order or regulation of his department, to exclude from the mails any species of newspapers, magazines, or pamphlets. Such a power vested in the head of this department would be fearfully dangerous, and has been properly withheld." Then, he revealed the low estate to which federal authority had sunk under Andrew Jackson and the degree of subserviency to the slightest whims of the slaveholders by saying: "By no act or direction of mine, official or private, could I be induced to aid, knowingly, in giving circulation to papers of this description, directly or indirectly. We owe an obligation to the laws, but a higher one to the communities in which we live, and if the former be perverted to destroy the latter, it is patriotism to disregard them. Entertaining these views, I cannot sanction and will not condemn the step you have taken."[9]

This was a masterpiece of evasion, duplicity, and neglect of duty. Furthermore, it was an abject surrender of governmental authority. There might be some question as to whether Calhoun had won on the tariff issue; there was no question about this victory. Kendall went on to say: "There is reason to doubt whether these abolitionists have a right to make use of the mails of the United States to convey their publications into the states where their circulation is forbidden by law; and it is by no means certain that the mail carriers and Postmasters are secure from the penalties of the law [death in some states, penitentiary sentences in others] if they knowingly carry, distribute, or hand them out." The Southern state legislatures had not asked for federal legislation to suppress these publications; they had made their demands upon the Northern state legislatures. They did not want federal action, they wanted federal inaction, and that is what they got.

William Leggett, editor of the New York *Evening Post,* representing the view of many editors who, like himself, were not antislavery men, said: "Neither the General Post Office, nor the General Government itself, possesses any power to prohibit the transportation by mail of abolition tracts. On the contrary it is the bounden duty of the Government to protect the abolitionists in their constitutional right of free discussion, and opposed, sincerely and zealously as we are, to their doctrines and practice, we should be still more opposed to any infringement of their political or civil rights. If the Government once begins to discriminate as to what is orthodox and what heterodox in opinion, what is safe and what is unsafe in its tendency, farewell, a long farewell, to our freedom."[10]

No efforts whatever were made to punish Hayne and others for robbing the mails in Charleston. The postmaster general ordered all postal authorities to obey state laws with regard to antislavery literature. Even after Congress imposed heavy penalties upon postmasters who refused to deliver mail, no action was taken. Postmasters from one end of the slave states to the other, with few exceptions, destroyed antislavery literature which came into their hands. Their duty to do so, as required by state law, was reaffirmed by Postmaster General Holt, as late as Buchanan's administration. Slaveholders had kept the masses ignorant by refusing to establish public schools. They had kept the slaves ignorant by imposing heavy penalties upon anyone who taught them to read. They drove everyone who criticized slavery out of the slave states and suppressed all antislavery newspapers. They now stopped all antislavery publications from coming into the South by censoring the United States mails. It is a fair conclusion that not one person in one thousand in the slave states ever heard or read an antislavery argument or had even the slightest idea of

what the antislavery people were talking about.

President Andrew Jackson was just as ignorant of the issues involved. He accepted without the slightest hesitation the charge that antislavery publications addressed to prominent Southerners were designed to stir up the slaves to insurrection. He so far forgot the principles of democratic government and the dignity of his official position as to compliment persons who had "given so strong and impressive a tone to the sentiments entertained against the proceedings of the misguided persons who have engaged in these unconstitutional and wicked attempts," meaning, of course, he congratulated those who mobbed antislavery lecturers, destroyed printing presses, and broke up peaceable assemblages of people. He did not condone withholding of mail from addressees, but he took no action to prevent Kendall from doing so. He recommended that postmasters list the names of everyone subscribing to antislavery publications and publish them in the newspapers "for there are few so hardened in villainy, as to withstand the frowns of all good men."

Jackson then all but spoiled Calhoun's program of subordinating federal power to that of the states. He asked Congress, December 7, 1835, for legislation to prohibit the sending of incendiary literature through the mails into the South. Calhoun threw his full weight against such legislation. He recognized it as a step in the direction of greater federal power. The federal government should recognize the power of the states to exclude incendiary publications and assist them in doing so. A move in any other direction would deprive the South of the power to protect itself against a flood of antislavery literature.

Jackson did not get legislation to exclude, and Calhoun did not get legislation making mail carriers and postmasters subject to state laws. An amendment was offered to the bill for the reorganization of the Post Office Department, May 25, 1836, which would have done both of these things. It was promptly challenged as censorship of the press and was immediately rejected.[11] The Act for Reorganization as then passed provided $500 fine and six months imprisonment for any postmaster convicted of detaining letters, packages, pamphlets, or newspapers to prevent or delay delivery (Section 32).[12] Laws, unfortunately, meant nothing to Kendall. He had referred to the Constitution as a compact. He had said the states were justified in taking "any measures necessary" to exclude antislavery literature. He deplored his lack of legal authority to exclude by departmental regulation. He had virtually invited the states to take punitive action against postmasters and mailmen who delivered the publications. He informed postmasters that it was their duty to examine newspapers, to determine if they were incendiary in character, and detain them as a "voluntary" act.[13] Kendall defended his position in an elaborate argument. In substance, he held that persons who would be subject to severe penalties extending to life imprisonment or even death in every slave state, if they resided therein and spoke or wrote against slavery, should not be permitted to use the government mail service to disseminate their inflammatory literature in those states without risk to themselves; that the federal government was obligated to suppress insurrections and therefore to prevent distribution of literature through the mails which would precipitate slave revolts; and exclusion of antislavery literature would protect the mail service against destruction by mobs and make possible speedy and safe delivery of legitimate correspondence.[14]

Calhoun, in one grand flourish, then sought to sanctify this prostration of federal power by offering his Resolutions of 1837 in the Senate. The several states, said Calhoun, formed the Union to increase their security from foreign and domestic dangers and to strengthen and make more secure their institutions. They did not delegate to the general government, but retained, each to itself, control over these domestic institutions. "Any intermeddling of any one or more States, or a combination of their citizens, with the domestic institutions and policy of the others, on any ground or under any pretext whatever, political, moral or religious, with a view to their alteration, or subversion, is an assumption of superiority not warranted by the Constitution, insulting to the States interfered with, tending to endanger their domestic peace and tranquility, subversive of the objects for which the Constitution was formed, and, by necessary consequence, tending to weaken and destroy the Union itself."

He added that the federal government was obligated to promote the security and prosperity of the several states, to use its powers to uphold and strengthen their respective domestic institutions, and to resist all efforts of one section to use it as an instrument of attack upon the institutions of another section. Slavery was an important domestic institution of the Southern states previous to adoption of the Constitution. Attacks upon it by the citizens of other states were a violation of the terms of the compact. Any agitation for or action toward abolishing slavery in the District of Columbia or in the territories, or excluding a slave state from the Union, would be contrary to equality of the states and destroy the Union.

Calhoun was speaking for the slaveholders. They were denying the right of any man to raise his voice against slavery. They were denying the right of anyone to advocate congressional exclusion of slavery from the District of Columbia or the territories. Congress, they insisted, could take no action with respect to slavery except to strengthen, defend, and extend it. It must, therefore, use its full power to counteract antislavery agitation. To question the righteousness of slavery was to violate the moral obligations assumed by the founding fathers and their descendants in perpetuity.[15]

Northern state legislatures refused to suppress antislavery publications, and they refused to outlaw antislavery societies. There was no evidence, and there is no evidence available today, of any intention on the part of antislavery people to encourage slave insurrections. Antislavery literature sent into the South was not addressed to slaves but to responsible white people, especially to men in the professions and in public office. Slaves could not read in any case, and inflammatory antislavery literature was almost nonexistent. The American Anti-Slavery Society urged congressional committees to examine their headquarters, challenging them to find a single publication to support the charges of incendiarism.

The question of state punitive action against antislavery men and measures in response to Southern demands was discussed in all Northern legislatures. Ohio was a key state in the controversy, and there Governor Robert Lucas, staunch Jacksonian Democrat, although condemning antislavery agitation, ruled out of consideration as unconstitutional either legislation or extradition. The language of the state constitution protecting freedom of speech and of the press was so emphatic and direct that there could have been no argument. It said further: "No person shall be liable to transportation out of this state for any offense committed within the state." The Southern requests were discussed fully in legislative committee, but no act was presented for passage. Maine, New

Hampshire, Vermont, and Connecticut also refused to act without contests.

In Pennsylvania the Southern demands were denounced by Governor Joseph Ritner and by the chairman of the legislative committee, Thaddeus Stevens, but not before retiring Governor George Wolf had denounced the antislavery movement as "the offspring of fanaticism of the most dangerous and alarming character," and had indirectly endorsed mob violence with two suggestions: that it "be left to public opinion alone to check and control the further progress of this misdirected enthusiasm," and that a firm expression of opinion by the legislature with reference to this "highly dangerous" movement be made to give "tone and expression to public sentiment."[16] In New York, Governor William L. Marcy was caught between the demands of party solidarity on the one hand and antislavery power on the other. Marcy shuddered at the thought of offending the South. But New York was the headquarters of the American Anti-Slavery Society, and most antislavery publications were printed there. Finally, he condemned antislavery men in language worthy of a slaveholder in his message to the legislature, but he refused the demand of Governor John Gayle of Alabama that Robert G. Williams, publishing agent of the American Anti-Slavery Society, be delivered to that state as a fugitive from justice.[17] The statement in the *Emancipator* upon which the grand jury and governor of Alabama demanded the surrender of Williams was: "God commands and all nature cries out that man should not be held as property. The system of making men property has plunged 2,250,000 of our fellow countrymen into the deepest physical and moral degradation, and they are every moment sinking deeper."[18]

The idea that a citizen of a Northern state, who published antislavery literature which was sent into a slave state, was equally guilty of inciting insurrection as any person living within the slave state, and should be subject to extradition and punishment within the slave state under the laws, was made in all seriousness and was universally supported in the South. It shows how warped judgments had become. The legislature refused to support Marcy's position, and passed no legislation.[19]

The real test came in Massachusetts, because Garrison's *Liberator* was published in Boston. Governor Edward Everett, hopelessly ignorant of what had been happening, apparently blamed the antislavery people for mob action. He then repeated the assertion that has become through the years one of the cornerstones of Southern mythology: that Southern liberals were moving that section rapidly toward emancipation when antislavery agitation began in the North and reversed the trend in the South. Everett referred the resolutions of the slave states to the legislature, but did not request legislation.

It is not likely that the legislature would have passed any punitive laws in view of the extraordinary courtesies shown to Angelina Grimké and Henry B. Stanton within the year, but the Massachusetts Anti-Slavery Society asked the legislative committee for a hearing, which was granted. Antislavery people, they explained, sought complete, immediate abolition of slavery. They relied entirely upon moral suasion and education and appealed only to free persons, not to slaves. They examined slavery in the light of Christian faith and pronounced it a sin. They had a right to do so, "a right," said the committee, "conferred upon us by our creator—a right enforced by his explicit command, 'to plead for the oppressed'—a right most solemnly asserted by the founders of our Republic—a right exercised by our fellow-citizens from the first moment of our national existence—a right which our national and state constitutions explicitly guaranteed to us and to all the free people of the land."[20]

The committee challenged anyone to find encouragement to violence or insurrection in antislavery publications.[21]

They called attention to the fact that the very people in the South who were loudly protesting against the circulation of antislavery literature as likely to excite slave insurrections were at the same time printing in their own papers and shouting from the house tops the strongest passages from such literature in order to crystallize public opinion against the societies. They denied that any publications had ever been sent to slaves, or any agents sent among them. They denied any claim to federal jurisdiction over slavery in the states.

The committee quoted the guarantees of freedom of speech and of the press contained in the federal and several state constitutions, including those of the Southern states. They cited the clear violations of these constitutional guarantees by the laws of the Southern states, and the defense of such laws as an exercise of legislative authority "to suppress whatever discussions or publications shall be deemed subversive of the public safety or peace."[22] They denied that legislative bodies possessed any such discretionary powers, because to acknowledge discretionary power is to sanction unlimited power. They quoted the scintillating paragraph from Rhode Island's guarantee of religious freedom: "To suffer the civil magistrate to intrude his power into the field of opinion, and restrain the profession or propagation of principles, on supposition of their ill tendency, is a dangerous fallacy, which at once destroys all religious liberty, because he, being of course judge of that tendency, will make his opinions the rule of judgment, and approve or condemn the sentiments of others, only as they shall square with, or differ from his own. It is time enough for the rightful purposes of civil government, for its officers to interfere, when principles break forth into overt acts against peace and order; and finally, truth is great, and will prevail, if left to herself; she is the proper and sufficient antagonist of error, and has nothing to fear from the conflict, unless by human interference disarmed of her natural weapons, free argument and debate; errors ceasing to be dangerous when truth is permitted freely to combat them."[23]

The committee discussed the Southern claims that antislavery activities were in violation of the principles of international law, of the common law, and of the constitutional compact. They cited the complete absence of any evidence of a compact in the Constitution and the proceedings of the ratifying conventions that people should not speak or write against slavery. They referred to the antislavery activities of men like John Jay, Benjamin Franklin, and Benjamin Rush, to the antislavery pronouncements of men like Thomas Jefferson and William Pinckney, and to the abolition of slavery in several states after the Constitution was adopted. They insisted the Union was formed to secure more effectually the liberties of the people, whereas the Southern claims embraced the theory of restricted liberty for the sake of Union. They quoted at length from Calhoun's speech against President Jackson's request for legislation abridging freedom of the press.

The committee then made its contribution to the rapidly evolving doctrine of the Higher Law: "We claim . . . that Abolitionists and Anti-Slavery Societies are guilty of nothing more nor less, than a consistent vindication and exercise of the fundamental, inherent, and inalienable rights of man, which no human Constitutions can either originate or annul, though they may protect or infringe . . . are engaged in a work, without which the liberties of mankind in general, and of our laboring population at the North in particular, can never be secured . . . Cannot be proscribed, either by penal enactments or legislative censure, without a proscription of the first principles of republican freedom . . . fatal, of necessity to the liberties and sovereignty of the people.

"Our doctrine of inalienable rights is the doctrine of our National Declaration of Independence . . . of the Bible. We maintain this doctrine because it is unalterable Truth . . . a cardinal principle of the Christian religion from the practical operation of which its incomparable morality results."[24]

Any laws, explained the committee, which punished men for maintaining and defending this doctrine would run counter to the basic principle of Christianity and of civil and religious freedom and would establish dangerous precedents. Any resolutions of censure would be even worse, because expressions of opinion concerning the past conduct of citizens are not the function of legislatures, and in this case would only contribute to popular hatred of antislavery men and measures. Neither laws nor censure could possibly silence the opponents of slavery or arrest the progress of antislavery principles.

Finally, the committee asserted an eternal conflict between free labor and slave labor, quoting at great length the infamous speech of Governor McDuffie of South Carolina, in which he declared slavery to be "the cornerstone of our Republican edifice." They spoke out strongly against the inability of antislavery men and free Negroes to travel in the South, against kidnapping under the operation of the fugitive slave law, and against the practice of offering rewards at the South for the abduction of Northern men.

THE PRUDENCE CRANDALL CASE

Chapter 25

Refusal of Northern state legislatures to follow the example of those in the slave states in suppressing antislavery publications and organizations did not wholly sustain the basic democratic principle of free enquiry and discussion. People always have found it easy to crucify those who differ with them. They never succeed in suppressing ideas in this way, but they never fail to try, and they seem to get a sadistic pleasure from the effort. Such was the public attitude toward the slaves and the free Negroes and their antislavery friends. Great souls must always bear a certain amount of rudeness and disrespect. The liberals, the humanitarians, the intellectuals, the philanthropists, and practitioners of Christian benevolence of the 1830's were no exception. The American people in 1830, certainly, were an ill-mannered lot, and when slaveholders, men in high public office, and political newspapers chanted a hymn of hate, ill manners turned to brutality. The shame of what happened then will always be with us. It could not have happened if public officials had performed the most elementary duty of protecting persons and property. They did not do so. The caprice of public opinion in a given community at a given time took from the law control of the affairs of men. The result was either mob violence or legal persecution, or both.

The first outburst of public hostility toward Negroes and their antislavery friends to attract national attention was the Prudence Crandall Case at Canterbury, Connecticut.[1] Miss Crandall, in January 1833, admitted to her private school for young ladies seventeen-year-old Sarah Harris, daughter of a highly respected local Negro family. The white pupils made the adjustment easily enough, but some white parents and others protested. Miss Crandall then closed her school to white girls and opened it to *Negro girls only* in April 1833. The students were recruited from substantial Negro families in Boston, New York, Philadelphia, and Providence, with the aid of a group of prominent men of both races, including Samuel E. Cornish, George Bourne, James Forten, Samuel J. May, Simeon S. Jocelyn, and Arnold Buffum.[2]

Sentiment in the town against Miss Crandall was whipped into a frenzy by Andrew T. Judson, ambitious local politician and guiding genius of the local colonization society. This was a continuation of the battle against Jocelyn's project at New Haven, but one step farther down the ladder toward barbarism. Judson and his cohorts remonstrated with Miss Crandall. They dumped a load of manure in her well. They refused to sell her supplies and threatened her father and brother with mob violence, fine, and imprisonment if they continued to bring her food from their nearby farm. They piled refuse from a slaughter house on her front porch. They called a town meeting, refused to permit Samuel J. May and Arnold Buffum to speak in her behalf, and resolved to oppose the school "at all hazards." They tried to buy her out. They stoned her and her pupils on the street. They shut them out of the church services. They pelted the house with rotten eggs. The doctors refused medical care to Miss Crandall when she was ill.

They prepared to whip the girl pupils in the public square under the provisions of the vagrancy laws and were stopped from doing so only because Samuel J. May posted bond of $10,000 provided by prominent men of Brooklyn. Judson then secured passage of a state law forbidding the harboring, boarding, or instruction in any manner or form whatsoever of any "person of color" not an inhabitant of the state "without the consent in writing, first obtained, of a majority of the Civil Authority, and also of the Select Men of the town." The law did not apply to public schools, nor to incorporated academies and colleges. The penalty for the first offense was a fine of $100, for the second offense $200, and for each succeeding offense double the amount of the preceding one.

There was no question about Miss Crandall's violation of the law. There was serious question about the constitutionality of the law. Miss Crandall was arrested, and Rufus Adams, justice of the peace, ordered her to trial before the county court. This being a trial in the court of public opinion, as well as in a court of law, she refused to post bond and was detained in jail until it was posted by antislavery friends and advisers. She was then tried before Judge Eaton of the county court, August 23, 1833. Andrew T. Judson conducted the prosecution; Calvin Goddard, Henry Strong, and W. W. Ellsworth the defense. Arthur Tappan paid the cost of the defense. The jury failed three times to reach a verdict. Miss Crandall was then tried again, this time before the notoriously reactionary professor of law and chief justice of the State Supreme Court, David Daggett, whose knowledge of history was very bad, and whose hostility toward Negroes, defense of slavery, and support of the Connecticut Black Law not only unfitted him for the bench in any cases involving these issues but blackened an otherwise creditable, though not distinguished, record of public service.

Miss Crandall was convicted, but she was convicted because of Daggett's charge to the jury, in which he declared that Negroes were not citizens of the United States. Said he: "It would be a perversion of terms, and the well-known rule of construction to say that slaves, free blacks or Indians, were citizens within the meaning of that term, as used in the Constitution. God forbid that I should add to the degradation of this race of men; but I am bound, by my duty, to say they are not citizens."[3] Daggett had played a leading part in preventing establishment of the Negro college in New Haven, where he was professor of law. Now, as judge, he gave a future chief justice of the

United States a judicial precedent for the notorious Dred Scott decision. The proceedings were set aside on technical grounds by the Court of Errors, the full court revolting against the decision, but being unwilling apparently to reverse it in the existing excitement.

Miss Crandall's school was then set on fire, and an unsuccessful attempt was made to foist the blame upon a Negro friend of the school. Finally, every window and window frame in the building was broken out by a mob during the night. Miss Crandall then closed her school on insistence of the Reverend Calvin Philleo, whom she had recently married. They went to northern Illinois, where all of her remaining years she taught Negro children. Her brother, who had stood loyally by her at Canterbury, was arrested on a trumped-up charge of distributing antislavery literature in Washington, D. C. He was held in jail before trial for nearly a year. He was acquitted, but never recovered his health and died in 1836. Andrew T. Judson realized his ambition of going to Congress, but was defeated for re-election. The tide of public opinion was already running heavily against such men. The chairman of the Senate committee which wrote the notorious black law, Phillip Pearl, was converted by Theodore Weld in 1837 and said: "I could weep tears of blood for the part I took in that matter. I now regard that law as utterly abominable. The truth is my prejudices against that poor persecuted class of people were so violent as to blind me to the dictates of common humanity and justice." He led the successful movement for repeal of the law in 1838.[4] Prudence Philleo lived through the war, the emancipation of the slaves, and the enfranchisement of the Negroes in Connecticut, but her greatest joy must have come from a Connecticut pension and erasure from the record of her conviction of 1834 on petitions signed and promoted by the nephew of Andrew T. Judson.

The trial of Miss Crandall on the charge of harboring, boarding, and instructing colored persons not inhabitants of the state of Connecticut, in violation of state law, is one of our most important cases in the history of the antislavery movement. The history of the case begins with the Declaration of Independence. The founding fathers based their action upon the doctrine of inalienable rights, conferred by the Creator, and possessed in common and on equal terms by all men. They established a general government of such nature as seemed best suited to the maintenance of those rights. It was a Republican government, the true foundation of which is, in the words of Jefferson, "the equal rights of every citizen, in his person and property, and in their management." The state of Massachusetts, for example, wrote into her Bill of Rights the first sentence of the Declaration of Independence, and, in a judicial decision the soundness of which was never questioned, it was held to have abolished every vestige of slavery in the state. The people of *that* state, at least, approved the doctrine that slavery and the foundation principles of the nation were incompatible. The House of Representatives said in 1839: "Since the spirit of the Revolution broke the chains of slavery in Massachusetts, no inequality of civil rights has here existed."[5]

The intellectual giants of the Revolution then framed the Articles of Confederation and, finally, the Constitution. If they had expressly stated that the Declaration of Independence was a part of the fundamental law of the land, every vestige of slavery must have been destroyed immediately. The more advanced antislavery men held that they *were* inseparable, Alvan Stewart saying in 1838: "To tolerate slavery a single year in one of these states, after this Declaration of Independence, was a base hypocrisy, a violation of our engagements to mankind, and to God."[6] There was such a storm of protest over omission of a Bill of Rights from the Constitution that the first ten amendments were promptly added. In the Constitution itself, Article IV, Section 2, it was stated: "The citizens of each State shall be entitled to all Privileges and Immunities of Citizens in the several states," and in the Amendments, Article V, it was said that no person should "be deprived of life, liberty, or property, without due process of law." Antislavery men insisted that all men were equal in the sight of God; and, by virtue of the Declaration, were equal under the Constitution and laws of the United States. They insisted that privileges and immunities were the natural right of man. Finally, they insisted that free Negroes were citizens; some insisted that slaves were citizens.

The Prudence Crandall case occurred midway between two learned pronouncements on this important subject. The first, pertaining to United States citizenship, was by John Sergeant of Pennsylvania in the Missouri debates. Speaking of the rights and privileges of a citizen of the United

COLORED SCHOOLS BROKEN UP, IN THE FREE STATES.
When schools have been established for colored scholars, the law-makers and the mob have combined to destroy them ;—as at Canterbury, Ct., at Canaan, N. H., Aug. 10, 1835, at Zanesville and Brown Co., Ohio, in 1836.

IMMEDIATE EMANCIPATION.

Aug. 1, 1834, 30,000 slaves were emancipated in Antigua. Without any apprenticeship, or system of preparation, preceding the act, the chains were broken at a stroke, and they all went out FREE ! It is now four years since these 30,000 slaves were "turned loose" among 2,000 whites, their former masters. These masters fought against the emancipation bill with all their force and fury. They remonstrated with the British Government—conjured and threatened,—protested that emancipation would ruin the island, that the emancipated slaves would never work—would turn vagabonds, butcher the whites and flood the island with beggary and crime. Their strong beseechings availed as little as their threats, and croakings about ruin. The Emancipation Act, unintimidated by the bluster, traversed quietly through its successive stages up to the royal sanction, and became the law of the land. When the slaveholders of Antigua saw that abolition was *inevitable*, they at once resolved to substitute immediate, unconditional, and entire emancipation for the gradual process contemplated by the Act. Well, what has been the result ? Read the following testimony of the very men who, but little more than four years ago, denounced and laughed to scorn the idea of abolishing slavery, and called it folly, fanaticism, and insanity. We quote from the work of Messrs. Thome and Kimball, lately published, the written testimony of many of the first men in Antigua,—some of whom were among the largest slaveholders before August, 1834. It proves, among other points, that

EMANCIPATED SLAVES ARE PEACEABLE.

TESTIMONY. "*There is no feeling of insecurity.* A stronger proof of this cannot be given than *the dispensing, within five months after emancipation, with the Christmas guards, which had been uninterruptedly kept up for nearly one hundred years*—during the whole time of slavery.

"I have *never head of any instance of revenge* for former injuries." *James Scotland, Sen. Esq.*

"Insurrection or revenge *is in no case dreaded.* My family go to sleep every night with the doors unlocked. There is not the *slightest* feeling of insecurity—quite the contrary. Property is more secure, *for all idea of insurrection is abolished forever.*" *Hon. N. Nugent. Speaker of the House of Assembly.*

"There has been no instance of personal violence since freedom. I have not heard of a single case of even *meditated* revenge." *Dr. Daniell, member of the Council, and Attorney for six estates.*

"Emancipation has banished the *fear* of insurrections, incendiarism, &c." *Mr. Favey, Manager of Lavicount's.*

"I have never heard of an instance of violence or revenge on the part of the negroes." *Rev. Mr. Morrish, Moravian Missionary.*

Opposition to the education of Negro children is one of the most difficult to understand of all inherent acts of meanness.

States, he said: "They are the same throughout the United States. They are, therefore, independent of local rights, or those which depend upon residence in a particular place. An inhabitant of a State has certain privileges arising from his inhabitancy of the State. An inhabitant of a Territory, too, has certain privileges, which arise from his living in a Territory. A citizen of the United States who resides neither in a State nor Territory but is out of the limits of the Union, enjoys neither the privileges of a State or Territory; but he possesses the rights, privileges, and immunities of a citizen of the United States, which are common to all the three descriptions of persons . . . He carries them with him wherever he goes; if he is in a state, he may add to them State privileges; if he is in a Territory, he may enjoy the rights of an inhabitant of a Territory; in either, or beyond the limits of both, he is still a citizen of the United States, and upon an equal footing with any other citizen."[7]

The second statement was by the New York *Evening Post,* in 1849, when Secretary of State John Clayton refused a passport to a Negro of Philadelphia on the grounds that passports were not granted to persons of color. Said the *Post:* "A more flagrant outrage upon the rights of an American citizen was never perpetrated in this country, out of the State of South Carolina. There are, in more than half the States of this Union, many thousands of men, recognized by the laws of those States as citizens, entitled, before the law, to enforce all the rights and privileges of citizenship in their respective States, who, by Mr. Clayton, are denied the protection of the American flag the moment they put their feet upon foreign soil . . . The State of New York extends the privileges of citizenship to persons of color. Within her bounds reside many thousands such citizens. By the Constitution of the United States these citizens are entitled to all the privileges and immunities of citizens in the several states . . . Mr. Clayton has . . . no more authority to deny the protection of the American government to a man with a dark skin than to a man with red hair, or with a pug nose, or crippled, or distinguished in any other way, by some physical peculiarity . . . If any such precedents exist, in our judgment, it is just as disgraceful now to follow them as it was originally to establish them. An act so clearly wrong cannot be palliated, much less justified by usage."[8]

The founding fathers provided that the Constitution of the United States should be the supreme law of the land and subject to interpretation by the courts. They provided also for an amending process. This was the basis for two parallel processes: judicial statesmanship and spiritual and intellectual ferment. I mean by judicial statesmanship that the function of the federal courts included the establishment of precedents, the definition of rights, the enforcement of the law, and the establishment of a system of jurisprudence for the regulation of society. I mean by intellectual and spiritual ferment that out of the experiences, the aspirations, and the faith of the people come new ideas, ideas that are discussed in the family circle, the club, the church, the political convention, wherever and however there is a meeting of minds. Ideas are refined by this discussion, ultimately stated in classic form, translated into law, and sometimes written into the Constitution or immortalized in the literature and political institutions of the world.

The two processes are closely interrelated, never completely separate. They converge in the court room for judgment as to the rights of the individual with reference to the law and the Constitution. It is the most solemn, sometimes the most sublime, moment in the lives of our people, for here their government protects the individual in his inalienable rights, however strong, or mighty, or determined his oppressors. The decision in any given case may affect the lives of millions, or determine the destiny of a nation. Such was the Crandall case. The decision may be followed by appeal to a higher court for a contrary interpretation of the law or the Constitution, or by a campaign to secure repeal of the law, or by recourse to the amending process, or by the slower, more dignified method of changing the philosophy of the court by appointments. In any case, intellectual ferment is intensified, for the will of the people must ultimately prevail. Such, again, was the result of the Crandall case.

The basic issue in this case was the doctrine of biological inequality and racial inferiority of the Negro. No one said so, but it was a contest of colonization philosophy *versus* antislavery philosophy, to determine whether the heavy hand of the law should be added to the prejudices of the people to crush and drive out of the country the free Negro population; or whether the great truths of the Declaration should prevail through the Constitution to aid an humble people in their terrifying struggle to live and be free. The prosecution clearly understood the issue. Judson, stating the case for the prosecution, prefaced his argument by expressing satisfaction with attendance of Negro children at the district schools, and denying either approval of slavery or opposition *per se* to educating Negroes. Having performed this perfunctory ablution, he then stated as facts, directly or by implication, certain false assumptions that were used to prejudice every case against Negroes and their antislavery friends.[9]

1. That slavery was recognized by the Constitution of the United States, and each state was at liberty to have slavery or not as it chose.

2. That whoever sought to educate Negroes was actually preparing them to go as antislavery missionaries to foment insurrection in the slave states.

3. That all antislavery men were hostile to the Constitution because it recognized slavery and desired a dissolution of the Union, in short, all of them were Garrisonians.

4. That slavery was no concern to the people of the nonslaveholding states, and anyone interested in changing the status of the slaves should go to slave states and address their arguments to the slave state governments. Failure to do so was evidence either of cowardice or deception.

He concluded his remarks to the jury, however, with a bold defense of race prejudice and an appeal to the fears of amalgamation, saying: "It was a nation of *white men,* who formed and have administered our government, and every American should indulge that *pride* and *honor,* which is falsely called prejudice, and teach it to his children. Nothing else will preserve the *American name,* or the *American character.* Who of you would like to see the glory of this nation stripped away, and given to another race of men . . . The present is a scheme, cunningly devised, to destroy the rich inheritance left by your fathers. The *professed object* is to educate the blacks, but the real object is to make the people yield their assent by degrees, to this universal amalgamation of the two races, and have the African race placed on the footing of perfect equality with the Americans."[10]

The defense rested its case upon the proposition that the pupils in Miss Crandall's school were citizens of the several states of the United States,

and, as such, were protected against the Connecticut Black Law by Article IV, Section 2 of the Constitution of the United States: "The citizens of each state shall be entitled to all privileges and immunities of citizens in the several states." The question of whether Negroes were citizens had been thoroughly debated in Congress during the Missouri contest. It was now debated in a court of law.

The prosecution (Judson) denied that "colored persons" were citizens within the meaning of the term "citizen" as used in the Constitution, but did not permit himself to be drawn into a definition of colored person. In his eagerness to sustain the constitutionality of the Connecticut law, however, Judson made an important concession to the basic antislavery principle of reciprocal duties and protection. This clause of the Constitution, he maintained, applied to action by the United States government and not to the laws of the sovereign states. It meant, he said, "that by the laws of Congress, equal and exact justice should be measured out alike to the citizens of all the States, because those citizens are all equally bound to sustain that government, and therefore have equal claims to the distribution of its favors and blessings."[11]

Judson insisted, however, that the men who framed the Constitution did not intend to include Negroes under the term citizen, but he was very confused as to the attributes of citizenship and the meaning of privileges and immunities. He argued that alien Negroes could not be naturalized, and, regardless of their place of residence in this country, could not enjoy "privileges and immunities with white citizens." This left unanswered the status of Negroes born in this country. It ignored the claim of antislavery men that "privileges and immunities" was the constitutional term applied to the natural rights of man, and that the principal function of all government was the protection of these natural rights. Judson also erroneously insisted that the elective franchise was a privilege and immunity of the highest order and that limitation of the franchise to white males by the slave states and by Ohio, Indiana, Illinois, and Connecticut proved lack of citizenship on the part of Negroes. He went farther and insisted that these provisions of the state constitutions were void if Negroes were citizens.

The antislavery position, or defense, was stated by Ellsworth and Goddard. They were distinguished attorneys, but their efforts were feeble indeed compared with what Stanton and Weld, who would today stand high in the ranks of scholars in the field of constitutional history, would have done. Ellsworth argued that citizens of other states could not be prohibited from residing in Connecticut to study since the pursuit of knowledge was open to all of the citizens of Connecticut. If Connecticut could exclude colored citizens of other states, it could exclude white citizens, and, said Ellsworth, "no such barrier can be erected against the citizens of this Union." Here, again, was the old question of the Missouri contest: were Negroes citizens, could they be excluded from a state, driven out of a state, or special conditions be placed on their residence?

"The criterion of citizenship," said Ellsworth, "in the view of my friend from Canterbury [Judson] is complexion; in mine, it is birth and naturalization."[12] Persons born in the United States were citizens. Goddard pursued this point still further, and emphasized that never since the adoption of the Constitution had the question ever been brought to judicial determination of whether "free, native inhabitants of the United States were citizens, and entitled to the privileges of citizens." "The term citizen," he said, "is, under a republican government, what the term *subject* is under a monarchy; it embraces high and low—rich and poor—male and female—white and colored—a general term which includes the whole republican family—all who are free and live under the same government, and owe to it permanent allegiance—subject to its duties—entitled to its privileges."[13] "The revolution," he said, "produced a change in all the free inhabitants of the United States—all the citizens of the several States became citizens of the United States. They were *subjects* of Great Britain—they became *citizens* of the United States from the very nature of our government." Said Ellsworth: "I deny that it [a state] can prohibit a 'citizen of the United States' from entering this state and remaining in it . . . If he has fled from justice, and is demanded, under the Constitution, he must be delivered up, but while he is here, unoffending, the state cannot drive him out, nor make it penal to supply his necessities here; it could, were it not for the Constitution of the United States: he is a citizen, and that is his protection."[14]

This language of the attorneys has often been interpreted as sustaining the doctrine, then prevalent, that United States citizenship derived from state citizenship. Viewed in the knowledge of antislavery doctrine—and these men were speaking for antislavery people—that interpretation simply is not correct, and men like Stanton and Weld, who were masters of argumentation, would never have left any doubts about the matter. What Goddard and Ellsworth were saying, and what all antislavery men said, was that all subjects of Great Britain residing in the colonies and remaining there ceased to be subjects of Great Britain and became citizens of a new Republican nation. The transformation of colonies into states made them citizens of the several states and subject to the jurisdiction of their laws. The organization of the Confederation gave them also a common citizenship, if, indeed, this did not occur with the signing of the Declaration of Independence, and the adoption of the Constitution of the United States —the supreme law of the land—made their status as citizens of the United States paramount, protected them against encroachments upon their natural rights, and gave them complete freedom to go and reside in whatever state they pleased, subject only to the authority of that state government within the limits of its powers on an equal basis with the citizens of that state. When this was denied, as it was by the highest court in the land in 1857, the antislavery people wrote the Fourteenth Amendment to put an end to the argument.

Persons born in the United States being citizens, Negroes were citizens. They fought in the Revolution, drew pensions, could be tried for treason, could sue and be sued in the federal courts. The Declaration of Independence made no distinctions on the basis of color, nor did state Bills of Rights. The Negro population was represented in Congress, and denial of the franchise to Negroes in some states no more divested them of citizenship than it did women and children.

Ellsworth met forthrightly the charge of the prosecution that those who were interested in Negro education were seeking to achieve equality of the races. It was a cardinal principle of the antislavery creed and was never denied. The object of the Connecticut law, said Ellsworth, was to "extinguish the light of knowledge; to fasten chains and ignorance upon those, whom the God of all has made equal with ourselves; whose future destiny is as high; whose hopes are as dear as ours."[15] He quoted the law of Louisiana: "That whosoever shall make use of language, in any public discourse, from the bar, the bench, the pulpit, the stage or any other place whatsoever; shall make use of language in any private discourses, or shall make use of signs or actions having a tendency to produce discontent among the colored population, shall suffer imprisonment at hard labor, not less than three years, nor more than twenty-one years or *death* at the *direction* of the court." He compared the Connecticut law to this, to the Virginia law which forbade all meetings of free Negroes for purposes of instruction, and to the North Carolina and Georgia laws which made entry into their ports of free Negroes a crime. These, he said, "are a specimen of the disgusting and unrighteous authority, to which the gentleman from Canterbury refers to sanction this law."

Finally, Ellsworth rested his case upon the antislavery interpretation of privileges and immunities. "Will it be asserted," he asked, "that education is not one of the fundamental rights, included in the broad words 'privileges' and 'immunities' . . . Education, is the first and fundamental pillar on which our free institutions rest—the last privilege we will give up."[16]

The Crandall case gave cohesion to antislavery principles in so far as they pertained to constitutional law for the first time since the Missouri debates, and for the first time in a court room. It did not add much to, nor change, those principles with regard to United States citizenship, privileges and immunities, allegiance and protection, equality before the law. It helped to popularize them; it gave them added respectability. The misfortune of the entire episode was the fact that Daggett was only nominally a judge in this case. Only a man blinded by race prejudice could have denied the citizenship of free Negroes. Yet, his charge to the jury gave comfort and satisfaction to purveyors of racial hatred, and the reversal of Prudence Crandall's conviction by the Court of Errors went unnoticed by the public. One can, in retrospect, only exclaim with William Leggett: "What a mysterious thing this federal compact must be, which enjoins so much by its spirit that is wholly omitted in its language—nay not only omitted, but which is directly contrary to some of its express provisions."[17]

How can it be done?
Mobs were social monsters. Neither schools, churches, printing presses, nor homes were spared.

LYNCH LAW

Chapter 26

William Leggett, writing in the New York *Evening Post*, July 11, 1834, made a most significant pronouncement, saying: "We may keep a vigilant eye upon them [abolitionists] and procure them to be indicted and visited with legal punishment whenever their proceedings become obnoxious to the law. But till then *they are entitled to all the privileges and immunities of American Citizens, and have a right to be protected in their persons and property against all assailants whatsoever.*" [1]

This editorial comment was occasioned by a riot on the previous day in New York City. There had been earlier instances of mob violence. When the organizational meeting of the New York City Anti-Slavery Society had been announced for October 2, 1833, a mob had taken possession of Clinton Hall, and the meeting had been held in Chatham Street Chapel. In that event the mob had been summoned by placards which read: "Notice —to all persons from the South—All persons interested in the subject of a meeting called by J. Leavitt, W. Greene, W. Goodell, J. Rankin, Lewis Tappan, at Clinton Hall, this evening at 7 o'clock, are requested to attend at the same hour and place. Many Southerners." Another had read: "All citizens who may feel disposed to manifest the true feeling of the state on this subject are requested to attend." [2]

Opposition to the American Anti-Slavery Society, which was organized two months later, continued to build up during the winter and early summer; and, beginning July 10, 1834, the longest of all riots on record against antislavery people occurred in the city. The colonization society

was deeply involved in the affair. [3] The mob first met at Chatham Street Chapel where antislavery meetings were customarily held. It organized and passed resolutions approving the colonization society. It then fanned out through the city committing acts of violence against the Negroes themselves. Lewis Tappan suffered substantial losses. His home was plundered, and his furniture was piled in the yard and burned. The mercantile establishment of the Tappan brothers was invaded, but, being business property, was protected by the police. [4] The churches of the Reverend A. L. Cox and Reverend H. G. Ludlow were gutted of all furniture, benches, and pulpits. [5] Three Negro churches were damaged. The furniture and organ of St. Phillips African Episcopal Church were burned. A school house, a barbershop, and at least twenty homes, all belonging to Negroes, were destroyed. The Negro homes were so completely wrecked that the owners had to apply to charity for the necessaries of life. [6] Order was not restored until the governor sent troops into the city.

It was in the midst of this riot that Leggett had written his editorial in reference to the privileges and immunities—including, among other natural rights, the right to protection of persons and property—of American citizens. The following day, July 12, 1834, he said: "The fury of demons seems to have entered into the breasts of our misguided populace. Like those ferocious animals which, having once tasted blood, are seized with an insatiable thirst for gore, they have had an appetite awakened for outrage, which nothing but the most extensive and indiscriminate destruction seems capable of appeasing. The cabin of the poor negro, and the temples dedicated to the service of the living God, are alike the objects of their blind fury. The rights of private and public property, the obligations of law, the authority of its ministers, and even the power of the military, are all equally spurned by these audacious sons of riot and disorder."[7]

There were riots in Philadelphia at irregular intervals from 1829 to 1849. The most tragic was in August 1834, shortly after the riot in New York City. It started with an argument at an amusement house frequented chiefly by Negroes. The building was totally destroyed.[8] The next evening a Negro Presbyterian church and a lodging house for Negroes were wrecked. Then the rioting spread and forty-five homes were destroyed. The mob entered the homes, smashed the breakable furniture, ripped open the feather beds, and scattered everything into the street. The treatment of the occupants is almost unbelievable. In one case a corpse was thrown from a bed to the floor, and a dead child tossed about and its mother cruelly abused. A cripple, unable to escape, was mercilessly beaten.[9] Property damage amounted to thousands of dollars. One Negro was killed. There is no question about the origin of the orgy. It began with a colonization meeting and was well planned—so well planned, in fact, that lights were placed in the windows of white homes so the rioters would not molest them. The riot was thereafter designated the Passover riot.[10]

The following year, 1835, another riot was occasioned by the murder of one Robert R. Stewart by his Negro servant. The motive was unknown, but its effect on public opinion by the time newspapers had elaborated on the crime was so great that a riot was directed against Negroes in general. Negro homes were invaded and the inmates beaten. Furniture was destroyed; houses were burned. A half hundred Negroes finally barricaded themselves in a building, heavily armed and prepared to defend themselves to the end. The police interfered at this point and restored order.[11]

The extent to which antislavery lecturers were mobbed is almost incredible. Literally hundreds of mobs formed, did their dirty work, and then disbanded. The brunt of this kind of brutality was borne by Theodore Weld, Henry B. Stanton, and the other pioneer lecturers from Lane Seminary. Their accounts of what happened in Ohio,

particularly, are so much a part of the early movement as to divert attention from more important aspects of their work. Samuel Galloway, writing from Springfield, Ohio, to Weld, August 9, 1835, said: "Before you went to Putnam, I was enabled to trace you by the outbreakings of public sentiment (as the Negro haters say), since that time your course has been unknown."[12]

These young men encountered hostility everywhere, but with courage, meekness, and apostolic devotion. Two accounts, by the men themselves, are sufficient to tell the story. Writing from Putnam, Ohio, March 2, 1835, Weld said: "The Presbyterian minister, Mr. Benton, said among his people that I was a rebel, had made all the mischief at Lane Seminary, and surely a man should not be countenanced who was such a disturber of the peace. Further, he said that the distinguished faculty at Lane Seminary had felt themselves impelled from solemn sense of duty to warn the public against me, declaring in their official capacity that I was a remarkable instance of monomania. The Presbyterian Church was shut against me. Finally, the vestry room of the Episcopal Church was procured. At the second lecture the mob gathered and threw stones and eggs through the window . . . The next day the mob were so loud in threats that the trustees of the church did not feel at liberty to grant the use of the vestry. The next night I lectured in a store room in the center of the village. Stones and clubs flew merrily against the shutters. At the close as I came out, curses were showered in profusion. Lamp black, nails, pockets full of stones and eggs had been provided for the occasion, and many had disguised their persons, smeared their faces, etc., to avoid recognition. Next evening same state of things, with increase of violent demonstrations. The next, such was the uproar that a number of gentlemen insisted upon forming an escort and seeing me safe to my lodging. This state of things lasted until I had lectured seven times, then hushed down, and for the latter part of the course had a smooth sea."[13]

At Willoughby, the Methodist minister declared that he would stand in the door of his church with a club to keep James A. Thome from lecturing, so Thome moved on to Middlebury, from which place he wrote: "Last evening Middlebury puked. Spasmodic heavings and retchings were manifest during the whole day, but Brother Alvord proceeded to lecture . . . All was still until about

Marius R. Robinson

eight o'clock when in came a broadside of Eggs, Glass, egg shells, whites and yolks flew on every side. Br. Alvord's fact book received an egg just in its bowels, and I doubt whether one in the House escaped a spattering. I have been trying to clean off this morning, but can't get off the stink."

Said Alvord:

"Thome dodged like a stoned gander. He brought up at length against the side of the desk, cocked his eye and stood gazing upward at the flying missiles as they streamed in ropy masses through the house . . . The mob threatens dreadfully today. There are a few determined men here, but the mob are set on by men of influence most of whom are church members. Abolitionists heretofore in this place have always been mobbed out. We must try to carry the day this time if possible."[14]

At Zanesville, Weld could not secure so much as a shanty in which to lecture. At Putnam he was mobbed and every kind of outrage was committed against the Negroes as a consequence of his inviting them to attend his lectures. They were turned

out of employment, men were prosecuted under the vandal laws for employing them, and the entire population was thrown into a frenzy of fear as houses were torn down in profusion. A Negro appeared shortly afterward as a delegate to the antislavery convention, but a committee of the Negro population came to Weld in agony and terror. "They begged that he [the Negro] might be prevailed upon not to go into the convention, as it would not only peril his life, but would bring down upon the colored people the vengeance of the mob."[15]

The Ohio Anti-Slavery Convention of 1836 was held at Granville. Every tavernkeeper within a radius of twenty miles sought to discourage delegates from attending with prophecies of certain death by mob violence. A schoolhouse in which Thome attempted to lecture two miles south of Granville was almost totally destroyed. Four express coaches were sent to St. Albans, Mount Vernon, and Newark by the most respectable citizens of the town to bring in ruffians from those points. A bloody battle ensued in which numerous casualties were inflicted, and finally the delegates to the convention rode away on their horses amid a shower of eggs and curses without a single prominent citizen willing to utter a protest.[16]

Marius Robinson gave a lecture at Berlin, Ohio, in June 1837. The following day, he was kidnapped, carried a mile out of town, tarred and feathered, then hauled ten miles away in a wagon and dumped beside the road. He was so seriously injured in this attack that he never completely recovered.[17] At Troy, New York, almost the entire city screamed in protest when Weld came to lecture. They stoned him until he felt certain death was near, but he refused to leave. Finally, the city authorities, fearful that he would be killed, drove him out. When George Thompson, recognized leader of the movement in England, came to this country at Garrison's request, he was insulted everywhere. He went to Boston to lecture to the Female Anti-Slavery Society, October 21, 1835. A huge mob assembled, but Thompson had fled from the city. The women's meeting was dispersed, and Garrison was flushed from his hiding place. He did not suffer bodily harm, but considerable loss of dignity, when rescued by the mayor and detained in jail until the mob spirit quieted down.[18]

On October 21, 1835, about six hundred antislavery men from all parts of the state of New

York assembled at Utica to form the New York Anti-Slavery Society. Few organizational meetings ever brought together so distinguished a group of men. The common council chamber had been obtained for the convention. Previous to the date of the convention a protest meeting was arranged by Samuel Beardsley, who was reported by Samuel J. May to have said that "the disgrace of having an Abolition Convention held in the city is a deeper one than that of twenty mobs, and that it would be better to have Utica razed to its foundations, or to have it destroyed like Sodom and Gommorah, than to have the convention meet here."[19] This was an invitation to mob violence, and a mob took possession of the courtroom which had been granted by the common council for the meeting. This had come to be standard procedure.

Deprived in this fashion of their meeting place in Utica, the antislavery delegates secured the use of the Second Presbyterian Church. Their meeting had scarcely begun—Alvan Stewart was reading a draft of the proposed constitution—when the mob, organized around a committee of twenty-five persons, pounded on the doors for admission. The constitution was adopted before the ruffians gained entrance, but they drove the delegates from the church, followed them to their rooming houses, and did not desist until all had left the city. The leader of this mob, and the man who inspired it, was Samuel Beardsley, who is described in the *Dictionary of American Biography* "as a progressive leader and defender of free speech and of the right of petition." He had been a member of Congress, and a United States attorney. He was a close personal friend and confidential adviser of President Andrew Jackson. Two weeks after his service in Utica, as a reward, he was appointed attorney general of New York by Governor William L. Marcy, and subsequently became chief justice of the New York Supreme Court. The disrupted convention was invited to Peterboro by Gerrit Smith, who promptly and publicly disavowed all connection with the colonization movement. The convention completed its organization at Peterboro. Smith became one of the stalwart antislavery advocates.

James G. Birney, driven out of Kentucky, finally established his *Philanthropist* at Cincinnati in January 1836.[20] So much excitement had been created by Lane Seminary and Danville events that he decided to have the actual publishing done at New Richmond until April 1836. Even

"LAWLESS" BURNING OF MEN "BY THE MANY."

April 28, 1836, in St. Louis, Mo., a black man named McIntosh, who had stabbed an officer, that had arrested him, was seized by the multitude, and fastened to a tree *in the midst of the city*, in the open day, and in the presence of an immense throng of citizens, was burnt to death. The Alton (Ill.) Telegraph, in its account of the scene says:

"All was silent while they were piling wood around their victim; when the flames seized upon him he uttered an awful howl, attempted to sing and pray, and then hung his head and suffered in silence, except in the following instance:—After the flames had surrounded their prey, his eyes burnt out of his head, and his mouth seemingly parched to a cinder, some one in the crowd, proposed to put an end to his misery by shooting him, when it was replied, 'that would be of no use, since he was already out of pain.' 'No, no,' said the wretch, I am suffering as much as ever; shoot me, shoot me.' 'No, no,' said one, 'he shall not be shot. *I would sooner slacken the fire, if that would increase his misery;*' and the man who said this was, as we understand, an OFFICER OF JUSTICE."

The St. Louis correspondent of a New York paper adds:—"The shrieks and groans of the victim were loud and piercing, and to observe one limb after another drop into the fire was awful indeed. I visited the place this morning; only a part of his head and body were left."

Hon. Luke E. Lawless, Judge, of the Circuit Court of Missouri, at its session, in St. Louis, some months after, decided that since the burning of McIntosh was the act, directly or by countenance, of a *majority* of citizens, it is a 'case which transcends the jurisdiction,' of the Grand Jury!

The 'New Orleans Post,' of June 7, 1836, publishes the following:—

"We understand, that a negro man was lately condemned, by the mob, to be BURNED OVER A SLOW FIRE, which was put into execution at Grand Gulf, Mississippi, for murdering a black woman and her master."

"Tuscaloosa, Ala., June 20, 1827.—Last week a Mr. M'Neilly charged a slave with theft. M'Neilly, and his brother, seized him, and were about to chastise him, when the negro stabbed M'Neilly. The negro was taken before a justice, who *waived his authority*. A crowd collected, *and he acted as president of the mob*, and put the vote, when it was decided he should be immediately *burnt to death*." He was led to the tree, a large quantity of pine knots placed around him, the fatal torch applied to the pile, and the miserable being was in a short time burned to ashes. This is the SECOND negro who has been THUS put to death, without judge or Jury, in this county."—African Observer, for August, 1827.

McIntosh was removed from jail and burned. Lovejoy's criticism of Judge Lawless' charge to the grand jury was the beginning of his own trouble.

before he had begun publication the mayor of the town, reinforced by the chief of police, called upon Birney and assured him of mob violence if he went ahead with plans to publish.

Slowly but surely the political newspapers of Cincinnati whipped up the spirit of mob violence. A meeting was held in the courthouse on January 22, presided over by Mayor Samuel W. Davies, assisted by Postmaster William Burke and Jacob Burnet, United States senator, president of the colonization society, former justice of the Supreme Court of Ohio, former president of the Cincinnati branch of the Second United States Bank, and member of the French Academy of Science. There were speeches charging Birney with incendiarism and treason. Birney was present and replied in an impassioned defense that quieted the opposition for a time. The *Philanthropist* was moved to Cincinnati and became the official organ of the Ohio Anti-Slavery Society.

Trouble began again in July 1836.[21] The establishment where the *Philanthropist* was printed was pillaged, and the Anti-Slavery Society had to post a guarantee against loss of $2,000 to continue printing.[22] Appeals to mob violence and warnings to Birney were posted about the city on numerous occasions.[23] The press sunk to the level of personal insults. Finally, a meeting was called at the Lower Market House to decide whether the "voice of the community" would permit the publication or distribution of antislavery papers in the city. Postmaster Burke presided, assisted by Nicholas Longworth, reputedly the largest property owner in the city; Josiah Lawrence and Robert Buchanan, presidents of Cincinnati's two largest banks; and David Disney, former speaker of the Ohio House of Representatives. These men and others, constituting a committee of twelve, waited upon representatives of the antislavery society, including Birney, to secure discontinuance

of his publication as the only alternative to its destruction by force. The demand was rejected, of course, and the mob was assembled on the night of July 30.

The mob was regularly organized, with a president and secretary, and resolved that the press should be destroyed and Birney notified to leave the city in twenty-four hours. The press building was then invaded, the types scattered, the press broken and thrown into the river. The Negro section of the city was then invaded. The interiors of some houses were wrecked, other houses were torn down. The pillaging went on for four hours before Mayor Davies, who was present as a sort of general supervisor, admonished the crowd: "We have done enough for one night. The abolitionists themselves must be convinced by this time what public sentiment is, and that it will not do any longer to disregard or set it at naught." The following day, the mayor himself led an unsuccessful search for Birney with evident intentions of doing him bodily harm.[24]

Charles Hammond, editor of the Cincinnati *Gazette*, took the lead in restoring order and in the defense of civil rights. Salmon P. Chase, at that time a young attorney, soon to become prominent in the Liberty Party, and later secretary of the Treasury and chief justice of the United States, enlisted in the antislavery movement at this time. William Birney, a close associate of Chase, went on to become head of Negro troops in the Civil War and beloved by all of that race. William T. Allan and others at Oberlin, who had participated in the Lane Seminary debate, broke away from Finney's influence and went out to work primarily in the antislavery movement. Above everything else, it gave Birney undisputed leadership of the main stream of antislavery action, and it was a powerful stimulant to the growing belief in the necessity of direct political action.

Birney brought Gamaliel Bailey into prominence as associate editor of the *Philanthropist*, then went to New York as corresponding secretary of the American Anti-Slavery Society. There was no further violence of consequence until 1841, when the press was destroyed a third time. The trouble is said to have started with a minor quarrel between a party of Irish and some Negroes. The entire city was soon in the hands of a mob, and by the end of the third day, many Negroes had taken refuge in the surrounding hills. The *Philanthropist* press was broken and thrown into

the river. Several Negroes were killed, many wounded. There were Kentuckians in the mob, as before, and influential people in the city gave their encouragement.

Closely associated with the Danville-Cincinnati violence of 1835–36 were riots in Missouri and Illinois. The Reverend David Nelson was the first victim. Nelson grew up in east Tennessee, in the area so strongly identified with the work of Samuel Doak, Elihu Embree, and Benjamin Lundy. Ultimately, he became a Presbyterian minister, pastor of the Church at Danville, Kentucky. He was then an antislavery colonizationist. He freed his slaves and sent them to Liberia. Then, in 1830 he went to Palmyra, Missouri, where he founded Marion College, a theological school after the manner of Oneida Institute and Lane Seminary. Five years later he became an agent of the American Anti-Slavery Society, published a blistering antislavery indictment under the title "Last Advice to My Old and Beloved Congregation at Danville, Kentucky," and wrote *The Cause and Cure of Infidelity* of which the American Tract Society distributed more than 100,000 copies. He also became vice-president of the American Anti-Slavery Society.[25]

At a camp-meeting near the college, May 22, 1836, Nelson read an offer of one of his parishioners to contribute $10,000 toward a fund for compensated emancipation and an appeal for funds. That man was violently assailed and the service broke up in a riot. One man was killed. A committee of citizens waited on Nelson and demanded that he leave the state immediately, never to return. A. C. Garrett, superintendent of the college farm, was also driven out of the state. The faculty of the college was forced to forbid "all discussions and public meetings amongst the students, upon the subject of domestic slavery." Nelson fled to Quincy, Illinois.[26]

Meanwhile, a convert of Nelson's was having trouble in St. Louis. Elijah P. Lovejoy, a school teacher of St. Louis, had been converted by Nelson in 1832, and after work at Princeton had been licensed as a Presbyterian minister.[27] He returned to St. Louis in the autumn of 1833 as an agent of the American Home Missionary Society and editor of the St. Louis *Observer*. It was inevitable that he should analyze and criticize the institution of slavery, inevitable also that the citizens of this slaveholding city should demand silence. Lovejoy's defense of civil rights—freedom of speech,

Burning of Pennsylvania Hall

press, and petition—became more vigorous as opposition increased. The crisis came in May, 1836.

A mob had removed a Negro from the jail in
St. Louis and burned him at the stake. Lovejoy
reported the event under the caption "Awful Murder and Savage Barbarity." His printing establishment was damaged first on May 23 in retalia-
tion. The grand jury called to investigate the
lynching was instructed by Judge Luke E. Lawless to bring indictments only if a few individuals
were found to have been involved. He also blamed
the mob action on Lovejoy's criticism of slavery.
Lovejoy was in process of moving his paper to
Alton, Illinois, but severely criticized this obvious
subserviency to mob rule in his last issue of the
paper. His press was moved to Alton, but was
almost immediately destroyed by men who followed him up the river from St. Louis.

In Illinois, Lovejoy was among friends and sympathizers. There had been a considerable influx
of antislavery men from New England, from the
slave states, and from the fertile area of southern
Ohio and Kentucky. The southern Presbyterians
had come by way of Brown County, Ohio, and

Gilliland's church at Red Oak. James Buchanan,
who left Danville with Birney, and went to Oberlin, was in Carlinville. Gideon Blackburn, another
student of Samuel Doak and former president of
Centre College, and James H. Dickey from the
Chillicothe Presbytery, were all in the area. Add
to these David Nelson and Edward Beecher, president of the only college in the state, and one has
a formidable group of intellectuals, humanitarians, and, withal, influential men.

Publication of the *Observer* at Alton began in
September 1836, and continued without interruption for some months. Its circulation increased
from one thousand to seventeen hundred from
November 1836 to March 1837. In January 1837
legislative committees reported upon the demands
of southern states that antislavery publications be
suppressed. The reports were strongly proslavery
in tone and almost open invitations to violence.
They repeated the old story of how antislavery
societies had reversed the trend toward emancipation and fastened the chains of slavery more
securely upon the "black man," had been responsible for all of the mob violence, had threatened

to violate the sacred rights of private property, and were about to deluge the country in blood and disrupt the Union. They eulogized the colonization society. They called upon public opinion to "firmly and powerfully rebuke" all antislavery activities. They resolved that "the right of property in slaves is secured to the slaveholding states by the Federal Constitution, and that they cannot be deprived of that right without their consent."[28] In a House of Representatives where seventy-seven men voted against antislavery societies, against congressional power to abolish slavery in the territories and in the District of Columbia, and for the sanctity of slave property, and only six men voted to the contrary, Abraham Lincoln was one of the six, and he formally insisted by resolution, that slavery was unjust and impolitic and that Congress did have the power to abolish slavery in the territories and in the District of Columbia. Anyone who says Lincoln was not an antislavery man—and as early as 1836—has read history to no purpose.

By the summer of 1837 the Alton *Observer* was as important to the liberal movement as Birney's *Philanthropist* at Cincinnati.[29] Antislavery societies in Illinois were multiplying rapidly and were continuing their indictment of slavery with a powerful defense of free speech, press, and assembly. A very high percentage of these people actually were from slave country originally. Call them pilgrims, or call them exiles, they were as determined to prevent the spread of slavery to the territories, to new states, and to Texas, and to abolish slavery in the District of Columbia and the slave trade, as they were to defend their civil rights. The two were inseparable everywhere. Organization on a statewide basis to consolidate and coordinate their strength was inevitable.

The battle was joined at mere mention of need for a state society. The colonizationists organized the opposition. First, there was the committee of protest, then the mob. The press of the *Observer* was destroyed August 21, 1837. A new press was brought in from Cincinnati, but it, too, was thrown into the river before it could be installed. All the forces of colonization and proslavery were marshaled at Upper Alton to disrupt the antislavery convention called for October 26, 1837.[30] Meeting after meeting was held to discredit Lovejoy and drive him from the city. Finally, an armed mob surrounded the warehouse where Lovejoy and others were guarding a new press. The building

A MINISTER ARRESTED FOR PREACHING AGAINST SIN.

Dec. 14, 1835, Rev. George Storrs, who was invited to address the Anti-Slavery Society at Northfield, N. H., was dragged from his knees while at prayer by *Sam'l Tilton* deputy sheriff. He was also arrested in the pulpit, March 31, 1836, (fast day,) at Pittsfield, N. H., by the authority of a writ issued by *Moses Norris, Esq.*, Gov. Isaac Hill sanctioned the outrage by reappointing Norris.

of the whites in the adjacent settlements MANIFEST a RESTLESS DESIRE to obtain them." "April 27, 1835. The negroes in the nation DREAD the idea of being sold from their present state of ease and comparative liberty to bondage and hard labor under overseers on sugar and cotton plantations. They have always had a great influence on the Indians. An Indian would almost as soon sell his child as his slave." John Lee Williams, in his "Florida," published in 1837,though evidently disposed to conceal the worst part of the truth, says : " *Great exertions* have been made to get the Indian negroes away, by FALSE CLAIMS, and MANY negroes have been taken away by FORCE and FRAUD." The Washington correspondent of the N. Y. Journal of Commerce, June 3, 1836, says it was stated on the floor of Congress and uncontradicted, that our Government recognized the claim of the slaveholders, and SENT AGENTS TO KIDNAP THE CHILDREN OF THE SEMINOLES. Jan. 27, 1835, Gen. Thompson called for more forces, and the war begun. It has been protracted on one side, by the desperation of fugitive slaves, preferring death to slavery ; and the following, from a Mobile paper of March 28, 1838, shows why it is continued on the other. " It is the *power to entice away and instruct in bush-fighting so many of our slaves* that we would wish to annihilate. These Seminoles cannot remain in the peninsula of Florida, without threatening the internal safety of the south." Southern men have estimated the expense of this war at **$20,000,000!!!** Of its destruction to life, the Army and Navy Chronicle says : " *Apprised* as we have been of the DEADLY service in Florida in which our gallant army has been, since 1835, engaged, we were not a little SURPRISED to learn the GREAT MORTALITY among its officers and men."

Freemen of the north, have you done enough for slavery in Florida ? Will you strangle the honor and prosperity of your country, and bury them with your children's liberty ? Let the north open her dumb mouth,—cut the string of her tied tongue—rebuke in thunder her doughfaced politicians, and make them warning beacons to the betrayers of liberty, in all coming time,—a certain sign of perdition to all political Judases, who impiously sell their MASTERS. Let the PEOPLE rescue Florida from slavery, and secure it for LIBERTY.

COLONIZATION.

At a public meeting in Philadelphia, May, 1838, Rev. R. J. Breckenridge said their cause was " too great to be managed on any ONE set of PRINCIPLES." Accordingly its friends deny, in one place, what they assert in another. Thus :

" Into their accounts, the subject of emancipation does not enter at all."—*African Repository*, (the Society's official organ,) *vol.* 4. *p.* 306.

" Our efforts, our money, our plans, ALL contemplate emancipation."—*Address of Colonizationists to citizens of Washington Co.. Pa* , 1836.

The Reverend George Storrs was charged with being a common railer and brawler, was convicted by three magistrates, and was sentenced to hard labor for three months. He was arrested in church and dragged from the pulpit.

was fired. Lovejoy was killed as he emerged from the burning building. The press was destroyed.[31]

Lovejoy was a kindly, Christian man. His antislavery creed embraced four cardinal principles: that all men are created equal and endowed with certain inalienable rights which are not abrogated by the color of one's skin; that slavery was a legalized system of injustice and a sin; that all persons born of slave mothers are born free and, if held in slavery, the sin is that of the slaveholder, not of his fathers; and emancipation to be of value to the slave must be freely and voluntarily given by the master.[32] Said David Root: "*Rights and immunities* dear to all have been outraged. He stood as the representative of the Constitution of our country, as the representative of the freedom of speech, the liberty of the press, the rights of conscience, the obligation of civil government and the claims of suffering humanity, and in his death they have all been cloven down."[33]

Pennsylvania Hall was built in Philadelphia during the winter of 1837–38. It was built by subscription at a cost of $40,000, and dedicated to free speech in extensive ceremonies beginning May 14, 1838. Long and careful preparations were made for the dedication ceremonies, leading orators of the antislavery movement being invited to attend. Theodore Weld, his voice gone, sent to the managers his regrets at being unable to speak in this "Temple of Freedom." It was, he said, "the first and only one in a republic of fifteen millions consecrated to Free Discussion and Equal Rights . . . God grant that your Pennsylvania Hall may be *free* indeed." "The empty name," he continued, "is everywhere,—*free* government, *free* news, *free* speech, *free* schools, *free* churches. Hollow counterfeits all! Free! It is the climax of irony, and its million echoes are hisses and jeers, even from the earth's ends . . . Words are the signs of *things*. The substance has gone! Let fools and madmen clutch at shadows."[34]

Weld had braved the fury of mobs from one end of the country to another. He knew whereof he spoke. Judge William Jay of New York called it an "astounding fact" that in Philadelphia, of all places, it was found necessary to build a building "in which the rights of man may be discussed, and the freedom of speech and the press advocated."[35] John Quincy Adams refused to come, probably because of the city's reputation for mob violence. Thomas Morris was unable to be present, and William Slade, Gerrit Smith, and Thad-

deus Stevens.[36] Many distinguished antislavery men and women, however, were present and spoke, including Arnold Buffum, C. C. Burleigh, William H. Burleigh, Alvan Stewart, Alanson St. Clair, and William L. Garrison.

"This is the home of the stranger," said Alvan Stewart, "the resting-place of the fugitive, the slave's audience chamber. Here the cause of the slave, the Seminole, and the Cherokee shall be heard. Here, on this rostrum, the advocates of holy justice, and Heaven-descended humanity, shall stand and plead for poor insulted man; here with boldness shall they untwist the guilty texture of those laws which from generation to generation have bound men in the dungeons of despair . . . Let this Hall be a moral furnace, in which the fires of free discussion shall burn night and day, and purify public opinion of the base alloy of expediency, and all those inversions of truth, by which first principles are surrendered in subserviency to popular prejudice, or crime."[37]

Instead of a "moral furnace," the hall became a fiery furnace three days after it was opened. The antislavery people were numerous enough to control elections in many areas of the country, and as William Jay had written, as a group, had never been surpassed "in rectitude of intention, disinterestedness of motive, and purity of life." Yet, as Jay went on to say, "are they hunted as felons at the South, and at the North are abandoned to the mercy of mobs, and as we are taught by the civil authorities at Alton, may be murdered with impunity."[38] Placards had been posted in the city before the dedication ceremonies began, summoning a mob. Procedure was no different in this case from many others in the East. Once aroused, in characteristic mob fashion, ever-increasing bands of excited men cared little for property, and, unfortunately, little for human life. They broke up antislavery meetings, abused lecturers, terrified audiences; they also roamed through cities destroying homes, churches, and people. In this case, a meeting was broken up on the afternoon of May 16. The trustees appealed to the sheriff, to the mayor, and the chief of police. The keys of the building were given to the mayor. He had them in his pocket when the mob broke down the doors, demolished and set fire to the furniture, and then burned the building.[39] He stood and watched the building burn. The fire department made little effort to put out the fire.

The city council subsequently appointed a committee to investigate the affair, and the report, more clearly than any other adopted at any time, placed the blame for mob action upon the victims of the mob and repeated the absurd claim that mobs represented the will of the community. It said that the "excitement was occasioned by the determination of the owners of the building, and their friends, to persevere in openly promulgating in it doctrines repulsive to the moral sense of a large majority of our community . . . heedless of the dangers which they were encountering, or reckless of its consequences to the peace and order of the city."[40] It is a singular fact that this doctrine was widely expounded by public officials from the President of the United States down to this humble city council of Philadelphia—singular, because it was so contrary to morality, to every conceivable concept of civil rights, and to the principles of municipal law.

Northern colonizationists and the Democratic newspapers raised the issue of amalgamation, as usual, saying that the sensibilities of the people were offended by the association of Negroes and whites together in the meetings and on the streets of the city. This was not unusual, but in this instance it brought sharp rebuttal from Charles Hammond, editor of the *Cincinnati Daily Gazette,* who insisted that slaveholders were not hostile to antislavery men because their moral sense was offended, but because their interests were threatened. Southern men, he insisted, made their colored mistresses members of their domestic establishments. He continued: "No moral sense feels outraged at this. And a strong illustration is at hand, in the fact that the individual that now occupies the second office in the government, was selected for and chosen to that high station, with a full knowledge, on the part of the whole community, that he had married as his wife his own slave, and openly sustained his connubial relation with her. That he had educated his daughters of mixed blood, in the best fashion of the country, and had secured for them white men as husbands! To this individual a very large numerical vote was given in Philadelphia to place him where he now is."[41]

Death of Elijah P. Lovejoy
Three of Lovejoy's presses had been destroyed by mobs. In defense of the fourth, the famous preacher and editor was killed, November 7, 1837.

THE HIGHER LAW

Chapter 27

There were several frightening aspects to the mob violence against Negroes and their antislavery friends. Committees of vigilance, composed of prominent citizens—bankers, lawyers, merchants, newspaper editors, preachers, public officials— were formed to sit in judgment and to inflict punishment upon men and women who had violated no law. These committees gathered to themselves ruffians, sadists, and scoundrels of every sort. Such people are ever present, ever eager to satisfy their own perverted instincts, and ever scornful of both human and divine law. The respectable men went as far as necessary to identify the objects of their displeasure and then remained in the shadows while peaceable assemblages of men and women were disrupted, distinguished visitors were driven from the community, printing presses were destroyed, schools were closed, churches, private homes, and public buildings were burned, the mails were pillaged, and men were beaten, stoned, hanged, and shot. This was lynch law; it was unrestrained sadism on a grand scale; it was anarchy; it was a complete annihilation of the basic principles of democracy; it was desecration of the most sacred guarantees of the Constitution, both federal and state.

On January 2, 1833, Reverend William Peabody made a remarkably cogent statement in Boston: "It is not an easy thing, nor a trifling privilege, to be free. What is a free state? It is one which lives under the government of laws and not of men; it is one in which all are equal, as respects their civil rights; it is one, in which the liberty of each is abridged as little as possible, and his re-sponsibility extended as far as possible; it is one, which gives the widest range to the moral and intellectual powers, while it restrains and governs injurious passions; it is one, in which the prosperity of the state depends upon the conduct and character of its individual members."[1]

One of the most important functions of the President of the United States, indeed of all public officials to a degree commensurate with the importance of their office, is to provide leadership in the discussion of important issues and in the formulation of public policy. The prestige of their office adds great weight to their opinions. They must lead in the definition of public policy—that is, in *enacting laws*. Here is a case in which they gave a diabolical twist to the final step of this democratic process, and instead of upholding the majesty of the law by requesting legislation they urged the people to supply the deficiencies of existing law by mob violence. They called this strong, or emphatic, or unmistakable expressions of public sentiment—the will of the community. They rationalized their own cowardly evasions of responsibility to protect persons and property by saying that there are times when officers of the law have an obligation to the community in which they live superior to those of the law itself.

These men sought to ease their own consciences and to justify their actions before the public, perhaps even in the annals of history, by charging the guilt of a mob to its victims. This was almost universal, from the President and senators, on through governors, judges, mayors, and police of-

The *Leeds Juvenile Series* consisted of thirteen separate pamphlets.

ficials. After Lovejoy was murdered a grand jury indicted the defenders of the press, including the owner of the warehouse which the mob had set on fire, for having "unlawfully, riotously, and wantonly, and in a violent and tumultuous manner resisted and opposed an attempt . . . to break up and destroy a printing press." They were brought to trial, but the petit jury refused to convict. This attempt to cast the blame upon antislavery men was a monstrous perversion of justice. It could only be done by a studied campaign of slander, sly insinuations of mental disorders, and charges of extreme radicalism. It was easy, on the other hand, to arouse passions against the Negro because of the widespread belief in racial inferiority and the pitiless campaign of the colonizationists. The men who did these things were politicians, mostly Democrats, utterly and completely subservient to a slaveholding President

and the slaveholding leadership of their party, and eager for judgeships, contracts, or other perquisites of party regularity. They were aided and abetted by businessmen who had important commercial ties with the South, by the colonization societies, and by the political press. The New York *Courier* and *Enquirer* denounced antislavery men as "a club of villains who ought not be allowed the liberty to hold a public meeting." Similar statements without number may be found in the New York *Commercial Advertiser*, the Boston *Gazette*, the Hartford *Times*, and the Philadelphia *Enquirer*.

Passions were inflamed, also, by pamphleteers, both Northern and Southern. Two widely distributed pamphlets were one by Richard Yeardon in Charleston, South Carolina, and one by Jacobus Flournoy in New York. Yeardon spoke of the antislavery people as "misguided fanatics, who, in the reckless prosecution of their views of false philanthropy, would apply the torch to our dwellings, and the knife to our throats." In the fashion of the day, he said: "At the North, they have raised the mob against the property and lives of their sable *proteges*, and at the South they have only added to the rigor of the *Code noir*, caused a repeal of the laws permitting emancipation, and in numerous other particulars abridged the enjoyment of former privileges." Yeardon then went on to insist on the right of the South to demand the surrender of antislavery men for trial in the South, the exclusion of antislavery literature from the mails, and legislation to suppress antislavery societies. "We take the ground," said he, "that the non-slave-holding states have not the right of discussing the practical question of emancipation, and the agitation of the abstract question of slavery is, therefore, worse than idle, and positively mischievous."[2] Flournoy's pamphlet, published in New York, was a terrible attack upon Negroes as subhuman beings, lower than all other races of man, and fit only for slavery of the worst kind. He insisted upon their proverbial ignorance, brutal passions, lewdness, obscenity, animal appetites, viciousness, illegitimacy. He called them cumbersome, ignorant, and perverse, wicked fellows and wenches, pests of white men, agents of Satan.[3]

Simon Clough, a preacher of Fall River, Massachusetts, attacked the American Anti-Slavery Society in a pamphlet in which he denounced Negroes as the dregs of humanity.[4] An attorney of

New Haven took the position that "inequality is inseparable from our social conditon. Human rights in society are relative, not absolute; and every living creature should be intrusted with so much liberty as is for the general good, and no more."[5] Richard H. Colfax went all the way in his appeal for more rigorous treatment of Negroes, both slave and free, by insisting they were not human beings. They were, he insisted, "exactly intermediate between the superior order of beasts, such as elephant, dog, or Orang Outang; and Europeans or white men."[6] Edmund Bellinger went the limit in the South, in his appeal for harsher treatment of antislavery men. Threatening Civil War, he said: "If any man at the South makes but a movement toward emancipation—general or particular—immediate or remote—he is faithless to the duty which he owes to his slaves—faithless to the duty which he owes to his state—faithless to the duty which he owes to his God."[7] Such was the general sanction of the principle that the tastes or prejudices of the majority should be the measure of the rights of the minority.

Antislavery men were contending for two principles of democratic life, both essential to progress: the dignity and equality of all men, and the right of free inquiry and discussion. They were deeply concerned, also, about the way in which attacks upon the federal government were undermining the foundations of all law and order. The ultimate victory in these three areas is to be found in the Fourteenth Amendment, the defense of the Union in 1861, and the higher law doctrine. It is with the latter that we are primarily interested in 1835–37. What is the right of free enquiry and discussion which the abolitionists so strenuously defended, where did it originate, and by what power was it granted?

Faced with the threat of legislative proscription, antislavery men claimed the protection of the Bills of Rights in their federal and state constitutions. The provisions of state constitutions, briefly quoted here, were brought to the attention of legislative committees and of the people in every possible way:

Maine: Every citizen may freely speak, write and publish his sentiments on any subject, being responsible for the abuse of this liberty.

Massachusetts: The liberty of the press is essential to the security of freedom in a state; it ought not, therefore, to be restrained in this Commonwealth.

New Hampshire: The liberty of the press is essential to the security of freedom in a state; it ought, therefore, to be inviolably preserved.

Vermont: The people have a right to freedom of speech, and of writing and publishing their sentiments concerning the transactions of government, and therefore the freedom of the press ought not to be restrained.

Connecticut: No law shall ever be passed to curtail or restrain the liberty of speech or of the press.

New York: Every citizen may freely speak, write and publish his sentiments on all subjects, being responsible for the abuse of that right.

Pennsylvania: The free communication of thoughts and opinions is one of the invaluable rights of man; and every citizen may freely speak, write and print on any subject, being responsible for the abuse of that liberty.

Indiana and Illinois: The free communication of thoughts and opinions is one of the invaluable rights of man; and every citizen may freely speak, write, and print on any subject, being responsible for the abuse of that liberty.

Ohio: Every citizen has an indisputable right to speak, write or print upon any subject, as he thinks proper, being liable for the abuse of that liberty.[8]

Federal Constitution, Article I (Amendments): Congress shall make no law respecting an establishment of religion, or prohibiting the free exercise thereof; or abridging the freedom of speech, or of the press; or the right of the people peaceably to assemble, and to petition the government for a redress of grievances.

All of the Constitutional guarantees, of course, were designed to protect individual rights from legislation by hostile majorities. No state legislature violated them, nor did Congress, by new legislation, although the special anti-Negro or "Black Laws" still on the statute books of some Northern states were clear violations and still had to be repealed. Antislavery men, however, went beyond these constitutional guarantees. They had to do so for two reasons: because these Constitutional restraints operated upon legislative bodies, and not upon all branches of the government, and because of imperfect understanding of a citizen's rights and responsibilities in relation to two governments, state and federal.

The Constitution, they said, was not the whole of the fundamental law, but only a part thereof.

The fundamental law, as a minimum, certainly embraced the Declaration of Independence and the Ordinance of 1787. The Declaration advertised to the world the principles upon which we were establishing a new nation. It brought other men and other nations to our support, providing the margin of victory. It secured a place for us in the family of nations. It swept through the world of arbitrary power, implementing and inspiring men in their quest for freedom and justice. It was intended to give character and direction to the policies of the new nation, which had already come into being with the association. It might not always be possible for every executive and every justice, and every legislator to act in perfect harmony with those principles, but certainly no public official, no branch of the government, above all, no court in its interpretations of the Constitution, should ever do violence to them.

The foundation principle of our fundamental law was that all men are created equal and endowed by their Creator with certain inalienable rights. We established government to make those rights secure. The rights themselves, and corresponding duties, derive from the nature of the human mind and the relationship between God and man and cannot be destroyed by human government. They are not derived from conventions, compacts, or laws. They are not immunities and privileges which were granted, could have been withheld, or may be taken away by any man, men, or constituted authority, nor does membership in any organization or association with any institution divest man of them.[9] "Our political and constitutional rights, so called," said Gerrit Smith, "are but the natural and inherent rights of man, asserted, carried out, and secured by modes of human contrivance. To no human charter am I indebted for my rights. They pertain to my original constitution; and I read them in that Book of books, which is the great Charter of man's rights. No the constitution of my nation and state create none of my rights. They do, at the most, but recognize what it was not theirs to give. My reason, therefore, for loving a republican form of government, and for preferring it to any other is, not that it clothes me with rights which these withhold from me; but that it makes fewer encroachments than they do on the rights which God gave me . . . It is not then to the constitution of my nation and state, that I am indebted for the right of free discussion; though I am thankful for the glorious defense with which those instruments surround that right. This right is, for the most part, defended on the ground, that it is given to us by our political constitutions; and that it was purchased for us by the blood and toil of our fathers. Now, I wish to see its defense placed on its true and infinitely higher ground; on the ground that God gave it to us; and that he who violates or betrays it, is guilty, not alone of dishonoring the laws of his country and the blood and toil and memory of his fathers; but he is guilty also of making war upon God's plan of man's constitution and endowment; and of attempting to narrow down and destroy that dignity with which God invested him when he made him in his own image."[10]

Why did Smith single out this right of free enquiry and discussion as an inalienable right? Because it is the cornerstone of the democratic edifice. Jefferson spoke of life, liberty, and the pursuit of happiness, but only as *being among* the inalienable rights. He left room for others, and the use of man's intelligence was certainly one. These men were fighting for principles as truly as men had fought for principles at the time of the Revolution. They were in a new and strange situation: a situation in which self-constituted tribunals, or lawless assemblages of men, set themselves above the laws of the land and wreaked their vengeance upon those who incurred their displeasure. Almost without exception these committees were organized by prominent men in a cool, calculating, and deliberate fashion. The large city newspapers encouraged them. Congress condemned their victims by refusing to entertain their petitions. The President of the United States threw his personal and official prestige against them by recommending congressional legislation to deny them the use of the mails. Governors recommended repressive legislation. Mayors and police stood by and watched the burning of Pennsylvania Hall, the killing of Lovejoy, the pillaging of innumerable newspaper establishments. No one was ever punished for these offenses, nor for the thousands of acts of violence against antislavery lecturers and free Negroes. No one bothered to bring indictments against them—juries would not have convicted if they had done so.

Southerners had completely abolished free enquiry and discussion of slavery. They controlled the party which controlled the government. They had struck down the right of petition, challenged the supremacy of the federal government, and devised an ingenious theory of concurrent majority which would have reduced public policies to the moral standards of whatever section possessed the lowest cultural level in the nation. They were denying with increasing vehemence the principle of universal manhood suffrage. They were denouncing the Declaration of Independence and the Virginia Declaration of Rights as glittering generalities. They were defending, for all time to come, a system of human bondage which reeked of bigotry, race prejudice, and inhumanity. The antislavery men were fighting for the basic principle of democracy: the exaltation of the individual, recognition of his natural rights, and protection against restraints by the government and his fellowmen that he might develop his talents to the utmost of his ability. In short, they were fighting to free four million men, women, and children from slavery, and a half million more from the cruel oppression of the Northern black laws and spoilation by their neighbors. They were fighting for justice and equality under the law for all men They were fighting for the survival of law itself, for this was a contest between government by law and government by man.

"The liberty to know, to utter, to argue freely, according to the dictates of conscience, we prize above all liberties," they said, "without *this,* the inalienable right to *life* would be worthless, to *liberty* unmeaning, to the *pursuit of happiness* unavailing." Man, said they, is a free moral agent, endowed with certain attributes, certain rights, and certain responsibilities by the creative act of God. These rights and responsibilities are reciprocal. A man possesses his rights by the law of nature—natural law, natural rights. They pertain to his original constitution; they are a birthright; they cannot be separated from accountable agency; and to lose them is to lose a part of oneself. The Supreme Ruler of the universe cannot take them away without "repealing the law of our moral agency or reducing us to our primitive nothing." Man cannot abandon them, nor voluntarily surrender them, without "unfitting himself for the designs of his existence."[11]

The right of the individual to inquire freely into all subjects and to communicate freely his ideas to others is God's instrument for renovating the world." Man was given the power to think, and he must use that power to free the human race from fear and from those restraints which prevent full expression of intellectual and moral powers. He must be free from restraints to contemplate the sublime thoughts of all ages, to engage in contemporary discussions of principles of right conduct, to anticipate posterity's judgments on moral questions, and to use his influence in directing aright the slow-moving current of human destiny. Either man must use this ability to reason, to know, to feel, to act by choice, or surrender his right to live.

Free discussion, said Weld, "is the acting out of the command: *Prove all things.* It is inquiry after immutable truth, whether embodied in the word, or hid in the works of God, or branching out through the relations and duties of man. We are bound to conduct this search, *wherever it may lead,* and to adopt the conclusions to which it may bring us. And, whereas, the single object of ascertaining truth is to learn *how to act,* we are bound to do at once whatever truth dictates to be done." "If God," said Smith, "made me to be one of his instruments for carrying forward the salvation of the world, then is the right of free discussion among my inherent rights, then may I, must I, speak of sin, any sin, every sin that comes in my way." Said Lovejoy, standing in the shadow of death, "you may hang me up, as the mob hung up the individuals at Vicksburgh! You may burn me at the stake, as they did McIntosh at St. Louis; or, you may tar and feather me, or throw me into the Mississippi, as you have threatened to do; but you cannot disgrace me. I, and I alone, can disgrace myself; and the deepest of all disgrace would be, at a time like this, to deny my Master by forsaking his cause . . . I dare not flee away from Alton. Should I attempt it, I should feel that the angel of the Lord with his flaming sword, was pursuing me wherever I went . . . the contest has commenced here; and here it must be finished . . . If I fall, my grave shall be made in Alton."[12]

Said Weld: "Let every abolitionist debate the matter once for all, and settle it with himself whether he is an abolitionist from *impulse* or principle—whether he can lie upon the rack—and clasp the faggot—and tread with steady step the scaffold—whether he can stand at the post of duty and having done all and suffered all, stand—and if cloven down, fall and die a martyr not accepting deliverance."[13]

So it was that natural law and moral law—natural rights and moral obligations—became one and the same in the antislavery movement. Freedom of individuals to perform all the obligations arising out of the relationships between persons and between persons and God is what they called the *natural rights of man*. The natural law and the moral law lead to the same basic concept in all human relationships: the equality of all men in the eyes of God. The first words and the most important words of the Declaration had been an affirmation of human equality and of the natural rights of man. It was no accident, therefore, that the First Amendment should have been a guarantee of those rights, nor that men like David Rice in Kentucky should have stoutly and clearly stated the amenability of legislative bodies to the moral law, nor that antislavery men in widely separated areas should have reaffirmed it with such clarity and unanimity. The Declaration became the most quoted of all documents for thirty years. This was the higher law.

Interwoven into all of the demands for suppression of antislavery men and measures was the argument that they were seeking to overthrow an ancient institution, one which was endorsed by the Scriptures, recognized by the Constitution, and imbedded in the structure of southern society, and that it was a domestic institution of the South, which was of no concern whatever to the people of the nonslaveholding states. This has been one of the most persistent and widely accepted themes of Southern mythology. Actually, of course, that the whole of the people in the nation had a vital interest in the enslavement of 3,500,000 persons was perfectly obvious.

Slavery weakened the nation, and was a menace to its peace and safety. Every citizen of the United States had a vital interest in its defense against a foreign aggressor and was liable to military service in putting down slave insurrections.

The people of the nonslaveholding states were deeply involved by the rendition of fugitive slaves. The peace of hundreds of Northern communities was disturbed by Southern slaveholders coming among them and seizing alleged fugitives. These unfortunate persons, as a minimum, were carried before their courts, lodged in their jails, and driven over their highways. Often, far too often, they were free citizens and respectable citizens of their states, being kidnapped and carried away into slavery. The people also were involved by

the federal control of the territories. Having rid their own states of slavery, they were not disposed to have their children burdened with the problem in new states. Their votes entered into both the control of the territories and the admission of states. Furthermore, the government which did these things also conducted foreign affairs, and it was their government as much as it was that of the slave states. The same applied to the District of Columbia which was solely and completely under the control of Congress.

Men reared in the slave country, deeply indoctrinated with the defense of slavery as a positive good to both races, firm in the conviction that it must be protected and perpetuated, and convinced of the biological inequality and racial inferiority of the Negro, were members of Congress, judges of the Supreme Court, and presidents of the United States. They held prominent positions in the churches, in the colleges, and in political parties. In these positions they exercised authority, within their sphere of authority, over the entire nation and determined or helped to determine its policies, its educational philosophy, and its religious doctrines.

Slavery disrupted the entire normal process of communication and transportation. Negro citizens of the free states could not exercise their constitutional right of going from one state to another without the ever-present danger of being taken into custody and sold into slavery. White citizens of free states, known to be opposed to slavery, were almost certain to be imprisoned or killed if they ventured into the slave states. All references to slavery were deleted by publishers from books to be offered for sale in the South and from magazines and from the literature of the American Tract Society.

Finally, the United States did not live in a world apart from other nations; could not do so any more than the slave states could live in a world apart from the free states. It alone of all the great nations retained slavery. It was peculiarly an American institution. It was hostile to the genius of our people and contrary to the principles of individual freedom we so loudly proclaimed. Other people scorned us for it, questioned our sincerity, and held us under suspicion in their dealings with us.

THE CAPITAL OF THE NATION

Chapter 28

What then of the District of Columbia, where the authority of the states did not extend, where men from all sections must meet in Congress to determine the policies of the nation, and where the most humble citizen must go to seek justice in the highest court in the land? There were slaves in the nation's capital city. They were bought and sold there and transported to and from and through the city both by their owners and in the commercial slave trade. There were pens, privately owned, in the District, for their detention. There were black laws, harsh and offensive to common decency, which set the free Negroes apart, and there was prejudice against them among the people as cruel as in the slave states, for the District lay between Maryland and Virginia, currently sources of supply for the lower South.[1] The slave states insisted that Congress could not abolish, restrict, or otherwise interfere with slavery in the District of Columbia without the consent of Maryland and Virginia. In fact, by 1836 they were claiming almost exclusive control of the District and denying the right of anyone in the nation to petition Congress for the abolition of slavery in the District.

On August 10, 1835, Reuben Crandall was arrested in the District of Columbia, thrown into jail, and kept there until April 15, 1836, despite all efforts to obtain his release. Francis Scott Key, United States attorney for the District of Columbia, author of the "Star Spangled Banner," and brother-in-law of Roger B. Taney, initiated proceedings against Crandall and conducted the prosecution.[2] Crandall was the brother of Prudence

Crandall. He had studied medicine with Dr. Harris who had refused to minister to Prudence after she admitted Negroes to her school. Crandall was a physician of excellent reputation. He had come to Washington to lecture on botany. Andrew T. Judson, who had led the prosecution and the persecution of Prudence, was now in Congress and testified in strong terms for Reuben. So, too, did the president of the Washington Medical College. Judson claimed that Reuben went from New York to Canterbury to put a stop to the educational activities of his sister. The biographer of Prudence indicates that he was sympathetic and helpful.[3] It is of little consequence. He was not an active antislavery agent, perhaps not even a devotee of the cause. He did not go to Washington to distribute antislavery literature, and no evidence was presented that he had actively done so or that he had any contact with slaves or free Negroes or communications with antislavery men while in Washington. On the other hand, his relationship to Prudence, her relationship with William Lloyd Garrison and Arthur Tappan, and the wide interest in her trial must have accounted for his having been kept under surveillance and the discovery that he had antislavery literature in his possession.

Crandall was charged, under the common law of libel, with having published papers calculated and intended to excite insurrection and rebellion, the charge being based upon the fact that he had the published pamphlets in his possession and, second, that he or someone else had written upon them the words "read and circulate." This indictment for a seditious libel at common law, according to the defense, was the first of that description ever brought up for judicial decision, entirely new to the courts of the United States. The published report spoke of it as "the first case of a man charged with endeavoring to excite insurrection among slaves and the free colored population that was ever brought before a judicial tribunal."[4] District Attorney Key called it "a case to try the question, whether our institutions have any means of legal defense against a set of men of most horrid principles, whose means of attack upon us are insurrection, tumult, and violence."[5]

The act of "publishing" must, in this case, be understood as *having put into the hands of a third party* the libelous and seditious literature. The defense, therefore, correctly contended that the publications—*The Anti-Slavery Reporter,* the *Emancipator,* and *Human Rights*—"themselves must be calculated to excite insurrection among the blacks, and contempt of government among the whites; and the mode and manner of the publication must be such as to justify the supposition that the publisher intended to produce this effect."[6]

In the first instance, then, the quality and character of antislavery literature were on trial. In fact, the indictment as presented at the opening of the trial embraced copious extracts from such publications, including the famous declaration of intent: "Our plan of emancipation is simply this— to promulgate the doctrine of human rights in high places and low places, and all places where there are human beings—to whisper it in chimney corners, and to proclaim it from the house tops, yea, from the mountain tops—to pour it out like water from the pulpit and the press—to raise it up with all the force of the inner man from infancy to gray hairs—to give line upon line, precept upon precept, till it forms one of the foundation principles and parts indestructible of the public soul."[7] In the end, the defense presented an even greater selection from the speeches and publications of the colonizationists, including a quotation of some length from a speech by District Attorney Key at the eleventh anniversary of the American Colonization Society. They insisted these speeches, many by slaveholders, were as much calculated to excite sedition as those quoted in the indictment. They showed that the headquarters of the American Colonization Society were in Washington, that all publications of the American Anti-Slavery Society were sent there in exchange and frequently loaned to other persons to be read, that these same publications were always sent to members of Congress, and that they were frequently quoted in the *African Repository,* official organ of the colonization society.

So it was, in this important trial, that antislavery men and measures, rather than Reuben Crandall, were under indictment and prosecuted by colonizationist Francis Scott Key. "I call your attention to the libels and to their tendency," said he. "The Colonization Society published them only to denounce them. The Colonization Society only contemplates free negroes, and has nothing to do with slavery." The inference was clear. Colonizationists would rid the country of Negroes; abolitionists would free the slaves. Key expanded this charge to the limit: "In one instant the chains of the slaves must snap asunder. Without delay, and without preparation, he becomes a citizen, a legislator, goes to the polls, and appoints *our* rulers . . . Are you willing, Gentlemen, to abandon your country; to permit it to be taken from you, and occupied by the abolitionist, according to whose taste it is to associate, and amalgamate with the negro."[8] Finally, not the least of the charges lodged against Crandall during the proceedings was that he was a Northern man, who had come, not on private business to the nation's capital, but to disturb the peace by his presence in a community where slavery was recognized by law. "Have we then," said Mr. Coxe, his defense attorney, "lived to see the day when in a court of justice, in the federal city, under the very eyes of Congress, and of the National government, it can be urged against an individual arraigned at the criminal bar, as a circumstance of aggravation, or as a just ground for suspicion, that the individual comes from the North or the South, from the East or the West? But we *were* told that the Northern men were interlopers and intruders amongst us."[9]

Crandall was acquitted by the jury, but died shortly afterward from neglect during his long detention in jail. Neither his acquittal nor his death is of much consequence in the history of this strange event. The evidence is clear that he could not have been acquitted if he could have been shown to be a member of an antislavery society. R. R. Gurley and Benjamin Lundy, two colonizationist editors of the District, could publish and distribute whatever they pleased, but membership in an antislavery society was regarded as *prima facie* evidence of intent to incite insurrection. A bitter contest to drive slavery out of the nation's capital and break the hold of the slave power upon the government was now inevitable. Its imperiousness knew no bounds; it had gone too far.

Petitions for the abolition of slavery in the District of Columbia had been going to Congress since Washington's administration. It was an important activity of the old abolition societies of the Eastern states, but petitions came also from all parts of the country in ever-increasing numbers. There were other petitions of sorts, at all times, touching upon the foreign slave trade, the domestic or interstate slave trade, and slavery in the territories, but slavery and the slave trade in the District of Columbia, in the capital city of a nation dedicated to freedom, was especially disconcerting. It was the one place where people from all parts of the country and the people's representatives came into intimate contact with the hated institution. Petitions for its abolition there, while partaking of the more general public policy characteristic of other petitions, were not unlike petitions for redress of personal grievance.

Antislavery people had won the long contest for suppression of the African slave trade. They had successfully maintained the power of Congress to exclude slavery from the territories and *had excluded* it from the vastly larger portion of the Louisiana Purchase. The one victory had followed the other in rapid succession, and then the Missouri contest had merged into the struggle for use of the public lands to finance a program of gradual emancipation and colonization. Northern state legislatures, led by Ohio, had initiated and supported the proposal; Southern state legislatures had reacted violently against it. The decline of the colonization movement had begun at this point. Antislavery men opposed both gradual emancipation and colonization. Their organization represented a forward advance from the halfway measures of the older abolition societies and the anti-Negro philosophy of the colonizationists. It intensified the demand that slavery be circumscribed and put in course of ultimate extinction.

The battle of legislative resolutions (1824–26) had been followed immediately by an accelerated petition campaign for the abolition of slavery in the District of Columbia. These petitions had reached Congress in such great numbers in 1828–29 that some response in the House had been imperative. Representative Charles Miner of West Chester, Pennsylvania, had offered resolutions in the House for abolition of slavery in the District on May 13, 1826, without success. On January 6, 1829, he had again requested an investigation of the slave trade in the District and the laws pertaining to slavery, and an inquiry into the expediency of gradual abolition of slavery. The committee on the District of Columbia had been instructed to do these things by votes of 120 to 59, and 114 to 66, and there the matter had rested.[10]

Miner had supported his request with facts obtained by personal investigation. Commercial slave traders had established their headquarters in the District. They were using both public and privately owned prisons in their operations, 452 slaves for sale and 290 alleged fugitives having been lodged in the public jail between 1824 and 1828. Citing the case of a woman and three children he had found there, Miner said: "She was a slave, but had married a man who was free. By him she had eight or nine children. Moved by natural affection, the father labored to support the children, but, as they attained an age to be valuable in the market, perhaps ten or twelve, the master sold them. One after another was taken away and sold to the slave dealers. She had now come to an age to be no longer profitable as a breeder, and her master had separated her from her husband and all the associations of life, and sent her and her children to your prison for sale. She was waiting for a purchaser, and seemed to me to be more heart-broken than any creature I had ever seen . . . Of the four hundred fifty others, I know nothing. I see no reason to suppose that there were not many cases of equal cruelty."[11]

Miner then had talked of the 290 alleged fugitives, many of whom were free men, taken up and lodged in prison, and finally sold. "It seems to me a hardship," said Miner, "that persons born free in New York, Pennsylvania, or elsewhere, who perhaps never thought of a certificate of freedom, should, without any charge of a crime, if they come within this District, be thrown into prison . . . A free man, poor, friendless, and ignorant, so arrested and confined in a cell of little more than ten feet square, would have but slight chance of asserting his rights."[12] He had cited the cases of five men sold in 1827. No one knew why, no one knew where the money went. Then he had piled case upon case, argument upon argument, and the whole was a shocking record of fraud, injustice, and cruelty.

Finally, Miner had presented the record of protest: the remonstrance of the District grand jury in 1802, the bitter attack in the House by Randolph of Virginia in 1816, the crusade of the Alexandria *Gazette* in 1827. He read from the newspapers of the District advertisements for slaves wanted by the traders and for slave auctions. He spoke of the protests from the legislature of Pennsylvania, of the petition signed by 1,000 inhabitants of the District, of the flood of petitions from all parts of the country. Why this concern of the people? Because, said Miner, "We are acknowledgedly the principal republic on the globe. Justice and equal rights are professedly at the foundation of our Government . . . Despotism must look with keen desire for our failure; the friends of civil liberty look with not less anxious hope for our prosperity and success. If we fail the great cause of freedom will be lost forever. As we succeed, the sacred principles of the rights of man gain strength and will extend their influence.[13]

Each year thereafter the number of petitions increased. They represent a growing interest in public policy with regard to slavery; a real concern over failure to humanize the system, a determination to prevent its expansion, a protest against the brutality of the fugitive slave law and the interstate slave trade. These petitions must have continued to flow to Congress under normal circumstances, because memorials are a natural expression of community solidarity. They give a sense of importance and achievement to the petitioners. They make organizational effort worth while. And, in this case, whether they influenced Congress or not, the person to person, house to house canvass for signatures in a local community kept the issue alive.

The American Anti-Slavery Society was not slow to grasp the importance of petitions to the growth of its local organizations. It did not initiate the practice; it could not have arrested it. Organized antislavery effort and petitions to Congress grew together; fortunately so, because Congressional debates on slavery provided almost the only way to get antislavery arguments before the people of the South. Southern congressmen knew this to be so, and they would neither permit themselves to be drawn into debate on the issue of slavery nor permit the petitions to become a part of the printed record.

A special committee in the House of Representatives, appointed on February 8, 1836, under the chairmanship of Henry L. Pinckney of South Carolina, recommended the following resolution: "That all petitions, memorials, resolutions, propositions, or papers, relating in any way, or to any extent whatever, to the subject of slavery, or the abolition of slavery, shall, without being either printed or referred, be laid upon the table, and that no further action whatever shall be had thereon."[14] This resolution was adopted by the House May 26, 1836, by a vote of 117 to 68. Pinckney was former owner and editor of the Charleston *Mercury*, violent protagonist of state rights and nullification; but a severe quarrel had erupted between him and Calhoun.

Pinckney took the position that Congress *did not have any power* under the Constitution to interfere with slavery in the States, but he said that "Congress *ought not to interfere* in any way with slavery in the District of Columbia." His appeal to expediency was the only defensible position for the South to take. Calhoun wanted to add insult to injury in both houses of Congress by having petitions summarily rejected, and went so far as to denounce Pinckney as a traitor to the South. His argument, which could not be defended on any grounds, was that Congress had no power to abolish slavery in the District of Columbia. Wise of Virginia and Thompson of South Carolina were most violent in their denunciation of the report and of Pinckney's position. Thompson said: "Instead of a cool, firm, and fixed purpose to stand on the rights, the chartered rights, of the South, what have we? An abandonment of those rights, stale homilies about union and fanaticism; puerile rhetoric, and jesuitical sophistry."[15]

More stringent gag resolutions, therefore, were passed each year thereafter, the fifth one, January 28, 1840, becoming a standing rule and remaining in force until December 2, 1844.[16] It could not have been passed except for the votes representing slaves. It resolved: "That upon the presentation of any memorial or petition praying for the abolition of slavery or the slave trade in any District, Territory, or State of the Union, and upon the presentation of any resolution, or other paper touching that subject, the *reception* of such memorial, petition, resolution, or paper, shall be considered as objected to, and the *question of its reception* shall be laid on the table, without debate, or further action thereon"; and "That no petition, memorial, resolution, or other paper praying the abolition of slavery in the District of

Columbia, or any State or Territory, or the slave trade between the States or Territories of the United States in which it now exists, shall be received by this House, or entertained in any way whatever."

Whether this series of rules constituted denial of the right of petition in a technical sense or not, the incontrovertible fact remains, it effectively prevented debate and publication of petitions.

The Pinckney resolution brought John Quincy Adams out into the open on the slavery question. Adams was shrewd, calculating, brilliant, and unsurpassed in his time for devoted public service. He was a man of integrity. He was a man of noble character, instinctively opposed to slavery and its evil consequences, but restrained by Garrison's vagaries from earlier association with the organized movement. He denounced the Pinckney resolution as "a direct violation of the Constitution of the United States, the rules of this House, and the rights of my constituents." It was that and more. It was a refusal by the majority in the House to countenance discussion or any type of consideration, in committee or otherwise, of a most vital area of public policy. The question of whether the seat of government belonged to the people of the United States or to the slaveholders was now before the people. Men suspected of antislavery principles could not go there without being put under surveillance; and, if found with antislavery literature in their possession, being tossed into jail. Free Negroes could not go there without danger of being sold into slavery. Representatives of the people could only take their seats in the House, restrained and muzzled.

A flood of protests, in the form of memorials, flowed into state legislatures. In Massachusetts the legislature appointed a committee of fourteen to consider all memorials on the subject of slavery. These memorials, almost without exception, requested the legislature to declare that Congress had power under the Constitution and should use it to abolish slavery and the slave trade in the District of Columbia; to request the "utmost exertions" of senators and representatives from Massachusetts to secure such legislation; and to protest, in the name of the people, against the Pinckney resolution.

Henry B. Stanton, in charge of public relations for the American Anti-Slavery Society, and most successful advocate before legislative bodies, appeared before the committee, the entire legisla-

ture and hundreds of spectators on the evening of February 23, 1837, the afternoon of February 24, and again in the evening of that day. He spoke one and one-half hours the first night, three hours the following afternoon, and more than an hour that evening, when he collapsed from exhaustion. The legislative committee requested that the testimony be continued. Theodore Weld was summoned from New York City to carry on the discussion but was completely and permanently incapacitated by a throat ailment. Stanton's speech is generally regarded as one of the greatest single efforts of that period of our history and was confined largely to the power and duty of Congress immediately to abolish slavery and the slave trade in the District of Columbia.[17]

Stanton's impressive array of testimony by statesmen and state legislatures in support of congressional power need not detain us. More important was his constitutional argument, based upon Article 1, Section 8, of the Constitution, that "the Congress shall have power to exercise exclusive legislation, in all cases whatsoever, over such district as may . . . become the seat of the government of the United States." Congress, having full legislative power over the District, may abolish slavery there in the same manner as the legislatures of Pennsylvania, Connecticut, Rhode Island, New York, and New Jersey had abolished slavery in those states. "Slavery is the creature of law," said Stanton. "Let them repeal these laws, and it is no longer legal; in other words, is *abolished* . . . Repeal these statutes, and the great fundamental principles, on which the common law is based, would batter down the walls of this American Bastile."[18]

Stanton presented the acts of cession of Maryland to show that the District was ceded to the "Congress and Government of the United States, in full and absolute right, and exclusive jurisdiction"; that there were no reservations; that the laws of Virginia and Maryland ceased to have effect at the time of cession; and that on July 16, 1790, Congress provided for the laws of those states to remain in effect in the District "until Congress shall otherwise provide." Slavery, therefore, existed in the District by direct force of Congressional law. If there were any compact or understanding aside from the Constitution itself, declared Stanton, it was "not a *pro*-slavery, but an *anti*-slavery compact," as shown by the assurances given in Northern ratifying conventions that the foreign slave trade would be completely stopped after twenty years and that no new slave states would be admitted, and by the immediate progression of emancipation in the several states. "And, by the great mass of the country," said Stanton, "it was hoped, believed, and understood, that long, long ere this, the last vestige of slavery was to have rotted in a dishonored grave." [19]

Continuing the second day, Stanton insisted that Congress should abolish slavery and the slave trade in the District of Columbia; but he insisted, also, that the real issue was much more important. "The cause of freedom throughout the world," he said, "the honor of God's law, will be deeply affected by your deliberations. The interests here involved, are co-extensive with human hopes and human happiness; wide as the universe, lasting as eternity, high as heaven . . . the slave, the master, this Commonwealth, the nation, the world, Jehovah himself, demand that we deliberate patiently, cautiously, impartially." [20]

Stanton's indictment of slavery literally sparkled with cogent and unanswerable statements of fact:

"Slavery is a system at war with natural justice and moral equity . . . a political and moral wrong, a sin against man and God . . . It robs men of their distinctive characteristics as rational and immortal beings, and makes them things . . . God gave to man his faculties to be employed in the promotion of his own happiness . . . [slaves] are permitted to live only as appendages to the existence of others . . . and so far as it is in the power of human legislation to do it, are divested of every right, natural, social, intellectual, political and moral, and are crowded out of God's creation into the chaos of an anomalous existence . . . it is an inflexible and universal rule of slave law, that the testimony of a colored person, whether bond or free, cannot be received against a white person . . . That the lust of power, and the love of gain, should so corrode the human heart, that man should traffic in the sinews of his brother, is the wonder of fiends . . . The record of its cruelty is written in tears and blood. In savage atrocity, it yields not to the African slave trade . . . As to the immediate investment of the slaves with the elective franchise, and other more conventional rights, we leave that to the wisdom of Congress. We only say, let there be no tests on account of *color*. Let the quality of the brains, and the color of the heart, be the standards, rather than the color of the skin, and the texture of the hair." [21]

Stanton then went on to discuss the vicious consequences of having slavery in the nation's Capital, impairing as it did the "freedom of locomotion, of speech, of the press, of debate, which are necessary to transact the public business of the nation." [22] He pointed out that free Negro citizens could not go there without danger of being seized and sold; that Dr. Reuben Crandall of New York was held in jail there for eight months and then tried as an incendiary, when there was not a shred of evidence against him; that in this trial Ransom G. Williams of New York was summoned as a witness but was warned by members of Congress not to come because his life was in danger, the governor of Alabama having demanded of the governor of New York his surrender as an incendiary; that William Ellery Channing had been denounced on the floor of Congress, and John Quincy Adams threatened by Waddy Thompson of South Carolina and the latter urged by the Charleston *Mercury* to assassinate him. "Shall our Representatives deliberate with threats of indictment in their ears," asked Stanton, "and gags in their mouths, and cords around their necks, and the Assassin's steel at their backs?" [23]

"A Wise Providence," said Stanton, "has so ordered, that perfect freedom and absolute slavery cannot, for a long time, co-exist on the same soil . . . rather let us attempt to mingle light and shade, heat and cold, sickness and health, right and wrong, heaven and hell, than hope that freedom of speech, of debate, and the press can dwell in the District of Columbia, or in this nation, while slavery is tolerated." [24]

Stanton dwelt long upon the injury of slavery to our national reputation, bringing contempt upon our professions of equality, exposing us to charges of hypocrisy, and denying us any claim to moral leadership in man's long struggle against oppression. "The citizens of this nation," he said, "have deep responsibilities, as republicans, as Christians, as citizens of the world. Our character and reputation, are moral capital, loaned us by God, to be invested for the political and moral renovation of the human race." [25] It was imperative, he argued, that the free states repudiate, in every possible way and immediately, the Pinckney report which had been adopted by Congress, because it contained a strong defense of slavery as "a wise and benevolent institution." Having been adopted by the House of Representatives,

Southern Negro quarter

Southern cotton plantation

it went out to the world as "the voice of America." Thus, at one and the same time, it had uttered a "foul libel upon our freedom and our religion," and denied the sacred right of petition.

Threats of disunion, if slavery should be abolished in the District of Columbia, were dismissed by Stanton as very unlikely, because disunion would not lessen antislavery agitation, nor facilitate the return of fugitives, nor prevent insurrections. Should the South attempt disunion "the whole weight of the General Government will be precipitated upon her head."[26]

The powerfully persuasive voice of Weld had broken under the infernal torture of mob violence and the strain of lecturing for hours at a time, night after night, under all sorts of conditions; but Weld could write as brilliantly as he could lecture. He now published in the New York *Evening Post* his examination of the power of Congress to abolish slavery and the slave trade in the District of Columbia.[27] The constitutional provision: "The Congress shall have power to exercise exclusive legislation, in all Cases whatsoever, over such District" was incapable of misconstruction. There were no restraints upon congressional power, and because of that grant of unlimited power, George Mason, Patrick Henry, and others in the Virginia Convention had vigorously opposed ratification. Their objections had not prevailed. Madison had said in the forty-third number of the *Federalist:* "The indispensable necessity of complete authority at the seat of government, carries its own evidence with it."[28] The only question, therefore, was whether abolition of slavery was within the legitimate scope of legislative power.

Weld took the position that slavery could be abolished by legislative action because it was the creature of statute law. This was not new theory. Antislavery men had maintained from the beginning of the contest, and would unto the end, that slavery was complete subjection of one man to the will of another, established by force, maintained by force, and recognized and sustained by law. Slaveholders tried, without complete success, to establish the principle that slavery was based in the common law, and, therefore, was not subject to legislative authority because slaves were property and the definition of what constituted property was an exercise of sovereign power. Slavery, therefore, could be abolished only by action of a state constitutional convention.

Weld's contribution lay first in his historical treatment of the subject. He cited one act of emancipation after another to show that every civilized nation had abolished slavery by legislative act; and that, in this country, Pennsylvania (1780), Connecticut (1784), Rhode Island (1784), New York (1799), New Jersey (1804) all had abolished slavery by act of state legislatures.[29] He showed that legislatures in the remaining slave states had abolished slavery in its parts and could do so in its entirety. Virginia (1792), for instance, had provided freedom for slaves brought into and kept in the state for one year. South Carolina's legislature had forbade an owner to work a slave more than fifteen hours a day. Why then could if not limit hours of work to ten or five or none? Georgia's legislature had limited work to six days a week. Why could it not say three or two? Immoderate correction was prohibited in North Carolina, humane treatment was acquired in Mississippi. Could these legislatures not define immoderate correction and humane treatment in such manner as to make control of slaves impossible? Thus, Weld anticipated the argument of Stephen A. Douglas in his defense of popular sovereignty by two decades.[30]

Weld then discussed the common law argument. "The common law knows no slaves," he said. "Its principles annihilate slavery wherever they touch it. It is a universal, unconditional, abolition act. Wherever slavery is a legal system, it is so only by *statute* law, and in violation of common law. The declaration of Lord Chief Justice Holt, that 'by the common law no man can have property in another,' is an acknowledged axiom, and based upon the well known common law definition of property. The subjects of dominion or property are *things,* as contra-distinguished from persons." Weld went on to show that the constitution of the United States does not recognize slaves as property but as persons. This is true in apportionment, and in the provision for the return of fugitives. Slaves are tried in the courts as persons and punished as persons, "even though loaded with cruel disabilities in courts of law."[31]

Finally, Weld touched upon two aspects of the problem soon to be paramount in all discussions. Slaveholders were claiming that emancipation by legislative act constituted depriving persons of property without due process of law. The Constitution said: "No person shall be deprived of life, liberty, or property without due process of law." All slaves had been deprived of liberty by laws, and if that legislation was due process then laws freeing the slaves were due process. If legislation is not due process then every slave was deprived of his freedom unconstitutionally and was free by constitutional provision. "A legislative act" [of emancipation], said Weld, "changes the condition of the slave—makes him his own *proprietor* instead of the property of another. It determines a question of original right between two classes of persons—doing an act of justice to one, and restraining the other from acts of injustice; or, in other words, preventing one from robbing the other, by granting to the injured party the protection of just and equitable laws."[32] Finally, with almost prophetic vision, Weld said: "It has been shown already that *allegiance* is exacted of the slave. Is the government of the United States unable to grant *protection* where it exacts *allegiance?* It is an axiom of the civilized world, and a maxim even with savages, that allegiance and protection are reciprocal and correlative. Are principles powerless with us which exact homage of barbarians? *Protection is the* CONSTITUTIONAL RIGHT *of every human being under the exclusive legislation of Congress who has not forfeited it by crime."[33]

PETITIONS

Chapter 29

The brightest years of the antislavery enlightenment were 1837 to 1839, despite adoption in the House of Representatives of the Pinckney report and in the Senate of Calhoun's resolutions. Stanton's powerful speech before the Massachusetts legislature was followed by an intensified petition campaign, and by publication of four special treatises: Weld's *American Slavery As It Is,* Birney's *Correspondence with F. H. Elmore of South Carolina,* Thome and Kimball's *Emancipation in the West Indies,* and Beriah Green's *Chattel Principle.*

The Constitution forbids Congress to make any law "abridging the freedom of speech, or of the press; or the right of the people peaceably to assemble and to petition the government for a redress of grievances." The Pinckney report of May 26, 1836, and those other gag resolutions which followed it, would seem to have been clear violations of this constitutional provision, but they were rules of procedure, not laws governing individual conduct, and who was to say to the House that it must do thus and so. Because only the sovereign people at the ballot box could control Congress (and ultimately that was the solution of this problem) did not justify the House in passing the Pinckney report. It was not legal or illegal. It was not constitutional or unconstitutional. It was tyranny.

Anyone who permits himself to become involved in the abstract questions of what constitutes the right of petition, and whether these petitions should have been referred to a committee for systematic tabulation and periodic report, fails to grasp the hateful significance of the Pinckney re-

port.[1] The rule of procedure was preceded by a lengthy defense of slavery. They were inseparable. That report said: "They rejoice" (meaning the Committee and the House when it passed the report); "They rejoice, therefore, that the great body of the people of the non-slaveholding states, have come forward, as they have done, in the true spirit of American patriotism, to maintain their constitutional obligations to their southern brethren, and to arrest the disturbance of the public peace."

The report was then, first of all, a deliberate encouragement to mob violence. Never before, nor since, in this land of free institutions, has the rule of impartial law been so threatened by mobs as at this time. Force had triumphed over law everywhere in the land for many months and the contest had scarcely begun. The slave power, and its Northern allies, the colonizationists, who wanted to use mobs to put down discussion, insisted that mob violence was an expression of the will of the people. They insisted that the inalienable rights of individuals might be infringed at any time by this expressed will of a community. They insisted that the victims were responsible for the "excitement," in any given case. Every one of these perversions of truth and justice was wrapped up in this report. They were labeled patriotism. They were soon to be repeated and emphasized by the postmaster general and the President of the United States.

The report went on to say: "Every true patriot must be aware that a crisis has now arrived in the political condition of the country, in which neutrality would be criminal, and in which he must determine between the suppression of abolition, and the destruction of the Union, and take his stand accordingly, for or against his country." The report was then, in the second place, a repetition and endorsement of the slanderous charge that a discussion of slavery at the North was a threat to the Union. All of the talk about the Union being dissolved was by Southerners, and if it were to be dissolved, of course, they would do it. In one sweeping sentence, the report exonerated them, apparently justified their threats of disunion, and said that to save the Union freedom of speech and of the press and of antislavery organizations, men and measures must be suppressed. This was Calhoun's future Resolutions of 1837 in capsule form.

The report went on with a direct, and grossly vulgar, defense of slavery. Emancipation of the slaves would be impracticable, undesirable, impossible. It would be impracticable because slaves were a valuable species of property. Slaveholders would have to be paid full market value and such a sum of money could never be raised. It would be undesirable because the Negroes were an improvident, shiftless, lazy lot of people who would not be able to provide for themselves and would be an intolerable nuisance and burden upon society. Agriculture and commerce would steadily decline. It would be impossible because the two races could not live together on any basis except that of slavery for the Negro. Slavery was a humane and Christian institution. It was being condemned unjustly by fanatical and misguided persons whose continued activity would destroy the Union.

Pinckney said very frankly in the House that his first great object was "to arrest discussion of the subject of slavery within these walls," because slavery was inviolable, antislavery men were fanatics, and perpetual slavery was the price of continued Union. Men could not have the Union without slavery. They must make their choice. Whether or not the right of petition was denied, it was abridged, and freedom of debate was stricken down on the most vital question ever embraced in the determination of domestic policy. No one made any effort to provide an analysis of the petitions and presentation of their substance to the House. The whole purpose of the gag was to suppress their content and prevent its ever seeing the light of day. The report went out to the country,

and to foreign countries as a statement of public policy. It could not be allowed to go unchallenged.

Beyond these very obvious reasons for continuing and intensifying the petition campaign were other practical considerations. Petitions, as has been said, gave to the local antislavery societies a common area of endeavor and to the movement as a whole a cohesion and solidarity. They provided an opportunity for intimate personal discussion of slavery and public policy greatly to be desired. That discussion swelled into a mighty chorus of protest. The issue penetrated farm homes, workshops, and school rooms. Circulating petitions was peculiarly a woman's work. It gave them an opportunity, despite their inability to vote, to participate largely in political affairs, and they were not happy about having the results of their labors end up under the table instead of on the table in Congress.

It was not really clear to people in farm communities that Southern slaveholders had anything to do with mob violence in the North, but it was perfectly obvious that they instigated the gag rule. This was not a matter of slaveholders *versus* slaves. This was a direct issue between slaveholders and Northern free men. The Pinckney report for the first time, in a way that penetrated even remote communities, shouted the threat of disunion. When Southerners like Calhoun, McDuffie, and Wise insisted that the discussion of slavery would dissolve the Union, they pronounced the death sentence on slavery. It was asking just a little too much, as Calhoun did in the Senate, for them to believe that Providence brought the two races together on the basis of slavery in this country.

Finally, Alanson St. Clair explained as cogently as anyone the importance of the petition campaign when he said: "Petition and the ballot-box are the hands on the great public clock, to show the antislavery time of day. Just so far as our moral measures prepare the nation for emancipation, men will be elected and legislatures petitioned for this purpose; and when the people are but once ready to vote for such men as will go for emancipation, and to instruct them accordingly, the work will be done, and not before."[2]

There were four men in Congress willing to champion the right of petition during the early phases of the contest: Senator Thomas Morris of Ohio, and Representatives John Quincy Adams of Massachusetts, William Slade of Vermont, and

Joshua Giddings of Ohio. Morris and Adams were not thoroughgoing antislavery men; Slade and Giddings were antislavery stalwarts. Morris was a Democrat, the others were Whigs. Adams took a prominent part in the petition struggle, and it has given him an undeserved prominence in the history of the antislavery movement. He was at times very feeble, illogical, and inconsistent, and he was a politician. He fearlessly defended the constitutional right of petition, but does not deserve a very high place on the list of antislavery men. He *opposed* slavery, but frankly said that he would not vote to abolish it in the territories nor in the District of Columbia. His argument was that public opinion was opposed; in short, he would vote according to majority opinion, no matter how morally wrong it was.

Adams also favored compensated emancipation, utterly oblivious to the post-emancipation problem of justice and equality under the law for Negroes if a property right in slaves were recognized. He insisted that the growth of antislavery societies had weakened the prospects for the abolition of slavery. He took the position that questioning of candidates for public office was "very questionable, with reference to the freedom of elections." He insisted that Florida must come into the Union as a slave state by the terms of the treaty of cession; yet he voted against the admission of Arkansas because her constitution forbade the legislature ever to abolish slavery. He would not vote to abolish slavery where established, without compensation and without consent of the owner.[3]

Adams' position was important in the decision to turn to political organization. He admitted "that freedom is the natural and inalienable right of man, and that by the laws of nature, and of nature's God, an immortal soul cannot be made a chattel." Antislavery men said that if slavery was wrong everywhere and always, Congress was responsible in its collective capacity for allowing it to continue in the territories, and each member was responsible individually if he did not speak against it. It was not a question of what a man in public life could do, but what he ought to do. No reform could ever be accomplished by legislation if the minority voted according to the opinions of the majority rather than on the basis of right. Unless a man were governed by his own moral convictions, minority influence could never be felt.

Senator Morris insisted that the Fugitive Slave Act of 1793 was unconstitutional. He frequently raised the questions of whether a slave could commit treason against the United States, and whether Congress could draft slaves into the armed services, holding that if they could the federal government had complete power to abolish slavery. "I have," he said, "always believed slavery to be wrong, in principle, in practice, in every country, and under every condition of things. So radically wrong, that no time, place, or circumstances can palliate it, or give it even the appearance of being right; and that American slavery is the most obnoxious of its kind, a libel upon our republican institutions, and ruinous to the best interests of our country. I have repeatedly asserted that the framers of the Constitution of the United States intended that its whole moral power should operate to the extinguishment of slavery in the country, and that it no where guarantees the existence of slavery, or the right of the master to the slave."[4] Beyond that Morris was strictly a states-rights Democrat.

He agreed that slavery was created by state law; that the Constitution of the United States did not prohibit it or guarantee it; that Congress had no power to free the slaves in the several states; that Congress had the power to abolish slavery in the District of Columbia; that Congress should not exercise that power but should remove the seat of government to the free states; that Congress probably did not have the right to refuse admission to a slave state; that it could and should prohibit slavery in the territories; that the power of Congress ceased when a state was created, and could not prevent a state from legalizing slavery after admission. He would not vote to abolish slavery in the District of Columbia; he would vote to admit a slave state.

William Slade came to Congress from Vermont in 1831. Six years later, in the midst of the fearful contest over civil rights, James G. Birney said: "Should the slaveholders succeed in banishing liberty from the free states, the last refuge would be in the hearts and hills of these noble Vermonters."[5] Meanwhile, the Vermont Anti-Slavery Society had been organized in May, 1834. There had been some mild disturbances in connection with antislavery meetings, particularly those of Samuel J. May, but the state was as thoroughly antislavery as any in the Union. When the argument over petitions erupted in the winter of 1835–36, Slade was the one man in the House of Representatives willing to receive and read these petitions, saying: "Sir, we must not bury these petitions . . . such a policy will certainly defeat itself . . . the spirit of free enquiry is the master spirit of the age. It bows to the authority of truth and reason and Revelation; but it bows to nothing else. It must have free course, and it will have it; giving life and soul and energy to the march of liberal principles, and destined to shake every institution of earth which does not recognize the 'inalienable rights' of man, and bow to the supremacy of just and equal laws. And Sir, it shall move onward, and onward, until every kindred and tongue and people under Heaven shall acknowledge and glory in the truth that 'all men are created equal.'"[6] Slade believed in gradual emancipation, but he favored the abolition of slavery in the District of Columbia and introduced the first bill to that effect in the House, in December 1837.

Joshua R. Giddings, giant, broad-shouldered, deep-chested young attorney of Jefferson, Ohio, went to Congress in 1838. He, like Morris of Ohio, had educated himself while wresting a living from the soil. He had the advantage not only of an early contact with the master mind among pioneer abolitionists—Theodore D. Weld—but of living in the Western Reserve, where President Charles B. Storrs and Professors Beriah Green and Elizur Wright had early converted Hudson College into a citadel for free discussion of all public questions and where the antislavery agents trained by Weld had done their earliest and some of their most effective work. Giddings, when he went to Congress, immediately threw himself into the struggle for freedom of debate and the right of petition on all subjects in Congress. He had as deep and sincere abhorrence of slavery as any man in the movement, a solid antislavery constituency, and a willingness to legislate against slavery at every opportunity.

The petition campaign was Whittier's contribution to the antislavery movement. He was closely associated with its operation from the beginning, with Stanton and Weld carrying the burden of directing it after the annual meeting of the American Anti-Slavery Society in 1837. *The organized campaign, therefore, followed the adoption of the first gag rule rather than preceding it. The gag rule was responsible for the organized petition campaign; not the reverse as has commonly been supposed.* Petitions were printed and sent out to local societies from the New York office, but thousands, also, were drawn up locally, signed, and sent to the district's congressman. An enormous number of the latter were consigned to waste baskets by hostile representatives. Most of the petitions were circulated by women, and when signed were channeled back through the state societies or the American Anti-Slavery Society to a congressman who could be trusted.

The third session of the Twenty-fifth Congress, December 1838 to March 1839, is probably the most valuable for a study of what happened. There were eight different petitions dealing with slavery: (1) for the abolition of slavery in the District of Columbia, (2) for the abolition of slavery in the territories, (3) for the prohibition of the interstate slave trade, (4) against the admission of any new slave state, (5) against the annexation of Texas, (6) for recognition of the Republic of Haiti, (7) to rescind the gag (Atherton) resolution of December 1838, and (8) to remove the seat of government to a free state. The first, second, and third were often presented in combination, with one set of signatures, and four, five, and six were also often combined. There were occasional petitions for the education of Negroes, for a general emancipation act by Congress, for the repeal of all territorial laws restricting free colored persons, and for more effective suppression of the African slave trade. Finally, there was a famous Fathers and Rulers petition circulated and signed only by women.

Birney, in his correspondence with Elmore in 1838, had placed the total number of signatures at 500,000, about equally divided between men and women. The larger number by far were 130,-246 for abolition of slavery in the District of Columbia, and 182,392 against the annexation of Texas. There were 31,836 for repeal of the gag resolution, 22,161 against the admission of more slave states, 23,405 for abolition of the interstate slave trade, and 21,212 for abolition of slavery in the territories.[7] These were the figures for the period between January 18, 1837, and March 1838. They did not include petitions sent directly to congressmen and not tabulated. There must have been many such.

In the third session of the Twenty-fifth Congress as indicated above (December, 1838–March, 1839), 1,496 petitions were presented in the House of Representatives. Some of them embraced a single subject, some were multiple petitions. Had they been separated into single units, there would have been a total of 3,335 documents. They were signed by 101,850 persons, but there was, of course, a duplication of names and a total of 163,-845 signatures. The largest number of petitions came from New York (362), Massachusetts (346), Vermont (177), Ohio (171), Pennsylvania (117), and Maine (113). In the West, Michigan and Illinois each sent 23, and Indiana 14. There were 71 from New Hampshire, 58 from Connecticut, 20 from Rhode Island, and 14 from New Jersey.

These petitions show a great deal of discrimination on the part of the petitioners. Sometimes three petitions were combined over one set of signatures. Sometimes they would be signed separately and fastened together for transmission to the House. In these cases, there was a wide variation in names, some people signing one and not another. There is no indication, as charged in the House, that long lists of names were written in by one person or that all members of an antislavery society automatically signed whatever was placed before them for their signatures. The petition which received the most support—80,755 signatures—was that for the abolition of slavery and the slave trade in the District of Columbia. Abolition of the interstate slave trade was second with 54,547, exclusion of slavery from the territories was third with 48,575, exclusion of Texas was fourth with 44,427, and prohibition of slavery in new states was fifth with 44,126. By the time of the Twenty-sixth Congress, anti-Texas petitions were outnumbering all others combined. John Quincy Adams presented the majority of the petitions (693). William Slade presented 430, and a number of other members a total of 373. Of the latter number, the newly elected Joshua Giddings of Ohio brought in 42, but the fact that eleven other men presented from 15 to 30 each, and as many more at least a half-dozen, indicates an increasing willingness to risk the penalties of party discipline.

What of these petitions as antislavery literature? They were read by more people, probably, than any other publications. Whether congressmen ever read any of them or not, all antislavery people did, and hundreds of thousands of others to whom appeals were made for signatures. The most popular of all petitions through the years was the Fathers and Rulers of our Country, designed entirely for the signatures of women. The copy here reproduced has as its first two signa-tures those of the wives of James Gilliland, beloved pastor of Red Oak Church, and John B. Mahan, later kidnapped and taken to Kentucky for trial for aiding fugitives, both of Brown County, Ohio. The Women's Anti-Slavery Convention of 1839 said of circulating petitions: "It is our only means of direct political action. It is not ours to fill the offices of government, or to assist in the election of those who will fill them. We do not enact or enforce the laws of the land. The only direct influence which we can exert upon our Legislatures, is by protests and petitions."[8]

Another petition, exclusively for women, was printed and widely circulated by the Ohio Anti-Slavery Society in 1836–37, praying for the abolition of slavery and the slave trade in the District of Columbia. Speaking of slavery as "unjust and cruel in its operations to one portion of our fellow-creatures, pernicious in its effects to all where it is practiced, and a heinous sin against God," they asked for speedy abolition of slavery in the District because it entailed "accumulated woes on thousands of native-born citizens, who are entitled to the protection of our enlightened government by the declared rights of the nation"; because of the stigma cast upon our national character by allowing a trade in Washington which had been denounced as piracy if practiced on the high seas; and because of attendant evils, including the imprisonment and sale of free persons and of women and children. Finally, and most emphatically, they asked "for the freedom of the slaves in the said District and for the protection of the laws to be extended to them, as to *other citizens of the United States*."[9]

Another petition flowed into Congress from all parts of the free states, signed by both men and women, asking for abolition in the District "because slavery is unjust, violating the rights both of God and man; because it corrupts public morals; because it is oppressive to the honest free laborer, and tends to make labor disreputable as well as unprofitable; because it brands our nation before the world as cruel and hypocritical; because persons are imprisoned in the District on mere suspicion of being 'runaways,' and not being proved to be such, are sold into perpetual slavery for the payment of their jail fee; because while slavery continues there must of necessity be a slave trade; a trade which has, by a solemn act of Congress, been declared PIRACY, when carried on upon the ocean; because its existence in a District, over which Congress has the right of exclusive legislation in all cases whatsoever, involves the whole nation in the sin of slaveholding . . . because it is demanded by the enlightened sentiment of the civilized world, by the principles of the revolution, and by humanity."[10] Citizenship was referred to again in a petition circulated everywhere which said: "The same acts, which when committed against strangers on a foreign coast, your honorable bodies have branded as the worst of infamous crimes, are licensed by your authority and abetted by your officers against our fellow citizens."[11]

Still another petition on the same general subject insisted that it was the duty of those who had the power to comply with the principles of the Declaration of Independence, and "restore to the slaves their liberty, and place them under the full protection, as well as the control of impartial law." Since Congress possessed exclusive power over the District of Columbia, and the most important function of government was to secure to its subjects the free enjoyments of their natural rights, it should abolish, not the slave trade, but slavery in the District because "where men are not objects of property, there they will not be bought and sold." It also said, with obvious reference to the Pinckney report which denied the expediency and the Calhoun doctrine which denied the right even of discussing abolition in the District: "It would wipe off a reproach from our national character. In the reputation of his country, *every* citizen is interested; a majority of the people therefore have a right to impose upon the District of Columbia such domestic institutions as shall accord with our national profession of republicanism. It need not be said that the existence of slavery there is a stigma upon the whole nation. It holds in disrepute our Declaration of equal rights, and stamps with the brand of hypocrisy our pretensions to be the friends and supporters of true liberty." Then, once more, on the point of citizenship: "He [God] has no attributes which can take sides with a nation, which by law makes merchandise of its *native born citizens*."[12]

Finally, a memorial, printed and circulated in Vermont, dealt only with the practice of arresting free Negroes in the District of Columbia, committing them to prison on the presumption they were slaves, holding them incommunicado; and, then, since they had not proved their freedom, selling them "into bondage to pay the costs occa-

sioned by the *suspicion* that they are not entitled to that liberty with which the declaration of independence declares *all men* to be endowed." The issue here raised in 1841 (Twenty-sixth Congress) was fully applicable to the bitter contest over the Fugitive Slave Act which began ten years later; and in the memorial is a clear and simple statement of free-state position at that later date: "That the existence, within the Capital of the republic of the United States, of laws so abhorrent to humanity—to the principles of natural justice and to the genius and spirit of free institutions, is well calculated, not only to diminish the reverence and attachment which all true friends of republican freedom should feel for their country and its laws, but also to disgrace us deeply and indelibly disgrace us as a nation—in the eyes of the world, appears too plain to your memorialists to require anything more than a simple statement of the facts, to substantiate. Your memorialists, therefore, *earnestly, firmly, but respectfully* ask your honorable bodies immediately to pass such laws as shall prohibit the local authorities from imprisoning as slaves, persons of color, claiming to be free, in the absence of satisfactory evidence before a judicial tribunal, that they are slaves, so that the presumption shall always be in favor of freedom rather than slavery."[13]

One petition, printed and circulated by the American Anti-Slavery Society in 1836, requested Congressional action for emancipation in the District of Columbia, and the territories of Arkansas and Florida, affecting about thirty thousand of "our countrymen, who though charged with no crime, and in violation of the fundamental principles of our national existence, are held in a state of bondage the most cruel and exacting." The petition implored Congress "to enact just and equal laws for the protection of all persons within the limits of your exclusive jurisdiction, securing to them the enjoyment of the inalienable rights of man"; and, also, "prohibit a traffic in living men, women and children, which in defiance of the laws of God, and the universally acknowledged principles of human rights, is now extensively prosecuted from one state to another of this union."[14]

Another petition, printed and circulated in Philadelphia, protested specifically against the admission of Arkansas with a constitution which prohibited the state legislature from emancipating any slave without consent of the owner, and from preventing persons coming into the state from any other state with their slaves. "From any view which we have been able to take of the subject," said the petition, "we cannot perceive it to be the conventional right of those now interested in the holding of slaves, to ask a virtual appropriation of the national domain for the enjoyment of such a species of property, against the conscience of the nation and of the World, and to the prevention of its occupancy, as would otherwise be the case, by a dense, industrious, and intelligent race of Freemen."[15]

The use of short petitions, of a few lines only, began in the Twenty-fourth Congress, and continued thereafter in very large numbers. The women of the country, acknowledging their exclusion from "party and political strife," nevertheless requested that slavery be abolished in the District of Columbia and announced their intention of presenting the petition every year as a sort of memorial to having done what they could.[16] Another general petition pointed out that Congress, if it did not abolish slavery in the District of Columbia, was using its power of exclusive legislation to perpetuate slavery and the slave trade in the nation's capital.[17] Another petition simply requested Congress to abolish slavery in the District of Columbia and the territories and to suppress the interstate slave trade.[18]

The petition from Pittsburgh requested emancipation in the District of Columbia: "Because, slavery is unjust in depriving the honest laborer of his wages . . . tyrannical and consequently cruel, subjecting the slave to the irresponsible will of the master, and making him, often times, the victim of cruelty too shocking to be witnessed by an undisciplined mind . . . a flagrant violation of the only perfect rule of human intercourse 'Whatever ye would that men should do to you do ye even so to them' . . . a practical contradiction of the foundation principles of our free institutions "That all men are born FREE AND EQUAL . . . and makes us a by-word and hissing among the nations of Europe."[19] The women of Massachusetts emphasized the manner in which slavery degraded women, tearing wives from husbands and mothers from children and depriving them of the protection of husbands and fathers.

"History would blush for American women," said they, "if, under such circumstances, they ever allowed the voice of expostulation and entreaty to cease throughout the land."[20]

By the time of the Twenty-fifth Congress, 1839–40, petitions were ordinarily very short and printed in series. A typical example is one dealing with Texas: "The undersigned citizens of _____ in the State of _____ respectfully pray your honorable body, promptly to reject all proposals for the annexation of Texas to this Union, from whatever source they may come."[21] There was not a great deal of variation in anti-Texas petitions, but they far surpassed all others combined both in number of petitions and number of signatures. They went to the House of Representatives, to the Senate, to governors, and to state legislatures. Some of them included a protest against admission into the Union of any slave state. Annexation of Texas was opposed because its independence had not been acknowledged and annexation would probably lead to war with Mexico, its constitution sanctioned slavery, its vast area and its continuation as slave country would give control of the nation to the slave power, and subordinate the interests of the free states, particularly of free labor, the foundation of their wealth and prosperity.[22]

Protests against the annexation of Texas, and pleas for the abolition of slavery in the District of Columbia, were equaled by prayers for the regulation of commerce among the states, so as to prohibit the domestic slave trade and assure admission of none but nonslaveholding states in the future. These petitions regarding the interstate slave trade and admission of states multiplied in variety and volume in the Twenty-sixth Congress, all of them clearly demanding restriction of slavery to the area where it already existed. There were petitions, also, for a constitutional amendment abolishing slavery throughout the nation, and assuring Congress that petitions would continue in increasing numbers until the nation ceased to countenance the "cowardly invasion of the most sacred rights of the feeble and defenseless of both sexes . . . robbery of the produce of the poor man's sweat and toil . . . and sacrilegious inroads upon the peace and purity of domestic life."[23]

AMERICAN SLAVERY AS IT IS

Chapter 30

American Slavery As It Is is history—well written and well documented. It is an encyclopedia of knowledge. It is a book of horrors. It is the greatest of the antislavery pamphlets; in all probability, the most crushing indictment of any institution ever written. It was written by Theodore Weld, who said in the introduction:

"We will prove that the slaves in the United States are treated with barbarous inhumanity; that they are overworked, underfed, wretchedly clad and lodged, and have insufficient sleep; that they are often made to wear round their necks iron collars armed with prongs, to drag heavy chains and weights at their feet while working in the field, and to wear yokes, and bells, and iron horns; that they are often kept confined in the stocks day and night for weeks together, made to wear gags in their mouths for hours or days, have some of their front teeth torn out or broken off, that they may be easily detected when they run away; that they are frequently flogged with terrible severity, have red pepper rubbed into their lacerated flesh, and hot brine, spirits of turpentine, etc. poured over the gashes to increase the torture; that they are often stripped naked, their backs and limbs cut with knives, bruised and mangled by scores and hundreds of blows with the paddle, and terribly torn by the claws of cats, drawn over them by their tormentors; that they are often hunted with bloodhounds and shot down like beasts, or torn in pieces by dogs; that they are often suspended by the arms and whipped and beaten till they faint, and when, revived by restoratives, beaten again till they faint and some-times till they die; that their ears are often cut off, their eyes knocked out, their bones broken, their flesh branded with red hot irons; that they are maimed, mutilated and burned to death over slow fires . . . we will establish all these facts by the testimony of scores and hundreds of eye witnesses, by the testimony of *slaveholders* in all parts of the slave states, by slaveholding members of Congress and of state legislatures, by ambassadors to foreign courts, by judges, by doctors of divinity, and clergymen of all denominations, by merchants, mechanics, lawyers and physicians, by presidents and professors in college and professional seminaries, by planters, overseers and drivers. We shall show, not merely that such deeds are committed, but that they are frequent; not done in corners, but before the sun; not in one of the slave states, but in all of them; not perpetrated by brutal overseers and drivers merely, but by magistrates, by legislators, by professors of religion, by preachers of the gospel, by governors of states, by gentlemen of property and standing, and by delicate females moving in the highest circles of society."[1]

Weld did exactly what he said here he was going to do. He wrote to all antislavery men who, to his knowledge, had been born and reared in the South or had resided there for a number of years. He sought the names of others, but required that the testimony of any man unknown to some one of the executive group—Birney, Stanton, Tappan, Weld—submit supporting affidavits, and these were scrupulously checked for proof of the man's character and veracity. These testimonials were

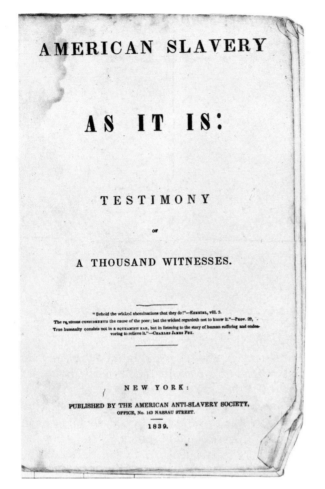

AMERICAN SLAVERY

AS IT IS:

TESTIMONY

OR

A THOUSAND WITNESSES.

"Behold the wicked abominations that they do!"—EZEKIEL, viii. 9.
The righteous considereth the cause of the poor; but the wicked regardeth not to know it."—PROV. 29,
True humanity consists not in a squeamish ear, but in listening to the story of human suffering and endeavoring to relieve it."—CHARLES JAMES FOX.

NEW YORK:

PUBLISHED BY THE AMERICAN ANTI-SLAVERY SOCIETY,
OFFICE, No. 143 NASSAU STREET.

1839.

The most devastating of all indictments of slavery.

checked word for word; they named names, dates, and places. Every testimonial was preceded by a full statement of the man's education, residence, public position, time and place of residence in the South. There was testimony from all of the prominent Southerners in the antislavery movement like Sarah and Angelina Grimké, John Rankin, William Ladd, William Allan, and Philemon Bliss. There were well written, moderate narratives from preachers of every denomination, public officials, merchants, and others, presently living in the free states, who had been born and reared in slave states, or had resided for periods as long as thirty years in states from Virginia to South Carolina to Texas. There were elaborate quotations from judicial decisions and laws, from the works of men like George Whitefield, John Woolman, and Anthony Benezet,[2] from the speeches of southern members of Congress, and from the

speeches and writings of prominent slaveholding members of the colonization society.

The most important testimony, however, was that gleaned from the files of Southern newspapers. Weld bought the files of the New York Commercial Reading Room from 1837 to 1839. This was to be slavery as it is, not slavery as it was. Twenty thousand copies of such widely scattered and prominent papers as the New Orleans *Bee*, Charleston *Courier*, Charleston *Mercury*, Vicksburg *Sentinel*, Huntsville *Democrat*, Memphis *Enquirer*, Montgomery *Advertiser*, Raleigh *Standard*, and Mobile *Register*, were searched for advertisements, speeches, court trials, and other evidence of the treatment of slaves.[3]

The book, then, constituted an anthology of testimony from the slave country, by slaveholders or former slaveholders. It is as close as history can come to the facts, because it was compiled from the statements of men who knew slavery, who had come North because they could not witness its cruelties and remain silent, and who were now in a position to speak freely. Some of it was letters these men had previously written to friends in the North while still living in the South. Much of it was the revealing testimony of such ordinary things as advertisements for fugitive slaves. The great mass of evidence as to treatment of slaves, of course, is lost. Diaries and plantation records are largely worthless because slaveholders never kept a record of their own evil ways, and that applies especially to overseers who were responsible to their employers. There seldom were white witnesses to what occurred, and those who suffered carried their awful memories to the grave. Suffice it to say that this was a record of facts. A check of more than 60 per cent of the documentary evidence here presented, extending over a period of thirty years, has not revealed a single misstatement or error. Weld himself was an extremely careful editor. In addition, he required every member of the executive committee to read the manuscript with care, and he then submitted it for final searching criticism to Judge William Jay.

Weld wrote about the *system* of slavery. Brutality was inherent in the system. Slaveholders failed to humanize it because they could not do so without dissembling the psychological basis upon which the regime rested. State laws said slaves were property; the Constitution of the United States said they were persons. Slaveholders, legislators, and judges were forever trying to make property out of them. It conditioned their thinking, their attitudes, their treatment of the slaves. They simply did not regard them as human beings. Weld cited the decision of the Supreme Court of South Carolina in the case of State *versus* Cheatwood: "The criminal offense of assault and battery cannot, at common law, be committed on the person of a slave. For, notwithstanding for some purposes a slave is regarded in law as a person, yet generally he is a mere chattel personal, and his right of personal protection belongs to his master . . . a slave is not generally regarded as legally capable of being within the peace of the state." He also cited State *versus* Mann (North Carolina) in which the Supreme Court of that state said a slaveowner could not be indicted for shooting a female slave who had broken loose when he was whipping her.[4]

Being property, slaves were treated as "livestock." Slaveholders called their children "increase," spoke of the mothers as "breeders," gave the term "drivers" to men set over them at work, advertised and sold them with cattle and hogs, and treated them far worse, because laws, custom, court decisions, and all the force in the world could not rob them of the attributes of human beings. Weld quoted the case of a large South Carolina planter who said "I never lose a day's work; it is an established rule on my plantations that the tasks of all the sick negroes shall be done by those who are well in addition to their own";[5] and the statement of the lieutenant governor of South Carolina: "I consider imprisonment in the stocks at night, with or without hard labor in the day, as a powerful auxiliary in the case of good government . . . there is no punishment to which the slave looks with more horror";[6] and reprinted from the Charleston *Mercury* the following advertisement: "*Negroes for sale. A Girl* about twenty years of age (raised in Virginia), and her two female children, one four and the other two years old—is remarkably strong and healthy—never having had a day's sickness, with the exception of the small pox, in her life. The children are fine and healthy. She is very prolific in her generating qualities, and affords a rare opportunity to any person who wishes to raise a family of strong and healthy servants for their own use."

"Though great cruelties have always been inflicted by men upon brutes," said Weld, "yet incomparably the most horrid ever perpetrated, have been those of men upon *their own species*

One of the many pictorial representations of slavery published by the American Anti-Slavery Society.

. . . It is impossible for cattle to excite in men such tempests of fury as men excite in each other . . . The greatest provocation to human nature is *opposition to its will* . . . The idea of *property* having a will, and that too in opposition to the will of its *owner*, and counteracting it, is a stimulant of terrible power to the most relentless human passions; and from the nature of slavery, and the constitution of the human mind, this fierce stimulant must, with various degrees of strength, act upon slaveholders almost without ceasing."[7]

Because slavery was the complete subjection of one man to the will of another, established by force and sustained by law, and because there were millions of slaves, resistance to the master's will, however slight or passive, had to be broken as an example for group control. Said Weld: "If a slave runs away and is caught, his master flogs him with terrible severity, not merely to gratify his resentment, and to keep him from running away again, but as a warning to others. So in every case of disobedience, neglect, stubbornness, unfaithfulness, indolence, insolence, theft, feigned sickness, when his directions are forgotten, or his wishes crossed, or his property injured, or left exposed, or his work ill-executed, the master is tempted to inflict cruelties, not merely to wreak his own vengeance upon him, and to make the slave more circumspect in future, but to sustain his authority over the other slaves, to restrain them from like practices, and to preserve his own property."[8]

This, of course, was but half the story. All members of slaveholding families, often girls and boys in their teens, too young to have developed self-discipline, could and did order punishment of both men and women for trivial offenses. Slaves had no defense against lying and deceit by both whites and other slaves. The purchase price alone determined who might be a slaveholder. There were no standards of character, intelligence, or integrity for slaveholding. There were no public or private agencies charged with responsibility for the slave's welfare. His lot depended entirely upon the character of his owner; and there were just as many sadists in the world then as there are now, a fair sprinkling of them in the ranks of slaveholders. Owners were absent from plantations a great deal, sometimes for long periods of time, and overseers were ignorant, mercurial, and brutal. They went armed as a rule, always carried whips, and were as free to use one as the other.

W Stands for **Woman.** In Slavery-life,
Full many are mothers, but no one is wife.
For decency's sake, form of wedding there is,
But the parties are claimed by the master as his;
And the children are sold, and the father is sold
To this or that trader, "to have and to hold;"
And the woman is whipped, for the motherly moan
And the cry of a heart that is left all alone.
O master all monstrous! is conscience amiss
In dooming the sham of a wedding like this!

Certain Southern ladies claimed, not long since, that they care as tenderly for slave mothers as Northern ladies care for poor white mothers. "Possibly that is true," was the reply, "but Northern ladies do not afterwards sell the baby!"—Besides this, it is the *money-interest* of Southerners to look well to the increase of their *property*, whereas a true humanity, as a principle, underlies and quickens the charitable attention of Northern ladies, above referred to.

The brunt of all the cruelties and wickedness of a system of human bondage fell upon the slave women.

Some slaves were whipped on every plantation nearly every day of the year. Thirty-nine lashes was considered moderate punishment. Their wrists were tied together, drawn over their knees, and a stick then passed over the arms and under the knees. Absolutely helpless, they were then beaten with a paddle. Their arms were drawn up by a rope thrown over a beam or the limb of a tree, until they stood on tiptoe, and they were lashed with a cowhide. They were spread-eagled on a ladder, or on the ground, with ankles and wrists tied to pegs, and then whipped. They were sent to the public jail to be whipped.

The slave had no recourse against intolerable conditions except perilous flight. Runaway slaves were hunted with bloodhounds. Men went hunting fugitives with dogs and guns in the same spirit they hunt coons and quail. The fugitives were frequently outlawed, which seemed to have been as casual as placing an advertisement in a newspaper offering a reward for the slave, dead or alive. They were decapitated and their heads carried home for the reward. Often, they were burned at the stake. Sometimes they were left lying where they were killed.[9] If slaves were prone to run away, they were made to work in chains, iron collars, and leg irons. Weld presented thirty advertisements similar to the following: "Detained at the police jail, the negro wench Myra—has several marks of lashing, and has irons on her feet."[10] He said there were scores of such notices by jailors and owners in Southern papers every month. Actually, there were hundreds. Many fugitives remained away and died in the swamps. Some who returned or were captured were branded with hot irons, or by having one or two teeth knocked out, or by having their ears cropped. Weld listed 144 advertisements from the papers in a two-year period for fugitives who had gunshot wounds; brands on the cheeks, forehead, arms, or breasts; dog bites; cropped ears; eyes missing; and broken bones.[11] All slaves were subject to chastisement by anyone who caught them off their owner's property without a written permit. Such a high proportion of advertisements for fugitives spoke of severe and permanent scars from the whip that the prevalence of brutal whippings is an inescapable conclusion.

"To disbelieve that arbitrary power naturally and habitually perpetrates cruelties, where it can do it with impunity, is not only ignorance of man, but of things," said Weld. "Arbitrary power is to the mind what alcohol is to the body; it intoxicates. Man loves power. It is perhaps the strongest human passion; and the more absolute the power, the stronger the desire for it; and the more it is desired, the more its exercise is enjoyed . . . The fact that a person intensely desires power over others, *without restraint*, shows the absolute necessity of restraint . . . That American slaveholders possess a power over their slaves which is virtually absolute, none will deny . . . such power . . . canot but be abused."[12]

Slaveholding blunted the feelings toward the slave of everyone connected with the institution, to such a degree that they actually believed the slaves were kindly treated. The constant exercise of arbitrary power, the constant repetition of injustices and punishments, the acceptance of the property-right dogma, the propensity to rationalize one's conduct all made the most cruel treatment seem like gentleness to slaveholders.[13] Said Weld: "Remember, also, that a part of this good treatment of which slaveholders boast, is plundering the slaves of all their inalienable rights, of the ownership of their own bodies, of the use of their own limbs and muscles, of all their time, liberty, and earnings, of the free exercise of choice, of the rights of marriage and parental authority, of legal protection, of the right to be, to do, to go, to stay, to think, to feel, to work, to rest, to eat, to sleep, to learn, to teach, to earn money, and to expend it, to visit, and to be visited, to speak, to be silent, to worship according to conscience, in fine, *their right to be protected by just and equal laws, and to be amenable to such only.*"[14]

No myth was more frequently repeated during the days of slavery and afterward than that slaves were well treated and well provided for because they were valuable property. Weld argued that it was to the best interests of a good many people in the world—drunkards, gluttons, spendthrifts, and so forth—to curb one appetite or another, but that the whole history of man was a "record of real interests sacrificed to present gratification," that lust, pride, anger, exercise of power were a great deal stronger than pecuniary interest, that slaveholders were notoriously extravagant, and that there were a thousand ways to be inhumane and cruel to slaves without impairing their ability to work and their sale value.

Purely from the standpoint of economic interest it would be far better to shorten the lives of slaves who were old and unable to work, or were

Common mode of whipping with a paddle

incurably diseased or injured, or were blind, deaf, dumb, or otherwise handicapped. It would be better to allow feeble infants to die, in some regions to buy rather than rear slaves, to punish brutally incorrigible and runaway slaves as a deterrent to others since they were of little value, and to overwork and underfeed hired slaves. It was well known that overseers' wages were frequently proportioned to the size of crops raised, which was nothing less than placing a premium on driving the slaves to the limit of endurance. Weld estimated the number of these classes of slaves at more than one million.[15]

Slaves had no protection against abuse. Slave codes were designed for the protection of society, not for the protection of the slave from injustices at the hands of his owner. The great body of law, both common and statute, and the courts, the instruments of its operation, to which men have looked since time immemorial for the administration of justice and for protection of their most elementary human rights, simply did not exist for the slaves. They sometimes enjoyed privileges, but never rights. This lack of legal protection for the slave was the greatest single indictment against the institution, and it is a matter of record that

it was not remedied in any respect while slavery survived.

Slavery was established and sustained by law. Specifically, all children born of slave mothers were reduced to slavery by law. The law protected a master's slave property against trespass by another, but it did not protect the slave against rape or assault, even to death, by the master. It denied them the right of trial by jury. It forbade them to assemble for worship or social intercourse. It forbade them to read or write or to possess anything written or printed. It left them to the tender mercies of their owners in matters of food, clothing, and shelter. It denied them the right to testify against a white man. It denied them the right of legal marriages, and slave marriages were generally a matter of indifference to owners.

Miscegenation was so common as to be regarded as a matter of personal choice, little noticed by the public. Its prevalence leads to the inescapable conclusion that it was the basis—unspoken, to be sure—of much of the defense of the institution. Hiram White, of Illinois, who had lived thirty-two years in North Carolina, said: "Amalgamation was common. There was scarce a family of slaves that had females of mature age where there were not some mulatto children."[16] Abundant evidence showed that white men lived openly with their slaves, and that female slaves were forced to serve owners, owners' sons, overseers, and anyone else in a position to take advantage of them. Worse still, the children from these unions were sold with impunity and forced back into the Negro race and slavery.

Slave families were broken up indiscriminately by sale, and both men and women were beaten nigh to death, sometimes killed as fugitives, for thereafter seeking out their mates. The law was completely indifferent as to these things. It gave every white man the right to kill a slave who struck him, however great the provocation; in short, it denied to the slave the right to protect himself, his wife, or his children. It gave every white man the right to kill any slave who had been declared an outlaw by his owner.

The worst of all features of the law was that which denied slaves the right to testify against a white man. Said Weld: "Injuries must be legally *proved* before they can be legally *redressed;* to deprive men of the power of proving their injuries, is itself the greatest of all injuries; for it not only exposes to all, but invites them, by a virtual guarantee of immunity, and is thus the author of all injuries.[17]

In those cases in which the law took cognizance of slave offenses against society, the penalties were excessively severe, there being more than seventy capital crimes in Virginia and thirty in Mississippi. The slaves were denied every means of becoming acquainted with the provisions of these laws except the examples of punishment for their violation. The law of slavery, said Weld, "tramples on all those fundamental principles of right, justice, and equity, which are recognized as sacred by all civilized nations." Categorically, it placed restraints and onerous exactions upon the slaves, but gave them no protection; it imposed upon three million *innocent* persons one of the most severe punishments for crime, denial of freedom for life; it punished by death exercise of the most sacred and elementary human rights: self-preservation and self-defense; it denied protection to those who needed it most, who had no protection deriving from birth, position, wealth, friends, and influence; and it failed completely, in the case of slaves, in its grand object of protecting man's natural rights.

Taking cognizance of food, shelter, and cloth-

ing, Weld compared the rations of slaves to those of the army and navy of the United States, the armies of Europe, and the inmates of prisons in the United States and Great Britain. The daily ration of the army was one and three-sixteenths pounds of bread, one and a quarter pounds of beef; and at the rate of eight quarts of beans, eight pounds of sugar, four pounds of coffee, and two quarts of salt to every hundred rations. The French army ration allowed one pound of beef and one and a half pounds of bread. The average penitentiary allowance was one pound of meat, one pound of bread, and one pound of vegetables. The basic ration of slaves was one peck of corn per week from March until August. They ground this themselves, on the plantation hand mill, into grits or meal. The remainder of the year, they got sweet potatoes or rice. Occasionally, there was a meat allowance and molasses. On the small plantations, and for the house servants, there were vegetables in season. The great mass of supporting evidence was that the diet was greatly deficient in meat and vegetables, that it was deadly monotonous and lacking in both quality and quantity, that the food was poorly cooked and was eaten under unfavorable conditions, that no attention was given to the dietary needs of pregnant women or those who were ill, and that most slaves, particularly field hands, were hungry all of their lives.[18]

Slaves were poorly housed and inadequately clothed. A high percentage of the children went naked, and both men and women partially so in the summer months. In winter they suffered severely from cold and inclement weather.[19] There was no standard for dwellings. Sometimes they were huts, sometimes log cabins, sometimes of frame and clapboards, almost always without floors, and with rare exceptions without windows and furniture. Slaves slept on straw—like animals —or old rags on the dirt floor. They worked long hours, especially in the sugar country, and elsewhere during the cotton picking and ginning season. They worked in the rice fields and swamps, where it was said white men could not survive. They worked so incessantly in unhealthful conditions and without proper nourishment, in the Southeast and Southwest, that births did not equal deaths and imports from the breeding states were necessary to sustain the slave population. Some slaves near cities were allowed to cut wood at night or gather moss to sell in exchange for clothes, but of the nearly three million slaves, the percentage must have been small indeed. Many slaves were hired out, others were allowed to find their own occupations and turn their earnings over to their owners.[20]

Valuable information was presented with regard to slave trading and slave breeding. The number of slaves smuggled into the United States annually in violation of the federal law was estimated by one Southern congressman at 13,000, and by another at 15,000. These estimates were also given by a planter of Louisiana to Harriet Martineau.[21] If they were correct, the total number of slaves imported in each ten-year period was 150,000. Supporting testimony showed there

were slaves who could not speak English on plantations everywhere in the lower South. The number of free Negroes kidnapped in the Northern states and carried off to the South every year, or "shanghaied" and sold when they ventured into the South, was estimated at hundreds. Judge George M. Stroud said those kidnapped in Philadelphia, mostly children, numbered more than thirty in a two-year period.[22]

American Slavery As It Is sold more copies than any other antislavery pamphlet ever written: more than 100,000 copies within a year. The British and Foreign Anti-Slavery Society distributed it to government officials, libraries, and schools. William Jay sent a copy to every lawyer in New York City.

Making sure muscles are taut

BIRNEY AND THOME

Chapter 31

John C. Calhoun by 1838 was the recognized leader of the proslavery forces in Congress and chief architect of the constitutional theory by which they hoped to perpetuate slavery *ad infinitum*. The American Anti-Slavery Society frequently sent its publications to senators and representatives, and one such missive—*Why Work for the Slave*—sent to Calhoun resulted in formation of a committee of Southern representatives to seek general information about the activities of antislavery societies.[1] F. H. Elmore of South Carolina, on behalf of the committee, addressed to James G. Birney, corresponding secretary of the society, the following series of questions:[2]

1. How many societies, affiliated with that of which you are the Corresponding Secretary, are there in the United States? And how many members belong to them in the aggregate?

2. Are there any other societies similar to yours and not affiliated with it in the United States? and how many, and what is the aggregate of their members?

3. Have you affiliation, intercourse, or connection with any similar societies out of the United States, and in what countries?

4. Do your or similar societies exist in the Colleges and other Literary institutions of the nonslaveholding States, and to what extent?

5. What do you estimate the numbers of those who co-operate in this matter at? What proportion do they bear in the population of the Northern states, and what in the middle nonslaveholding states? Are they increasing, and at what rate?

6. What is the object your associations aim at? Does it extend to the abolition of slavery only in the District of Columbia, or in the whole slave country?

7. By what means and under what power do you propose to carry your views into effect?

8. What has been for three years past, the annual income of your societies? And how is it raised?

9. In what ways and to what purposes do you apply these funds?

10. How many printing presses and periodical publications have you?

11. To what classes of persons do you address your publications, and are they addressed to the judgment, the imagination, or the feelings?

12. Do you propagate your doctrines by any other means than oral and written discussions—for instance, by prints and pictures in manufactures—say pocket handkerchiefs, etc.? Pray, state the various modes.

13. Are your hopes and expectations increased or lessened by the events of the last year, and, especially, by the action of this Congress? And will your exertions be relaxed or increased?

14. Have you any permanent fund, and how much?

Birney was the best qualified man in the movement to answer these questions. He was a former slaveholder, thoroughly familiar with every phase of the antislavery movement, moderate and dignified in everything he did, trained in the law, a close student of constitutional government, and

Slave sale

leader of the political action forces. He could answer some of the questions briefly, and did so. There were, he said, as of May each year, 225 antislavery societies in 1835; 527 in 1836; 1,006 in 1837; and an estimated 1,406 in 1838.[3] The total number of members was 112,000 as a minimum. Some put it as high as 150,000. The movement had now become so general that organization of local societies was no longer thought to be essential and was not being pressed. Of societies not affiliated with the American Anti-Slavery Society, there were a number of Methodist organizations, the Illinois Anti-Slavery Society which had been organized just prior to Lovejoy's murder and had not met since that event, the Delaware Society which had just been organized, the Manumission Society of New York City of which John Jay and Alexander Hamilton had been the first two presidents, and the Pennsylvania Abolition Society, founded by Benjamin Franklin and Benjamin Rush. These old societies of the convention period, Birney explained, were now engaged almost entirely in rescuing kidnapped persons and others illegally held in bondage.

There were two societies in Canada which were affiliated with the American Anti-Slavery Society, and the Society maintained an agent in Upper Canada for "the moral and intellectual elevation of the ten thousand colored people there; most of whom have escaped from slavery in this Republic, to enjoy freedom under the protection of a Monarchy." There were numerous societies in Great Britain working for the abolition of the apprentice system in her colonies, one in England promoting worldwide abolition of slavery, a French society for the abolition of slavery (1834), and the Haitian Abolition Society (1836), but none of these was affiliated with the American Anti-Slavery Society.

The governing bodies of the colleges and seminaries had tried, with some success, to suppress antislavery discussions by the students, for various reasons. "One of them," said Birney, "is to conciliate the wealthy of the south, that they may send their sons to the north, to swell the college catalogues . . . in this we have a manifestation of that aristocratic pride, which, feeling itself honored by having entrusted to its charge the sons of distant, opulent, and distinguished planters, fails not to dull everything like sympathy for those whose unpaid toil supplies the means so lavishly expended in educating southern youth at northern colleges." This situation was rapidly changing because the murder of Lovejoy, the attacks upon freedom of speech and the press, and "prostration of the right of petition in Congress" were of the utmost concern to intellectual and religious students, and their influence throughout the country was tremendous.[4] Without mentioning their names Birney then referred to the Lane Seminary group, particularly to Thome and Kimball and their work on the West Indies, and to Stanton and his persuasive arguments before the Massachusetts legislature.

The number of members in the several societies, as stated conservatively at 115,000, was about equal to those ready to join societies when an opportunity presented, there being many communities where there were none, and about one-fourth to one-sixth as many more ready to join in the defense of civil rights. There was a larger proportion of active antislavery men in the whole population of Massachusetts and Vermont than elsewhere: about one in thirty. In Rhode Island the practice of questioning candidates had been fully applied in the 1838 election. William Sprague was elected governor. He had answered all questions put to him by the Rhode Island Anti-Slavery Society, strongly supporting the abolition of slavery and the slave trade in the District of Columbia, and the abolition of the interstate slave trade, condemning congressional abridgement of the right of petition, advocating jury trials for all fugitive slaves, opposing the annexation of Texas, and all attempts of any sort to prevent peaceable assembly for the discussion of any subject—moral, political, or religious—and, by implication, opposing temporary residence within the state of slaveholders with their slaves.[5]

In Connecticut great progress had been made. In response to petitions from antislavery men the legislature had repealed the black law, which had been passed for the suppression of Prudence Crandall's school. It had provided jury trial for fugitive slaves. It had approved the *power* and *duty* of Congress to abolish slavery in the District of Columbia. It had passed resolutions against the annexation of Texas. It had condemned the gag rule in Congress. In the courts a slave brought from Georgia had been freed by the supreme court, two antiabolition rioters had been fined $20 each and sent to prison for six months, and 1,700 voters had joined in organizing a state antislavery society. In New York conditions had changed greatly since the riots of 1833 and 1834. Said Birney: "Many of the merchants and mechanics are favorable to our cause; gentlemen of the bar, especially the younger and more growing ones, are directing their attention to it; twenty-one of our city ministers are professed abolitionists; the churches are beginning to be more accessible to us; our meetings are held in them openly, attract large numbers, are unmolested; and the abolitionists sometimes hear themselves commended in other assemblies, not only for their honest *intentions,* but for their *respectability* and *intelligence.*"[6]

In Pennsylvania the Democratic party in power had followed the lead of North Carolina and Tennessee in depriving Negroes of the franchise which they had long enjoyed, "a pernicious, a profitless violation of great principles," said Birney, "a vulgar defiance of the advancing spirit of humanity and justice, a relapse into the by-gone darkness of a barbarous age." In Ohio, as in Rhode Island, antislavery people could now control elections. The constitution of the state condemned slavery in strong terms and forbade any amendment to introduce slavery at any future time.

The antislavery movement, Birney explained, had made remarkable progress in view of the limited means at its disposal and the intense opposition it encountered in the beginning. It expected to persuade slaveholders to abolish slavery completely in the United States. Meanwhile, it would continue to work for Congressional legislation to stop the interstate slave trade, to abolish slavery in the District of Columbia, and to prevent its extension to new states and territories. It would continue to aid and encourage the intellectual, moral, and religious improvement of the Negroes, to eliminate race prejudice, and to secure recognition of their complete equality with the whites in civil and religious privileges. It would continue to seek reform within the churches in relation to slavery. Its funds for these purposes were limited. The American Anti-Slavery Society had $10,000 in 1834–35, $25,000 in 1835–36, and $44,000 in 1836–37.[7] This did not include expenditures of state and local societies, nor the subscription fees for antislavery newspapers, nor gifts for special printing by auxiliaries. The total of all expenditures by the several organizations was greater than by any other benevolent society. The money was given by all classes of people, largely in small amounts. It was used for lectures and agents, for printing disquisitions on all aspects of the problem—religious, constitutional, political, legal, economic—and for the maintenance of three secretaries and for office staff. The number of permanent agents had been greatly reduced from its maximum of sixty in 1837, but the number of lawyers, preachers, and ministers serving as local agents had greatly increased. These were paid no salaries, but were allowed expense money on request.[8]

Events of the preceding year had not been unexpected by antislavery men and were very little different from what they had been experiencing for three years. There was no particular reason for antislavery men to be discouraged because they fully understood the enormity of the evil of slavery. The influence of slavery had reached into the institutional life of the country and had dulled the finer sensibilities of the people, with great harm to the cause of human rights. It had contaminated the churches of the slave states until they had endorsed the dogma that slavery was a divine institution. Preachers no longer condemned slavery. They had joined with members of their churches of all denominations in interfering with the mails and in such violations of personal rights as the Dresser episode. They had helped to popularize the false notion that the slaves, most of whom were held by their own parishioners, were contented and happy, when facts proved that slavery was "replete with torment and horrors—the direst form of oppression that upheaves itself before the sun."[9]

It had been asserted and reasserted long and loudly even in Congress that slavery had produced in the South the highest degree of culture ever known to man. Multitudes at the North had come to believe it. Antislavery men knew that the tendency of slavery "was to produce, on the part of the whites, looseness of morals, disdain of the wholesome restraints of law, and a ferocity of temper, found, only in solitary instances, in those countries where slavery is unknown."[10] Northern people now questioned the "purity" of a society which held its own offspring of mixed blood as slaves, and a hospitality grounded on slave labor, and a chivalry which held all visitors under suspicion, illegally imported slaves from Africa, scourged and hanged friendless strangers without

recourse to law, and summarily executed both slaves and free Negroes with untold cruelty and torture. "Southern chivalry," said Birney, "will soon be regarded as one of the by-gone fooleries of a less intelligent and less virtuous age . . . giving place to the more reasonable idea, that the denial of wages to the laborer, the selling of men and women, the whipping of husbands and wives in each other's presence, to compel them to unrequited toil, the deliberate attempt to extinguish mind, and, consequently, to destroy the soul—is among the highest offenses against God and man —unspeakably mean and ungentlemanly."[11]

Antislavery men had been apprehensive from the first about the power of slavery in the government and its ever-present threat to the Constitution. They had great affection for the Constitution, and veneration for the men who framed it. Those men who framed the Constitution had known that slavery was unprofitable; that it was being abolished in one state after another; that the current of universal liberty was running strong; that freedom of speech and the press were secure; that Congress could stop the importation of slaves from Africa; that losses were so great as to destroy the system if replacements were denied; that Congress could prevent slaves from being carried from one state to another, and to the territories, and could deny the admission of any state "whose form of government was repugnant to the principles of liberty set forth in that of the United States."[12] Congress had exercised only one of these powers—then thought to have been the most important. It had made the foreign slave trade illegal. Actually, the prohibition of the African slave trade had only transferred the source of supply to America and had increased the number of slaves by increasing the price to the point of encouraging slave breeding in Virginia and Maryland.

Slavery had risen to undreamed-of power by intimidation and corruption. Slavery had been allowed to enter the territories. New slave states had been admitted to the Union. It was not until Missouri had applied for admission that there had been a fair test of strength between the friends of slavery and the friends of freedom. Slavery had won because freedom had been betrayed by "one whose raiment, the remainder of his days, ought to be sackcloth and ashes—because of the disgrace he has continued on the name of his country, and the consequent injury that he has inflicted on the cause of Freedom throughout the world . . . THE SANC-

TION OF THE NATION WAS GIVEN TO SLAVERY."[13]

Emboldened by their successes, the slaveholders now had discarded all pretenses, had repudiated their former admissions that slavery was a political and moral evil, and were seeking to consolidate their political power by the admission of Texas into the Union. Calhoun had said in the Senate, January 10, 1838: "Many in the South once believed that it [slavery] was a moral and political evil; *that* folly and delusion are gone. We see it now in its true light, and regard it as the most safe and stable basis for free institutions in the world." Hammond had said in the House of Representatives, February 1, 1836: "I do firmly believe, that domestic slavery, regulated as ours is, produces the highest toned, the purest, best organization of society, that has ever existed on the face of the earth." Presbyteries, Baptist Associations, and Methodist conferences of South Carolina and Georgia had endorsed slavery as a Christian institution.

Antislavery men had considered the threat of disunion by the South and were not inclined to believe the South would resort to such a measure. Leading men in the slave states, in both state and church, knew the antislavery movement was not promoting violence either directly or indirectly. They objected to a discussion of slavery, and they knew full well that dissolution of the Union would precipitate vigorous discussion on a worldwide scale and to their own disadvantage. The people of the South would then know what antislavery men were talking about. "Now we cannot reach them," said Birney, "then, it would be otherwise. The united power of the large slaveholders would not be able longer to keep them in ignorance. If the Union were dissolved, they *would* know the cause, and discuss it, and condemn it."[14] Disunion would increase the danger of slave insurrection. It would so antagonize the Northern people as to afford all possible aid and encouragement to fugitive slaves. It would drive out of the South a large class of yeoman farmers who would not remain permanently in a nation founded upon slavery.

Slavery would not survive in an independent South. The power of the several European nations —England, France, Spain, Portugal—had sustained slavery in their American possessions. Independence from the mother country had been followed in every case by freedom for the slaves, except in the Southern states of the United States, where it

survived because of the power of the national government drawn from the free states. Slavery was distinctly an American institution, and the full moral force of the civilized world would be marshaled against the South if she separated from the North in order to perpetuate it. Separation would soon lead to war, and war would immediately pose the threat of slave insurrections.

More important than all of these things, in some respects, was the lack of solidarity among the slave states. Maryland, Virginia, Kentucky, and east Tennessee were farming states. All states below Tennessee were planting, slave-buying states. Sentiment in favor of emancipation in the upper South was still strong enough to prevent those states from uniting with the plantation states in "making slavery the *perpetual bond* of a new political organization." Certainly, these farming states would prefer the "privileges of the Union to the privilege of perpetual slaveholding." Separation of the two sections of the Union would not be possible in any but a political sense. "There will be no chasm," said Birney, "no rent made in the earth between the two sections. The natural and ideal boundaries will remain unaltered. Mason and Dixon's line will not become a wall of adamant that can neither be undermined nor surmounted. The Ohio River will not be converted into flame, or into another Styx, denying a passage to every living thing . . . The complicated ties of commerce could not suddenly be unloosed . . . The newspapers of the North—its magazines, its Quarterlies, its Monthlies, would be more sought after by the readers of the South than they now are; and the Southern journals would become doubly interesting to us. There would be the same lust for our Northern summers and your Southern winters . . . the same desire of marrying and of being given in marriage that now exists between North and South. Really . . . it would seem like a poor exchange for the South, to give up all these pleasant and profitable relations and connections for the privilege of enslaving an equal number of their fellow creatures."[15]

The South was threatening disunion, Birney argued, because she had always had her way by doing so. Missouri had been admitted as a slave state, the Indians had been driven out of the South, the tariff had been modified, all because of the dire threats of disunion by the South. Again, they had threatened disunion unless freedom of speech and of the press were put down in the

North, and mobs had acted with the "promptness of commission-merchants" to break up assemblies, stone citizens, and destroy printing presses. They threatened disunion if slavery were abolished in the District of Columbia, and they threatened disunion if Northern congressmen read petitions for the abolition of slavery and the slave trade in the District of Columbia and the interstate slave trade, so fifty Northern Congressmen voted to submerge the right of petition. The South had gained so much, so easily, and so often, that she certainly would continue her bluster and her threats until she persuaded herself she was serious about breaking up the Union, and perhaps destroy herself. Nothing would prevent it except firmness on the part of the North in maintaining the principles on which the nation was founded.

The legislatures of the Northern states were showing the influence of strong public sentiment in this respect. The legislature of Vermont in 1836 had denied the right of either state governments or the federal government to abridge free expression of opinion or its exclusion from the mails and had affirmed the power of Congress to abolish slavery in the District of Columbia. In November 1837, the legislature had protested against the annexation of Texas and the admission of any more slave states, and had reaffirmed the power of Congress to abolish slavery and the slave trade in the District of Columbia, and the House of Representatives had favored action by Congress to abolish the interstate slave trade. In Massachusetts, where Governor Everett had severely censured antislavery activity, and the legislative committee had recommended disavowal of the right of any citizen to agitate against slavery, the legislature had not acted upon the recommendations. The subject had been fully debated in the subsequent election campaign, and the new legislature, by a vote of 378 to 16 in the House and with only two dissenting votes in the Senate, had condemned the gag resolution of Congress as "an assumption of power and authority at variance with the spirit and intent of the Constitution of the United States, and injurious to the cause of freedom and free institutions; that it does violence to the inherent, absolute, and inalienable rights of men; and that it tends, essentially, to impair those fundamental principles of national justice and natural law which are antecedent to any written constitutions of government, independent of them all, and essential to the security

of freedom in a state."[16] The present legislature also had protested against annexation of Texas.

Antislavery men were not discouraged by the action of the Congress in refusing to consider their petitions. They knew that the people were sound, and "still cherish, as their fathers did, the right of petition—the freedom of the press—the freedom of speech—the rights of conscience; that they love the liberty of the North more than they love the slavery of the South."[17] Congressional resolutions meant very little. Senators and representatives could be dismissed; Congress would discover that the people could not be controlled by resolutions. They had sent petitions to Congress signed by 37,000 persons after the resolution of May 1836, by 110,000 after the resolution of January 1837, and by 500,000 in the Congress of 1838. Even this was of little consequence over the long view, for senators and representatives would soon be going to Congress who would not need petitions; they would know what their constituents expected of them with regard to slavery before they left home.

Elmore acknowledged Birney's reply to his inquiries. Speaking of the 4,500,000 inhabitants of the slave states, he said: "Christians and civilized, they are now industrious, prosperous, and happy; but should your scheme of abolition prevail, it will bring upon them overwhelming ruin, and misery unutterable. The two races cannot exist together upon terms of equality—the extirpation of one and the ruin of the other *would be inevitable.*"[18] "The Negroes lived in peace," Birney said, "wherever they had been freed and given legal equality. It is the *denial* of this that produces discontent. Men will never be satisfied without it. Let the slaveholders consult the irreversible laws of the human mind—make a full concession of right to those from whom they have withheld it, and they will be blessed with a peace, political, social, moral, beyond their present conceptions; without such concessions they never can possess it . . . If *justice* be done, all necessity for the extirpation of any part of the people will at once be removed. Baptisms *of blood* are seen only when humanity has failed in her offices, and the suffering discern hope only in the brute efforts of despair."[19]

The American Anti-Slavery Society had just published another of its special books: *Emancipation in the West Indies.*[20] James A. Thome and J. Horace Kimball, two of the seventy agents, had been sent there in 1836 by the executive committee to report on conditions after three years of emancipation. Thome was one of the best known of the Southerners in the movement. Most of the work fell to him because Kimball, editor of the *Herald of Freedom,* was very ill, was unable to complete the tour, and died of tuberculosis soon after his return. Thome had gone to Antigua, which had adopted complete, immediate emancipation; to Barbadoes, where the apprenticeship system had been put into operation; and to Jamaica, where the planters had been bitterly opposed to emancipation and were not giving any co-operation in the apprenticeship program. Weld had to rewrite Thome's manuscript and check every word of it for accuracy, but, when finished, it was as complete an analysis of the *Negro in Emancipation* as his *American Slavery As It Is* had been of the *Negro in slavery.* The first edition was 2,500 copies, the second 100,000, and it went through many editions.

The book went far beyond the observations and judgments of Thome and Kimball. It consisted of conversations with governors and police officials; with attorneys, physicians, and preachers; with plantation managers and teachers; and also of a wealth of letters and other documentary evidence. In short, it embraced the most accurate testimony available concerning the adaptation of the Negroes to freedom: their obedience to law and their general conduct, their education and religious instruction, their morality and temperance, their labor under the wage system, their family life, and their ability to assume personal responsibilities.

In general, proof was overwhelming that immediate emancipation was put into effect without any sort of disorder, that it had worked far better than the apprentice system, and that there was no *need* for preparation for freedom. Reverend M.

Banks of Bartholomew's said on that point, "one of the grossest of all absurdities was that of *preparing men for freedom* . . . Some pretend that immediate emancipation is unsafe, but it was evident to him that if men *are peaceable while they are slaves,* they might be trusted in any other condition, for they could not possibly be placed in one more aggravating. If *slavery* is a safe system, *freedom* surely will be. There can be no better evidence that a people are prepared for liberty, *than their patient endurance of slavery.*"[21]

The evidence also showed that freemen worked better than slaves, and plantation managers were completely satisfied in that respect, that racial prejudice was diminishing, that there was a great relaxation from the tensions of previous years arising from the fear of insurrections and incendiarism, and that the free Negroes were making remarkable cultural progress. All of this was in spite of the fact that emancipation had been accomplished by Act of Parliament over the bitter protests of the slaveowners, where the freed slaves greatly outnumbered the white population, and where, because of owner absenteeism, the people in charge of plantations were not qualified to give much assistance in the transition period.

The book had an enormous sale because it proved the safety and practicability of emancipation without colonization. All the talk about massacres and bloodshed and complete economic ruin in event of emancipation was shown to be false. If emancipation of a million slaves in the British possessions could be carried out with public safety, and in peace, if the Negroes, once free, could make such amazing progress in a period of three years, then there was no reason to fear emancipation in the United States. Neither was there any doubt but that slavery was doomed throughout the civilized world.

GENERAL LITERATURE

Chapter 32

The antislavery publications included principally books, pamphlets, tracts, broadsides, and newspapers, of which there are in all several thousand titles. These were published by a great many people in a great many places.

Birney probably was about right in saying there were "upwards of a hundred" antislavery newspapers in 1839, but the list of important papers —permanent, well edited, influential—extending through the foundation years 1828 to 1840 was not large. There were not more than a dozen papers, nor more than a dozen editors in all, but every one of the editors made a singular contribution to the cause. Birney himself founded and edited the *Philanthropist* at New Richmond and Cincinnati in January 1836. Gamaliel Bailey joined him the following May. Bailey, son of a Methodist preacher of New Jersey, was both a physician and school teacher before he identified himself with the Lane Seminary rebels and taught during their period of informal study after they withdrew from Lane and before they went to Oberlin. He became editor of the paper when Birney went to New York in September 1837 as corresponding secretary of the American Anti-Slavery Society. When the Tappans, through the American and Foreign Anti-Slavery Society, established the *National Era* in Washington, D. C., in 1847, Bailey was selected as editor because of his literary ability, fair-minded tolerance, good business judgment, and integrity. He continued in that post until his death in 1859.

Bailey brought in as his associate editor Daniel Reaves Goodloe, a native North Carolinian, who

had left his state because of opposition to slavery. Goodloe succeeded to the editorship when Bailey died. Goodloe was a close friend of Horace Greeley, wrote extensively for the *Tribune*, and was active in Lincoln's emancipation program. Bailey also associated John Greenleaf Whittier with the *Era* as corresponding editor, and first published *Uncle Tom's Cabin*, written by the wife of his old associate at Lane Seminary. He published, both at Cincinnati and at Washington, D. C., a long series of specially written articles on various aspects of the slavery question under the general title of *Facts for the People*. The *Philanthropist* was the official organ of the Ohio Anti-Slavery Society.[1] The *Anti-Slavery Bugle* was founded at New Lisbon, Ohio, in June 1845, by B. S. Jones and his wife, Elizabeth H. Jones, and was edited by them until 1849, then by Marius Robinson at Salem, Ohio, until 1861. It was the organ of the state society after the *Philanthropist*, but by that time antislavery effort was concentrated in the Liberty Party, and the *Bugle* and those people still active in the society were Garrisonians.

A second key journalistic pilgrimage, beginning in the critical period and moving through all phases of the movement, was that of William Goodell. He was a native of New York, a man of extraordinary literary talent, an earnest and kindly humanitarian, and, like Birney, deeply concerned with the constitutional crisis of his time. He left a short business career in 1826 to become editor of the *Investigator and General Intelligencer* in Providence, Rhode Island. This general reform journal was combined with the *National*

Philanthropist of Boston and was moved to New York in 1830, as the *Genius of Temperance*. Goodell had been a director of the New York Mercantile Library Association for several years. He now became one of the small group of men who laid the foundations of the organized antislavery movement between 1831 and 1833. He assumed complete responsibility for the *Emancipator* and edited that official organ of the American Anti-Slavery Society until 1836. He then went to Utica as editor of the *Friend of Man*, organ of the New York State Anti-Slavery Society. He remained in this post for six years, made a major contribution to the organization of political action, and wrote a number of powerful treatises.[2] He was one of the stalwarts in the movement until emancipation.

Charles C. Burleigh, and his brother William Henry Burleigh, farm boys of Connecticut, together wrote a brilliant chapter in the antislavery movement. Both of them came into the contest by way of the Prudence Crandall persecution. Samuel J. May put them into the editorship of Arthur Tappan's paper, the *Unionist,* which had been established at Brooklyn, Connecticut, to defend Prudence and secure repeal of the Black Law. Charles abandoned a promising career in the legal profession to continue his antislavery work. Both of the brothers were members of the famous "seventy" agents.

Charles Burleigh continued his editorial work as successor to Lundy and Whittier. Benjamin Lundy had published the *Genius of Universal Emancipation* until 1835. Then, in August 1836, he began publishing in Philadelphia the *National Enquirer and Constitutional Advocate of Universal Liberty.* Whittier succeeded Lundy as editor in March 1838 and changed the name of the paper to the *Pennsylvania Freeman.* The editorial offices of the paper were in Pennsylvania Hall when it was burned May 17, 1838, and all of Lundy's vast antislavery collection, papers, and files of the *Genius* were burned. Lundy then went to Illinois and re-established the *Genius* at Lowell, where he published twelve numbers before his death in 1839. Whittier gave up the editorship of the *Freeman* because of ill-health in February 1840, and Charles Burleigh took his place. The *Freeman* was the official publication of the old Pennsylvania Society for the Abolition of Slavery, after 1844 of the eastern district of the Pennsylvania Anti-Slavery Society. Charles was a brilliant lecturer and writer, but did not publish

Fugitives had to be surrendered up on demand, and the shadow of the slave catcher darkened many doorways.

outside the columns of his paper.[3] He became corresponding secretary of the American Anti-Slavery Society in 1859, wrote the reports of the society for the years 1859, 1860, and 1861, and published one lecture titled *No Slave Hunting in the Old Bay State*. He was one of the most conscientious and accurate workers in the movement. He was tall and slender with strongly marked features, a careless dresser, wearing a frock coat without buttons, steel-gray satinette pantaloons, turned-down shirt collar, and a black cravat tied sailor fashion, but he could hold an audience breathless for hours with his amusing, persuasive argumentation.

William Henry Burleigh went to Pittsburgh in 1837, where he edited the *Christian Witness* and continued to lecture, maintaining a close personal relationship with Francis J. LeMoyne. In 1843 the Connecticut Anti-Slavery Society took him to Hartford as editor of their official publication, the *Christian Freeman*. The name of the paper was changed in February 1848 to the *Charter Oak*. It was known as an antislavery family newspaper. Burleigh went to Albany in 1849 as lecturer, editor, and corresponding secretary of the New York State Temperance Society.

One of the stalwarts of the American Anti-Slavery Society whose career like that of Goodell extended through every phase of the movement was Joshua Leavitt. He had gone to New York in 1828, where he became secretary of the Seaman's Friend Society and then editor of the New York *Evangelist*. He was secretary also of the Society for Promoting Manual Labor in Literary Institutions, which sent Theodore Weld west in 1831. He had written against slavery in the columns of the *Christian Spectator* since 1825 and was a member of the powerful New York committee from the beginning of the organized movement. When Goodell gave up the editorship of the *Emancipator* to go to Utica in 1836, the executive committee turned to Amos A. Phelps, who was lecturing in Connecticut. Elizur Wright said: "After thorough search we could find none, except Bro. P. whom we dare *trust*. We have some regrets about spoiling a *lecturer*, when editors are so much plentier. But Br. P. is not after all a Demosthenes—he is logical, mathematical, convincing, but not passionate, moving, electrifying. His talents of all kinds, we think, will have full play here, and we *must* have him *now*."[4] Phelps was forced to return to his home in Boston after a time because of

his wife's illness. Leavitt had been forced by the panic and depression to sell the *Evangelist*. The executive committee, therefore, brought Leavitt into the main office and gave him the editorship of the *Emancipator*.

The *Emancipator* was the official organ of the American Anti-Slavery Society and had a subscription list of slightly less than four thousand. In the twelve months ending in May 1838, 217,000 single copies were printed. Everything pertinent to the progress of emancipation in England and the United States and its impact upon the churches and political institutions was fully reported. Its editorials were not always scintillating, but its coverage was complete and accurate. Elizur Wright, the only corresponding secretary of the society until 1837, was in charge of publications. He designed and published for two years, beginning in October 1835, the *Quarterly Anti-Slavery Magazine* for educators, students, and professional men. He said to Weld: "We want to concentrate the best minds of the abolition host, and bring out a work which shall tell with overwhelming force upon our Seminaries and upon our reading and

William Goodell

thinking men."[5] The monthly publication of the society was *Human Rights*. It was a four-page folio, filled with facts and arguments for the general reader. It was popular and much quoted. In 1838, 190,000 single copies were printed.

Elizur Wright said to Weld, also in June 1835: "We are now making arrangements with all possible expedition to use the press on a larger scale—shall issue gratuitously from 20,000 to 50,000 of some publication or other every week. What seems now the greatest difficulty is to get the *names* of the right persons to whom we send them. We want names of *inquiring, candid, reading* men who are not abolitionists."[6] The publications he was talking about were *The Anti-Slavery Record* and *The Slave's Friend*. The *Record* was a small magazine with excellent woodcuts, containing, principally, extracts from other publications. There were thirty-six issues published between January 1835 and December 1837. The *Slave's Friend* was a children's magazine. Birney described it as "replete with facts relating to slavery and with accounts of hair-breadth escapes of slaves from their masters and pursuers that rarely fail to impart the most thrilling interest to its little readers."[7] Both of these publications were distributed freely without charge, and they, together with Weld's *Bible Argument*, found their way into the schools and colleges everywhere. In September 1835 Wright said the society was publishing each month 15,000 *Emancipators*, 20,000 *Human Rights*, 25,000 *Anti-Slavery Records*, and 12,500 *Slave's Friend*.[8] In the year ending May 11, 1838, the society published 7,877 bound volumes, 47,250 tracts and pamphlets, 4,100 circulars, 10,490 prints, 9,000 *Quarterly Anti-Slavery Magazine*, 131,050 *Slave's Friend*, 189,400 *Human Rights*, and 217,000 *Emancipator*. Tracts and pamphlets increased to 250,-000 in 1840. In addition, 40,000 copies yearly of pictorial representations were published.

The *Emancipator* cost two dollars a year, *Human Rights* twenty-five cents, the *Anti-Slavery Record* twenty cents, and the *Slave's Friend* for children eighty cents per hundred pieces. The executive committee of the New York State Anti-Slavery Society in March 1838 recommended appointment of one man and one woman in each school district by the local societies to compile lists of heads of families and the names of every person over eighteen years of age. The societies were to purchase an *Anti-Slavery Almanac* for every family, sell as many as possible for six cents

The New York nine months' law permitted temporary residence by a slaveowner with his slaves for that period of time.

A NORTHERN FREEMAN ENSLAVED BY NORTHERN HANDS.

Nov. 20, 1836, (Sunday,) Peter John Lee, a free colored man of Westchester Co., N. Y., was kidnapped by Tobias Boudinot, E. K. Waddy, John Lyon, and Daniel D. Nash, of N. Y., city, and hurried away from his wife and children into slavery. One went up to shake hands with him, while the others were ready to use the gag and chain. See Emancipator, March 16, and May 4, 1837. This is not a rare case. Many northern freeman have been enslaved, in some cases under color of law. Oct. 26, 1836, a man named Frank, who was born in Pa., and lived free in Ohio, was hurried into slavery by an Ohio Justice of the Peace. When offered for sale in Louisiana, he so clearly stated the facts that a *slaveholding* court declared him FREE—thus giving a withering rebuke to northern servility.

"Throughout the island the estates were never in a more advanced state than they now are. I have frequently adopted the job system—the negroes accomplished twice as much as when they worked for daily wages, *because they made more money.* On some days they would make three times the ordinary wages."—*Dr. Daniell.*

"On my estate, cultivation is more forward than *ever* it has been at the same season. The laborers have *done well.*"—*Mr. Favey, of Lavicount's estate.*

"Emancipation has almost wholly put an end to the practice of *skulking*, or pretending to be sick."—*James Howell, Esq.*

"I find my people much more disposed to work than they formerly were. The habit of feigning sickness to get rid of going to the field, is completely broken up. My people say, 'they have not time to be sick now.' My cultivation has *never* been so far advanced at the same season. I have been encouraged by the *increasing industry* of my people to bring several additional acres under cultivation."—*Mr. Hatley.*

"I get my work done better than formerly, and with incomparably more cheerfulness. My estate was never in a finer state of cultivation, though I employ *fewer* laborers than during slavery."—*D. Cranstoun, Esq.*

EMANCIPATED SLAVES ARE EASILY CONTROLLED BY LAW.

TESTIMONY. "I have found that the negroes are readily controlled by *law.*"—*David Cranstoun, Esq.*

"They are as pliant to the hand of legislation, as any people."—*Wesleyan Miss'y.*

"Aggression on private property, such as breaking into houses, cutting canes, &c., are *decidedly fewer* than formerly."—*Dr. Daniell.*

Messrs. Thome and Kimball add: "Similar sentiments were expressed by the Governor, Hon. N. Nugent, R. B. Eldridge, Esq., Dr. Ferguson, James Scotland, Jr., Esq., and numerous other planters, managers, &c."

In connection with the above, we present extracts of a letter from the SUPERINTENDENT OF THE POLICE, addressed to us, dated St. John's, Feb. 9, 1837.

"The laborers have conducted themselves generally in a highly satisfactory manner to all the authorities. They are peaceable, orderly, and civil. ☞ *A due fear of, and a prompt obedience to the authority of the magistrates, is a prominent feature of the lower orders.* To judge of the past and present state of society throughout the island, I presume that *the lives and properties of all classes are as secure in this, as in any other portion of his Majesty's dominions.*" R. S. WICKHAM, *Superintendent of police.*

Kidnapping never ceased, because the risks were less than ordinary horse stealing and the profits were greater.

each, and give away the remainder. They were also to purchase a circulating library for each school district including Jay's *Inquiry* (thirty-seven cents), *Testimony of God Against Slavery* (twenty-five cents), Whittier's *Poems* (thirty-seven and one-half cents), Sunderland's *Appeal* (thirty-seven and one-half cents), Child's *Appeal* (thirty-seven and one-half cents), the *Anti-Slavery Record* (Vol. I, twenty-five cents), Bourne's *Picture of Slavery* (fifty cents), Rankin's *Letters* (twenty-five cents). School houses were to be used for meetings, school teachers were to be used as librarians, and every person in the community was to be asked to sign a petition.

There were other papers, of course, and other editors. Elijah P. Lovejoy's St. Louis *Observer,* from 1833 to 1836, and his *Alton Observer,* from September 1836 to August 1837, compared favorably with the *Philanthropist* in the importance of its location. The two papers differed greatly for two reasons. Birney was a lawyer, Lovejoy was a preacher. Birney stuck to his antislavery publishing, Lovejoy deviated to denounce war, intemperance, and Catholicism. There were three Negro editors of importance during the 1830's: John B. Russwurm, graduate of Bowdoin, who founded *Freedom's Journal* in New York City in 1827, Charles B. Ray, educated at Wesleyan University, who edited the *Colored American* in New York in 1838–39, and James McCune Smith, educated in the African Free School of New York City and recipient of three degrees from the University of Glasgow, who wrote for the *Emancipator* and was editor of the *Colored American* for some time.

In New Hampshire, at Concord, the *Herald of Freedom* was published from March 1835 to October 1846, was edited in succession by Joseph H. Kimball (1836–37), N. P. Rodgers (1839–44), and Parker Pillsbury (1845–46), and was the organ of the New Hampshire Anti-Slavery Society after 1840. The Maine Anti-Slavery Society published the *Advocate of Freedom* from 1838 to 1841. In Vermont, at Brandon, the *Vermont Telegraph* was established as a Baptist journal in 1828, but was purchased by Orion S. Murray in 1834 and continued as an antislavery paper until 1843. Finally, in New York City, LaRoy Sunderland preached antislavery doctrine to the Methodists with *Zion's Watchman* from 1836 to 1842.

The American Anti-Slavery Society published the *Anti-Slavery Examiner* as an elite series of monographs, irregularly, as they were completed.

These included, before 1840, Angelina Grimké's *Appeal to the Christian Women of the South*, Weld's *Bible Argument Against Slavery*, his *Power of Congress over the District of Columbia*, and *American Slavery As It Is*, Thome and Kimball's *Emancipation in the West Indies*, Beriah Green's *Chattel Principle*, the *Birney-Elmore Correspondence*, two letters by Gerrit Smith, and Thomas Morris' famous speech in the Senate, February 9, 1839, in reply to Henry Clay. The society also published or republished, before 1840, Birney's *Letter on Colonization*, and *Letters to Ministers and Elders*, Duncan's *Treatise on Slavery*, Heyrich's *Immediate, Not Gradual Abolition*, Jay's *Inquiry*, and *View of the Action of the Federal Government*.

Newspapers and solid treatises of the above list far surpassed all other publications in importance. They were factual, accurate, and logical. They appealed to conscience and intellect, and this was, first, last, and always, a great religious and intellectual crusade for social reform. Other publications—almanacs, sermons, tracts, and so forth—drew heavily upon them for facts and arguments. They were the sort of literature that found its way to the tables of doctors, lawyers, college professors, and preachers. The best of them, by far, were in print by the end of the critical period or first decade of organized effort. Along with these publications in importance must be listed petitions and Congressional speeches. Petitions, as we have seen, were circulated in far-flung communities, read and discussed and signed at social gatherings, in country stores, and at prayer meetings by some people, at least, who never read. Not all, but nearly all, of the Congressional speeches came after 1840. They were important. Novels came after 1850. They were not important. Not many antislavery people would have anything to do with them. They converted very few people to antislavery principles.

Every home had its Bible and its almanac, and the evangelistic movement of the 1820's had accustomed everyone to the distribution of tracts. The New York executive committee, therefore, published a series of almanacs and a series of miniature tracts. The idea of almanacs probably originated with Nathaniel Southard, one of the "seventy" and an assistant in the New York editorial offices. They were published each year from 1836 to 1844, Weld preparing those of 1839, 1840, and 1841, and David Lee Child the last three.

Twelve *Miniature Anti-Slavery Tracts*, of sixteen or twenty-four pages each, were published between 1837 and 1839. They dealt with such subjects as race prejudice, moral condition of the slaves, and colonization. The almanacs proved so popular that they were continued as *The Liberty Almanac* from 1844 to 1852 by the American and Foreign Anti-Slavery Society, which was principally the original New York executive committee or political action group. The almanacs contain a greater amount of antislavery principles, fact, argument, and anecdotes than can be found anywhere else. The pictures were apt, striking, each a sermon in itself—regarded as harsh, severe by some, but calculated to tell a powerful truth.

There were other ways of preachment, and none was neglected. Birney, in his correspondence with Elmore, said: "Female abolitionists often unite in sewing societies. They meet together, usually once a week or fortnight, and labor through the afternoon, with their own hands, to furnish means for advancing the cause of the slave. One of the company reads passages from the Bible, or some religious book, whilst the others are engaged at their work. The articles they prepare, especially if they be of the 'fancy' kind, are often ornamented with handsomely executed emblems, underwritten with appropriate mottoes. The picture of a slave kneeling and supplicating, in the words, '*Am I not a man and a brother?*' is an example. The mottoes or sentences are, however, most generally selected from the Scriptures; either appealing to human sympathy in behalf of human suffering, or breathing forth God's tender compassion for the oppressed, or proclaiming in thunder tones, his avenging justice on the oppressor."

Birney quoted some of the mottoes, then went on to say: "Fairs, for the sale of articles fabricated by the hands of the females, and recommended by such pictures and sentences as those quoted above, are held in many of our cities and large towns. Crowds frequent them, to purchase; hundreds of dollars are thus realized to be appropriated to the anti-slavery cause; and, from the cheap rate at which the articles are sold, vast numbers of them are scattered far and wide over the country. Besides these, if we except various drawings or pictures on paper . . . such as the Slave-market in the District of Columbia, with members of Congress attending it . . . I am apprised of no other means of propagating our doctrines than by oral and written discussion."[9]

ANTI-SLAVERY WAFERS,

Designed to further the Cause of Emancipation, by continually exposing the Sin of Slavery.

Price One Halfpenny, or Three Shillings per 100. Published by H. Armour, 54 South Bridge, Edinburgh.

A man may sell himself to work for another, but he cannot sell himself to be a slave. *Blackstone.*	All men are created free and equal, and have an inalienable right to liberty. *Fundamental Principle of American Government.*	He that holds another man as property, is more detestable than the robber and the assassin combined. *Thomas Day, 1776.*	The negroes are destitute of the Gospel, and ever will be, under the present state of things.—*Synod of South Carolina and Georgia, 1834.*	*ANTI-SLAVERY.* The righteous considereth the cause of the poor; but the wicked regardeth not to know it. *Prov. xxix. 7.*
Those are man-stealers who abduct, keep, sell, or buy slaves. *Grotius, 1650.*	Men-buyers are exactly on a level with Men-stealers. *Rev. J. Wesley, 1777.*	Slaves are liable, as chattels, to be sold by the master at his pleasure, and may be taken in execution for debt. *Kentucky Law of Descent.*	To be a slave, is to be denied the privilege of reading the Gospel of the Son of God. *Elijah P. Lovejoy, 1837.*	Shall the throne of iniquity have fellowship with thee, which frameth mischief by a law. *Psalm xciv. 20.*
Slaveholding is injustice which no considerations of policy can extenuate. *Bishop Horsley, 1785.*	I thought it my duty to expose the monstrous impiety and cruelty, not only of the slave-trade, but of slave-holding itself, in whatever form it is found. *Gran. Sharpe, 1787.*	Time has proved that slavery and education are incompatible." *Cassius M. Clay, 1845.*	To be a slave, is to be shut out from all enjoyment in this world, and all hope in the next. *Elijah P. Lovejoy, 1837.*	*Anti-slavery.*—Who will stand up for me against the evil-doers, or who will stand up for me against the workers of iniquity. *Psalm xciv. 16.*
Man-stealers! the worst of thieves: in comparison of whom, highway robbers and housebreakers are innocent. *Rev. J. Wesley, 1777.*	Liberty is the right of every human creature as soon as he breathes the vital air: and no human law can deprive him of that right. *Rev. J. Wesley, 1777.*	All meetings of slaves, at any meeting-house or school, for learning to read or write, shall be deemed unlawful. *Virginia Code, 1819.*	Negroes are not free agents, have no personal liberty, no faculty of acquiring property, but are themselves property, at the will of their masters. *Patterson, in Convent. 1787.*	*ANTI-SLAVERY.* Woe unto him that useth his neighbour's service without wages, and giveth him not for his work. *Jer. xxii. 13.*
The children of men are by nature free, and cannot without injustice be either reduced to or held in slavery. *Judge Jay, 1786.*	The owners of slaves are licensed robbers, and not the just proprietors of what they claim. *Mr. Rice, Kentucky, 1780.*	The Christian religion classes man-stealers with murderers of fathers and mothers. *Bishop Porteous.*	Why ought slavery to be abolished? Because it is incurable injustice. *William Pitt.*	*ANTI-SLAVERY.* THOU SHALT NOT STEAL. *Ex. xx. 15.*
The Almighty God has no attribute that can take sides with Slaveholders *Thomas Jefferson.*	To hold a man in slavery is to be every day guilty of robbing him of his liberty, or of manstealing. *Jonathan Edwards, 1791.*	He that stealeth a man, and selleth him, or if he be found in his hand, he shall surely be put to death. *Exodus xxi. 16*	Let sorrow bathe each blushing cheek, Bend piteous o'er the tortured slave, Whose wrongs compassion cannot speak, Whose only refuge is the grave. *Mrs. Morton.*	There are Three Millions of Slaves in the United States of *Christian (?)* America.
ANTI-SLAVERY. Be not partakers of other men's sins.	*ANTI-SLAVERY.* Remember them that are in bonds as bound with them. *Heb. xiii. 3.*	*Anti-slavery.*—Love worketh no ill to his neighbour, therefore Love is the fulfilling of the Law. *Rom. xiii. 10.*	*ANTI-SLAVERY.* God hath made of one blood all nations. *Acts xvii. 26.*	Is not every slave a brother or a sister, ought we not then to seek for immediate, universal, and unconditional EMANCIPATION.
Anti-slavery. Where the Spirit of the Lord is, there is liberty. *2 Cor. iii. 17.*	Proclaim liberty to the captive, and the opening of the prison doors to them that are bound. *Isaiah lx. 1.*	Pure religion and undefiled before God and the Father is this, to visit the fatherless and the widows in their affliction, and to keep himself unspotted from the world.	*Anti-slavery.* Whatsoever ye would that men should do unto you, do ye even so to them. *Matt. vii. 12.*	Oppression is the forerunner of revolution, are not Slaveholders then tampering with the internal peace of America?
Anti-slavery. Woe unto him that buildeth his house by unrighteousness. *Bible.*	Every slaveholder is guilty of reducing human beings to the condition of brutes and things.	All who fellowship with slaveholders are abettors and promoters of theft, robbery, and concubinage.	There is no respect of persons with God. *Rom. ii. 11.* In the churches of the U. S. separate pews are generally provided for the negroes.	The slave can do nothing, possess nothing, nor acquire anything but what must belong to his master. *Louisiana Civil Code.*
There are Seven Millions of Slaves in the World, held by professedly Christian nations	*Anti-slavery.* In Christian America there is no Marriage for the Slaves.	In America Slaves are joined to Churches, as members, to enhance their price on the auction-block.	Thou shalt love thy neighbour as thyself. *Matthew, xxii. 39.*	In America 30,000 slaves are members of the Presbyterian Church, and these men and women have no legal marriage.
NO UNION with SLAVEHOLDERS.	Is not this the fast that I have chosen, to loose the bands of wickedness, to undo the heavy burdens, and to let the oppressed go free, and that ye break every yoke.	Is every Free Church to have a SLAVE STONE in it?— *Rev. Dr. Duncan of the Free Church.*	Slaves shall be deemed, held, taken, reputed, and judged in law to be chattels personal. *South Carolina Code.*	Every slave in America is a stolen man or woman—every slaveholder is a man-stealer.
While men despise fraud, and loathe rapine, and abhor blood, they shall reject with indignation the wild and guilty phantasy, that man can hold property in man. *Brougham.*	My God what wish can prosper, or what prayer, For those who deal in cargoes of despair; Or drive a loathsome traffic, gauge and span, And buy the muscles and the bones of man. *Cowper.*	Are we then fanatics? Are we enthusiasts? Because we say to all Slaveholders, Do not rob, Do not murder. *Charles James Fox.*	Have we separated ourselves from our moderate brethren to form an alliance with manstealers. *Rev. H. Grey, Moderator of the Free Church General Assembly for 1846.*	Slaves regard all instruction, addressed especially to themselves, as a device of their masters, to make them more obedient and profitable to them. Such are the workings of slavery.

Anti-slavery wafers, bearing quotations from the Bible and from the writings of distinguished statesmen and philosophers, were intended for use as seals, principally on envelopes. The purpose was to bring to the attention of people repeatedly the evils of slavery.

Typical of the pictorial publications was the twenty by twenty-seven inch sheet *Slave Market of America.* On this large poster were:

1) Three quotations from the Bible: "All Things whatsoever ye would that men should do to you, do you even so to them, for this is the law and the prophets"; "And they sighed by reason of the bondage, and they cried, and their cry came up unto God by reason of the bondage, and God heard their groaning"; and "Thus saith the Lord, execute judgment in the morning, and deliver him that is spoiled out of the hands of the oppressor, lest my fury go out like fire, and burn that none can quench it, because of the evil of your doings."

2) The foundation sentence from the Declaration of Independence—"We hold these truths to be self-evident;—That all men are created equal; that they are endowed by their Creator with certain inalienable rights; that among these are life, liberty, and the pursuit of happiness."

3) Three quotations from the Constitution: "The citizens of each state shall be entitled to all the privileges and immunities of citizens of the several states"; "Congress shall make no law abridging the freedom of speech or of the press, or of the right of the people peaceably to assemble, and to petition the government for a redress of grievances"; "Congress shall have power to exercise exclusive legislation, in all cases whatsoever, over such district (not exceeding ten miles square) as may, by cession of particular states and the acceptance of Congress, become the seat of government of the United States."

4) The guarantees of freedom of the press contained in all of the several state constitutions.

5) The names of every member of the House of Representatives, listed alphabetically by states, who had voted for the resolution of February 8, 1836, "That in the opinion of this House Congress ought not in any way to interfere with slavery in the District of Columbia."

6) Nine pictures, showing the "Reading of the Declaration of Independence"; the location of the public prison in Washington, D. C.; a coffle of slaves being driven past the Capitol Building; the jail in Alexandria; the "Sale of a Free Citizen to Pay His Jail Fees" at the Washington jail; Fanny Jackson and her three children in jail, where they had been held nine months; the slave detention house of the traders J. W. Neal and Co.; a slave ship leaving Alexandria for New Orleans with a cargo of slaves; and the Franklin and Armfield's slave prison.

7) A considerable array of facts, advertisements, and so forth, explanatory of the pictures.[10]

Other pictures published and sold for a few pennies or distributed free of charge were the "Attack upon the Post Office in Charleston," the scene of a public hanging by a mob, a female slave in chains kneeling under the caption "An American Woman," separation of husband and wife by sale, the public whipping of Amos Dresser, the destruction of a printing press by a mob, the pillaging of a school for Negro girls, a kidnapping scene, and the burning of McIntosh in St. Louis.

The use of quotations from the Bible and statements about slavery by famous people and authorities in state and church was so effective as to constitute the most important appeal to the general public. They were used as texts for sermons, as captions for pictures, on all sorts of fancy needlework, and on seals the size of large postage stamps for use on envelopes such as Red Cross and Christmas seals are used today. Fairs at which all sorts of agricultural commodities, mechanical devices, needlework, clothing, and gift books were sold were being held as early as 1834. Birney, in his correspondence with Elmore, listed, among others, the following as Biblical quotations frequently used by the ladies in their art work:[11]

"Blessed is he that considereth the poor."

"Defend the poor and fatherless; do justice to the afflicted and needy. Deliver the poor and the needy; rid him out of the hand of the wicked."

"Open thy mouth for the dumb, plead the cause of the poor and needy."

"Blessed are the merciful, for they shall obtain mercy."

"First be reconciled to thy brother, and then come and offer thy gift."

"Thou shalt love thy neighbor as thyself."[12]

"All things whatsoever ye would that men should do to you, do ye even so to them."[13]

"He hath sent me to heal the broken-hearted, to preach deliverance to the captives, to set at liberty them that are bruised."

"Rob not the poor because he is poor, neither oppress the afflicted in the gate; for the Lord will plead their cause, and spoil the soul of those that spoiled them."

"Wo[e] unto him that buildeth his house by unrighteousness, and his chambers by wrong; that useth his neighbor's service without wages, and giveth him not for his work."[14]

Antislavery wafers may have been introduced into this country by Henry C. Wright, a thorough Garrisonian, whom Whittier described as a man of "startling opinions" and Weld denounced as "itching to be known" beyond any other man he had ever seen. Wright published a number of pamphlets in England in 1845–46 which contained most of the quotations used on the wafers and mistakes of dates, spelling, and sources are identical in many instances. The quotations from the Bible are, in many cases, no doubt because of the small size of the wafers, not complete. The important ones were as follows:

"Where the spirit of the Lord is, there is liberty, 2 Cor[inthians] iii, 17."

"He that stealeth a man, and selleth him, or if he be found in his hand, he shall surely be put to death, Exodus, xxi, 16."

"God hath made of one blood all nations. Acts, xvii, 26."

"Shall the throne of iniquity have fellowship with thee, which frameth mischief by a law. Psalm xciv, 20."

"Proclaim liberty to the captive, and the opening of the prison doors to them that are bound. Isaiah, lx[i], 1."

The non-Biblical quotations, while accurately conveying the meaning of the source, often presented flagrant alterations in wording and sometimes errors of citation. The New York executive committee would never have permitted this sort of sloppy editing, which is further evidence of its origin through Wright and his British associates. A typical example is: "Man-stealers! The worst of thieves; in comparison of whom, highway robbers and housebreakers are innocent. Rev. J. Wesley, 1777." This quotation was taken from one of Wright's pamphlets.[15] What Wesley did say in his *Thoughts on Slavery* (1774) was far more severe than this simple condemnation:

"And this equally concerns every gentleman that has an estate in our American plantations; yea, all slaveholders of whatever rank and degree: seeing *men-buyers* are exactly on a level with *men-stealers*. Indeed you say, 'I pay honestly for my goods; and I am not concerned to know how they are come by.' Nay but you are: you are deeply concerned to know they are honestly come by. Otherwise you are partaker with a thief, and are not a jot honester than he. But you know they

are not honestly come by; you known they are procured by means nothing near so innocent as picking pockets, housebreaking, or robbery upon the highway. You know they are procured by a deliberate series of more complicated villainy (of fraud, robbery, and murder) than was ever practised either by Mahometans or Pagans, in particular by murders of all kinds; by the blood of the innocent poured upon the ground like water. Now it is *your* money that pays the merchant, and through him the captain, and the African butchers. *You* are therefore guilty, yea principally guilty, of all these frauds, robberies, and murders. You are the spring that puts all the rest in motion: they would not stir a step without *you:* therefore, the blood of all these wretches who die before their time, whether in the country or elsewhere, lies upon *your* head. 'The blood of my brother' (for whether thou wilt believe it or not, such he is in the sight of Him that made him) 'crieth against thee from the earth,' from the ship, and from the waters. Oh, whatever it costs, put a stop to its cry before it be too late: instantly, at any price, were it half of your goods, deliver thyself from the blood-guiltiness! Thy hands, thy bed, thy furniture, thy house, thy lands, are at present stained with blood. Surely it is enough, accumulate no more guilt: spill no more blood of the innocent! Do not hire another to shed blood; do not pay him for doing it: Whether you are a Christian or not, show yourself a man! Be not more savage than a lion or a bear!"[16] Other quotations follow:

1) Liberty is the right of every human creature as soon as he breathes the vital air; and no human law can deprive him of that right (which he derives from the law of nature)."[17]

2) (And Whereas,) "the children of men are by nature [equally] free, and cannot without injustice be either reduced to or held in slavery. Judge Jay, 1786 [1784]."[18]

3) "The Almighty God has no attribute that can take sides with slaveholders. Thomas Jefferson."[19]

4) "There is a law above all the enactments of human codes—the same throughout the world, the same in all times . . . it is the law written by the finger of God on the heart of man; and by that law, unchangeable and eternal; while men despise *fraud*, and loathe *rapine*, and abhor *blood*, they will reject with indignation the wild and guilty phantasy, that man can hold property in man. Brougham."[20]

5) "(And) to hold a man in (a state of) slavery (who has a right to liberty) is to be every day guilty of robbing him of his liberty, or of man-stealing. Jonathan Edwards, 1791."[21]

There were also quotations from William Cowper's poem "Charity,"[22] from Thomas Day's poem "The Dying Negro,"[23] and Sarah Wentworth Morton's poem "The African Chief."[24] There were statements from the speeches of William Pitt, from the *Commentaries* of Blackstone, from the works of Hugo Grotius, and from the pronouncements of Samuel Horsley, bishop of Rochester, and Beibly Porteus, bishop of London and chaplain to the king.

Antislavery tracts, of course, could be printed cheaply and distributed widely without much effort. There never was any continuity of subject matter or uniformity of quality in any series. The New England Anti-Slavery Tract Association published a series of fourteen tracts of four, eight, or twelve pages. There were poems by Longfellow, a discussion of fugitive slaves by Weld, an appeal to the ministers of the churches by Goodell, an exposé of race prejudice by Clarkson and others. The Garrisonians, after they took the headquarters of the society to Boston in 1840, were not active for a time, but in 1855–56 they published a series of twenty tracts, including among others discussions of the interstate slave trade by John G. Palfrey, of Jamaica by Richard Hildreth, of slavery and the North by Charles C. Burleigh, of the Fugitive Slave Law by Samuel J. May, and of slavery and the Bible by Charles Beecher. They then published a new series of twenty-five tracts in 1860–61, of unusual length, some as long as forty-eight pages. Nearly one-half of these were by Garrison himself, but Wendell Phillips discussed the philosophy of the abolition movement, Lydia Maria Child explained the duty of disobeying the Fugitive Slave Law, and William Ellery Channing wrote a tribute to antislavery men for their vindication of freedom of speech.

The finest of all tracts published were by the Anti-Slavery Society of Leeds, England, for distribution at home and in the United States. The series of eighty-two tracts was mostly of one or two pages each, published in 1853.[25] A second series of thirteen tracts, mostly of twelve pages, and containing exceedingly fine woodcuts, was published in 1856. These tracts were primarily for youngsters, but were designed to capture the interest of everyone. There was an abridged edition of *Uncle Tom's Cabin*, and stories of escapes from

slavery, branding of slaves, separation of families, the slave trade, slave auctions, kidnappings, slave breeding, and others.

The most active group of antislavery women was in Boston, closely associated with Garrison and his advocacy of women's rights. Maria Weston Chapman, assisted by her sister, Anne Warren Weston, edited annually, beginning in 1839, a gift book of antislavery poems and prose sketches under the general title *The Liberty Bell*.[26] Maria Weston Chapman, wife of a wealthy Boston merchant, was an uncompromising, militant, Garrisonian abolitionist. John Greenleaf Whittier called her Garrison's "evil genius" and refused ever to contribute to the gift books, even though his poems frequently were published in the *Liberator*. *The Liberty Bell*, therefore, was important as a yearly testimonial to the most extreme antislavery principles.[27] It was important because contributions to its pages came from the British Isles, France, Sweden, Haiti, and Cuba, nearly one-half of the contributing authors being distinguished foreigners, and antislavery workers in Dublin, Edinburgh, London, Liverpool, and Leeds. A few, but very few, of the American contributions came from outside New England.

The extracts from speeches, the letters, essays, and some poems were vehement denunciations of the churches and government of the United States, and of Southerners and their sympathizers. Some of these came from England and Ireland, some were written by William Lloyd Garrison, Samuel J. May, Parker Pillsbury, Theodore Parker, and Wendell Phillips. In Garrison's contribution were his references to the Constitution as an "atrocious compromise," a "libel of Democracy which was stained with human blood," and a "covenant with death and an agreement with Hell . . . and accursed be the American Union as a stupendous Republican imposture." Samuel J. May in his essay "Our National Idolatry" declared that the Union was an "idol of the people worshipped above God" and the Constitution a "sin framed by law." At a later date, after the compromise of 1850, Garrison referred to Daniel Webster as "the Great Apostate," and Maria Weston Chapman in the essay "Necrology" referred to him as a "brilliantly endowed but a feeble-souled man."[28]

Poems in *The Liberty Bell* were by Bernard Barton, the Quaker poet of Suffolk, England; Elizabeth Barrett Browning, whose poems "The Runaway Slave at Pilgrim's Point" and "A Curse for a Nation" were written specifically for the gift book; Henry Wadsworth Longfellow, James Russell Lowell, and others of New England. The subject matter of the poems and of the stories was the tragedy of the slaves' existence, the detrimental effect of slavery on master and slave, and the intellectual and moral equality of Negroes and whites.

The testimonials were usually contributed by famous French leaders in literary, political, and scientific circles: Jean Jacques Ampère, scientist and literary critic; François Arago, astronomer, physicist and politician; Gustave de Beaumont, author; Madame Belloc, author and translator of

Harriet Beecher Stowe's *Uncle Tom's Cabin;* Emile de Girardin, journalist; Jules Janin, literary critic; Jules Michelet, historian; and a powerful group of political leaders who pressed for abolition of slavery in French colonies, including Baron de Staël-Holstein, Charles Forbes Montalembert, Count Charles Rémusat, Victor Schoelcher, and Alexis de Tocqueville. The contributions of these men were in the tone of aid and encouragement to antislavery men in the United States and had none of the cynical, sharp criticism so characteristic of the English and Irish essayists.

One stage in the emergence of the Free Soil party from the campaign of 1848.

MADISON COUNTY
and the adjoining Counties!
AWAKE!

The friends of Freedom and of righteous Government -- the enemies of land-monopoly and tariffs, and secret societies -- are invited to come by thousands to the Meeting, which is to be held in Peterboro, Wednesday 1st day of September next, and which is to begin at precisely 9 o'clock A. M.

Beriah Green, William Goodell, John Thomas, and other distinguished speakers from abroad, are expected to address the Meeting.--- Such an opportunity to hear great truths, eloquently spoken, seldom occurs. Let all, who can, improve it.

The Inn-keeper, Mr. Hyde, will have dinner ready at 1-2 past 12.

August 12, 1847.

WOMEN IN THE MOVEMENT

Chapter 33

Women made a very positive contribution to the abolition of slavery, a contribution which was obscured by controversy over participation by women in public affairs and by the efforts of Garrison, Henry C. Wright, and others to promote women's rights at the expense of the antislavery effort.

Lucretia Mott of Philadelphia, a member of the Hicksite group of Friends, was present at the organization of the American Anti-Slavery Society. She spoke, on invitation of the president, Beriah Green, to the question of the Declaration of Sentiments. None of the women present, however, was invited to sign the declaration or to join the society. They *were* urged to form female antislavery societies.[1] There was no dissent from this action, although it represented somewhat of an innovation with regard to participation by women in public activities.

Lucretia Mott had preached in Friends' meetings as early as 1818, but Sarah Grimké ran into trouble in her attempt to do so.[2] Angelina Grimké then wrote her appeal to Southern women and Sarah Grimké her epistle to Southern clergymen and trouble began on all sides.[3] The executive committee of the American Anti-Slavery Society was dubious about the propriety of women speaking, but Wright, Stanton, and Weld were too powerful for any adverse action, although the society never gave the two sisters any financial support.[4] In its 1837 report to the society, the committee said: "The Committee cannot omit to mention . . . the important aid the cause has received from two sisters, from Charleston, S. C. . . . Let them hold

on their course, till universal womanhood is rallied in behalf of the bleeding victims of wrong."[5]

The Grimké sisters had attended the agents' convention in New York City and had spoken to women's meetings there. They then went to Massachusetts by invitation of the Massachusetts Anti-Slavery Society, where Angelina lectured with such effectiveness that men poured into the meeting house in spite of the old taboo against women speaking to mixed audiences. Angelina, with the encouragement of Stanton, then spoke before the legislative committee on petitions, and ended her tour in triumph with a series of lectures at the Odeon in Boston.[6] Sarah, writing to Weld, said: "A few words will tell all. The end crowned all, full of solemn pathos and deep feeling. I remembered what Jesus says—'If they hear not Moses and the Prophets neither will they hear tho one rise from the dead.' John Tappan was there. A lady told me he said a fire had been kindled which would never go out."[7]

Angelina, who had been married to Theodore Weld shortly before, made her last appearance as a public speaker at the second national convention of antislavery women, May 17, 1838. The convention met in Pennsylvania Hall, Philadelphia, and Angelina spoke as the mob gathered for the destruction of the recently dedicated building. The mob was not directed at her personally, nor did it represent particular hostility to women. It was, as we have seen, only one of the many acts of violence against antislavery people.[8] Abby Kelly spoke before a mixed assembly of men and women for the first time at this same meeting. Weld heard her address and urged her to abandon teaching in order to lecture in the antislavery cause. Garrison quotes him as saying: "Abby, if you don't, God will smite you."[9] She began lecturing in the spring of 1839, being the first woman, after the Grimké sisters, to do so, and became a leader in the American Anti-Slavery Society after women were admitted in 1839. Samuel J. May said of her work: "Her knowledge of the subject was complete, her facts pertinent, her arguments forceable, her criticisms were keen, her condemnation was terrible. Few of our agents of either sex did more work while her strength lasted, or did it better."[10]

Sharp criticism of Angelina Grimké began as soon as she started her lecture tour. Some of it came from people who were slow to accept a larger participation by women in public affairs. Much of it was artificially stimulated by colonizationists and proslavery forces who sought to confuse the public by introducing extraneous issues into the slavery controversy. Even more of it came from antislavery men, not because they were opposed to the emergence of women into a larger field of usefulness, but because Garrison, Henry C. Wright, and others were retarding the antislavery movement by promoting all sorts of ideas, including militant feminism, through the antislavery press.

The emerging controversy threw the ranks of the clergy into confusion and was responsible for some angry words among antislavery leaders. Samuel J. May, who became a staunch advocate of admitting women into the American Anti-Slavery Society without prejudice, was initially sharply critical in a letter to Angelina Grimké: "I hear you have been addressing promiscuous audiences. I am astonished; it is in such utter violation of all that we have considered proper and decorous and becoming in your sex! Nevertheless, I am satisfied that it is a prejudice, and I beg you to come to my home [South Scituate] and assist me as soon as possible to trample it under my feet."[11] Sarah Grimké said that at Uxbridge the Congregational minister read the notice of a meeting at which Angelina was to speak "at the request of one of the Deacons, but added many strictures on the sin of women's preaching, and urged his hearers to absent themselves."[12]

Amos Phelps, one of the first to hear Angelina speak, wrote a "long, kind, admonitory letter" to the sisters, urging them to cease talking to mixed audiences, and debated seriously in his own mind his duty to make public protest against their activity.[13] Phelps and May, of course, were antislavery stalwarts. Many among the clergy were not, and church men all over the country, clergy and laymen, openly condemned the public participation of women in the movement. In general, orthodoxy recognized the propriety of women singing but not praying in church services, of answering questions in Bible classes and catechism, but not of teaching, preaching, or groaning.

In 1837, a portion of the clergy of Massachusetts issued a pastoral letter to the churches under their care warning them against the "dangers which at present seem to threaten the female character with widespread and permanent injury." They said specifically: "We cannot but regret the mistaken conduct of those who encourage females to bear an obtrusive and ostentatious part in measures of reform, and countenance any of that sex who so far forgot themselves as to itinerate in the character of public lecturers and teachers."[14]

Opposition to women lecturing in public was so strong that many people regarded women who were willing to do so as unnatural. Weld wrote to Angelina Grimké just before their marriage: "Nine tenths of the community verily believe that you are utterly spoiled for domestic life. A man of whom I hoped better things and who really has great respect for your principles and character said he did not believe it possible for a woman of your sentiments and practice as to the sphere of woman to be anything but 'an obtrusive noisy clamorer' in the domestic circle 'repelled and repelling.' He said he could admire your talents and your principles for he did believe you honest, but it was *impossible* for a man of high and pure feeling ever to *marry* you. He said that nature recoiled at it."[15] Even Anne Warren Weston told Angelina: "Yet I have believed you had thrown yourself *entirely* beyond the ordinary lot of woman and *no man* would wish to have such a wife."[16] This was important not as a matter of personal happiness and domestic tranquility for the Welds; it was a question of dissension in the churches and antislavery societies with which we shall deal after we recount the broad scope of the contribution of women to the cause. It was more important, furthermore, in the East than in Ohio, Indiana, Illinois, and Michigan, where the antislavery work of men and of women was more closely correlated.

The first female antislavery society of record was formed at Reading, Massachusetts, in March 1833. The second was a female juvenile society in Utica, New York, in April 1833. Several other societies were formed that year previous to the organization of the American Anti-Slavery Society: one at Boston in October, another at Hudson, New York, in November, and, two in December, one at Amesbury, Massachusetts, and the other at Philadelphia.[17] The American Anti-Slavery Society, as we have seen, did not invite women to join, although some were present at the organization meeting, but it did encourage the formation of women's antislavery societies. Such societies were organized during 1834 in Maine, New Hampshire, Massachusetts, Rhode Island, Pennsylvania, and Michigan.[18]

The most active of the women's societies in the East were those in New York, Philadelphia, and Boston. There are no printed records of the New York society, but the activities of all were about the same. The Boston Female Anti-Slavery Society began its work in October 1833 with only twelve members. The history of the society from its beginning differed from others only in its sponsorship of money-making projects. All women's societies circulated antislavery literature and petitions, some became expert in other activities, and the Boston group, as we have seen, conducted annual fairs with special emphasis upon the printing and sale of the *Liberty Bell*. The money derived from these fairs was given to the state societies, or to the American Anti-Slavery Society, or was used to purchase and distribute literature, or to

FAIR.

The Ladies (of color) of the town of Frankfort propose giving a **FAIR**, at the house of Mrs. **RILLA HARRIS**, (*alias*, Simpson,) on Thursday evening next, for benevolent purposes, under the superintendence of Mrs. Rilla Harris.

All the delicacies of the season will be served up in the most palatable style----such as *Ice Creams, Cakes, Lemonades, Jellies, Fruits, Nuts, &c. &c.*

It is hoped, as the proceeds are to be applied to benevolent purposes, that the citizens generally will turn out and aid in the enterprise.

JULY 6, 1847.

The box supper and the ice cream social of modern times were preceded by the ladies' fairs. Usually fancy needlework, etc., was sold.

hire an antislavery agent, or to pay the expenses of lecturers.[19] The Boston society held its first fair in 1835, the Philadelphia society in 1836.

These very colorful fairs were an important social activity not only in the larger cities where the fairs were held but in the small towns and in faraway places in the British Isles from which women's societies sent contributions.[20] Some antislavery people opposed the fairs. Theodore Weld was so hostile to ostentatious display and to anything in the nature of quest for notoriety that he would not attend conventions nor permit his reports and letters to be published. He said in 1837 that all the fairs he had seen "really grieved and indeed quite disgusted" him.[21] Nevertheless, the fairs made money, the one in Boston in 1837 accounting for five hundred of the society's fourteen-hundred-dollar income that year, and furnishing about one-third of the income of the Massachusetts Anti-Slavery Society in 1843 and about one-half in 1845.[22] It was also said that many converts to the antislavery cause were secured at the fairs, especially among the young people who came to enjoy the social atmosphere. The best of the antislavery lecturers spoke at the fairs in the evenings.[23]

In the winter of 1836–37 Lewis Tappan suggested to the Boston society that a national meeting of women should be held. There was an exchange of letters among the various women's societies, and the Women's Anti-Slavery Society of New York City issued a call for a general antislavery convention of American women to be held there May 9–12. Some three hundred women from ten states attended the meeting, some from as far west as Ohio. The purpose of the meeting was to plan the petition campaign, the most important of all women's part in the movement. There was serious discussion of whether a national women's antislavery society should be organized, but it was unanimously agreed that an annual convention would accomplish the objectives of a society without its cumbersome machinery.[24]

The most important action of the convention—indeed, one of the most important events in the entire history of the antislavery movement—was publication of "An Appeal to the Women of the Nominally Free States." This was prepared and presented by Angelina Grimké, over whose activities as a public speaker the storm of protest was about to break. No one, not even Lucretia Mott, who had spoken at the organization of the American Anti-Slavery Society, understood so well as she the inseparable character of the contests for freedom of the slave and emancipation of women. It was a struggle for human rights; not man's, not woman's, but the equal rights of all human beings whatever their nationality, color, or sex. Man had arrogated to himself, by denying the franchise to women, stifling their voices, and circumscribing their freedom, control of the state, the church, the schools, the morality and health of society, and the legal control of woman's status as a mother, wife, widow, and daughter. Both women and slaves were robbed of rights; the slave being annihilated as a man and reduced to the status of a thing, a chattel, property; woman being robbed of her natural, personal rights in part and almost entirely of her relative rights.

The "Appeal" which Angelina wrote and the women gathered here published to the world was a challenge to every woman to work for emancipation of the slaves, and by so doing to demonstrate to a world dominated by men the right of women to free equality with men. The Grimké sisters, by their courageous entry into the antislavery movement, by their writings, and by their public speaking around New York, by their dignity and humility and brilliance, had demonstrated that sex neither qualified nor disqualified any person for the performance of duties. Endorsement by the convention of the "Appeal" was essentially an endorsement of the principle. The sisters went from the convention to Massachusetts where, on every possible occasion, they defended not only the right of the slave to freedom but the right of women to be regarded as responsible beings, entitled to participate in discussing public affairs, in enacting the laws, administering justice, and preaching the gospel.

In the "Appeal" Angelina had said: "Every citizen should feel an interest in the political concerns of the country, because the honor, happiness, and well-being of every class are bound up in its politics, government and laws. Are we aliens because we are women? Are we bereft of citizenship because we are the mothers, wives, and daughters of a mighty people?"[25] Women, she argued, were the victims of slavery. They were also slaveholders. They used the products of slave labor. They apologized for slavery. They held deep-rooted prejudices against Negroes. They lent aid to the colonization movement. Women, therefore, ought to organize themselves into antislavery societies, familiarize themselves with every aspect of the slavery question, distribute antislavery literature, refrain from using the products of slave labor, aid and comfort the distressed among free Negroes, and in every possible way aid in the cause of emancipation.[26]

Later, when her lectures to mixed audiences, the protests of the New England clergymen, and Garrison had aroused the country to a discussion of the province of women, she said: "This will soon be an absorbing topic. It must be discussed whether women are responsible beings; whether there are male and female virtues, male and female moral duties. My belief is that there is no difference . . . whatever is morally right for a man to do is morally right for a woman to do . . . woman is not to be as she has been a mere second-hand agent in the regeneration of the world, but the acknowledged equal and co-worker with man."[27] Preachers, suffering already from a decay of deference to the pastoral office, thought otherwise.

The Second Anti-Slavery Convention of American Women was held at Philadelphia, May 15–18, 1838, in Pennsylvania Hall, which was burned by a mob during the meeting. The convention was forced to hold its final session in a schoolroom, Temperance Hall having been refused to the women by its managers.[28] Public sentiment in the city continued so hostile that the third convention, May 1–3, 1839, was unable to secure even a church for its meeting and had recourse to the hall of the Pennsylvania Riding School. This, the last of the conventions, was not well attended. Most of those present came from Pennsylvania and Massachusetts, with a few only from Rhode Island, New York, and New Jersey.[29] Garrison had taken a considerable number of the New England women to the New York meeting of the American Anti-Slavery Society, where a bitter argument over the right of women to vote and hold office in the convention occurred.[30] These three national conventions of the women were important because of the petition campaign, and because they gave encouragement and solidarity to the participation of women in the movement in the face of hostile sentiment. The 1840 convention, which was to have met in Boston, did not convene because the 1840 convention of the American Anti-Slavery Society admitted women to membership and equal voting privileges with men.

The participation of women in the movement in the West was quite different, but more difficult to trace because the records of the meetings were not published. The difficulty of travel and communication and the common burden shared by men and women in the newer regions led to a joint effort in the cause of emancipation. Men and women both attended the first anniversary convention in Ohio, at Granville, in May 1836, and women were members and officers in the Ohio societies from the first. James A. Thome said there were forty women delegates of a total of 200 in the 1836 convention.[31] Moreover, women in the West not only carried the burden of the petition campaign, they played an important role, sometimes a dominant one, in the work of the underground railroad. The entire burden of feeding, clothing, and nursing fugitives fell to them. In Ohio, at least, their contribution was as great as that of women in the East, and their sacrifices were greater.

The Logan Female Anti-Slavery Society in Lenawee County, Michigan Territory, organized by Elizabeth Chandler and Laura Haviland on October 8, 1832, may well have been the earliest women's society in the Old Northwest. Both were Quaker ladies. Elizabeth Chandler had come west from Philadelphia, where she had belonged to a free produce society and had written for Lundy's *Genius of Universal Emancipation*. She continued to write, especially poetry, until her death in 1834 at the early age of twenty-six. Laura Haviland, wife of an ardent Quaker, had come from New York to Lenawee County. She and her husband, Charles Haviland, founded Raisin Institute and admitted both Negroes and whites. They severed their relations with the Society of Friends in 1839. Combined in the work of these two women, then, were education of Negroes, antislavery publications, and organized effort in assistance to fugitives.[32]

The first recorded Female Anti-Slavery Society of Ohio was that of Muskingum County, which was formed in April 1835 with 52 charter members. The Granville Female Anti-Slavery Society was formed in June of the same year with 40 members, the Mount Vernon Female Anti-Slavery Society in August with 20 members, the Ashtabula County Female Anti-Slavery Society in September with 224 members, and the Oberlin Female and Oberlin Young Ladies Anti-Slavery Societies in December, with 48 and 86 members, respectively.[33] The Lane Rebels organized societies all over Ohio in 1836, at Middlebury, Canton, Elyria, Geneva, Madison, St. Albans, and elsewhere, some of them with more than one hundred charter members, and in 1837 at Cincinnati and Unionville.[34] These societies were all auxiliary to the American Anti-Slavery Society, but the women also attended and participated in the conventions with men and were as often as not present at the many mobbings in that area.[35]

Organization of women's antislavery societies began in Indiana among the Quakers about 1839, and in Michigan somewhat later with intensive effort about 1844. These so-called Female Benevolent and Anti-Slavery societies did not differ from the earlier societies of Ohio. The antislavery impulse in the 1830's was flowing through the American Anti-Slavery Society and the women's societies of Ohio were formed as auxiliaries to it. The antislavery impulse in the 1840's was flowing through the Liberty Party, and the Indiana-Michigan women's societies were formed as auxiliaries and in conjunction with it. The first women's societies in Indiana were formed in Jefferson, Wayne, Union, and Henry counties, beginning in January 1839. The Indiana societies promoted the free labor produce movement largely due to the Quaker influence. Levi Coffin, who was active in the early phases of the movement in Indiana, promoted the circulation of antislavery literature. This was easy to do because Whittier and Weld had established a library system by which a selected, bound, and boxed collection of literature was sold to state and local societies at a standard price. The ladies' societies went beyond this, however, and made such extensive collections of their own that the state became known for its great number of library (female antislavery) societies. The societies in Indiana not only sent petitions to Congress for the abolition of slavery in the District of Columbia and the exclusion of slave states, but were very active in petitioning the state legislature for repeal of the black laws and for extension to fugitive slaves of jury trial and other safeguards of due process. In Michigan the state antislavery society was formed in November 1839. There were nineteen local societies in Detroit and fifteen in Lenawee County by 1838. These were nearly all mixed societies. The society formed at Young's Prairie in April 1843 had four women on its seven-member executive committee. Women were in complete control of the state society by the 1850's.

The Lane Seminary students had engaged in extensive social service work among the Negroes in Cincinnati, but Weld wrote Lewis Tappan in March, 1834: "In visiting among the blacks, and mingling with them, we have all felt the great importance of another species of instrumentality in raising them, which was not within our reach. I mean a SELECT FEMALE SCHOOL. We know of no female, except Miss Crandall, who has resolution and self-denial enough to engage in the enterprise."[36] Tappan made a plea for volunteers for this missionary effort in the New York Evangelist, and financed the trip west for Phebe Mathews, Emeline Bishop, and Susan Lowe. They were later joined by Lucy Wright and Mary Ann Fletcher. These girls came to be known in intimate antislavery circles as the "Cincinnati Sisters." They assisted in the Sabbath schools and day schools of Augustus Wattles and Marius Robinson and carried on a labor of love among the Negroes. Theodore Weld, in his obituary notice of Phebe Mathews Weed, described her work in the schools, then said: "Her heart turned especially to the lowest class of the colored people; among whom she prosecuted her heavenly mission whenever she could snatch a brief respite from her stated labors. Often, when exhausted by overtoil, and weak from fasting and insufficient sleep, she treaded obscure lanes and dingy passages, stooping into cellars and climbing to garrets, kneeling on damp floors at dying beds, and weeping with those that wept, in sheds and hovels. She perfectly identified herself with the scorned and persecuted class for whom she was spent. She lived in their families, made them her companions, linked herself to their lot, shared with them their burdens and their bonds, and meekly bowed her head with theirs to the storm that swept over them."[37]

Some of the ladies of Cincinnati aided in the initial work and raised some funds for the schools, but finances were limited and the young ladies had to live in cramped quarters, rely for food on the generosity of their Negro friends, and subsist at times on bread and water. After the Lane students went to Oberlin, the sisters carried on their work with great difficulty, each of their schools being in a different part of the city, and that of one having eighty-five students, ranging from little girls to married women. They encountered so much hostility—mobs threatening to tear down the houses in which they lived—that they abandoned the schools and went to Oberlin some time in 1836. Phebe Mathews married Edward Weed and accompanied him on his lecture tours in Ohio. Susan Lowe married Augustus Wattles and helped him found a trade school for Negroes in Indiana.

Antislavery doctrine was introduced directly into the public schools by women teachers and text-book writers, and there was considerable discussion in the American Anti-Slavery Society about exclusion of antislavery passages by publishers of books revised under pressure from the slave states.[38] Lindley Murray's *English Reader,* for example, contained one of Cowper's antislavery poems, Peter Parley's *Method of Telling About Geography to Children* had an illustrated account of slave catching on the Guinea Coast, and Moses Severance's *The American Manual, or New English Reader,* contained Bryant's "The African Chief." Many of the teachers coming from New England and all of those trained at Oberlin were strongly opposed to slavery.

Not many women entered upon the difficult work of lecturing in the tradition of Sarah and Angelina Grimké. Abigail Kelly Foster began her active service in 1839, following the second anti-slavery convention of American women at which she had been encouraged by Theodore Weld. During the 1840's she was an agent of the American Anti-Slavery Society and lectured in New England, western New York, Michigan, and Ohio.[39] She was a very effective lecturer, at times vehement, and never moderate. Her appointment to the executive committee of the American Anti-Slavery Society in 1839 was the occasion, though not the cause, for the split in the society. She was one of the women who went to the world anti-slavery convention in London in 1840, without invitation, with unfortunate consequences to the cause. She served as a general financial agent of the society after 1853, but devoted an increasing amount of her time and effort to fighting the legal and economic disabilities under which women lived and worked.

Sallie Holley, a graduate of Oberlin College, became a lecturer in 1851 and continued to lecture in the West until the Civil War. She was the opposite of Abby Kelly in her approach, being a very devout Christian and never dealing in personalities or denouncing churches, clergy, and politicians. In short, she was much less of a Garrisonian.[40] Caroline Putnam accompanied her on her lecture tours, distributing antislavery literature as a colporteur.[41] Lucy Stone, more famous for her activities in the women's rights movement, also served as an agent after 1850. She, too, was a graduate of Oberlin, and an ardent opponent of slavery.

Antislavery literature was written by nearly all of those women who were prominent in the activities of state and local societies, and many women wrote against slavery who were not connected with any antislavery organization. Margaret Chandler began writing for Lundy's *Genius of Universal Emancipation* in 1829. Lundy claimed she was the *first* woman in the country to make slavery the principal theme of her writing. Lundy collected and published her essays and letters after her death in 1834. Lydia Maria Child was the most versatile of the women authors. She published books on numerous subjects, but slavery was her principal concern, and she not only sacrificed a promising literary career, but gave up social prominence as well, to devote her life to the cause of emancipation. She was very unlike most Garrisonians, in fact very similar to Theodore Weld in her aversion to personal publicity.[42] She came into the movement, however, through the influence of Garrison in 1831.[43] Two years later she wrote *An Appeal in Favor of That Class of Americans Called Africans.* A copy of the book which she presented to the Boston Athenaeum was thrown out and her library privileges were withdrawn in consequence. This was one of the books first recommended to agents of the American Anti-Slavery Society.[44] Weld wanted her to become one of the agents of the American Anti-Slavery Society, but she refused. She wrote for the *Liberty Bell,* was elected to the executive committee of the American Anti-Slavery Society in 1840, and became editor of the *American Anti-Slavery Standard* in New York in 1841. The best of her other works on slavery was a recommendation that the United States follow the West Indian plan of emancipation, published in 1860.[45]

AMERICAN AND FOREIGN ANTI-SLAVERY SOCIETY

Chapter 34

We have seen that the participation of women in the antislavery movement caused serious differences of opinion among antislavery men in the East. This was not true of the West, where women were present at the formation of the various state antislavery societies and attended conventions religiously. By the 1850's they had assumed leadership in these societies. It is a significant fact that only one delegate from Michigan and Illinois voted for the denial of votes to women in the 1839 meeting of the American Anti-Slavery Society.[1] That was in harmony with the equalitarianism of the western region. Women were coworkers, not subordinates. They shared every part of the perils, the responsibilities, and the pleasures of building a new civilization. Women in the East were more sophisticated, and those who ventured into public affairs were considered fanatics. This was not true in the West. There were some objections raised against women participating in some activities, but in the antislavery movement they were invited to assume leadership, as shown by the many resolutions to that end in the state conventions. There were women's local societies, but they were so closely affiliated with the men's groups that they held no conventions as in the East but came together in the state organizations.

The second important difference between the two regions was the underground railroad which, as we shall see, was largely operative west of the mountains. An underground railway station was a friendly home where fugitives were concealed until they could be moved northward. It was risky business because it was against the law. It was laborious business because the fugitives had to be fed and nursed, sometimes for days, and clothed. The women in the societies combined their efforts to prepare clothing. They conducted fairs for money to buy shoes and other articles which could not be made. The Boston ladies sold gift books to get money to send out lecturers; the Western women sewed rag carpet and sold it to buy shoes for barefooted fugitives. Practically every article of clothing otherwise was spun and woven in their homes, and they moved 40,000 fugitives through Ohio between 1830 and 1860.[2]

The third important difference between the two regions was that the Liberty Party, organized in 1839, came out of the West. In the East, particularly in Boston, the women were closely associated with Garrison and his anti-Constitution, anti-government, anti-political action vagaries. Women in the West could not vote, but they did not subscribe to that sort of nonsense, and they moved naturally and easily from circulating petitions to supporting the Liberty Party along with their menfolk. Moreover, they later moved right on into the Civil War with their fairs and their sewing to provide vegetables and hospital supplies for the Western armies. In 1839 they were not identified with Garrisonian radicalism, and were maintaining a close association with the men in the movement, and this was regarded as both expedient and proper.

In the East, when the churchmen launched an attack against the Grimké sisters, the executive committee of the American Anti-Slavery Society took no part in the argument. Every one of these men was devoting his time, and money, and the best years of his life to emancipation of the slaves, and not one of them was willing to see any deviation from the main objective, or dilution of effort, or dissension within the ranks of antislavery men by the raising of extraneous issues regardless of merit. Stanton, Weld, and Whittier, all staunch believers in the right of a woman to speak in public, insisted that by speaking, as brilliantly as Angelina was speaking, a more effective argument was being presented than could be presented by any amount of disputation. They insisted, further, that to take notice of the Pastoral Letter and of the Clerical Appeal,[3] signed by only five men, was to magnify it out of all proportion to its real importance, and to attack the clergy generally and the churches because of it was only to borrow trouble.

Garrison, notoriously intolerant even toward his strongest friends, eager for notoriety and adulation, and, according to some observers, sustained by controversy, militantly defended the right of women to full equality. He attacked the clergy through his *Liberator,* and then he attacked the executive committee of the American Anti-Slavery Society because it did not attack the clergy through the *Emancipator.*[4] Lewis Tappan replied to Garrison, in a private letter, that an attack by five ministers was a minor matter, requiring no reply.[5] The executive committee pleaded with him to leave extraneous issues alone while the question of slavery was still not settled. Elizur Wright wrote to him: "Still do I beg of you, as a brother, to let other subjects alone till *slavery* is finished, *because* this is the work you have taken in hand, it is the most pressing, and needs your whole energy."[6] It was in vain. He continued to agitate for equality for women, sometimes to the total exclusion of slavery from his columns, and finally brought the question to a series of tests by pressing the issue in any convention with which he was connected. He secured the admission of women delegates to the Worcester Convention of 1837. He then split the Massachusetts Convention of 1839 with a resolution admitting women to equal privileges of voting and holding office.[7] Finally, he prepared to press the issue in the American Anti-Slavery Convention.

The conclusion, then, is inescapable that the woman question was a false issue. For any man to deny that slavery and subordination of women equally violated the basic natural rights of the

American Anti-Slavery almanacs were followed by Liberty almanacs after the American and Foreign Anti-Slavery Society was organized in 1840.

Harriet Beecher Stowe
The author of *Uncle Tom's Cabin* learned her lessons about slavery at the Lane Seminary debates, but she forgot some of them when she became a colonizationist. Whether she or the antislavery cause profited most from her writing is a moot question.

individual was to confess ignorance of fundamental principles. The great triumvirate of Birney-Stanton-Weld had too much intelligence and too much character to argue about it. The enormous contribution of women to the cause of emancipation and aid to fugitives and free Negroes was plain for all to see. No one could argue about that and no one did. Men and women worked closely together in the West. The men in control of the American Anti-Slavery Society in New York had no quarrel with any antislavery activity of women. Some New England clergy, but not all of them by any means, publicly denied the propriety of women speaking to mixed audiences. Some antislavery men denied the propriety of women serving on committees with men. The board in control—Birney-Stanton-Weld-Wright-Whittier—simply did not want to take cognizance of criticism by a portion of the clergy. They tried to prevent Garrison from doing so. One can almost hear them say "a curse on both your houses."[8]

All of this leads to a second inescapable conclusion. The question of the degree to which women were to share in the conduct of the antislavery societies would not of itself have split the organization, but Garrison's antigovernment, proslavery constitution, and disunion principles could and

did do so. His tying together of his support of various unpopular reforms with emancipation was distressing to many antislavery people. His brawling with the clergy alienated many orthodox Christians, especially when he became an anti-Sabbatarian.[9] His castigation of the martyred Lovejoy and his friends for defending his press against mob violence seemed to encourage disrespect for the law. Finally, he agreed with the slaveholders that the Constitution of the United States was a proslavery document—"A covenant with death and an agreement with hell"—a fixation which ultimately led him in 1854 to burn it publicly; he supported separation from the slave states with as much earnestness as Calhoun argued for secession from the Union, and he denounced everyone who voted, held office, or performed any of the other obligations of intelligent citizenship. This was anarchy and disunion.[10] More than that, it was abysmal ignorance or complete disregard of the fact that slavery was established and sustained by law, that legal protection of the civil rights of Negroes was desperately needed, and that the only actual gains against slavery had been by political action. In fact, when one considers Garrison's acceptance of the Constitution as a proslavery document, the Bible as sustaining slavery, and the wisdom of disunion, and his opposition to political action against slavery, one wonders why the slaveholders did not welcome him with open arms into their own camp.

It is noteworthy—in fact, it is imperative to a correct understanding of the schism—to remember that the slow-moving but ever-expanding antislavery movement, going back to Revolutionary days, had been *political*. The impulse it had received from Christian benevolence in the decade ending in 1839 was now exhausted. Hundreds of thousands now felt deeply the moral and political evil of slavery, but this great reservoir of moral power could be used against slavery only at the ballot box. Stanton and Birney, in charge of agents and public relations, had placed renewed emphasis upon political action after 1836. The entire petition campaign was designed to secure legislation by Congress and state legislatures. Agents gave less and less time to organizing societies and much more to influencing state and local elections. They questioned candidates in what was a fairly effective campaign of pressure politics. They sought repeal of the discriminatory black laws. They elected a few congressmen and a few governors. They expected every antislavery man to do his duty at the ballot box.

There was something tragic about Garrison's feeble effort to change the whole course and character of the antislavery movement. His heresies were not acceptable to the great body of antislavery men, and he lost ground constantly after 1840. He did create a great deal of confusion and bitterness, however, and he became president and remained president of the American Anti-Slavery Society for a quarter of a century. He accomplished this by the simple expedient of flooding the conventions, first of the Massachusetts Anti-Slavery Society, then of the American Anti-Slavery Society, with women delegates from Boston and Lynn.[11] It was a hollow victory. The American Anti-Slavery Society was henceforth but a shadow of what it had been.

Henry B. Stanton, the soul of honor, the keenest observer in antislavery circles, and a greater power in Massachusetts than Garrison himself, wrote to Birney privately about the Massachusetts meeting, where he and Phelps fought a losing battle against Garrison's nongovernment dogma: "A resolution, declaring it to be the duty of such abolitionists as can conscientiously exercise the elective franchise, to go to the polls and vote for the slave, was strenuously opposed by him, and voted down . . . the Society hauled down its flag and run [*sic*] up the crazy banner of the non-government heresy, and we had to rally around or be ostracized. The split is wide, and can never be closed up . . . Our cause in this State is ruined unless we can separate the A. S. Society from everything which does not belong to it . . . Don't be alarmed about Mass. Abolitionism. It is sound. The *pledged* [Garrisonian] delegates from Lynn and Boston carried through the report and voted down political action. But Lynn and Boston are not all the Commonwealth. If they were, the whole abolition fabric in the State would be in ruins, and we would be compelled to erect a new Society out of the fragments."[12] A new society was organized, under the leadership of Amos Phelps, and named the Massachusetts Abolition Society. It established a new paper, the *Massachusetts Abolitionist*, as its official organ, and brought Elizur Wright from New York as editor. The orthodox ministers most strongly opposed to Garrison were Amos Phelps, C. T. Torrey, Orange Scott, Elizur Wright, C. P. Grosvenor, and George Allen.[13]

Garrison then moved to gain control of the American Anti-Slavery Society by bringing to the 1840 convention in New York 464 delegates from Massachusetts.[14] That was almost half the total number of delegates present at the convention. Even so, he won by only a slender margin, on the more or less fictional issue of appointing women to committees.[15] Abby Kelly, who once went to jail for refusing to pay taxes because she could not vote and made a habit of walking into church services and starting to lecture on slavery while the minister was preaching, was appointed to the business committee. The men on the committee, including Lewis Tappan and Amos Phelps, promptly resigned. Later, Lucretia Mott, Lydia Maria Child, and Maria W. Chapman were elected to the executive committee. The old committee had transferred the *Emancipator* to the New York City Anti-Slavery Society some weeks before the convention. It had no other current publications, and no money in the treasury. Garrison went back to Boston with only a name.[16]

How could the men who had built an organization of such power and prestige have permitted it to fall under the control of Garrison and a few women from Boston? The answer is simple. The old organization no longer served their purpose. They had created a new one—the Liberty Party—

during the preceding year to take its place. They now walked out of the old edifice, some with reluctance, some with regrets; and knowing from experience the difficulty of reorientation, they organized a new society to do those things a political party could not do.

Three hundred members of the convention, representing eleven states, withdrew and formed the American and Foreign Anti-Slavery Society. Almost without exception, they were men who had formed the Liberty Party, and with few exceptions they included all of the stalwarts in the movement during the preceding decade. The officers were Arthur Tappan, president; James G. Birney and Henry B. Stanton, secretaries; and Lewis Tappan, treasurer. The executive committee was composed of the officers and William Jackson, John Greenleaf Whittier, Gerrit Smith, Judge William Jay, Joshua Leavitt, Thomas Morris, William H. Brisbane, and Edward Beecher.[17]

Henceforth, the Garrisonian influence dwindled day by day. His numerous vagaries so offended the moral and religious sensibilities of antislavery men that few remained loyal to him except the Hicksite Friends.[18] There were so many people opposed to slavery, and so many well-organized local societies, that there was no longer need of proselyting for converts. The problem was now quite different, and far from easy solution: marshaling the antislavery hosts for political, legal, and judicial assault upon slavery. This was begun by the Liberty Party and the American and Foreign Anti-Slavery Society. Garrison raged against both, and it is a moot question whether his opposition was a help or a hindrance to the cause. Meanwhile, however, there was the World Anti-Slavery Convention in London, England. Friends of the slave had been summoned from every nation to meet there in June 1840. This, as events occurred, was immediately following the rupture in the American Anti-Slavery Society.

Acting upon the invitation from the British, the new (Garrisonian) Anti-Slavery Society appointed Lucretia Mott as one of its delegates. The Massachusetts Anti-Slavery Society, also Garrisonian, appointed Harriet Martineau, Maria W. Chapman, Lydia Maria Child, Abby Kelly, and Emily Winslow. The Pennsylvania Anti-Slavery Society, Eastern Branch, at Philadelphia, decided to send Mary Green, Sarah Pugh, Abby Kimber, and Elizabeth Neal. When word reached the British and Foreign Anti-Slavery Society that women delegates were likely to be sent, that society issued a circular requesting the "names of the *gentlemen*" who were to represent the American societies. This was followed by a personal protest from Joseph Sturge, who feared the disruption of the London Convention.[19] The Philadelphia executive committee revoked its commission to women delegates on receipt of Sturge's letter, but women delegates from the societies dominated by Garrison went to London. The question of admitting them immediately arose, since the executive committee of the British and Foreign Anti-Slavery Society had not placed their names on the membership list. Wendell Phillips moved that a membership committee be appointed with instructions "to include all names of all persons bearing credentials from any anti-slavery society." The ensuing debate was a repetition of what had been said in the American Anti-Slavery Society, but the motion was overwhelmingly defeated. Garrison, who arrived late, refused to take his seat in the convention; but, according to Elizabeth Cady Stanton, took advantage of a social gathering to promote his various interests. "This," said she, "was his first appearance and he was received with many cheers, but oh! how soon by his want of judgment did he change the current of feeling in his audience. A general look of disappointment was visible among the English ere he had spoken long."[20] This was the last conflict on the woman question, and it marks the beginning of Garrison's decline.

The preamble of the constitution of the American and Foreign Anti-Slavery Society, after the manner of the old Union Humane Society of Ohio, organized by Benjamin Lundy in 1815, began by quoting the immortal lines from the Declaration of Independence asserting the inalienable rights of man, and the Biblical admonition to love one's neighbors as oneself. It spoke of the three million people held in slavery, and the widespread practice of buying and selling human beings contrary to the right of every person, irrespective of color, to equality and impartial justice in the land of his birth and residence. It denounced as sinful both race prejudice and colonization.

The purpose of the society was to abolish slavery, and to promote security, protection, and improvement of free Negroes. Slavery was to be abolished by moral, religious, and pacific means, but every person enjoying the franchise was enjoined to vote against slaveholders and for legislation to abolish slavery, to extend the franchise to free Negroes, and to restrain lawless invasions of personal and property rights. The society would circulate literature, correspond with antislavery men throughout the world, encourage the use of free produce, and encourage clerical support of antislavery measures.

The society was controlled, financed, and directed largely by Lewis Tappan. It was closely allied with the British and Foreign Anti-Slavery Society in matters relating to fugitives in Canada, the coastal slave trade, and foreign missions. The British Society sometimes gave financial aid to the American Society, but Tappan was opposed to the solicitation of funds abroad. He urged the British to boycott cotton produced by slave labor, to aid fugitives in Canada, to refuse fellowship with slaveholders, and to continue efforts for complete emancipation, civil rights, and religious freedom jointly throughout the world. The two societies jointly promoted world antislavery conventions, lecturers, and publications.

The society appointed a committee to raise funds for missionary work, then organized the American Missionary Society in September 1846, by bringing together the Amistad Commission, the Union Missionary Society, the Western Evangelical Missionary Society, and the Commission for the West Indian Missionaries. The importance of the society's missionary work lay in its bitter opposition to appointment of missionaries who were slaveholders and the use for missionary activity of contributions from churches in the slave states.[21]

Garrison had broken completely with the churches, and antislavery preachers found it extremely difficult to encourage the work of the Liberty Party. The American and Foreign Anti-Slavery Society criticized the churches, severely at times, but there was no open break with them and relationships remained fairly peaceful if not always cordial. In the beginning the society merely urged ecclesiastical bodies to support antislavery reforms and to provide for the religious instruction of Negroes. Later, it sought greater uniformity in refusing communion to slaveholders, and in not permitting ministers from churches of the slave states to preach. Finally, it supported a movement for complete independence of Northern churches from those of the slave states. Slavery was held to be utterly incompatible with the Christian faith. Slaves must be made men before they could be made Christians.[22]

The society made no radical departure from the basic principles of the former American Anti-Slavery Society, maintaining firm opposition to colonization, to compensated emancipation, and to all the Garrisonian heresies pertaining to the Constitution and the Union. It was closely allied to the Liberty Party, and its activities were largely concerned with legislation, foreign policy, and court cases. Its work centered in Washington, D. C., through the organized efforts of antislavery members of Congress and through the *National Era,* established by the society and edited by Gamaliel Bailey.

Publications of the society were very irregular. The official organ was the *American and Foreign Anti-Slavery Reporter.* The *Liberty Almanac* was published by the society to promote the Liberty Party. It contained party platforms and election statistics not ordinarily available elsewhere. In some ways, the general publications resembled those of the old Tract Society. There were several series of Liberty Tracts and Anti-Slavery tracts.[23] There was a children's series and a Sabbath school series, and for adults a pamphlet series and a historical series. There were annual reports written by Lewis Tappan. There were special publications, some of which were widely distributed on a world-wide basis. Four of these were addressed to the Christians of the United States, to the Friends of Liberty, to the inhabitants of New Mexico and California, and to the nonslaveholders of the South.

The last of these, written by Lewis Tappan, appears in retrospect to have been the most important of all. It was the most important because it was addressed to nonslaveholding Southerners, and slaveholders feared, above everything else in the world, introduction of controversy into the slave states. They feared nonslaveholders far more than they feared slaves. In the end, they feared a Republican administration at Washington would build up its party at the South. This pamphlet was not so well written as many others—Weld's *American Slavery As It Is,* for example—nor so heavily documented, but it was designed to convince nonslaveholding white men in the South that slavery was injuring them and that they had the political power to do something about it if they wished. The key to the entire argument was the statement: "When an infant will bring one hundred, and a man from four hundred to a thousand dollars in the market, slaves are not commodities to be found in the cabins of the poor."[24]

Slaveholders, explained Tappan, were largely a landed aristocracy, always seeking to identify their own interests with the public welfare. They were but a small portion of the people, yet they talked as if their interests were those of the entire population. They did this to conceal their numerical inferiority. They talked about slavery being the institution of the South; actually it was the institution of only a small portion of the people of the South. They magnified its importance constantly. Governor George McDuffie called it the cornerstone of our republican institutions, and a committee of the South Carolina legislature (1842) spoke of it "as an ancient-domestic institution cherished in the hearts of the people at the South, the eradication of which would demolish our whole system of policy, domestic, social, and political."[25]

Slavery had retarded the South. In population, the free states had increased 38 per cent between 1830 and 1840, the slave states 23 per cent, and the difference was due to the fact that slavery drove enterprising white men out and kept emigrants from the free states and from Europe from coming. Kentucky, almost equal to, in fact a little larger than, Ohio, and separated from it only by a river, had 180,612 people to Ohio's 45,000 in 1800, but in 1840 Kentucky had only 597,000 (14.2 to the square mile) to Ohio's 1,519,000 (38.8 to the square mile). The Louisville *Journal* said of this: "The most potent cause of the more rapid advancement of Cincinnati than Louisville is the absence of slavery." Cassius M. Clay had said in the Kentucky legislature: "The world is teeming with improved machinery, the combined development of science and art. To us it is all lost; we are comparatively living in centuries that are gone; we cannot make it, we cannot use it when made." Thomas F. Marshall of Kentucky, comparing the population of Virginia and New York (1840) to the great advantage of the latter, said: "There is but one explanation of the facts I have shown. The clog that has stayed the march of her [Virginia] people, the incubus that has weighed down her enterprise, strangled her commerce, kept sealed her exhaustless fountains of mineral wealth, and paralyzed her arts, manufactures, and improvement, is Negro slavery." Other comparisons equally favorable to the free states were made between Massachusetts and Maryland, Michigan and Arkansas, and Alabama and Illinois.[26]

In the matter of education, Tappan pointed out, comparisons were even more favorable to the North. Education emancipates the poor man, elevates the masses, diminishes the influence and power of wealth, birth, and position. The South had never provided an education for its poor sons, being dominated by the spirit of Governor Berkley of Virginia, who said in 1671: "I thank God that there are no free schools nor printing presses, and I hope we shall not have them these hundred years." There were no free public schools in the South; they were everywhere in the free states. The census of 1840 gave the statistics of persons over twenty years of age who were not able to read and write. The lowest percentage was in Connecticut where there was one illiterate to every 568 persons. In all of the New England states the highest percentage was 1 to 108, in Maine. It was 1 to 97 in Michigan, and only 1 to 56 in New York with all its foreign-born. It was 1 to 43 in Ohio. The best of the slave states was Louisiana with 1 to 38½. Georgia had 1 to 13; and North Carolina 1 to 7. Only two of the free states were higher than the best of the slave states, Indiana having 1 to 18 and Illinois 1 to 17. In the public schools of Ohio alone there were 51,812 students, and in all of the slave states combined only 35,580. Governor James Clark of Kentucky had said in 1837 that one-third of all adults in the state could not write their names, and 1,047 men of the 4,614 applying for marriage licenses in Virginia in 1837 could not write.[27]

The South had little manufacturing, said Tappan, to provide the comforts of life or regular and profitable employment. Slavery had attached a stigma to honest toil. Production of cotton was the great industry, and it was produced by slave labor, offering little opportunity for employment to free white men. Slaveholders invested in land and slaves and in every possible way discouraged industrial development. They had contempt for the man who worked; they feared the working man; they feared a lessening of their own authority and prestige; they constantly tried to prove the superiority of slave labor to free labor. Tappan presented quotation after quotation from Southern men in public life and from Southern newspapers showing their contempt for men who worked with their hands, their opposition to permitting such persons to participate in public affairs, their fear of universal manhood suffrage unless all manual labor were performed by slaves, their belief that education unfitted the laborer for his station in life, and that the man who had to work with his hands had no time for improvement of his mind.[28]

In the field of religion and morality, Tappan said most of the clergy were slaveholders, personally interested in the continuance of slavery and ever ready to defend it by the Scriptures. This was a peculiarly American feature of the institution, the preachers of the West Indies never having defended it as a Christian institution. He quoted John Quincy Adams to the effect that the spirit of slavery "has crept into the philosophical chairs of the schools. Its cloven hoof has ascended the pulpits of the churches—Professors of Colleges teach it as a lesson of morals—writers of the Gospel seek and profess to find sanction for it in the word of God."[29]

The slave system had lowered the standard of morality to the point where life was cheap. Men did not hesitate to kill at the slightest provocation. In Congress slaveholders had threatened antislavery members with death repeatedly. Tappan cited case after case of this sort. Their profane, vulgar, threatening language in Congress was applauded by their constituents. Yet, there were men in the South who deplored the low state of morality. The governor of Kentucky said to the legislature in 1837: "We long to see the day when the law will assert its majesty and stop the wanton destruction of life which almost daily occurs within the jurisdiction of this commonwealth. Men slaughter each other with almost perfect impunity."

The Charleston *Courier* (1835) threatened all antislavery men with hanging and burning, the Augusta *Chronicle* with instant death, the New Orleans *True American* with burning at the stake. The Columbus, South Carolina, *Telescope* said "that the question of slavery is not and shall not be open to discussion," and anyone attempting to lecture on the evils of slavery should have "his tongue cut out and cast upon the dunghill." Slaveholders were arrogating to themselves the authority to speak in this manner as an expression of public sentiment. They were sitting in judgment upon men without legal authority to do so. They burned a Negro at Tuscaloosa, June 20, 1827, another at St. Louis, April 28, 1836, another at Hot Springs, Arkansas, October 29, 1836, and still another at Natchez, June 16, 1842. The Georgia legislature offered $5,000 for William Lloyd Garrison. The *Federal Union*, a newspaper at Milledgeville, February 1, 1836, carried an offer of $10,000 for the kidnapping of Amos A. Phelps. A committee of vigilance in the Parish of East Feliciana offered, in the Louisiana *Journal*, October 15, 1835, $50,000 for Arthur Tappan; the citizens of Mount Meigs, Alabama, August 3, 1836, offered $50,000 for Arthur Tappan or LeRoy Sunderland.[30]

Worst of all, the press was silenced on the subject of slavery. Said Tappan: "Every measure of policy may be advocated, except that of free labor; every question of right may be examined, except that of a man to himself; every dogma in theology may be propagated, except that of the sinfulness of the slave code. The very instant the press ventures beyond the prescribed limits, the constitutional barriers erected for its protection sink into the dust, and a censorship, the more stern and vindictive from being illegal, crushes it into submission."[31]

THE LIBERTY PARTY

Chapter 35

It is a singular fact that the Declaration of Sentiments of the American Anti-Slavery Society ended with the statement: "We also maintain that there are, at the present time, the highest obligations resting upon the people of the free states, to remove slavery by moral and political action." The meaning of that clause is to be found, not in the many bitter arguments of later days, but in the history of the movement before the society was organized and its Declaration of Sentiments was written.

Slavery had been abolished in eight states by constitutional provisions or by acts of state legislatures. No one denied that it could be abolished in the remaining states in the same way, though most Southerners held that it could be done only by constitutional conventions and not by legislatures.

Slavery had been abolished in the Northwest Territory and in that part of the Louisiana territory north of 36° 30′. It had been allowed to survive in the Florida Purchase and in the Territory of Arkansas, and Louisiana, Arkansas, and Missouri had been admitted as slave states by free action of Congress. There was argument on three main questions in this field of political action: Could Congress exclude slavery from the territories? It had done so. Could Congress exclude slave states from the Union? It had not done so. Could Congress bind states to remain free as a condition of admission? It had done so, but slaveholders denied the restraints were binding. These questions had to be decided by congressional action—perhaps by judicial interpretation. They had

been subjects of political agitation and provided a continuing field for political action.

The Constitution gave Congress power to abolish the foreign slave trade. It had done so, but insufficient legislation or lax law enforcement had permitted importations in violation of the law. The Constitution gave Congress exclusive control over interstate commerce, and in all probability interstate commerce embraced the commercial slave trade if not migrations. The latter seemed to have been placed under Congressional control by the clause pertaining to the foreign slave trade. This was a second broad field for Congressional legislation, though no action had been taken relative to the interstate trade.

The Constitution denied freedom to slaves by virtue of the laws of states to which they might escape. The provision was not a clear grant of power to Congress, and the law which the Congress had enacted nearly a half century before seemed to violate due process and actually did subject every free person of color to the danger of being kidnapped and sold into slavery. Political action in this field involved legislatures, Congress, and the courts because of state legislation designed to supplement the deficiencies of the federal law and to protect the civil rights of the individuals.

The Constitution gave to Congress exclusive control over the District of Columbia. Slavery and the slave trade were allowed to continue there by inaction of Congress. Only Calhoun extremists denied the power of Congress to abolish both, though many Southerners denied the expediency of doing so. Congress had refused to allow the reading, printing, or discussion of petitions or memorials relating to slavery, in violation of all precedent, probably in disregard of basic constitutional principles. Hundreds of thousands of antislavery men and women had been asked to sign memorials to Congress concerning these matters; most of them had done so in the most intense and concerted political activity of the decade.

The whole question of attributes, privileges, and immunities of citizens of the United States was confused and clearly in need of legislation or judicial determination or both. Congress had covered the subject rather thoroughly in the Missouri debates, without arriving at any clear definition of citizenship, or apparently any agreement as to the citizenship status of free Negroes. This was destined to be a subject of bitter debate in the ensuing decade. Slavery also was inextricably tied into the conduct of foreign affairs and vitally affected our relations with Great Britain, Spain, and Mexico.

The field of political action, as it existed, was still greater. "Political action," said John Pierpont, "in the broad sense already assigned to that phrase, embraces all that we do in reference to human laws: not only the enacting, the judicial declaring or exposition, and the executive administration or application and enforcing of laws; but also all steps or measures that, as Citizens, we adopt, either independently or in association with those whose sympathies and preferences are the same as our own, with a view to seeing that proper men are chosen to enact, declare, or administer them; nor yet this only, but it also includes all that we will ourselves do, as subjects upon whom those laws are to act; as whether we will or will not obey them; whether we will or will not, if we can change them; or, if this cannot be done, whether we will or will not break or even resist them."[1]

Many a sharp encounter between the antislavery forces and proslavery forces had taken place in state legislatures, Congress, state conventions, the Federal Convention of 1787 and the ratifying conventions, state and federal courts, party caucuses, party conventions, and in political campaigns. The advantage in the over-all contest had been with the antislavery forces, but they had not been strong enough to win a clear-cut victory in the Missouri contest. Now, in 1840, they were strong enough to do a good many things if they could consolidate their potential political power. Those many things in the field of political action embraced more than legislation *for this was revolution again in its finest form.* It was an appeal to the principles of the higher law. "Whenever there is collision between the municipal and moral law, the moral law is paramount," said Pierpont.[2]

The question was not one of political action but of the best line of procedure in the field of political action. Antislavery men had hoped to achieve their objective of complete emancipation by persuading slaveholders to manumit their slaves or Southern states to emancipate them; in short, to achieve by a vigorous campaign of enlightened discussion a resurgence of the revolutionary trend toward complete emancipation. They had been excluded from the South by mob violence and criminal law. Their publications had been excluded from the South by intimidation of the Post Office Department into compliance with local police regulations. Their petitions to Congress had been rejected, and all discussion of the subject in Congress had been interdicted. The Presbyterian, Baptist, and Methodist churches—perhaps we should say institutionalized religion—had not been very cordial. The same was true of the Whig and Democratic parties. All were national institutions in which slaveholders wielded power; in the case of parties, power out of all proportion to their numbers. It was clear by 1839 that pressure within these organizations by antislavery men would split them along sectional lines. No organization to which slaveholders belonged could ever be used to combat slavery.

Antislavery men, for the most part, were Whigs, and Whigs, in Jackson's day, did not vote the Democratic ticket however great the provocation. Pressure politics, therefore, based upon questioning of candidates, had failed.[3] The New Hampshire Anti-Slavery Convention of 1838 had resolved "that election to political office confers peculiar power to oppose or favor the abolition of slavery in the country, and . . . all abolitionists having the right of suffrage, have an important political duty to perform," and "that no man can receive the vote of a consistent abolitionist, unless his character as well as his professions gives assurance of his acting in favor of the abolition of slavery."[4] There were hundreds of such resolutions, and some antislavery men were elected, but only to be confronted by party discipline and the demand for party regularity.

There were two cases which illustrate the situation. William L. Marcy, Democrat, was governor of New York. He had sought, unsuccessfully, penal laws against antislavery activities. William H. Seward, Whig, was his opponent in the gubernatorial election. These men were asked three questions by Gerrit Smith and William Jay on instructions from the state antislavery society: Whether they favored trial by jury for alleged fugitives, removal of special qualifications for Negro voters, and repeal of the nine-months law which permitted slaves to be brought into the state for that period of time. Marcy was discourteous, almost abusive in his reply. There were not many antislavery men in his party. Seward was adroit. Most antislavery men were Whigs, though not all Whigs were antislavery men. Seward, however, was far from ready to take a position independent of his party, saying: "You must be aware, gentlemen, that the Convention which has designated me as a representative of the Whig party in this state, in the approaching election, has done so without any reference to the subjects indicated in your inquiries, and that those subjects enter not at all into the political creed of that large body of freemen, whose candidate I have become. Persons selected as the representatives of political principles, can have no right to compromise their constituents by the expression of opinions on other subjects than those in reference to which the selections were made."[5] A strong effort was then made to persuade antislavery men to withhold their votes from both Marcy and Seward, but without success, and Seward was elected. Later, when a new antislavery political party approached its ultimate goal of controlling the federal government, Seward had so far given lip service to its principles as to be considered a leading candidate for its presidential nomination and was regarded by the Southerners as the perfect embodiment of antislavery philosophy.

The second case was that of Thomas Morris, Democrat, of Ohio. Morris had studied law at night while making a living as a frontier brickmaker for a family of eleven children. He had served fifteen terms in the state legislature between 1806 and 1833 and was elected to the United States Senate by the legislature in 1832. Morris was a strong antislavery man, the only one in the Senate dur-

ing the petition struggle. He introduced petitions for the abolition of slavery in the District of Columbia, and he fought bitterly against Calhoun's Resolutions of 1837. This was political suicide for a Democrat, because the slaveholders were in control of the party. Morris was not re-elected to the Senate in 1838. On February 9, 1839, he delivered a masterful defense of the civil rights of antislavery men in debate with Henry Clay and returned to Ohio, as he said, to aid in "rekindling the beacon fires of liberty on every hill" in his state.[6] A party which could make a trained seal out of William L. Marcy and remove from the Senate a truly great public servant like Morris, all at the behest of slaveholders, was not likely to incorporate antislavery principles into its platform.

One might argue that what was needed was such a refreshment of antislavery fervor as would constrain every man in public life to act against slavery regardless of party affiliations. But the deference of Seward to political expediency, and the proscription of Morris, clearly indicated the overwhelming odds against success. Organized political action through the agency of a new party seemed to be the only solution. It seemed to be, also, the only possible answer to Garrison's antigovernment position. Theodore Weld remained aloof for a little while, but not for long. Julius LeMoyne was saddened by the turn of events. Arthur Tappan and Lewis Tappan worked through the American and Foreign Anti-Slavery Society. The other great leaders of the preceding ten years, and some powerful younger men, set themselves to the task with tenfold more promise of success than had favored the little group of antislavery apostles in 1829.

The executive committee of the American Anti-Slavery Society in May, 1839, said: "The Committee would solemnly inquire, whether it is not time for every man who regards the eternal laws of right and wrong, which God has imposed upon the moral universe, to cast off the cords which slavery has thrown around us all, whether they be political or ecclesiastical." Stanton discussed before the convention the scope of legislation needed in the several states, with emphasis upon repeal of the discriminatory laws known as "black laws," freedom for all slaves brought into free states, and jury trial for all alleged fugitives, and then said that if the full weight of Northern political power, properly used, could not put an end to slavery: "We will alter the Constitution and

Myron and Sallie Holley
Distinguished father and daughter.

bring slavery in the States within the range of federal legislation, and then annihilate it at one blow." It was then agreed to hold a convention at Albany in July to discuss the principles "which relate to the proper exercise of the right of suffrage by citizens of the free states."

This action by the 1839 convention was clearly indicative of a trend toward intensified political action. It left unanswered two significant questions: Should an independent political party be organized? and What were the limits of the Constitutional power of Congress over slavery? Alvan Stewart of Utica, New York, emerged as a national figure at this point. He had called the convention which organized the New York State Anti-Slavery Society at Utica, August 21, 1835, and he served as president of that society for many years. He was an able speaker, and an extremely capable lawyer.[7] He was the first man to advocate publicly a new political party. He was the first man to argue that the federal government had power under the Constitution to abolish slavery in the slave states. He said at the Pennsylvania Hall

dedication: "To tolerate slavery a single year in one of these states, after this Declaration of Independence, was a base hypocrisy, a violation of our engagements to mankind, and to God. They [those who signed] said: 'And for the support of this Declaration, with a firm reliance on the protection of Divine Providence, we mutually pledge to each other our lives, our fortunes, and our sacred honor.' This awful and solemn *promise* made in behalf of liberty, to all persons in this land, in the presence of mankind and the great Jehovah, in that awful moment of a nation's agony and peril, stands *unredeemed, uncancelled,* and *unsatisfied;* sixty-one years and three hundred and fifteen days have gone to join the years and days beyond the flood; every year, every month, yea, every day and hour, have gone to the Judge of all the earth, clamoring long and loud, for the execution of this vow."[8]

The question of the power of the federal government with regard to slavery had brought Alvan Stewart and William Jay into sharp debate as early as the 1838 Convention of the American

Anti-Slavery Society. The great weakness of the constitution of the society finally had caused trouble: "We fully and unanimously recognize the sovereignty of each State, to legislate exclusively on the subject of slavery which is tolerated within its limits; we consider that Congress, under the present national compact, has no right to interfere with any of the slave States in relation to this momentous subject." This deference to state rights on the slavery question assumed more and more importance as antislavery men were excluded from the South, the controversy became bitter in Congress, and Calhoun fashioned his decentralization philosophy for the protection of slavery. Alvan Stewart went into the 1838 Convention of the American Anti-Slavery Society determined to get the above clause stricken from the constitution. He had majority support but failed of the two-thirds majority required, due to the opposition of Judge William Jay.[9] Jay then withdrew from the society because of its advanced position, but he was far more disturbed by Garrison's no-human-government vagaries than by Stewart's consolidation doctrines.[10] He joined the American and Foreign Anti-Slavery Society, when it was formed, and contributed to the *Reporter*. He also continued to work independently for the cause. He was very reluctant to join the Liberty Party, but did so after a time and was the candidate of the party for the governorship of New York state.

Stewart's constitutional theory deserves far more attention than historians have given it, not only because his power and influence were great among antislavery men, but in relation to developing ideas of constitutional guarantees. In general, he believed, as Franklin had believed, that Congress should go to the very verge of its legislative powers, war powers, and treaty-making powers to put slavery in course of extinction. Beyond that, he held three theories: First, that "The Constitution of the United States is an Anti-Slavery document, in its general spirit and tendencies; and under other auspices and circumstances would have been called a great act of universal emancipation, and have set every slave free in the land, being paramount law, without doing the thousandth part of violence in construction which has been done by a slaveholding interpretation."[11] This was exactly what Birney and others had said in the higher law doctrine: the same generation of men who had fought the Revolution and had given the Declaration of Independence to the

world could not possibly have written a *proslavery* constitution so utterly at variance with the principles of the Declaration, as was claimed by the slave power.

Second, slavery violated Article IV, Section 4, of the Constitution, which said "The United States shall guarantee to every State in this Union a Republican Form of Government." That, said Stewart, "is a standing covenant against slavery . . . for the very idea of a republican form of government holds all persons under it equal in the eyes of the law."[12] Speaking before the Supreme Court of the State of New Jersey, in 1845, he said: "The form of a State government may be republican in its constitution, but legislation may spring up in that State, by which one half of the people may assume to own the other half, in direct hostility to a republican form of government, and the United States is then bound, by some exercise of sovereign power, to restore to the people . . . a republican form of government, either by legislation in Congress or by the exercise of judicial power through the Federal or State judiciaries . . . Give me a republican form of government in the Constitution and the legislation of a State, and I defy any man to hold a human being in that State as a slave, according to the law of that country, until the meaning of language is revolutionized."[13] All state laws establishing or sustaining slavery, therefore, according to Stewart were unconstitutional from the adoption of the constitution.

Third, said Stewart: "The word person, in the Constitution of the United States, means a human being possessed of the natural rights of life, liberty, and the pursuit of happiness. The word person means a human being in the fullness of his natural rights, and nothing more . . . a Constitution springs from our weakness and need of protection, and is a covenant of the whole people with each person, and of each person with the whole people, for the protection of our natural rights, of life, liberty, and the pursuit of happiness."[14] If, then, argued Stewart, the Constitution of the United States stripped one-sixth of all the people of their natural rights, and the people had so understood it, not a single state north of Delaware would have considered seriously its adoption. Slavery clearly violated the provision that no person should be deprived of life, liberty, or property without due process of law. Slaves, then, were free by virtue of the original Declaration of Independence, by the constitutional guarantee of a republican form of government to each state, and by the due process clause of the Fifth Amendment.[15] Birney, Jay, and others felt that Stewart's position was too far advanced, but none among them would have argued with Stanton about ultimate resort to constitutional amendment if existing powers of the general government were found to be inadequate for the object in view.

The vast majority of antislavery men were Whigs. They had long maintained a working coalition with the Southern Whigs, but they did not have a national party in the true sense of the word. The party was less able to discipline its members than was the Democratic party; therefore, it was more vulnerable to internal dissension and more likely to fall apart. Its Northern membership was strongly antislavery because the movement was an intellectual and religious crusade for social reform, and the professional classes, business men, and large property owners were Whigs. The inevitable tendency of these men, also, was toward an increase in the powers of the federal government. By 1840 there were four strong antislavery Whigs in Congress: John Quincy Adams of Massachusetts, William Slade of Vermont, Seth M. Gates of Western New York, and Joshua R. Giddings of Ohio. There were no antislavery Whigs in the Senate, and no antislavery men of either party in the Senate after Morris was purged by the Democrats. Whig party leaders were well aware of the danger which threatened their party both from insurgency and from organization of a new antislavery party which would draw its membership from their own adherents. It was this which inspired Henry Clay's speech in the Senate in February 1839, to which the purged Morris had made his eloquent response. Morris was destined to be the candidate of the Liberty Party for the vice-presidency.

Grass roots support for a new political party was strong in upstate New York, where Charles Grandison Finney had begun his great religious revival. Weld had come from this area and had spent much of his time and energy as a lecturer there. Beriah Green had been for years at Oneida. It was the country of Alvan Stewart and Myron Holley, of Gerrit Smith and William Goodell. Alvan Stewart had been the most consistent and powerful force in the New York State Anti-Slavery Society from the beginning. Myron Holley had long been prominent in state politics. Elizur Wright said the basis of Holley's religion was the

Declaration of Independence rather than the Bible. He had not been thoroughly aroused until Clay made his speech against political activities of antislavery men. Then, on July 4, 1839, he lashed out at the subserviency to the slave power of both the old line parties. During the next few months he worked for independent nominations by antislavery men through the columns of his newspaper, the Rochester *Freeman,* and in the many county antislavery conventions.[16]

The convention called by the American Anti-Slavery Society to meet at Albany, July 31, 1839, reaffirmed the duty of all antislavery men to vote, and to vote only for men who favored emancipation of the slaves. This was a signal defeat for Garrison, who mistook the abuses and perversions of government for government itself. He gained control of the American Anti-Slavery Society in 1840, as we have seen, but nine-tenths of all antislavery men rejected and ignored his plea to refrain from voting even when they retained a nominal membership in the society.

The Albany convention did not endorse independent nominations or organization of a new party, but it stated the need for organized political action in strong terms. "The Congress of the United States," it said, "to whose legislation the whole nation is subject, is composed, to a great and controlling extent, of the representatives of a people who are not themselves free; of legislators who neither enjoy nor permit liberty at home, who neither embrace nor understand the principles of liberty and inalienable rights, as laid down in the Declaration of Independence, and who cannot be supposed to seek or desire more liberty for the people of the North than is enjoyed by their own constituents at the South."[17]

The slave power was waging a determined war on the liberties of the people in the free states, embracing an expressed desire by men like Calhoun and McDuffie, to enslave white laborers, rewards for abduction of Northern citizens, demands for the suppression of antislavery societies, pillaging of the mails, and stifling of debate in Congress. In foreign affairs there were appointments of slaveholders to important diplomatic posts, refusal to recognize Haiti, plots against Cuba, and failure to suppress the African slave trade. "Slavery cannot maintain itself in a free country," said the convention, "except by making continual encroachments on liberty. There can be no compromise. There is no standing still, no middle way or middle ground. No man can be considered an efficient opponent of the political ascendancy of the Slave Power, who is not willing to engage in direct, open and determined efforts for the abolition of slavery itself . . . Shorn of political power, slavery would fall by its own weight, and die of its own imbecility. And the political power of slavery is only to be met by political action on the part of the true friends of liberty."[18]

A convention was then held at Cleveland, October 23, 1839. Myron Holley was there, served as temporary chairman, and worked diligently for organization of a new party. Stanton came from Massachusetts, still opposed to precipitate action despite Elizur Wright's plea for organization. Gamaliel Bailey, editor of the *Philanthropist,* was there, and he, too, was opposed to independent nominations, even more strongly than Stanton. The convention refused to endorse Holley's resolutions for nominations or for a new party, and still another convention was called, this time for November 13, at Warsaw, New York. This convention, attended by more than five hundred prominent antislavery men, did not formally organize a party, but it did make nominations: James G. Birney for president and Francis J. LeMoyne for vice-president. Myron Holley was given the responsibility of communicating with the nominees.

Shortly after the nominations at Warsaw, Gamaliel Bailey wrote to Birney: "I see you are divided among yourselves on the subject of separate political organization. What pity the notion was ever talked about. I go, as you know, tooth and nail against it. If ever we are to get along, as an association, harmoniously together, we must abstain from new projects—so it seems to me. I can not but think, that the majority of Abolitionists are opposed to the experiment. Why then should its friends so pertinaciously insist on it?"[19] F. Julius LeMoyne wrote to Birney in much the same tone. He did not rule out the need for independent nominations at some later date, but insisted the action at Warsaw was inexpedient and premature and refused to permit his name to be used. His reasons for wanting further discussion and deliberation were: that most antislavery men were presently opposed to direct action and it would, therefore, increase the divisions and distractions caused by such issues as equality of women, peace, and no human government; that the number of men who would support immedi-

ate action was too small to give it respectability; and that changing the character of the movement from religious to political would introduce all the evils inseparable from political parties into the movement.[20]

Birney then wrote to the Holley committee declining the nomination for the presidency. The action at Warsaw, he explained, had not united antislavery men as he had hoped it would. There still was too much difference of opinion among them, as revealed by the vigorous discussion in the antislavery press.[21] He followed this letter with a more informal one in which he said that far too many prominent men thought better nominations could have been made.[22] Holley agreed that someone else must be found as a vice-presidential candidate, but insisted that the movement for independent political action must go forward and that Birney's nomination must be reaffirmed.[23] He believed that the lack of enthusiasm for the new movement was evidence of far greater support of Garrison's no-human-government heresy than was thought.

In retrospect, there is something refreshing about Holley's objectivity. The Warsaw convention had stated cogently and emphatically that, since slavery was the creature of statute law, it could be abolished only by legislative action, and since it was just as criminal to vote at the ballot box for a candidate who was not opposed to slavery as for that candidate to vote for slavery and against freedom in an assembly, it was the Christian duty of all free men to organize and join in support of an antislavery political party.[24] Whether the Whigs or Democrats would offer candidates in 1840 that antislavery men could conscientiously support, whether issues other than slavery would hold men in line on election day, whether Garrison's opposition to all human government would force antislavery men to reorganize at the 1840 convention were among the questions which would soon be answered.

Birney, writing to Amos Phelps in February, said: "But if it should turn out, that the control of the Society should pass into the hands of the non-resistants [Garrisonians], it will at once fix its doom. It will be the dissolution of the whole concern. The men who are to carry this cause will never unite with them. In that event—which, by the by, I do not now much fear—a new organization will, of course, be necessary, and it can at once be entered on."[25] Stanton reported from Massachusetts in March that the drive for independent political action was strengthening Garrison because practically all antislavery men in that state were Whigs and nineteen-twentieths were opposed to independent nominations. "The Whig Abolitionists," he said, "will go for Harrison despite conscience, consistency, denunciation, and rebuke . . . The Whigs now think there is a good prospect of success. They would wade to their armpits in molten lava to drive Van Buren from power . . . Our strongest abolition friends swear they will take the liberty to make one more effort to displace Van Buren, and whatever is the result they will then go with us. *They speak truly.*"[26] Bailey, writing from Cincinnati, argued strongly that it was better to support Harrison than to make independent nominations, and argued that Thomas Corwin received the Whig nomination for governor because he would get the votes of antislavery men.[27] Both Stanton and Bailey undoubtedly were correct. The frenzy of the 1840 campaign is traditional in American history, especially among the Whigs, and there can be no doubt about antislavery influence in Whig nominations. In the executive committee of the American Anti-Slavery Society, Tappan was opposed to political action, Birney and Stanton wanted to delay nominations, Leavitt and Wright were for immediate action.

The antislavery men of western New York settled the whole matter by calling another convention in Arcade, in Genesee County, New York, January 28–29, 1840. Myron Holley, William L. Chaplin, and Gerrit Smith were now the leaders in the movement. There were between six and seven hundred men from western New York and adjacent Pennsylvania at the convention. Many had been opposed to a political party, and many more to independent nominations until after the 1840 elections. Holley said that he had never seen so many men change their minds so rapidly. In any case the convention unanimously approved both a party and nominations of candidates for office, condemned both Harrison and Van Buren as unacceptable, and severely criticized ministers who refused to pray and preach against slavery. The convention also issued a call for another meeting at Albany on April 1. One week after the Arcade convention, William Goodell published in the *Friend of Man* a letter from Gerrit Smith in

which he spoke of the party, still in its formative stages, as the Liberty Party.[28]

The Albany meeting was known as the National Convention of Friends of Immediate Emancipation. It convened in spite of almost impassable roads, with 121 delegates present, mostly from New York. The leaders and officers of the convention were Alvan Stewart, Benjamin Shaw of Vermont, Ichabod Codding of Maine, Charles T. Torrey of Massachusetts, Joshua Leavitt, Myron Holley, Elizur Wright, Gerrit Smith, and William Goodell.[29] Whittier and Thomas Earle of Pennsylvania were not present but both sent letters of approval.[30] The opposition was led by Nathan S. S. Beman of Troy, recognized leader of New School Presbyterians and stepfather of William L. Yancey, later the orator of secession. Torrey presented the resolutions and defended them vigorously. The vote was close. With fifty-five not voting, independent nominations were approved forty-three to thirty-three. James G. Birney and Thomas Earle were chosen as candidates for president and vice-president of the United States. The platform pledged the party to oppose slavery to the full extent of legislative power under the Constitution, with particular emphasis upon abolition of slavery in the District of Columbia and of the interstate slave trade.

Thus was organized by a majority of ten in a convention of less than one hundred men, against strong opposition, the political party which was to gain control of the government within twenty years. In the campaign of 1840 it bore different names in different places, but principally was known as the Liberty Party or Human Rights Party. Garrison fought it always because he was an anarchist and wanted to break up the Union instead of strengthening it by ridding it of slavery. The party had no local organization; in most cases, no nominations for local offices. It was seldom placed on the ballots. Its candidate for the presidency was in England attending the World Anti-Slavery Convention from May until November. Most antislavery men were caught up in the wildest political brawl between Whigs and Democrats in history. Birney received 7,059 votes, counted and reported. That insignificant number of votes has turned the attention of historians away from the most important event after the formation of the American Anti-Slavery Society in 1833.

THE LIBERTY PARTY
(CONTINUED)

Chapter 36

The Liberty Party and its affiliate, the American and Foreign Anti-Slavery Society, superseded the American Anti-Slavery Society in 1840. Garrison fumed in Boston, but his fulminations meant little west of the Hudson, where the equality of women was accepted and political action was regarded as a necessity. The platform of the party may be found in Birney's letter of acceptance: "The security—of life—of liberty—of civil and religious privileges—of the rights of conscience—of the right to use our own faculties for the promotion of our own happiness—of free locomotion—all these, together with the defense of the barriers and outposts thrown around them by the laws constitute the highest concerns of a government. These, for the last six years, we have seen invaded one after another—the administration aiding in the onset—till the *feeling of security* for any of them has well nigh expired. A censorship of the mail is usurped by the deputy postmasters throughout more than half the country, and approved by the administration under which it takes place. The pillage of the Post Office is perpetrated in one of our principal cities, and its contents made a bonfire of in the public square;—no one is brought in question for the outrage. Free speech and debate on the most important subject that now agitates the country, is rendered impossible in our national legislature; the *right* of the people to petition Congress for a redress of grievances is formally abolished by their own servants! And shall we sit down and dispute about the currency, about a sub-treasury or a no-sub-treasury, a bank or no-

bank, while such outrages on constitutional and essential rights are enacting before our eyes?"[1]

The platform of the party, also, is to be found in the character of the man who was its candidate for the presidency. He had sacrificed a promising political career, a rich monetary inheritance, and life in the land of his own people. He had associated himself with an almost universally despised group of humanitarians and braved the fury of countless mobs to uphold the priceless heritage of free enquiry and discussion. Antislavery men were not fools—they were men of wealth, education, respectability, and intelligence—and, of all the giant intellects among them, none moved with more dignity, nor spoke with more moderation, yet with more Christian charity. He was endowed, not only with a brilliant intellect, but with a warm humanitarianism and a great courage. In the fullness of manhood and professional attainment, he had dedicated his all to achieving and preserving unimpaired equality for all men before the law.

Antislavery men from Benezet to Birney had espoused the doctrine of natural rights. All persons were born free, and slavery was contrary to natural law, contrary to moral law, contrary to the fundamental law of the land. Slavery must be contained. Somehow it must be abolished. It must be kept out of the territories. It must be abolished in the District of Columbia. There must be no more slave states created, and Texas must be excluded. The interstate slave trade must be abolished. Government at all levels must be made to perform its primary function of protecting the

THE LIBERTY PARTY 299

natural (civil) rights of all persons regardless of wealth, position, or color, simply because they are human rights. Free enquiry and discussion must be restored, in and out of legislative halls. The individual must be free to go and come as he pleased. The power and prestige of the federal government must be restored. The Union must be preserved. This was the hard core of political action subscribed to by nine-tenths of the antislavery men in the country regardless of party affiliation. Convincing these men that independent political action was necessary was quite another matter.

It seemed downright vulgar to ask a good Whig to desert his party in 1840; something even worse to ask him to vote for two life-long Democrats, one of whom—Thomas Earle of Pennsylvania— had edited a free-trade, Democratic newspaper.[2] Most antislavery men were Whigs, but there were a goodly number of Democrats too, and they were equally faithful to party affiliations. Men were born into a political party, the same as they were born into a church, and, if anything, were more faithful to party platforms than to church disciplines. They knew party leaders deferred to the wishes of slaveholders both in the selection of candidates and in the writing of platforms. They were willing to embarrass candidates by asking questions, to work and to vote for the nomination of antislavery men for local and state offices, even for Congress, within their party organizations. They were willing to petition Congress to act against slavery to the full limits of its powers, but they were reluctant to do anything which might endanger party solidarity. When they cast a vote in a presidential election they wanted it to be something more than a protest vote. They wanted it to count for or against the bank, the tariff, and internal improvements. The leaders of the Liberty Party understood this fully. Pressure politics was impossible, because men would not switch from one party to the other.

Effective organization of the Liberty Party did not begin until *after* the election of 1840. The party had originated in upstate New York, and only there did it get much beyond its formative stages during the 1840 campaign. Myron Holley gave his fortune and his life to the cause, dying the following year from complete physical exhaustion. Liberty Party ballots, not always complete, were presented to the voters in all nonslaveholding states except Rhode Island and Indiana, but

only about 7,000 votes were cast for the party's presidential candidate.[3]

This election marked the beginning of twenty years of party reorganization. "Nothing short of miracles, constant miracles, and such as the world has never seen," said Weld, "can keep at bay the two great antagonist forces . . . They must drive against each other, till *one* of them goes to the bottom. *Events,* the master of men, have for years been silently but without a moment's pause, settling the basis of two great parties, the nucleus of one slavery, of the other freedom."[4] This continued to be true. There has been a tendency among historians to belittle the political action of the antislavery men in 1839–40, just as there has been a tendency to think of William L. Garrison as the great leader of the antislavery movement after 1840. *Neither is true.* In fact, nothing could be farther from the truth.

Only about one-tenth of the antislavery men paid any attention to Garrison. The other nine-tenths were honest, law-abiding, patriotic citizens, determined to uphold law and preserve the Union. Their leaders organized a political party. They launched it without any sacrifice of principles to vote-getting expediency. They were not politicians. They were not interested in coalitions. They were not interested in compromise. They were Christians, many of them ministers, and, until the first reorganization, religion and politics formed an integral union, with religious convictions governing political activities. Their new party did not disintegrate and disappear after the meager showing in 1840. It began a steady rise in influence and voting strength. The leaders worked without ceasing, giving of their time and talents and money, calling conventions, establishing newspapers, transforming into political reality their ideals and aspirations. They had to find the basis for union in their party of all antislavery men. In doing so they reorganized the party twice, each time under a new name, but they never surrendered their principles and they doubled their vote on the average every two years from 1840 to 1856.

They did not have to convert the nonbelievers to antislavery principles, although their party rallies and conventions differed little, sometimes not at all, from their former antislavery conventions. *They had to wean antislavery men away from the Whig and Democratic parties.* In short, they had to destroy those old-line parties and break the hold of the slaveholders upon the government by depriving them of the votes of Northern antislavery men. The Whig party was vulnerable because most staunch antislavery men were Whigs. It was vulnerable, also, because it was a coalition. There was a sharp cleavage between Northern and Southern Whigs on two issues of this dual revolution: freedom *versus* slavery, and national solidarity *versus* state rights and disunion. The party nominated William Henry Harrison and John Tyler in 1840, and antislavery men supported the ticket. It is not likely the rank and file of antislavery Whigs would have voted the Liberty ticket had it been fully organized. They had to be humiliated, chagrined, almost convicted of sin, to surrender their worship of party labels.

In the complexity of events during the ensuing four years, the progress of political action against slavery rapidly accelerated. Once the hypnotic effects of campaign oratory had worn off, thousands of Whigs went back to antislavery interests and associations. In New Hampshire, for instance, an election early in 1841 showed an increase of Liberty Party votes from the 1840 total of 111 to more than 2,000.[5] Antislavery men were emphasizing local and state elections, building their party at the grass roots level, nominating candidates for every office from local drain commissioner and school supervisor to governor, and demanding forthright opposition to slavery from all.[6] Their local organizations were good and they were permanent.[7] Local organizations being the foundation of national party strength, Liberty Party gains at the local level seriously weakened the Whig party, and they made it impossible for Northern Democrats, antislavery or otherwise, to continue to maintain solidarity with Southern pro-slavery leaders.

Disaster overtook the Whig Party soon after the election of 1840. Harrison's death brought John Tyler into the presidency. Harrison's record with regard to slavery expansion was not good, but Tyler brazenly supported annexation of Texas in order to strengthen slavery. He was, moreover, a strong exponent of state rights. No antislavery man could possibly support his policies; none could fail to see the folly of remaining in a party which had to accommodate its principles and its nominations to slaveholding membership. Antislavery men continued to drift out of the party in ever-increasing numbers during Tyler's administration. They had to come, if at all,

into the Liberty Party on the solid ground of antislavery doctrine. Birney was inflexible on that point, as hard and unyielding as granite, and it was his greatest contribution. The pressure upon antislavery Whigs in Congress was agonizing. They were forced into insurgency against party leadership.

The Liberty Party was a militant antislavery organization. A national convention was held in New York City on May 12–13, 1841. Alvan Stewart presided, and Alvan Stewart believed, without any reservation whatever, that every slave in the country had been freed by the Declaration of Independence, and, regardless of that point, that every child born thereafter of slave parents was born free because freedom was the natural state of all persons born into this world and laws enslaving free persons were unconstitutional. Alvan Stewart and everyone else in the party subscribed to the higher-law doctrine and quoted the Declaration of Independence as often as they did the Bible. Levi Coffin of Indiana, head of the underground railroad, which operated entirely by the philosophy of the higher law, was one of the secretaries of the convention. William Goodell, who wrote the "Address to the People," and Joshua Leavitt, one of the secretaries, were senior members of a venerable and devoted group of pioneers in the movement. Birney was renominated for the presidency and Thomas Morris was nominated for the vice-presidency. Goodell's address reaffirmed the demand for immediate emancipation, full equality for Negroes in educational opportunity and exercise of the franchise, exclusion of slavery from the territories, economic policies designed to enhance the prosperity of free labor and relieve it from both the stigma and competition of slave labor, retributive justice to the slaves at the time of emancipation, and election of the president and vice-president by popular vote.[8]

Birney had taken advanced ground in England in criticism of the churches and later in a western New York conference of Presbyterian and Congregational churches, condemning, among other things, their laxity in support of antislavery measures, their maintenance of Negro pews, their acceptance of money from slaveholders, and their continued communion with slaveholders and slaveholding ministers.[9] His letter of acceptance was a severe, though eminently fair, indictment of national policy since the founding of the Republic. The object of the party, he explained, was to achieve "Liberty—the liberty that is twin born with justice—the liberty that respects and protects the rights, not of the weak only, or of the strong only, but of the weak and the strong; and simply because they are human rights. We contend for liberty as she presents herself in the Declaration of American Independence—asserting that all men are created equal, that they are entitled to life, liberty, and the pursuit of happiness, and treating these rights as the gift of the Creator to man as man—therefore inalienable. In this, her clearest manifestation to the world, our countrymen have admired, not received her. We struggle for her reception, her installation, and the protection of every human being in the land by just and impartial laws."

Our policies and our lack of a generous love of liberty, Birney thought, would leave us far behind other nations in the race of civilization. The Revolution had freed us from colonial dependence, but not from slavery nor from the spirit of oppression and hypocrisy. His indictment followed the lines of the petition campaign: continuation of the African slave trade for twenty years, and then of a domestic trade equally evil in character; compulsory return from the free states of fugitive men, women, and children without due process of law, thus converting the entire area of the free states into hunting grounds for human prey; guaranty of the full power of the Union to suppress slave uprisings, even though inspired by unbearable cruelty; establishment of slavery and the slave trade by act of Congress in the District of Columbia; recognition of Texan independence, while spurning all intercourse with Haiti; constant denunciation of antislavery men in Congress as traitors, incendiaries, and fanatics; and denial of the Constitutional right of petition in both houses; such widespread mob violence against antislavery men and Negroes, destruction of newspapers, churches, homes, and schools, as to constitute anarchy.

"A law abiding people," said Birney, "under honest rulers must in the long run be a safe and prosperous people . . . But a people whose rulers and leaders have cast off reverence for human laws, always preceded by casting off reverence for laws of still higher obligation—such people can not be in a more pitiable and hopeless condition . . . Law has lost its honor; it is in the dust; none do it reverence; its authority to restrain, to punish, to protect, is mocked at. A new power,

more prompt and energetic, has risen up, that has pushed Law from her seat; one that tolerates no dissent; that declares Law unnecessary—smelling of by-gone ages; that rises up against all Laws and constitutions too, *the solemn enactments of the people;* not caring formally to repeal them, but setting them aside at pleasure. Public opinion, not law, is henceforward to regulate the rights and duties, the obligations and privileges of Americans." [10]

Birney spoke for the Liberty Party leaders, who saw no distinction between political and moral evils. [11] Their party was the party of human rights, fighting oppression in every form, be it economic, political, or religious. Their party discussions were religious in character. Their methods were those of the old antislavery society. In New York, for example, the leaders were Alvan Stewart, Gerrit Smith, Joshua Leavitt, William Goodell, Myron Holley, until his death, and Birney until he moved to Bay City, Michigan. William Jay was their candidate for governor. In Massachusetts, there were Elizur Wright, Henry B. Stanton, John Greenleaf Whittier, John Pierpont, and Samuel E. Sewall. In Maine, Austin Willey, a Congregational minister and editor of the *Advocate of Freedom,* Samuel Fessenden, a prominent lawyer, and General James Appleton were leaders in a group largely composed of ministers. The Pennsylvania leaders were Thomas Earle, Francis J. LeMoyne, and William H. Burleigh. Preachers in the party were legion, and all the members of the party were church members. Liberty men were religious politicians, and clerical members considered it a duty to preach politics, pray politics, and actively engage in politics. [12]

The great question of the terms on which all antislavery men would unite for political action was clarified by the campaign of 1844. The controlling centers of political power in the emerging contest were rapidly shifting to the West, in the nonslaveholding states, to Ohio, Michigan, and Illinois. The long range significance of early antislavery effort in Ohio was already apparent. It was the most thoroughly antislavery of all the states and at the center of unyielding nationalism. Salmon P. Chase, Gamaliel Bailey, and others, staunch antislavery men, had been reluctant, nevertheless, to sever old party affiliations. They now were overanxious to enlarge the Liberty Party's platform of principles and to nominate a prominent politician, perhaps even to sacrifice principles for success. They were, in short, impatient and ambitious, disturbed mightily that antislavery Whigs like Giddings and Seward refused to desert their party, and like all late comers, anxious to demonstrate their superior wisdom. Chase and Bailey, certainly, were willing to desert the master who had taught them the antislavery alphabet. They opposed Birney's renomination, presented his legal arguments to the public as their own, sought to discredit him by questioning his support of democratic processes, and lamented his prominence as a reformer rather than as a statesman.[13] Chase was the leader of the Ohio group, which included Samuel Lewis, former state superintendent of schools and a well-known orator; Leicester King, antislavery legislator and justice; and Edward Wade. Birney, Leavitt, Smith, Stewart, Stanton, and others refused to yield, and the campaign of 1844 became as much a contest between Whigs and Liberty men as between Whigs and Democrats.[14]

There were no less than 500,000 antislavery men eligible to vote in the country. Some, though not many, followed Garrison and refused to vote. They agreed with the slaveholders that the constitution was a proslavery document. They were disunionists and may be written off completely as far as the political history of the antislavery movement is concerned. The vast majority of the antislavery men belonged to two groups with reference to constitutional interpretation. Liberty Party men, first, last, and always, who subscribed to the higher-law doctrine, insisted the constitution must be interpreted in the light of the Declaration of Independence and was, therefore, antislavery; they argued that slavery, being contrary both to moral law and natural law, could have no legal existence.[15] Other Liberty Party men and antislavery Whigs and Democrats insisted slavery was the creature of statute (or municipal) law and could have no legal existence outside state limits. It should be abolished in the District of Columbia and in the territories, and no new slave state should be created. Slaves escaping from the limits of slave state authority were free men. The interstate slave trade should be abolished.

Gerrit Smith said in 1850—and he could just as well have said it in 1840: "There is a large class of voters who hate slavery; and who are entirely convinced, that the Whig and Democratic Parties will not overthrow it; but who, nevertheless,

cannot bring themselves to join a party so stringent in its principles, and so radical and comprehensive in its reformatory aim, and, hence, so limited in its actual and prospective numbers, as is the Liberty party. They will prefer to form a party on some midway ground between the Democratic and Whig parties on the one hand, and the Liberty party on the other. Such a party, combining in itself more of the element of principle than exists in the Democratic and Whig parties, with more of the element of numbers than exists in the Liberty party, and being, therefore, attractive both to the men of conscience and morality and to the lovers of majorities and offices, will give promise to its founders of becoming a triumphant party."

Reorganization along these lines came about as a result of the campaign of 1844.[16] There were at least four major developments:

Liberty party candidates were questioned regarding their attitude toward the bank, the tariff, the public lands, and so forth, even as they in previous campaigns had questioned the Whigs and Democrats. They could not evade important issues of domestic policy, and it was to Birney's credit that he did not attempt to do so, but his opposition to a protective tariff and to a national bank, for example, did not please everyone. Many party men doubted the good sense, and certainly the expediency, of doing on other issues what Whigs had been doing on slavery: seeking harmony by avoiding discussion. It might establish a coalition but never build a party. It was increasingly clear as the campaign progressed that the party must, in the future, define its position on all matters of public policy and do so in its platform.[17]

The Whig Party was at war with itself, torn asunder by internecine strife. Southern Whigs were pledged to the annexation of Texas. Antislavery Whigs, though not all Northern Whigs, opposed annexation. There were substantial and well-sustained reasons for annexation entirely apart from slavery; but very many Southern Democrats and Whigs, including President Tyler, demanded it as a great boon to the solidarity and extension of slavery and the slave power in the nation. Clay, possibly by preconvention understanding with Van Buren and after his nomination, tried to avoid the subject. He could not do so because the Democratic candidate, James K. Polk, was defining in broad outlines a bold expansion policy. Antislavery Whigs who voted for him did so in spite of his record on slavery and in disregard of Birney's scathing exposé in *Headlands in the Life of Henry Clay.*

John Quincy Adams and Joshua Giddings had behaved admirably in defense of the right of petition. Antislavery men recognized their contributions and supported both at the polls, even though Adams opposed immediate emancipation and refused to vote for abolition of slavery in the District of Columbia and in the territories, and Giddings refused to leave his moorings in the Whig Party. But Birney relentlessly berated Adams for his refusal to act against slavery, and he showed not the slightest signs of mercy in dealing with Henry Clay, who refused to recognize slavery as a moral question.[18] Clay was a pillar of the colonization society, a devotee of the doctrine of racial inequality, a slavery expansionist. He proudly asserted that slavery in his own establishment was preferable to the freedom of wage earners at the North. Birney denounced him as a slaveholder, a duelist, and a gambler.[19]

Whig party leaders, fighting desperately to keep their ranks intact, published in their newspapers reprints of a completely spurious edition of the Genesee County *Democrat* containing forged letters purporting to show that Birney had entered into a corrupt bargain with the Democrats. Copies of this forgery were prepared in Detroit for mailing to Whig newspapers and were carried to Columbus by an apparently innocent person from Chillicothe, Ohio, where they were mailed according to instructions. They were reprinted all over the country, too late for any refutation or denial of authenticity to reach the public. Whig newspapers would not have carried denials in any case, because they refused ever after to print apologies or even the laboriously gathered legal evidence of forgery. Thousands of Liberty Party men went to their graves believing that Birney had betrayed the cause. More thousands remained away from the polls on election day.[20] But, enough voted for Birney to give Polk the thirty-six electoral votes from New York state and the election.

It was ironical, but it was providential. The masses once more had confounded their leaders. Election of the militant expansionist, James K. Polk, was nothing less than a summons to the battlefield of all available proslavery and antislavery forces, because, war or no war, the South was determined to have Texas—for Texas divided would counterbalance a goodly number of new

free states—and was determined to have California, perhaps everything north of the Rio Grande. Suddenly, the issues of a bank and a protective tariff seemed less important. Polk's expansion policy and certainty of a rush of settlers to a vast new national domain brought principles, politicians, and governmental policies to a crisis from which there was no escape.

Van Buren's temporizing attitude toward annexation of Texas had cost him the Democratic nomination. Upstate New York was the last place in the country where a Democrat could afford to defend the proslavery militancy of Democratic leadership. Van Buren left the party, and, with him, many antislavery Democrats. It was the first serious defection from the Democratic Party. Reorganization of antislavery forces moved forward at once. The Ohio and Michigan groups took the lead. Gamaliel Bailey and Salmon P. Chase, through the columns of the *Philanthropist* at Cincinnati, and Theodore Foster and Guy Beckley, with the *Signal of Liberty* at Ann Arbor, published the first halting suggestions for a new platform. A Southern and Western Liberty Convention was held at Cincinnati, June 10–13, 1845. Two thousand antislavery men of all parties were present. Birney was chairman of the convention and Salmon P. Chase wrote the address to the public. All were agreed that the Constitution was not a proslavery document.[21] Goodell, Smith, and others, representing the original political action group, held a convention at Macedon Lock, New York, in June 1847 and endorsed the more advanced position that the Constitution was an antislavery document and that Congress could abolish slavery in the states. Gerrit Smith was the choice of the convention for president. The convention said: "We hold slavery to be illegal and unconstitutional, and that the Federal Government is bound to secure its abolition by the guaranty, to every State in this Union, of a republican form of government. If the South demurs, let her, peacefully, withdraw from the Union." The convention then made the first statement in regard to free homesteads: "Along with the abolition of all other monopolies, we would restrict within reasonable bounds, the extent to which individuals, corporations, or the government, should hold property in land, providing an opportunity for all to become possessors of the soil, and thus enjoy (without its being contested) the original right of every human being to enjoy a portion of the earth's surface, and breathe its free air. To this end, we would also have the public lands thrown open to actual settlers, free of cost, and every man's homestead held inalienable, except with his own consent, not being liable to seizure and sale for debt."[22]

A third convention was held at Buffalo in October, 1847, where the more moderate view that Congress could not directly interfere with slavery in the states was endorsed, and John P. Hale of New Hampshire was nominated for president. Finally, at Buffalo in August 1848, practically all antislavery groups, including Liberty Party men, Van Buren Democrats, and even more Whigs united under the name of "Free Soil" and nominated Van Buren for the presidency.

This was not an absorption of the Liberty Party by the Whigs or the Democrats. It was an expansion of the Liberty Party under a new name. No one surrendered his antislavery principles or modified his antislavery principles or his constitutional theories. The movement of antislavery men continued to be from the Whig and Democratic parties to the Free Soil Party, not the opposite. The number of new adherents to antislavery principles continued to increase, not decrease. Each individual antislavery man became stronger, not weaker, in his convictions with the passing of time. In short, the reorganization of political action against slavery under a new name represented progress, aggressiveness, and renewed strength. None of those people disappeared who believed that Congress could abolish slavery everywhere. They were only a few in 1833, now they were a formidable group. The entire body of antislavery men was not so far advanced in 1848, but they all stood solidly together on the oldest and most venerable antislavery principle of Congressional exclusion of slavery from the territories, on the principle of free enquiry and discussion in defense of which antislavery men had suffered much, and on the principle of placing slavery in course of ultimate extinction at the earliest practical moment and by the most practicable means. Moreover, they accepted as the two most advanced weapons in their battle to wrest control of the government from the slaveholders the theory of inevitable conflict between slave labor and free labor and the wisdom and equity of free homesteads.

The fugitive

FUGITIVE SLAVES AND THE PEOPLE

Chapter 37

No laws of Congress ever produced more bitterness and widespread disobedience than the fugitive slave laws. No other laws of Congress, probably, ever were so wicked in their consequences, and it is doubtful if any other ever was held by the people to be so flagrantly unconstitutional. The question of why Article 4, Section 2,[1] was inserted in the Constitution becomes superficial when one remembers the widespread belief, testified to by most honorable men and affirmed in ratifying conventions everywhere except in the southernmost states, that slavery was expected to disappear at an early date, and when one remembers also, as generally agreed by all, that every state possessed the power to protect persons within its jurisdiction and none had been obliged to permit the capture of alleged fugitives under the Articles of Confederation. If the clause was a grant of power to the federal government to return fugitives and a denial to the states of a power to protect persons within their jurisdiction, as the courts ultimately claimed, it placed a heavy responsibility upon Congress, if and when it implemented the clause by legislation, to provide every safeguard against kidnapping. Congress failed to do so, thus placing an equally heavy responsibility upon the courts to declare the Act of 1793 unconstitutional.

The request for federal legislation did not originate in a slave state but in Pennsylvania, and it did not arise from a case of recovery but from a case of kidnapping.[2] There was every reason, therefore, for Congress to have passed an antikidnapping law. Instead, it passed a law for the recovery of fugitive slaves.[3] Antislavery resistance to the law was based upon the fact that the clause in the Constitution and the law of 1793 were both contrary to the moral law and to the natural law. This doctrine of the moral law went back in antislavery tradition at least to the days of Woolman and Benezet, for the Quakers of that day emphasized the command, "Thou shalt not deliver unto the master the servant which is escaped from his master unto thee; he shall dwell with thee, even among you, in that place which he shall choose, in one of thy gates where it liketh him best, thou shalt not oppress him," and the golden rule, "All things whatsoever ye would that men should do unto you, do ye even so to them, for this is the law and the prophets." By the time of David Rice and David Barrow, it was clearly and universally believed among antislavery men that no legislative body could enact an enforceable law which was contrary to the law of God as revealed in the Word or in the immutable laws of nature. This firm conviction was reinforced by the theory of natural rights as enshrined in the Declaration of Independence, to which no constitution or law within the framework of our political institutions could do violence and command obedience.[4]

The clause in the Constitution was wrong. It legalized kidnapping. The men who wrote it into the Constitution were so ashamed of it that they said "persons held to service or labor" instead of "slaves." James Iredell said so in the North Carolina ratifying convention. The law of 1793 was wrong. Slaves were men and endowed with the same natural rights as other men.[5] They had a right to be free. It was wrong to deliver them up when they attained freedom by flight. Whether the Act of 1793 was constitutional or not was beside the point. The Constitution itself was wrong. Lest the reader at this point fall into the error of thinking the recovery of fugitives was a humane and dignified legal procedure, it must be said that it was bloody business. Slaves, from colonial days, fled to the swamps, or to the Indian tribes, or to Spanish Florida, or to Northern colonies and states, and on into Canada. They were men, and men cannot long be denied freedom without resistance or flight.[6] They did not escape easily before 1820, and thousands thereafter failed in the attempt every year. All of them suffered untold hardships; many died in the undertaking before reaching the comparative safety of the free states. This matter is so important in the history of the contest that the following legal notice from the North Carolina newspapers is reproduced in full:

"State of North Carolina
Lenoir County

"Whereas, complaint hath been this day made to us, two of the Justices of the Peace for the said county, by William D. Cobb, of Jones County, that two negro slaves belonging to him, named *Ben*, commonly known by the name of Bea Fox, and Rigdon, have absented themselves from their said master's service, and are lurking about in the counties of Lenoir and Jones, committing acts of felony. These are in the name of the state to command the said slaves forthwith to surrender themselves and turn home to their said master. And we do hereby also require the Sheriff of said county of Lenoir, to make diligent search and pursuit after the above mentioned slaves, and them having found, to apprehend and secure so they may be conveyed to their said master, or otherwise discharged as the law directs. And the said Sheriff is hereby empowered to raise and take with him such power of his county as he shall think fit for the apprehension of said slaves. And we do hereby, by virtue of an act of the assembly of this state concerning servants and slaves, intimate and declare if the said slaves do not surrender themselves and return home to their masters immediately after the publication of these presents, that any person may kill and destroy said slaves by such means as he or they think fit, without accusation or impeachment of any crime or offense for so doing, or without incurring any penalty or forfeiture thereby.

Given under our hands and seals, this 12th November, 1836.

B. Coleman, J.P.
Jas. Jones, J.P."

"200 *Dollars Reward*—Ran away from the subscriber, about three years ago, a certain negro named Ben, commonly known by the name of Bea Fox. He is about 5 feet 5 or 6 inches high, chunky made, yellow complexion, and had but one eye. Also, one other negro, by the name of Rigdon, who ran away on the 8th of this month. He is stout made, tall, and very black, with large lips.

"I will give the reward of one hundred dollars for each of the above negroes to be delivered to me or confined in the jail of Lenoir or Jones County, or for the killing of them, so that I can see them.[7] Masters of vessels and all others, are cautioned against harboring, employing, or carrying them away under the penalty of the law. November 12, 1836.[8]   W. D. Cobb"

Slaveowner shooting a fugitive slave

This, of course, was a death warrant, issued by the alleged owner of the fugitives, inviting all and sundry persons to murder them and offering two hundred dollars for the execution. The slaves could not read the command to return, and there was not one chance in a thousand of it ever coming to their attention. Descriptions were so meager that hundreds of Negroes could have been mistaken for the fugitives. This was the kind of business the federal government got itself into at the behest of slaveholders.

The federal law provided that when a person held to labor escaped into another state, the person to whom the labor was due, or his agent, might seize the alleged fugitive, take him before any circuit or district judge of the United States, or any county, city, or municipal judge, and prove to the satisfaction of the judge, either by oral testimony or affidavit, that the person seized did owe him service or labor, and receive a certificate of removal to his home state.[9] A magistrate's hearing was thus substituted for a jury trial, and the choice of freedom or eternal slavery for men, women, and children was left to the judgment of one man, ordinarily a justice of the peace, who might be ignorant, or venal, or prejudiced.[10] Moreover, the owner, kidnapper, pursuer, whatever he might be, could of his own free will choose the magistrate he thought most likely to do his bidding.

In consequence of the omission from this law of any safeguards against disturbances of the peace, or against kidnapping of free Negroes—safeguards commonly spoken of as due process of law, particularly writs of habeas corpus, legal counsel, trial by jury, and testimony of witnesses—antislavery men waged a relentless battle for the enactment of a body of legislation to supplement the deficiencies of the federal law. It was apparent at a very early date that the freedom of any person brought before a magistrate would depend upon that gentleman's personal philosophy. In Vermont, Judge Theophilus Harrington refused to return an alleged fugitive, saying that he would not accept as evidence of ownership anything short of a bill of sale from God Almighty.[11] Other justices insisted that in any case involving the question of a Negro's freedom the burden of proof rested upon the Negro. He must present positive evidence of freedom. In short, color was a presumption of slavery. This was the prevailing philosophy of courts in the slave states,

and it became the philosophy of the federal courts after 1831. There were plenty of slaves who could pass for white persons and thousands of free whites in the North who were darker than an equal number of slaves in the South. Color was a poor safeguard of freedom. Indiana, Illinois, and Pennsylvania all had early laws which, in effect, provided jury trials in fugitive slave cases.[12] The Pennsylvania Act of 1826 came before the Supreme Court of the United States in the case of *Prigg* v. *Pennsylvania* (1842). Justice Joseph Story wrote the decision of the Court, stating four fundamental principles: [13]

The Fugitive Slave Act of 1793 was constitutional.

The power to legislate on the subject was not concurrent but exclusively a power of Congress. All state laws touching the subject, therefore, whether designed to assist or to hinder the return of fugitives, were unconstitutional.

The Act of 1793 was valid insofar as it conferred authority upon state magistrates. State officials might exercise the authority conferred upon them unless prohibited by state legislation, but states were not bound to enforce federal statutes and might prohibit their officials from acting under the law.

Slaveholders must have the right to seize and remove their slaves without process or warrant.

Chief Justice Roger B. Taney, as vigorous now in defense of the slaveholder's property rights as he had been in denouncing slavery in 1818, and still adhering to the colonization theory that Negroes must remain in slavery or be removed from the country, completely rejected the danger of enslaving free Negroes and declared the states must assist in enforcement of the federal law. Justice John McLean of Ohio insisted that the rights of free Negroes must not be jeopardized in the process of returning fugitives. Alleged fugitives must not be removed from the state by force without presentation of proof of ownership. Presumption of slavery because of color must not determine the fate of alleged fugitives.

The states shortly began to take full advantage of Story's dictum that they were not obliged to enforce federal statutes and passed an even more extensive body of personal liberty laws.[14] Moreover, even where such statutes did not hinder the return of fugitives, local and county judges, particularly justices of the peace, being answerable to the people of the local community in which

The Christiana tragedy
A body of slave catchers and Negroes met in bloody encounter in Lancaster County, Pennsylvania, in 1851.

they lived, became increasingly reluctant to return alleged fugitives. The underground railroad was functioning thoroughly and almost openly in many areas. Finally, slaveholders and their agents were easily spotted when they came into a community and just as easily thwarted, if not actually intimidated. If slave owners apprehended their runaways before they became settled residents of Northern communities their chances of recovery were good before 1850, not otherwise and not after that date. Justice McLean had jurisdiction over the Third Circuit, including Ohio, Indiana, Illinois, and Kentucky. This was the area through which most fugitives escaped and where people were inclined to use force to protect the free Negroes after the Prigg decision. McLean, who was very critical of the doctrine laid down in that decision and who had warned his colleagues on the bench that it would lead to widespread violence, allowed the use of the writ of habeas corpus in fugitive slave cases as the only effective safeguard against kidnapping.

All of this led to a demand by the slaveholders for a more effective system of recovery. They were given an amendment to the Act of 1793, known as the Fugitive Slave Act of 1850. This amendment did not add any of the elements of due process to the procedure of recovery. It still permitted slaveholders or their agents to arrest fugitives without legal process and without warrants, but it placed the main burden of enforcing the act upon United States commissioners and marshals. The commissioners were given concurrent powers with circuit and district judges in fugitive slave cases. Commissioners were to issue warrants for the arrests. United States marshals were to make the arrests and were liable to $1,000 fine for nonperformance of duty and to civil suits for the value of slaves lost from their custody. Anyone obstructing the recovery of a fugitive or assisting a fugitive to escape was liable to a fine of $1,000 and a prison sentence of six months. The testimony of the alleged fugitive was not to be admitted as evidence. The fee of the commissioner if the alleged fugitive were surrendered to the claimant was twice the amount of the fee if the claim should be denied.

The personal liberty laws passed during the preceding decade were now expanded to the point where many of them clearly nullified the federal statute. Public attorneys were charged with the responsibility of defending all persons arrested as fugitive slaves in Maine, New Hampshire, Vermont, Massachusetts, New York, Michigan, and Wisconsin. In Massachusetts, the governor was required to appoint state commissioners in each county for this purpose. In Wisconsin an elaborate system was devised by law for alerting public attorneys to impending arrests. The states paid the costs of all such defense actions. The use of all public buildings, jails or otherwise, and state or county, was denied for the detention of fugitives in Maine, New Hampshire, Vermont, Massachusetts, Rhode Island, Michigan, Pennsylvania, and Ohio. All public officials were forbidden to arrest or to aid in arresting alleged fugitives by Maine, Vermont, Massachusetts, Connecticut, Rhode Island, New Jersey, Michigan, New York, Pennsylvania, and Wisconsin, and some states forbade citizens to lend assistance. Antikidnapping laws placed heavy penalties upon anyone who unlawfully seized another person as a fugitive. Maine fixed the punishment at five years and $1,000 fine, Massachusetts and Connecticut at a maximum of five years and $5,000 fine, Rhode Island and New York at ten years, Illinois at seven years, Wisconsin at two years and $1,000, and Indiana at fourteen years and $5,000. If slaveholders brought slaves into Maine, Vermont, New York, or Michigan, the slaves were free, and if the slaveholder attempted thereafter to exercise authority he was subject to fine and imprisonment of one year and $1,000 in Maine, fifteen years and $2,000 in Vermont, and ten years and $1,000 in Michigan. Habeas corpus acts provided jury trials in Vermont, Massachusetts, New York, New Jersey, Pennsylvania, Michigan, Wisconsin, Connecticut, and Rhode Island. In Vermont, anyone seizing or confining an alleged fugitive was subject to ten years' imprisonment and $1,000 fine. In Connecticut, testimony as to service or labor due was invalid unless supported by two witnesses. No slaveholder could come into Illinois and seize a fugitive without action by court officials. No slave and no free person could be taken forcibly from the state of New Jersey on

penalty of five years' imprisonment and $1,000 fine.

This widespread legislative opposition to federal law can only be understood in the light of the hateful significance of the law. Every single judicial decision upholding the constitutionality of the Fugitive Slave Act was based in part on the assertion that slaves (meaning Negroes) were not party to the Constitution. This was assertion, not historical fact. It emanated from prejudice, not from logic. It simply was not true. Negroes were citizens, and a well-reasoned case can be made to show that slaves became citizens as soon as they became free, if indeed they were not citizens while still in slavery. Every man, woman, and child in the free states, black, white, red, or yellow, insofar as the provisions of these laws and the recovery process provided were concerned, were liable to be seized and carried South into slavery. The judges begged the question constantly until one wonders if this were not a form of national insanity that pervaded even the courtrooms. Slaves were not being brought before the magistrates. Slaves were not being seized and carried away. Persons were being given a trial—a hearing, if you please—to determine if they were slaves: that is, had been slaves of the claimant. Anyone who thought the judgment of a local justice of the peace—and judgment based upon the oral testimony of some stranger who suddenly appeared before him—was competent to determine whether a person should be dragged off to a lifetime of servitude and perpetual servitude for all his descendants—and that, too, without reference to family, property, and status in the community—was in the judgment of the common man a consummate fool and unfit to be either judge or a congressman.

Worse still was the fact that the federal law clothed every slaveholder, and everyone callous enough to claim that he was a slaveholder, and every agent of a slaveholder with power of arrest. Yet arrest was not the correct word. The law said "to seize or arrest," and it meant to seize since warrants were not necessary. How compatible was this sort of thing with the dignity and security of civilized human beings: to have a few thousand slaveholders clothed with authority to roam around seizing people and dragging them before a justice of the peace? It was an open invitation to kidnapping, made possible and made profitable by the interstate slave trade. Antislavery men were determined to put an end to both these evils. The law, too, offered every commissioner an extra five dollars' bounty for every person sent into slavery, and it violated every principle of common decency and due process in taking away a man's life without allowing him to speak in his own defense.

"What would James Madison and his noble compeers have thought of themselves, and their posterity," asked Charles Beecher, "had they been told the day would come, when the sanction of their names should be invoked upon a law that bribes judges with a paltry five dollars for every man condemned to slavery; and fines every citizen a thousand dollars for giving that fugitive a supper and a bed . . . This law then is wrong in the sight of God and man—it is an unexampled climax of sin. It is the monster iniquity of the present age, and it will stand forever on the page of history, as the vilest monument of infamy of the nineteenth century . . . nations afar off pause awhile from their worship of blocks of wood and stone, to ask what will those Christians do next."[15]

Here was its most offensive feature to antislavery men. They were compelled by heavy fines to obey it; they were counseled by conservative men to obey it because it was the law; yet obedience was equivalent to a denial of Christ himself. Suppose, Charles Beecher explained, a fugitive mother and child should come knocking at your door of a winter night pleading for aid. "What does the law require of you?" he asked. "What must you do, to obey the law? What is obedience to law? You must shut your door in her face, or you must take her captive, and shut her up until the hounds of officers can come up. This is obedience; and if you do not do this you are a law-breaker. If you give her a crust of bread, you break the law. If you give her a shawl, a cloak; if you let her warm herself by your fire an hour, and depart, you break the law. If you give her a night's rest, and let her go, you break the law. If you show her any kindness, any mercy, if you treat her as Christ treated you, if you do to her as you would wish to be done by, you have broken the law."[16]

Christians could not obey the law while seeking its repeal. They made a fine distinction between laws which injured themselves and laws which commanded them to do wrong. "I may disapprove a law, I may think it unwise, injudicious, and even unjust in its bearings on me, and on my interests," said Beecher, "and yet it may not re-

quire me to *do anything* positively wrong. I may submit to such a law, innocently, because I wrong nobody. But here is a law which commands me to *sin* positively and without apology. It commands me, when fully obeyed, to deny Christ, to renounce and abjure Christ's law, to trample under foot Christ's spirit, and to remand Christ's flesh and blood into cruel bondage. A law which does me some injury is one thing. A law which makes me do wrong is another. The first I may submit to while seeking its repeal. To the latter I must not give place by subjection . . . those men who clamor for blind obedience to all law—right or wrong—are striking at the throne of God . . . he who obeys this wicked law because it is law, has the double guilt, not only of the thing itself done, which is diabolical, but also of proving traitor to the cause of liberty of conscience and the right of private judgment . . . It is a complete shipwreck of every principle of religious liberty for which our fathers ever contended; it is a barefaced dereliction of every position of the Reformation, and a giving up of everything which as Protestants and as republicans we have ever held dear. If this law is to be obeyed merely because it is law, no matter how diabolical its spirit, then farewell to liberty, farewell to religion. There is henceforth no barrier to the encroachment of corruption."[17]

"*Disobey this Law,*" said Beecher, and his admonition was echoed and re-echoed across the land. "If you have ever dreamed of obeying it, repent before God, and ask his forgiveness. I counsel no violence. I suggest no warlike measures of resistance. I incite no man to deeds of blood. I speak as the minister of the Prince of Peace. As much as lieth in you, live peaceably with all men . . . But if a fugitive claim your help on his journey, break the law and give it him. The law is broken as thoroughly by *indirectly* aiding his escape as *directly*, for both are penal. Therefore break the law, and help him on his way, *directly* if you can, *indirectly* if you must. Feed him, clothe him, harbor him, by day and by night, and conceal him from his pursuers and from the officers of the law. If you are summoned to aid in his capture, refuse to obey. If you are commanded by the officer to lay hands on the fugitive, decline to comply . . . If they fine you, and imprison you, take joyfully the spoiling of your goods, wear gladly your chain, and in the last day you shall be rewarded for your fidelity to

God. Do not think any true disgrace can attach to such penalties. It is the devil, and the devil's people only, who enact, enforce, or respect such penalties."[18]

The pleas of men like Beecher did not fall on deaf ears. The Act of 1850 was important on several counts. It provided a common ground upon which antislavery men of all shades of opinion and men who had never taken an active part in the movement could meet. In that respect it was a continuation of the civil rights issue, because lawyers emphasized the impossibility of protecting free persons from kidnapping without a jury trial. The law was a threat to the natural (constitutional) rights of all men. It provided a constantly recurring reminder of the evils of slavery little less effective than the petition campaign. Some sort of arbitrary action and violence connected with enforcement was brought to the attention of the people every day, and it tended to emphasize the claim of antislavery men that there could be no peace or safety for anyone until slavery was abolished. It got antislavery princi-

ples into the courts and shattered the almost impervious protective shell of legal dogma. The judiciary and the lawyers began to understand what was going on in the minds of the people.

There was a unity on why the Act was unconstitutional—more unity than there had ever before been on any aspect of the slavery question. The law of 1850 continued the previous evil of private arrests without warrants, meaning forcible seizures; summary trials by one person;[19] *ex-parte* (one-sided) testimony; disregard of all extenuating circumstances; lack of safeguards against kidnapping. In addition, this law struck down the writ of habeas corpus. It gave judicial powers to nonjudicial officials.[20] It compelled every person to aid in recovery of fugitives. It made the recovery of fugitives a charge against the public treasury.[21]

Kindly people everywhere were convinced that free Negroes were being kidnapped, that perjury was being committed in the recovery of fugitives, that the law withheld from the Negro the basic constitutional safeguards of freedom. They knew many Negroes were disappearing in the stillness

Fugitives escaping from the eastern shore of Maryland

A group of twenty-eight fugitives from Cambridge, Maryland.

A bold stroke for freedom
Fugitives from Loudoun County, Virginia, who fled on Christmas Eve, 1855.

of the night. They saw multitudes of them flee-ing to Canada. They saw the look of fear upon the faces of decent, law-abiding people of their own communities. They heard their preachers tell them that if the general law of Christianity—to do unto others as they would that others should do unto them—did not teach them how to treat a poor fugitive, to remember such commands as "Deliver the poor and needy—rid them out of the hands of the wicked." "Whoso stoppeth his ears at the cry of the poor—he also shall cry himself, but shall not be heard." "Take counsel—execute judgment—hide the outcasts—let mine outcasts dwell with thee—be thou a covert to them, from the face of the spoiler." "Remember them that are in bonds, as bound with them."[22]

Systematic organization for aiding fugitives be-gan among the Quakers in the East before the adoption of the Constitution and continued among those people in Philadelphia, New Jersey, and southeastern Pennsylvania until the Civil War.[23] This was the area where, in early years, there were

the largest number of fugitives and the strongest antislavery sentiment. New York joined in the movement at an early date. It is estimated that more than 9,000 fugitives were helped to freedom through the branches of the underground railroad north of Philadelphia before 1860. The main lines of flight, however, were through western Pennsyl-vania, Ohio, or Indiana, to Lake Erie, the Niagara River, or Detroit. There was some traffic from Iowa and Illinois to Chicago and Lake Michigan. The vast majority of the fugitives crossed from Virginia or Kentucky into Ohio, which had a boundary of nearly 400 miles along these two slave states, or they came from Kentucky into Indiana and moved north across Lake Erie or by way of Detroit into Canada.

In the early years, before the system was well organized, fugitives were fed and clothed, then given directions to follow the North Star and sent on alone to the next town. That was about all the aid needed because they were seldom pursued. They were told always to ask for Quaker families,

Fugitive escaping the pursuit of bloodhounds.
Only an agile fugitive could thus escape injury by dogs.

because Quakers never refused them food and shelter. In fact, fugitives often traveled from Quaker family to Quaker family, and in this way the system of organized aid began. When women and children came to be numbered among the fugitives, they were taken on horseback, in wagons, or on boats to the next stop, never more than a day's journey away. Communication and transportation were difficult. The risks involved on the part of those who joined in the work were great. It had to be done in secret. Only those who were resourceful and courageous participated, and they did it because they were making a tangible stroke against slavery, aiding the oppressed, and engaging in a highly romantic enterprise. Most of them were Quakers and Presbyterians, but there were some Baptists, Methodists, Episcopalians, and Catholics. They were farmers, preachers, and physicians. Nearly all of them were Liberty–Free Soil–Republican Party members, and an amazing number rose to high positions in state and federal governments. One of the most active members in

Michigan, for example, was Jacob M. Howard, elected as a Whig to Congress in 1840, later as a Republican to the Senate, who was a member of the joint committee on reconstruction and introduced the Thirteenth Amendment into the Senate.

Persons in charge of the work in each community provided food, clothing, and shelter for the fugitives. Women's antislavery societies organized sewing circles to provide clothing. Local agents were prepared to receive fugitives at any time, but vigilance committees were organized to warn them of probable arrivals. They were secreted in livery stables, in attics, in storerooms, under featherbeds, in secret passages, in all sorts of out of the way places. They were disguised in various ways, nursed through long and serious illnesses, moved on at night. They were carried by wagon, by boat, and by train. Routes of travel were changed at a moment's notice, and when fugitives settled down in the free states it was along the underground railroad routes, so as to get away quickly when necessary. Not until the late 1850's, with a feeling of greater security, did they move away from these railroad stations.

The most dangerous part of the work was going into the South, supplying slaves with food and directions on how to get to the free states. Negroes did a great deal of this work because it was easier for them to convince the slaves of the possibility of escape. The most famous of the Negro guides was Harriet Tubman, called the "Moses" of her people and once introduced to Wendell Phillips by John Brown as "one of the best and bravest persons on this continent." She was born a slave in Maryland and worked as a beast in the field. She escaped and devoted her life to aiding the escape of slaves, to serving the Army as a spy under General Hunter, and finally to supporting the indigent and aged. She had no formal education, but she was shrewd and uncommonly strong. She made nineteen excursions into the slave states and led 300 slaves to freedom. She always started on Saturday night in order to be far gone before an alarm could be sounded. She hired Negroes to tear down and destroy all notices of escapees. She threatened to kill any fugitive that attempted to turn back, and none ever did so. In this way she was able to avoid publicity and detection. Slaveholders offered a total of $40,000 for her dead or alive.

The most tragic case of a white man engaged in this work was perhaps that of Calvin Fairbanks, who was imprisoned for nearly seventeen years in Kentucky. He dedicated his life to moving slaves from Virginia and Kentucky into Ohio, where Levi Coffin and others took charge of them. One of the slaves was Lewis Hayden, later a member of the Massachusetts legislature. For this offense Fairbanks was sent to prison in Louisville for fifteen years, but served only for four (1845–49), being pardoned by Governor John J. Crittenden. He went to Oberlin, but returned to Kentucky to aid two women and a child to escape. He was pursued, kidnapped at Jeffersonville, Indiana, taken to Kentucky, and sent to the state penitentiary for fifteen years. He was placed in a cell seven and one-half feet long by three and one-half feet wide and whipped almost daily. Sometimes he worked with twenty-five pound bars fastened to his ankles. He was released, a broken man, in 1864.

Little wonder that entire communities sprang to the defense of famished, terrified, half-clothed fugitives who came their way. Said Walt Whitman:

The fugitive slave came to my house and stopt outside,
I heard his motions crackling in the twigs of the woodpile,
Through the swung door of the kitchen I saw him limpsy and weak,
And went where he sat on a log and led him in and assured him,
And brought water and filled a tub for his sweated body and bruis'd feet,
And gave him a room that entered from my own, and gave him some coarse clean clothes,
And remember perfectly well his revolving eyes and his awkwardness,
And remember putting plasters on the galls of his neck and ankles;
He staid with me a week before he was recuperated and passed north,
I had him sit next me at my table, my fire-lock lean'd in the corner.[24]

FUGITIVE SLAVES AND THE LAW

Chapter 38

Antislavery philosophy in regard to the constitutional rights and legal status of the Negro held that slavery was the complete subjection of one man to the will of another by force, the exercise of which was sanctioned by the statute law of the colonies and the subsequent states; that slaves were recognized as property in the states still sanctioning slavery, but not in the nonslaveholding states and not, and deliberately not, in the Constitution of the United States; that in the slave states, where slavery was perpetual, again by statute law, slavery was equated to race and made a system of racial adjustment.

Antislavery men insisted that all of these laws were contrary to the principles of the Declaration of Independence; that Negroes were persons entitled to all the natural rights of man, to equality before the law, and to all the safeguards of due process; that when they passed beyond the limits of the state whose laws authorized their forcible subjection they were free men, because freedom was the natural state of all men.

The question, of course, was whether this Declaration, this statement of natural law, this magnificent definition of manhood, did or did not have constitutional force. The slaveholders said it did not, federal judges said it did not, but it had given greater solidarity and completeness to man's quest for freedom and justice than any other document ever written. It had cut away from slavery every single shred of philosophical support. It has been truly said: "The United States of America came into being with the Declaration of Independence, and for nearly two centuries the people have carried closer to their hearts than any other treasure the testament of faith therein contained." It was true in 1787, and it was true in 1850, as it is today. It was true, that is, where there was no slavery, with its doctrine of racial inferiority to stultify the minds and souls of men. Whether at the time of the Revolution Negroes were considered a special class of inferior beings or not—and there is precious little evidence for such assertions—the Northern people quickly came to respect them as persons, and a very great percentage of the people to treat them as equals insofar as all of their natural rights were concerned. If this were not true in 1820, then dozens of people representing great constituencies stood up in Congress and in pulpits all over the land and lied, and if it were true in 1820 it had been largely true in 1787, for the institutions of a people and the attitudes which sustain them do not change so quickly.

In the slaveholding states slaves were property by force of statute law, and Negroes were slaves unless they could prove the contrary. In the North they were persons, regardless of status elsewhere and despite all legal subtleties, and every person was free until proved otherwise by positive evidence. All Negroes, all antislavery whites, and, ultimately, the Northern people generally demanded that legislative bodies and the courts recognize the rights of slaves as persons. Slaveholders fought stubbornly to keep slaves property, no matter where they were taken or fled. The conflict raged in the courts, in the judicial cases involving fugitives, free Negroes, and their friends.

Arrival of a party at League Island
Fugitives from Norfolk, Virginia, arriving in Philadelphia in July 1856.

This question first caused trouble in the matter of transit through free states by slaveholders with their slaves and temporary residence by slaveholders in free states with their slaves. It must be remembered with regard to slaves taken into free states and then taken back to slave states that very few ever obtained freedom because of their ignorance, their lack of legal standing, and their lack of friends who cared or dared enough to press for their freedom in the courts; but, in the relatively few cases of early years, decisions were handed down directly contrary to the dictum of the Supreme Court of the United States in both the Prigg case of 1842 and the Dred Scott case of 1857. If the owner had become a *fully established resident* of a free state or of the Northwest Territory before states were created, the slaves, even though voluntarily returning to a slave state, were free.[1]

Why was this so? Because a slave never could do anything voluntarily, except in legal fiction; freedom should always take precedence over bondage in cases of doubt; slavery existed only by municipal (positive local) law, and residence by

the owner with his slave in a state or territory where there were no such laws gave the slave freedom; and, once free, he could not again be enslaved. In *Harry and Others* v. *Decker and Hopkins*, the Court said: "Slavery is condemned by reason and the laws of nature. It exists and can only exist, through municipal regulations, and in matters of doubt, is it not an unquestioned rule, that courts must lean in favorem vitae et libertatis." These cases were in state courts.[2] They may rightfully be presumed to reflect more closely the will of the people than contrary decisions at a later period by federal judges who were appointed by a political party in which slaveholders provided intellectual leadership. These decisions would have freed every person ever kidnapped and carried South, also, if only there had been some kind of machinery in the slave states for the protection of slaves. There was none. They would not have freed slaves who accompanied owners on temporary sojourns in the free states. They would not have given freedom to returned fugitives. They would not have applied in cases where antislavery men claimed that slaves were free once beyond the limits and authority of a slave state, or by positive authority of a free state.

Temporary residence was something else again, and here there was even stronger support for freedom. The Northern states had freed their own slaves, in every case by firm declaration of the natural right of all persons to freedom and equality. Bringing slaves into these states under any circumstances was a technical violation of the law, and an affront to the basic philosophy of the people. It also compounded the difficulties of gradual emancipation. Pennsylvania had a law permitting temporary residence with slaves for nine months, New York for six months. These were special exemptions to prevent municipal (state) law from freeing the slaves. Antislavery men worked diligently for the repeal of all such laws. The problem presented by the presence of these slaves in a free state was whether they should be treated as slave property or as men. Ellis Gray Loring of Massachusetts stated the problem graphically by asking if the law of slavery prevailed and gave the master the "right absolutely to direct the slave's locomotion; to confine his person; to exact his labor without wages; and to force him out of Massachusetts by any degree of personal violence which may be required. If the slave should marry here, he must of course be separated from his wife. Can he make a contract? Will his marriage be valid, or will it be void and his children illegitimate? Are the children born here of a slave mother, to be also slaves? Or will their father, if he should be a free citizen of Massachusetts, be entitled to his own children? If the slave sees a crime committed by his master, shall he be admitted as a witness? And if he shall testify against his master, what treatment may he expect upon his return to the slave state? If a slave is slandered in Massachusetts, has he a remedy? If he is assaulted by a stranger, has he an action as a *person*, or does the action belong to his master as for an injury to property? May the master be bound to keep the peace toward his slave? If the slave refuses to leave the State, may the master justify an assault and battery upon him?"[3]

An answer to these questions propounded by Loring was not easily given; nor to the further and equally pertinent question of what constituted residence. Was it being in a free state for any other purpose than passing through?[4] Was it six months? three months? a matter of days or of

hours? There was only one answer so far as antislavery people were concerned: slaves who set foot on free soil were free. Northern state courts increasingly freed such slaves during the 1850's, Justice Ozias Bowen of Ohio saying in 1856: "Strengthened, therefore, as we find the case to be, by the clearest principles of natural law, and by the decisions of courts of high character, we have no hesitation in arriving at the conclusion that Poindexter, in coming into this State by the consent and license of his master, obtained thereby the freedom of which he had been deprived by local municipal legislation. His servitude from that hour ceased, and there is no law which can bring into operation the right of slavery when once destroyed."[5] Later, Justice P. J. Mitchell of the New York Supreme Court declared that slaves in transit from Virginia to New York City for shipment by boat to Savannah and New Orleans were free when they entered New York state because slavery was contrary to the natural right of freedom, originating in force and sustained by force of municipal law which does not operate beyond the limits of a state; slaves were free immediately when they passed beyond the limits of the jurisdiction of Virginia, free also by the laws of New York because there were no constitutional restraints upon that state except in the matter of fugitives.[6] William M. Evarts, representing the state of New York, said: "The status of slavery is not a natural relation, but is contrary to nature, and at every moment it subsists, it is an ever new and active violation of the law of nature. It originates in mere predominance of physical force, and is continued by mere predominance of social force or municipal law. Whenever and wherever the physical force in the one stage, or the social force or municipal law in the other stage, fails, the *status* falls, for it has nothing to rest upon."

Meanwhile, the federal courts had followed a narrow and totally unrealistic line of reasoning in such cases. District Judge Read said in 1845 that masters lost all control of their slaves if they brought them into free states unless the slaves returned voluntarily to a slave state.[7] Justice John McLean of the United States Supreme Court freed slaves who had been forcibly returned to slave states, but said there was some question if they would be entitled to freedom had they returned voluntarily.[8] Slaves, of course, never did anything voluntarily. The will of the master was the will of the slave. That was a well-recognized legal principle in the slave states, and every judge who spoke of voluntary return knew it. Judges knew, also, and the people of the free states knew that free Negroes could not enter South Carolina, Georgia, Virginia, Arkansas, North Carolina, Mississippi, or Tennessee. State laws forbade them to do so and provided for their sale as slaves if apprehended. Under these laws no slave could gain freedom by virtue of residency in free states whether they returned voluntarily or were carried back by force. Length of time in a free state did not matter. Whether the owner established residence in the free states, or not, did not matter. So said the courts of Kentucky in 1850, and the Supreme Court approved in denying jurisdiction and approved again in the Dred Scott decision.[9]

We pass now to judicial dictum concerning *fugitives and fugitive slave laws*. Neither the act of 1793 nor the act of 1850 applied to slaves brought into free states by their owners, but only if and when slaves came into the free states without their masters' consent.[10] Before 1820 the return of fugitives was routine procedure, but the courts protected free Negroes more carefully than in later years. Chief Justice Kinsey of New Jersey declared in 1795 that anyone claiming another person as a slave must prove good title, and mere possession was not proof of title. Said he: "It is not incumbent on the negro to prove himself absolutely a freeman; it is sufficient if he disproves the right of the person who claims him."[11] As more and more slaves became free under the gradual emancipation acts of the Northern states and numbers of easily kidnapped children multiplied, this repudiation of the principle that a Negro was presumed to be a slave unless he could prove otherwise became universal in all Northern states. It could not have been any other way.

The courts of the states which did not emancipate at the time of the Revolution held that color was a presumption of slavery, and that a Negro must present positive proof of freedom in all cases. They also held that slaveholders possessed the right under the common law to reclaim their slaves at any and all times exactly as they reclaimed a horse that had strayed away. The superior courts, federal and state, generally followed the courts of the slave states after 1830. This change in the attitude of the federal courts after 1830 came precisely at the time of Andrew Jackson's administration when the slave power was making its supreme effort to bend every agency

of government, federal and state, to its will. It lost the battle so far as Northern state governments were concerned because the Northern people, freeing themselves of the last vestiges of slavery, moved forward in a vast liberal reform movement. It won in the federal government because the slaveholders controlled the Democratic party, and its victory extended to the courts. Slaveholders, from the beginning, had sought greater federal control of the return of fugitives. This they fully achieved in the Act of 1850. They sought application to the entire country of presumption of slavery on the basis of color. This they fully achieved in the Dred Scott decision.

There was no previous basis in federal courts for the acceptance of the philosophy of slavery in lieu of the philosophy of freedom; no indication that the common law of recapture—which was Southern law—should be applied to the free states on the basis of constitutional interpretation. This was done by the judges. Why it was done remains a subject for future research, *but it was done*. The argument was presented that slave states would not have become parties to the Constitution unless their property in slaves had been protected. The Constitution, it was said, could not have been adopted without it.[12] This philosophy of slaveholders that the supreme law of the land recognized the right of one man to hold another in bondage and that his right to do so must be protected from violation at all costs was abhorrent to the prevailing philosophy of natural rights and justice in the nonslaveholding states. Slaveholders not only insisted that a Negro be presumed to be a slave unless he could prove by positive evidence that he was free, but that all cases of doubt must be resolved in favor of the alleged owner. They insisted upon their right to come into the free states, seize any Negro, and keep him until he proved his freedom.[13] This, of course, was impossible for the Negro to do once he was taken into a slave state. They even insisted upon the right to go on the property and into the house of another person without permission to seize a fugitive. By 1842 the courts allowed them to carry alleged fugitives out of a free state without a certificate of removal, and after the Prigg decision they came across into the free states with impunity in pursuit of fugitives, seized them, and returned home without ever going near a magistrate.

Taney had said in that decision that a free Negro was an anomaly in American society, and his rights must remain subordinate to the good of society. The people of the free states insisted that the rights of persons, regardless of color, must be protected whether slaveholders recovered so-called property or not, and the principle that a person could not be property became a legal concept. The slaveholders insisted, and the federal courts agreed, that slaves were property, that all Negroes were presumed to be slaves, and that they had no constitutional rights.

Slaveholders under the act of 1793 were allowed to seize slaves without a warrant and without the presence of a civil officer. The only issue before the magistrate at the hearing after the seizure was one of identity, and that could be determined in a summary manner. Bushrod Washington, justice of the Supreme Court (1798–1829), seems to have exercised care to protect free persons.[14] Justice John McLean, at a later date, did likewise; but magistrates did not have to do so. The people of the free states demanded writs of habeas corpus and jury trials as the only safeguard against enslavement of free citizens of their states. The slaveholders insisted, and Chief Justice Taney agreed, that a trial would entail excessive costs on the part of the claimant, and that the Constitution gave said claimant a right to immediate recovery which neither state nor federal law could impair. The courts upheld this argument. Trial by jury was not argued by counsel or considered by the court in *Prigg* v. *Pennsylvania*, but the question was certainly embraced in the decision because Prigg had seized a fugitive without process and had carried her away without any certificate from a magistrate or judge in the state of Pennsylvania. The court declared he had a right to do so by virtue of the Constitution and the Act of 1793. All of this action by the courts embraced the concept that Negroes were presumed to be slaves, ignored the inability of free Negroes to obtain justice in the courts of the slave states, and subordinated human rights to property rights.

Perhaps the most wicked part of this whole business was the utterly callous disregard of gradual emancipation. A number of Northern states, particularly New York, Pennsylvania, and New Jersey, had been slave states and had embarked upon programs of gradual emancipation with legal safeguards against re-enslavement and kidnapping. All of these laws were made inoperative by the summary procedures under the Fugitive Slave Act. Then, in the New York Court of Errors in 1834, state laws *authorizing* seizure and return of fugitives were declared to be unconstitutional on the grounds that Congress had the sole right to legislate.[15] Some years later, in *Prigg* v. *Pennsylvania,* the whole argument about authority not being expressly granted to Congress nor expressly prohibited to the states, and about the rights of Negroes wrongfully seized and of states whose laws were being violated, was resolved by the Supreme Court of the United States, and resolved on the side of slavery. The power to legislate lay exclusively with Congress, and all state legislation touching the subject was unconstitutional.

Penalties for harboring and concealing fugitives were severe. John Van Zandt, a former Kentuckian and an active participant in underground railroad operations, was apprehended near Cincinnati with nine fugitives in his wagon. One of the fugitives escaped, and Van Zandt was sued for $500 by action of debt, and for damages for the loss and temporary absence of his property by the owner as provided in the Act of 1793. The case was tried in the United States Circuit Court, then by appeal in the Supreme Court. William H. Seward and Salmon P. Chase, two future members of Lincoln's Cabinet, were the defense lawyers. They lost the case but won wide renown. Van Zandt died in May 1847, before the case was concluded, the administrators of his estate having to pay costs of $1,000 and judgment of $1,700.[16]

In 1845 Jane and Harrison Garretson and four children escaped from their owner in Kentucky. They were apprehended on February 28 at the home of Parish in Sandusky. He refused to deliver them to the agent and they escaped to Canada. The owner, one Driskill, brought action under the provisions of the Act of 1793 and was awarded $500.[17] In 1848 a suit was brought in Pennsylvania against Kaufman and others who had assisted twelve slaves to escape by concealing them in a barn. The owner was awarded $2,800.[18] In another case four slaves who had been apprehended at Cassopolis, Michigan, were rescued near South Bend, Indiana, and given certificates of freedom. The owner was awarded $2,850.[19] Slaveowners who were manhandled or arrested for the recovery of fugitives were awarded damages of $4,000 in Pennsylvania and $6,000 in Michigan.[20]

Slaveholders had previously attempted to obtain extradition of those who aided escape of fugitives. The question of whether it was an extraditable offense was one for Northern governors rather than for federal judges to decide, and the governors were far more responsive to the will of the people. In 1834 the officers of the schooner "Susan," returning from Georgia, allowed a Negro stowaway to escape upon reaching a port in Maine. The governor of Georgia sent a requisition to the governor of Maine, asking extradition of the officers of the "Susan," charging that they were fugitives from justice under the laws of Georgia. Extradition was refused on the grounds that the officers had not fled from justice, having left Georgia before being charged with the offense. In 1839 members of the crew of the "Robert Center" assisted slaves to escape from Norfolk, Virginia. Governor Seward refused to surrender them, because New York law did not recognize property in man, and the legislature enacted a law granting fugitives trial by jury.[21] Virginia retaliated by providing special inspection of all vessels leaving her ports for New York. Governor Bell of Ohio refused to surrender fifteen persons

in 1848 who had assisted a fugitive to escape from Kentucky on the grounds Ohio law did not recognize property in man. John Mahan, at an earlier date, had been surrendered to Kentucky, and a friend who had posted bond to pay any damages awarded against him had been required to pay $1,600.[22] *This was the only case* in which a Northern governor allowed the extradition of a person accused of aiding the escape of a fugitive slave.

Then came the fugitive slave act of 1850. Commissioners were to be appointed by the circuit and district courts of the United States. These commissioners, who were allowed concurrent jurisdiction with judges, were entitled, upon satisfactory proof having been made, to grant certificates to the claimants authorizing the return of the fugitives. In order to insure perfect co-operation and enforcement, the marshals and their deputies were commanded to obey such warrants on the penalty of a maximum fine of $1,000 which would be given to the claimant. If the fugitive escaped after the arrest, with or without the con-

Desperate conflict in a barn

Capture of Robert Jackson, fugitive from Harpers Ferry in 1853, as recorded by Still.

sent of the federal marshals, such marshals would be held liable to prosecution by the claimant for the full value of the fugitive. Then, in order to protect the marshals, they were given the power to appoint assistants at any time deemed necessary. They were given authority to summon the aid of bystanders or to appoint a *posse comitatus* whenever necessary. The claimant could procure a warrant or seize without one. Proof could be presented orally or in writing. No testimony by alleged fugitives was allowable. A maximum fine of $1,000 and imprisonment not exceeding six months was provided for anyone who hindered the arrest of a fugitive, attempted to rescue him from the custody of the claimant or marshal, or in any manner hampered the process of rendition. Such persons were liable also for civil damages up to $1,000 for each slave lost.

Every item in this law was challenged in the courts, and it was sustained in its entirety. No federal court ever declared the act unconstitutional.[23] In every case sharply defined principles abhorrent to the champions of freedom were sustained by the federal courts. There was bitter criticism of the penalties imposed upon men for acts of Christian charity, and of the attempt by the government to define disobedience of the law as treason, but these were not the important things. The key to opposition lay in the summary hearing before commissioners. Appointment of commissioners was challenged because the Constitution limits the exercise of judicial powers to organized courts of justice, composed of judges holding office during good behavior and receiving fixed salaries for their services. The most any federal court ever would admit was that the inquiry made by the commissioners had a judicial flavor of the sort exercised by examiners of the patent office. They insisted that the legal force of a certificate issued by a commissioner lay merely in its authorization to remove the alleged fugitive named in it from one state to another. The disposition made of the alleged fugitive depended entirely upon the law of the state to which he was being taken. Stephen A. Douglas, devious as always, insisted that the fugitive had a right to a jury trial in the home state of his claimant, and that the hearing only established identity, not whether the man was a slave or not.

The hearing, of course, did not establish anything with certainty except that the alleged fugitive, *slave or free, was doomed to eternal servi-* *tude.* The whole business was a shameful perversion of justice, a lie and a deception, and ample grounds for revolution in any age and in any civilized country. There is a good deal to be learned from an analysis of the opposition to this law, and one emerges from such an examination with great respect for the old-line antislavery men. There is occasional evidence of the Garrisonian argument that the Constitution was a pro-slavery document. There was occasional emphasis at the other extreme on state rights philosophy. But the great body of antislavery argument moved along the lines of nationalism, antislavery interpretation of the Constitution, and complete emancipation by political action at the earliest possible moment. The law must be contested in the courts. It must be repealed, but the problem must be solved within the framework of the national government.

Antislavery men argued for equality of all men in the endowment and the enjoyment of natural rights. They believed the primary function of gov-

William Still

United States slave trade, 1830

ernment to be the protection and security of those rights.[24] They insisted that Negroes were persons entitled to all constitutional guarantees of free men *wherever federal law operated,* and that they could only be considered slaves within the narrow field of operation of state law.[25] If this were not so, it should be so. They insisted also that the term citizen meant what they were later to say in the Fourteenth Amendment it meant. In the language of the American and Foreign Antislavery Society: "Free inhabitants born within the United States, or naturalized under the laws of Congress. If a slave, born in the United States be manumitted or otherwise discharged from bondage, or if a black man be born within the United States and born free, he becomes thenceforward a citizen."[26] Citizenship did not depend upon rights recognized, but upon the place of birth. All Negro freemen in 1787 and all born free or emancipated thereafter were citizens no matter how much they were discriminated against.

Antislavery men, therefore, refused to concede inferiority of the Negro, color as a presumption of slavery, or application *only* of the law of property in fugitive slave cases. The equality of all men had been carefully safeguarded by the fathers of the Constitution, who had refused to recognize slaves as property in the Constitution. Whether

fugitives or *free men,* therefore, everyone seized by the peculiar operations of the law was entitled to stand before the bar of justice fully clothed with all the constitutional safeguards of individual freedom.[27]

There were Northerners, multitudes of them in fact, who agreed with the slaveholders that slaves were not party to the Constitution and that slaveowners were entitled to recover fugitives, but they insisted upon protecting free men regardless of color. All persons removed must be proved slaves. Free men must not be taken. They must be tried before their freedom was taken away, and the trial must be in the nonslaveholding states where the presumption of freedom prevailed, not in the slave states where the possibility of trial was almost nonexistent and the presumption of slavery prevailed.

The Fugitive Slave Act of 1850 drove these two groups together in resistance to the extension of slave law into the Northern states by way of the federal Constitution and judicial interpretation. Denial to the alleged fugitive of all constitutional safeguards of freedom placed every person in jeopardy, and all the legal arguments and judicial pronouncements did not balance the evidence of continued kidnapping.[28] Chief Justice Whiton of the Wisconsin Supreme Court, who was not an antislavery man, said in the celebrated *Booth* case: "We do not propose to discuss the question whether a slave escaping from the state where he is held to service or labor, into a state where slavery does not exist, thereby becomes free by virtue of the local law, subject only to be delivered up to be returned again to servitude, as it is a question not necessarily involved in the consideration of the subject before us. But we propose to examine the operation of the act upon a free citizen of a free state, and to show that by it such a person may be deprived of his liberty without due process of law."[29] Said E. C. Larned: "It is the making a man a slave at all without the verdict of a jury upon the fact of freedom of which we complain." Said Robert Rantoul: "Due process of law is meant to distinguish the careful, guarded, strict, precise manner known to the English law, from the summary military process used in time of war. There can, therefore, be no doubt that a person held to service is, by due process of law, entitled to his trial by jury."[30]

With regard to the authority of the Supreme Court, the hard phalanx of old antislavery men who were pushing the issue of slavery to a conclusion never wavered. Men like Gerrit Smith, Salmon P. Chase, William Birney, William H. Seward never denied the authority of the court. They did deny—and *this is important in connection with secession in 1861*—that the decision of the court was correct in this case, or unchangeable. Said Gerrit Smith: "I cheerfully submit the general proposition, that the decisions of the supreme judiciary are to be regarded as conclusive, at least for many years. But I deny that decisions of any, even the highest, earthly tribunal, against fundamental, unchangeable, eternal human rights are ever, even for one moment, to be regarded as final and unalterable."[31] The way to correct the errors of the court was through the ballot box. This was the position of all political action antislavery men, probably nine-tenths of the whole.

The Garrisonian extremists, constituting a very decided minority of antislavery men, took a very different position. James Mott said in 1855 that whether the Constitution was a "supreme law or a binding treaty, it is in our view an abominable thing, with which we cannot, as honest and honorable men, have anything to do, except to seek its destruction."[32] Wendell Phillips, as great an orator of disunion as William L. Yancey ever was, though with far more purity of heart, had said in

1848, and he never deviated from the position: "I love these men; [Jay, Adams, Lee, Morris, Martin, Sherman, Wilson] I hate their work. I respect their memory; I reject their deeds. I trust their hearts; I distrust their heads. We are not greater than they, but we live after them; we stand on the shoulders of 50 years, and are therefore wiser. They tried to do well. They failed. I am sorry. We will try to do better. They are dead, but we live. We will break the chains. Till a purified soil south of Mason's and Dixon's line shall call the sisterhood together and make us a nation of freemen, the abolitionist who loves his father must be a traitor to the institutions of America. The abolitionist who loves his country is bound to be a traitor to the constitution. He is bound to trample it underfoot for the cause of justice and the slave . . . I will not guarantee the slave in rebellion; neither will I guarantee the master in oppression. We ask for a dissolution of the union because it is our duty to cease sinning, and that can be done in no way but by leaping out of this network which the Constitution has woven."[33]

Charles Sumner of Massachusetts denied that the Supreme Court was the final arbiter in controversies involving constitutional interpretation. His philosophy was that of Andrew Jackson—that every public official takes an oath to support the Constitution as he understands it. Wisconsin Judges Abram D. Smith and Edward V. Whiton represented men who, regardless of their attitude toward slavery, used state rights arguments. Every fugitive must be protected by the legal machinery of the state against recapture. They followed the precedent of the Virginia and Kentucky resolutions. They got publicity as the Garrisonians got publicity and just about as much of a following. Most men preferred to disobey the law as individuals and suffer the consequences. Aid to fugitives was not an assertion of state rights.

There were many rescues of fugitives. A slave, Shadrach, was seized by his owner in Boston in October 1850 and carried before a United States commissioner. He was rescued and spirited away, antislavery men said, by Negroes. Five persons, including Elizur Wright, were tried but not convicted. Congress, incensed, gave the President authority to use the armed forces in such cases.[34] At Christiana, Lancaster County, Pennsylvania, there was a riot in 1851, by Negroes fighting for freedom. White men refused to aid the federal authorities, but took no part in the affair. The

Slave auction at Richmond
Human flesh was inspected as carefully as horseflesh by the buyer, perhaps more so. This sketch was made from life by Eyre Crowe.

owner of the alleged fugitives was killed; several men were wounded; all of the Negroes escaped. United States marines and police from Philadelphia then combed the area and arrested thirty-five Negroes and three white Quakers. They were tried on charges of treason, but were acquitted.[35]

In Syracuse, also in 1851, an attempt was made to recover a fugitive, Jerry, when a Liberty Party convention was being held in the city. A group of men, including Gerrit Smith and Samuel J. May, rescued him from jail and sent him to Canada. Several men, Negro and white, were indicted but only one Negro, Enoch Reed, was convicted. He died in prison during an appeal.[36] In Boston, in 1854, Anthony Burns was placed on shipboard for return to Virginia by United States Marines,

the Fourth Regiment of United States Artillery, and United States marshals, numbering in all about 1,100 armed men, at a cost to the government of an estimated $40,000 to $100,000. Six persons, including Theodore Parker, were brought to trial, but the case was dismissed.[37]

President Fillmore, the federal courts, the slave power, and many people of the free states insisted that people who gave food and shelter to fugitives, who aided them to avoid arrest, or rescued them from United States marshals, or encouraged others to do so were guilty of treason. It is true that there were thousands of public meetings which resolved to prevent enforcement of the Fugitive Slave Act, that the underground railroad was well organized, and that there were local vig-

Holy Bible.
Thou shalt not deliver unto the master his servant which has escaped from his master unto thee. He shall dwell with thee. Even among you in that place which he shall choose in one of thy gates where it liketh him best. Thou shalt not oppress him.
Deut XXIII 15.16

Effects of the Fugitive-Slave-Law.

Declaration of independence.
We hold that all men are created equal, that they are endowed by their Creator with certain unalienable rights, that among these are life, liberty and the pursuit of happiness.

ilance committees. It was also true that violence was, in every case, spontaneous, that Negroes themselves were heavily involved, and that white men who participated were prominent in their communities. Negroes needed protection. They could not get it from the government, so they got it from their friends and neighbors. Juries simply refused to take seriously the charge of treason. No one was ever convicted. Judges refused to take cognizance of the higher law doctrine, but the people accepted it, and Charles Sumner could say in the Senate: "By the Supreme Law which commands me to do no injustice, by the Comprehensive Christian Law of Brotherhood, and by the Constitution, which I have sworn to support, I am bound to disobey this act."[38]

It was sometimes easier to kill than to capture.

NEGRO LEADERS

Chapter 39

The Revolutionary period was the beginning of steady and remarkable progress for the Negroes. The three important centers for the development of leadership and institutional life among them were New York City with 14,000 free Negroes by 1830, Philadelphia with 9,700, and Boston with slightly less than 2,000. Other important centers were Providence, Albany, Newark and Pittsburgh. By 1830 there were 38,000 in Pennsylvania, 18,000 in New Jersey, 45,000 in New York, 8,000 in Connecticut, and 7,000 in Massachusetts. In this geographical area, between the time of the Revolution and the beginning of the organized antislavery movement, were developed the religious, educational, business, and social leaders. It was the period of gradual emancipation and of wholesale kidnappings.

To the South was the land of perpetual slavery, where the struggle to be free from physical bondage and from the mental and spiritual darkness of slavery has surpassed our ability to understand, but it seethed in the souls of the free Negroes, whose numbers were constantly augmented by fugitives. Once free from the deadening influence of slavery these people began life anew with spirit and zest and enthusiasm. There were among them many professional men, including preachers (some of white congregations), educators, lawyers, physicians. They owned property, engaged in business, paid taxes; and some were wealthy. They had fought in the Revolutionary armies, some free and some slave, and those who had been slaves had fought both for the freedom of their country and for their own personal freedom.

With the threat of permanent slavery to the South by kidnapping and the promise of permanent security to the North by flight to Canada; with the slave power gaining a greater stranglehold upon the federal government each passing year; with its Northern arm of colonization fomenting oppression in order to drive them out; and without protection from any agency of government: under these circumstances the free Negroes not only dedicated their lives and fortunes to elevating their own people but to protecting the fugitives and getting them to Canada. They fought for their own right to remain in the United States, and through it all they were a thousand times more loyal to the Constitution and the Union than white men of many times their numbers both North and South.

Schools, churches, and lodges were evidence of intellectual and social achievement, the church being the most important single element in Negro society. It was the strongest of their organizations, being a social institution, a religious center, a forum for the exchange of ideas, and a training center of leaders. Benezet's schools in Philadelphia continued to expand after his death.[1] African free schools were begun in New York before 1790. The first Negro schools were established in Boston in 1798. New York began state support for these schools in 1797, Pennsylvania in 1818, and Boston in 1820. All of this was a part of the broad program of the convention period of the antislav-

Douglass, Garnet, Brown, and Allen were among the anti-slavery great.

ery movement. In 1787 the Negroes withdrew from the St. George Methodist Episcopal Church in Philadelphia and founded the first Negro churches in that city: the St. Thomas African Episcopal Church under Absolom Jones, and the African Methodist Episcopal Church under Richard Allen. The latter became a powerful organization. Allen had worked as a circuit rider, and he and Daniel Coker, Negro Methodist of Baltimore, established circuits in New York, Pennsylvania, and Ohio before 1824. A similar movement in New York City led to the organization of the African Methodist Episcopal Zion Churches in 1821, and in Boston to the first African Baptist Church in 1806. The first Baptist Church was established in Philadelphia in 1809, and the African Presbyterian Church in Philadelphia in 1807, by John Gloucester, an ex-slave from Tennessee. Samuel E. Cornish, Presbyterian minister of Philadelphia, established the first Negro Presbyterian Church in New York in 1822. There were ten Methodist Churches, five Baptist, three Presbyterian, and one Episcopalian in Philadelphia by 1849.[2] In 1787 a group of Negroes in Boston organized a Masonic Lodge (African Lodge, No. 459 F. & A.M.) under a warrant from the Grand Master of England. A lodge was organized in Philadelphia in 1797, and then one in Providence. These three formed the African Grand Lodge in 1800. There were four lodges in Philadelphia by 1815, and there were forty-four beneficiary and mutual aid societies in that city by 1830.

The Negroes had made two important contributions to the antislavery movement by 1830. They had given positive proof of how utterly false was the doctrine of racial inferiority, and they had produced some excellent antislavery literature. It is possible here only to give examples of individual achievement. Benjamin Banneker, of pure African descent, was born in Maryland in 1730. His mother was born free, his father purchased his own freedom. Benjamin went to a country school for Negroes and was given access to the large library of one George Ellicott. He mastered Latin and Greek and had a good working knowledge of German and French. He became a student of astronomy and published almanacs annually in Philadelphia, 1792–95. He participated in the original survey of the District of Columbia. He was a devoted advocate of emancipation, but wrote no literature on the subject. He was cited in France, in Britain by Pitt, Wilber-

force, and Buxton, and by the American Anti-Slavery leaders many times as proof of the equality of the races.[3]

The antislavery societies published and sold *The Memoir and Poems of Phillis Wheatley.* The memoir was written by some one of the antislavery leaders, but the poems were the product of a precocious Boston slave girl of revolutionary days. She was brought from Africa to Boston at seven years of age and was sold to John Wheatley, a prosperous merchant of that city. Taken into the family and admitted to church, she became a pet of the entire congregation. Her poems, published when she was nineteen, were religious in character and were used to illustrate the intellectual capacities of the Negro.[4]

Theodore Weld, when he lectured in Ohio in the early days of the antislavery movement, used a small book of poems which he called the longings of a slave after liberty.[5]

> Oh, Heaven! and is there no relief
> This side the silent grave
> To soothe the pain—to quell the grief
> And anguish of the slave?

The poet was George Moses Horton, a slave belonging to James Horton of Chatham County, North Carolina.[6] George was allowed to hire his time to the students at Chapel Hill, for whom he composed love letters, poems, and witticisms. His poems first appeared in the *Raleigh Register* and were reprinted in the Boston papers. They were collected in 1829 and published under the title *The Hope of Liberty* to raise money to purchase George's freedom and send him to Liberia. The plan failed and his subsequent poems were wails of despair.

The first of the free Negro leaders was James Forten. He was born in Philadelphia in 1766 and was educated by Benezet until nine years of age. He went into the navy at fourteen as drummer boy on Decatur's ship "Royal Louis," was taken to England, and was sent back as an apprentice to a sailmaker in Philadelphia. He founded his own business eventually, employing forty white and Negro men. In 1814, Forten, Richard Allen, and Absolom Jones raised a force of 2,500 Negro volunteers to protect the city against the British. He always refused to supply any ship suspected of being used in the slave trade. It was he who purchased enough subscriptions to enable Garrison to found the *Liberator*, and he gave Garrison the necessary financial assistance to keep the paper from being discontinued in 1834. Forten died in 1842.

The Negro antislavery writers included John B. Russwurm, born in Jamaica in 1799 of a Negro mother and white father. He was educated in Canada and at Bowdoin, where he graduated in 1826. He established in New York, March 16, 1827, the first Negro newspaper, *Freedom's Journal*. It was renamed the *Rights of All* in March 1828 and was published until 1830. The paper carried a biography of Paul Cuffee, ship owner of Massachusetts who was a colonizationist, and who took thirty Negroes to Sierra Leone before his death in 1817. Russwurm was a staunch advocate of immediate emancipation, but his advocacy of colonization destroyed his influence among the Negroes, and he went to Liberia to superintend the schools. Included among the publications of this early period were *An Address To Those Who Keep Slaves and Approve the Practice* by Richard Allen and Absolom Jones in 1794, and a petition by the same men to the sixth Congress, which precipitated a two-day debate and led John Rutledge of South Carolina to denounce the entire discussion of slavery as unconstitutional.[7] Finally, when the Pennsylvania legislature proposed excluding Negro immigrants in 1813, James Forten wrote a series of letters under the signature "A Man of Color."

The transition from the earlier period to the militant antislavery movement was marked by publication of David Walker's *Appeal*. This pamphlet, as we said before, struck fear into the hearts of slaveholders. Benjamin Lundy condemned it as injuring the antislavery cause; even Garrison said it was injudicious. It is doubtful if either observation can be substantiated. Walker's mind was not trained, perhaps not disciplined, but that is precisely what made his *Appeal* one of the greatest pieces of antislavery literature. It was the primitive cry of anguish from a race oppressed. It was precisely what would have come from a million throats could they have been articulate and have been heard. It may have caused Walker's death. If so, no man ever died more nobly, because he left a legacy of raging hatred for slavery, for the degradation, wretchedness, and ignorance of his people, and for colonization, which was designed to rob them of their natural leaders. His mantle fell upon Henry Highland Garnet.

New leaders quickly gave new direction to the movement for social, economic, and intellectual

Phillis Wheatley
An English portrait of a famous poetess brought to America as a child by the slave traders.

improvement, and, in doing so, they consolidated Negro support of the militant antislavery, anticolonization movement. Negro conventions were held between 1830 and 1834 and at intervals thereafter throughout the country, but the idea of exclusive Negro institutions was falling into disfavor. It was too closely associated with segregation, and it gave a superficial respectability to the idea of colonization. Antislavery leaders of both races rejected it for united effort and sought to promote integration in the general community.[8]

Lewis Tappan, William L. Garrison, and Simeon S. Jocelyn were present at the 1831 Negro convention. The twelve men who formed the New England Anti-Slavery Society met in the schoolroom of the African Baptist Church in Boston. Garrison drew up the Declaration of Sentiments of the American Anti-Slavery Society at the home of the Negro dentist James McCrummell. There were always three Negroes on the twelve-man

Sojourner Truth

executive committee of that society. Theodore S. Wright and Samuel Cornish remained on the committee until 1839 and then served on the executive committee of the American and Foreign Anti-Slavery Society. Wright died in 1846, and Charles B. Ray took his place.

Theodore Weld said: "To make a distinction between a white man and a black on account of their color in organization is the very principle of slavery. Treatment according to worth irrespective of color is the doctrine."[9] The Oberlin Appeal to the Philanthropists of Great Britain[10] bore the signatures of the following Negroes: James Forten, James McCune Smith, Charles W. Gardner, Samuel Cornish, Robert Purvis, and Paul Williams. Weld wrote the Appeal, and he had said at the very beginning of the movement that it was essential "to testify in its corporate capacity that God had made all men of one blood."[11] The American and Foreign Anti-Slavery Society, with its emphasis on missionary work, attracted an able and experienced group of Negro ministers: Theodore S. Wright and Samuel E. Cornish, who served on the executive committee, both Presbyterian clergymen, Christopher Rush, who served with them,

bishop of the Zion Connection, Reverend James W. C. Pennington of Hartford representing the Union Missionary Society, and the distinguished Amos G. Beman of New Haven and Henry H. Garnet.[12] From first to last, the Negroes made a great contribution as lecturers, as authors, and as operators of the undergound railroad.

Some of these men were freeborn, most were fugitives. Their importance as lecturers was recognized from the first. Weld and Tappan were convinced that it was the best way to kill prejudice, and the Negroes emphasized in their lectures the danger of race prejudice continuing after emancipation.[13]

The two principal agents for the New York committee were Theodore S. Wright and Samuel Ringgold Ward. Ward was born a slave in Maryland in 1817 and escaped with his parents to New Jersey when he was three years old. He was educated in the New York City schools, appointed an agent of the American Anti-Slavery Society in 1839, and licensed to preach by the New York Congregational Association. He supported the Liberty Party, worked among the fugitives in Canada, conducted a lecture tour in Great Britain, and finally went to the West Indies. Frederick Douglass thought he was the leading speaker and most brilliant intellect among the Negroes. He was often called the Black Daniel Webster. He was said to have been blacker than coal, a fact that was emphasized because he was the pastor of a white congregation at South Butler, New York. Gerrit Smith had provided for his education.

Another agent was Lunsford Lane. He was born a slave in Raleigh, North Carolina, hired his time, and was able to purchase his freedom by manufacturing smoking tobacco. His business prospered, but before he was able to purchase his wife and children he was forced to leave the state. He returned for his family only to be brutally treated by a mob. The remainder of his life was spent in Oberlin and in Boston. He lectured for the American Anti-Slavery Society, and served as a nurse in the army during the Civil War.

Another prominent Negro speaker was Sojourner Truth, who had been born a slave in New York about 1797. She was sold several times, obtaining freedom only by the state emancipation act in 1829. She left New York in 1843, traveled through the free states for years, then settled in Battle Creek, Michigan, in 1856. She never learned to read or write, but she lectured effectively and informally wherever she happened to be at the time.

Charles Lenox Remond was born in Massachusetts of free parents in 1810. He received an excellent education and became an eloquent speaker, his ability as an orator being compared to that of Wendell Phillips. He became an agent of the Massachusetts Anti-Slavery Society in 1838, traveled through New England, New York, and Pennsylvania with Ichabod Codding, went to the World Anti-Slavery Convention in 1840, and lectured for eighteen months in the British Isles. He brought back from Ireland in 1841 a petition signed by 60,000 people asking the Irish in the United States to support the antislavery cause. Frederick Douglass had been engaged as a lecturer by the Massachusetts society during Remond's absence, and the two men toured New York, Pennsylvania, Ohio, and Indiana. Both were powerful opponents of race prejudice and perfect examples of racial equality.

It has often been said that Remond was overshadowed by Douglass, which may have been true to some extent, due to Remond's illness, but the two real competitors for influence among the Negroes were Douglass and Henry Highland Garnet. Douglass' mother was a Maryland slave, his father an unknown white man. He was born in 1817, and his childhood was unmistakably a period of cruelty, hard work, and hopelessness. He escaped to New York in 1838 and went to New Bedford, Massachusetts. In 1841 he spoke at a meeting of the Massachusetts Anti-Slavery Society in Nantucket. His speech was a simple narrative of his life as a slave. He was immediately employed as an agent of the society, and for a time was a strong advocate of Garrisonian anti-unionism.

Henry Highland Garnet was born in Maryland in 1815, a pure-blooded grandson of an African chief. His family escaped in 1824 and went to New York City. Henry went to the African free schools for three years, excelling in Latin and Greek. In 1835 he went to the Academy of the Reverend William Scales at Canaan, New Hampshire, which was pulled from its foundations and burned shortly afterward. He fled to Albany, and then to Whitesboro, New York, to study under Beriah Green at Oneida Institute. He went to Troy in 1840 to serve as pastor of the Negro

Frederick Douglass

Presbyterian Church and to conduct a school for Negro children, until 1843.

Douglass and Garnet met in bitter debate in the Negro convention at Buffalo in 1843. Garnet delivered an eloquent appeal to the slaves to rise in revolt. This was the first such appeal after that of David Walker fourteen years before, and the convention refused to publish it. John Brown had it printed and distributed at his own expense.

Said Garnet: "Two hundred and twenty-seven years ago the first of our injured race were brought to the shores of America . . . The first dealings they had with men calling themselves Christians exhibited to them the worst features of corrupt and sordid hearts; and convinced them that no cruelty is too great, no villainy and no robbery too abhorrent for even enlightened men to perform, when influenced by avarice and lust . . . Succeeding generations inherited their chains, and millions have come from eternity into time, and have returned again to the world of spirits, cursed and ruined by American slavery . . .

"Slavery! How much misery is comprehended in that single word. What mind is there that does not shrink from its direful effects? Unless the image of God be obliterated from the soul, all men cherish the love of liberty . . . In every man's mind the good seeds of liberty are planted, and he who brings his fellow down so low, as to make him contented with a condition of slavery, commits the highest crime against God and man. Brethren, your oppressors aim to do this. They endeavor to make you as much like brutes as possible. When they have blinded the eyes of your mind—when they have embittered the sweet waters of life—when they have shut out the light which shines from the word of God—then, and not till then, has American slavery done its perfect work.

"TO SUCH DEGRADATION IT IS SINFUL IN THE EXTREME FOR YOU TO MAKE VOLUNTARY SUBMISSION . . . THE DIABOLICAL INJUSTICE BY WHICH YOUR LIBERTIES ARE CLOVEN DOWN, NEITHER GOD NOR ANGELS, OR JUST MEN, COMMAND YOU TO SUFFER FOR A SINGLE MOMENT. THEREFORE IT IS YOUR SOLEMN AND IMPERATIVE DUTY TO USE EVERY MEANS, BOTH MORAL, INTELLECTUAL, AND PHYSICAL, THAT PROMISES SUCCESS. . . . Think of the undying glory that hangs around the ancient name of Africa—and forget not that you are native-born American citizens, and as such you are justly entitled to all the rights that are granted to the freest. Think how many tears you have poured out upon the soil which you have cultivated with unrequited toil and enriched with your blood; and then go to your lordly enslavers and tell them plainly, that you *are determined to be free.* Appeal to their sense of justice, and tell them that they have no more right to oppress you than you have to enslave them. Entreat them to remove the grievous burdens which they have imposed upon you, and to remunerate you for your labor. Promise them renewed diligence in the cultivation of the soil, if they will render to you an equivalent for your services. Point them to the increase of happiness and prosperity in the British West Indies since the Act of Emancipation. Tell them in language which they cannot misunderstand of the exceeding sinfulness of slavery, and of a future judgment, and of the righteous retributions of an indignant God. Inform them that all you desire is *freedom,* and that nothing else will suffice. Do this, and forever after cease to toil for the heartless tyrants, who give you no other reward but stripes and abuse. If they commence work of death, they, and not you, will be responsible for the consequences. You had far better all die—*die immediately,* than live slaves, and entail your wretchedness upon your posterity. If you would be free in this generation, here is your only hope. However much you and all of us may desire it, there is not much hope of redemption without the shedding of blood. If you must bleed, let it all come at once—rather *die freemen than live to be slaves* . . . In the name of the merciful God,

Charles Lenox Remond

Henry Highland Garnet

Robert Purvis

and by all that life is worth, let it no longer be a debatable question, whether it is better to choose *liberty or death.*"[14]

Douglass then addressed the convention in more moderate tone and was thereafter recognized as the more influential of the two men. Two years later Douglass wrote the narrative of his own life which Wendell Phillips advised him to burn and which so compromised his safety that he fled to England. He was there eighteen months, lecturing and associating as an equal with distinguished men. He returned with enough money to purchase his freedom and to start *The North Star* at Rochester. He was now mature and independent enough to free himself from the vagaries of Garrison and to ignore Garrison's bitter opposition to a Negro newspaper.[15]

Garnet, meanwhile, went strongly into religious work, but continued to support the antislavery cause. He went to England in 1850, and, speaking French and German fluently, spent considerable time lecturing on the continent as well as in the British Isles, during the next three years. Douglass and Garnet both strongly supported political action, working for the Liberty Party candidates. Douglass, editor of *The North Star* for seventeen years, was a close associate of Gerrit Smith, Horace Mann, Salmon P. Chase, Charles Sumner, and William H. Seward.[16] Douglass, despite Garrison's ill-concealed effort to destroy him, never permitted himself to engage in acrimonious controversy. He and Garnet both strongly supported the government during the Civil War, and both played an active role in policies regarding emancipation and the freedmen. Garnet preached the sermon before the House of Representatives commemorating passage of the Thirteenth Amendment.

There was in the East, also, a group of very able and zealous men whose major contribution was in the rescue of fugitives. Robert Purvis, of English-Negro, Moorish-Jewish ancestry, was born free in South Carolina in 1810. Brought to the North in 1819, he was given a good education, and graduated from Amherst. He was very fair and could easily have passed as a white man, but he identified his life with the Negroes of Philadelphia.[17] He was intellectually brilliant, wealthy, and the son-in-law of James Forten. He had read Torrey's *Portraiture of Slavery* as a boy and was well acquainted with Benjamin Lundy.[18] He helped organize the American Anti-Slavery Soci-

ety and the Pennsylvania Anti-Slavery Society and was closely associated with Garrison and Wendell Phillips. Practically his entire life was devoted to the work of the underground railroad. In Philadelphia, also in the 1850's, was William Still, who was born in New Jersey in 1821. His father purchased his freedom, but his mother was a fugitive. William worked on a farm for a time, then went to Philadelphia in 1844 and worked as a clerk for the Pennsylvania Anti-Slavery Society. He became corresponding secretary of the Philadelphia branch of the underground railroad and kept a record of the experiences of all fugitives who came through the city, publishing it in 1872.[19] His life after the war was devoted to welfare work among the Negroes and to fighting discrimination.

New York City had three very able leaders. James McCune Smith, born in 1813 of slaves in New York, had been educated abroad at the University of Glasgow and held the degrees of A.B., M.A., and M.D. (1837) from that institution. He was a practicing physician of distinction, a life-long foe of colonization, a prolific writer on the subject of racial equality, an able speaker, and in every sense the leader of the Negroes in that city. Charles B. Ray, born in Massachusetts in 1807, graduated from Wesleyan University in 1832. He became a merchant in New York City, was chairman of the city vigilance committee, secretary of the state vigilance committee, and editor of the *Colored American* from 1839 to 1842. He was pastor of the Bethesda Congregational Church for twenty-two years. These men were ably assisted in the work of the underground railroad by David Ruggles, a fearless publisher and bookseller, who is said to have transported 600 fugitives to safety and who never turned aside to avoid a pamphlet controversy.[20]

One of the Negroes' most significant contributions was the slave narrative, a very distinctive type of literature. There had been the earlier type of biographical sketches, written by others than the Negro, such as Margaret Matilda Odell's *Memoir and Poems of Phillis Wheatley.*[21] There had been fictional narratives, such as Richard Hildreth's *The Slave; or, Memoirs of Archy Moore.*[22] There had been dictated narratives, such as the *Narrative of David Barrett* by Hiram Wilson.[23] The more important *true narratives*, however, grew out of the lectures of fugitive slaves. These show the blackest pages of American history, the very depths of depravity to which the slave system had sunk, and they were heard by thousands in addition to those who read them. The first of these has already been mentioned: *Narrative of the Life of Frederick Douglass.*[24] There were four others.

William Wells Brown was born in Lexington, Kentucky, not later than 1816. He was said to have been the grandson of Daniel Boone. Matters of such delicacy are hard to prove. His mother was a slave, his father a white slaveholder. He was made a companion of his master's nephew, and the family moved to St. Louis. The lad was fair and was so often taken to be his master's son that he was hired out to a slave trader, sold to a merchant, and then sold to a river-boat captain. He escaped into Ohio in 1834, was given refuge by a Quaker, Wells Brown, and assumed his benefactor's name in gratitude. He reached Cleveland, went to work on a lake steamer, and in one year helped sixty fugitives to Canada. He worked on the lake from 1834 to 1843, gradually acquiring an education and—like the vast majority of the Negro leaders—mastering the principles of temperance, peace, and women's rights. The New York Anti-Slavery Society appointed him an agent in 1843, and for six years he was associated with the New York and Massachusetts societies. He then went to Great Britain, lectured in the British Isles for five years, visited the continent four times, and wrote three books. On his return, he contributed regularly to the London *Daily News,* to *Frederick Douglass' Paper,* and to the *National Anti-Slavery Standard.* His writings were of the first order, and he was held in high regard as a speaker, historian, and man both here and abroad.

His *Narrative of William Wells Brown, A Fugitive Slave,* was published in 1847.[25]

Jermain Wesley Loguen, as he finally came to be known, was born in Tennessee of a white slaveholding father and a Negro mother who had been kidnapped in Ohio. This woman's daughter was sold away from her, her son fled to the North, and her owner refused to sell her to that son unless he would also pay for his own freedom, which he had attained by flight. The lad escaped through Kentucky and Indiana to Detroit and Canada, saved some money, and learned to read. He went to Rochester to work, and then to study under Beriah Green at Oneida. He became an elder in the African Methodist Episcopal Zion Church, served pastorates at Ithaca, Syracuse, and Troy, and in 1868 was elected bishop. The Liberty Party men of western New York were attracted by his ability as a speaker when he was raising money for his church in Syracuse. They promptly brought him into the campaign for Birney. He became a close friend of Gerrit Smith, and in one way or another aided hundreds of fugitives. He was indicted for participation in the Jerry Rescue (1851) and fled to Canada. His *Narrative* was published in 1859.[26]

James W. C. Pennington was born a slave in Maryland in 1809. His master lived in Washington County, where the Reverend Jacob Gruber had run afoul of the law in 1819. Trained as a stone mason and blacksmith, cruelly treated, and kept in complete ignorance, he ran away in 1830, was given refuge by a Pennsylvania Quaker, and sent to Long Island. He received enough education to teach in the Negro schools. He then studied theology in New Haven and was pastor of the African Congregational Church at Hartford from 1840 to 1847. He spent some time in Europe during this period, lecturing in London, Paris, and Brussels and receiving a doctor of divinity degree from Heidelberg University. His freedom was purchased from his former master after the Fugitive Slave Act of 1850 was passed. His narrative, *The Fugitive Blacksmith,* was published in 1849.[27]

William Wells Brown

J. W. Pennington

HERE THE SLAVE FOUND FREEDOM

Chapter 40

There is a bronze plaque on the Dominion Bank Building of Windsor, Ontario, which bears the following inscription: "Here the Slave Found Freedom. Before the United States Civil War of 1861–65, Windsor was an important terminal of the underground railroad. Escaping from bondage thousands of fugitive slaves from the South, men, women, and children landing near this spot found in Canada friends, freedom, protection under the British flag."

Most of these people went to Canada after 1850, but some had been going since Revolutionary days. Upper Canada provided for gradual abolition of slavery on July 9, 1793, the year Congress passed the infamous Fugitive Slave Act, and from that date until the Civil War the flight of slaves from the United States never quite ceased. Slavery was completely abolished there by parliamentary act of 1833.[1] There were not more than one thousand Negroes, slave and free, in the whole of Canada when the War of 1812 began, but many were carried away from the United States ports by British warships, some to the Bahamas and Bermuda, but a goodly number to Nova Scotia and New Brunswick. Henry Clay said the number was 3,601; we accepted payment for 1,650.[2] There is no way of knowing how many of these refugees actually went to Canada, but some did, and this became common knowledge among the slaves. Henry Clay, secretary of state in 1826, requested extradition of fugitives. The British government refused on the ground that property in human beings was not recognized by the laws of Canada and every slave entering the

province became free immediately whether he had been brought there or had come of his own accord.[3] Canada, thereafter, was the one certain haven of refuge.

Most of the fugitives entered Essex and Kent counties, Ontario, by way of Detroit, and there in Amherstburg still stands the old Negro Baptist Church, built of timbers cut and squared by men who had worn the fetters of slavery. The auction block, the slave pens, and the prisons, with their separation of families and all else that was involved in the nefarious traffic in human flesh, had driven them into a stroke for freedom.[4] Certainly, no engine of torture was ever more demoralizing than the sale of men and women as cattle of the field, and certainly also, if better reasons for flight were needed, the scars of brutal beatings which so many bore were silent testimony that they were ample. The New Orleans *Commercial Bulletin*, December 19, 1860, said that 1,500 slaves had escaped annually to the free states and Canada during the previous fifty years. It was a conservative estimate.

Many of the Negroes living in the free states were fugitives at all times. Some remained there; some passed on to Canada after gaining a competence, or at times of peril. Some of the Negroes in the free states were free by virtue of state emancipation acts, or by manumission, or by being born free. It would have taken a great deal more brains than United States commissioners possessed to have sorted all these people out. There were many times in the 1820's and 1830's, during the era of mob violence, when free Negroes went to Canada in large numbers. For example, in the spring of 1829, enough Negroes left Cincinnati to found the town of Wilberforce, near London, Ontario.[5] Not all who left Cincinnati went to Canada, but the Negro population of that city decreased by 50 per cent in three years. Antislavery leaders of both races opposed such migrations, for the same reasons they opposed expatriation to Africa or Haiti or anywhere else, but of the refugees going to Canada always some were free Negroes from the nonslaveholding states. The Negro population of Canada, therefore, consisted of a few from the old French regime, slaves direct from the slave states, free Negroes who had left the free states, and fugitives who had lingered perhaps for years in the free states, feeling safe until the Fugitive Slave Act of 1850.

An investigation of the condition and prospects of the Negro population in Upper Canada by the American Anti-Slavery Society disclosed a population of ten thousand in 1837.[6] Two qualified observers, Isaac Rice, missionary at Amherstburg, and Hiram Wilson, at Dawn, placed the number in Upper Canada at 20,000 in 1850. Samuel J. May, who traveled through the province, agreed on this estimate, but William Wells Brown claimed there were 25,000.[7] The Reverend William Mitchell, a Negro missionary of Toronto, estimated that not less than 1,200 refugees reached that area every year. Levi Coffin said there were 40,000 in the whole of Canada in 1844.[8] We know that no less than 3,000 reached there within three months after the Fugitive Slave Act of 1850 was passed. They streamed in from all parts of the free states; and, by 1860, there were 60,000 Negroes in Upper Canada alone, of whom 45,000 were fugitive slaves.

The flight of fugitives and migration of free Negroes in such vast numbers was amazing, and it was tragic. Suddenly the entire Negro population of the free states had been placed in peril. Every Negro was a potential victim of kidnappers, for there were commercial slave catchers in the North who specialized in "recovering fugitives" for a commission, promising that if a description were given they would find a Negro to fit it. Fear was not lessened by numbers. All who were fugitives were terrified, and the flight was something of a mass migration. Three hundred persons crossed the river at Detroit in one day, one Negro Baptist Church losing 84 members.[9] In May 1851 Henry Bibb said 4,000 fugitives had

come into Upper Canada in less than a year.[10] Hiram Wilson said his churches were thronged with fugitives. A Pittsburgh news item in the *Liberator* stated: "Nearly all the waiters in the hotels have fled to Canada. Sunday, thirty fled; on Monday, forty; on Tuesday, fifty; on Wednesday, thirty; and up to this time the number that has left will not fall short of 300. They went in large bodies armed with pistols and bowie knives, determined to die rather than be captured."[11] More than 130 communicants of one Baptist church in Buffalo fled, and in Rochester the pastor and 114 members of one church.[12] This fear did not diminish through the years. At Chicago in 1861, almost on the eve of war, more than 100 Negroes left on one train following the arrest of a fugitive.[13]

Those fugitives who moved north through New England went to the Province of Quebec, mostly to Montreal. A few went by boat from New England to New Brunswick, Nova Scotia, and Cape Breton. Most fugitives, however, went to the interlake region of Upper Canada. It was the safest place, and the most easily reached. It was bounded on the east by New York, on the west by Michigan, and on the south by Ohio and Pennsylvania. The densest settlements were in the counties of Essex and Kent, bordering on the Detroit River and Lake St. Clair. On the western end of the marginal strip facing Lake Erie were Windsor, Sandwich, Amherstburg (Fort Malden), New Canaan, Colchester, and Buxton, fed through Detroit and across Lake Erie. At the eastern end were Fort Erie, St. Catherines, Niagara, Hamilton, and Toronto. In the Thames Valley were Chatham, Dresden, Dawn, Sydenham, London, and Wilberforce.[14] The natural tendency was to go to the towns, where relief and employment could be found, and these were the commercial ports on the lakes. Amherstburg was considered the terminus of the underground railroad.

The Negroes encountered some prejudice in Canada, though slight in comparison to that in the United States. Frederick Douglass, speaking of the contrast, said: "It is astonishing that people living within a stone's throw of each other should be so opposite in their tastes, feelings, and principles."[15] The Negroes had legal protection, and they were fully conscious of that fact. Prejudice which has no legal support is not difficult to meet. They did not go to Canada, nor remain there, to enjoy political rights. They went for the right to live as free persons—to be unmolested members of their community. They had the right because neither the provincial government, nor the imperial government, nor the courts would surrender them to any claimant. Personal freedom was a jealously guarded right in the British Empire, and that fact provided temporary refuge for many slaves who returned to the United States at the end of the Civil War. Canada also granted citizenship to the Negro on the same terms as any other immigrant, making no distinction on account of color. If the Negro fulfilled the proper qualifications, he was eligible for the elective franchise and for office holding. Fugitives voted, and sometimes their votes were decisive in elections. They also served on juries.[16]

In Canada there were organized refugee settlements for a few. Those Negroes who left Cincinnati in 1829 because enforcement of the black law threw them out of work secured 25,000 acres near London and founded the Wilberforce colony. They established schools, built Methodist and Baptist churches, and organized a temperance society. Their schools were so good that many white children attended. The colony, however, encountered difficulties due to conflict of interests in the board of management, and most of its members were absorbed in other communities.[17]

A second colony was at Dawn. Hiram Wilson, one of the Lane Seminary students, worked as an antislavery agent in Ohio for a year, then went to Canada to work among the fugitive slaves. He was commissioned by the American Anti-Slavery Society as one of the "seventy" and traveled over the whole of Upper Canada, studying the condition of the Negroes and assembling pertinent information about education, working conditions, and religious activities. He founded the British-American Manual Labor Institute on 300 acres at Dawn, near Dresden. There came to work with him after a time the fugitive Josiah Henson. Henson, who was said to have been the original "Uncle Tom," was born a slave in Maryland in 1789. His father beat an overseer who had assaulted the lad's mother and was, in turn, castrated. Josiah himself, at a later date, was injured for life for offending an overseer. He went to Kentucky on a mission of trust for his master, was denied the privilege of purchasing his freedom, and was sent to the slave market in New Orleans. He fled with his wife and four children and reached Canada by way of Cincinnati and Buffalo. He went to Dawn in 1842, and three times to England,

where he was greatly honored. Neither he nor Wilson possessed the business ability to make the institute a success. Wilson and his wife moved to St. Catherines about 1850, where they continued to work among the fugitives until the Civil War.[18]

The most successful of the colonies was the Buxton settlement in Kent County, under the management of the Elgin Association. In population, in material wealth, and in general organization it was outstanding. It was founded and managed by Reverend William King, a well-educated Scotch Presbyterian minister from Louisiana. The nucleus of his colony was a group of fifteen slaves, valued at $9,000, whom he had acquired by marriage. He took them to Canada in 1848–49, where they automatically became free. His plan was to establish homes and provide for their education. He formed the Elgin Association for the purchase of land, in order to keep out speculators, August 10, 1850. Nine thousand acres were acquired, and sold to the individual families in fifty-acre plots at $2.50 per acre. There were 200 families in the

Henry Bibb

settlement by 1856 and a total of 1,000 people by 1860. The farms were well stocked, the farmers thrifty and highly respectable. They had, in addition, a sawmill, a brickyard, and a pearl ash factory. King always exhibited the colony as absolute proof that a group of Negroes could make progress equal to any group of white people if given an opportunity.[19]

A group of antislavery men in or near Detroit organized the Refugee Home Society, May 21, 1851.[20] This society established the Refugee Home Settlement in the township of Sandwich, south of Windsor. The original plan was to purchase 50,-000 acres, but not more than 5,000 seem to have been acquired. This was divided into twenty-five-acre plots for sale to individual families, each receiving five of the acres free if the land was cleared within three years. One-third of all revenues was to be used for educational purposes. No settler could sell his land in less than fifteen years, and, if abandoned, it reverted to the society.[21] Mrs. Laura Haviland taught in the schools of the colony for several years.

The fugitive Henry Bibb was closely associated with the Refugee Home Settlement. Bibb was born a slave in Kentucky. Denied an education himself, he was hired out for ten years to earn the money to send his master's daughters to finishing schools. He tried to escape first at ten years of age, was captured, and was sold and resold. He finally escaped to Cincinnati in 1837, and went to Perrysburg for the winter. He went back to the slave states to free his wife, was captured and sold into the Red River country as the slave of an Indian, and escaped again through Indian Territory and Missouri to Detroit. A born orator, he lectured in Ohio and Michigan for the Liberty Party with S. B. Treadwell and Amos Dresser. He lectured first at Adrian, Michigan, in May 1844 and then spent the years 1846 and 1847 in New York and New England. The Michigan antislavery leaders refused to permit him to risk capture again and sent their own men to the South in an unsuccessful effort to recover his wife. He went to Canada after the passage of the Fugitive Slave Act of 1850 and established the *Voice of the Fugitive* at Sandwich. It is a chronicle of all important activities concerning the fugitive group in Canada, including frequent reports of the number of Negroes who crossed the Detroit River. His paper was read widely by the refugees. He took an active part in the work of the Canadian Anti-Slav-

Josiah Henson ("Uncle Tom")

ery Society and traveled widely through the refugee communities, lecturing on slavery and the problems of the Negro in exile. His *Narrative* ranks with those of Douglass, Brown, and Pennington as the four most important.[22]

Refugees not a part of colonies, and most were not, led more independent lives, usually as farmers. Most of them had always lived close to the soil, and Bibb was convinced they should settle on farms. Many of them did so. They hired out to Canadian farmers. They rented farms. They cleared the land, providing a labor force for the frontier areas of Canada. They introduced tobacco culture in southern Ontario.[23] They could purchase timber lands for two to four dollars an acre from the government or from private land speculators, and their farms were usually of about fifty acres. Their houses were log cabins. They were thrifty and hard working by all accounts. In the cities they worked in hotels, in domestic service, in the trades, and in road and railroad construction. They were skilled carpenters and blacksmiths.[24]

Negroes in Canada were troubled by the same problems of policy as in the United States. The first of these was financial aid. It was easy for the antislavery people to be generous, and they were generous as fugitives moved along toward Canada. James M. Ashley of Ohio, who later introduced the Thirteenth Amendment into Congress, was active in the underground railroad and dealt generously with all who came through Toledo. Joshua Giddings said in Congress: "Gentlemen will bear with me when I assure them and the President that I have seen as many as nine fugitives dining at one time in my own house . . . I fed them, I clothed them, gave them money for their journey and sent them on their way rejoicing."[25] Gerrit Smith's home at Peterboro, New York, was always a safe haven for fugitives, and none ever left without some material assistance.

Erastus Hussey was the agent at Battle Creek, Michigan. He assisted more than one thousand fugitives between 1840 and the Civil War, hiding them in a livery stable, in a room over his store, and in the basement of his home. He had to provide food for these fugitives, which was not always a simple matter. He said in his memoirs: "At one time forty-five came upon us in a bunch. It was when the Kentucky slave owners made a raid upon the famous Quaker settlement in Cass County. One night a man by the name of Richard Dillingham came to my house and informed me that there would be forty-five fugitives and nine guards here in two hours. What to do I did not know. My wife was sick in bed. I met Abel Densmore, then Silas Dodge and Samuel Strauther, and we talked the matter over . . . Lester Buckley owned a small unoccupied dwelling house . . . Buckley was a Whig, but sympathized with us. He said we could have the use of the building. There happened to be a stove in the house. I got some wood and then went over to Elijah T. Mott's mill . . . and he gave me sixty pounds of flour. Silas Dodge went to a grocery store and bought some potatoes and Densmore got some pork. We heard them coming over the West Main Street Bridge. Everybody had heard of their coming and every man, woman and child in the city was upon the street and it looked as if a circus was coming to town. It was a lovely moonlight night. There were nine white men with them who acted as guards. Ahead of them rode Zack Shugart, the old Quaker, with his broad-brimmed white hat and mounted upon a fine horse—he always had good horses. He met me in front of my house and shook hands with me. I told him of my arrange-

ments. He took off his white hat and with a military air and voice said: 'Right about face!' They all about-faced and marched down to the house and took possession . . . The next morning the majority of them went on to Canada."[26]

No secrecy here; no question of cost; no fear of arrest. This was a community affair. A very high percentage of the fugitives moved through Michigan. The hayloft of a famous old livery stable at the corner of State and Griswold in Detroit was always full of Negroes waiting to be conveyed across the river. They were taken by boat to a point opposite Woodward Avenue to a warehouse where the Dominion Bank Building now stands. In 1852 the Detroit vigilance committee moved 1,200 across the river. When the route through Kalamazoo, Jackson, and Ann Arbor was closed, fugitives were taken through Lansing and Flint to Port Huron, and then across to the Dawn settlement. Supplies, of course, flowed into all of these settlements from Michigan, including money, seeds, fruit trees, books, and other supplies for the schools. They went mostly to transients, that is, to newly arrived refugees. Once established, the Negroes resented financial and other gifts. Generosity, beyond a certain point, discouraged thrift. Fugitives had to become economically independent; their salvation depended upon it. Evidence is overwhelming that they fully realized the fact.

There was organized in 1854 in Malden, and then in other communities, an organization known as the "True Band Association." It was a mutual aid society with all members pledged to help each other when in distress. It was designed to encourage education for the children by improving the schools and keeping regular attendance. It was a concerted effort to find ways of eradicating prejudice. Above all else, it sought unity and self-containment.[27] There were, for example, in Sandwich Township, 500 Negroes, with a day school, a Sabbath school, two Baptist churches, and one Methodist church. In Chatham there were 1,200 Negroes, with two Methodist and two Baptist churches. The association sought to counteract the factionalism by uniting the churches. It insisted that all begging for outside aid be abolished and that funds be raised among themselves for the care of the sick and the indigent.

The second question of policy was that of segregation versus integration, and it involved colonies and schools. Fortunately, they were spared the most disorganizing of all issues among the Negroes of the United States: that of deciding between Garrison's moral suasion and Birney's political action. They did not have to worry about integration of Negroes and whites in antislavery societies. They fully accepted, as in the United States, equality of the sexes in all of their activities. Schools and settlements, however, were real problems.

In the United States, integration leaders were opposed to building Negro churches and Negro schools because it fostered the spirit of prejudice. William Lloyd Garrison and Wendell Phillips, and the Negroes David Ruggles, William Whipper, and James Forten, for example, refused to recognize any special needs and problems of the Negro people requiring separate organization.[28] They encouraged the Negro to become part and parcel of a general community. The national convention movement was disrupted by the issue, with the Garrisonians pulling away, forming the American Moral Reform Society, and publishing their own paper, the *National Reformer*, under the editorship of William Whipper. Many of them felt that attendance at exclusive Negro meetings was a tacit acceptance of segregation.[29] They insisted that the Negro people go only to those schools and churches open to both races. The Garrisonians supported this position through the *Liberator* and *National Anti-Slavery Standard*.

The idea of a manual labor college for Negroes had been approved by the first Negro Convention, at Philadelphia, in 1831, but the college was not established because of the hostility of the citizens of New Haven. Negroes were divided on the issue from that time. By 1850 Douglass had abandoned the Garrisonian viewpoint and had come to believe in the wisdom of Negro Manual Labor colleges. It was difficult for Negroes to find employment. They could not become apprentices because there were so few Negro craftsmen and white craftsmen were reluctant to take Negroes in service. An industrial college would introduce young men to the trades and promote self-reliance. The presence of an "industrious, enterprising, upright, thrifty, and intelligent free black population would be a killing refutation of slavery."[30] This was the thought of Douglass, of James McCune Smith, and of James Pennington. The convention of 1848, in Cleveland, took issue with the Garrisonian moral reformers who insisted on immediate and complete integration. In

an address to the colored people of the United States, it said: "Never refuse to act with a white society or institution because it is white, or a black one, because it is black. But act with all men without distinction of color." It urged a change as fast as possible from those employments associated only with Negroes because by such association they had been degraded in the mind of the public.[31] They did not name these employments, but this convention differed widely from previous ones where preachers, teachers, and other professional men predominated. There were sixty-one delegates present, among them, printers, carpenters, blacksmiths, shoemakers, engineers, dentists, gunsmiths, editors, tailors, merchants, wheelwrights, painters, farmers, physicians, plasterers, masons, clergymen, barbers, hairdressers, coopers, livery-stable keepers, and grocers.[32]

Division of opinion in Canada was not very much different, except there were no antislavery societies or Negro conventions, nor were there trained leaders to contend for position and influence. There was a high percentage of adults among the refugees. Most of them had little, if any, formal education. Church schools, therefore, were tremendously important because they pro-

William Whipper

vided education for adults. As elsewhere among Negroes, there were those who favored separate schools for the children and those who strenuously opposed such schools. They possessed the legal right to send their children to the public schools and did so increasingly until separate schools practically ceased to exist. There was severe criticism of colonies, because they represented segregation in the same manner as separate schools. Refugees succeeded best when they were scattered and formed a small proportion of the whole community. Colonies made for more rapid progress, but they represented in a very real way a period of apprenticeship, prolonged dependence, and retarded self-reliance. They seemed almost necessary in the beginning because of the complete destitution of the refugees. Most of the fugitives were entirely penniless when they reached Canada, especially in the early years. Few, even of the refugees from the free states, possessed more than enough for a month's subsistence. They became independent, however, very quickly, even under adverse circumstances. They chafed under the restraints of the colonies, especially that at Buxton, which seemed to be the most successful.

There was some prejudice, but little agree-

ment upon how much or upon the reason for it. The city of London had several hundred Negroes in its population of 12,000. They owned property, some of them thousands of dollars' worth. They had no schools of their own, because the public schools were open to them, but attendance was poor because of prejudice against them on the part of the whites. A preacher by the name of Proudfoot is quoted as saying: "The prejudice against colored people is growing here. But it is not a British feeling; it does not spring from our people, but from your people coming over here. There are many Americans here, and great deference is paid to their feelings."[33] A Negro, A. T. Jones, said there was more prejudice in London than in the United States and that it would be a great deal worse but for the protection of the law. The headmaster of the school said it originated with the parents and that the white children refused to play with the Negro children.[34] A preacher, S. R. Ward, said it did not exist among the better class of white people but among the unskilled labor class who were thrown into economic competition with the Negroes. Benjamin Drew says there was prejudice in Sandwich but that the entire township would rise up to protect

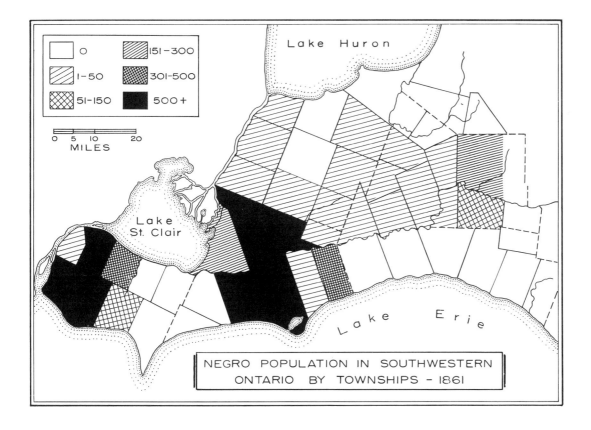

NEGRO POPULATION IN SOUTHWESTERN ONTARIO BY TOWNSHIPS - 1861

a Negro against recapture by a slaveholder.[35] The town clerk of Windsor said there was discrimination there in the selection of jurors. One Negro woman of St. Catherines said there was more prejudice there than in New York state, and another that the one restraint upon prejudice was equality under the law. There were no interracial marriages, though these were not forbidden by law.

An Anti-Slavery Society of Canada was formed on March 24, 1851. Its two most prominent sponsors were Charles Stuart, who had written the basic exposé of the colonization scheme, and George Brown, editor of the Toronto *Globe*. The society was strongly opposed to the principle of colonization and to the activities of the American Colonization Society. It disavowed any purpose to aid fugitives in their flight to Canada, being careful to avoid violating the laws of the United States. It did, however, and this was its chief purpose, extend aid to refugees in Canada, seeking to provide employment, establish adult evening classes, and combat prejudice.[36]

Taken in its entirety, the record of the fugitives discloses that they came out of the very depths of degradation and oppression, adjusted to the status of freedom without preliminary training, and were thrifty, honorable, intelligent citizens in the Northern states and in Canada. A remarkable number of them displayed intellectual capacity of the highest order, attaining distinction in the professions, on the lecture platforms, and in journalism. They went to Canada, not as *émigrés,* but as refugees seeking temporary asylum, expecting some day to return, yet performing all the obligations of intelligent citizenship during their residence; even though born in slavery and suffering great injustices and cruelties, they were devoted to the United States and reluctant to leave its soil.

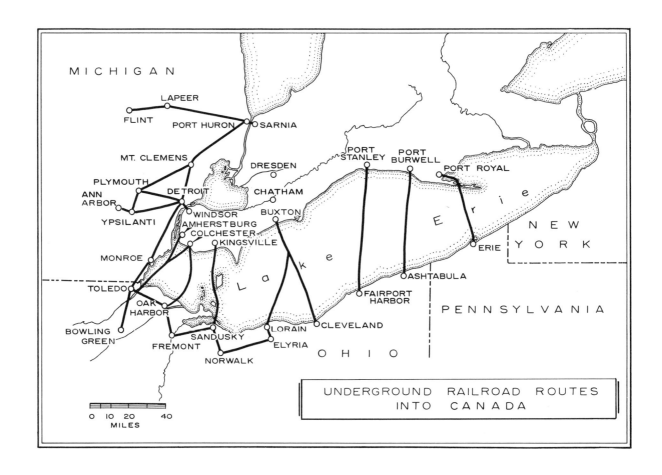

UNDERGROUND RAILROAD ROUTES INTO CANADA

THE CHURCHES

Chapter 41

"The abolitionist . . . looks upon the institutions of his country, religious and political, as forming the character of her great men . . . when we have pronounced these two words [religion and politics], we have expressed every thing that gives pressure to American thought. Now, Religion is the most productive, the most efficient, the deepest idea, and the foundation of American thought and American institutions." So said Wendell Phillips in 1848.[1]

Repetitious examination of political and ecclesiastical literature discloses a sharp decline of spirited defense of individual freedom after 1800, in no particular more clearly evident than in the attitude of the agencies of state and church toward slavery. Slavery was a waning institution at the time of the Revolution, and it was recognized as such in the fundamental law, if indeed it was recognized at all. In a manner of speaking, it crept into the Constitutional Convention by the back door, but was held in such disrepute as not even to have been addressed by its proper name.

The lamentable fact is, however, that despite the most terrible denunciations to which the English language lends itself, by the greatest among statesmen, philosophers, and churchmen of two continents, and in the Constitutional Convention and ratifying conventions, and in the councils of the several churches, neither the government nor the church ever completely divorced itself from slavery or took an uncompromising position with regard to it.[2] The great leaders in both areas were honest in their abhorrence of the institution, but they did not strike it down. They temporized.

Then the fervor of their reforming zeal lessened. Their social and economic environment changed. The principle of *gradualism* which they applied both in state and church did not work. The spirit of liberty lessened. Sound public morality declined, and wealth became more attractive than humanity. Property rights became more important than human rights. Slavery was resuscitated, and presently represented great wealth and political power. It had a stranglehold on political parties and upon the church. It reversed national policy. Apathy toward it turned to apology and defense. The rulers in the church interpreted the Bible in the light of their own prejudices, and the rulers in the state interpreted the Declaration and the Constitution in the same manner. These great charters of human freedom and Western liberalism had to be rescued by greater men of lesser public stature or they would have been completely trampled underfoot.

William and Mary College gave a doctor of laws degree to Granville Sharp in 1791, the man who had taught the courts of England why no man could stand upon her soil and be a slave. The Sommersett decision was the greatest single personal achievement in the long struggle against slavery. In 1835 Granville Sharp's writings would have been confiscated in Virginia, and he himself might well have been hanged without indictment and without trial.

The Methodist Episcopal Church in 1780 condemned slavery as "contrary to the laws of God, man, and nature, and hurtful to society; contrary to the dictates of conscience and pure religion and doing that which we would not others should do to us or ours."[3] Four years later, all slaveholders were given twelve months to dispose of their slaves or quietly withdraw from the church, and all who disposed of them in any way except by giving them their freedom were to be expelled from the church.[4] John Wesley condemned slavery as the "sum of all villainies." Ministers were required to circulate his tract on slavery. In 1801 the rule of 1785 was reaffirmed, and the annual conferences were directed to circulate petitions to the legislatures of the several states for gradual emancipation.[5]

It was at this point that the departure from correct understanding began in the church. Here were the two fatal errors. Circulating petitions to legislatures was nothing more and nothing less than abandonment of the power and duty of the church to direct the moral reformation of slaveholders by condemning slaveholding as a sin. This was no mere academic question. It was fatal to the church and a death blow to democracy. Henceforth, the church considered slavery a political question. It forgot about, and never wanted to be reminded of, the sin of slaveholding. No one will ever understand this terrifying struggle over a century and a half, and perhaps forever, in this country, who misses this point, for the Methodists were not alone. The same thing happened in the other churches. Sectarian rivalries for wealth and numbers caused a sacrifice of principles. Slaveholders were patronized by both Methodists and Presbyterians. The position of both churches may be said to have been that sins which were a part of society or were sanctioned by the government were not personal sins and should not be treated as such by the church. This meant that accountability of the individual ceased insofar as all evil acts were created or allowed by civil government.

There is a gulf as wide and deep as the ocean between the Quaker practice of individual repentance, manumission, and retributive justice on the one hand, and emancipation by political action on the other. The failure of the churches at this point in our history forced the country to turn to political action against slavery, and political action destroyed slavery as a system but left the hearts of the slaveholders unregenerate and left oppression of the free Negro little less of an evil than slavery had been.

By 1836 the reversal of Methodist church policy from that of an earlier date was so complete that the General Conference, meeting in Cincinnati, condemned two members for lecturing in the city in favor of emancipation, and disclaimed "any right, wish, or intention to interfere in the civil and political relation between master and slave as it exists in the slaveholding states of this Union." Having abandoned its own power to legislate in the field of individual morality, it now denied to its ministers the right to condemn political immorality.[6]

Nor was this the end. In a pastoral address to the churches, the conference said that the question of slavery was a political one belonging entirely to the state legislatures and admonished all members of the church "to abstain from all abolition movements and associations, and to refrain from patronizing any of their publications." In response to this pastoral letter the annual conferences in the two key states in the antislavery movement, Ohio and New York, came dangerously close to joining in the subordination of civil rights to the pleasure of mobs. The Ohio Annual Conference resolved that "those brethren and citizens of the North who resist the abolition movement with firmness and moderation are the true friends of the church"; and the New York Conference threatened with disciplinary action anyone supporting in any way the publication or distribution of LaRoy Sunderland's *Zion's Watchman.* The several Southern conferences resolved that slavery was "not a moral evil," or a proper subject "for the action of the church." Finally, the General Conference of 1840 denied the right of any Negro member to give testimony in the church courts if the laws of his state forbade him to do so in the civil courts.[7]

The antislavery movement in the Presbyterian Church extended back to the *Address to the Inhabitants of the British Colonies in America* of the distinguished Benjamin Rush of Philadelphia in 1773. Intensity of agitation in the synods and general assemblies of the church fluctuated from then until 1861. Public avowals appeared in the minutes of the General Assembly from time to time, but long periods of silence intervened. The Synod of New York and Philadelphia expressed strong condemnation of slavery in 1787. Then the General Assembly of 1794 adopted a catechism which classified manstealers with murderers and whoremongers and defined manstealers as men who brought human beings into slavery and retained them in it. This was quietly dropped from the Confession of Faith in 1816. Two years later, however, the General Assembly passed the following resolution: "We consider the voluntary enslaving of one part of the human race by another, as a gross violation of the most precious and sacred rights of human nature; as utterly inconsistent with the law of God, which requires us to love our neighbors as ourselves; and as totally irreconcilable with the spirit and principles of the Gospel of Christ, which enjoins that all things whatsoever ye would that men should do to you do ye even so to them."[8]

This was the point at which the Presbyterian church faltered. In spite of its previous declarations against slavery, it had never disciplined any slaveholding members. Now it endorsed the program of the Colonization Society which had been formed in 1817, and it continued to support expatriation of the Negro until the antislavery societies were formed in 1831–33. The publication of Birney's *Letter on Colonization,* the Lane Seminary debate, Stuart's pamphlets, and other expressions of anticolonization principles then forced men to take a definite stand on antislavery principles. The Synod of Kentucky, where slavery was as mild as anywhere in the country, said: "There is not a village or road that does not behold the sad procession of manacled outcasts, whose chains and mournful countenances tell that they are exiled by force from all that their hearts hold dear. Our church, years ago, raised its voice of solemn warning against this flagrant violation of every principle of mercy, justice, and humanity. Yet we blush to announce to you, that this warning has been often disregarded even by those who hold to our communion. Cases have occurred in our own denomination where professors of the religion of mercy have torn the mother from the children and sent her into a merciless and returnless exile. Yet acts of discipline have rarely followed such conduct."[9]

The question of slavery was not the sole cause, but a heavily contributing factor, of a separation in the church between 1836 and 1838. The General Assembly followed the party line of the slave power in 1836 at Pittsburgh and declared that it was not proper for ecclesiastical bodies to interfere with an institution connected with the laws of the states. In 1837 it expelled four Northern antislavery synods called New School Presbyterians containing 60,000 members. When separation was completed the following year it was not entirely along antislavery-proslavery lines. There were three slavery presbyteries in the New School church and between thirty and forty in the Old School church. The Old School General Assembly refused to discuss the subject from that time forward. The New School General Assembly referred the subject to the presbyteries, but censured those, in 1843, which had excluded slaveholders from communion. Moreover, the New School continually expressed a willingness to reunite and commune with the Old School, and by 1850 it had twenty slaveholding presbyteries with 20,000 members in the slave states. Despite the many distinguished antislavery men in the Presbyterian church, therefore, the church as a whole after 1818 apologized for slavery, avoided discussion under the pretexts of saving the Union or church unity, or insisted slavery was a political question. It did not legislate against it.

Neither the Congregationalists nor the Baptists had an ecclesiastical body with jurisdiction over the whole country, nor did the Congregationalists have any churches in slaveholding states as did the Baptists, Methodists, and Presbyterians. The Congregationalists were closely affiliated with the Presbyterians through their associations of ministers. Congregational and Presbyterian ministers moved rather freely from one church to the other, and the two churches were close to each other in creed, forms of worship, and ministerial training. It was claimed that New England Congregational ministers who had transferred and New England school teachers were staple exports to the Southern states, where they became proslavery, and that the commercial intercourse, intermarriages, and other invisible bonds between the two sections were a constant pressure to modify antislavery pronouncements by the New England clergy.

Two of the early antislavery divines whose works were never challenged and who stand preeminent still among the country's greatest theologians were Congregationalists. Jonathan Edwards said: "While you hold your Negroes in slavery, you do wrong, exceedingly wrong; you do not as you would men should do to you; you commit sin in the sight of God; you daily violate the plain rights of mankind, and that in a higher degree than if you committed theft or robbery." [10] Samuel Hopkins said: "Slavery is, in every instance, wrong, unrighteous, and oppressive; a very great and crying sin, there being nothing equal to it on the face of the earth." [11] Jonas Clark, of equal fame, said: "In heathen countries, Slavery was in some sort excusable; but among Christians, it is an enormity and a crime, for which perdition has scarcely an adequate state of punishment." Clark was a classic example of the fact that every champion of emancipation at the time of the Revolution was a champion of liberty. The idea that slavery was a political question never bothered the churchmen of England and the British colonies. The church had tremendous influence in stamping out slavery in the British Empire. In 1840 the Congregational Union of Scotland said to Christians in the United States: "It is with disappointment and distress, and shame . . . that we look at so large a body of professing Christians in your country at this moment consigning their fellow men, some of whom are professors of the same faith with themselves, to the wrongs and indignities of hopeless bondage." [12]

There were many strong men from the Congregational churches who supported the antislavery movement, but there were others who were proslavery or only mildly opposed, who held that slavery in itself was not sinful, only the abuse of the master-servant relationship. A leading proslavery advocate was Moses Stuart, professor of sacred literature at Andover Theological Seminary. Stuart's power was great, for he is said to have taught 1,500 men who entered the ministry and seventy who became affiliated with colleges as professors or presidents. He was one of those New England preachers who eulogized Daniel Webster for his part in securing passage of the Fugitive Slave Act of 1850—a group which included Professors Leonard Woods and Ralph Emerson of the same seminary, and President Jared Sparks of Harvard University.

The Baptists had no supervision by conferences, bishops, and general assemblies, as did the Methodists and Presbyterians. The Philadelphia Association, representing fifty churches in Pennsylvania, New York, New Jersey, Connecticut, Virginia, and Maryland, in 1789 endorsed the work of the abolition societies then being founded in these several states. [13] The Baptists of Virginia, in the same year, resolved: "That slavery is a violent deprivation of the rights of nature and incon-

sistent with a republican government and therefore recommend it to our brethren to make use of every legal means to extirpate this horrid evil from the land." [14] In 1805 the Elkhorn Association of Kentucky said: "This Association judges it improper for ministers, churches, or associations to meddle with emancipation from slavery, or any other political subject, and as such, we advise ministers and churches to have nothing to do therewith, in religious capacities." [15]

These two opposite views pretty well represent the situation in the Baptist church. The church was strong in the Philadelphia area, with few slaves, at an early date; but the church as a whole in colonial days had been fighting for ecclesiastical freedom and was committed to a policy of noninterference in civil affairs. Northern Baptists supported the emancipation acts. Southern Baptists were helpless. Many of them freed their slaves. Others kept their slaves, sought refuge in the Old Testament, and fell in line with the proslavery contention that slavery was a matter for civil jurisprudence. There was active antislavery sentiment in Virginia and Pennsylvania between the Revolution and 1810. There was some in the West after that date, but little in the East again for twenty-five years. The Baptist James Lemen, prominent in Virginia, went to Illinois. Others freed their slaves as soon as the Virginia law of 1782 made it possible, including Robert Carter who owned more than 600. David Barrow went to Kentucky. The importance of Barrow's work in that state and of Lemen's organization, Friends of Humanity, in Illinois, can not be minimized, but the fact remains that Kentucky Baptists as a whole were very unwilling to be disturbed over slavery, and did not hesitate to expel Barrow for preaching against it. [16]

In South Carolina one-third of all Baptist laymen and preachers alike were slaveholders. [17] The Charleston Baptists Association in 1835 sent a memorial to the legislature of South Carolina, saying "that the said association does not consider that the holy scriptures have made the fact of slavery a question of morals at all . . . The question, it is believed, is purely one of political economy." Richard Furman, the recognized leader of Southern Baptists, wrote one of the classic statements of the positive good of slavery, *Views of the Baptists Relative to the Coloured Population of the United States,* and when he died shortly afterward his estate was sold at auction and was ad-

21st JULY.

In pursuance of a deed of trust executed to me by Walter B. Morris on the 2d day of June, 1840, and acknowledged and recorded the 5th day of September, 1840, I will on Thursday, the 21st day of July next, proceed to sell to the highest bidder, at the Sumner Mills, for purposes therein specified, six negroes, one man, two women and two children, *for cash.* Also 20 shares in the Gallatin Turnpike Company, Horses, Cows, and Cart, Beds and Bedding, Bedsteads, Beaureaus, Tables, Chairs, Carpets, Maps, Books, say 1500 volumes, with a great variety of furniture, &c. &c. mentioned in said deed of trust. All sums under five dollars, cash, over that sum, on a credit of twelve months; notes with approved security will be required.

April 18th, 1842.   GEO. A. WILLIE, *Trustee.*

☞I would take this occasion to say to my friends and the public generally, that I should be pleased to see them at the *Sumner Mills* on the day of sale.

Very respectfully,   WALTER B. MORRIS.

Bill of sale

vertised as "a plantation or tract of land on and in the Wataree Swamp. A tract of the first quality of fine land, on the waters of Black River. A lot of land in the town of Camden. A Library of miscellaneous Character, Chiefly Theological. 27 NEGROES, some of them very prime. Two mules, one horse, and an old wagon."[18]

Not only were slaveholders members and preachers and officeholders in the three great Protestant churches in the slave states, slaves themselves were members of the churches. In 1840 there were an estimated 80,000 slave members of the Methodist church, an equal number in the Baptist church, and 40,000 in the others, including the more aristocratic Presbyterian and Episcopal churches.[19] Slaves who were church members belonged to the same church as their masters as a general rule. It was problematical, and still is, if

such arrangement were for any other purpose than to permit an outlet for the slaves' religious emotions while at the same time keeping them under rigorous supervision, for they were not allowed to read and were rarely given religious instruction. They were sold as freely as other slaves. They went through the form of marriage, but it was not legal and it was not sacred to anyone. Married female slaves were violated the same as unmarried female slaves, and it was no greater offense than trespass on someone else's property. The Savannah River Baptist Association of Ministers was asked in 1835 whether slaves, if separated by sale, could marry again, and said that "such separation among persons situated as our slaves are, is civilly a separation by death . . . The slaves are not free agents, and a dissolution by death is not more entirely without their consent and beyond their control than by such separation."[20] This, of course, was accommodation to the rules of slavery which forced cohabitation and violated marriages at will. Slave members were not allowed to testify against whites in the church courts, but they were tried in such courts as shown by the case of a Kentucky female slave who was expelled from the church for saying that slaveholders were not Christians.[21]

In the Methodist, Baptist, Presbyterian, and Episcopal churches, slaves in the South and free Negroes in the North who belonged to white churches sat in a particular part of the church designated the Negro pew. They could sit nowhere else even though invited to do so and regardless of whether or not they were members or visiting ministers of Negro churches. This practice was not as rigid in the free states as in the slave states, but it was never condemned by the ruling bodies of the churches. Moreover, special areas were set aside in the burial grounds for Negroes. In the South the churches in their corporate capacity owned slaves, hired them out to support their ministers, and sold them at will at public auctions. Monies from their sale frequently were willed to the support of churches and foreign missions. The Baptist churches owned more slaves than those of any other denomination, as many as 1,200 in some cases being owned by a single church, and 125,000 by the several churches of that denomination.[22]

Churches which owned slaves in their corporate capacity could hardly have been expected to punish individuals for owning slaves, and they did not do so. Like political parties, they wanted unity. Individual members of the churches in the slave states were not alike in their attitude toward slavery. A great many left it alone. Some opposed it mildly. Now and again someone opposed it vehemently, but most people of any standing and competence owned slaves and rationalized their conduct as best they could. Fewer than one-third of the people in the slave states had any direct connection with slavery, but the Reverend James Smylie of Mississippi declared: "If slavery be a sin, and if advertising and apprehending slaves, with a view of restoring them to their masters, is a direct violation of the divine law, and if the buying, and selling, and holding slaves for the sake of gain, is a heinous sin and scandal, then verily, three-fourths of all the Methodists, Episcopalians, Baptists, and Presbyterians,

in eleven States of the Union, are of the Devil."[23]

Associations of ministers, conferences, assemblies, and all other governing bodies suppressed all inquiries, memorials, and petitions in order to preserve harmony. None of them ever condemned slavery. None of them ever expelled slaveholders. None of them ever established any rules or regulations of personal conduct toward slaves. None of them ever remonstrated against harsh and restrictive legislation or memorialized for its repeal. None of them ever insisted upon the right of a slave, member of a church or otherwise, to read the Scriptures, and that in the face of indisputable fact that the burning desire to read the Bible was the greatest single stimulus to education in our history. On the contrary, they defended slavery as a Christian institution, contributed to the suppression of civil rights, and violently denounced all antislavery activities. Wherever the spiritual leaders of a people forego the exercise of their most important function, to condemn corruption and tyranny in government and in law, a curse, indeed, has fallen upon that people.

Fortunately, in the North there were individual preachers and congregations opposed to slavery and determined to do something about it. The Society of Friends excluded all slaveholders. They had produced the first of the great treatises against slavery, and, from time to time after the Revolution, a Quaker would write another pamphlet.[24] They were the predominant group in the underground railroad, but they did not participate, at least with any enthusiasm, in political action. The United Brethren Church in Maryland and Virginia, both slave states, would not allow slaveholders to be members. The Reformed Presbyterians, to which Alexander McLeod belonged, abolished slavery in 1802, and the decision made it difficult for its members to continue living in the slave states. Many of them came north and west to Ohio and Indiana. The roster of distinguished Presbyterian and Congregational ministers who preached and wrote against slavery, as we have seen, was very long, including among others such men as Samuel Doak, George Bourne, David Rice, and John Rankin. But there were three proslavery Presbyterian journals in the North: the Philadelphia *Presbyterian*, the *Princeton Review*, and the *New York Observer;* and all the combined efforts of antislavery men could not break the power of slavery in the General Assembly.

Separation came first in the Baptist and Methodist churches. The Free Will Baptists led the way. Founded by Benjamin Randall in 1780, they had 130 churches, 6,000 members, and 110 ministers by 1808, most of them in Maine, New Hampshire, Vermont, New York, and Ohio. The seat of the denomination was in Dover, New Hampshire, and the denominational newspaper was the *Morning Star*. John Marks, editor of the paper from 1832 to 1835, and his successor, William Burr, were both strongly antislavery. Year after year in their annual conferences the church condemned slavery as a sin, deplored its toleration by other denominations, supported antislavery societies, and refused membership to anyone claiming the right of property in his fellow man. John Marks traveled widely, lecturing and forming antislavery societies. He wrote to the World Anti-Slavery Convention in 1840: "As a people we [Free Will Baptists] mourn that the church in this land is so deeply involved in the sin of slavery, and have endeavored to keep our garments pure and unspotted from its foul stains. We neither receive into our churches, nor at the communion table, *any* whose hands are polluted with slavery. Our Board of Foreign Missions refuses to receive any donation or bequest from slaveholders, on the principle that their wealth is the wages of iniquity, and the price of blood."[25] The church expanded rapidly into Maine and Michigan, numbering 60,000 members by 1845. They generally agreed to abandon party allegiance when necessary to vote for righteous men as the only security for free government. Their preachers urged them to do so.[26] They served as agents of state antislavery societies, and they organized antislavery societies of their own after 1840 to promote political action.

In 1845 the Baptist denomination separated into two branches over the question of slavery, insofar as churches independent of each other in regard to ecclesiastical jurisdiction could separate. They had held a General Convention every three years to direct the Baptist Home Missionary Society and the American and Foreign Bible Society. In April 1840 an American Baptist Anti-Slavery Convention had been called in New York City, and another shortly afterward at Warsaw, New York. The Warsaw convention had been presided over by Elon Galusha, a strong antislavery man and vice-president of the Baptist Board of Foreign Missions. Finally, in 1843 an American Baptist Free Mission Society was organized, ad-mitting no slaveholders and recognizing no distinction based on color. By 1845 the antislavery people were strong enough to prevent a slaveholder of Georgia from being appointed as a home missionary. The Baptists of Maine, New York, Vermont, and Michigan designated that none of their contributions were to go to missionaries who held slaves, and Alabama demanded a statement of policy with regard to appointing slaveholders. The executive board of the society replied that it would not appoint slaveholders. In May 1845, therefore, a Southern convention was held, the society separated, and all co-operative enterprises between the churches of the two sections came to an end.

The antislavery movement among Methodists centered largely in New England. Orange Scott and LaRoy Sunderland had organized the first Methodist Anti-Slavery Society in New York in 1833. George Storrs was the leader of the movement in New Hampshire. Sunderland began publication of the *Zion's Watchman* in 1836. Then the General Conference stepped in and removed Scott from his position as presiding elder, refused to license several antislavery men as preachers, and forbade Methodists to lend support to Sunderland's paper. Antislavery Methodists in Ohio, Michigan, and western Pennsylvania withdrew from the church and organized as Wesleyan Methodists at Utica, New York, in 1843. The church forbade all connection with slavery. In 1844 a Georgia bishop of the Methodist church married a woman who owned slaves and was suspended until he disposed of them. Southern Methodists then withdrew and established the Southern Methodist Church.

Attempts were made at interdenominational organization. An Evangelical Union Anti-Slavery Society, with James G. Birney as president, was formed at Broadway Hall in New York City, January 11, 1839. It was interdenominational, and its object was to purify the churches on the slavery question. Some years later, a great Christian Anti-Slavery Convention was held in Cincinnati. All such attempts at union came to nothing. The two factors which contributed most to the growth of antislavery sentiment in the churches were the efforts of the government to enforce the Fugitive Slave Act and the Kansas-Nebraska Act of 1854. The latter, especially, produced violent reaction among the clergy of the several denominations.[27]

LABOR

Chapter 42

The American Antislavery Society at the time of organization said: "Every man has the right to his own body; to the products of his labor; to the protection of the common advantages of society." It then resolved to buy the produce of free labor instead of slave labor.[1] This economic approach to the problem of how to abolish slavery had been made as early as the religious approach, and in the end was just as ineffective. Slaveholders weathered the threat to their pocketbooks about as easily as the threat to their salvation.

Sometime about 1791 a movement began in England to refrain from the use of anything produced by slave labor in order that slavery might thereby be made so unprofitable as to disappear.[2] This was the free produce movement, thoroughly sound in its conception when West Indian sugar was the chief product of slave labor, but thoroughly ineffective when cotton became the staple crop of the American South. Clarkson said at the height of the debate over the slave trade in the House of Commons that people of all classes in every town in England had given up the use of sugar, as many as 500 in some towns and 300,000 in all.[3] Most of the Quakers in England supported the movement, and in the United States it was primarily a Quaker movement.[4] A society was organized at one time to promote the use of maple sugar in place of cane sugar. It was estimated that 263,000 acres of sugar brush would supply the needs of the entire country.[5] The third convention of the abolition societies, meeting in Philadelphia in 1796, urged the members of the several societies to promote the buying of free labor produce.[6] The movement continued in both England and the United States during the early years of the nineteenth century. A leading Quaker in 1853 argued that three-fourths of the slaves were engaged in supplying the English mills with cotton, and if the British market were closed three-fourths of the land devoted to cotton culture would revert to wilderness and the planters would be bankrupted.[7]

People were urged to refrain from using the products of slave labor that they might not partake of other men's sins. Samuel Rhoads and Elihu Burritt both argued that such produce was the fruit of robbery perpetrated on the slave every day and that its voluntary consumption was participation in the awful sin of holding men in bondage. Christians should practice their professions.[8] Every Christian man, woman, and child in England and the United States should and could refrain from the use of rice, sugar, and cotton. Angelina Grimké wrote a detailed explanation to Lewis Tappan in 1841 of the sin of using cotton goods.[9] She also forbade Theodore Weld to buy mattress ticking produced by slave labor for their home.[10] She said to Tappan: "If every bale of cotton and every piece of calico were stained with the sweat and blood which has flowed so freely in raising the raw material, who would be found ready to receive, and manufacture, and vend, and wear the fabric into which slave grown cotton has been wrought?" Elizabeth Margaret Chandler spoke in a more personal way in her poem "Slave Produce":

Look! they are robes from a foreign loom,
Delicate, light as the rose leaf's bloom;
Stainless and pure in their snowy tint,
As the drift unmarked by a footstep's print.
Surely such garment should fitting be,
For women's softness and purity.

Yet fling them off from thy shrinking limb,
For sighs have rendered their brightness dim,
And many a mother's shriek and groan,
And many a daughter's burning moan,
And many a sob of wild despair,
From woman's heart, is lingering there.[11]

The movement failed of general support largely because substitutes like silk, linen, and wool were very expensive, substitutes were difficult to obtain, and cotton fabrics represented more free labor in the processing and manufacture than they did slave labor in the growing of cotton.[12] The principal reason for its failure, however, was that antislavery people were reluctant to destroy slavery by any other method than moral suasion. The ultimate consequences of turning aside from moral condemnation of slaveholders and their political and ecclesiastical supporters restrained the antislavery societies from giving the movement full support. What could be gained in the battle for human rights by forcing slaveholders to abandon slavery from economic necessity? It was an honorable thing to refrain from using the products of slave labor as a personal protest, but it would be fatal to rely upon this method alone or to divert any considerable part of their effort to it.

Antislavery societies, therefore, spoke out in favor of abstention, but they did not promote the establishment of free produce stores. The American convention consistently recommended to the members of the several abolition societies the use of free labor produce.[13] The American Anti-Slavery Society in 1836 adopted a resolution of Gerrit Smith's urging members prayerfully to consider whether they could "innocently make an ordinary use of, or be concerned in, the traffic of the productions of slave labor.[14] Antislavery women at their convention in 1837 reminded all women that the products of slave labor, which they used in their homes almost daily, had cost the slave "his unrequited toil, his blood, and his tears." They were asked to take the same firm stand against the use of these products as their fathers had taken against the use of products which Great Britain had unjustly taxed.[15]

The American and Foreign Anti-Slavery Society, in its constitution, endorsed the use of free produce.[16] In 1847 the executive committee urged the British government to develop cotton production in India and in Africa. The Manchester, England, society went further and urged English merchants to break off all commerce with slaveholders.[17] The London society (1847) warned cotton growers in the United States to look toward emancipation before it was too late. "There is now growing up here," they said, "a deep conviction that we ought to get rid of slavery in America by going to India for our cotton."[18] Successful experiments in the growth of cotton were conducted in 1845–46 in southern India, in 1847 in Australia, and in 1849 in the British West Indies.[19] Two British manufacturing firms guaranteed their cloth to have been produced from cotton grown by free labor, and 60,000 British women petitioned the Queen to banish from the royal household everything produced by slave labor.[20]

The two most active centers of the movement in the United States were Philadelphia and Cincinnati. Philadelphia was the headquarters of the old abolition societies and a stronghold of the Society of Friends. The American Free Produce Association was organized there in 1839. Its purpose in general terms was to make it easier for the wage earner to compete with slave labor.[21] The society did not prosper, although it arranged for the manufacture and wholesale distribution of muslin, gingham, bed-ticking, drilling, Canton flannel, calico, and cotton yarns.[22] In June 1845 the Free Produce Association of Friends of Philadelphia Yearly Meeting was organized. The association appointed a committee to secure information concerning the means by which free goods could be obtained in commercial channels.[23] It created a capital fund for the purchase of free cotton and its manufacture. It sent agents into the Southern states to investigate the supply of free cotton. Numerous men in Mississippi, Georgia, and Tennessee agreed to collect and ship such cotton, with sworn affidavits that it was free grown, and with the name and residence of the grower of every bale. Great difficulty, however, was experienced in carrying it through the mills without contamination by other cotton.

In the West activity centered in a Free Produce Association of Friends of Ohio Yearly Meeting, organized at Mount Pleasant, and a Western Free Produce Association organized at Salem, Indiana, both in 1846. The Salem association opened a store in Cincinnati with a capital investment of

$3,000. Levi Coffin of Salem reluctantly agreed to go to Cincinnati and began operations in April 1847. His greatest difficulty was in securing enough stock in New York and Philadelphia to fill orders. Samuel Rhoads of the Philadelphia society authorized him to purchase a cotton gin and ship it to William McCray in Mississippi and to employ Nathan Thomas to go South and see that all arrangements with planters were carried out. All free cotton within reach of the gin was purchased. It was shipped to Memphis to a merchant who used no slave labor. It was shipped up the river on boats that used no slaves to Cincinnati, where it was manufactured. The cost was so great, however, that Coffin's personal resources were completely exhausted and the enterprise came to an end after about ten years.

Men who worked for wages in shops and factories, in services, and as unskilled laborers exhibited an almost callous unconcern toward the entire antislavery movement until about 1845. This indifference may have been the result, in part, of the refusal of the hard core of antislavery men to dilute or confuse their main efforts by discussing other issues. They would neither oppose nor support women's rights, and they would neither oppose nor support labor reforms, not because they were conservative aristocrats but because they had dedicated their lives to abolishing slavery and firmly believed that slavery was the great obstruction to all social progress. One would have expected the Garrisonians to champion the demands of the increasingly class-conscious wage earners; but Garrison was hostile to labor and may well have driven labor leaders away from support of the antislavery movement.[24]

White laborers, both North and South, believed that emancipation would throw them into competition with an enormous supply of Negro labor. Unskilled labor was already conscious of the growing numbers of Negroes in the cities. Colonizationists played upon these fears constantly, not only intensifying race hatred among a poorly educated class, but increasing their unreasoned opposition to emancipation. George Henry Evans, an agrarian and editor of labor publications, charged antislavery men with a desire to reduce "both northern workers and southern slaves to the lowest level of wage dependence and to anarchical competition with each other for the privilege of doing the drudgery of capital."[25] Henry Field James, in 1856, called antislavery men "midas-

eared Mammonites" who wanted to bring Southern slaves into the North to "compete with and assist in reducing the wages of the white laborer."[26]

Such bitter opposition was rare. There were not many such publications, but they do indicate that many wage earners looked askance at the antislavery movement. For the most part their attitude was one of indifference—a lack of interest on the part of men deeply concerned about their own emancipation through trade unions, ten-hour days, mechanics-lien laws, anti-garnishee legislation, prohibition of child labor, free homesteads, antimonopoly laws, and public schools. George Henry Evans carried on a sharp exchange of letters in the public press with Gerrit Smith about wage slavery and bond slavery, insisting, as did a large group of Southern proslavery writers, that the slaves were better off than the Northern wage earners. It must be remembered, of course, that their arguments were narrowly economic, and that the Northern laboring men were opposed to slavery, as Evans said, "in every form; the slavery of might and the slavery of want . . . the slavery of the mind and the slavery of the body." He insisted that crowded cities, rent exactions, disease, crime, and prostitution went hand in hand with the wage system and were more destructive of life, health, and happiness than the labor system of the South.[27] Even Horace Greeley could say that if he were less concerned about slavery in the South than some, it was because he saw so much in New York which had first claim upon his interest.

The preoccupation of labor with its own welfare became less exclusive as the antislavery movement progressed, and the arguments of antislavery writers were increasingly effective. William Ellery Channing wrote that the greatest and most elementary property right was that of an individual to his own mental and physical capacities. Most people possessed nothing but their energy and ability to do certain things well. Slavery deprived them of the fruits of their labor, was robbery of the first magnitude, and was destructive of all property rights.[28] The deception embodied in the term wage slaves was exposed. There were injustices and there were inequalities of wealth, but there was *equality of rights*. A man worked for someone else today and hired others to work for him tomorrow. The worker could always claim protection of the law in this relationship if there was occasion for it. He could work for someone else. He could work for himself. No one could rob him of his wife, or children, or freedom to speak as he pleased and to go where he pleased. To call this slavery was sheer nonsense.[29]

It was of the utmost importance for individuals to know that they were making some definite contribution to the welfare of their fellow men and that their contributions were recognized and appreciated. Pride in one's work was essential to maintenance of the dignity of labor. Slavery had created a deep contempt for labor in the slave states. Physical toil was looked upon with scorn. It was ridiculed and despised by white men, and poor men had long been leaving the slave states to escape the humiliation of having to work. That same situation would soon exist everywhere in the country unless slavery were abolished. It could not be corrected in the presence of slavery, because the poor man, working with his hands, was reduced to the same low estate as the slave and was unable to improve his standard of living. Rather than suffer the humiliation of working where it was not honorable to work, men preferred to live on the barest margin of subsistence.[30]

This appeal to Northern labor was very important because it was also directed to the nonslaveholding Southerner. It must never be forgotten that slaveholders fled from the Union in 1860–61 in a last desperate gamble to preserve slavery. They had three great fears: that a world-wide boycott of the products of slave labor would destroy them economically, that a reorganized Supreme Court would find the power of Congress to abolish slavery, and that the nonslaveholders of the South would turn against them. This argument of the antislavery men dealt with the third of these areas and was largely anticipated by the slaveholders in their suppression of all discussion touching upon slavery. It was emphasized that the white man who labored in the South was held in contempt. No one in the North, regardless of wealth, would consider it disgraceful to engage in physical labor, and no one was restrained from working by feeling that it was dishonorable. The great wealth of the Northern states derived from their teeming population of free laborers and consumers; the poverty of the slave states from the migration of their free laborers to the North and West.[31]

This argument finally gained acceptance and support by nonslaveholders who saw that slavery was bringing complete ruin to the South. Once a region of great natural advantages and endless opportunity, the South had been reduced by slavery, except for the slaveholders, to a region of ignorance and poverty. Hinton Rowan Helper, who hated slavery for what it was doing to the nonslaveholders, used statistics to show that even in agricultural pursuits the free states had far outstripped the slave states. His conclusions were that free labor was "far more respectable, profitable, and productive than slave labor." "In the South, unfortunately," he said, "no kind of labor is either free or respectable."[32] Charles Francis Adams argued that the South would never be able to attain a high degree of culture because of its agrarian economy. It was impossible, he insisted, for manufacturing to develop on a large scale because the working force was slaves and had to be kept ignorant for disciplinary reasons. Workers could not acquire the knowledge necessary to operate complicated tools and machines. Without industry the slave states would remain economically depressed and culturally stagnant.[33]

Southern apologists defended slavery with arguments which, however satisfactory and comforting to themselves, did as much to promote emancipation as anything the antislavery people ever said. "Look at the sick and infirm slave on the one hand with his family and his friends around him," said one, "under the superintending care of a kind master and mistress, and compare it with the forlorn and wretched condition of the pauper poor, now swelling the burdens of every other civilized population upon earth save our own."[34] His advice, and he was not alone, was that the laborer could better his condition only by placing himself under the care and in the possession of a benevolent master. The idea that a worker could rise in society by his own efforts was a fantasy. Workers would always be cruelly treated and friendless until they became slaves.

This argument was presented finally in classic form in the poem The Hireling and the Slave. The wage earner was here presented, with great passion, as suffering agonies to the very day of his death, and in contrast, the slave as a pampered, loved, and carefree member of society.[35] Champions of slavery then went one step farther and warned the property owners and professional men that the working class, discontented and embittered, was on the verge of seizing control of the government and would destroy republican institutions. They argued against universal manhood suffrage. They said that in other nations large military establishments were necessary to control the ignorant and poverty-stricken rabble. They urged the same measures in the free states. They pointed with pride to the fact that the slave states were not confronted with the problem, because the slaves, who were the laborers of the South, had no political privileges. Unlike Northern laborers, they posed no threat to the dominance of the upper classes.[36] This attempt to discredit the antislavery movement, by implying that it was setting in motion a great social upheaval at the North, was a complete failure. It has, of course, a historical value, as revealing how completely the slave system had enmeshed the South in a form of social insanity. One page of Theodore Weld's American Slavery As It Is tore the argument to shreds, and time after time master minds from colonial days forward had explained the horrors with which any free man would shrink from thought of enslavement for himself and his family; yet here were men trying to persuade several million freeborn and intelligent artisans and farm boys that slavery was a positive good for the laboring man and the salvation of democracy.

The actual relationship of the wage earner to slavery was not a happy one. The South had less than 10 per cent of the nation's manufactures, so that the total number of factory workers was relatively small, and there were no trade unions. Slaves constituted the bulk of the labor force, outnumbering white wage earners by four to one, and the latter simply could not compete with slaves hired out by their masters. By 1847 they were complaining that slavery was reducing the working population "to a state of physical debility, moral decay, and hopeless idleness, which must lead them to complete degradation or desperate revolt." Northern wage earners did not have to compete against slave labor but against free Negro labor. Immigrant German and Irish laborers, unskilled for the most part, had to compete against slave labor in the South and free Negro labor in the North.[37]

The only way a Southern wage earner could escape from the vicious competition of slavery was to move his family to the free states. Thousands of them did so, taking with them a bitter hatred of slavery. Most of them, however, remained in the South, first hating the slaves, then hating the slave system. Opposition to slavery per se was fully developed between 1845 and 1850,

and at the same time a very great fear of an industrial labor force developed among the champions of the slave system. Christopher G. Memminger, later secretary of the Treasury of the Confederate States, wrote: "I find an opinion gaining ground that slaves ought to be excluded from mechanical pursuits and everything but agriculture, so as to have their places filled with whites . . . Drive our negro mechanics and all sorts of operatives from our cities, and who must take their places? The same men who make the cry in the Northern cities against the tyranny of Capital . . . and would soon raise here the cry against the Negro and be hot Abolitionists. And every one of these men would have a vote."[38] Hinton Rowan Helper pointed out that even though there was a greater density of population in the free states, labor could command double the wages which prevailed in the South because in the slave country the cost of free labor was determined by the cost of competitive slave labor. Even in industry slaves were preferred. They were cheaper and they could not strike. They were introduced into the Tredagar iron works of Richmond as strikebreakers, and when white wage earners protested, as they did in increasing numbers, they were held in little less suspicion than abolitionists.[39] Employers simply would not bargain because of the ease with which they could hire slave replacements.

Southern wage earners such as mechanics, carpenters, bricklayers, coopers, and wheelwrights, who lived in the semirural areas, were far more vulnerable to the competition of slave labor than factory workers. By the mid-1840's enough slaves were trained in these special skills to supply the needs of plantation operations and provide a surplus for hire. Only in the cities, of which there were not many, could free artisans escape this ruinous competition, and that only by organization. Time after time they protested to city councils and state governments, but the protests bear an unmistakable hostility to Negro labor, be it free or slave, rather than to the evil of slavery.[40] The unskilled worker was in an even worse position than the factory worker or the independent craftsman. The wages and the hours of work of the common day laborers were determined by the standards of slavery. Manual labor in itself was a badge of servility. Their standard of living was low, and their standard of work was low. Their hatred, like that of the skilled craftsman, was directed against the slave, yet eventually and inevitably against slavery. Many of them were German and Irish immigrants who were by instinct opposed to all forms of oppression.

In retrospect, then, it may be said that antislavery leaders had indifferent success in their appeal to labor during the first two decades of the movement. The sin and injustice of slavery were acknowledged by the vast majority of workers, but they had problems of their own and the relationship between slavery and their own problems was not nearly so clear as the threat of competition posed by emancipation. They had to be shown how slavery was injuring them. They had to be convinced that men who were working to free the slaves were not their own oppressors. That is what makes renewed emphasis upon the territorial question so important.

George Henry Evans, editor of the first labor publications in the country, went back to New York from his farm in 1843 and renewed publication of the *Working Man's Advocate*. He had been arguing for free homesteads since the 1820's. In the early years of the antislavery movement he had talked of wage slavery and the need of providing free lands before freeing the slaves—to prevent emancipation becoming an exchange of one type of slavery for another. By 1845 he was engaged in a powerful crusade for free land and free labor, and free land translated into free homesteads made sense both to labor and homestead farmers. The movement spread throughout the country and was supported by the new wave of German immigrants.

Evans had no connection with antislavery societies. His agrarian movement reached maturity when the main stream of antislavery was flowing through the Liberty and then the Free Soil parties. He had long been opposed to slavery. Emancipation of the slaves was a major part of his general program. He insisted, in fact, that land reform would lead quickly to abolition of slavery, but that it should come first to protect Northern workers against depressed wages when emancipated slaves entered the labor market. "Man's right to life," he said, "is the source of all other rights. Since he lives, he has a right to be. This implies a right to use the materials of nature necessary for being. These are light, air, water, and soil. These are man's natural material rights. All others, such as liberty, labor, capital, and education are acquired."[41] He insisted upon free homesteads of not less than 160 acres before emancipation and offered the votes of labor to any party which agreed to this plan of political action. On this basis he must be recognized as one of the outstanding antislavery leaders during the last ten years of his life.[42] The wisdom and equity of free homesteads, as we have seen, was added to the antislavery creed by the Buffalo convention of 1848. The other concept, though not entirely new, emphasized from that time forward was the inevitable conflict between slave labor and free labor.

It had been said in the first days of the organized antislavery movement that the struggle was between free labor and slave labor, that they could not both survive in the same nation, and that the slaves would gain their freedom or the Northern wage earners would lose their freedom. It was said a thousand times, in as many different ways. Labor heard, but was reluctant to believe, until the philosophy of slavery was presented to them by the political newspapers and the political leaders of the 1850's. We can select almost at random from the many statements. Said Harper: "It is the order of nature and of God that the being of superior faculties and knowledge, and therefore of superior powers, should control and dispose of those who are inferior. It is as much in the order of nature that men should enslave each other as that animals should prey upon each other."[43] Said Fitzhugh: "We deem this peculiar question of negro slavery of very little importance. The issue is made throughout the world on the general subject of slavery in the abstract. The argument has commenced. One set of ideas will govern and control after a while the civilized world. Slavery will everywhere be abolished, or everywhere be reinstituted."[44] Said the Richmond *Enquirer*: "The great evil of Northern free society is that it is burdened with a servile class of mechanics and laborers unfit for self-government, and yet clothed with the attributes and powers of citizens. Master and slave is a relation as necessary as that of parent and child; and the northern states will yet have to introduce it. Slavery is the natural and normal condition of the laboring man, whether white or black."[45]

While the newspapers were printing and reprinting the philosophy of slavery, William H. Seward and Abraham Lincoln became official spokesmen of the antislavery party for the cause of free labor. Abraham Lincoln delivered his House Divided speech at the Republican state convention at

Springfield, Illinois, June 16, 1858. Seward delivered his equally famous Irrepressible Conflict speech at Rochester, October 25, 1858. Said Lincoln: "Either the opponents of slavery will arrest the further spread of it, and place it where the public mind shall rest in the belief that it is in course of ultimate extinction, or its advocates will push it forward until it shall become alike lawful in all the States old as well as new, North as well as South."[46] Said Seward, speaking of the collision between free labor and slave labor brought on by increasing social unity and consolidation: "They who think it is accidental, unnecessary, the work of interested or fanatical agitators, and therefore ephemeral, mistake the case altogether. It is an irrepressible conflict between opposing and enduring forces, and it means that the United States must and will, sooner or later, become either entirely a slaveholding nation, or entirely a free-labor nation. Either the cotton and rice fields of South Carolina and the sugar plantations of Louisiana will ultimately be tilled by free labor and Charleston and New Orleans become marts for legitimate merchandise alone, or else the rye-fields and wheat fields of Massachusetts and New York must again be surrendered by their farmers to slave culture and to the production of slaves, and Boston and New York become once more markets for trade in the bodies and souls of men."[47]

Reading the Emancipation Proclamation

FREE SOIL

Chapter 43

Whatever hopes the leaders of the Whigs and Democrats may have had of maintaining party solidarity were dashed by the aggression of the slave power. There seemed to be no end to its demands, no limits to its pretensions. Resistance to its greed and its vanity, in the end, provided the broad base for political unity of antislavery men. *Free Soil, Free Speech, Free Labor,* and *Free Men,* which they inscribed upon their banner at Buffalo in 1847, had depth and meaning, because the slave power controlled the government, and the slave power had many of the basic characteristics of a modern totalitarianism system.

It held three and one-half million human beings in abject, perpetual slavery, denying to them all hope of redemption.

It had suppressed free enquiry and discussion, denying by law and by violence in the slave states the right to express other than support for slavery, in private conversations, in print, in the pulpit, and in courts of justice.

It had distorted the teachings of Jesus into seeming support of oppression by a strange exegesis and had prostituted the church to its support.

It had exerted powerful pressure to subordinate freedom of speech, of the press, and of assembly in the free states to the support of slavery and oppression of free Negroes.

It had compelled thousands of clergy in the churches to abandon their ancient prerogative and solemn obligation of denouncing sin and oppression in both private and public life.

It had brought great pressure upon all publishing houses to drop from their lists all books and to delete from others all passages critical of slavery.

It had openly defied the law in its control of the executive branch of the federal government by extracting from the mails and destroying antislavery literature.

It had struck down the right of petition in order to prevent criticism of slavery in the most numerous branch of the national legislature.

It was denying the validity of universal manhood suffrage, and particularly of the right of men who worked for wages to participate in government.

It was declaiming the superior virtues of slavery over freedom for the laboring man, thus advocating degradation and further denial of privilege instead of social justice.

It was insisting that the full power of the government, sustained by the wealth, manpower, and intelligence of all the people, be dedicated to defending, strengthening, and perpetuating slavery.

It demanded that slaveholders be allowed to roam at will through the free states, picking up whatever Negroes took their fancy, and carrying them off to slavery.

It demanded recognition by the courts of the principle that color was presumptive of servitude.

It demanded punishment of all persons who extended aid and comfort to fugitives.

It denied that Negroes could be citizens and excluded them from the slave states.

It denied the right of states which had freed their slaves, and of those which always had been nonslaveholding, to protect their citizens against kidnapping by due process of law.

ISAAC and ROSA, Emancipated Slave Children,
From the Free Schools of Louisiana,
Photographed by KIMBALL, 477 Broadway. N.Y.
Entered according to Act of Congress, in the year 1863 by GEO. H.
HANKS, in the Clerk's Office of the U. S. for the Sou. Dist. of N.Y.

It had aided and abetted the revolt of Texas from Mexico in order to re-establish slavery in that area.

It had annexed Texas to the United States by the highly questionable procedure of joint resolution, for the avowed purpose of providing a new market for human flesh, increasing the number of slave states, and strengthening the power of slavery.

It had conducted a frenzied campaign of villification against Great Britain because she recognized the right of persons to assert their freedom, once they were beyond the limits of state law and on the high seas.

It had welcomed war with Mexico that more and more territory might be brought within the orbit of an expanding slave empire.

It was demanding the dedication of all the vast national domain to slavery rather than to freedom.

It was threatening, over and over again, to break up the Union and form an independent Confederacy based upon slavery unless it could have its way without let or hindrance.

Antislavery men added nothing to their platform of principles after the Buffalo convention of October 1847. They had turned to political action by combining their voting strength in a party of their own in 1840. This was the only way in which any man could cast his vote against slavery, because all of the slaveholders were in either the Democrat or Whig parties, and those parties accommodated their expressed principles and legislative programs to the desires of the slaveholders. Convincing antislavery men that this was true and weaning them away from lifelong party allegiance was something of a problem.

Votes cast for Liberty Party and Free Soil Party candidates between 1840 and 1852 have no relationship to antislavery strength in the country. It is highly probable that antislavery men could have taken control of the government ten years before they did so, if they had united. There is no room for argument here. Hundreds of thousands of staunch antislavery men voted for Whigs and Democrats. That is precisely what gives meaning to the Liberty and Free Soil parties. Day after day and month after month, antislavery Whigs and Democrats in public office were forced into a more emphatic defense of their principles in party caucuses and in the halls of Congress. It became increasingly difficult for them to work with their colleagues from the slave states, and day by day those Southerners were forced into a more determined defense of their own position. The question was how long the two old-line parties could stand the internal pressure. All the antislavery party had to do was maintain vitality and respectability. Antislavery men in the other parties would come to it when their working alliances with the slave power were no longer defensible before their constituents.

It is not possible to say that *all* antislavery men believed alike on the particulars of a legislative program, but there were four broad areas within which there was general agreement.

They believed the primary function of government to be that of providing security for the natural and equal rights of all persons. These had been invaded by irresponsible mobs for a decade, in some areas by the government itself.

They rejected the thesis that slavery was national, was recognized by the Constitution, and was entitled to protection by all the powers of the government. It had no national character except in the expansive concepts of its protagonists. It was an exercise of force, recognized and sustained by state law. It must be contained within the limits of the states. It could have no existence elsewhere.

They believed the greatest of all crimes would be further expansion of slavery. It must be kept out of the territories. There must be no more slave states. It must be abolished in the District of Columbia. The buying and selling of human beings in interstate commerce must stop.

They were strong Union men. The Union must be preserved. The power and prestige of the federal government must be restored. There must be no acceptance of devices to provide local autonomy and thus escape from the operation of the moral law as revealed in the national conscience.

Antislavery men had opposed the annexation of Texas as basically immoral—the beginning of a national career of war, crime, and aggression that would carry us to the Isthmus of Panama or beyond—and well it might had it not been for their strong opposition. They prophesied freely that it would lead to war with Mexico, perhaps with Great Britain, and John Quincy Adams confided to his diary a fear of the conquest of Mexico and the West Indies, the loss of individual freedom, and the development of a monarchy. Benjamin Lundy, whose knowledge of Texas was as great as that of any man in the country, wrote that annexation would lead very soon to a dissolution of

the Union and a confederation of the slaveholding states.[1]

Antislavery men had no need to formulate either a policy or a constitutional theory about slavery in the territory we obviously intended to take at the conclusion of the war. The Congress had excluded slavery from the Northwest Territory in 1787, and from the major portion of the Louisiana Purchase in 1820, and would have excluded it from Arkansas and Florida except for the representatives of slaves. David Wilmot presented the venerable principle of Congressional exclusion in the House of Representatives in 1846, and it passed by a vote of eighty-five to seventy-nine, the negatives including all the votes cast for the slaves. Congress adjourned before a vote could be taken in the Senate.

Lewis Cass, leading candidate of the Democrats for the presidential nomination, broke new ground in the territorial dispute with what may be called either the constitutional theory or the practical expedient of nonintervention. The people who might go to the territories to live should be left free to determine the nature of their own institutional development. His exposition was published as the Nicholson Letter, December 24, 1847.[2]

William L. Yancey of Alabama, the orator of secession, had resigned from Congress on September 1, 1846. He wrote his Alabama Platform in 1848.[3] This was a statement of abstract principles far in advance of any previous pronouncements, and the first step in the timetable of aggression by the slave power. It was the basic document in what the slave power chose to call Southern rights, and was variously restated many times, particularly in the Davis Resolutions, the Dred Scott Decision, and the Southern Rights Platform of 1860. In substance it said that slaves were property, and definition of what constituted property was an exercise of sovereign power belonging exclusively to a state constitutional convention. This had no basis in historical fact, because five great states had abolished slavery by acts of their legislatures. Yancey's theory also embraced the premise that the territories were the common property of the several states and that congressional power over them was limited to the protection of persons and property while they remained in territorial status. Any citizen of any state, therefore, could go to the territories, taking with him any species of property recognized by his state, and look to the federal government for protection in the enjoyment of that property until a constitutional convention met to frame a constitution for admission of the territory into the Union as a state.

This was revolutionary doctrine, and its explosive force was no less than frightening to party managers. The Democratic Party, even in Alabama, shied away from it, and the Democratic National Convention at Baltimore rejected it by a vote of 216 to 36. Northern leaders of the party could not endorse it. Stephen A. Douglas gave his own interpretation of nonintervention, insisting that those people who went to the territories carried the right of self-government with them and could legislate on all subjects as soon as a territorial legislature met. This was the doctrine of popular sovereignty. Southern rights men insisted that if Congress could not exclude slavery from the territories a territorial legislature, the creature of Congress, could not do so. The Yancey platform of principles became the creed of the Southern rights men, both Whigs and Democrats. It is not too much to say it became the creed of the slave states by 1860.

The time was long past when the free states would have accepted the doctrine of Congressional protection, in fact they *never* would have done so—in 1787, or 1820, or 1848. President Taylor, Southern Whig and Louisiana slaveholder, refused to promise a veto of the Wilmot Proviso excluding slavery from the newly acquired territory, if it should pass. Southern Whigs and Southern Democrats united in strong support of slavery expansion, throwing Congress into turmoil, but when Calhoun called a caucus of Southern members of Congress in January, 1849, only a minority was willing to sign an address to the people of the South urging the formation of a Southern sectional party and strongly hinting at the necessity for disunion. There was no disagreement thereafter between Southern Whigs and Southern Democrats on the principles of the Southern rights platform as expounded by Yancey and Calhoun so far as slavery and the right of secession were concerned, but there was a strong disagreement on what, if anything, would justify a resort to secession.

The Congress which met in December 1849 was forced by circumstances to make some hard decisions, at least from the standpoint of party harmony. Antislavery men from the North were inflexible in support of Congressional exclusion. The weight of constitutional theory, legislative precedent, and moral responsibility were heavily on their side. So, too, were numbers, if representation of slaves were disregarded. Southern Democrats were crusading for recruits to the revolutionary doctrine of Congressional protection and threatening disunion if denied the full measure of acceptance. Southern Whigs and Northern Democrats united to define public policy in such a way as to silence the slavery controversy and save their political alliances. They did badly in the attempt because the spirit of man is such that the longing for freedom can be neither crushed nor compromised. Not a single item in the congressional acts of 1850 constitutes an acknowledgment of the evils of slavery, or even of the incompatibility of slavery and democracy. Not a single one constitutes progression in the program of emancipation, except that California came into the Union as a nonslaveholding state.

It was with the greatest difficulty that the territories of New Mexico and Utah were organized, each with the provision that it was to be admitted to the Union eventually "with or without slavery, as their constitution may prescribe at the time of admission." That was exactly what Yancey and Calhoun, and all other Southern rights men said. The question of whether a territorial legislature could exclude slavery or pass unfriendly legislation, as Douglas claimed, was left unanswered. The country, to all intents and purposes, was committed to the slaveholders' creed. Slavery might not expand, but Congressional action was not going to stand in its way. The same Congress passed the amendment to the Fugitive Slave Act of 1793. That act, as we have seen, was an abject surrender to the greed of slaveholders of the most precious safeguards of freedom. All Negroes, citizens or not, were exposed to the tender mercies of kidnappers as a matter of *national policy.*

Northern Democrats tried to save themselves and their party by an appeal to the principle of self-determination. They called it popular sovereignty. They talked about the first settlers being able to determine the future of a territory as if it were a highly antislavery technique. The simple fact was, however, that having rejected the constitutional principle of Congressional exclusion with regard to Utah and New Mexico, they could not retain it with regard to the vast and fertile Missouri Valley. The Missouri Compromise, so-called, must be repealed.

Franklin Pierce was elected President of the United States in 1852. His support by the Southern-rights members of his party was due to his long record of hostility to antislavery men and measures. He had never failed to bait and harass them if opportunity offered. He did not fail as President to give free reign to the pretensions of the slave power. Antislavery men must be silenced. They must be crushed. They must be convicted of treason if they resisted the fugitive slave laws. Either the man was ignorant of the strength of antislavery sentiment, or his prejudices were intensified by a feeling of overconfidence, or he was overawed by the strength of the slave power. Leading members of his Cabinet and his diplomatic corps were proslavery imperialists. His first and his last pronouncements as President were in defense of the new national policy. Slaveholders were free to roam at will over the whole of the national domain.

Three attempts were made in the short space of four years to expand the area of slaveholding to imperial dimensions, one only was successful. Pierre Soule of Louisiana, next to Jefferson Davis the strongest of Calhoun's successors as a leader of states rights and a violent proslavery imperialist, was sent as minister to Spain, and probably went there determined to secure Cuba for the United States. Secretary of State Marcy, as we have seen, had a most unsavory record of hostility to antislavery men. He did not encourage Soule to go beyond the legitimate field of diplomacy to acquire Cuba, but Soule thought he had done so, and both Pierce and Marcy were aware of, if not sympathetic to, Soule's aggressiveness. The important point is that Soule, James Buchanan, minister to Great Britain, and John Y. Mason, minister to France, met at Ostend, and then at Aix-la-Chapelle in October 1854 and prepared a report known as the Ostend Manifesto.

This remarkable document dwelt upon the relationship of Cuba to the security of the United States, and particularly upon the danger of a slave insurrection which would spread to the mainland. We must have Cuba. We must have it immediately. We would pay a very handsome price for it. We would support an insurrection to gain it. We would be justified in seizing it "if Spain, dead to the voice of her own interest, and actuated by stubborn pride and a false sense of honor, should refuse" to sell. Then came an extraordinary statement: "We should . . . be recreant to our duty, be unworthy of our gallant forefathers, and commit base treason against our posterity should we permit Cuba to be Africanized and become a second St. Domingo, with all its attendant horrors to the white race, and suffer the flames to extend to our own neighboring shores seriously to endanger or actually to consume the fair fabric of our Union. We fear the course and current of events are rapidly tending toward such a catastrophe." This pledge of fealty to the slave power won Buchanan the next Democratic nomination for the presidency. It discredited Soule and prompted his recall.

The second effort to acquire more slave territory was directed at Mexico. There is no way of knowing how much of that unfortunate country the United States might have retained at the end of the Mexican War had opposition to the expansion of slavery been less. Pierce sent James Gadsden of Florida and South Carolina to Mexico at the behest of Jefferson Davis, secretary of war, for the specific purpose of purchasing enough land south of the Gila River for a railroad route to the Pacific Coast. Gadsden went, not as the representative of a peaceful, friendly people, but as the agent of special interests bent on getting as much slave territory as possible by extravagant use of money and intimidation. He reported that much of northern Mexico, including Lower California, Tamaulipas, and Chihuahua, was within our reach. He was instructed to buy as much as possible for $50,000,-000. Neither the people of Mexico nor the antislavery people of the United States would have any part of such highhanded business. Gadsden's purchase was whittled down to a mere 30,000 square miles, for which we paid $10,000,000 and Santa Anna went into exile.

Unable to intimidate Spain or Mexico, or to buy from either for $50,000,000 more land for slave states to the south, the Pierce administration turned to a consummation of the betrayal of 1850. Congress did not have the power under the Constitution to exclude slavery from the territories. The principle of congressional exclusion had been superseded by nonintervention as applied in the territorial acts of 1850. Exclusion of slavery from the Louisiana Purchase, north of 36° 30', by the act of 1820, was unconstitutional. The act must be repealed. The settlers going into the area must have perfect freedom to determine the nature of their own institutional development. The Kansas-Nebraska Bill, declaring the Missouri restriction inoperative and void, was arranged by Jefferson Davis and Stephen A. Douglas, the two sectional leaders of the Democratic Party, and was forced through Congress with full administrative support. It received a majority of only thirteen votes in the House of Representatives. Once more, it was the votes of men representing the slave that provided the margin of success for the slave power.

When the two houses of Congress passed the Kansas-Nebraska Act they did everything but set the date for the emancipation of the slaves. The slave power had gone too far. This vast area of fertile land had long been dedicated to freedom. Men from all over the land, as we have seen, had talked for years about the pressure upon homestead farmers to get away from the slave country, on into the free West. They had done so in ever-increasing numbers. The farmers of the Ohio Valley and Great Lakes area expected their sons and

daughters to go to this region west of the Mississippi and establish homes. Their concern over the cultural environment which would develop there was as great as the concern of New England had been in respect to the Ohio Valley. Labor was only now, but with the enthusiasm of new converts, rushing to the support of the antislavery movement because the promise of free homesteads in the national domain held out some hope of escape from urban insecurity.

The contest in Congress over the fugitive slave and territorial acts of 1850 had completely disrupted the Whig Party. The Kansas-Nebraska Act drove Northern antislavery Democrats out of *their* party. Somehow, the repeal of the 1820 restriction seemed more reprehensible than anything else that had been done. Northern Democrats tried to save their political fortunes by emphasizing the power of the first settlers to keep slavery out of the territories. Southern Democrats denied the power to a territorial legislature and turned on Douglas furiously because of his doctrine of popular sovereignty. The ensuing controversy split the party.

Come and join us brothers

Negroes, former slaves and otherwise, were brought into the army in large numbers in the winter of 1862-63. No one could longer question their citizenship.

Parties, like people, grow old, but they do not die so easily. Senators Salmon P. Chase and Charles Sumner, Representatives Joshua Giddings, Edward Wade, and Gerrit Smith, and others, issued an *Appeal of the Independent Democrats in Congress to the People of the United States. Shall Slavery Be Permitted in Nebraska?* It was published in the *National Era* and in the New York *Tribune,* and as a pamphlet. The Kansas-Nebraska Bill was denounced "as a gross violation of a sacred pledge; as a criminal betrayal of precious rights; as part and parcel of an atrocious plot to exclude from a vast unoccupied region immigrants from the Old World and free laborers from our own States, and convert it into a dreary region of despotism, inhabited by masters and slaves." Then, after reviewing the history of Congressional exclusion and warning against the separation of the nonslaveholding states from the West by a band of slave territory, the appeal made a most formidable antislavery pronouncement:

"We appeal to the people. We warn you that the dearest interests of freedom and the Union are in imminent peril. Demagogues may tell you that the Union can be maintained only by submitting to the demands of slavery. We tell you that the Union can only be maintained by the full recognition of the just claims of freedom and man. The Union was formed to establish justice and secure the blessings of liberty. When it fails to accomplish these ends it will be worthless, and when it becomes worthless it cannot long endure.

"We entreat you to be mindful of that fundamental maxim of Democracy—EQUAL RIGHTS AND EXACT JUSTICE FOR ALL MEN. Do not submit to become agents in extending legalized oppression and systematized injustice over a vast territory yet exempt from these terrible evils.

"We implore Christians and Christian ministers to interpose. Their divine religion requires them to behold in every man a brother, and to labor for the advancement and regeneration of the human race.

"Whatever apologies may be offered for the toleration of slavery in the States, none can be offered for its extension into Territories where it does not exist, and where that extension involves the repeal of ancient law and the violation of solemn compact."

The North already was seething with bitter opposition to the Fugitive Slave Act. Now petitions poured in upon Congress again on the territorial question, and this time they came from ministerial associations and church antislavery societies, and from labor. There was no need to seek converts. People had been petitioning and protesting for decades against expansion of slavery. They had won a partial victory in 1820, only to have it repudiated after thirty-four years by faithless public servants. Douglas was burned in effigy in a thousand communities, and for the first time in his life he found it impossible to control an assembled audience in Chicago.

The reorganization and expansion of the antislavery political party in 1848 had brought Liberty Party men, Van Buren Democrats, and even more Whigs together under the name "Free Soil." Now the Free Soilers were joined by a host of old-line Whigs and antislavery Democrats. The fusion began in 1854. It was spontaneous, almost universal in the free states. No one needs argue about where the Republican Party was organized. The first national convention under the new name was at Pittsburgh in 1856, but the Republican Party was the old Free Soil Party, just as the Free Soil Party had been the Liberty Party, in each case with accretions of antislavery men who had broken away from the Whigs and the Democrats. Except for the Garrisonians, who spurned their responsibilities at the ballot box, all antislavery men were in the Republican Party by 1860.

The last of the antislavery men came over to the Republican Party for two very obvious reasons. The Supreme Court had handed down the Dred Scott Decision in 1857. That decision was a full and complete endorsement of Southern rights. The people of the United States in Congress assembled could not prohibit the expansion of slavery to the territories. The decision was wrong on every point, and it smacked of collusion between judges and politicians. The Whig Party no longer existed. The Republican Party provided the only effective opposition to the Democrats. The slave power was not completely within the Democratic Party but the larger part of it was, and the leaders of the Southern Rights Democrats, almost without exception, were on record as favoring secession if and when a Republican president should be elected. Republicans were determined that slavery should be excluded from the territories and were prepared to appoint justices to the Supreme Court who would find in the Constitution the Congressional power of exclusion. They were determined, also, to preserve the Union.

THE ROAD TO FREEDOM

Chapter 44

Abolition of slavery was a long, slow, agonizing process, achieved in a manner contrary to the best judgment of antislavery men, and never fully completed. Freedom by manumission was commonplace. Individual slaves, from early colonial days, were given certificates of freedom as a reward for long and faithful service in return for some particular acts of devotion, because they were children of the master, because they had passed the age of productive labor, and probably for many other reasons in individual cases. Many slaveholders also freed their slaves because of a conviction that slavery was morally wrong, and many more, not because of a sense of moral obligation, but because they could afford to indulge in generous humanitarianism. These acts of manumission sometimes were completed during a man's lifetime, but more often by his last will and testament.

Freedom was very often obtained by purchase. There is not very much room here for commendation of the master, but, considering the high percentage of slaves who were hired out by their owners and the wretched state of their existence, there was a degree of contrition in the heart of the man who permitted all or a portion of the slave's earnings to count for his redemption. Sometimes, as we have seen, such slaves were allowed to go over into a free state to work. A great many, having bought themselves, then turned to the purchase of their wives and children or other relations, giving a lifetime of hard labor to secure that which, as a nation, we had said was a gift of God to every man.

A third way to freedom was by perilous flight. The *slave system* was designed to prevent escape. Slaves inclined to brood over their bondage or to show a spirit of resistance sooner or later were sold into the deep South, from whence the road to free soil was long and tortuous. It required great endurance and skill to outdistance the hound dogs and the armed hounds of hell who took them out for a sporting venture or a piece of silver. It required rare discernment to know whom to approach for aid when it seemed that every man's hand was against you. It required extreme wariness to move in secret where every white man was invested with legal authority to search, to chastise, and perhaps to kill, and every road might well be patrolled by armed men.

Escape from bondage, but not to freedom, could be obtained also by suicide. An enormous number of slaves took this way out. Official and unofficial accounts of the African slave trade and of slavery in the West Indies dwell at length upon it, and newspaper accounts prove it to have been a common occurrence in the United States. Slaves killed themselves and their children so frequently that the total number who were killed in flight or committed suicide equaled the number who escaped, and the two combined was five times the number who were freed by manumission.

Society never encouraged manumission. State laws were not uniform, except in the sense of discouraging the practice. They forbade manumission except by special consent of the state legislature. They required bond by the grantor that the manumitted slave would never become a public charge. They required the freed slave to leave the parish or the state within a specified time—three months to a year—under penalty of being sold for failure to do so. They made every Negro liable to seizure and sale who could not present positive proof of freedom. They provided that a manumitted slave might thereafter be seized and sold to satisfy the claims of his former owner's creditors, and for debts incurred after the date of manumission. They imposed the most onerous restrictions upon the free Negroes to drive them out of the state or back into slavery, allowing them no formal education and little freedom of movement.

Emancipation or freedom by law, with or without consent of the master, took two forms. The only states which ever emancipated all slaves at once were Vermont, New Hampshire, and Massachusetts. In those three states the original constitutions freed all slaves and were so interpreted by the courts. No other state ever adopted immediate emancipation. Connecticut, Rhode Island, New York, Pennsylvania, and New Jersey provided by action of their respective state legislatures that children born of slave mothers thereafter were to be free at a specified age. Only at later dates did the legislatures free all slaves still living. They did, however, make every effort to protect the emancipated slave from re-enslavement by kidnapping, and in no state where slaves were given their freedom by law was the possibility of re-enslavement ever admitted.

Thereafter, for a half-century following the action of these Eastern states, emancipation was discussed, but never seriously by those who had the power to act. Two conditions always were attached to any proposal: compensation to the master and colonization. Jefferson wanted to write into the constitution of Virginia in 1777 a program of gradual emancipation, freeing all children born to slaves after a certain date, educating them at public expense until the females were eighteen years of age and males twenty-one, and colonizing them abroad in a protectorate of the United States. St. George Tucker rejected that plan as excessively costly. Instead, he suggested freeing all females when they reached twenty-eight years of age, and then treating all free Negroes so cruelly that they would flee from the country without cost to anyone. Thomas Jefferson Randolph, at the time of the 1832 debates in Virginia, wanted all slave children born after July 4, 1840, to become the property of the state at the ages of eighteen and twenty-

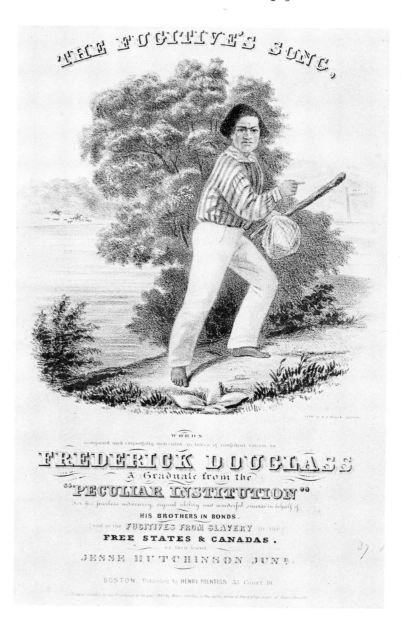

A song dedicated to fugitive slaves by Jesse Hutchinson in 1845.

one, and to be hired out until the income from their labor was sufficient to pay the cost of colonization.[1] The proposal was rejected, as was every plan for the use of the public lands or of money from the federal or state treasuries for colonization. The argument in Virginia, and it was not different elsewhere, was that the cost of compensated emancipation at $200 for each of the 470,000 slaves would be $94,000,000, and the cost of colonization $15,000,000. Such an expenditure being unmanageable, it was inexpedient to discuss the subject of emancipation.

Randolph's plan for hiring out the slaves for money to pay the cost of colonization was not different in any important respect from that of Henry Clay, who wanted to set a distant date, 1855 or 1860, and free all slaves born after that date when they reached the age of twenty-five years, but to add another three years of hired labor for the benefit of the state to pay for colonization.[2]

There is no record of any support in the slave states at any time for emancipation. The slaveholders talked about compensation, but only to show that the cost of emancipation would be prohibitive, never as something they would support. They talked about colonization, but not compulsory colonization even of free Negroes. That would have led to terrific opposition and directly to a test in the courts or to the use of public funds and complete emancipation. Slaveholders wanted no part of either, so they talked of colonization, as they talked of compensation, to confuse and confound the issue of emancipation. They would have gone to war to prevent the purchase and colonization of the slaves just as quickly as they later went to war to prevent emancipation. They never would have surrendered their labor supply nor the political power derived from the slaves.

Admitting, then, that the slaves were held in bondage by virtue of state law and that the federal government could not interfere with slavery in the states, how was slavery to be abolished? Antislavery men with few exceptions believed in restricting it to as small an area as was compatible with federal authority. They would exclude it from the territories, from the District of Columbia, and from federal forts and arsenals. They would abolish the interstate slave trade. It is doubtful if many of them in 1830 would have gone beyond these restrictive measures. The entire history of the movement reveals a horror of insurrection and an aversion to compulsion. Antislavery men wanted

acceptance of the principle that slavery was contrary to natural law, to moral law, and to the fundamental law of the nation. They wanted it as an assurance of full citizenship for the Negro after emancipation. They could not get it by purchasing the freedom of the slaves or by compulsion. They were shocked and disillusioned by the refusal of slaveholders to permit discussion. They then turned to two ideas, because there was no other way. One was emancipation by amendment of the federal constitution, the other was emancipation by exercise of the war powers.

Slaves had been finding freedom and losing freedom in war for a long time. The British gave freedom to those who joined them, bearing arms, during the Revolution, but did not go so far as to encourage a servile insurrection. They carried many away from the plantations, whether to freedom remains unanswered. General Cornwallis raided Thomas Jefferson's plantation in June 1781. Jefferson, who was in France at the time, said: "He destroyed all my growing crops of corn and tobacco; he burned all my barns . . . having first taken what corn he wanted; he used . . . all my stock of cattle, sheep, and hogs, for the sustenance of his army . . . and he burned all the fences on the plantation, so as to leave it an absolute waste. He carried off also about thirty slaves. Had this been to give them their freedom, he would have done right."[3] Jefferson's loss was only one of many up and down the coast. Many of the states gave freedom to slaves who enlisted in their armed forces, some paid the owners for their freedom, and some paid pensions to the veterans in addition to giving them freedom.

It is a singular fact that fugitives in Canada fought in the British forces against the United States, free Negroes in Baltimore and elsewhere fought equally well against the invading British armies, and hundreds of slaves fled to the British warships and were carried away to freedom. The most amazing performance of all, however, was at New Orleans, where Andrew Jackson was so hard pressed to mount a defense that he called for support of both pirates and slaves.

In 1840 Henry Highland Garnet, then a relatively young man from Oneida Institute, stepped to the platform of the American Antislavery Society Convention and presented a resolution: "That all the rights and immunities of American citizens are justly due to the people of color, who ever have been and still are willing to contribute their full share to enrich and to defend our common country." Speaking to that resolution, he told of the service of Negroes in the wars of the Revolution and 1812. He quoted the proclamation of Jackson to the Negroes of his victorious force: "I knew well how you loved your native country, and that you had, as well as ourselves, to defend what man holds most dear, parents, relations, wives, children, and property. You have done more than I expected. In addition to those previous qualifications I before knew you to possess, I found, moreover, a noble enthusiasm which leads to the performance of great things." "Such," said Garnet, "is the language of slaveholders when they would have colored men stand in the front of battle." Then he continued: "Sir, in consideration of the toils of our fathers in both wars, we claim the right of American citizenship. We claim it, but shall we ever enjoy it? Our ancestors fought and bled for it, but I will leave it with this assembly to decide whether they fought and bled as wise men or as fools. They have gone to their rest, many of them with their brows all marked with wounds received in fighting the battles of liberty, while their backs were furrowed by the cruel scourge. Unfortunate men."4

Meanwhile, following close upon the War of 1812, had come the Missouri debates. John Quincy Adams, secretary of state, recorded in his diary a conversation with John C. Calhoun, February 24, 1820, in which Calhoun made reference to a possible dissolution of the Union and an alliance of the slave states with Great Britain. Said Adams: "I pressed the conversation no further; but if the dissolution of the Union should result, from the slave question, it is as obvious as anything that can be forseen of futurity, that it must shortly afterward be followed by the universal emancipation of the slaves."5 Some months later, he wrote: "If slavery be the destined sword in the hand of the destroying angel which is to sever the ties of this Union, the same sword will cut in sunder the bonds of slavery itself. A dissolution of the Union for the cause of slavery would be followed by a servile war in the slave-holding states, combined with a war between the two severed portions of the Union. It seems to me that its result must be the extirpation of slavery from this whole continent; and, calamitous and desolating as this course of events in its progress must be, so glorious would be its final issue, that, as God shall judge me, I dare not say that it is not to be desired."6

Adams was in the House of Representatives in 1836. Texas was fighting for independence, the crucial battle of San Jacinto being fought on April 21 of that year. One month later (May 26) the Pinckney report eulogizing slavery and imposing the gag rule so far as antislavery discussion was concerned was adopted by the House of Representatives. In the course of the debates Adams dwelt at length upon the Texas revolution, the insecurity of slavery in time of war, the danger of war with Great Britain, France, and Mexico, and the possibility of a slave insurrection. He made very clear that while the peace-time powers of Congress and the chief executive are limited by provisions within the Constitution itself, the war powers are limited only by the "laws and usages of nations." He then propounded and answered a simple question: "Do you imagine that your Congress will have no constitutional authority to interfere with the institution of slavery in any way in the States of this confederacy? Sir, they must and will interfere with it—perhaps to sustain it by war; perhaps to abolish it by treaties of peace; and they will not only possess the constitutional power so to interfere, but they will be bound in duty to do it by the express provisions of the Constitution itself. From the instant that your slaveholding States become the theatre of war, civil, servile, or foreign, from that instant the war powers of Congress extend to interference with the institution of slavery in every way by which it can be interfered with, from a claim of indemnity for slaves taken or destroyed, to the cession of the State burdened with slavery to a foreign power."7

Adams' peroration was a brilliant and exceedingly caustic indictment of the action of Alabama and Georgia, sustained by the general government, in breaking up established Indian policy and driving the civilized tribes west of the Mississippi. "There you have undertaken to lead the willing and to drive the reluctant," said he, "by fraud or by force, by treaty or by the sword and the rifle, all the remnants of the Seminoles, of the Creeks, of the Cherokees, of the Choctaws, and of how many other tribes I cannot now stop to enumerate . . . Of the immediate causes of the war we are not yet fully informed; but I fear you will find them . . . in the last agonies of a people, forcibly torn and driven from the soil which they had inherited from their fathers . . . it is in the last conclusive struggles of their despair that this war has originated."8

It was the Indian wars in Florida that opened a new and interesting chapter in the controversy over slavery and the powers of the federal government. Joshua Giddings took the floor in the House of Representatives, February 9, 1841, to denounce the Seminole War which had been in progress for five years. His argument, replete with documentary evidence, showed that Congress had appropriated $250,000 in 1821 to pay Georgia slaveholders for slaves who had fled to the Seminole tribes of Florida between 1770 and 1790; that an unused portion of this sum, amounting to $141,000, was prorated to these slaveholders by special act of Congress as "compensation for the offspring which they would have borne their masters, had they remained in servitude"; that the fugitives had intermarried with the Seminoles, and the latter could not come out of the swamps without surrendering their wives and children to slavery; that bloodhounds were imported from Cuba at a cost of $5,000 to track them down; that by order of the commanding General all Negroes, cattle, and horses belonging to the Indians were the property of the Army unit capturing them; that $20 each was paid to the soldiers from the United States Treasury for more than 500 of these slaves, who were turned over to claimants. Said Giddings: "Our officers and soldiers became slave catchers, companions of the most degraded class of human beings who disgrace that slave cursed region. With the assistance of bloodhounds, they tracked the flying bondsman over hill and dale, through swamp and everglade, until his weary limbs could sustain him no longer." Giddings insisted that the federal government had no constitutional power to use the Army for the recovery of fugitives, or to use public funds to purchase them from their captors. "The slaves of the South are held in bondage by State laws," said he. "Slavery itself is a State institution, with which this government cannot rightfully interfere, either to sustain or to abolish it."[9]

A few months after this discussion on October 27, 1841, the "Creole" sailed from Hampton Roads for New Orleans with a cargo of 135 slaves. The slaves overpowered the crew and took possession of the ship. One passenger was killed. Persuaded that the ship's larder would not sustain them on a voyage to Africa, the slaves put into the port of Nassau. British officials held nineteen of them for trial on a charge of murder. The rest of them were set free. President John Tyler, Secretary of State Daniel Webster, the minister to England, Edward Everett, goaded by Calhoun, and not an antislavery man among them, joined in a grand chorus of demands for their return.[10]

James G. Birney wrote an article on the case for the New York *American,* which Seth M. Gates and Joshua Giddings used as the basis for a series of resolutions introduced into the House of Representatives by Giddings. The principle was precisely that presented in the fugitive slave cases and by Giddings in his speech on the Seminole War. It was that slavery was the creature of state (municipal) law. A state had exclusive jurisdiction over slavery within its own limits, no power over it, within the limits of the states, having been surrendered to the federal government. Some states supported slavery, others had rid themselves of it completely. The latter had a perfect right to be free from involvement in the support of slavery. The federal government possessed no power to involve the people of the nonslaveholding states in such support. Slavery could not exist outside the limits of a slave state because the authority of a state could not extend beyond its own limits. Once beyond the limits of a slave state, the slave stood in the character of a *person* under the Constitution of the United States, entitled to assert and to maintain his natural right to freedom. In the Creole case, the ship on the high seas had a United States character, the laws of Virginia did not apply, and the slaves were entitled to assert their freedom.[11]

Theodore Weld had gone to Washington, December 30, 1841, at the behest of antislavery congressmen to do research for them in the Library of Congress. Day after day he counseled them on history, antislavery principles, and parliamentary procedure. Whatever they needed for debate, they got. Joshua Leavitt was there, also, for the *Emancipator.* Day after day John Quincy Adams and Joshua Giddings drove the Southern congressmen into a frenzy of hatred and vituperation by arguments they could not answer. They talked of expulsion. They tried desperately to censure Adams and failed. Finally, Northern Whigs, angered by the refusal of Giddings to bow to party discipline, joined with the Southerners in forcing through the House a resolution censuring him. He promptly resigned, stood for re-election, and was returned to Congress by an overwhelming majority. The power of the Whig Party was broken, and with *its* solidarity gone the gag resolution survived less than three years.

"EMANCIPATION"

Adams had not been satisfied with the Giddings resolutions, saying in his diary: "Mr. Giddings came to inquire the precise extent to which I hold the subject of slavery in the states subject to jurisdiction of the National Government; and I explained it to him. In the case of a servile war, involving the free states of the Union, the question of emancipation would necessarily be the issue of the conflict. All war must end in peace, and peace must be concluded by treaty. Of such a treaty, partial or universal emancipation would probably form an essential, and the power of the President and the Senate of the United States over it would be coextensive with the war."[12] Giddings was reluctant to confuse the principle of peace-time powers by discussing war powers. Adams was fearful that the resolutions as presented would be cited at a later date as a denial of war powers. Speaking in Congress again, therefore, April 15, 1842, he made one of the most important pronouncements in the whole history of the antislavery movement.

"I will now tell this House," said Adams, "my constituents and the world of mankind, that the resolution against which I would have voted was that in which he [Giddings] declares that what are called the slave states have the exclusive right of consultation on the subject of slavery. For that resolution I never would vote, because I believe that it is not just, and does not contain Constitutional doctrine. I believe that so long as the slave states are able to sustain their institutions without going abroad or calling upon other parts of the Union to aid them or act on the subject, so long I will consent never to interfere . . . but if they come to the free States and say to them, You must help us to keep down our slaves, you must aid us in an insurrection and a civil war; then I say that with that call comes a full and plenary power to this House and to the Senate over the whole subject. It is a war power. I say it is a war power; and when your country is actually in war, whether it be a war of invasion or a war of insurrection, Congress has power to carry on the war, and must carry it on according to the laws of war; and by the laws of war an invaded country has all its laws and municipal institutions swept by the board, and martial law takes the place of them . . . the moment you place a military commander in a district which is the theatre of war, the laws of war apply to that district. I might furnish a thousand proofs to show that the pretensions of gentlemen to the sanctity of their municipal institutions, under a state of actual invasion and of actual war, whether servile, civil, or foreign, is wholly unfounded; and that the laws of war do, in all such cases, take precedence. I lay this down as the law of nations. I say that the military authority takes for the time the place of all municipal institutions, and of slavery among the rest; and that, under that state of things, so far from its being true that the States where slavery exists have the exclusive management of the subject, *not only the President of the United States, but the Commander of the army, has power to order the universal emancipation of the slaves.*"[13]

The first organized campaign by the antislavery men for political action was underway when Adams made his historic remarks. All hope of persuading slaveholders voluntarily to emancipate the slaves was gone. There was no other way to universal emancipation except control of the government, restrictive legislation to force slavery back into the states which sustained it, and constitutional amendment, with exercise of the war powers if the opportunity should arise. Antislavery men were pretty thoroughly agreed on this by 1860. There was nothing new, or strange, or extreme about the so-called radical program of the war years, and there was no unnecessary delay in putting it into effect.

When the antislavery men took control of the presidency and the Congress in March, 1861, they faced an appalling situation: bankrupt treasury and impaired credit with tremendous expenditures required, an almost nonexistent and hopelessly inefficient Army, a Navy scattered over the high seas, a rebellion of no mean proportions, and every branch of government service shot through and through by treason. In spite of the difficulties they got a new diplomatic corps into operation, a blockade established, and large armies into the field within twelve months—all without serious disruption of normal peace-time economy. In fact, by February the armies were ready to move, and, in the West, Fort Donelson, Fort Henry, Island

No. 10, Shiloh, and New Orleans were history in about twelve months after the inauguration.

During those critical months the entire emancipation program outlined by the antislavery men in the 1830's and 1840's was launched. All the precedents of interfering with slavery when operating in slave areas as established in previous wars by British and South American naval commanders and generals and by Generals Andrew Jackson, Edmund Gaines, Winfield Scott, and Thomas Jesup, as outlined in detail in Congress by Adams and Giddings, Sumner, and others, were followed by the commanders of the Union armies.

Exercise of the war powers to abolish slavery was initiated by General Benjamin Butler, May 24, 1861, less than three months after Lincoln's inauguration, when he refused to surrender fugitives coming within his lines. They were, he said, contraband of war. On July 30 he took a second step, as did General John C. Fremont in Missouri. Butler reported to Secretary of War Cameron that he had fugitive slaves to the number of 300 men, 175 women, 225 children under ten years of age, and 175 children between ten and eighteen years of age. His judgment was that, having been abandoned by their owners, they were in the status of free persons. This was sound antislavery doctrine; slaves were held by force, whether they escaped from it by flight or by flight of their masters made no difference, they were again in their natural state of freedom. Butler then made this significant statement: "In a loyal State I would put down a servile insurrection. In a state of rebellion I would confiscate that which was used to oppose my arms, and take all that property, which constituted the wealth of that State, and furnished the means by which the war is prosecuted, besides being the cause of the war; and if, in so doing, it should be objected that human beings were brought to the free enjoyment of life, liberty, and the pursuit of happiness, such objection might not require much consideration."[14]

On the same day that Butler addressed his letter to Secretary Cameron, General Fremont, in command of the Department of the West, proclaimed martial law in the state of Missouri, a loyal slave state with a strong secessionist minority of people. All persons captured with arms within the area of military occupation were liable to summary execution. The property of persons in armed resistance to the United States was declared forfeit, and their slaves, if they had any, were de-

Primary School for Freedmen, Vicksburg—classroom

Freedom to know is the greatest of all man's natural rights.
The contest for human rights in this country began there,
and there it will end.

clared free.[15] This order was modified by President Lincoln, but one week after it was issued, on August 6, 1861, Congress passed the first Confiscation Act, making subject to seizure all property used in aid of the rebellion. This action by the generals and by Congress a few weeks after Lincoln's inauguration, and months before there was an important military engagement sealed the doom of slavery. Newspapers discussed Fremont's proclamation and reprinted the speeches on slavery and the war powers by Adams and Giddings.[16]

Winter came, and the armies were ordered to move by February 22. The government was ready to do the job that had been waiting a long time. On March 6, 1862, with Forts Donelson and Henry captured, but with Shiloh a month away, Lincoln proposed compensated emancipation in the *loyal* slave states. One week later (March 13, 1862) Congress prohibited the return of fugitives to any but loyal slave masters, all others to be free. Even then they were debating complete emancipation. Shiloh was fought and won April 6 and 7. General David Hunter, closer to Lincoln than any other general, in command of the Department of the South, captured Fort Pulaski on April 11 and on the following day issued an order freeing all slaves who had come into the possession of his troops and followed it, May 9, with another freeing all slaves in his department.

Congress on April 16 abolished slavery in the District of Columbia, providing compensation not to exceed $300 per slave. On May 20 Congress passed the Homestead Act, a most important item in the antislavery program, making available 160 acres of land in the public domain to any person over twenty-one years of age who was a citizen or had declared intention to become a citizen and had never borne arms against the government. On the same day Congress provided full co-operation with Great Britain in suppressing the African slave trade, and on June 19 it abolished slavery in all of the territories without compensation to the owners. One week later (June 27) Charles Sumner gave a memorable speech in the Senate, reviewing fully the Adams speeches of May 25, 1836, June 7, 1841, and April 15, 1842.[17] Two weeks later, on July 13, 1862, Lincoln forewarned Secretaries Seward and Welles that he was considering an emancipation proclamation, and he read it to his Cabinet on July 22, 1862. Congress did exactly the same thing at the same time. The Treason Act or Second Confiscation Act was passed July 17, providing, among other things, freedom for the slaves of all persons participating in the rebellion as the armies regained control.[18]

Nothing short of the full power of the government, used to the point of extermination, ever could have restored slavery after July 1862. The Thirteenth Amendment and the legislative acts of the several states were of little significance over the long view. They simply reaffirmed an established fact and prevented any possible confusion from recourse by slaveholders to court action. The Republican Party was controlled by men who were determined to abolish slavery at the earliest practicable moment. There was complete co-ordination by the Congress, the President, and the field commanders of the Army, all operating under the war powers to that end. None of the three could have prevented emancipation. Had there been no laws, no presidential proclamations, no general orders, every slave would have been free as the armies moved because the owners fled and subjection by force was ended. That is how the slaves became free in such numbers as to impede the progress of the armies. Lincoln's proclamation simply restored the balance of the war's objectives—nationalism and freedom—in the eyes of the world.

NOTES

Chapter 1

Perpetual Servitude

1 Slavery in international law is discussed in John Codman Hurd, *The Law of Freedom and Bondage in the United States* (2 vols., Boston, 1858–62), I, pp. 151–65.

2 Dwight L. Dumond, *Antislavery Origins of the Civil War in the United States*, Commonwealth Foundation Lectures, University College, London, 1938–39 (Ann Arbor, 1939), p. 52.

3 The controversy over slavery produced several legal treatises on the subject which must be consulted by the serious student in addition to the many compilations of the laws: Thomas R. R. Cobb, *An Inquiry into the Law of Negro Slavery in the United States of America* (Philadelphia, 1858); William Goodell, *The American Slave Code in Theory and Practice; Its Distinctive Features Shown by Its Statutes, Judicial Decisions, and Illustrative Facts* (New York, 1853); Richard Hildreth, *Despotism in America; an Inquiry into the Nature, Results, and Legal Basis of the Slave-Holding System in the United States* (Boston, 1854); John Codman Hurd, *The Law of Freedom and Bondage in the United States* (2 vols., Boston, 1858–62); George M. Stroud, *A Sketch of the Laws Relating to Slavery in the Several States of the United States of America* (Philadelphia, 1827. Second edition with additions; Philadelphia, 1856); Jacob D. Wheeler, *A Practical Treatise on the Law of Slavery. Being a Compilation of All the Decisions Made on That Subject, in the Several Courts of the United States and State Courts* (New York, 1837).

4 William Agutter, *The Abolition of the Slave Trade Considered from a Religious Point of View. A Sermon Preached before the Corporation of the City of Oxford, at St. Martin's Church, on Sunday, February 3, 1788* (London, 1788), p. 14.

5 Agutter was a very learned man; and he had a wide acquaintance with men who knew Africa and the slave trade. He said this: "In the extensive kingdoms of Africa, the most horrid wars, rapine, and desolation have been encouraged for more than 200 years, to promote this trade in human blood. Some are entrapped by deceit, but the generality are seized by violence. Their fields are desolated; their houses are burnt with fire. The mild and peaceable Negro is driven from his comfortable home; torn from all the tender connections of social life; branded with a hot iron; confined on shipboard amidst chains and nakedness, filth and pestilence. There they are crowded in such numbers, and treated with such cruelty, that death brings a happy release unto thousands . . . For those who escape the dangers of the sea, and endure the hardships of the voyage, new calamities are reserved in store, when they arrive at their places of destination." *Ibid.*, p. 17.

6 See indirect references to the question in cases involving recovery of property values of slaves not in England in *Butts* v. *Penny*, 1667, 83 *English Reports* 518; also in *Gelly* v. *Cleve*, 1694, 91 *English Reports*, 994. See also reference to the subject in Daines Barrington, *Observations upon the Statutes, Chiefly the More Ancient, from Magna Charta to the Twenty-First of James the First* (second edition; Dublin, 1767).

7 *Smith* v. *Brown and Cooper*, 91 English Reports 566.

8 The decision in the *Sommersett Case* is in 98 *English Reports*, 509. See also Francis Hargrave, *An Argument in the Case of James Sommersett, a Negro, Lately Determined by the Court of the King's Bench: Wherein It Is Attempted to Demonstrate the Present Unlawfulness of Domestic Slavery in England. To Which Is Prefixed a State of the Case. By Mr. Hargrave, One of the Counsel for the Negro* (London, printed for the author, 1772).

9 One would be hard pressed to find an apologist for slavery who failed to blame the British for imposing slavery upon America. Some early antislavery writers did likewise. See John Atwood, *The Blessings of Freedom Illustrated and the Horrors of Slavery Delineated* (Boston, 1824).

10 William Blackstone, *Commentaries on the Laws of England in Four Books*. Edited by Thomas M. Cooley (2 vols., Chicago, 1884), I, p. 107; Joseph Story, *Commentaries on the Conflict of Laws* (third edition; Boston, 1846), p. 164.

11 Edward Channing, *A History of the United States* (6 vols., New York, 1905–32), II, pp. 413–16; Joseph Story, *Commentaries on the Conflict of Laws* (third edition; Boston, 1846), pp. 175–76.

12 See James Kent, *Commentaries on American Law* (second edition; 4 vols., New York, 1832), I, p. 471; *Commonwealth v. Aves* (1836), Octavius Pickering, *Reports of Cases Argued and Determined in the Supreme Judicial Court of Massachusetts* (24 vols., Boston, 1826–42), XVIII, pp. 193–225; *Jackson v. Bullock* (1837), Thomas M. Day, *Reports of Cases Argued and Determined in the Supreme Court of Errors of Connecticut* (21 vols., New York, 1924–25), XII, pp. 38–69.

13 Volumes could be written on this one aspect of the controversy, and much will be said about it later. David Barrow, *Involuntary, Unmerited, Perpetual, Absolute, Hereditary Slavery, Examined; on the Principles of Nature, Reason, Justice, Policy, and Scripture* (Lexington, 1808), said: "The God of Nature, it seems, made no *slaves;* but the laws of men have created them—and have rightly named them *slaves!*"

14 *Ibid.*, p. vi.

15 D. B. Warden, in his introduction to the distinguished work of Henri Grégoire, *An Enquiry Concerning the Intellectual and Moral Faculties, and Literature of Negroes; Followed with an Account of the Life and Works of Fifteen Negroes and Mulattoes, Distinguished in Science, Literature, and the Arts.* Translated by D. B. Warden, secretary to the American Legation at Paris (Brooklyn, 1810), p. 10, says: "I recollect to have heard the celebrated professor Millar, of the University of Glasgow, observe, in his course of civil law, 'that the mind revolts at the idea of a *serious* discussion on the subject of slavery. Every individual, whatever be his country or complexion, is entitled to freedom. The happiness of the poor man is of as much importance as that of the rich. No man has a right to reduce another to the condition of the brute. No individual can sell his liberty. The bargain is unequal, and ought to be broken. Negro slavery is contrary to the sentiments of humanity and the principles of justice.'"

16 William Waller Hening (ed.), *The Statutes at Large; Being A Collection of All the Laws of Virginia from the First Session of the Legislature in the Year 1619* (13 vols., Richmond, 1810–23), II, p. 170.

17 John Codman Hurd, *The Law of Freedom and Bondage in the United States*, I, p. 303.

18 Charles Lincoln, William Johnson, and Ansel Northrup (eds.), *The Colonial Laws of New York from the Year 1664 to the Revolution* (5 vols., Albany, 1894), I, p. 598. Massachusetts courts followed the principle without statute law. See an order of the General Court in 1716 in Ellis Ames and Abner C. Goodell (eds.), *The Acts and Resolves Public and Private of the Province of the Massachusetts Bay* (21 vols., Boston, 1869–1922), IX, p. 492.

19 William L. Saunders (ed.), *The Colonial Records of North Carolina* (10 vols., Raleigh, 1886–90), I, p. 294; John Codman Hurd, *The Law of Freedom and Bondage in the United States*, I, p. 294.

20 William H. Browne (ed.), *Archives of Maryland* (32 vols., Baltimore, 1883–1912), I, p. 553; John Codman Hurd, *The Law of Freedom and Bondage in the United States*, I, p. 249.

21 John Codman Hurd, *The Law of Freedom and Bondage in the United States*, I, p. 294.

22 Most slave codes were written before 1715 when figures compiled for the Board of Trade showed the following white and Negro populations:

Colony	White	Negro
New Hampshire	9,500	150
Massachusetts	94,000	2,000
Rhode Island	8,500	500
Connecticut	46,000	1,500
New York	27,000	4,000
New Jersey	21,000	1,500
Pennsylvania and Delaware	43,300	2,500
Maryland	40,700	9,500
Virginia	72,000	23,000
North Carolina	7,500	3,700
South Carolina	6,250	10,500

23 The first South Carolina "Act for the better ordering of slaves" was passed in 1690 as a temporary measure. It was re-enacted in part from time to time until the basic law of 1712. See Thomas Cooper and David J. McCord (eds.), *The Statutes at Large of South Carolina* (10 vols., Columbia, 1836–41), II, p. 49, 121, 182, 401; VII, pp. 352–65, 397–421. See also John Codman Hurd, *The Law of Freedom and Bondage in the United States*, I, pp. 297–309.

24 John Codman Hurd, *The Law of Freedom and Bondage in the United States*, I, pp. 228–54.

25 "Proceedings of the General Court of Assizes Held in the City of New York, October 6, 1680 to October 6, 1682," *New York Historical Society Collections, 1912* (New York, 1868–), XLV, pp. 37–38.

26 Charles Lincoln, William Johnson, and Ansel Northrup (eds.), *The Colonial Laws of New York from the Year 1664 to the Revolution*, I, p. 154.

27 *Ibid.*, pp. 598, 765–66.

28 Aaron Leaming and Jacob Spicer (eds.), *The Grants, Concessions, and Original Constitutions of the Province of New Jersey* (Philadelphia, 1752, and Sommerville, N. J., 1881), pp. 356–57.

29 *Acts of the General Assembly of the Province of New Jersey from the Surrender of the Government to Queen Anne on the 17th Day of April, 1702, to the 14th Day of January, 1776* (Burlington, 1776), p. 308.

30 John Codman Hurd, *The Law of Freedom and Bondage in the United States*, I, p. 284.

31 *Charter to William Penn and Laws of the Province of Pennsylvania Passed Between the Years 1682 and 1700* (Harrisburg, 1879), pp. 151–53, 211–13.

32 James T. Mitchell and Henry Flanders (eds.), *The Statutes at Large of Pennsylvania from 1682 to 1801* (18 vols., Harrisburg, 1896–1915), II, pp. 77–78.

33 William H. Whitmore (ed.), *Colonial Laws of Massachusetts Reprinted from the Edition of 1672, with Supplements Through 1686* (Boston, 1889), p. 281; J. H. Trumbull and C. J. Hoadley (eds.), *The Public Records of the Colony of Connecticut* [1636–1776] (15 vols., Hartford, 1850–90), IV, p. 40.

34 Ellis Ames and Abner C. Goodell (eds.), *The Acts and*

Resolves Public and Private of the Province of Massachusetts Bay, I, p. 154; J. H. Trumbull and C. J. Hoadley (eds.), *The Public Records of the Colony of Connecticut*, V, p. 52.

35 Sidney R. Rider (ed.), *The Charter and the Acts and Laws of His Majesties Colony of Rhode Island and Providence Plantations in America, 1719* (Providence, 1895), pp. 101–2.

36 John Noble and John R. Cronin (eds.), *Records of the Court of Assistants of the Colony of the Massachusetts Bay* (3 vols., Boston, 1901–28), I, pp. 25, 74, 197, 304–5, 321.

37 *Acts and Laws of His Majesty's Colony of Rhode Island and Providence Plantations in New England, in America* (Newport, 1745), pp. 263–64.

38 Ellis Ames and Abner C. Goodell (eds.), *Acts and Resolves Public and Private of the Province of the Massachusetts Bay*, I, p. 578.

39 Nathan Dane, *A General Abridgement and Digest of American Law with Occasional Notes and Comments* (9 vols., Boston, 1823–29), II, p. 313; Tapping Reeve, *The Law of Baron and Femme; of Parent and Child; of Guardian and Ward; of Master and Servant; and of the Powers of Court of Chancery; with an Essay on the Terms Heir, Heirs of the Body* (New Haven, 1816), pp. 340–41.

40 Ellis Ames and Abner C. Goodell (eds.), *Acts and Resolves, Public and Private, of the Province of Massachusetts Bay*, I, p. 519.

41 John R. Bartlett (ed.), *Records of the Colony of Rhode Island and Providence Plantations* (10 vols., Providence, 1856–65), IV, pp. 415–16.

42 Charles Lincoln, William Johnson, and Ansel Northrup (eds.), *The Colonial Laws of New York from the Year 1664 to the Revolution*, I, pp. 922–23.

43 James T. Mitchell and Henry Flanders (eds.), *The Statutes at Large of Pennsylvania from 1682 to 1801*, IV, p. 61.

Chapter 2
Foundations of Freedom

1 A descendant of Sewall's, Samuel Edmund Sewall, helped to found the New England Anti-Slavery Society and gave both advice and financial aid to William Lloyd Garrison in regard to the *Liberator*. He advocated a program of gradual emancipation and second-class citizenship for the freed slaves. See *Remarks on Slavery in the United States. From the Christian Examiner*, II, No. 3 (Boston, 1827).

2 Thomas E. Drake, *Quakers and Slavery in America* (New Haven, 1950), p. 5. This monograph, by a very distinguished scholar, is one of the best in the literature of American history.

3 George Kieth, *An Exhortation & Caution to Friends Concerning Buying or Keeping Negroes, Given the 13th Day of the 8th Month, 1693* [Philadelphia, 1693].

4 Ralph Sandiford, *A Brief Examination of the Practice of the Times, by the Foregoing and the Present Dispensation* [Philadelphia], 1729. Published in a second edition: *The Mystery of Iniquity; in a Brief Examination of the Practice of the Times, by the Foregoing and the Present Dispensation* (Philadelphia, 1730).

5 Benjamin Lay, *All Slave-Keepers That Keep the Innocent in Bondage, Apostates . . . The Leaders of the People Cause Them to Err. Written for a General Service, by Him That Truly and Sincerely Desires the Present and Eternal Welfare and Happiness of All Mankind . . . As His Own Soul* (Philadelphia, 1737).

6 Thomas E. Drake, *Quakers and Slavery in America*, p. 51.

7 John Woolman, *Some Considerations on the Keeping of Negroes; Recommended to the Professors of Christianity of Every Denomination* (Philadelphia, 1754); and *Considerations on Keeping Negroes; Recommended to the Professors of Christianity of Every Denomination, Part Second* (Philadelphia, 1762). These were published in a new edition in Philadelphia in 1774; and in 1794 was published *A Journal of the Life, Gospel Labours, and Christian Experiences of That Faithful Minister of Jesus Christ, John Woolman, Late of Mount Holly, in the Province of New Jersey, North America* (Dublin, 1794). All of his works passed through many editions.

8 See the bibliography for Benezet's many publications. In his *Caution and Warning to Great Britain and Her Colonies*, he drew upon James Foster's *Discourses on Natural Religion and Social Virtue*, Francis Hutcheson's *System of Moral Philosophy*, and George Wallis' *System of the Laws of Scotland*. His *Brief Considerations on Slavery, and the Expediency of Its Abolition, with Some Hints on the Means Whereby It May Be Gradually Effected* (Burlington, 1773) suggested gradual emancipation, with masters freeing their slaves between the ages of twenty-one and fifty, and paying the public a stipulated sum for every year they held them over age twenty-one.

9 John Wesley, *Thoughts upon Slavery* (London, 1774). Reprinted in New York in 1834.

10 James Otis, *The Rights of the British Colonies Asserted and Proved* (Boston, 1764), p. 43.

11 It should be said at this point that Jefferson condemned slavery, but it cannot be shown that he, or Washington, or Madison, or Monroe ever tried very hard to do anything about it. Jefferson elaborated on his belief that Negroes could never equal the whites under the same set of circumstances. He refused to accept evidence—and it was abundant—to the contrary, and was condemned for it by the antislavery men of his own period.

12 Quoted in Lydia Maria Child, *The Evils of Slavery, and the Cure of Slavery; the First Proved by the Opinions of Southerners Themselves, the Last Shown by Historical Evidence* (Newburyport, 1836), p. 3.

13 Hugh H. Brackenridge, *Modern Chivalry* (2 vols., Philadelphia, 1792), pp. 146–47.

14 Benezet and Woolman encountered some published opposition, none of it substantial. An anonymous pamphlet, attempting to prove Negroes were stupid people, incapable of reason or improvement, was published under the title *Personal Slavery Established by the Suffrages of Custom and Right Reason. Being a Full Answer to the Gloomy and Visionary Referies of All the Fanatical and Visionary Reveries, of All the Fanatical and Enthusiastical Writers on That Subject* (Philadelphia, 1773).

15 Benjamin Rush, *An Address to the Inhabitants of the British Settlements in America, upon Slave Keeping* (Philadelphia, 1773), pp. 2–3.

16 *Ibid.*, pp. 5–7.

17 *Ibid.*, p. 9.

18 *Ibid.*, pp. 13–14.

19 *Ibid.*, p. 16.

20 *Ibid.*, p. 30.

21 Samuel Hopkins, *A Dialogue Concerning the Slavery of the Africans; Shewing It to Be the Duty and Interest of the American Colonies to Emancipate All Their African Slaves; with an Address to the Owners of Such Slaves. Dedicated to the Honorable the Continental Congress* (Norwich, 1776), p. 6.

22 *Ibid.*, p. 17. One of the earliest expositions of the effects of the slave trade upon Africa itself was by Bishop William Warburton in what is said to have been the first direct assault upon slavery in England. *In A Sermon Preached Before the Incorporated Society for the Propagation of the Gospel in Foreign Parts; at Their Anniversary Meeting in the Parish Church of St. Mary-le-Bow, on Friday, February 21, 1766* (London, 1766), he said: "But who are they that have set on foot this general Hunting. Are they not these very civilized violators of humanity, themselves? Who tempt the weak appetites, and provoke the wild passions of the fiercer Savages to prey upon the rest," p. 28. Grégoire said, in the same manner: "The Europeans, to procure slaves there, create and perpetuate a state of constant warfare. Those regions are poisoned by their strong liquors, by every species of debauch, of rapacity, cruelty and seduction." *An Enquiry Concerning the Intellectual and Moral Faculties, and Literature of Negroes . . . Translated by D. B. Warden, Secretary to the American Legation in Paris* (Brooklyn, 1810), p. 50.

23 Samuel Hopkins, *A Dialogue Concerning the Slavery of the Africans . . . ,* p. 34.

24 *Ibid.*, p. 44.

25 Isaiah 2: 16–18.

26 Jeremiah 7: 5–7.

27 Ezekiel 22: 29–31.

28 David Rice, *Slavery Inconsistent with Justice and Good Policy; Proved by a Speech Delivered in the Convention Held at Danville, Kentucky* (Philadelphia, 1792), p. 14.

29 [David Cooper], *A Serious Address to the Rulers of America on the Inconsistency of Their Conduct Respecting Slavery: Forming a Contrast Between the Encroachments of England on American Liberty and American Injustice in Tolerating Slavery* (Trenton, 1783).

30 Worthington C. Ford (ed.), *Journals of the Continental Congress, 1774–1789* (34 vols., Washington, 1904–37), II, p. 140.

31 *Ibid.*

32 [David Cooper], *A Serious Address to the Rulers of America on the Inconsistency of Their Conduct Respecting Slavery: . . . ,* p. 24. See also *A Letter from ——, in London to His Friends in America on the Subject of the Slave-Trade; Together with Some Extracts, from Approved Authors of Matter of Fact Confirming the Principles Contained in Said Letter* (New York, 1784). This is a severe criticism of Americans for continuing to hold slaves after winning a war for their own political freedom.

33 William Agutter, *The Abolition of the Slave Trade Considered in a Religious Point of View. A Sermon Preached Before the Corporation of the City of Oxford, at St. Martin's Church, on Sunday, February 3, 1788* (London, 1788), pp. 25–26.

Chapter 3
Impact of the Revolution

1 It is impossible to give accurate statistics for any period previous to the federal census of 1790. The following are from Evarts B. Greene and Virginia D. Harrington, *American Population Before the Federal Census of 1790* (New York, 1932), *passim.*

Year	Colony	Total	White	Negro
1775	New Hampshire	81,050	80,394	656
1776	Massachusetts	338,667	333,418	5,249
1774	Connecticut	197,806	191,342	6,464
1774	Rhode Island	59,678	54,435	3,761
1776	New York	191,741	169,148	21,993
1784	New Jersey	150,435	139,934	10,501
1775	Pennsylvania	302,000	300,000	2,000
1775	Delaware	30,000	------	------
1782	Maryland	254,050	170,688	83,362
1782	Virginia	567,614	296,852	270,762
1786	North Carolina	224,000	164,000	60,000
1775	South Carolina	174,000	70,000	104,000
1774	Georgia	32,000	17,000	15,000

2 A. A. Liscomb and A. L. Berg (eds.), *The Writings of Thomas Jefferson* (20 vols., Washington, 1903–4), I, p. 34.

3 *Ibid.*, I, p. 201.

4 *Ibid.*, II, pp. 226.

5 *Ibid.*, II, p. 227.

6 *Dictionary of American Biography* (20 vols., New York, 1928–37), XII, p. 364.

7 Jonathan Elliot (ed.), *The Debates in the Several State Conventions, on the Adoption of the Federal Constitution, as Recommended by the General Convention at Philadelphia in 1787. Together with the Journal of the Federal Convention . . . and Other Illustrations of the Constitution* (second edition; 5 vols., Philadelphia, 1836), V, p. 458. Hereinafter cited as *Elliot's Debates.*

8 *Ibid.*, III, p. 452.

9 *Ibid.*, V, pp. 392–93.

10 *Ibid.*, V, p. 457.

11 Judge St. George Tucker to Dr. Jeremy Belknap, January 24, 1795, in Massachusetts Historical Society, *Collections* (Fifth Series), III, p. 379.

12 For examples of such laws, see Virginia (1723 and 1727) William W. Hening (ed.), *The Statutes at Large, Being a Collection of All the Laws of Virginia from the First Session of the Legislature in the Year 1619* (13 vols., Richmond, 1819–23), IV, pp. 118, 182; Pennsylvania (1710) Samuel Hazard (ed.), *Colonial Records of Pennsylvania* (16 vols., Harrisburg, 1838–53), II, 530. Other Colonial prohibitory laws disallowed or vetoed included South Carolina (1760), Delaware (1775), New Jersey (1763), and Massachusetts (1771).

13 Francis Newton Thorpe (ed.), *The Federal and State Constitutions, Colonial Charters, and Other Organic Laws* (7 vols., Washington, 1909), VI, pp. 3739–40; John H. Watson, "In re Vermont Constitution of 1777, as Regards Its Adoption, and Its Declaration Forbidding Slavery, and the Subsequent Existence of Slavery within the Territory of the Sovereign State," in Vermont Historical Society, *Proceedings*, 1919–20, pp. 227–56.

14 *Selectmen v. Jacob*, Royall Tyler, *Reports of Cases Argued and Determined in the Supreme Court of Judicature of the State of Vermont* (2 vols., New York, 1809–10), II, p. 200.

15 William Slade (ed.), *Vermont State Papers, Being a Collection of Records and Documents Together with the Laws from the Year 1779 to 1786* (Middlebury, 1823), pp. 505–6.

16 Francis Newton Thorpe (ed.), *The Federal and State Constitutions, Colonial Charters, and Other Organic Laws*, IV, pp. 2453–54.

17 *Ibid.* The degree to which the philosophy of men coincided with these documents or was derived from them is shown by the powerful treatise of James Duncan of Indiana, *A Treatise on Slavery. In Which Is Shown Forth the Evil of Slaveholding Both from the Light of Nature and Divine Revelation* (Vevay, Ind., 1824), pp. 23–24.

18 Nathaniel Bouton (ed.), *Documents and Records Relating to Towns in New Hampshire with an Appendix Embracing the Constitutional Conventions of 1778–1779; and of 1781–1783; and the State Constitution of 1784* (Concord, 1875), p. 897.

19 Charles Francis Adams (ed.), *The Works of John Adams, Second President of the United States; with a Life of the Author by His Grandson Charles Francis Adams* (10 vols., Boston, 1850–56), II, p. 200; Nathan Dane, *A General Abridgement and Digest of American Law, with Occasional Notes and Comments* (2 vols., Boston, 1823), II, pp. 426–27; George Henry Moore, *Notes on the History of Slavery in Massachusetts* (New York, 1866), pp. 111–23.

20 See *Winchendon v. Hatfield* (1808), Donald A. Tyng, *Reports of Cases Argued and Determined in the Supreme Judicial Court of Massachusetts* (16 vols., Boston, 1811–37), IV, p. 128.

21 *Journal of the Convention for Framing a Constitution of Government for the State of Massachusetts Bay, September 1, 1779, to June 16, 1780* (Boston, 1832), Appendix, p. 257.

22 *Commonwealth v. Jennison*, in Massachusetts Historical Society, *Proceedings*, XIII, p. 296.

23 *Commonwealth v. Aves* (1836), Octavius Pickering, *Reports of Cases Argued and Determined in the Supreme Judicial Court of Massachusetts* (24 vols., Boston, 1826–42), XVIII, p. 193.

24 *Parsons v. Trask* (1856), Horace Gray, Jr., *Reports of Cases Argued and Determined in the Supreme Judicial Court of Massachusetts* (16 vols., Boston, 1863–71), VII, p. 478.

25 *Acts and Laws of Massachusetts Passed by the General Court, 1788*, pp. 672–73.

26 John R. Bartlett (ed.), *Records of the Colony of Rhode Island and Providence Plantations* (10 vols., Providence, 1856–65), VII, p. 251.

27 *Ibid.*, p. 253.

28 *Acts and Laws Made and Passed by the General Court or Assembly of His Majesty's English Colony of Connecticut in New England* (New London, 1774), pp. 403–4.

29 John R. Bartlett (ed.), *Records of the Colony of Rhode Island and Providence Plantations*, VIII, p. 618.

30 *Ibid.*, X, pp. 7–8. This act provided for maintenance and education of the children and maintenance of freed slaves under forty years of age by the respective towns, but the provision was repealed the following year.

31 Charles J. Hoadley (ed.), *The Public Records of the State of Connecticut* (3 vols., Hartford, 1894–1922), I, p. 415. *Acts and Laws of the State of Connecticut in America, May, 1792* (Hartford, 1796), p. 421.

32 Zephaniah Swift, *A System of the Laws of the State of Connecticut* (2 vols., Windham, 1795), II, pp. 348–49.

33 *Ibid.*, p. 348.

34 John W. Purdon (ed.), *A Digest of the Laws of Pennsylvania from the Year One Thousand Seven Hundred, to the Seventh Day of April, One Thousand Eight Hundred and Thirty* (Philadelphia, 1831), pp. 4–5.

35 James T. Mitchell and Henry Flanders (eds.), *The Statutes at Large of Pennsylvania from 1682 to 1801* (18 vols., Harrisburg, 1896–1915), X, pp. 70–73.

36 *Ibid.*, XIII, p. 54.

37 *Ibid.*, XIII, pp. 55–56.

38 Charles Lincoln, William Johnson, and Ansel Northrup (eds.), *The Colonial Laws of New York from the Year 1664 to the Revolution* (5 vols., Albany, 1894), V, 533–34.

39 *Laws of the State of New York Passed at the Sessions of the Legislature Held in the Years 1777 to 1801* (5 vols., Albany, 1886–87), III, pp. 121, 676.

40 *Ibid.*, p. 677.

41 *Acts of the General Assembly of the State of New Jersey, First Session to the Eighty-fourth, 1778–1860*, Tenth Assembly, First Session, pp. 239–40.

42 *Ibid.*, Thirteenth Assembly, First Session, pp. 486–88.

43 See General Gage's proclamation, December 30, 1764, *American State Papers, Public Lands*, II, p. 209.

44 William W. Hening (ed.), *The Statutes at Large; Being a Collection of All the Laws of Virginia from the First Session of the Legislature in the Year 1619*, IX, p. 552.

45 Francis Newton Thorpe (ed.), *The Federal and State Constitutions, Colonial Charters, and Other Organic Laws*, II, p. 956.

Chapter 4
Slavery and the Constitution

1 *Elliot's Debates*, IV, p. 176.
2 *Ibid*, V, p. 161.
3 *Ibid.*, V, p. 478.
4 *Ibid.*, V, p. 181.
5 *Ibid.*, V, p. 393.
6 *Ibid.*
7 *Ibid.*, IV, p. 285.
8 *Ibid.*, V, pp. 459–60.
9 *Ibid.*, V, p. 457.
10 *Ibid.*, V, p. 460.

11 *Ibid.*, V, p. 393.
12 *Ibid.*, V, p. 461.
13 *Ibid.*, V, p. 459.
14 *Ibid.*, V, p. 160.
15 *Ibid.*, V, p. 459.
16 *Ibid.*, V, p. 458.
17 *Ibid.*, V, p. 393.
18 *Ibid.*, IV, pp. 285–86.
19 *Ibid.*, V, p. 489.
20 *Ibid.*, V, p. 492.
21 *Ibid.*, II, p. 452.
22 *Ibid.*, II, p. 115.
23 *Ibid.*, II, p. 41.
24 See also Max Farrand, *The Records of the Federal Convention of 1787* (4 vols., New Haven, 1937), III, p. 161.
25 *Ibid.*, III, p. 453.
26 *Ibid.*, IV, p. 286.

Chapter 5
Gradual Emancipation

1 *Constitution of the Pennsylvania Society for Promoting the Abolition of Slavery, and Relief of Free Negroes Unlawfully Held in Bondage; Enlarged at Philadelphia, April 23d, 1787* [Philadelphia, 1788].
2 *Constitution of a Society [Providence] for Abolishing the Slave Trade* (Providence, 1789).
3 *Constitution of the Connecticut Society for the Promotion of Freedom, and for the Relief of Persons Holden in Bondage* (New Haven, 1795).
4 Zephaniah Swift, *An Oration on Domestic Slavery, Delivered at the North Meeting House in Hartford, on the 12th Day of May A.D. 1791* (Hartford, 1791). Swift was later chief justice of the State.
5 Jonathan Edwards, *The Injustice and Impolicy of the Slave Trade, and of the Slavery of the Africans: Illustrated in a Sermon Preached Before the Connecticut Society for the Promotion of Freedom, and for the Relief of Persons Unlawfully Holden in Bondage, at Their Annual Meeting in New Haven, September 15, 1791* (New Haven, 1791).
6 James Dana, *The African Slave Trade. A Discourse Delivered in the City of New Haven, September 9, 1790, Before the Connecticut Society for the Promotion of Freedom* (New Haven, 1791).
7 Noah Webster, *Effects of Slavery on Morals and Industry* (Hartford, 1793).
8 Theodore Dwight, *An Oration, Spoken Before the Connecticut Society for the Promotion of Freedom and the Relief of Persons Unlawfully Holden in Bondage* (Hartford, 1794).
9 Noah Webster, *Effects of Slavery on Morals and Industry* (Hartford, 1793), p. 33.
10 *Constitution of the New York Society for Promoting the Manumission of Slaves and Protecting Such of Them as Have Been, or May Be Liberated* (New York, 1796).
11 *Constitution of the Delaware Society for Promoting the Abolition of Slavery and for the Relief and Protection of Free Blacks and People of Colour Unlawfully Held in Bondage or Otherwise Oppressed* (Wilmington, 1801).
12 *Constitution of the Maryland Society for Promoting the Abolition of Slavery, and the Relief of Free Negroes and Others Unlawfully Held in Bondage* (Baltimore, 1789).
13 *Constitution of the New Jersey Society for Promoting the Abolition of Slavery to Which Is Annexed Extracts from a Law of New Jersey Passed the 2d March, 1786, and Supplement to the Same, Passed the 26th November, 1788* (Burlington, 1793).
14 *Minutes of the Proceedings of a Convention of Delegates from the Abolition Societies Established in Different Parts of the United States Assembled at Philadelphia, on the First Day of January, One Thousand Seven Hundred and Ninety-Four, and Continued by Adjournment, until the Seventh Day of the Same Month, Inclusive* (Philadelphia, 1794).
15 No meetings were held in 1799 and 1802. The 1815 meeting was adjourned to 1816, and there were adjourned meetings in 1818, 1826, and 1828. See Bibliography, "American Convention."
16 James T. Mitchell and Henry Flanders (eds.), *The Statutes at Large of Pennsylvania from 1682 to 1801* (18 vols., Harrisburg, 1896–1915), X, pp. 67–71.
17 *Negro Flora v. Joseph Graisberry.* This very important case in the long view of slavery, like the contrary interpretation of the constitution of Massachusetts (*Commonwealth v. Jennison*), is not in the printed reports. See George M. Stroud, *A Sketch of the Laws Relating to Slavery in the Several States of the United States of America* (second edition, Philadelphia, 1856), p. 227.
18 *Respublica v. Negro Betsey* (1789), Alexander Dallas, *Reports of Cases Ruled and Adjudged in the Several Courts of the United States, and of Pennsylvania, Held at the Seat of the Federal Government* (4 vols., Philadelphia, 1790–1807), I, p. 469.
19 *Respublica v. Gaoler* (1794). Jasper Yeates, *Reports of Cases Adjudged in the Supreme Court of Pennsylvania* (4 vols., Philadelphia, 1817–19), I, p. 368.
20 *Wilson v. Belinda* (1817). Thomas Sergeant and William Rawle, *Reports of Cases Adjudged in the Supreme Court of Pennsylvania* (second edition, 17 vols., Philadelphia, 1841–51), III, p. 396.
21 *Commonwealth, ex rel. Jesse v. Craig* (1814). *Ibid.*, I, p. 23.
22 *Elson v. Wm. M'Colloch* (1804). Jasper Yeates, *Reports of Cases Adjudged in the Supreme Court of Pennsylvania* (4 vols., Philadelphia, 1817–19), IV, p. 115.
23 *Commonwealth v. Barker* (1824), Thomas Sergeant and William Rawle, *Reports of Cases Adjudged in the Supreme Court of Pennsylvania* (second edition, 17 vols., Philadelphia, 1841–51), XI, p. 360.
24 *Overseers of Ferguson v. Overseers of Buffaloe* (1820), *Ibid.*, VI, p. 102; *Ferris v. Henderson* et al (1849), J. Pringle Jones and R. C. McMurtrie, *Pennsylvania State Reports, Containing Cases Adjudged in the Supreme Court* (Philadelphia, 1883–), XII, p. 49.
25 *Commonwealth v. Smyth* (1809). Peter Browne, *Reports of Cases Adjudged in the Court of Common Pleas of the First Judicial District of Pennsylvania* (2 vols., St. Louis, 1871), I, p. 113.
26 *Commonwealth ex rel. Hall v. Cook* (1832). Frederick Watts, *Reports of Cases Argued and Determined in the Supreme Court of Pennsylvania* (10 vols., Philadelphia, 1834–41), I, p. 155.

27 *Butler v. Hopper* (1804). *The Federal Cases, Comprising Cases Argued and Determined in the Circuit and District Courts of the United States from the Earliest Times to the Beginning of the Federal Reporter* (30 vols., St. Paul, 1894–97), IV, p. 904.

28 *Commonwealth v. Holloway* (1816). Thomas Sergeant and William Rawle, *Reports of Cases Adjudged in the Supreme Court of Pennsylvania* (second edition, 17 vols., Philadelphia, 1841–51), II, p. 304.

29 *Miller v. Dwilling* (1826), *ibid.*, XIV, p. 442.

30 *Jackson v. Bullock* (1837). *Reports Containing Cases Argued and Determined in the Supreme Court of Errors of the State of Connecticut* (28 vols. Hartford, 1814–60), XII, p. 42.

31 *Public Acts of the State of Connecticut Passed by the General Assembly, May, 1848* (New Haven, 1848), p. 70.

32 *Public Laws of the State of Rhode Island and Providence Plantations* (Providence, 1844), p. 342.

33 *Laws of the State of New York Passed at the Sessions of the Legislature Held in the Years 1777 [to 1801] Inclusive, Being the First [to Twenty-Fourth] Sessions* (5 vols., Albany, 1886–87), IV, pp. 388–89.

34 *Laws of the State of New York Passed at the Twenty-Seventh Session of the Legislature: Begun and Held at the City of Albany the Thirty-First Day of January, 1804* (Albany, 1809), pp. 145–46.

35 *Laws of the State of New York Passed at the Second Meeting of the Twenty-Fourth Session of the Legislature, Begun and Held at the City of Albany the Twenty-Seventh Day of January 1801* (Albany, 1801), pp. 548–49.

36 *Fish v. Fisher* (1800). William Johnson, *Reports of Cases Argued and Determined in the Supreme Court of Judicature, and in the Court for the Trial of Impeachments and the Correction of Errors in the State of New York* (23 vols., New York, 1807–23), II, p. 89.

37 *In the Case of Tom, A Negro Man* (1810), *ibid.*, V, p. 365.

38 *Wells v. Lane* (1812), *ibid.*, IX, p. 144.

39 *Public Laws of the State of New York Passed at the Thirty-second Session of the Legislature* (Albany, 1809), p. 450; William P. Van Ness and John Woodworth (eds.), *Laws of the State of New York, Revised and Passed at the Thirty-sixth Session of the Legislature* (5 vols., Albany, 1813), II, p. 207.

40 *Griffin v. Potter* (1835). John L. Wendell, *Reports of Cases Argued and Determined in the Supreme Court of Judicature and in the Court for the Trial of Impeachments and the Correction of Errors of the State of New York* (26 vols. New York, 1872–83), XIV, p. 209.

41 See Cooley, *Slavery in New Jersey*, Johns Hopkins University, *Studies in Historical and Political Science*, XIV, p. 22.

42 See *State v. Frees* (1794). Richard S. Coxe, *Reports of Cases Argued and Determined in the Supreme Court of New Jersey from April Term, 1790 to November Term, 1795* (second edition, Newark, 1901), p. 299.

43 *State v. Administrators of Prall* (1790), *ibid.*, p. 4.

44 *State v. Pitney* (1793), *ibid.*, p. 192.

45 William Paterson (ed.), *Laws of the State of New Jersey Revised and Published under the Authority of the Legislature* (Newark, 1800), p. 313.

46 *Acts of the Twenty-eighth General Assembly of the State of New Jersey, at a Session Begun at Trenton, on Tuesday, the Twenty-fifth Day of October, One Thousand Eight Hundred and Three, and Continued by Adjournments. Being the Second Sitting* (Trenton, 1804), pp. 251–53.

47 *Acts of the General Assembly of the State of New Jersey*, Forty-third Assembly (Trenton, 1818), pp. 3–6.

48 *State v. Post* (1845). Robert D. Spencer, *Reports of Cases Determined in the Supreme Court of Judicature of the State of New Jersey* (second edition, Newark, 1901), p. 368.

49 *Minutes of the Proceedings of the Fourth Convention of Delegates from the Abolition Societies Established in Different Parts of the United States Assembled at Philadelphia, on the Third Day of May, One Thousand Seven Hundred and Ninety-seven, and Continued, by Adjournments, until the Ninth Day of the Same Month, Inclusive* (Philadelphia, 1797), pp. 38–39.

50 *Minutes of the Proceedings of a Convention of Delegates from the Abolition Societies Established in Different Parts of the United States Assembled at Philadelphia on the First Day of January, One Thousand Seven Hundred and Ninety-four . . .* (Philadelphia, 1794).

51 *Ibid.*, pp. 12–15.

52 *Minutes of the Proceedings of the Fourth Convention of Delegates from the Abolition Societies Established in Different Parts of the United States Assembled at Philadelphia on the Third Day of May, One Thousand Seven Hundred and Ninety-seven . . .* (Philadelphia, 1797).

53 *Ibid.*, pp. 31–34.

54 *Ibid.*, pp. 29–31.

Chapter 6
National Policy

1 Abolition Societies of the United States, "Address to the People of the United States," in *Minutes of the Proceedings of a Convention of Delegates from the Abolition Societies Established in Different Parts of the United States, Assembled at Philadelphia, on the First Day of January, One Thousand Seven Hundred and Ninety-four, and Continued by Adjournment, until the Seventh Day of the Same Month, Inclusive* (Philadelphia, 1794), pp. 22–25.

2 Signed: Benjamin Franklin, President, Philadelphia, February 3, 1790. *Annals of Congress*, 1 Cong., 2 Sess. (1789–91), p. 1240.

3 *Ibid.*, p. 1246.

4 *Annals of Congress*, 1 Cong., 2 Sess., pp. 1224–33; 1240–48.

5 *Ibid.*, p. 1229.

6 *Ibid.*, p. 1230.

7 *Ibid.*, p. 1226.

8 *Ibid.*, p. 1228.

9 *Ibid.*, p. 1241.

10 *Ibid.*, p. 1242.

11 *Ibid.*, p. 1246.

12 *Ibid.*

13 *Ibid.*, p. 1414.

14 *Ibid.*

15 *Ibid.,* p. 1474.

16 *Ibid.*

17 *Ibid.,* p. 1458.

18 *Ibid.,* pp. 1457–60.

19 Pennsylvania Society for Promoting the Abolition of Slavery, and the Relief of Free Negroes Unlawfully Held in Bondage, and for Improving the Condition of the African Race, *Memorials Presented to the Congress of the United States of America, by the Different Societies Instituted for Promoting the Abolition of Slavery, Etc., in the States of Rhode Island, Connecticut, New York, Pennsylvania, Maryland, and Virginia* (Philadelphia, 1792), p. 3.

20 *Ibid.,* pp. 24–26.

21 *Ibid.,* pp. 29–30.

22 *Annals of Congress,* 3 Cong., 1 Sess. (1793–1795), p. 1426.

23 See an excellent treatment of the origin of the Act by William R. Leslie, "A Study in the Origins of Interstate Rendition: The Big Beaver Creek Murders," in *American Historical Review,* LVII (October, 1951), pp. 63–76.

24 *Annals of Congress,* 2 Cong., 2 Sess. (1793), p. 1414.

25 *Annals of Congress,* 2 Cong., 2 Sess., p. 861.

26 David Rice, *Slavery Inconsistent with Justice and Good Policy; Proved by a Speech Delivered in the Convention Held at Danville, Kentucky* (Philadelphia, 1792), p. 3.

27 Salmon Portland Chase, *Reclamation of Fugitives from Service; an Argument for the Defendant Submitted to the Supreme Court of the United States, at the December Term, 1846 in the Case of Wharton Jones vs. John Vanzandt* (Cincinnati, 1847), p. 83.

28 David Rice, *Slavery Inconsistent with Justice and Good Policy . . . ,* pp. 4–6.

29 *Ibid.,* p. 8.

30 *Ibid.,* p. 10.

31 *Ibid.,* p. 11.

32 *Ibid.,* pp. 15–16.

33 *Ibid.,* p. 17. Joseph D. Learned, *A View of the Policy of Permitting Slaves in the States West of the Mississippi; Being a Letter to a Member of Congress* (Baltimore, 1820), takes the position that the Negro should be kept in slavery for the purpose of amalgamation. Learned was a lawyer.

Chapter 7
Slavery and Political Power

1 Documentary proof is overwhelming. A typical example is Thomas J. Randolph, *Speech . . . in the House of Delegates of Virginia on the Abolition of Slavery; Delivered Saturday, January 21, 1832* (Richmond, 1832).

2 Theodore Weld, *American Slavery As It Is: Testimony of a Thousand Witnesses* (New York, 1839), p. 182.

3 *Ibid.,* p. 183.

4 U. S. Bureau of the Census, *A Century of Population Growth; From the First Census of the United States to the Twelfth, 1790–1900* (Washington, D. C., 1909), p. 92.

5 In the House of Representatives the extra votes of the slave states numbered as low as seventeen in 1812 and as high as twenty-five in 1830.

6 New York and New Jersey were in process of emancipation and are here designated free states.

7 *Annals of Congress,* 9 Cong., 2 Sess., pp. 113–14, 151.

8 *Ibid.,* pp. 231–43.

9 *Ibid.,* pp. 265–66.

10 *Ibid.,* pp. 626–27. John Randolph said, in the course of this debate, that the slave states need never expect any help from the free states in event of a slave insurrection, and that all he, personally, hoped for was an attitude of neutrality.

11 *Annals of Congress,* 15 Cong., 2 Sess., II, p. 1222.

12 *Ibid.,* pp. 1273–74.

13 *Annals of Congress,* 16 Cong., 2 Sess., pp. 1586–87.

14 *Congressional Globe,* 33 Cong., 1 Sess., II, p. 1254.

Chapter 8
Foreign Slave Trade

1 *Minutes of the Proceedings of a Convention of Delegates from the Abolition Societies Established in Different Parts of the United States, Assembled at Philadelphia, on the First Day of January, One Thousand Seven Hundred and Ninety-four, and Continued by Adjournment, until the Seventh Day of the Same Month, Inclusive* (Philadelphia, 1794), pp. 22–25.

2 Warner Mifflin, *A Serious Expostulation with the Members of the House of Representatives of the United States* (Philadelphia, 1793).

3 Warner Mifflin, *The Defense of Warner Mifflin against Aspersions Cast on Him on Account of His Endeavors to Promote Righteousness, Mercy, and Peace among Mankind* (Philadelphia, 1796).

4 Timothy Dwight, *Greenfield Hill: A Poem in Seven Parts* (New York, 1794).

5 *Ibid.,* p. 38.

6 *Ibid.,* p. 40.

7 St. George Tucker, *A Dissertation on Slavery with a Proposal for the Gradual Abolition of It, in the State of Virginia* (Philadelphia, 1796), p. 10.

8 *Ibid.,* pp. 29–30.

9 Alexander McLeod, *Negro Slavery Unjustifiable. A Discourse by Alexander McLeod, A.M., Pastor of the Reformed Presbyterian Congregation in the City of New York* (New York, 1802).

10 Thomas Branagan, *A Preliminary Essay on the Oppression of the Exiled Sons of Africa. Consisting of Animadversions on the Impolicy and Barbarity of the Deleterious Commerce and Subsequent Slavery of the Human Species; to Which Is Added, a Desultory Letter Written to Napoleon Bonaparte, Anno Domini, 1801* (Philadelphia, 1804).

11 Thomas Branagan, *Avenia, or A Tragical Poem, on the Oppression of the Human Species; an Infringement on the Rights of Man* (Philadelphia, 1805).

12 Thomas Branagan, *The Penitential Tyrant: Or, the Slave Trader Reformed: A Pathetic Poem in Four Cantos* (Philadelphia, 1805).

13 Thomas Branagan, *Serious Remonstrance, Addressed to the Citizens of the Northern States, and Their Representatives; Being an Appeal to Their Natural Feelings and Common Sense; Consisting of Speculations and Animadversions, on the Recent Revival of the Slave Trade, in the American . . . Republic* (Philadelphia, 1805).

14 Thomas Branagan, *A Preliminary Essay . . . 1801*, p. 27.

15 *Ibid.*, p. 33.

16 St. George Tucker, attorney at Williamsburg and later professor of law at the College of William and Mary and eminent jurist, said in 1796: "Whilst America hath been the land of promise to Europeans, and their descendants, it hath been the vale of death to *millions* of the wretched sons of Africa." *A Dissertation on Slavery with a Proposal for the Gradual Abolition of It, . . .* p. 9.

17 Thomas Branagan, *A Preliminary Essay . . . 1801*, p. 33.

18 Thomas Branagan, *Avenia; Or A Tragical Poem in the State of Virginia*, pp. 311–13.

19 *Ibid.*, pp. 313–14.

20 *Ibid.*, p. 309.

21 John Parrish, *Remarks on the Slavery of the Black People; Addressed to the Citizens of the United States, Particularly to Those Who Are in Legislative or Executive Stations in the General or State Governments; and Also to Such Individuals as Hold Them in Bondage* (Philadelphia, 1806), p. 8.

22 *Ibid.*, p. 9.

23 *Annals of Congress*, 6 Cong., 1 Sess., *Appendix*, p. 1514.

24 *Ibid.*, 8 Cong., 1 Sess., p. 991.

25 *Ibid.*, 8 Cong., 1 Sess., p. 995.

26 *Ibid.*, 8 Cong., 1 Sess., p. 1004.

27 *Ibid.*, 8 Cong., 1 Sess., p. 1005.

28 *Ibid.*, 8 Cong., 1 Sess., p. 1010.

29 *Ibid.*, 8 Cong., 1 Sess., p. 1014.

30 *Ibid.*, 8 Cong., 1 Sess., p. 1020.

31 *Ibid.*, 8 Cong., 1 Sess., p. 1034.

32 *Ibid.*, 8 Cong., 1 Sess., p. 1036.

33 *Ibid.*, 9 Cong., 1 Sess., p. 374.

34 *Ibid.*, 8 Cong., 2 Sess., pp. 1221–22; *ibid.*, 9 Cong., 1 Sess., pp. 343, 348, 360; *ibid.*, 9 Cong., 2 Sess., p. 32.

35 *Ibid.*, 9 Cong., 1 Sess., p. 435.

36 *Ibid.*, 9 Cong., 1 Sess., p. 436.

37 *Ibid.*, 9 Cong., 1 Sess., p. 437.

38 Paul L. Ford (ed.), *Writings of Thomas Jefferson* (10 vols., New York, 1892–99), III, p. 421.

39 *Annals of Congress*, 9 Cong., 2 Sess., p. 174.

40 *Ibid.*, 9 Cong., 2 Sess., p. 190.

41 *Ibid.*, 9 Cong., 2 Sess., p. 201.

42 *Ibid.*, 9 Cong., 2 Sess., pp. 237–38.

43 *Ibid.*, 9 Cong., 2 Sess., pp. 265–66.

44 *Ibid.*, 9 Cong., 2 Sess., p. 266.

45 *Ibid.*, 9 Cong., 2 Sess., p. 478.

46 *Ibid.*, 9 Cong., 2 Sess., pp. 1266–70.

Chapter 9
Migrations to the Free States

1 Richard Furman, *Exposition of the Views of the Baptists Relative to the Coloured Population of the United States in a Communication to the Governor of South Carolina* (Charleston, 1823).

2 A South Carolinian [Frederick Dalche], *Practical Considerations Founded on the Scriptures, Relative to the Slave Population of South Carolina* (Charleston, 1823).

3 William Barlow, *Considerations on the Employment of the Press, as a Means of Diffusing the Principles of the*

Church with the Plan of a Society, and a Draft of a Proposed Constitution Adapted to That Object (Charleston, 1826).

4 Benjamin Seebohm (ed.), *Memoirs of the Life and Gospel Labours of Stephen Grellet* (2 vols., Philadelphia, 1877), II, pp. 157–58.

5 *Seventh Census of the United States: 1850*, p. 317.

6 John Hill Wheeler, *Historical Sketches of North Carolina from 1584 to 1851* (Philadelphia, 1851), p. 9.

7 Burton Alva Konkle, *John Motley Morehead and the Development of North Carolina* (Philadelphia, 1922), pp. 58, 65–75.

8 G[uion] Griffis Johnson, *Ante-Bellum North Carolina, A Social History* (Chapel Hill, 1937), p. 567.

9 Henry Ruffner, *Address to the People of West Virginia, Shewing that Slavery Is Injurious to the Public Welfare, and That It May Be Gradually Abolished, Without Detriment to the Rights and Interests of Slaveholders* (Lexington, 1847), p. 17.

10 For the history of the early antislavery movement in Kentucky, see Asa Earl Martin, *The Anti-Slavery Movement in Kentucky* (Louisville, 1918).

11 John H. Spencer, *A History of Kentucky Baptists from 1769 to 1885 Including More than 800 Biographical Sketches* (Cincinnati, 1886), p. 185.

12 Said the synod: "To preach publicly against slavery, in present circumstances, and to lay down as the duty of everyone, to liberate those who are under their care, is that which would lead to disorder and open the way to great confusion." William Henry Foote, *Sketches of North Carolina; Historical and Biographical Illustrations of the Principles of a Portion of Her Early Settlers* (New York, 1846), p. 293.

13 John Rankin, *Letters on American Slavery, Addressed to Mr. Thomas Rankin, Merchant at Middlebrook, Augusta County, Virginia* (Boston, 1833).

14 There were close family ties in this group. James H. Dickey and William Dickey were half-brothers. James H. Dickey and Samuel Crothers married sisters.

15 Willard C. MacNaul, *The Jefferson-Lemen Compact. The Relations of Thomas Jefferson and James Lemen in the Exclusion of Slavery from Illinois and the Northwest Territory with Related Documents, 1781–1818* (Chicago, 1915), p. 36.

16 Asa E. Martin, *The Anti-Slavery Movement in Kentucky Prior to 1850* (Filson Club Publications, No. 29), p. 42.

17 *Ibid.*, pp. 42–47.

Chapter 10
The Old Northwest

1 "Report of a Committee of the Delaware Society, Respecting the Constitutional Powers of Congress, to Prohibit or Restrict Slavery within the Territories Belonging to the United States, or New States on Their Admission into the Federal Compact," in *Minutes of the Sixteenth American Convention for Promoting the Abolition of Slavery and Improving the Condition of the African Race, Held at Philadelphia, on the Fifth of October, and the Tenth of November, 1819* (Philadelphia, 1819), pp. 19–20.

2 *Annals of Congress,* 8 Cong., 2 Sess., p. 996.

3 *Ibid.,* pp. 1596–97.

4 Francis Newton Thorpe, *The Federal and State Constitutions, Colonial Charters, and Other Organic Laws* (7 vols., Washington, 1909), II, p. 957.

5 *Ibid.,* p. 958.

6 Hunter Miller (ed.), *Treaties and Other International Acts of the United States of America, 1776–1863* (8 vols., Washington, 1931–48), II, p. 246.

7 Clarence W. Alvord (ed.), *Kaskaskia Records, 1778–1790,* in Illinois Historical Library, *Collections* (Springfield, 1909), V, pp. 488–93.

8 Worthington C. Ford (ed.), *Journals of the Continental Congress, 1774–1789* (34 vols., Washington, 1904–37), XXIV, p. 541.

9 William H. Smith (ed.), *The Life and Public Services of Arthur St. Clair with His Correspondence and Other Papers* (2 vols., Cincinnati, 1882), II, p. 245; Clarence E. Carter (ed.), *The Territorial Papers of the United States* (18 vols., Washington, 1934–52), II, p. 248.

10 The judges were Samuel H. Parsons of Massachusetts (1787–89), James M. Varnum of Rhode Island (1788–89), and John C. Symmes (1788–1802).

11 William H. Smith (ed.), *The Life and Public Services of Arthur St. Clair . . . ,* II, pp. 447–48.

12 *Journal of the Convention of the Territory of the United States Northwest of the Ohio, 1802,* p. 27.

13 Francis Newton Thorpe, *The Federal and State Constitutions, Colonial Charters, and Other Organic Laws,* V, p. 2909.

14 Jacob P. Dunn (ed.), *Slavery Petitions and Papers,* Indiana Historical Society, *Publications,* II, No. 2 (Indianapolis, 1894), pp. 447–62.

15 *Ibid.,* p. 471.

16 See Francis S. Philbrick (ed.), *The Laws of Indiana Territory, 1801–1809,* Illinois Historical Library, *Collections,* XXI (Springfield, 1930), pp. 42–69, 136–39.

17 Emma Lou Thornbrough's *The Negro in Indiana Before 1900* (Indianapolis, 1957) is a model of historical scholarship. The reader will find here the best short discussion of the violations of the Northwest Ordinance during the territorial period.

18 Francis S. Philbrick (ed.), *The Laws of Indiana Territory, 1801–1809,* pp. 203–4.

19 Francis Newton Thorpe, *The Federal and State Constitutions, Colonial Charters, and Other Organic Laws,* II, p. 1055.

20 *Ibid.,* p. 1068.

21 *The State v. Laselle* (1820), Isaac Blackford, *Reports of Cases Argued and Determined in the Supreme Court of Judicature of the State of Indiana; Containing the Cases from May Term, 1817, to November Term, 1847* (8 vols., Indianapolis, 1830–50), I, p. 60.

22 *Elizabeth Dennison et al* (1807), William W. Blume, *Transactions of the Supreme Court of the Territory of Michigan, 1805–1836* (6 vols., Ann Arbor, 1936–40), I, pp. 385–95.

23 Michigan Pioneer and Historical Society, *Collections,* XII, p. 652.

24 Francis Philbrick (ed.), *Pope's Digest, 1815* (2 vols., Springfield, 1938–40), II, pp. 33, 185–91, 473.

25 Francis Newton Thorpe, *The Federal and State Constitutions, Colonial Charters, and Other Organic Laws,* II, p. 969.

26 "Journal of the Convention [1818]," in Illinois State Historical Society, *Journal,* VI (1913–14), pp. 355–424.

27 *Annals of Congress,* 15 Cong., 2 Sess. (1818–19), I, pp. 306–7.

28 *Ibid.,* 15 Cong., 2 Sess., pp. 308–9.

29 *Ibid.,* 15 Cong., 2 Sess., p. 310.

30 *Ibid.,* 15 Cong., 2 Sess., pp. 310–11.

Chapter 11
The Missouri Contest

1 *Annals of Congress,* 16 Cong., 1 Sess. (1819–20), I, pp. 42–44.

2 *Ibid.,* 15 Cong., 2 Sess. (1818–19), I, p. 1170.

3 There was some effort made in the debate to belittle the opposition to slavery expansion as an effort of Federalists to recover ground lost in the War of 1812. Actually, little or no politics was involved. Tallmadge himself was a Democrat. There were only twenty-five Federalists in a total membership of one hundred eighty-six in the House of Representatives. Tallmadge did represent the Negroes and the Negro vote in New York, where they were well educated and politically active.

4 Quoted by Tallmadge, *Annals of Congress,* 15 Cong., 2 Sess. (1818–19), I, p. 1204; see also *ibid.,* II, p. 1437.

5 *Annals of Congress,* 16 Cong., 1 Sess. (1819–20), I, 129.

6 The meeting was held on the evening of November 16, 1819, in New York City. The principal addresses were by Peter Jay and John T. Irving. The address to the people was a simple explanation of the Constitutional principle of Congressional exclusion. See *Niles Weekly Register,* XVII (Sept. 1819–March, 1820), pp. 199–200.

7 The "little letter" was a remarkable document considering Jay had written the Constitution of New York and five numbers of *The Federalist,* and had served as Chief Justice both of New York and of the United States. He said: "To me the constitutional authority of the Congress to prohibit the migration and importation of slaves into any of the States, does not appear questionable. The first article of the Constitution specifies the legislative powers committed to the Congress. The ninth section of that article has these words:

"'The *migration* or *importation* of such *persons* as any of the *now existing* States shall think proper to admit, shall not be prohibited by the Congress prior to the year 1808. But a tax or duty may be imposed on such importations, not exceeding ten dollars for each person.'

"I understand the sense and meaning of this clause to be, that the power of the Congress, although competent to prohibit such migration and importation, was not to be exercised with respect to the *then existing* States (and them only) until the year 1808; but that Congress were at liberty to make such prohibition as to any new State, which might, in the *mean* time, be established, and further, that from and after *that period,* they were authorized to make such prohibition, as to all the States, whether new or old." Jay to Elias Boudinot,

November 17, 1819, Henry P. Johnson (ed.), *The Correspondence and Public Papers of John Jay* (4 vols., New York, 1890–93), IV, pp. 430–31.

Elias Boudinot had presided over a meeting at Burlington, New Jersey, August 30, 1819. He was a president of the Continental Congress, and one of the founders of the American Bible Society. Burlington is near Mount Holly, home of the pioneer abolitionist John Woolman. King was from Jamaica, Long Island.

8 *Annals of Congress*, 16 Cong., 1 Sess. (1819–20), I, pp. 419–20. Reference is to Marcus [pseud.]. *An Examination of the Expediency and Constitutionality of Prohibiting Slavery in the State of Missouri* (New York, 1819).

9 *Ibid.*, p. 160. Said Fuller of Massachusetts: "It is vain to attempt to stifle the public feeling and the public view. The freemen of our country can never be insensible, when the rights of a numerous portion of their fellow-creatures . . . are in controversy; they will never be silent, when the victims of oppression require an advocate." *Ibid.*, p. 1467.

10 *Ibid.*, p. 175. Said Prentis Miller of Massachusetts: "We are told, that if the friends of the amendment should obtain their object, and succeed in excluding slavery from Missouri and succeed in maintaining a principle that will exclude it from the extensive territory beyond the Mississippi, sectional jealousies and animosities will be the immediate consequence; the harmony of our great and happy family will be destroyed; commotion and Civil War may next present their horrors, and a dissolution of the Union may be the fatal result." *Annals of Congress*, 16 Cong., 1 Sess. (1819–20), I, pp. 176–77.

11 *Ibid.*, 15 Cong., 2 Sess. (1818–19), I, pp. 1205–6.

12 *Ibid.*, 16 Cong., 1 Sess. (1819–20), I, p. 1181.

13 *Ibid.*, 16 Cong., 1 Sess. (1819–20), I, p. 132.

14 See the statement of Walker, of Georgia, *ibid.*, 16 Cong., 1 Sess. (1819–20), I, p. 173.

15 *Ibid.*, p. 174.

16 *Ibid.*, 15 Cong., 2 Sess. (1818–19), I, p. 1188.

17 *Ibid.*, 15 Cong., 2 Sess. (1818–19), p. 1192.

18 *Ibid.*, 15 Cong., 2 Sess. (1818–19), p. 1170. Taylor, a Democrat, was later speaker of the House of Representatives.

19 *Ibid.*, 15 Cong., 2 Sess. (1818–19), II, p. 1174.

20 *Ibid.*, 16 Cong., 1 Sess. (1819–20), II, p. 1467.

21 *Ibid.*, 16 Cong., 1 Sess. (1819–20), I, p. 107.

22 *Ibid.*, 16 Cong., 1 Sess. (1819–20), I, pp. 202–3. "This Government, for the period of thirty years," said Lowrie, "by its acts, has sanctioned the construction contended for. Territories have been nurtured and protected through their infancy and youth, until, arriving at a proper age, they were admitted into the family of the Republic."

23 *Ibid.*, II, p. 1298.

24 *Ibid.*, 16 Cong., 1 Sess. (1819–20), II, p. 1201.

25 *Ibid.*, 16 Cong., 1 Sess. (1819–20), p. 130.

26 *Ibid.*, 16 Cong., 1 Sess. (1819–20), p. 139.

27 *Ibid.*, 16 Cong., 1 Sess. (1819–20), I, p. 399.

28 *Ibid.*, 15 Cong., 2 Sess. (1818–19), p. 1210.

29 *Ibid.*, 16 Cong., 1 Sess. (1819–20), II, p. 1201.

30 *Ibid.*, 15 Cong., 2 Sess. (1818–19), pp. 1433–35.

31 *Ibid.*, 16 Cong., 1 Sess. (1819–20), I, p. 105.

32 *Ibid.*, 16 Cong., 2 Sess. (1820–21), p. 44.

33 *Ibid.*, 16 Cong., 2 Sess. (1820–21), p. 535.

34 *Ibid.*, 16 Cong., 2 Sess. (1820–21), p. 599.

35 *Ibid.*, 16 Cong., 2 Sess. (1820–21), p. 93.

36 *Ibid.*, 16 Cong., 2 Sess. (1820–21), p. 530.

37 *Ibid.*, 16 Cong., 2 Sess. (1820–21), pp. 598–99.

38 *Ibid.*, 16 Cong., 2 Sess. (1820–21), p. 633.

39 *Ibid.*, 16 Cong., 2 Sess. (1820–21), p. 638.

Chapter 12
Insurrections

1 *Annals of Congress*, 8 Cong., 1 Sess., pp. 995–96.

2 William W. Hening (ed.), *The Statutes at Large; Being a Collection of All the Laws of Virginia from the First Session of the Legislature in the Year 1619* (Richmond, 1819–23), I, p. 364; II, p. 77.

3 *Ibid.*, III, p. 252.

4 George M. Stroud, *A Sketch of the Laws Relating to Slavery in the Several States of the United States of America* (second edition; Philadelphia, 1856), pp. 229–43.

5 Worthington C. Ford (ed.), *Journals of the Continental Congress, 1774–1789* (34 vols., Washington, 1904–37), IV, p. 60.

6 John R. Bartlett (ed.), *Records of the Colony of Rhode Island and Providence Plantations* (10 vols., Providence, 1856–65), VIII, pp. 359–61; X, p. 85.

7 William W. Hening (ed.), *The Statutes at Large; Being a Collection of All the Laws of Virginia . . .* , IX, p. 280.

8 *Laws of the State of New York Passed at the Sessions of the Legislature, 1777–1784*, p. 351.

9 See W. B. Hartgrove, "The Negro Soldier in the American Revolution," *The Journal of Negro History*, I (1916), pp. 110–31; George Henry Moore, "Historical Notes on the Employment of Negroes in the American Army of the Revolution," *The Magazine of History* (1907), pp. 13–21.

10 Thomas Clarkson, *An Essay on the Slavery and Commerce of the Human Species, Particularly the African* (London, 1786), *An Essay on the Impolicy of the African Slave Trade* (London, 1788), *An Essay on the Comparative Efficiency of Regulation or Abolition, as Applied to the Slave Trade* (London, 1789).

11 Granville Sharp, *A Representation of the Injustice and Dangerous Tendency of Tolerating Slavery* (London, 1769), *An Essay on Slavery* (Burlington, 1773), *The Just Limitations of Slavery in the Laws of God Compared with the Unbounded Claims of the African Traders and British American Slaveholders* (London, 1776), *The Law of Liberty* (London, 1776).

12 Anthony Benezet, *A Serious Address to the Rulers of America, on the Inconsistency of Their Conduct Respecting Slavery* (Trenton, 1783).

13 John Newton, *Thoughts upon the African Slave Trade* (London, 1788).

14 Thomas Day, *Four Tracts: Reflections upon the Present State of England, and the Independence of America. Reflections upon the Peace, the East-India Bill, and the Present Crisis. A Dialogue Between a Justice of the Peace and a Farmer. Fragment of an Original Letter on the Slavery of the Negroes* (London, 1785).

15 James F. Stanfield, *The Guinea Voyage. A Poem, in Three Books* (London, 1789).

16 William Belsham, *An Essay on the African Slave Trade* (Philadelphia, 1790).

17 *An Abstract of the Evidence Delivered Before a Select Committee of the House of Commons in the Years 1790, and 1791; on the Part of the Petitioners for the Abolition of the Slave Trade* (London, 1791).

18 A long and exhaustive review of the affair was made by the Virginia legislature, and the Senate Journal of that state for the years 1801–2 remains the best source of information. Efforts were made at the time to keep down excitement. Information was suppressed, and current newspaper accounts are not too reliable.

19 See, for example, Thomas Branagan, *A Preliminary Essay, on the Oppression of the Exiled Sons of Africa . . . 1801* (Philadelphia, 1804), pp. 133–63; Samuel Hopkins, *A Dialogue Concerning the Slavery of the Africans; Shewing It to Be the Duty and Interest of the American States to Emancipate All Their African Slaves* (New York, 1785); John Parrish, *Remarks on the Slavery of the Black People; Addressed to the Citizens of the United States, Particularly to Those Who Are in Legislative or Executive Stations in the General or State Governments; and Also to Such Individuals as Hold Them in Bondage* (Philadelphia, 1806), p. 38.

20 James Swan, *A Dissuasion to Great Britain and the Colonies, from the Slave-Trade to Africa, Shewing the Injustice Thereof* (Boston, 1772) is a remarkably fine presentation of slave-catching, and cruelties, denial of racial inferiority, and dire prophecy.

21 Theodore Dwight, *An Oration, Spoken Before "The Connecticut Society, for the Promotion of Freedom and the Relief of Persons Unlawfully Holden in Bondage." Convened at Hartford, on the 8th Day of May, A.D. 1794* (Hartford, 1794), p. 11.

22 *Ibid.*, p. 20.

23 *Minutes of the Proceedings of the Seventh Convention of Delegates from the Abolition Societies Established in Different Parts of the United States, Assembled in Philadelphia, on the Third Day of June, One Thousand Eight Hundred and One, and Continued by Adjournments until the Sixth Day of the Same Month, Inclusive* (Philadelphia, 1801), pp. 37–41.

24 *An Account of the Late Intended Insurrection Among a Portion of the Blacks of This City. Published by Authority of the Corporation of Charleston* (Charleston, 1822); Lionel H. Kennedy and Thomas Parker, *An Official Report of the Trials of Sundry Negroes Charged with an Attempt to Raise an Insurrection in South Carolina, Preceded by an Introduction and Narrative. And in an Appendix, A Report of the Trials of Four White Persons on Indictment for Attempting to Excite the Slaves to Insurrection* (Charleston, 1822).

25 David Walker, *Appeal in Four Articles, With a Preamble, to the Colored Citizens of the World, But in Particular to Those of the U. S., Written in Boston, Mass., Sept. 28th, 1829* (Boston, 1829). The second and third editions of this work, both published in 1830, bore the title *Walker's Appeal, in Four Articles: Together with a Preamble to the Colored Citizens of the World, But in Particular, and Very Expressly to Those of the United States of America. Written in Boston, in the State of Massachusetts, September 28, 1829*. Citations are to the third edition of eighty-eight pages.

26 *Ibid.*, p. 26.

27 *Ibid.*, p. 21.

28 *Ibid.*, p. 28.

29 *Ibid.*, p. 31.

30 *Ibid.*, p. 44.

31 Henry Highland Garnet, *Walker's Appeal, with a Brief Sketch of His Life. By Henry Highland Garnet, And also Garnet's Address to the Slaves of the United States of America* (New York, 1848).

Chapter 13
Free Negroes

1 See *The Emancipator*, April 30, 1820, pp. 8–9; and Robert A. White, *Elihu Embree, Agitator and Abolitionist* (Nashville, 1932), pp. 7–8.

2 Dwight L. Dumond, "The Fourteenth Amendment Trilogy in Historical Perspective," presented at the annual conference of the Federal Judges of the Sixth Circuit, April 19, 1957, in *Michigan Alumnus Quarterly Review*, Autumn, 1957, pp. 55–64.

3 *Acts and Resolves Passed by the General Assembly of the State of Vermont, at the October Session, 1858* (Bradford, 1858), p. 43; *Laws of New Hampshire Passed, June Session, 1857* (Concord, 1857), p. 1867.

4 John Codman Hurd, *The Law of Freedom and Bondage in the United States* (2 vols., Boston, 1858–62), II, p. 36.

5 *Laws of New Hampshire Passed, June Session, 1857* (Concord, 1857), p. 1900.

6 *Acts and Resolves Passed by the General Court of Massachusetts, in the Year 1859* (Boston, 1859), pp. 703–7.

7 *Journal of the Convention for Framing a Constitution of Government for the State of Massachusetts Bay, September 1, 1779 to June 16, 1780* (Boston, 1832), Appendix, p. 257.

8 James Truslow Adams, "Disfranchisement of Negroes in New England," *American Historical Review*, XXX (1925), pp. 543–47.

9 *Acts and Laws of the Commonwealth of Massachusetts Passed by the General Court, A.D. 1783 to 1789* (Boston, 1783—89), p. 439; *Acts and Resolves Passed by the Legislature of Massachusetts in the Year 1843* (Boston, 1843), p. 4.

10 *Acts and Laws of the Commonwealth of Massachusetts Passed by the General Court, A.D., 1783 to 1789, . . .* p. 682; John Codman Hurd, *The Law of Freedom and Bondage in the United States*, II, pp. 30–31.

11 James Truslow Adams, "Disfranchisement of Negroes in New England," p. 546.

12 *Public Acts, Passed by the General Assembly of the State of Connecticut, May Session, 1857* (Hartford, 1857), p. 12.

13 *Ibid.*, p. 162. The vote in the convention was 103 to 72. Negroes were excluded from the franchise in the state until 1876.

14 *The Public Laws of the State of Rhode Island and Providence Plantations, 1822* (Providence, 1822), pp. 89–90; *Journal of the Convention Assembled to Frame a*

Constitution for the State of Rhode Island, at Newport, September 12, 1842 (Providence, 1859), pp. 15–22; Francis Newton Thorpe, *The Federal and State Constitutions, Colonial Charters, and Other Organic Laws* (7 vols., Washington, 1909), VI, pp. 3224–25.

15 Alfred Billings Street, *The Council of Revision of the State of New York; Its History; A History of the Courts with Which Its Members Were Connected; Biographical Sketches of Its Members; and Its Vetoes* (Albany, 1859), pp. 268–69.

16 Francis Newton Thorpe, *The Federal and State Constitutions, Colonial Charters, and Other Organic Laws* (7 vols., Washington, 1909), V, pp. 2643, 2656. See, also, Leo H. Hersch, "The Negro and New York, 1783 to 1865," *Journal of Negro History*, XVI (1931), pp. 382–473.

17 Francis Newton Thorpe, *The Federal and State Constitutions, Colonial Charters, and Other Organic Laws*, V, pp. 2595, 4188. See, also, E. Raymond Turner, "Women's Suffrage in New Jersey, 1790–1807," Smith College, *Studies in History*, I, No. 4 (July, 1916), p. 170; Marion Thompson Wright, "Negro Suffrage in New Jersey, 1776–1873," *Journal of Negro History*, XXXIII (1948), pp. 168–224.

18 Francis Newton Thorpe, *The Federal and State Constitutions, Colonial Charters, and Other Organic Laws*, V, p. 3108; *Hobbs et al. v. Fogg*, in Fredrick Watts, *Reports of Cases Argued and Determined in the Supreme Court of Pennsylvania* (10 vols., Philadelphia, 1834–41), VI, p. 553. The decision of the court was an amazing performance, based upon the uncertain memory of a Philadelphia attorney concerning a decision of the High Court of Errors and Appeals about 1795. There was not even a written memorandum of the earlier decision. The "Appeal of Forty Thousand Citizens Threatened with Disfranchisement, to the People of Pennsylvania," in *The Pennsylvania Freeman*, March 29, 1838, is indispensable.

19 Francis Newton Thorpe, *The Federal and State Constitutions, Colonial Charters, and Other Organic Laws*, V, p. 2907.

20 For the constitutions of the several states, see *ibid.*: (Indiana, 1816) II, p. 1067; (Michigan, 1837) IV, p. 1932; (Wisconsin, 1848) VII, p. 4080; (Illinois, 1818) II, p. 975.

21 *Acts of the State of Ohio, First Session of the General Assembly, 1803* (Chillicothe, 1803), I, p. 44.

22 *Laws of the Territory of Michigan* (4 vols., Lansing, 1871–84), I, p. 490; Thomas M. Cooley (ed.), *Compiled Laws of the State of Michigan* (2 vols., Lansing, 1857), II, p. 1189; *Acts of the Legislature of Wisconsin, Passed During the Winter Session of 1837–8, And the Special Session of June, 1838* (Burlington, 1838), p. 252; *The Revised Statutes of the State of Wisconsin, 1858* (Chicago, 1858), p. 655.

23 *Revised Code of Laws of Illinois Enacted by the Fifth General Assembly, at Their Session Held at Vandalia, 1827* (Vandalia, 1827), p. 251.

24 Francis S. Philbrick (ed.), *The Laws of Indiana Territory, 1801–1809*, Illinois Historical Library, *Collections*, XXI (Springfield, 1930), p. 40.

25 *Laws of the State of Indiana Passed and Published at the Second Session of the General Assembly* (Corydon, 1818), p. 39.

26 *Laws Passed by the First General Assembly of the State of Illinois, at Their Second Session, Held at Kaskaskia, 1819* (Kaskaskia, 1819), p. 143.

27 *Acts Passed at the First Session of the Fifth General Assembly of the State of Ohio, 1806* (Chillicothe, 1807), V, p. 54.

28 *Laws of the State of Indiana Passed at the Thirty-Seventh Session of the General Assembly, Begun on the Sixth Day of January, 1853* (Indianapolis, 1853), p. 60.

29 *The Statutes at Large of Pennsylvania from 1682 to 1801* (16 vols., Harrisburg, 1896–1915), X, p. 72.

30 *The Public Laws of the State of Rhode Island and Providence Plantations, January, 1798* (Providence, 1798), p. 483.

31 *Laws of the State of Indiana Passed and Published at the Second Session of the General Assembly* (Corydon, 1818), p. 94; *ibid., Fourth Session* (Corydon, 1820), p. 7; *ibid., Twenty-fourth Session* (Indianapolis, 1840), pp. 32–33.

32 *The Revised Statutes of the State of Michigan Passed at the Adjourned Session of 1837, and the Regular Session of 1838* (Detroit, 1838), p. 334.

33 *The Revised Code of Laws of Illinois* (Shawneetown, 1829), p. 111.

34 *Acts of the State of Ohio, Second Session of the General Assembly* (Chillicothe, n.d.), II, p. 64; *Acts Passed at the First Session of the Fifth General Assembly of the State of Ohio* [1806] (Chillicothe, 1807), V, pp. 53–54.

35 *Laws Passed by the First General Assembly of the State of Illinois at Their Second Session, Held at Kaskaskia, 1819*, p. 354; M. Mc. Fishback, "Illinois Legislation on Slavery and Free Negroes, 1818–1865," Illinois State Historical Society *Transactions*, IX (1904), pp. 414–32.

36 *The Revised Laws of Indiana* (Indianapolis, 1831), p. 375; Francis Newton Thorpe, *The Federal and State Constitutions, Colonial Charters, and Other Organic Laws*, II, pp. 1009, 1089.

37 John Hutchinson, *Mississippi Code, 1798–1848* (Jackson, 1848), p. 523; *Revised Code of the Statute Laws of the State of Mississippi* (Jackson, 1857), p. 236; Harry Toulmin, *A Digest of the Laws of the State of Alabama* (New York, 1823), p. 632.

38 John Hutchinson, *Mississippi Code, 1798–1848*, p. 523; Harry Toulmin, *A Digest of the Laws of the State of Alabama*, p. 644.

39 William C. Dawson, *A Compilation of the Laws of the State of Georgia from 1819 through 1829* (Milledgeville, 1831), pp. 411–12.

40 *Revised Code of the Statute Laws of the State of Mississippi* (Jackson, 1857), p. 255.

41 John Hutchinson, *Mississippi Code, 1798–1848*, p. 528.

42 Joseph Brevard, *An Alphabetical Digest of the Public Statute Law of South Carolina* (3 vols., Charleston, 1814), II, pp. 254–55.

43 *Revised Code of the Statute Laws of the State of Mississippi*, p. 254.

44 *Ibid.*, p. 510; Horatio Marbury and William H. Crawford (eds.), *A Digest of the Laws of the State of Georgia, 1755 to 1800* (Savannah, 1802), pp. 429–30; Benjamin James, *A Digest of the Laws of South Carolina to 1822* (Columbia, 1822), pp. 394–95.

45 *Ibid.*; L. Q. C. Lamar (ed.), *A Compilation of the Laws*

of the State of Georgia, 1800–1819 (Augusta, 1821), pp. 797–800.

46 Joseph Brevard, *An Alphabetical Digest of the Public Statute Law of South Carolina,* II, pp. 254–55, 260–61; Oliver H. Prince (ed.), *A Digest of the Laws of the State of Georgia to December, 1837* (second edition; Athens, 1837), pp. 808, 811–12.

47 John Hutchinson, *Mississippi Code, 1798–1848,* pp. 240, 510, 517; *Revised Code of the Statute Laws of the State of Mississippi* (Jackson, 1857), pp. 254–55; L. Q. C. Lamar (ed.), *A Compilation of the Laws of the State of Georgia, 1800–1819,* pp. 804–5; Joseph Brevard, *An Alphabetical Digest of the Public Statute Law of South Carolina,* II, p. 233.

48 L. Q. C. Lamar, *A Compilation of the Laws of the State of Georgia, 1808–1819,* pp. 811–12.

49 *Revised Code of the Statute Laws of the State of Mississippi* (Jackson, 1857), p. 236.

50 Harry Toulmin, *A Digest of the Laws of the State of Alabama,* pp. 644–46.

51 Joseph Brevard, *An Alphabetical Digest of the Public Statute Law of South Carolina,* pp. 250, 256–62.

Chapter 14
Colonization

1 Jedediah Morse, *The American Geography; or, A View of the Present Situation of the United States of America* (Elizabeth Town, 1789), p. 67. Morse's *Geography* was an important antislavery publication because of its wide circulation over a long period. Only a few paragraphs were devoted to slavery but they were sharply critical and incisive. For example: "The Africans are said to be inferior in point of sense, understanding, sentiment and feeling to white people. Hence the one infers a right to enslave the other. The African labours night and day to collect a small pittance to purchase the freedom of his child. The white man begets his likeness, and with much indifference and indignity of soul, sees his offspring in bondage and misery, and makes not one effort to redeem his own blood. Choice food for satire! Wide field for burlesque! Noble game for wit! Sad cause for pity to bleed, and for humanity to weep!" *Ibid.,* p. 66.

2 Albert Henry Smyth (ed.), *The Writings of Benjamin Franklin* (10 vols., New York, 1905–7), X, pp. 66–69. Franklin's plan, adopted by the Pennsylvania Society, *ibid.,* pp. 127–29, was to establish a committee of twenty-four persons which should resolve itself into a Committee of Inspection, a Committee of Guardians, a Committee of Education, and a Committee of Employment.

3 *The First Annual Report of the American Society for Colonizing the Free People of Color, of the United States; and the Proceedings of the Society at Their Annual Meeting in the City of Washington, on the First Day of January, 1818* (Washington, City, 1818), p. 3.

4 Charles Francis Adams (ed.), *Memoirs of John Quincy Adams, Comprising Portions of His Diary from 1795 to 1848* (12 vols., Philadelphia, 1874–77), IV, p. 293.

5 *Ibid.,* p. 292.

6 *Annals of Congress,* 15 Cong. 2 Sess., II, pp. 544–46.

7 *Minutes of a Special Meeting of the Fifteenth American Convention for Promoting the Abolition of Slavery, and Improving the Condition of the African Race, Assembled at Philadelphia, on the Tenth Day of December, 1818, and Continued by Adjournment until the Fifteenth Day of the Same Month, Inclusive* (Philadelphia, 1818), p. 49.

8 *Minutes of the Seventeenth Session of the American Convention for Promoting the Abolition of Slavery, and Improving the Condition of the African Race, Convened at Philadelphia, on the Third Day of October, 1821* (Philadelphia, 1821), p. 57. Said the Convention: "We think it worthy of consideration, how far any measure should be recommended that may tend to draw from our country the most industrious, moral, and respectable of its colored population, and thus deprive others, less improved, of the benefit of their example and advice . . . Deeply injured as they have been by the whites, the coloured people certainly claim from us some degree of retributive justice."

9 *Ibid.,* pp. 50–55.

10 *The First Annual Report of the American Society for Colonizing the Free People of Color, of the United States,* p. 18.

11 *Ibid.,* pp. 30–31.

12 *The African Repository and Colonial Journal* (68 vols., Washington, 1825–1889), IV, p. 118.

13 *The African Repository and Colonial Journal,* VII, p. 29.

14 Herman V. Ames (ed.), *State Documents on Federal Relations: the States and the United States* (Philadelphia, 1904), V, pp. 11–12.

15 *Register of Debates in Congress,* 18 Cong., 2 Sess., I, p. 623.

16 Jefferson to Jared Sparks, February 4, 1824, in A. A. Liscomb and A. L. Berg (eds.), *The Writings of Thomas Jefferson* (20 vols., Washington, 1903), XVI, pp. 8–14.

17 James Madison to Thomas R. Dun, February 23, 1833, in Gaillard Hunt (ed.), *The Writings of James Madison* (9 vols., New York, 1900–1910), IX, pp. 498–502.

18 *House Documents,* 19 Cong., 2 Sess., Doc. No. 64.

19 Herman V. Ames (ed.), *State Documents on Federal Relations: The States and the United States,* No. 5, p. 15.

20 Georgia, December 7, 1824; Mississippi, February 1, 1825; Louisiana, February 16, 1826, and Alabama, January 1, 1827.

21 *Register of Debates in Congress,* 18 Cong., 2 Sess., pp. 696–97.

22 Herman V. Ames (ed.), *State Documents on Federal Relations: The States and the United States,* No. 5, p. 17.

23 *Register of Debates in Congress,* 19 Cong., 2 Sess., p. 289.

24 *Ibid.,* p. 329.

Chapter 15
Voices from the West

1 See Asa Earl Martin, *The Antislavery Movement in Kentucky Prior to 1850.* Filson Club Publication, No. 29 (Louisville, 1918), pp. 20, 38–47.

2 David Barrow, *Involuntary, Unmerited, Perpetual, Absolute, Hereditary, Slavery Examined; on the Principles*

of *Nature, Reason, Justice, Policy, and Scripture* (Lexington, 1808), p. 12.

3 *Ibid.*, p. 13. The "Grand Charter" reference is to the Book of Genesis, 1:28.

4 *Ibid.*, p. 17.

5 *Ibid.*, p. 19.

6 *Ibid.*, p. 20.

7 *Ibid.*, pp. 21–22.

8 *Ibid.*, p. 23.

9 John Rankin, *Letters on American Slavery, Addressed to Mr. Thomas Rankin, Merchant at Middlebrook, Augusta Co., Va.* (fifth edition; Boston, 1838), p. 6.

10 *Ibid.*, p. 10.

11 *Ibid.*, p. 16.

12 *Ibid.*, p. 21.

13 *Ibid.*, p. 26.

14 *Ibid.*, pp. 32–70.

15 *Ibid.*, p. 71.

16 See *The History of Brown County, Ohio* (Chicago, 1883), p. 174; Henry Howe, *Historical Collections of Ohio* (2 vols., Cincinnati, 1907), II, pp. 328–41; *The Friend of Man*, October 6, 1836.

17 For the life and labors of Charles Osborn, see *Journal of That Faithful Servant of Christ, Charles Osborn, Containing an Account of Many of His Travels and Labors in the Work of the Ministry* (Cincinnati, 1854); Asa Earl Martin, "The Anti-Slavery Societies of Tennessee," *Tennessee Historical Magazine*, I (December, 1915), pp. 261–81; and Asa Earl Martin, "Pioneer Anti-Slavery Press," *Mississippi Valley Historical Review*, II (March, 1916), pp. 509–28. *The Emancipator* (1932 reprint), April 30, 1820, pp. 10–12, and May 31, 1820, contains a history of the organization and the constitution of the society.

18 Lundy's papers were destroyed in the burning of Pennsylvania Hall. The main facts of his life may be had from Thomas Earle, *The Life, Travels and Opinions of Benjamin Lundy, Including His Journeys to Texas and Mexico; with a Sketch of Contemporary Events, and a Notice of the Revolution in Hayti* (Philadelphia, 1847); Fred Landon, "Benjamin Lundy, Abolitionist," *Dalhousie Review*, July 1927; George A. Lawrence, "Benjamin Lundy, A Pioneer of Freedom," Illinois State Historical Society, *Transactions*, XVIII (1913), pp. 36–51; Lundy Memorial Committee of the John Swaney School Alumni and Society of Friends, *A Memorial to Benjamin Lundy on the Occasion of the Centennial of His Death*—1939.

19 A communication from a meeting of eight Local Union Humane Societies at Mt. Pleasant, July 7, 1819, was presented by Thomas H. Genin. A communication from the Kentucky Abolition Society, signed by David Barrow, was also received by the Convention. *Minutes of the Sixteenth American Convention for Promoting the Abolition of Slavery and Improving the Condition of the African Race, Held in Philadelphia, on the Fifth of October, and the Tenth of November, 1819* (Philadelphia, 1819).

20 See Thomas Earle, *The Life, Travels and Opinions of Benjamin Lundy*, pp. 13–14. Article 2 of the constitution of the Manumission Society of Tennessee said: "That no member vote for governor, or any legislator,

unless we believe him to be in favor of emancipation." *The Emancipator*, April 30, 1820, p. 11.

21 Mrs. Elizabeth Heyrich, *Immediate, Not Gradual Abolition; or, An Inquiry into the Shortest, Safest, and Most Effectual Means of Getting Rid of West Indian Slavery* (London, 1824), pp. 5–6.

22 *Ibid.*, p. 6.

23 *Ibid.*, p. 9.

24 *Ibid.*, p. 10.

25 *Ibid.*, p. 11.

26 *Ibid.*, p. 14.

27 *Ibid.*, p. 15.

28 James Duncan, *A Treatise on Slavery. In Which Is Shown Forth the Evil of Slaveholding Both from the Light of Nature and Divine Revelation* (Vevay, Indiana, 1824), pp. 17–18.

29 *Ibid.*, pp. 23–24.

30 *Ibid.*, p. 25.

31 *Ibid.*, pp. 25–26.

32 *Ibid.*, pp. 27–39.

33 *Ibid.*, p. 52.

34 *Ibid.*, pp. 72–74.

Chapter 16
Pulpit and Courtroom: An Anthology

1 David Martin, *Trial of Rev. Jacob Gruber, Minister in the Methodist Episcopal Church, at the March Term, 1819, in the Frederick County Court, for a Misdemeanor* (Fredericktown, 1819).

2 *Ibid.*, p. 33.

3 *Ibid.*

4 *Ibid.*, pp. 36–39.

5 *Ibid.*, pp. 40–43.

6 *Ibid.*, pp. 65–66.

7 *Ibid.*, p. 69.

8 *Ibid.*, p. 72.

9 *Ibid.*

10 *Ibid.*, pp. 77–78.

11 *Ibid.*, p. 84.

12 *Ibid.*, pp. 88–89.

13 *Ibid.*, p. 90.

14 *Ibid.*, pp. 100–101.

15 The quotation was taken from James Beattie, *Elements of Moral Science* (Edinburgh, 1793), pp. 155–223. Beattie was professor of moral philosophy and "logick" in Marischal College, Aberdeen. Those portions in brackets were omitted at the trial.

16 Josephus Wheaton, *The Equality of Mankind and the Evils of Slavery Illustrated. A Sermon Delivered on the Day of the Annual Fast, April 6, 1820* (Boston, 1820).

17 *Ibid.*, p. 4.

18 *Ibid.*, p. 5.

19 *Ibid.*, pp. 5–6.

20 *Ibid.*, pp. 6–7.

21 *Ibid.*, p. 7.

22 *Ibid.*, pp. 8–9.

23 *Ibid.*, pp. 9–10.

24 *Ibid.*, p. 11.

25 *Ibid.*, pp. 12–20.

26 *Ibid.*, p. 22.

Chapter 17
Impulses for Reform

1 Dwight L. Dumond, "The Mississippi: Valley of Decision," *The Mississippi Valley Historical Review*, XXXVI (June, 1949), pp. 3–26.

2 Edward Beecher, *Narrative of Riots at Alton: In Connection with the Death of Rev. Elijah P. Lovejoy* (Alton, 1838), p. 101.

3 J. L. Tracy to Weld, Nov. 24, 1831, in Gilbert H. Barnes and Dwight L. Dumond, *Letters of Theodore Dwight Weld, Angelina Grimké Weld, and Sarah Grimké, 1822–1844* (2 vols., New York, 1934), I, p. 57.

4 *A Statement of the Reasons Which Induced the Students of Lane Seminary to Dissolve Their Connection with That Institution* (Cincinnati, 1834), p. 3.

5 See Charles Grandison Finney, *Lectures on Revivals of Religion* (new edition; Oberlin, 1868); and *Lectures to Professing Christians. Delivered in the City of New York, in the Years 1836 and 1837* (New York, 1837).

6 Samuel Gosnell Green, *The Story of the Religious Tract Society for One Hundred Years* (London, 1899), p. 4.

7 *Ibid.*, p. 18.

8 Reverend Justin Edwards was corresponding secretary of the society. William Allen Hallock, *Light and Love: A Sketch of the Life of Reverend Justin Edwards, the Advocate of Temperance, Sabbath, and the Bible* (New York, 1855). See also Charles Ray Keller, *The Second Great Awakening in Connecticut* (New Haven, 1942), p. 120.

9 Elizabeth Twaddell, "The American Tract Society from 1814–1860," in *Church History*, XV (June, 1946), pp. 116–32.

10 *Second Annual Report of the American Tract Society, Instituted at New York, 1825, with Lists of Auxiliaries and Benefactors, the Publications of the Society, etc.* (New York, 1827), pp. 8–9; *Fourth Annual Report of the American Tract Society, Instituted at New York, 1825, Presented, May, 1829, with Lists of Auxiliaries and Benefactors, the Publications of the Society, etc.* (New York, 1829, pp. 11–15).

11 It published in German, Dutch, Choctaw, Chippewa, Hawaiian, Russian, Greek, Armenian, Arabic, Burmese, Siamese, Assamese, and Chinese. By 1851 the society had a standard library of twenty-four volumes. Volumes one to nine, literature of the Seventeenth Century; ten to twelve, literature of the Eighteenth Century; thirteen to sixteen, treatises on Christian Evidences; seventeen to twenty, Christian memoirs; twenty-one to twenty-four, D'Aubignes' *History of the Reformation*.

12 William Warren Sweet, *Religion in the Development of American Culture, 1765–1840* (New York, 1952), p. 187.

13 Henry B. Stanton to Birney, March 21, 1840, in Dwight L. Dumond, *Letters of James Gillespie Birney, 1831–1857* (2 vols., New York, 1938), I, pp. 541–42.

14 In addition to the Annual Reports of the Society, see C. H. Whipple, *The American Tract Society* (Boston, 1859); S. W. S. Dutton, "The American Tract Society," *The New Englander*, III, pp. 372–83; William L. Kingsley, "The American Tract Society," *The New Englander*, XVI, pp. 612–45; Lawrence Thompson, "The Printing and Publishing Activities of the American Tract Society from 1825–1850," in Bibliographical Society of America, *Papers*, XXXV (Second Quarter, 1941), pp. 81–114.

15 The monthly visitation system is described in *Fourth Annual Report of the American Tract Society*, p. 29.

16 For the duties of the agents, see *Twenty-Sixth Annual Report of the American Tract Society, Presented at New York, May 12, 1851* (New York, 1851), p. 35.

17 American Tract Society, *Toils and Triumphs of Union Missionary Colportage for Twenty-Five Years* (New York, n.d.), pp. 1–10. See also Works Progress Administration, *New Jersey Historical Survey, Colporteur Reports to the American Tract Society, 1841–1846* (Newark, 1940).

Chapter 18
Lane Seminary

1 See G. F. Wright, *Charles Grandison Finney* (Boston, 1893), pp. 140–41. 150–52; Gilbert H. Barnes and Dwight L. Dumond, *Letters of Theodore Dwight Weld, Angelina Grimké Weld, and Sarah Grimké, 1822–1844* (2 vols., New York, 1934), I, 243–44; and Finney to Weld, July 21, 1836, *ibid.*, I, 318–19.

2 *First Annual Report of the Society for Promoting Manual Labor in Literary Institutions, Including the Report of Their General Agent, Theodore D. Weld* (New York, 1833), pp. 1–10.

3 Beriah Green (1795–1874) studied Theology at Middlebury College, preached in Vermont and Maine, and became professor of sacred literature in Western Reserve College in 1830. In late 1832, he preached four sermons in the college chapel in which he took strong ground against slavery. They attracted so much attention that he became president of Oneida Institute and was honored by the presidency of the organizational meeting of the American Anti-Slavery Society. Oneida Institute closed in 1843 and Green became pastor of a local Congregational church organized on antislavery principles. His most important writings were: *Four Sermons, Preached in the Chapel of the Western Reserve College, on Lord's Day, November 18th and 25th, and December 2nd and 9th, 1832* (Cleveland, 1833), *The Chattel Principle the Abhorrence of Jesus Christ and the Apostles: or, No Refuge for American Slavery in the New Testament* (New York, 1839), and *Sketches of the Life and Writings of James Gillespie Birney* (Utica, 1844).

4 See Weld to Lewis Tappan, March 18, 1834, Gilbert H. Barnes and Dwight L. Dumond, *Letters of Theodore Dwight Weld, Angelina Grimké Weld and Sarah Grimké, 1822–1844*, I, pp. 132–35.

5 Gilbert H. Barnes, *The Antislavery Impulse, 1830–1844* (New York, 1933), pp. 70–73.

6 Huntington Lyman, in his speech at the opening of the Oberlin Semi-Centennial in 1883, said Weld spoke six evenings for a total of eighteen hours, but Henry B. Stanton said, in a letter to the *New York Evangelist* at the close of the discussion, that it was four evenings. Stanton was probably correct because Lyman's testimony was not given until after the lapse of half a cen-

tury. Weld was inclined to agree with Stanton, although his memory had failed him on this point. Barnes says Allan led off the debate, but evidence is otherwise.

7 W. G. Ballantine (ed.), *The Oberlin Jubilee, 1833–1883* (Oberlin, 1883), p. 62.

8 See Beecher's statement in *The Friend of Man*, September 15, 1836. Also Asa Mahan, *Autobiography, Intellectual, Moral and Spiritual* (London, 1882), p. 178.

9 The statement of the faculty is in *Fifth Annual Report of the Trustees of the Officers and Students* (Cincinnati, 1834). See also *A Statement of the Reasons which Induced the Students of Lane Seminary to Dissolve Their Connection with That Institution* (Cincinnati, 1834).

10 *A Statement of the Reasons Which Induced the Students of Lane Seminary to Dissolve Their Connection with That Institution* (Cincinnati, 1834).

11 *Ibid.*, pp. 5–9.

12 Oberlin's intimate connection with the antislavery movement gave it one of the three finest collections of antislavery literature. The others are the Samuel J. May Collection at Cornell University and the William Birney Collection at Johns Hopkins University. For the Oberlin Collection, see Julian S. Fowler (ed.), *A Classified Catalogue of the Collection of Antislavery Propaganda in the Oberlin College Library*. Oberlin College Library, *Bulletin*, II, No. 3.

13 Theodore D. Weld, Sereno W. Streeter, Edward Weed, Henry B. Stanton, Huntington Lyman, James A. Thome, John W. Alvord, Marius R. Robinson, George Whipple, William T. Allan.

It is little wonder that these men completely abolitionized Ohio. It was a remarkably fine group of lecturers.

14 See Gilbert H. Barnes and Dwight L. Dumond, *Letters of Theodore Dwight Weld, Angelina Grimké Weld, and Sarah Grimké, 1822–1844*, I, p. 123; *The Emancipator*, January 19, March 2, May 4, and July 29, 1837; *The Friend of Man*, February 1, and March 22, 1837.

15 N. D. Harris, *History of Negro Servitude in Illinois, and of the Slavery Agitation in That State, 1719–1864* (Chicago, 1904), pp. 139–42.

16 Various steps in Alvord's antislavery career may be traced in the *Emancipator* for January, 1836; *Report of the First Anniversary of the Ohio Anti-Slavery Society, Held Near Granville, on the Twenty-Seventh and Twenty-Eighth of April, 1836* (Cincinnati, 1836); Gilbert H. Barnes and Dwight L. Dumond, *Letters of Theodore Dwight Weld, Angelina Grimké Weld, and Sarah Grimké*, I, pp. 299–301, 327, 536, 695–97; C. K. Whipple, *The American Tract Society, Boston* (Boston, 1859); American Tract Society, *Fifty-Second Annual Report* (Boston, 1866), pp. 3–4.

17 The Ohio State Anti-Slavery Society, "Report on the Condition of the People of Color in the State of Ohio." Reprinted from the *Proceedings of the Ohio Anti-Slavery Convention, Held at Putnam, on the 22d, 23d, and 24th of April, 1835* (Putnam, 1835). This report was signed by A. Wattles, J. W. Alvord, S. Wells, H. Lyman, M. R. Robinson; but it was written by Wattles. Robinson had been with him from the beginning in Cincinnati. Alvord, Wells, and Lyman had assisted. See, also, Gilbert H. Barnes, *The Antislavery Impulse, 1830–1844*, pp. 68, 226.

18 Gilbert H. Barnes and Dwight L. Dumond, *Letters of Theodore D. Weld, Angelina Grimké Weld, and Sarah Grimké*, I, p. 182; *The Emancipator*, September 22, 1836.

19 There are many references to Wilson's work. Josiah Henson, *Truth Stranger Than Fiction* (Boston, 1858), pp. 167–71; William H. Siebert, *The Underground Railroad from Slavery to Freedom* (New York, 1898), p. 199; Carter G. Woodson, *The Education of the Negro Prior to 1861* (New York, 1915), p. 25; *Pennsylvania Freeman*, January 13, 1848; the *Emancipator*, February 22, 1837, October 5, 1837; Fred Landon, *The Work of the American Missionary Association Among the Negro Refugees in Canada West, 1848–1864* (Toronto, 1924), pp. 5–6. There are numerous letters of his in the *Journal of Negro History*, XII (April, 1927), pp. 248–52; XIV (July, 1929), pp. 347–49. There is also a considerable correspondence in the Miscellaneous Correspondence File of the Treasurer's Office, Oberlin College.

20 See Gilbert H. Barnes and Dwight L. Dumond, *Letters of Theodore D. Weld, Angelina Grimké Weld, and Sarah Grimké*, I, pp. 181, 256–59, 281–86; II, pp. 751–52, 822–23; *Emancipator*, April, 1836; *Pennsylvania Freeman*, December 10, 1846; J. H. Fairchild, *Oberlin: The Colony and the College, 1833–1883* (Oberlin, 1883), p. 290.

21 See *Dictionary of American Biography*, II, pp. 375–76.

Chapter 19
William Lloyd Garrison

1 Fred Landon, "The Diary of Benjamin Lundy Written during His Journey through Upper Canada—January, 1832," Ontario Historical Society, *Papers and Records*, XIX (1922), pp. 110–33; Thomas Earle, *The Life, Travels and Opinions of Benjamin Lundy, Including His Journeys to Texas and Mexico; with a Sketch of Contemporary Events, and a Notice of the Revolution in Hayti* (Philadelphia, 1847); Fred Landon, "Benjamin Lundy, Abolitionist," *Dalhousie Review*, July, 1927; George A. Lawrence, "Benjamin Lundy, a Pioneer of Freedom," Illinois State Historical Society, *Transactions*, XVIII (1913), pp. 36–51; Lundy Memorial Committee of the John Swaney School Alumni and Society of Friends, *A Memorial to Benjamin Lundy on the Occasion of the Centennial of His Death*, 1939.

2 She discussed her plan with Madison and Jefferson: (1) The federal government to provide land acreage for Negro co-operative farms, (2) two hundred slaves to be assigned to each and provided with food, clothing, and an education, (3) profits, after maintenance, to be used to purchase freedom of slaves and their families. Her experimental co-operative near Memphis graduated one group to Haiti at the end of five years, but opposition forced its abandonment in 1829.

3 Board of Managers [Appointed by the State] for Removing the Free People of Color, *Colonization of the Free Colored Population of Maryland, and of Such Slaves As May Hereafter Become Free. Statement of Facts, for the Use of Those Who Have Not Yet Reflected on This Important Subject* (Baltimore, 1832); and

News from Africa. A Collection of Facts, Relating to the Colony in Liberia, for the Information of the Free People of Color in Maryland (Baltimore, 1832). See also [William Lloyd Garrison], *The Maryland Scheme of Expatriation Examined by a Friend of Liberty* (Boston, 1834).

4 William Goodell, though denied a college education by poverty, was a man of great intellectual ability. He was a founder of the New York City Mercantile Library Association and editor of the *Genius of Temperance* in that city after 1830. He helped organize the American Antislavery Society in 1833, edited its official organ, the *Emancipator*, lectured for the society, and then took charge of the *Friend of Man*, official organ of the New York State Antislavery Society in 1836. Goodell was not a good lecturer, but a sound and exceedingly good writer. He was not a Garrisonian. He firmly adhered to the Constitution and the Union and belonged to the Birney Political Action group. His writings include (short titles) *The American Slave Code in Theory and Practice* (New York, 1853), *The Constitutional Duty of the Federal Government To Abolish American Slavery* (New York, 1855), *Slavery and Anti-Slavery* (New York, 1852), *Views of American Constitutional Law, in Its Bearing upon American Slavery* (Utica, 1844).

5 Wendell P. Garrison and Francis J. Garrison, *William Lloyd Garrison, 1805–1879: The Story of His Life, Told by His Children* (4 vols., New York, 1885–89), I, pp. 108–9.

6 *Ibid.*, pp. 127–37.

7 See William Lloyd Garrison, *Thoughts on African Colonization; or, An Impartial Exhibition of the Doctrines, Principles and Purposes of the American Colonization Society Together with the Resolutions, Addresses, and Remonstrances of the Free People of Color* (Boston, 1832). Also, Louis R. Mehlinger, "The Attitude of the Free Negro Toward African Colonization," *The Journal of Negro History*, I (July, 1916), pp. 276–301.

8 Thomas Earle, *The Life, Travels and Opinions of Benjamin Lundy, Including His Journeys to Texas and Mexico . . .* , p. 29.

9 [William Lloyd Garrison], *A Brief Sketch of the Trial of William Lloyd Garrison, for an Alleged Libel on Francis Todd, of Newburyport, Mass[achusetts]* (Boston, 1834), p. 7.

10 Samuel J. May (1797–1871), a Unitarian minister, was a graduate of Harvard College and Divinity School. He became interested in antislavery from reading John Rankin's *Letters* in 1820, and his interest was reinforced when Lundy spoke in his church at Brooklyn, Connecticut, on his second New England visit (1828). He was a great humanitarian, with interests as broad as those of Garrison, but he was of kind and gentle nature and in the end opposed to war. He was a member of the organizational meetings of the American Anti-Slavery Society and the New England Anti-Slavery Society. He was general agent of the latter organization for eighteen years and an agent of the American Anti-Slavery Society in 1834 and 1835. He was mobbed in Vermont and was rescued on one occasion by Whittier's sister. At Syracuse, New York, he was active in the underground railway. His collection of antislavery literature is in the Cornell University Library.

11 William Lloyd Garrison, *An Address Delivered Before the Free People of Color, in Philadelphia, New York, and Other Cities, During the Month of June, 1831* (third edition; Boston, 1831), pp. 21–22.

12 *Freedom's Journal*, March 16, 1827. Negroes were admonished to educate their children, read good literature, practice economy, strive for full civil rights, and vote whenever possible.

13 Allen Johnson and Dumas Malone (eds.), *Dictionary of American Biography* (22 vols., New York, 1928–44), I, pp. 204–5. Allen said in a letter, published in *Freedom's Journal*, November 2, 1827: "This land which we have watered with our *tears* and our *blood* is now our *mother country* and we are well satisfied to stay where wisdom abounds, and the gospel is free."

14 *Ibid.*, VI, pp. 536–37.

15 Charles H. Wesley, *Richard Allen: Apostle of Freedom* (Washington, 1935), pp. 160–61. Herbert Aptheker (ed.), *A Documentary History of the Negro People in the United States* (New York, 1951), p. 71.

16 For the Philadelphia meeting, August 10, 1817, see James Forten and Russell Perrott, "An Address to the Humane and Benevolent Inhabitants of the City and County of Philadelphia," in Carter G. Woodson, *Negro Orators and Their Orations* (Washington, D. C., 1925), pp. 51–55; see also Samuel E. Cornish, *The Colonization Scheme Considered, in Its Rejection by the Colored People—In Its Tendency To Uphold Caste—In Its Unfitness for Christianizing and Civilizing the Aborigines of Africa, and for Putting a Stop To the African Slave Trade; in a Letter to the Hon. Theodore Frelinghuysen and the Hon. Benjamin F. Butler* (Newark, 1840).

17 "Public Warning to Cincinnati Negroes and Commentary on Their Reaction," *Journal of Negro History*, VIII (July, 1923), pp. 331–32.

18 John W. Cromwell, *The Negro in American History; Men and Women Eminent in the Evolution of the American of African Descent* (Washington, D. C., 1914), pp. 28–29.

19 "Constitution of the Society of Free Persons of Colour . . . in the United States," in Herbert Aptheker (ed.), *A Documentary History of the Negro People in the United States* (New York, 1951), pp. 104–7.

20 *Freedom's Journal*, March 16, 1827.

21 *Ibid.*, September 24, 1831.

22 Lewis Tappan, *The Life of Arthur Tappan* (New York, 1871), pp. 146–50. See also [Simeon S. Jocelyn], *College for Colored Youth. An Account of the New Haven City Meeting and Resolutions, with Recommendations of the College, and Strictures upon the Doings of New Haven* (New York, 1831).

23 The 1831 convention had said: "If we must be sacrificed to their philanthropy, we would rather die at home. Many of our fathers, and some of us, have fought and bled for liberty, independence and peace which you now enjoy; and, surely, it would be ungenerous and unfeeling in you to deny us a humble and quiet grave in that country which gave us birth." William Lloyd Garrison, *Thoughts on African Colonization; or, An Impartial Exhibition of the Doctrines, Principles, and Purposes of the American Colonization Society Together with the Resolutions, Addresses and Remon-*

strances of the Free People of Color (Boston, 1832), part 2, p. 71.

24 "Minutes and Proceedings of the Third Annual Convention of the Free Persons of Color," in Herbert Aptheker (ed.), *A Documentary History of the Negro People in the United States* (New York, 1951), pp. 141–42.

25 *First Annual Report of the American Anti-Slavery Society; with the Speeches Delivered at the Anniversary Meeting, Held in Chatham Street Chapel, in the City of New York, on the Sixth of May, 1834, and by Adjournment on the Eighth, in the Rev. Dr. Lansing's Church; and the Minutes of the Meetings of the Society for Business* (New York, 1834), p. 47.

26 The *Liberator*, August 1, 1835; William C. Nell, *The Colored Patriots of the American Revolution, with an Additional Survey of the Condition and Prospects of Colored Americans* (Boston, 1855), pp. 345–55.

27 William L. Garrison, Oliver Johnson, Robert B. Hall, Arnold Buffum, William J. Snelling, John E. Fuller, Moses Thacher, Joshua Coffin, Stillman B. Newcomb, Benjamin E. Bacon, Isaac Knapp, Henry K. Stockton.

28 William Lloyd Garrison, *Thoughts on African Colonization. . . .*

Chapter 20
The American Anti-Slavery Society

1 Gilbert H. Barnes, *The Antislavery Impulse* (New York, 1933), p. 35.

2 George Bourne, *The Book and Slavery Irreconcilable* (Philadelphia, 1816), p. 3. Other antislavery books include, principally, *Picture of Slavery in the United States of America* (Middletown, Conn., 1834), *Slavery Illustrated in Its Effects upon Woman and Domestic Society* (Boston, 1837), and *A Condensed Anti-Slavery Bible Argument; by a Citizen of Virginia* (New York, 1845).

3 Leavitt was trained in the law as well as divinity. He was a Congregationalist, a man of definite convictions, and, in antislavery circles, an exponent of direct political action.

4 Details of Weld's career may be found in Gilbert H. Barnes and Dwight L. Dumond (eds.), *Letters of Theodore Dwight Weld, Angelina Grimké Weld, and Sarah Grimké, 1822–1844* (2 vols., New York, 1934); Gilbert H. Barnes, *The Antislavery Impulse* (New York, 1933); and Benjamin P. Thomas, *Theodore Weld, Crusader for Freedom* (New Brunswick, 1950).

5 Details of Birney's career may be found in Dwight L. Dumond (ed.), *Letters of James G. Birney, 1831–1857* (2 vols., New York, 1938); Betty Fladeland, *James Gillespie Birney: Slaveholder to Abolitionist* (Ithaca, 1955).

6 Wright's best writing was done as editor of the *Quarterly Anti-Slavery Magazine, 1835–1837*. He was strongly in favor of direct political action, but had no official position after the schism in 1839. He later turned his attention to life insurance, in which field his reputation largely lies.

7 *First Annual Report of the American Anti-Slavery Society; with the Speeches Delivered at the Anniversary*

Meeting . . . and the Minutes of the Meetings of the Society for Business (New York, 1834), pp. 48–49.

8 James Gillespie Birney, *Letter on Colonization, Addressed to the Rev. Thornton J. Mills, Corresponding Secretary of the Kentucky Colonization Society* (New York, 1834); William Jay, *An Inquiry into the Character and Tendency of the American Colonization and American Anti-Slavery Societies* (New York, 1835). The latter work, of more than two hundred pages, went through ten editions before 1840.

9 *Minutes of the Twenty-First Biennial American Convention for Promoting the Abolition of Slavery and Improving the Condition of the African Race, Convened at the City of Washington, December 8, A.D. 1829* (Philadelphia, 1829).

10 The several documents pertaining to the organization of the society are as follows: *The Declaration of Sentiments and Constitution of the American Anti-Slavery Society, Adopted at the Formation of Said Society, in Philadelphia, on the 4th Day of December, 1833* (Penny Tract, No. 1) (New York, 1833); *The Constitution of the American Anti-Slavery Society; with the Declaration of the National Anti-Slavery Convention at Philadelphia, December, 1833, and the Address to the Public, Issued by the Executive Committee of the Society, in September, 1835* (New York, 1838); *First Annual Report of the American Anti-Slavery Society. . . .*

11 Elizur Wright to Weld, December 31, 1833, Gilbert H. Barnes and Dwight L. Dumond (eds.), *Letters of Theodore Dwight Weld, Angelina Grimké Weld, and Sarah Grimké, 1822–1844*, I, 121.

12 *Ibid.*

13 American Anti-Slavery Society, *Commission to Theodore D. Weld, ibid.*, I, p. 124.

14 Particular Instructions, *ibid.*, I, pp. 125–28.

15 Thomas Clarkson, *Thoughts on the Necessity of Improving the Condition of the Slaves in the British Colonies, with a View to Their Ultimate Emancipation; and on the Practicability, the Safety, and the Advantages of the Latter Measure* (London, 1833); Charles Stuart, *The West India Question . . . An Outline for Immediate Emancipation; and Remarks on Compensation* (London, 1832); Lydia Maria Child, *An Appeal in Favor of That Class of Americans Called Africans* (Boston, 1833); George M. Stroud, *A Sketch of the Laws Relating to Slavery in the Several States of the United States of America* (Philadelphia, 1827); John D. Paxton, *Letters on Slavery; Addressed to the Cumberland Congregation, Virginia* (Lexington, Ky., 1833); John Rankin, *Letters on American Slavery, Addressed to Mr. Thomas Rankin, Merchant at Middlebrook, Augusta County, Virginia* (Boston, 1833); David Lee Child, *The Despotism of Freedom, or the Tyranny and Cruelty of American Republican Slave-Masters, Shown To Be the Worst in the World* (Boston, 1833); William Lloyd Garrison, *Thoughts on African Colonization . . . Together with the Resolutions, Addresses and Remonstrances of the Free People of Color* (Boston, 1832).

16 Thompson came to the United States at Garrison's insistence prepared to remain three years. He should not have come. See Gilbert H. Barnes, *The Antislavery Impulse*, p. 225.

17 See *First Annual Report of the American Anti-Slavery Society*, p. 41.

18 See *Friend of Man*, October 13, 1836; Massena Goodrich, *Historical Sketch of the Town of Pawtucket* (Pawtucket, 1876), p. 178.

19 See Elizur Wright to Amos Phelps, March 3, 1834; and Charles Dennison to Elizur Wright, February 14, 1838, in Elizur Wright Papers, Library of Congress.

Chapter 21
Theodore Weld: The Agency System

1 Weld to Elizur Wright, March 2, 1835, Gilbert H. Barnes and Dwight L. Dumond (eds.), *Letters of Theodore Dwight Weld, Angelina Grimké Weld, and Sarah Grimké, 1822–1844* (2 vols., New York, 1934), I, pp. 205–8.

2 Weld to Elizur Wright, June 6, 1835, *Emancipator*, June 15, 1835; Gilbert H. Barnes and Dwight L. Dumond (eds.), *Letters of Theodore Dwight Weld, Angelina Grimké Weld, and Sarah Grimké, 1822–1844*, I, p. 224.

3 Weld wrote to Lewis Tappan, December 22, 1835, that Lyman would go to western New York. Said Weld: "He resided there many years, was a high military officer, postmaster, temperance lecturer, a leader in politics and universally known and respected throughout that region. As he had a large amount of *Capital in Character* invested *there* we thought he had better *go there* and trade on it for the cause." *Ibid.*, I, pp. 247–49.

4 Weld to Lewis Tappan, November 17, 1835, *ibid.*, I, pp. 242–45.

5 Sereno Streeter decided to preach, but later resumed work as an agent. See his letter to Weld, August 9, 1836, *ibid.*, I, pp. 325–26.

6 Foote had organized the first antislavery society in New York, at Oneida Institute, in January, 1833. See also, report of his lecture tour in *The Friend of Man*, February 8, 1837.

7 See the *Emancipator*, October 20, 1836; the *Philanthropist*, December 2, 1836; and Gilbert H. Barnes and Dwight L. Dumond (eds.), *Letters of Theodore Dwight Weld, Angelina Grimké Weld, and Sarah Grimké, 1822–1884*, I, p. 80.

8 *Ibid.*, I, p. 51.

9 *The Emancipator*, April 27, 1837; Jonathan Blanchard, *A Debate on Slavery; Held in the City of Cincinnati, on the First, Second, Third, and Sixth Days of October, 1845, upon the Question: Is Slavery in Itself Sinful, and the Relation Between Master and Slave, a Sinful Relation? Affirmative: Rev. J. Blanchard. Negative: N. L. Rice* (Cincinnati, 1846).

10 H. B. Stanton and Theodore Weld to Lewis Tappan, August 15, 1836, Gilbert H. Barnes and Dwight L. Dumond (eds.), *Letters of Theodore Dwight Weld, Angelina Grimké Weld, and Sarah Grimké, 1822–1844*, I, pp. 330–33; Samuel J. May, *Some Recollections of the Anti-Slavery Conflict* (Boston, 1869), p. 66; New York Tribune, March 20, 1871.

11 *The Emancipator*, April 27, 1827; *The Friend of Man*, March 15, 1837.

12 For Phillips' appointment, see Elizur Wright to Amos Phelps, September 2, 1837, Elizur Wright Papers.

13 See Henry B. Stanton and Theodore Weld to Lewis Tappan, August 15, 1836, Gilbert H. Barnes and Dwight L. Dumond (eds.), *Letters of Theodore Dwight Weld, Angelina Grimké Weld, and Sarah Grimké, 1822–1844*, I, pp. 330–33; *The Emancipator*, October 26, 1836, and January 12, 1837.

14 *The Friend of Man*, February 8, 1837, and March 29, 1837; Theophilus Packard, *A History of the Churches and Ministers, and of Franklin Association in Franklin County, Massachusetts* (Boston, 1854), p. 21.

15 See Henry Wyles Cushman, *A Historical and Biographical Genealogy of the Cushmans* (Boston, 1855), pp. 627–32; *The Friend of Man*, February 1, 1837, and May 10, 1837. The account of the Nashville brutality is given in Amos Dresser, *The Narrative of Amos Dresser, with Stone's Letters from Natchez,—an Obituary Notice of the Writer, and Two Letters from Tallahassee, Relating to the Treatment of Slaves* (New York, 1836); and in Amos Dresser, *Narrative of the Arrest, Lynch Law Trial, and Scourging of Amos Dresser at Nashville, Tennessee, August, 1835* (Oberlin, 1849).

16 See *American Anti-Slavery Society, Annual Report . . . by the Executive Committee, for the Year Ending May 1, 1859* (New York, 1860), pp. 135–36; Elizur Wright to Amos Phelps, September 12, 1837, Elizur Wright Papers; the *Liberator*, May 28, June 4, and June 18, 1858.

17 See Francis J. LeMoyne to Elizur Wright, October 17, 1837, Elizur Wright Papers; Myron Holley to Birney, January 1, 1840; Dwight L. Dumond (ed.), *Letters of James Gillespie Birney, 1831–1857* (2 vols., New York, 1938), I, pp. 518–19; Francis J. LeMoyne to Birney, December 10, 1839, *ibid.*, I, pp. 511–14; and Francis J. LeMoyne to Birney, March 24, 1840, *ibid.*, I, pp. 543–45.

18 Lucius C. Matlack, *The History of American Slavery and Methodism from 1780 to 1849* (New York, 1849), p. 162; *The Friend of Man*, January 14, 1837; Elizur Wright to Weld, April 21, 1836, Gilbert H. Barnes and Dwight L. Dumond (eds.), *Letters of Theodore Dwight Weld, Angelina Grimké Weld, and Sarah Grimké, 1822–1844*, I, 291–93; Elizur Wright to Weld, August 18, 1836, *ibid.*, I, 333–34.

19 *Second Annual Report of the American Anti-Slavery Society; with the Speeches Delivered at the Anniversary Meeting, Held in the City of New York, on the 12th May, 1835, and the Minutes of the Meetings of the Society for Business* (New York, 1835), p. 47; William Goodell, *Slavery and Anti-Slavery; A History of the Great Struggle in Both Hemispheres, with a View of the Slavery Question in the United States* (third edition, New York, 1855), p. 439; Lewis Tappan to Theodore Weld, March 10, 1836, Gilbert H. Barnes and Dwight L. Dumond (eds.), *Letters of Theodore Dwight Weld, Angelina Grimké Weld, and Sarah Grimké, 1822–1844*, I, pp. 275–77; *The Friend of Man*, February 1, 1837; *The Herald of Freedom*, September 17, 1836. See also George Storrs, *Mob, under Pretense of Law; or, the Arrest and Trial of Rev. George Storrs at Northfield, N.H., with the Circumstances Connected with That Affair and Remarks Thereon* (Concord, 1835).

20 Franklin P. Rice, *Reminiscences of the Reverend George Allen of Worcester with a Biographical Sketch and Notes* (Worcester, 1883), pp. 11–21; *The Friend of Man*, January 19, 1837; *The Emancipator*, May 26, 1836.

21 *The Friend of Man*, February 1, 1837; May 10, 1837; March 21, 1838.

22 Gilbert H. Barnes and Dwight L. Dumond (eds.), *Letters of Theodore Dwight Weld, Angelina Grimké Weld, and Sarah Grimké, 1822–1844*, I, p. 280; *The Friend of Man*, March 22, 1837.

23 Records of the Graduate School of Theology, Oberlin College.

24 A. P. Putnam (ed.), *Old Anti-Slavery Days* (Danvers, 1893), p. 14; *Friend of Man*, October 6, 1836, May 10, 1837.

25 James A. Thome to Weld, April 17, 1838, Gilbert H. Barnes and Dwight L. Dumond (eds.), *Letters of Theodore Dwight Weld, Angelina Grimké Weld, and Sarah Grimké, 1822–1844*, II, pp. 642–44; James A. Thome and J. Horace Kimball, *Emancipation in the West Indies. A Six Months Tour in Antigua, Barbadoes, and Jamaica, in the Year 1837* (New York, 1838).

26 *The Friend of Man*, February 1, 1837.

27 *Fourth Annual Report of the Board of Managers of the Massachusetts Anti-Slavery Society, with Some Account of the Annual Meeting, January 20, 1836* (Boston, 1836). Reports for 1833, 1834, and 1835 were under the name New England Anti-Slavery Society.

28 See *The True History of the Late Division in the Anti-Slavery Societies, Being Part of the Second Annual Report of the Executive Committee of the Massachusetts Abolition Society* (Boston, 1841); and *Formation of the Massachusetts Abolition Society* [Boston, 1839].

29 *The Report and Proceedings of the First Annual Meeting of the Providence Anti-Slavery Society, with a Brief Exposition of the Principles and Purposes of the Abolitionists* (Providence, 1833); *Proceedings of the Rhode Island Anti-Slavery Convention, Held in Providence, on the 2d, 3d and 4th of February, 1836* (Providence, 1836). The latter contains a "Declaration of Principles of the Rhode Island Anti-Slavery Society." It was in part almost identical with the statement of the Lane Seminary students, showing the influence of Stanton.

30 *First Annual Report of the Vermont Anti-Slavery Society, Presented at Middlebury, February 18, 1835* (Montpelier, 1835); *Proceedings of the New Hampshire Anti-Slavery Convention, Held in Concord, on the 11th & 12th of November, 1834* (Concord, 1834).

31 *Proceedings of the Ohio Anti-Slavery Convention, Held at Putnam on the Twenty-Second, Twenty-third, and Twenty-fourth of April, 1835* (Putnam, 1835).

32 *Address of the New York City Anti-Slavery Society to the People of the City of New York* (New York, 1833); *Proceedings of the New York Anti-Slavery Convention, Held at Utica, October 21, and New York Anti-Slavery State Society, Held at Peterboro, October 22, 1835* (Utica, 1835). See also *Preamble and Constitution of the New York Young Men's Anti-Slavery Society, Formed May 2, 1834* (New York, 1834).

33 *Proceedings of the Pennsylvania Convention Assembled To Organize a State Anti-Slavery Society, at Harrisburg, on the 31st of January and 1st, 2d, and 3d of February, 1837* (Philadelphia, 1837).

34 *Proceedings of the Anti-Slavery Convention of American Women Held in the City of New York, May 9th, 10th, 11th, and 12th, 1837* (New York, 1837).

35 *Report of the Proceedings of the Anti-Slavery State Convention, Held in Ann Arbor, Michigan, the Tenth and Eleventh of November, 1836* (Detroit, 1836); *Proceedings of the Illinois Anti-Slavery Convention Held at Upper Alton on the Twenty-Sixth, Twenty-Seventh, and Twenty-Eighth of October, 1837* (Alton, 1838); *Proceedings of the Indiana Convention Assembled To Organize a State Anti-Slavery Society, Held in Milton, Wayne Co., Sept. 12, 1838* (Cincinnati, 1838).

36 These were not always financed by the state society.

37 Elizur Wright's figures, given in the annual reports of the society, are only approximations.

Chapter 22
Angelina Grimké—Women's Rights

1 Catherine H. Birney, *Sarah and Angelina Grimké, the First American Women Advocates of Abolition and Woman's Rights* (Boston, 1885), pp. 156–57.

2 *The Works of Frederick Grimké* (2 vols., Columbus, 1871). This was, in part, a severe criticism of antislavery doctrine. Frederick was no reformer.

3 Catherine H. Birney, *Sarah and Angelina Grimké, the First American Women Advocates of Abolition and Woman's Rights*, pp. 85, 89–90.

4 September 19, 1835. This letter was published also as a broadside in Philadelphia, August 30, 1935, under the title *Slavery and the Boston Riot*.

5 A[ngelina] E. Grimké, *Appeal to the Christian Women of the South* (New York, 1836), reprinted in England with an introduction by George Thompson as *Slavery in America* (Edinburgh, 1837); Sarah Moore Grimké, *An Epistle to the Clergy of the Southern States* (New York, 1836).

6 Catherine H. Birney, *Sarah and Angelina Grimké, the First American Women Advocates of Abolition and Woman's Rights*, pp. 149–50. See Elizabeth Ladd, *Some Account of Lucy Cardwell, a Woman of Color Who Departed This Life on the 25th of the 3rd Month, 1824. Age 39 yrs.* (Philadelphia, 1824).

7 A[ngelina] E. Grimké, *Appeal to the Christian Women of the South*, p. 15.

8 *Ibid.*, p. 16.

9 *Ibid.*, p. 25.

10 *Ibid.*, p. 30.

11 Catherine E. Beecher, *An Essay on Slavery and Abolitionism with Reference to the Duty of American Females* (Philadelphia, 1837).

12 A[ngelina] E. Grimké, *Letters to Catherine E. Beecher, in Reply to an Essay on Slavery and Abolitionism, Addressed to A. E. Grimké* (Boston, 1838).

13 *Ibid.*, p. 4.

14 *Ibid.*, p. 7.

15 *Ibid.*, p. 8.

16 *Ibid.*, p. 9.

17 *Ibid.*, p. 10.

18 *Ibid.*, p. 12.
19 *Ibid.*, p. 14.
20 *Ibid.*, pp. 35–36.
21 *Ibid.*, p. 36.
22 See Catherine H. Birney, *Sarah and Angelina Grimké, the First American Women Advocates of Abolition and Woman's Rights*, pp. 157–95. There was later some confusion about this appointment. See Angelina Grimké to Weld, August 27, 1837, Gilbert H. Barnes and Dwight L. Dumond (eds.), *Letters of Theodore Dwight Weld, Angelina Grimké Weld, and Sarah Grimké, 1822–1844*, I, p. 441; and Weld to Sarah and Angelina Grimké, September 1, 1837, *ibid.*, pp. 442–45.

Chapter 23
James Gillespie Birney

1 The Birney Papers are in the William L. Clements Library, and those pertinent to his public career are in print: Dwight L. Dumond (ed.), *Letters of James Gillespie Birney, 1831–1857* (2 vols., New York, 1938). There is an excellent, short biography: Betty L. Fladeland, *James Gillespie Birney: Slaveholder to Abolitionist* (Ithaca, 1955).
2 David Rice, *Slavery Inconsistent with Justice and Good Policy; Proved by a Speech Delivered in the Convention at Danville, Kentucky* (Philadelphia, 1792).
3 Theodore Weld to James G. Birney, July 24, 1832, in Dwight L. Dumond (ed.), *Letters of James Gillespie Birney, 1831–1857*, I, pp. 12–13; and Weld to Birney, September 27, 1832, *ibid.*, I, pp. 26–29.
4 James G. Birney, Memoranda of Donations, Collections, Subscriptions, etc., for the American Colonization Society in Tennessee, Alabama, Mississippi, Louisiana, and Arkansas, Commencing September 15, 1832. Permanent agent for the Fifth District.
5 Manuscript lecture notes, and series of fifteen articles on colonization published in Huntsville *Democrat* during 1833, May 16 to August 15.
6 The above quotations are from the unpublished manuscript "To the Public, Colonization of the Free Colored People. No. 15." Opposition was so strong that this was never published. Another No. 15 was written in place of it.
7 "Constitution and Address of the Kentucky Society for the Gradual Relief of the State from Slavery," *Olive Branch–Extra*, December 24, 1833.
8 *Ibid.*
9 Elizabeth Heyrich, *Immediate, Not Gradual Abolition; or, An Inquiry into the Shortest, Safest, and Most Effectual Means of Getting Rid of West Indian Slavery* (Philadelphia, 1824).
10 Ralph R. Gurley to James G. Birney, December 17, 1833, Dwight L. Dumond (ed.), *Letters of James Gillespie Birney, 1831–1857*, I, pp. 110–11.
11 James G. Birney, *Letter on Colonization Addressed to the Rev. Thornton J. Mills, Corresponding Secretary of the Kentucky Colonization Society* (New York, 1834).
12 James G. Birney to Gerrit Smith, November 14, 1834, Dwight L. Dumond (ed.), *Letters of James Gillespie Birney, 1831–1857*, I, pp. 147–52.

13 James G. Birney, *Mr. Birney's Letter to the Churches; to the Ministers and Elders of the Presbyterian Church in Kentucky* (New York, 1834).
14 See Dwight L. Dumond (ed.), *Letters of James Gillespie Birney, 1831–1857*, I, p. 135.
15 Theodore D. Weld to Birney, October 20, 1834, *ibid.*, I, pp. 145–47; Elizur Wright to Weld, August 14, 1834, Gilbert H. Barnes and Dwight L. Dumond (eds.), *Letters of Theodore Dwight Weld, Angelina Grimké Weld, and Sarah Grimké, 1822–1844* (2 vols., New York, 1934), I, pp. 166–67.
16 *Proceedings of the Kentucky Anti-Slavery Society, Auxiliary to the American Anti-Slavery Society at Its First Meeting in Danville, Ky., March 19th, 1835* (Danville, 1835).
17 *Proceedings of the Ohio Anti-Slavery Convention, Held at Putnam on the Twenty-Second, Twenty-Third, and Twenty-Fourth of April, 1835* (Putnam, 1835); *Second Annual Report of the American Anti-Slavery Society, with the Speeches Delivered at the Anniversary Meeting, Held in the City of New York, on the 12th May, 1835* (New York, 1835).
18 *Ibid.*, p. 76.
19 Birney's powerful speech at the New York meeting was published in *ibid.*, pp. 3–11.
20 F. T. Taylor and others to Birney, July 12, 1835, Dwight L. Dumond (ed.), *Letters of James Gillespie Birney, 1831–1857*, I, pp. 197–200.
21 Birney to F. T. Taylor and others, July 22, 1835, *ibid.*, I, pp. 204–10.
22 Lexington *Intelligencer*, August 1, 1833.
23 Theodore D. Weld and H. C. Howells to Birney, August 4, 1835, Dwight L. Dumond (ed.), *Letters of James Gillespie Birney, 1831–1857*, I, pp. 227–30.
24 See, Birney to the Patrons of the *Philanthropist* [August, 1835], *ibid.*, I, pp. 232–35.

Chapter 24
Civil Rights

1 James G. Birney to Gerrit Smith, September 13, 1835, Dwight L. Dumond (ed.), *Letters of James Gillespie Birney, 1831–1857* (2 vols., New York, 1938), I, pp. 241–44.
2 Various interpretations of prejudice may be found as follows: Monroe N. Work, "The Life of Charles B. Ray," *Journal of Negro History*, IV, pp. 361–72; William Ellery Channing, *Remarks on the Slavery Question in a Letter to Jonathan Phillips* (Boston, 1839), p. 47; American Anti-Slavery Society, *Caste. Miniature Anti-Slavery Tract, No. 2* (New York, 1839).
3 *First Annual Report of the American Anti-Slavery Society; With the Speeches Delivered at the Anniversary Meeting . . . and the Minutes of the Meetings of the Society for Business* (New York, 1835), p. 24.
4 Theodore D. Weld to Angelina G. Weld, January 15, 1842, Gilbert H. Barnes and Dwight L. Dumond (eds.), *Letters of Theodore Dwight Weld, Angelina Grimké Weld, and Sarah Grimké, 1822–1844* (2 vols., New York, 1834), II, pp. 891–94.
5 Amos Dresser, *Narrative of the Arrest, Lynch Law Trial,*

and *Scourging of Amos Dresser at Nashville, Tennessee, August 1835* (Oberlin, 1849).

6 *Anti-Slavery Record* (January, 1835–December, 1837), I, pp. 404–5.

7 Speaking of the reward for Tappan, William Leggett said in the New York *Post,* August 26, 1835: "Has the violence of the South, its arrogant pretensious and menacing tone so overcrowded our spirits, that we would lamely submit to see our citizens snatched from the sanctuary of their homes, and carried off by midnight ruffians, to be burned at a stake, gibbeted on a tree, or butchered in some public place, without the slightest form of trial, and without even the allegation of crime?"

8 Inclosures in Massachusetts *House Report,* January 16, 1836.

9 See Amos Kendall to J. D. Townes, Chairman of Committee, Petersburg, Virginia, August 20, 1835, *Niles Weekly Register,* XLIX (Sept. 5, 1835), p. 7; and Amos Kendall to Samuel Gouverneur, postmaster of New York City Office, August 22, 1835, *ibid.,* pp. 8–9.

10 New York *Evening Post,* August 8, 1835, quoted in Theodore Sedgwick (ed.), *A Collection of the Political Writings of William Leggett* (2 vols., New York, 1840), I, pp. 10–11.

11 *Congressional Globe,* 24 Cong., 1 Sess., p. 481.

12 *Niles Register,* August 6, 1836.

13 See Amos Kendall to Samuel L. Gouverneur of New York, August 22, 1835, *Niles Register,* September 5, 1835.

14 See "Report of the Postmaster General," *House Documents,* 24 Cong., 1 Sess. (1835–36), I, Doc. No. 2, pp. 387–89.

15 *Congressional Globe,* 25 Cong., 2 Sess., p. 55.

16 Governor George Wolf's message, December 2, 1835, *Journal of the Senate of the Commonwealth of Pennsylvania Which Commenced in Harrisburg on the First Day of December, 1835,* I, p. 24.

17 A copy of the indictment by the circuit court of Tuscaloosa County and of Governor Gayle's demand upon Governor Marcy are to be found in *Remarks of Henry B. Stanton in Representatives Hall, on the 23d and 24th of February, 1837, before the Committee of the House of Representatives of Massachusetts, to Whom Was Referred Sundry Memorials on the Subject of Slavery* (Boston, 1837), pp. 40–41.

18 This was quoted by the grand jury and by the governor which gave it wide publicity in Alabama, and was re-quoted by Davis in the United States Senate in his speech supporting the post-office inquisition bill.

19 *Documents of the Senate of the State of New York, Fifty-ninth Session, 1836,* I, p. 37.

20 William Goodell, *A Full Statement of the Reasons Which Were in Part Offered to the Committee of the Legislature of Massachusetts, on the Fourth and Eighth of March, Showing Why There Should Be No Penal Laws Enacted, and No Condemnatory Resolutions Passed by the Legislature Respecting Abolitionists and Anti-Slavery Societies* (Boston, 1836), p. 5.

21 *Ibid.,* p. 7.

22 *Ibid.,* p. 10.

23 *Ibid.,* pp. 10–11.

24 *Ibid.,* pp. 17–18.

Chapter 25
The Prudence Crandall Case

1 Elizabeth Yates, *Prudence Crandall, Woman of Courage* (New York, 1955) is a charmingly written and wholly accurate account of that young lady's experience at Canterbury. See also [Chauncey F. Cleveland], *Report of the Arguments of Counsel in the Case of Prudence Crandall Pltf. in Error vs. State of Connecticut, before the Supreme Court of Errors, at Their Session at Brooklyn, July Term, 1834* (Boston 1834); and *Report of the Trial of Miss Prudence Crandall Before the County Court for Windham County, August Term, 1833, on an Information Charging Her with Teaching Colored Persons not Inhabitants of This State* (Brooklyn, 1833).

2 Girls named in the trial included M. E. Carter, Sarah Hammond, Ann Elizabeth Hammond, C. A. Weldon, Emila Willson, Eliza Weldon, C. G. Marshal, Maria Robinson, Elizabeth Henly, Theodosia DeGasse, and Ann Peterson. Samuel J. May and Arnold Buffum were refused permission to speak at the Canterbury town meeting. May was Unitarian minister at Brooklyn, Connecticut.

3 A brilliant critique of Daggett's charge to the jury was published by the eminent Judge William Jay, son of the first chief justice of the United States, in *Miscellaneous Writings on Slavery* (Boston, 1853), pp. 36–51. Either Daggett had never read the Congressional debates on Missouri, or he was lacking in comprehension.

4 Weld to Lewis Tappan, June 8, 1837, Gilbert H. Barnes and Dwight L. Dumond (eds.), *Letters of Theodore Dwight Weld, Angelina Grimké Weld, and Sarah Grimké, 1822–1844* (2 vols., New York, 1934), I, pp. 397–400.

5 The report continued: "The man of color may exercise the elective franchise, to the fullest extent, in the choice of his rulers. If possessing intelligence and integrity to secure the confidence of his fellow citizens, no restraint, save that of prejudice, prevents him from seeking the highest honors and holding the most elevated offices of church or state. No written rule excludes him from filling the seat of the chief magistrate, reclining on the cushioned dias of the senator, occupying the bench of the judiciary, or holding any post of civic or municipal distinction. His property is sacred; his house is walled about with the legal ramparts of the castled home; his offspring enjoy the common benefits of education with the children of other races. If he be deprived of any of the privileges of freedom, of any excitements of ambition, of any of the enjoyments of social happiness, it is by a power beyond that of the laws." Commonwealth of Massachusetts, *House Report No. 28, 1839* (February 25, 1839), p. 6.

6 [Samuel Webb], *History of Pennsylvania Hall, Which Was Destroyed by a Mob on the 17th of May, 1838* (Philadelphia, 1838).

7 *Annals of Congress,* 16 Cong., 1 Sess., I, pp. 1203–4.

8 As quoted in *Pennsylvania Freeman,* August 16, 1849.

9 *Andrew T.[hompson] Judson's Remarks to the Jury on the Trial of the Case: State v. P. Crandall, Superior Court, October Term, 1833, Windham County Court* (Hartford, 1833), pp. 3–4.

10 *Ibid.*, pp. 21–22.

11 *Ibid.*, p. 12.

12 *Report of the Trial of Miss Prudence Crandall, Before the County Court for Windham County* . . . , p. 8.

13 *Report of the Argument of Counsel, in the Case of Prudence Crandall, Pltf. in Error vs. State of Connecticut, Before the Supreme Court of Errors, at Their Session at Brooklyn, July Term, 1834* (Boston, 1834), pp. 24–25.

14 *Ibid.*

15 *Ibid.*, p. 11.

16 *Ibid.*, p. 12.

17 New York *Evening Post*, September 9, 1835, in Theodore Sedgwick, *A Collection of the Political Writings of William Leggett* (2 vols., New York, 1840), pp. 65–66.

Chapter 26
Lynch Law

1 Theodore Sedgwick, *A Collection of the Political Writings of William Leggett* (2 vols., New York, 1840), I, pp. 33–34.

2 *Boston Recorder*, October 9, 1833.

3 See William Jay, *Miscellaneous Writings on Slavery* (Boston, 1853), p. 116.

4 Lewis Tappan to Theodore Weld, July 10, 1834, Gilbert H. Barnes and Dwight L. Dumond (eds.), *Letters of Theodore Dwight Weld, Angelina Grimké Weld, and Sarah Grimké, 1822–1844* (2 vols., New York, 1934), I, p. 154.

5 The *Boston Recorder*, July 19, 1834, said bitterness against Ludlow was occasioned by his performing a mixed marriage.

6 See *The Presbyterian*, July 17, 1834; and *Boston Recorder*, July 19, 1834.

7 Theodore Sedgwick, *A Collection of the Political Writings of William Leggett*, pp. 34–35.

8 *Boston Recorder*, August 22, 1834.

9 William Jay, *Miscellaneous Writings on Slavery*, p. 394.

10 William Goodell, *Slavery and Anti-Slavery: A History of the Great Struggle in Both Hemispheres with a View of the Slavery Question in the United States* (New York, 1852), p. 405.

11 John Thomas Scharf, *History of Philadelphia* (Philadelphia, 1884), pp. 641–42, gives an interesting account of this riot.

12 Samuel Galloway to Weld, August 9, 1835, Gilbert H. Barnes and Dwight L. Dumond (eds.), *Letters of Theodore Dwight Weld, Angelina Grimké Weld, and Sarah Grimké, 1822–1844* (2 vols., New York, 1934), I, p. 229.

13 Weld to Elizur Wright, March 2, 1835, *ibid.*, I, pp. 205–8. See, also, Weld to Elizur Wright, October 6, 1835, *ibid.*, pp. 236–40; Weld to Rev. Ray Potter, June 11, 1836, *ibid.*, pp. 309–10.

14 James A. Thome and John W. Alvord to Weld, February 9, 1836, *ibid.*, I, pp. 256–62.

15 Weld to Lewis Tappan, March 9, 1836, *ibid.*, pp. 270–74.

16 James A. Thome to Weld, May 2, 1836, *ibid.*, pp. 298–302.

17 Charles Burleigh Galbreath, "Anti-Slavery Movement in Columbiana County," in *Ohio Archeological and Historical Quarterly*, XXX, pp. 355–95.

18 *Niles Register*, XLIX, p. 145.

19 Samuel J. May, *Some Recollections of the Anti-Slavery Conflict* (Boston, 1869), p. 164.

20 See Betty Fladeland, *James Gillespie Birney: Slaveholder to Abolitionist* (Ithaca, 1955), pp. 125–45.

21 *The Philanthropist*, July 15, 1836.

22 See Birney to Lewis Tappan, July 22, 1836, Dwight L. Dumond (ed.), *Letters of James Gillespie Birney, 1831–1857* (2 vols., New York, 1938), I, p. 345.

23 See one such poster in *ibid.*, I, p. 342.

24 A full account of the mob violence was carried in Hammond's *Cincinnati Gazette*. See, also, Beriah Green, *Sketches of the Life and Writings of James Gillespie Birney* (Utica, 1844), pp. 63–66; and William Birney, *James G. Birney and His Times* (New York, 1890), pp. 243–47.

25 See *Last Advice to My Old and Beloved Congregation, at Danville, Kentucky*. First published in *Western Luminary*, XII, No. 19.

26 Various accounts of the Nelson-Palmyra affair are available, but the most accurate is in the *Friend of Man*, June 23, 1836.

27 The most scholarly account of events leading up to Lovejoy's martyrdom is in Merton L. Dillon, *The Antislavery Movement in Illinois: 1809–1844* (Ann Arbor, 1951. University Microfilms). This work is indispensable to a student of the period and contains references to all the available source materials.

28 "Illinois Joint Select Committee on Southern Governors' Demands, 1837," in *Journal of the Senate of the Tenth General Assembly of the State of Illinois, at Their First Session, Begun and Held in the Town of Vandalia, December 5, 1836* (Vandalia, 1837), pp. 129, 130, 196–98.

29 For the events leading up to Lovejoy's death, see Edward Beecher, *Narrative of Riots at Alton: in Connection with the Death of Rev. Elijah P. Lovejoy* (Alton, 1838).

30 A. L. Bowen, "Antislavery Convention Held in Alton, Ill., Oct. 26–28, 1837," *Illinois State Historical Society Journal*, XX, pp. 329–56.

31 Joseph C. and Owen Lovejoy (eds.), *Memoirs of the Reverend Elijah P. Lovejoy; Who Was Murdered in Defense of the Liberty of the Press, at Alton, Illinois, Nov. 7, 1837* (New York, 1838), p. 268.

32 *Alton Observer*, July 20, 1837.

33 David Root, *A Memorial of the Martyred Lovejoy: in a Discourse by Rev. David Root, Delivered in Dover, New Hampshire* (Dover, 1838), p. 12.

34 Weld to Samuel Webb and William H. Scott, January 3, 1838, Gilbert H. Barnes and Dwight L. Dumond (eds.), *Letters of Theodore Dwight Weld, Angelina Grimké Weld, and Sarah Grimké, 1822–1844*, II, pp. 511–12.

35 Lewis C. Gunn of Philadelphia also testified to this fact. Speaking at the ceremonies, he said: "But, strange as it may seem, the churches and public halls of Philadelphia are closed against the advocates of human rights; and, I believe there is not a building in this city, except the one in which we are now assembled, large enough

to accommodate such a meeting as this, which could have been obtained for the advocacy even of that most valuable of all rights—the right of free discussion." [Samuel Webb], *History of Pennsylvania Hall, Which Was Destroyed by a Mob, on the 17th of May, 1838* (Philadelphia, 1838), p. 62.

36 See Thaddeus Stevens to Samuel Webb, May 4, 1838, The *Pennsylvania Freeman,* May 14, 1838.

37 [Samuel Webb], *History of Pennsylvania Hall Which Was Destroyed by a Mob on the 17th of May, 1838,* p. 113.

38 William Jay to Samuel Webb, January 3, 1838, *ibid.,* p. 9.

39 *Ibid.* See also *Sixth Annual Report of the Executive Committee of the American Anti-Slavery Society, with the Speeches Delivered at the Anniversary Meeting Held in the City of New York, on the 7th of May, 1839, and the Minutes of the Meetings of the Society for Business, Held on the Three Following Days* (New York, 1839), pp. 82–86.

40 "The Report in Council," in *Pennsylvania Freeman,* August 16, 1838.

41 Quoted in [Samuel Webb] *History of Pennsylvania Hall, Which Was Destroyed by a Mob on the 17th of May, 1838,* pp. 197–98. Reference is to Richard M. Johnson, Vice-President of the United States.

Chapter 27
The Higher Law

1 William Bourne Oliver Peabody, *The Duties and Dangers of Those Who Are Born Free. A Sermon Preached at the Annual Election, January 2, 1833, Before His Excellency Levi Lincoln, Governor. His Honor Thomas L. Winthrop, Lieutenant Governor, The Honorable Council, and the Legislature of Massachusetts* (Boston, 1833), p. 7.

2 Richard Yeardon, *The Amenability of Northern Incendiaries As Well to Southern As to Northern Laws, Without Prejudice to the Right of Free Discussion; to Which Is Added an Inquiry into the Lawfulness of Slavery, Under the Jews and Christian Dispensation Together with Other Views of the Same Subject* (Charleston, 1835), p. 5.

3 Jacobus Flournoy, *An Essay on the Origin, Habits, etc., of the African Race; Incidental to the Propriety of Having Nothing To Do with Negroes; Addressed to the Good People of the United States* (New York, 1835), pp. 5–7.

4 Simon Clough, *A Candid Appeal to the Citizens of the United States, Proving That the Doctrines Advanced and the Measures Pursued by the Abolitionists Relative to the Subject of Emancipation, Are Inconsistent with the Teachings and Directions of the Bible and That Those Clergymen Engaged in the Dissemination of These Principles Should Be Immediately Dismissed by Their Respective Congregations, as False Teachers* (New York, 1834).

5 W. P. N. Fitzgerald, *A Scriptural View of Slavery and Abolition* (New Haven, 1839).

6 Richard H. Colfax, *Evidence Against the Views of the Abolitionists, Consisting of Physical and Moral Proofs, of the Natural Inferiority of the Negroes* (New York, 1833).

7 Edmund Bellinger, *A Speech on the Subject of Slavery, Delivered 7th Septr, 1835, at a Public Meeting of the Citizens of Barnwell District, South Carolina* (Charleston, 1835).

8 This compilation is taken from the full provisions of all state constitutions as given in William Goodell, *A Full Statement of the Reasons Which Were in Part Offered to the Committee of the Legislature of Massachusetts, on the Fourth and Eighth of March, Showing Why There Should Be No Penal Laws Enacted, and No Condemnatory Resolutions Passed by the Legislature, Respecting Abolitionists and Anti-Slavery Societies* (Boston, 1836), pp. 38–40.

9 Charles Fitch, *An Address Delivered on the Fourth of July, 1836, at Pine Street Church, Boston, in the Morning, and at Salem in the Afternoon* (Boston, 1836), p. 4.

10 See *Proceedings of the New York Anti-Slavery Convention, Held at Utica, October 21, and New York State Anti-Slavery Society, Held at Peterboro, October 22, 1835* (Utica, 1835). Smith's speech was reprinted as a broadside in 1862 and widely distributed. Said Lovejoy: "I know that I have the right freely to speak and publish my sentiments, subject only to the laws of the land for the abuse of that right. This right was given me by my Maker; and is solemnly guaranteed to me by the Constitution of these United States and of this state." Edward Beecher, *Narrative of the Riots at Alton: In Connection with the Death of Rev. Elijah P. Lovejoy* (Alton, 1838), p. 86.

11 The three great treasures of this contest for the right of free enquiry and discussion are [Theodore D. Weld], *A Statement of the Reasons Which Induced the Students of Lane Seminary To Dissolve Their Connection with That Institution* (Cincinnati, 1834); Gerrit Smith, *Speech Before the New York Anti-Slavery Society at Peterboro, October 22, 1835* (printed separately as a broadside, and in *Proceedings of the New York Anti-Slavery Convention . . . 1835);* and Elijah P. Lovejoy's defense, as recorded in Edward Beecher, *Narrative of the Riots at Alton, . . .* Said Alvan Stewart, in Pennsylvania Hall the day before it was burned: "Therefore, as God had made man, he had a right to his own workmanship; and having conferred on man certain high powers, life, liberty, and the pursuit of happiness, which happiness consists in obeying his Creator's laws, this being could not abandon or surrender these rights to another human being, nor could another human being assume them." [Samuel Webb], *History of Pennsylvania Hall Which Was Destroyed by a Mob on the 17th of May, 1838* (Philadelphia, 1838), p. 103.

12 Edward Beecher, *Narrative of the Riots at Alton . . . ,* pp. 89–91. "Constitutions and laws may protect, but they do not bestow *human rights.* These are incident to and inseparable from human nature. They are the gift of God to man. They are indissolubly connected with our duties, and he who presumptuously interferes with one, does violence to the other." "Address of the Executive Committee of the Pennsylvania State Anti-Slavery Society, for the Eastern District," [Samuel

Webb], *History of Pennsylvania Hall Which Was Destroyed by a Mob* . . . , p. 153.

13 Weld to the Rev. Ray Potter, June 11, 1836, Gilbert H. Barnes and Dwight L. Dumond (eds.), *Letters of Theodore Dwight Weld, Angelina Grimké Weld, and Sarah Grimké, 1822–1844* (2 vols., New York, 1934), I, p. 310.

Chapter 28
The Capital and the Nation

1 Worthington G. Snethen, *The Black Code of the District of Columbia, in Force September 1, 1848* (New York, 1848), is a compilation of the laws of Maryland and the United States, and the Ordinances of Washington and of Georgetown, touching upon slaves and free Negroes.

2 There are two published reports of the trial, somewhat different in content, but consistent as to main features of the proceedings: *The Trial of Reuben Crandall, M.D., Charged with Publishing Seditious Libels, by Circulating the Publications of the American Anti-Slavery Society. Before the Circuit Court for the District of Columbia, Held at Washington, in April, 1836, Occupying the Court the Period of Ten Days* (New York, 1836); and *The Trial of Reuben Crandall, M.D., Charged with Publishing and Circulating Seditious and Incendiary Papers, etc., in the District of Columbia, with the Intent of Exciting Servile Insurrection. Carefully Reported, and Compiled from the Written Statements of the Court and the Counsel* (Washington, 1836).

3 Elizabeth Yates, *Prudence Crandall, Woman of Courage* (New York, 1955).

4 *The Trial of Reuben Crandall, M.D., Charged with Publishing and Circulating Seditious and Incendiary Papers* . . . , p. 3.

5 *Ibid.*, p. 46.

6 *Ibid.*, p. 43.

7 *Ibid.*, p. 7.

8 *The Trial of Reuben Crandall, M.D., Charged with Publishing and Circulating Seditious and Incendiary Papers* . . . , p. 46.

9 *Ibid.*, pp. 43–44.

10 *Congressional Debates*, 20 Cong., 2 Sess. (1828–29), p. 192.

11 *Congressional Debates*, 20 Cong., 2 Sess. (1828–1829), p. 176.

12 *Ibid.*, p. 176. For accounts of cruelties in the slave factories, of Washington, D. C., see J[ames] M[iller] M' Kim, *A Sketch of the Slave Trade in the District of Columbia, Contained in Two Letters Originally Published in the Emancipator* (Pittsburgh, 1838). See also Myron Holley, *An Address Delivered at Perry, New York, July 4, 1839* (Perry, 1839).

13 *Ibid.*, p. 179.

14 *Register of Debates in Congress*, XII (1836), p. 3757.

15 *Ibid.*, p. 3758.

16 See the Hawes Resolution, January 18, 1837, *Congressional Globe*, 24 Cong., 2 Sess., IV, p. 106, passed 129 to 69; the Patton Resolution, December 21, 1837, *ibid.*, 25 Cong., 2 Sess., VI, p. 45, passed 122 to 74; the Atherton Resolution, December 12, 1838, *ibid.*, 25 Cong., 3 Sess., VII, p. 28, passed 126 to 78; the Thomp-

son Resolution, *ibid.*, 26 Cong., 1 Sess., VIII, p. 150, passed 115 to 105.

17 Henry B. Stanton, *Remarks of Henry B. Stanton, in the Representatives' Hall, on the 23d and 24th of February, 1837, Before the Committee of the House of Representatives of Massachusetts, to Whom Was Referred Sundry Memorials on the Subject of Slavery* (Boston, 1837).

18 *Ibid.*, pp. 10–11.

19 Henry B. Stanton, *Remarks of Henry B. Stanton, in the Representatives' Hall, on the 23d and 24th of February, 1837* . . . , p. 19.

20 *Ibid.*, p. 23.

21 *Ibid.*, pp. 23–39.

22 *Ibid.*, p. 38.

23 *Ibid.*, p. 43.

24 *Ibid.*, p. 44.

25 *Ibid.*, pp. 51–52.

26 *Ibid.*, p. 75.

27 American Anti-Slavery Society, *The Anti-Slavery Examiner, No. 5.* [Theodore Dwight Weld], *The Power of Congress over the District of Columbia* (New York, 1838).

28 *Ibid.*, p. 4.

29 *Ibid.*, pp. 6–7.

30 *Ibid.*, pp. 7–8.

31 *Ibid.*, pp. 42–43.

32 *Ibid.*, p. 41. Weld here quoted from "Observations on the American Revolution" by the Continental Congress: "The great principle [of government] is and ever will remain in force, that men are by nature free; as accountable to him that made them; they must be so; and so long as we have any idea of divine justice, we must associate that of human freedom. Whether men can part with their liberty, is among the questions which have exercised the ablest writers; but it is conceded on all hands, that the right to be free can never be alienated—still less is it practicable for one generation to mortgage the privileges of another."

33 *Ibid.*, p. 45.

Chapter 29
Petitions

1 *House Reports*, 24 Cong., 1 Sess., III, No. 691, pp. 1–24.

2 Speech of Alanson St. Clair, in *History of Pennsylvania Hall, Which Was Destroyed by a Mob, on the 17th of May, 1838* (Philadelphia, 1838), p. 67.

3 *Ibid.*, pp. 11–12.

4 "Senator Morris' Address to the People of Ohio and Legislature of Ohio," in *Cincinnati Journal*, November 29, 1838.

5 Birney to Joshua Leavitt, October 30, 1937, *Philanthropist*, November 28, 1837.

6 *Register of Debates in Congress*, 24 Cong., 1 Sess., XII, p. 2062.

7 These are the figures for the number of petitioners given by Birney in *Correspondence Between the Hon. F. H. Elmore, One of the South Carolina Delegation in Congress, and James G. Birney, One of the Secretaries of the American Anti-Slavery Society* (New York, 1838), p. 65. These figures are incorrectly cited as petitions instead of petitioners in Russell B. Nye, *Fettered Freedom: Civil Liberties and the Slavery Controversy*

(East Lansing, 1949), p. 37, and are repeated by Samuel Flagg Bemis in *John Quincy Adams and the Union* (New York, 1956), p. 340, with the statement that they "indicate only the number of petitions, not the millions of signatures to them." There were, of course, no such numbers of signatures on any petitions.

8 *Proceedings of the Third Anti-Slavery Convention of American Women, Held in Philadelphia, May 1st, 2d, and 3d, 1839* (Philadelphia, 1839), pp. 26–27.

9 Females of the state of Ohio, *To the Honorable the Senate and House of Representatives of the United States of America, in Congress Assembled* [Twenty-fourth Congress].

10 Citizens of Jefferson County, State of Indiana, *Petition for the Abolition of Slavery in the District of Columbia* [Twenty-sixth Congress].

11 Citizens of Massachusetts, *To the Senate and House of Representatives of the United States in Congress Assembled, the Undersigned Citizens of Massachusetts Respectfully Represent* [Twenty-fourth Congress].

12 Citizens of the County of Wayne, Territory of Michigan, *Petition to the Honorable the Senate, and House of Representatives of the United States* [Twenty-fourth Congress].

13 Inhabitants of Chester, Vermont, *Memorial, to the Hon. the Senate and House of Representatives of the United States in Congress Assembled* [Twenty-sixth Congress].

14 Citizens of Philadelphia and vicinity, *To the Honorable the Senate and House of Representatives of the United States of America, in Congress Assembled* [Twenty-fourth Congress].

15 Citizens of Philadelphia, *To the Senate and House of Representatives of the United States of America, in Congress Assembled* [Twenty-fourth Congress].

16 Women of Rhode Island, *To the Honorable Senate and House of Representatives of the United States of America* [Twenty-fourth Congress].

17 Electors of Cuyahoga County, Ohio [to Twenty-fourth Congress].

18 Ladies of Bucks County, Pennsylvania, and Its Vicinity [to Twenty-fourth Congress].

19 Citizens of Pittsburgh and Vicinity to Twenty-fourth Congress.

20 *The Petition of the Undersigned Ladies of Massachusetts Respectfully Represents:* to Twenty-fourth Congress.

21 From Geauga County, Ohio.

22 Inhabitants of Farmington, Hartford County, Connecticut, *To the Senate and House of Representatives of the United States,* Twenty-fifth Congress.

23 Signed, and dated, Pittsburgh, Pennsylvania, January 11, 1838.

Chapter 30
American Slavery As It Is

1 [Theodore Weld], *American Slavery As It Is: Testimony of a Thousand Witnesses* (New York, 1839), p. 9.

2 George Whitefield, *To the Inhabitants of Maryland, Virginia, North and South Carolina, Concerning Their Negroes* (Philadelphia, 1740); John Woolman, *A Journal of the Life, Gospel Labours, and Christian Experiences of That Faithful Minister of Jesus Christ, John Woolman,*

Late of Mount-Holly, in the Province of New Jersey, North America (Dublin, 1794); Anthony Benezet, *A Caution and Warning to Great Britain, and Her Colonies . . . More Especially of Those in Power* (Philadelphia, 1767).

3 Among the other papers were the Alexandria (La.) *Planter's Intelligencer,* Fayetteville (N.C.) *Observer,* New Orleans *Commercial Bulletin,* Macon (Ga.) *Georgia Messenger,* Natchitoches (La.) *Herald,* Tuscaloosa (Ala.) *State Intelligencer,* Port Gibson *Correspondent,* Savannah *Republican,* Pensacola *Gazette,* Columbus (Ga.) *Southern Sun,* Grand Gulf *Advertiser,* Clinton (Miss.) *Gazette,* Knoxville (Tenn.) *Register,* and Jackson *Mississippian.*

4 [Theodore Weld], *American Slavery As It Is . . . ,* p. 143; State *vs.* Cheatwood (1834), W. R. Hill, *Reports of Cases at Law, Argued and Determined in the Court of Appeals of South Carolina* (3 vols., Charleston, 1857), II, p. 459; State *vs.* Mann (1829), Thomas P. Devereaux and William H. Battle, *Reports of Cases at Law Argued and Determined in the Supreme Court of North Carolina* (3 vols., Raleigh, 1837–40), I, p. 263.

5 Nathaniel Heyward of Combahee, South Carolina. [Theodore Weld], *American Slavery As It Is: Testimony of a Thousand Witnesses* (New York, 1839), p. 175.

6 Whitmarsh B. Seabrook speaking before the Agricultural Society of St. Johns, South Carolina.

7 [Theodore Weld], *American Slavery As It Is . . . ,* p. 111.

8 *Ibid.,* p. 112.

9 See the many cases cited in *ibid.,* pp. 155–61.

10 *Ibid.,* pp. 72–74.

11 *Ibid.,* pp. 77–84.

12 *Ibid.,* pp. 115–16. Another heavily documented, and much earlier, portrait of the horrors of slavery, of slaves, of bills of sale, and of fugitives was written in 1834 by a Quaker physician of Philadelphia: Edwin P. Atlee, *An Address Delivered Before the Female Anti-Slavery Society of Philadelphia, in the Session Room of the Second Presbyterian Church (on Cherry Street) in the First Month (January), 1834* (Philadelphia, 1834).

13 "It is the *novelty* of cruelty, rather than the *degree,* which repels most minds. Cruelty in a new form, however slight, will often pain a mind that is totally unmoved by the most horrible cruelties in a form to which it is accustomed." *Ibid.,* p. 125.

14 *Ibid.,* p. 123.

15 *Ibid.,* pp. 132–38.

16 *Ibid.,* p. 51.

17 *Ibid.,* pp. 148–49.

18 *Ibid.,* pp. 27–35.

19 *Ibid.,* pp. 40–43.

20 For the labor of slaves, see *ibid.,* pp. 35–40.

21 *Ibid.,* pp. 139–40.

22 *Ibid.,* p. 140.

Chapter 31
Birney and Thome

1 That, at least, is the excuse Elmore gave for writing to Birney. It is highly probable that there had been a good many caucuses of Southern members of Congress on petitions and Calhoun's resolutions.

2 American Anti-Slavery Society, *Correspondence Between the Hon. F. H. Elmore, One of the South Carolina Delegation in Congress, and James G. Birney, One of the Secretaries of the American Anti-Slavery Society. Anti-Slavery Examiner,* No. 8 (New York, 1838), p. 6.

3 Birney's reply was written March 8, 1838. There were 1,346 auxiliaries reported at the May meeting.

4 *Ibid.,* pp. 9–10.

5 See William Sprague to Oliver Johnson, March 28, 1838, in *ibid.,* Appendix B, pp. 56–57.

6 *Ibid.,* p. 13.

7 The society had some wealthy patrons: Arthur Tappan, the president; William Green, Jr., the treasurer; John Rankin of the executive committee; and Gerrit Smith were the most generous. Three-fourths of the money received from contributions, however, was collected in small amounts all over the country and forwarded to the New York office by the auxiliary societies. The sale of such publications as Weld's *American Slavery As It Is* brought in the dollar margin between comparative solvency and bankruptcy. The financial status of the society was accurately, though not always completely, reported from time to time in the *Anti-Slavery Record.*

8 Birney's discussion of antislavery publications was necessarily limited. Reference will be made to his answers on this point in the following chapters.

9 *Ibid.,* p. 26.

10 *Ibid.*

11 *Ibid.,* p. 28.

12 *Ibid.,* p. 29.

13 *Ibid.,* p. 32. Reference was to Henry Clay.

14 *Ibid.,* p. 36.

15 *Ibid.,* pp. 40–41.

16 *Ibid.,* p. 45.

17 *Ibid.,* p. 46.

18 *Ibid.,* p. 49.

19 *Ibid.,* p. 51.

20 James A. Thome and Horace J. Kimball, *Emancipation in the West Indies. A Six Months Tour in Antigua, Barbadoes and Jamaica, in the Year 1837* (New York, 1838).

21 *Ibid.,* pp. 76–77. The report of Thome and Kimball was strongly reinforced by publication of Sylvester Hovey, *Letters from the West Indies, Relating Especially to the Danish Island St. Croix, and to the British Islands Antigua, Barbadoes, and Jamaica* (New York, 1838). Hovey, professor of mathematics and natural philosophy at Amherst, made the survey for the American Union for the Relief and Improvement of the Colored Race.

Chapter 32
General Literature

1 The paper was titled the *Cincinnati Weekly Herald and Philanthropist,* 1843–46.

2 *Views of American Constitutional Law, in Its Bearing upon American Slavery* (Utica, 1844); *Come-Outerism, the Duty of Secession from a Corrupt Church* (New York, 1845); *Slavery and Anti-Slavery; A History of the Great Struggle in Both Hemispheres, with a View of the Slavery Question in the United States* (New York, 1852); *The American Slave Code in Theory and Practice: Its Distinctive Features Shown by Its Statutes, Judicial Decisions, and Illustrative Facts* (New York, 1853); and others. See Bibliography.

3 Burleigh wrote Anti-Slavery Tract No. 10, *Slavery and the North* (New York, 1855).

4 Elizur Wright to Weld, March 24, 1836, Gilbert H. Barnes and Dwight L. Dumond (eds.), *Letters of Theodore Dwight Weld, Angelina Grimké Weld, and Sarah Grimké, 1822–1844* (2 vols., New York, 1934), I, pp. 279–81.

5 Elizur Wright to Theodore Weld, June 10, 1835, *ibid.,* I, pp. 225–26.

6 *Ibid.*

7 *Correspondence Between the Hon. F. H. Elmore, One of the South Carolina Delegation in Congress, and James G. Birney, One of the Secretaries of the American Anti-Slavery Society* (New York, 1838), p. 19.

8 Elizur Wright to Weld, September 16, 1835, Gilbert H. Barnes and Dwight L. Dumond (eds.), *Letters of Theodore Dwight Weld, Angelina Grimké Weld, and Sarah Grimké, 1822–1844,* I, p. 231.

9 *The Anti-Slavery Examiner,* No. 8. *Correspondence Between the Hon. F. H. Elmore, One of the South Carolina Delegation in Congress, and James G. Birney, One of the Secretaries of the American Anti-Slavery Society* (New York, 1838), pp. 22–23.

10 Many of these pictures were used in the *Anti-Slavery Almanac* and in the *Emancipator.*

11 *The Anti-Slavery Examiner,* No. 8. *Correspondence Between the Hon. F. H. Elmore, One of the South Carolina Delegation in Congress, and James G. Birney . . . ,* p. 22.

12 Matthew 22: 29. Used also on wafers.

13 Matthew 7: 12. Used also on wafers.

14 Jeremiah 22: 13. Used also on two separate wafers.

15 Henry C. Wright, *American Slavery Proved To Be Theft and Robbery; with a Letter to Dr. Cunningham, Containing the Doctor's Apologies for Slavery, an Account of Eight Human Beings Sold by a Theological Seminary, and of the Sale of a Young Woman; and Also the Opinions of Thomas Clarkson and Dr. Andrew Thomson* (Edinburgh, 1845), p. 7.

16 *The Works of the Rev. John Wesley* (10 vols., New York, 1826–30), X, p. 504.

17 *Ibid.,* X, p. 504.

18 This quotation is from a newspaper notice of a deed of manumission, executed by John Jay in France in 1784, for a Negro boy named Benoit. See William Jay, *The Life of John Jay; with Selections from His Correspondence and Miscellaneous Papers* (2 vols., New York, 1833), I, 230.

19 This was a rephrasing of Jefferson's statement in *Notes on Virginia:* "The Almighty has no attribute which can take sides with us in such a contest."

20 Henry Peter Brougham, lord chancellor of Great Britain, spoke in the House of Commons, July 13, 1830, for abolition of slavery in the British Empire. The quotation is from that speech. See Henry P. Brougham, *Speeches of Henry Lord Brougham, upon Questions Relating to Public Rights, Duties, and Interests* (4 vols., Edinburgh, 1838), II, p. 155.

21 Jonathan Edwards, *The Injustice and Impolicy of the Slave Trade, and of the Slavery of the Africans: Illustrated in a Sermon Preached . . . September 15, 1791* (New Haven, 1791), pp. 24–25.

22 See *Poems by William Cowper, Esq. of the Inner Temple* (2 vols., Boston, 1826), I, p. 30.

23 Thomas Day, an English author and poet, strongly sympathized with the American revolutionaries. He condemned slavery in reply to a letter from Colonel John Laurens, son of the President of the Continental Congress. See Thomas Day, *The Dying Negro, A Poem by the Late Thomas Day and John Bucknell, Esquires. To Which Is Added a Fragment of a Letter on the Slavery of the Negroes* (London, 1793).

24 Sarah Wentworth Morton was a Boston poetess immediately following the Revolution. "The African Chief" was first published in the *Columbia Centinel*, June 8, 1792. It was widely reprinted, particularly into school readers, and was often quoted in antislavery literature.

25 See [Wilson Armistead], *Five Hundred Thousand Strokes for Freedom. A Series of Anti-Slavery Tracts, of Which Half a Million Are Now First Issued by the Friends of the Negro* (London, 1853).

26 For the general history of gift books, see Frederick W. Faxon, "Literary Annuals and Gift Books, American and English, A Bibliography," *Bulletin of Bibliography*, V (1908–11), p. 70; Ralph Thompson, *American Literary Annuals and Gift Books, 1825–1865* (New York, 1936).

27 *Liberator*, January 25, 1850.

28 See the *Liberty Bell* (1844), pp. 217–18; *ibid.* (1845), p. 220; *ibid.* (1843), pp. 136–37; *ibid.* (1847), p. 230.

Chapter 33
Women in the Movement

1 This was correct procedure for that day. Lucretia Mott later said: "I do not think it occurred to any one of us at that time, that there would be a propriety in our signing the document." *Proceedings of the American Anti-Slavery Society at Its Third Decade, Held in the City of Philadelphia, Dec. 3d & 4th, 1863* (New York, 1864), p. 41.

2 See Elizabeth Cady Stanton, "Lucretia Mott," in Elizabeth Cady Stanton, Susan B. Anthony, and Matilda J. Gage (eds.), *History of Woman Suffrage* (4 vols., New York, 1881), I, pp. 407–31 and Catherine H. Birney, *Sarah and Angelina Grimké, the First American Women Advocates of Abolition and Woman's Rights* (Boston, 1885), p. 153.

3 Angelina Emily Grimké, *Appeal to the Christian Women of the South* (New York, 1836); Sarah Moore Grimké, *An Epistle to the Clergy of the Southern States* (New York, 1836).

4 Wright probably overemphasized the opposition when he said at a later date: "The New York Board were so thoroughly imbued with Calvinistic prejudices that it came very near to throwing me overboard for encouraging Angelina Grimké to speak as well as write." Elizur Wright to Oliver Johnson, April 15, 1881, in Wendell Phillips Garrison and Francis Jackson Garrison, *William Lloyd Garrison, 1805–1879* (4 vols., New York, 1885–89), II, p. 318.

5 Fourth Annual Report of the American Anti-Slavery Society in *The Quarterly Anti-Slavery Magazine* (July, 1837), II, p. 352.

6 See particularly Sarah Grimké to Sarah Douglass, October 22, 1837, Gilbert H. Barnes and Dwight L. Dumond (eds.), *Letters of Theodore Dwight Weld, Angelina Grimké Weld, and Sarah Grimké, 1822–1844* (2 vols., New York, 1934), I, pp. 467–71; Angelina Grimké to Weld, February 11, 1838, *ibid.*, II, pp. 536–39; Angelina Grimké to Weld, February 22, 1838, *ibid.*, II, pp. 567–70.

7 Angelina and Sarah Grimké to Weld, April 29, 1838, *ibid.*, II, pp. 646–51.

8 Angelina's final address is in Elizabeth Cady Stanton, Susan B. Anthony, and Matilda J. Gage (eds.), *History of Woman Suffrage* (4 vols., New York, 1881), I, pp. 334–36.

9 See Wendell Phillips Garrison and Francis Jackson Garrison, *William Lloyd Garrison, 1805–1879*, II, p. 216 n.

10 Samuel J. May, *Some Recollections of the Anti-Slavery Conflict* (Boston, 1869), p. 244. Abby lectured from New England to Ohio. In 1845 she married Stephen Foster, another thoroughgoing Garrisonian. They were both controversial figures in the movement, being as violent as Garrison himself in their language. See also Elizabeth Cady Stanton, Susan B. Anthony, and Matilda J. Gage (eds.), *History of Woman Suffrage*, I, p. 40.

11 *Proceedings of the American Anti-Slavery Society at Its Third Decade . . .*, pp. 49–50.

12 Sarah Grimké to Sarah Douglass, October 22, 1837, Gilbert H. Barnes and Dwight L. Dumond (eds.), *Letters of Theodore Dwight Weld, Angelina Grimké Weld, and Sarah Grimké, 1822–1844*, I, pp. 467–71.

13 Sarah and Angelina Grimké to Henry C. Wright, August 12, 1837, *ibid.*, I, pp. 419–23; and, August 27, 1837, *ibid.*, I, pp. 436–41.

14 "A Pastoral Letter of the General Association of Massachusetts," quoted in *Right and Wrong in Boston. Annual Report of the Boston Female Anti-Slavery Society, with a Sketch of the Obstacles Thrown in Way of Emancipation by Certain Clerical Abolitionists and Advocates for the Subjection of Women, in 1837* (Boston, 1837), pp. 45–48. There are extracts from many sermons in *ibid.*, pp. 50–56.

15 Weld to Angelina Grimké, April 15, 1838, Gilbert H. Barnes and Dwight L. Dumond (eds.), *Letters of Theodore Dwight Weld, Angelina Grimké Weld, and Sarah Grimké, 1822–1844*, II, pp. 637–42.

16 Angelina Grimké to Weld, April 29, 1838, *ibid.*, II, pp. 646–51.

17 *The Third Annual Report of the American Anti-Slavery Society; with the Speeches Delivered at the Anniversary Meeting Held in the City of New York, on the 10th May, 1836, and the Minutes of the Meetings of the Society for Business* (New York), 1836, pp. 89–99, gives a list of the societies reported. It has some errors and probably is far from complete.

18 The Michigan society was organized by Elizabeth Margaret Chandler who lived on the Raisin River near Tecumseh. Laura S. Haviland was a charter member. This was the first antislavery society in Michigan. See Benjamin Lundy, *The Poetical Works of Elizabeth Mar-*

garet Chandler: With a Memoir of Her Life and Character (Philadelphia, 1845), p. 40; and Laura S. Haviland, *A Woman's Life-Work; Labors and Experiences of Laura S. Haviland* (Cincinnati, 1882), p. 32.

19 See Anne Warren Weston to Weld, February 24, 1836, Gilbert H. Barnes and Dwight L. Dumond (eds.), *Letters of Theodore Dwight Weld, Angelina Grimké Weld, and Sarah Grimké, 1822–1844*, I, pp. 267–69.

20 *Annual Report, Presented to the American Anti-Slavery Society, by the Executive Committee, at the Annual Meeting, Held in New York, May 9, 1855* (New York, 1855), p. 113; *Fourteenth Annual Report of the Massachusetts Anti-Slavery Society* (Boston, 1846), p. 60.

21 Weld to Sarah and Angelina Grimké, December 15, 1837, in Gilbert H. Barnes and Dwight L. Dumond (eds.), *Letters of Theodore Dwight Weld, Angelina Grimké Weld, and Sarah Grimké, 1822–1844*, I, pp. 490–96.

22 *Annual Report of the Boston Female Anti-Slavery Society, with a Sketch of the Obstacles Thrown in the Way of Emancipation . . .* , p. 90; *Eleventh Annual Report of the Massachusetts Anti-Slavery Society* (Boston, 1843), p. 85; *ibid.* (1845), p. 67.

23 See "Annals of Women's Anti-Slavery Societies," *Proceedings of the American Anti-Slavery Society at Its Third Decade, Held in the City of Philadelphia, December 3d & 4th, 1863* (New York, 1864), p. 128.

24 *The Genius of Universal Emancipation and Quarterly Anti-Slavery Review*, July, 1837.

25 *An Appeal to the Women of the Nominally Free States, Issued by an Anti-Slavery Convention of American Women, Held by Adjournments from the 9th to the 12th of May, 1837* (Boston, 1837), pp. 5–6.

26 *Ibid.*, p. 13.

27 Quoted in Theodore Weld to Susan B. Anthony, March 15, 1888, in *The Woman's Tribune*, April 3, 1888.

28 *Proceedings of the Anti-Slavery Convention of American Women Held in Philadelphia, May 15th, 16th, 17th and 18th, 1838* (Philadelphia, 1838); see also "Final Report of the Philadelphia Female Anti-Slavery Society," in Elizabeth Cady Stanton, Susan B. Anthony, and Matilda Joslyn Gage (eds.), *History of Woman Suffrage*, I, pp. 326–27.

29 *Proceedings of the Third Anti-Slavery Convention of American Women, Held in Philadelphia, May 1st, 2nd, and 3d, 1839* (Philadelphia, 1839).

30 *Sixth Annual Report of the Executive Committee of the American Anti-Slavery Society, with the Speeches Delivered at the Anniversary Meeting Held in the City of New York, on the 7th of May, 1839, and the Minutes of the Meetings of the Society for Business, Held on the Evening and the Three Following Days* (New York, 1839).

31 James A. Thome to Weld, May 2, 1836, Gilbert H. Barnes and Dwight L. Dumond (eds.), *Letters of Theodore Dwight Weld, Angelina Grimké Weld, and Sarah Grimké, 1822–1844*, I, pp. 298–302.

32 A passage from Elizabeth Chandler's work was often quoted in support of women's activity:

"When woman's heart is bleeding,
Shall woman's voice be hushed."

33 *Third Annual Report of the American Anti-Slavery Society . . .* , pp. 96–98.

34 *Fifth Annual Report of the Executive Committee of the American Anti-Slavery Society, with the Minutes of the Meetings of the Society for Business, and the Speeches Delivered at the Anniversary Meeting on the 8th May, 1838* (New York, 1838), p. 151.

35 See James A. Thome to Weld, May 2, 1836, Gilbert H. Barnes and Dwight L. Dumond (eds.), *Letters of Theodore Dwight Weld, Angelina Grimké Weld, and Sarah Grimké, 1822–1844*, I, pp. 298–302; Weld to Elizur Wright, October 6, 1835, *ibid.*, I, pp. 236–40.

36 Weld to Lewis Tappan, March 18, 1834, *ibid.*, I, pp. 132–35.

37 The Late Mrs. P. M. Weed, *ibid.*, II, pp. 995–99; *New York Evangelist*, February 8, 1844.

38 *Fourth Annual Report of the American Anti-Slavery Society; with the Speeches Delivered at the Anniversary Meeting Held in the City of New York, on the 9th May, 1837, and the Minutes of the Meetings of the Society for Business* (New York, 1837). Some publishing houses made public confessions of error and promised to delete antislavery material. These apologies were published in Southern newspapers. Not all of the publishers, however, bowed to the slaveholders' demands.

39 *Thirteenth Annual Report, Presented to the Massachusetts Anti-Slavery Society, by Its Board of Managers, January 22, 1845* (Boston, 1845), pp. 25, 36; *Annual Report, Presented to the American Anti-Slavery Society by the Executive Committee at the Annual Meeting Held in New York, May 9, 1855* (New York, 1855), pp. 111–12.

40 John White Chadwick, *A Life for Liberty. Anti-Slavery and Other Letters of Sallie Holley* (New York, 1899).

41 *Annual Report, Presented to the American Anti-Slavery Society by the Executive Committee, at the Annual Meeting Held in New York, May 7, 1856* (New York, 1856), p. 54.

42 See *Letters of Lydia Maria Child with a Biographical Introduction by John Greenleaf Whittier and an Appendix by Wendell Phillips* (Boston, 1883), p. 256.

43 Lydia Maria Child, *An Appeal in Favor of That Class of Americans Called Africans* (Boston, 1833), p. 150.

44 See Particular Instructions, Gilbert H. Barnes and Dwight L. Dumond (eds.), *Letters of Theodore Dwight Weld, Angelina Grimké Weld, and Sarah Grimké, 1822–1844*, I, pp. 125–28.

45 Lydia Maria Child, *The Right Way the Safe Way, Proved by Emancipation in the British West Indies, and Elsewhere* (New York, 1860).

Chapter 34
American & Foreign Anti-Slavery Society

1 *Sixth Annual Report of the Executive Committee of the American Anti-Slavery Society, with the Speeches Delivered at the Anniversary Meeting Held in the City of New York, on the 7th of May, 1839, and the Minutes of the Meetings of the Society for Business, Held on the Evening and the Three Following Days* (New York, 1839), p. 46.

2 William H. Siebert, *The Underground Railroad from Slavery to Freedom* (New York, 1899), p. 346.

3 The Clerical Appeal was a severe criticism of the methods of antislavery men, particularly of Garrison.

4 Garrison to G. W. Benson, September 16, 1837, Wendell P. Garrison and Francis J. Garrison, *William Lloyd Garrison, 1805–1879* (4 vols., New York, 1885–89), II, pp. 136–37, 162.

5 *Ibid.*, p. 165.

6 *Ibid.*, pp. 178–79.

7 *Seventh Annual Report of the Massachusetts Anti-Slavery Society, 1839* (Boston, 1839), p. 32.

8 There was no direct correlation between the argument over equality for women in the society and political action. William Jay, who led the fight against Alvan Stewart's constitutional principles, was also against Garrison on the woman question. Alvan Stewart, the extreme opposite of Garrison on political action, voted for admission of women. The Tappans were against both Garrison and Stewart.

9 The so-called "Come-Outer" movement led by Garrison opposed all American churches not only on the basis of their proslavery membership, but the institution of the church itself as a bulwark of American slavery. It held that the church must be destroyed before slavery could be abolished. It denounced the Sabbath as an institution of paganism, and the Bible as a proslavery document. In an address at Providence, July 4, 1837, Garrison declared that "the corruptions of the Church, so-called, are obviously more deep and incurable than those of the State." See *The Second Annual Report of the Massachusetts Abolition Society; Together with the Proceedings of the Second Annual Meeting, Held at Tremont Chapel, May 25, 1841* (Boston, 1841), p. 8. The Clerical Appeal was issued in answer to Garrison's heretical pronouncements.

10 The Garrisonians signed the following pledge: "We, the undersigned, to signify our abhorrence of injustice and oppression and to clear our skirts from innocent blood, do hereby pledge ourselves in all suitable ways to strive for peaceable dissolution of the Union, as the most consistent, feasible and efficient means of abolishing slavery." John B. Estlin, *A Brief Notice of American Slavery and the Abolition Movement* (London, 1853), pp. 29–31. The Garrisonian criticism of Lovejoy is presented in Leonard Worcester, *A Discourse on the Alton Outrage, Delivered at Peacham, Vermont, December 17, 1837* (Concord, 1838). Leonard Worcester and his brother, Noah Worcester, were peace advocates.

11 The defect in organization which gave Garrison his opportunity was no limitation on the number of voting delegates who could attend conventions.

12 Henry B. Stanton to Birney, Jan. 26, 1839, Dwight L. Dumond (ed.), *Letters of James Gillespie Birney, 1831–1857* (2 vols., New York, 1938), I, pp. 481–83.

13 The new society was organized by these men at Marlboro Chapel in Boston, May 27–29, 1839. It was recognized by the American Anti-Slavery Society on an equal basis with the Massachusetts Anti-Slavery Society. Massachusetts Abolition Society, *Formation of the Massachusetts Abolition Society* [Boston, 1839]; *The Second Annual Report of the Massachusetts Abolition Society.* . . .

14 Lewis Tappan, *Life of Arthur Tappan* (New York, 1871), p. 303.

15 In the *Philanthropist*, June 16, 1840, the causes were listed as nonresistance, antigovernment, woman's rights, denunciations of the clergy, personal ambition, sectarian affinities and prejudices. See, also, *Sixth Annual Report of the Executive Committee of the American Anti-Slavery Society* . . . , pp. 28–45; and remarks of Samuel J. May in *Proceedings of the American Anti-Slavery Society at Its Second Decade, Held in the City of Philadelphia, December 3rd, 4th, and 5th, 1853* (New York, 1854), p. 31.

16 There had been an extensive controversy over finances between the Board of Managers of the Massachusetts Anti-Slavery Society and the executive committee of the American Anti-Slavery Society. See Ellis Gray Loring to Birney, February 16, 1839, and note, Dwight L. Dumond (ed.), *Letters of James Gillespie Birney, 1831–1857* (2 vols., New York, 1938), I, pp. 483–84; and Henry B. Stanton to Birney, June 10, 1839, *ibid.*, I, pp. 489–91; Birney to Arnold Buffum, November 8, 1839, *ibid.*, I, pp. 502–5.

17 [Lewis Tappan], *An Address to the Anti-Slavery Christians of the United States* (New York, 1852) contains the Constitution of the society. See also James G. Birney, *A Letter on the Political Obligations of Abolitionists, by James G. Birney; with a Reply by William Lloyd Garrison* (Boston, 1839).

18 Lucretia Mott and Abby Kelly both belonged to this group.

19 Lewis Tappan to Weld, May 4, 1840, Gilbert H. Barnes and Dwight L. Dumond (eds.), *Letters of Theodore Dwight Weld, Angelina Grimké Weld, and Sarah Grimké, 1822–1844* (2 vols., New York, 1934), II, pp. 834–35; Wendell Phillips Garrison and Francis Jackson Garrison, *William Lloyd Garrison, 1805–1879* . . . , II, pp. 352–53.

20 Elizabeth Cady Stanton to Angelina Weld and Sarah Grimké, June 25, 1840, Gilbert H. Barnes and Dwight L. Dumond (eds.), *Letters of Theodore Dwight Weld, Angelina Grimké Weld, and Sarah Grimké, 1822–1844*, II, pp. 845–49.

21 *American and Foreign Anti-Slavery Reporter*, June 1842; *The [Seventh] Annual Report of the American and Foreign Anti-Slavery Society, Presented at the General Meeting Held in Broadway Tabernacle, May 11, 1847, with the Addresses, Resolutions, and Treasurer's Reports* (New York, 1847).

22 *American and Foreign Anti-Slavery Reporter*, May 1841, June 1842, May 1843, and January 1845.

23 These are very confused in the catalogues of all libraries, without exception.

24 [Lewis Tappan], *Address to the Non-Slaveholders of the South, on the Social and Political Evils of Slavery* (New York, 1843), p. 3. This appeal to nonslaveholding Southerners antedated Hinton Rowan Helper's *The Impending Crisis of the South; How to Meet It* by fifteen years.

25 *Ibid.*, pp. 4–5.

26 *Ibid.*, pp. 5–6.

27 *Ibid.*, pp. 6–7.

28 *Ibid.*, pp. 8–9.

29 *Ibid.*, p. 10.
30 *Ibid.*, pp. 12–16.
31 *Ibid.*, p. 19.

Chapter 35
The Liberty Party

1 John Pierpont, *Moral Rule of Political Action. A Discourse Delivered in Hollis Street Church, Sunday, January 27, 1839* (Boston, 1839), pp. 4–5.

2 Pierpont went on to say: "In all cases here supposed, it is not merely my right—it is my *duty*, as a true and faithful servant of God, to obey him in using my political influence, my elective franchise, in his service, by placing those in political office who, I believe, will be faithful in his cause;—in other words, I am bound to act in behalf of morality through political instrumentalities." *Ibid.*, p. 21. Pierpont was the grandfather of J. P. Morgan and a classmate of John C. Calhoun at Yale. He was a distinguished preacher and poet. His poetry was full of humor, biting sarcasm, and polished satire. An aristocracy of wealth sought unsuccessfully to drive him from his church because of his antislavery activities.

3 [William Foote], *An Examination of Mr. Bradish's Answer to the Interrogations Presented to Him by a Committee of the State Anti-Slavery Society, October 1, 1838* (Albany, 1838) contains the letters of Gerrit Smith and William Jay to Luther Bradish, candidate for the post of lieutenant governor of New York, his replies, and a criticism of the procedure.

4 *The Emancipator*, August 30, 1838.

5 *The Friend of Man, Extra*, October 26, 1838.

6 See Benjamin F. Morris, *The Life of Thomas Morris: Pioneer and Long a Legislator of Ohio, and United States Senator from 1832 to 1839* (Cincinnati, 1856).

7 Theodore Weld said of him: "Personally, I knew him less than I knew any other of the most prominent antislavery men of New York City, and State. Yet I knew enough of him to impress me as profoundly with the conviction of his rare powers, exhaustless versatility; that marvel of humor, ever fresh, ever at flood tide, and ever *his own* . . . but better far than all, that depth of pathos, those outwelling sympathies, never at ebb; that ever yearning heartache for the wronged; that moral courage that always dared yet never knew it dared; all these, with a kindred host come thronging around me at the thought of Alvan Stewart." Luther R. Marsh (ed.), *Writings and Speeches of Alvan Stewart on Slavery* (New York, 1860), p. 36.

8 [Samuel Webb] *History of Pennsylvania Hall, Which Was Destroyed by a Mob, on the 17th of May, 1838* (Philadelphia, 1838), pp. 108–9.

9 *Fifth Annual Report of the Executive Committee of the American Anti-Slavery Society, with the Minutes of the Meetings of the Society for Business, and the Speeches Delivered at the Anniversary Meeting on the 8th May, 1838* (New York, 1838).

10 Bayard Tuckerman, *William Jay and the Constitutional Movement for the Abolition of Slavery* (New York, 1893), pp. 86–111.

11 Alvan Stewart, *Argument in the Case of State vs. Edward Van Buren*, in Luther R. Marsh, *Writings and Speeches of Alvan Stewart on Slavery* (New York, 1860), p. 333.

12 Alvan Stewart to William L. Marsh, February, 1836, in *ibid.*, p. 82.

13 *Ibid.*, p. 338.

14 *Ibid.*, p. 339.

15 There were times when Stewart's indictment of slavery equaled anything ever said by Weld or Stanton. In his "Address to the Abolitionists of the State of New York, October, 1836," he said: "Yes, the twelve slave States of America are the headquarters of cruelty for the world; the residence of duelling, the native land of Lynch law, where its professors reside and its scholars practice. These States are the asylum of piracy, made respectable by the sanctions of law, where immortal minds are ruined, *in the wholesale*, by constitutional edicts; where the marriage contract is exchanged for wandering adultery. This is the land dedicated to amalgamation, where 500,000 mulattoes testify the affection and honorable love existing between the master and the female slave. This is the land where fathers sell children, and brothers and sisters sell brothers and sisters. This is the same land whose clergy have found a curious edition of the Bible, sustaining these acts upon the authority of Divine Commands . . . Here are the great man, woman and child flesh markets of the world. Immortal souls are the merchandise of the auction room. This is the land where Abolitionists are threatened, defamed, and put to death; this is the land which threatens the dissolution of the confederacy; this is the land of SLAVES." *Ibid.*, pp. 90–91.

16 The strong ground swell for political action in this area is fairly well revealed in John White Chadwick, *A Life for Liberty; Anti-Slavery and Other Letters of Sallie Holley* (New York, 1899); Elizur Wright, *Myron Holley; And What He Did for Liberty and True Religion* (Boston, 1882); and William Goodell, *Slavery and Anti-Slavery; A History of the Great Struggle in Both Hemispheres; with a View of the Slavery Question in the United States* (New York, 1885).

17 "Address of the National Convention of Abolitionists, Held at Albany, July 31, 1839, to the Citizens of the United States," in *Pennsylvania Freeman*, August 22, 1839.

18 *Ibid.*

19 Gamaliel Bailey to Birney, November 28, 1839, Dwight L. Dumond (ed.), *Letters of James Gillespie Birney, 1831–1857* (2 vols., New York, 1938), I, pp. 509–10.

20 F. Julius LeMoyne to Birney, December 10, 1839, *ibid.*, I, pp. 511–14.

21 James G. Birney to Myron Holley, Joshua H. Darling, and Josiah Andrews, December 17, 1839, *ibid.*, I, pp. 514–16.

22 James G. Birney to Myron Holley, December 26, 1839, *ibid.*, I, pp. 516–17.

23 Myron Holley to Birney, January 1, 1840, *ibid.*, I, pp. 518–19.

24 The resolutions may be found conveniently in *ibid.*, I, p. 512.

25 James G. Birney to Amos A. Phelps, February 4, 1840, *ibid.*, I, pp. 525–27.

26 Henry B. Stanton to Birney, March 21, 1840, *ibid.*, I,

pp. 541–43. This was the position of the Michigan men. In June 1839 the Michigan State Anti-Slavery Convention resolved "that moral influence, exercised in a spirit of kindness and Christian forbearance toward all concerned, remains, as it ever has been, the only appropriate means of accomplishing the anti-slavery enterprise." *Michigan Freeman*, June 18, 1839. By March 1840 they were strongly anti-Garrison, but favored delay as a matter of expediency. *Ibid.*, January 15, January 29, and March 4, 1840.

27 Gamaliel Bailey to Birney, February 21, 1840, Dwight L. Dumond (ed.), *Letters of James Gillespie Birney, 1831–1857* (2 vols., New York, 1938), pp. 531–32.

28 See *Michigan Freeman*, March 4, 1840; *ibid.*, March 18, 1840; and *Friend of Man*, February 8, 1840.

29 See Elizur Wright, *Myron Holley; and What He Did for Liberty and True Religion.*

30 *Pennsylvania Freeman*, April 23, 1840.

Chapter 36
The Liberty Party

1 Birney to Myron Holley, Joshua Leavitt, and Elizur Wright, May 11, 1840, Dwight L. Dumond (ed.), *Letters of James Gillespie Birney, 1831–1857* (2 vols., New York, 1938), I, pp. 562–74.

2 The best source of information about Earle is Edwin B. Bronner, *Thomas Earle As a Reformer* (Philadelphia, 1948). He was a Quaker, a Jeffersonian Democrat, and an attorney; a staunch advocate of universal suffrage, free trade, economy in government, and limitation of executive power. The Garrisonians threw him out of the American Anti-Slavery Society and the Pennsylvania Anti-Slavery Society, Eastern District, for his political activities.

3 See the files of the *Michigan Freeman*, the *Albany Patriot*, and the *Philanthropist* for the campaign. An old but still useful volume is Theodore C. Smith, *The Liberty and Free Soil Parties in the Northwest* (New York, 1897).

4 Theodore D. Weld to James G. Birney, January 22, 1842, Dwight L. Dumond (ed.), *Letters of James Gillespie Birney, 1831–1857*, II, p. 663.

5 *Signal of Liberty*, April 28, 1841.

6 "Address of the National Liberty Convention of 1841," in *Signal of Liberty*, September 15, 1841.

7 See *Signal of Liberty*, February 19, 1844.

8 *Signal of Liberty*, June 2 and 16, 1841.

9 *Signal of Liberty*, January 26, 1841.

10 Birney to Joshua Leavitt and others, January 10, 1842, Dwight L. Dumond (ed.), *Letters of James Gillespie Birney, 1831–1857*, II, pp. 645–56.

11 See "Liberty Address to the Voters of the Second Congressional District of Michigan," *Signal of Liberty*, June 12, 1843.

12 See remarks of Reverend Nathaniel Colver in *The Annual Report of the American and Foreign Anti-Slavery Society, Presented at the General Meeting, Held in Broadway Tabernacle, May 11, 1847, with the Addresses, Resolutions, and Treasurer's Report* (New York, 1847), pp. 25–26; Luther Rawson Marsh, *Writings and Speeches of Alvan Stewart on Slavery* (New York, 1860), pp. 40–49; *The Signal of Liberty*, June 30, 1841.

13 Salmon P. Chase to Birney, January 21, 1842, Dwight L. Dumond (ed.), *Letters of James Gillespie Birney, 1831–1857*, II, pp. 661–62.

14 James G. Birney to Salmon P. Chase, February 2, 1842, *ibid.*, II, pp. 670–72; Joshua Leavitt to Birney, February 14, 1842, *ibid.*, II, pp. 673–74; Alvan Stewart to Birney, April 14, 1842, *ibid.*, II, pp. 689–90.

15 See *ibid.*, I, Introduction, pp. 18–22. Birney, here, makes this significant statement of what a slave could prove in a court of law: "In the first place, he proves that *allegiance and protection* are inseparable. This doctrine is so well established, so generally—may I not say almost universally acknowledged—that the abundant proof of it contained in the best writers on public law is unnecessary. A slave, for instance, may be tried before a Court for robbing the United States Mail, or for piracy. We try him, because we demand from him allegiance. There is, on his part, a tacit condition that he will be subject to the laws. For this *allegiance* we owe him, what we refuse to pay, *protection*—'entire security.'"

16 Other outstanding leaders of the old antislavery group in the West included Zebina Eastman and Owen Lovejoy in Illinois, Arnold Buffum in Indiana, and Guy Beckley in Michigan. Eastman was editor of the *Western Citizen* and Beckley of the *Signal of Liberty*. Bailey edited the *Philanthropist* in Cincinnati; Charles T. Torrey the *Albany Patriot*; Joshua Leavitt the *Emancipator*; Elizur Wright the *Chronotype*; Austin Willey the Hallowell, Maine, *Liberty Standard*.

17 The best treatment of the Liberty Party campaign of 1844 is Betty Fladeland, *James G. Birney: Slaveholder and Abolitionist* (Ithaca, New York), pp. 227–51.

18 James G. Birney to Leicester King, January 1, 1844, in *Signal of Liberty*, January 29, 1844.

19 Birney's most important anti-Clay pronouncement was his "Headlands in the Life of Henry Clay," published serially in the *Emancipator* in September 1844. There were published during the campaign a number of pamphlets on the evils of dueling, probably because it was still prevalent in the South, and because James K. Polk had taken a firm and courageous stand against the practice.

20 All of the documents pertaining to the Garland Forgery are in the Dwight L. Dumond (ed.), *Letters of James Gillespie Birney, 1831–1857*, volume 2; and the best account of its aftermath, probably as much as will ever be known, is given in Betty Fladeland, *James G. Birney: Slaveholder and Abolitionist*, pp. 244–51.

21 *The Address of the Southern and Western Liberty Convention Held at Cincinnati, June 11 & 12, 1845, to the People of the United States* (New York, 1845).

22 William Goodell, *Address of the Macedon Convention; and Letters of Gerrit Smith* (Albany, 1847); and *Case for a National Nominating Convention* [June 8–20, 1847, at Macedon Lock, New York].

Chapter 37
Fugitive Slaves and the People

1 "No person held to service or labor in one State under the Laws thereof, escaping into another, shall, in consequence of any law or regulation therein, be dis-

charged from such service or labor, but shall be delivered up on claim of the party to whom such service or labor may be due."

2 See William R. Leslie, "A Study in the Origins of Interstate Rendition: The Big Beaver Creek Murders," *American Historical Review*, LVII (October, 1951), pp. 63–76.

3 George M. Stroud, *A Sketch of the Laws Relating to Slavery in the Several States of the United States of America* (second edition; Philadelphia, 1856), pp. 272–73.

4 Charles Olcott, *Two Lectures on the Subject of Slavery and Abolition* (Massillon, Ohio, 1838), p. 6.

5 Any argument in support of the natural rights of man is equally applicable to all persons of both sexes of all races and nationalities.

6 A special section of Southern newspapers was reserved for notices of runaways, headed by a small woodcut. The figure of a man was an energetic person striding along with a bundle of clothes tied to a stick and carried over his shoulder. The woman appeared to proceed more slowly. She was slightly stooped and carried her bundle of clothes at her side. Slavery was abolished in Mexico by presidential proclamation on September 15, 1829. Upper Canada (1793) provided for the freedom of all slave children at age twenty-five, and the British Emancipation Act of 1833 forbade all slavery in the Empire.

7 The South Carolinians, in the eighteenth century, paid the Indians twenty pounds for each scalp and two ears of fugitives captured beyond the Savannah River.

8 Reprinted in *Friend of Man*, March 22, 1837.

9 Stroud, in his *Laws Relating to Slavery*, p. 280, gave the following form of these certificates:

"I hereby certify that negro Betsy owes service to John Jones, of Savannah, state of Georgia; that she escaped from said state into the state of Pennsylvania; where she was arrested; and I hereby authorize said John Jones to use such reasonable force and restraint as may be necessary to take and remove her to the said state of Georgia."

10 The Bill of Rights of the Constitution of the United States guaranteed jury trial in all criminal cases and in civil cases where more than twenty dollars was involved, and that no person (not citizen, but person) could be deprived of life, liberty, or property, without due process of law. This was a federal guarantee of protection against any agency of government and was not meant to control only the federal government. If it was not so, then Taney was completely wrong in 1819, for no man ever said it was so in more simple, but eloquent, language.

11 Wilbur H. Siebert, *Vermont's Anti-Slavery and Underground Railroad Record* (Columbus, 1937), p. 5.

12 See William R. Leslie, "The Constitutional Significance of Indiana's Statute of 1824 on Fugitives from Labor," *The Journal of Southern History*, XIII (August, 1947), pp. 338–53; and "The Pennsylvania Fugitive Slave Act of 1826," *ibid.*, pp. 429–45.

13 Richard Peters, *Reports of Cases Argued and Adjudged in the Supreme Court of the United States, 1828–1842* (16 vols., New York, 1883–85), XVI (1842), pp. 424–73.

14 These laws forbidding the use of state law-enforcement machinery in the return of fugitives were passed in Vermont in 1842, Massachusetts in 1843, Connecticut in 1844, New Hampshire in 1846, Pennsylvania in 1847, and Rhode Island in 1848.

15 Charles Beecher, *The Duty of Disobedience to Wicked Laws, A Sermon on the Fugitive Slave Law* (New York, 1851), p. 12.

16 *Ibid.*, p. 14.

17 *Ibid.*, pp. 15–20.

18 *Ibid.*, pp. 21–22.

19 Those who supported the constitutionality of the law, like Stephen A. Douglas, insisted it was only a summary hearing to establish identity.

20 These were newly created officials, without precedents to guide them, possessing an administrative character yet performing judicial functions.

21 Even Gamaliel Bailey, editor of the *National Era* in Washington, D. C., spoke out strongly against the Act. *National Era*, September 26, 1850.

22 Gustavus L. Foster, *The Doctrine of Subjection to "The Powers That Be," in Its Application to the Fugitive Slave Law* (Jackson, Michigan, 1850).

23 Sympathy for the fugitive and clandestine aid to his escape were as old as slavery itself. Slaveholders, as we have seen, hated Quakers because of it and persecuted them whenever possible. The literature of this phase of the antislavery movement is abundant. See William Still, *The Underground Railroad* (Philadelphia, 1872); Levi Coffin, *Reminiscences of Levi Coffin* (Cincinnati, 1850); Marian McDougall, *Fugitive Slaves, 1619–1865* (Boston, 1891); Wilbur Siebert, *The Underground Railroad from Slavery to Freedom* (New York, 1899); Henrietta Buckmaster, *Let My People Go* (New York, 1941).

24 In "Song of Myself," in *Leaves of Grass*.

Chapter 38
Fugitive Slaves and the Law

1 *Bush's Representatives* v. *White and Wife*, 1825, Thomas B. Monroe, *Reports of Cases at Common Law and in Equity Argued and Decided in the Court of Appeals of the Commonwealth of Kentucky, 1824–1828* (7 vols., Cincinnati, 1850), III, pp. 75–79; *Harry and Others* v. *Decker and Hopkins*, 1818, R. J. Walker, *Reports of Cases Adjudged in the Supreme Court of Mississippi, 1818–1832* (Natchez, 1834), I, pp. 36–43; *Rankin* v. *Lydia*, 1820, Alexander K. Marshall, *Decisions of the Court of Appeals of Kentucky, 1817–1821* (3 vols., Cincinnati, 1848), II, pp. 813–21; *Winny* v. *Whitesides*, 1824, Louis Houck, *Reports of Cases Argued and Determined in the Supreme Court of the State of Missouri, 1821–1852* (15 vols., Cape Girardeau, 1870–72), I, pp. 259–61; *Lunsford* v. *Coquillon*, 1824, Francois-Xavier Martin, *Cases Argued and Determined in the Supreme Court of the State of Louisiana, 1823–1830* (8 vols., New Orleans, 1824–30), II, pp. 401–9.

2 My distinguished colleague, Professor William R. Leslie of the University of Michigan, for whose research I have the greatest respect, says that he has examined

over seven hundred cases in state courts which upheld this principle of the supremacy of universal freedom of man. It is strong supporting evidence of my previous contention that there is no basis for the idea so assiduously upheld by slaveholders and federal courts that Negroes were not parties to the Constitution, and not citizens of the states, and not intended to enjoy the guarantees of freedom and security contained in the Constitution. That is a fiction which further research will completely demolish.

3 *Commonwealth* v. *Aves*, 1836, in Octavius Pickering, *Reports of Cases Argued and Determined in the Superior Judicial Court of Massachusetts, 1822–1839* (24 vols., Boston, 1847), XVIII, p. 205.

4 In the case of *Daniel Wilson* v. *Edmund Melvin*, 1835, Justice Tomkins said that unnecessary delay in passing through a free state would free slaves. Louis Houck, *Reports of Cases Argued and Determined in the Supreme Court of the State of Missouri, 1821–1852*, IV, p. 350.

5 *Anderson* v. *Poindexter*, 1856, *Reports of Cases Argued and Determined in the Supreme Court of Ohio, 1821*, VI, p. 631. The Court said further in this case: "Its [slavery's] manacles instantly break asunder and crumble to dust, when he who has worn them obtains the liberty from his oppressor, and is afforded the opportunity by him of placing his feet upon our shore, and of breathing the air of freedom."

6 *Lemmon* v. *People*, 1860, Oliver L. Barbour, *Reports of Cases in Law and Equity in the Supreme Court of the State of New York, 1847–1874* (67 vols., New York, 1848–76), XXVI, pp. 270–88.

7 *State* v. *Hoppess*, 1845, *Western Law Journal*, II, p. 290.

8 *Vaughan* v. *Williams*, 1845, John McLean, *Reports Argued and Decided in the Circuit Court of the United States for the Seventh Circuit, 1829–1855* (6 vols., Cincinnati, 1840–66), III, p. 538.

9 *Strader, Gorman and Armstrong* v. *Graham*, 1850, Benjamin C. Howard, *Reports of Cases Argued and Adjudged in the Supreme Court of the United States, 1843–1860* (24 vols., Philadelphia, 1843–1937), X, p. 82.

10 *In re Susan*, 1823, *The Federal Cases, Comprising Cases Argued and Determined in the Circuit and District Courts of the United States from the Earliest Times to the Beginning of the Federal Reporter* (30 vols., St. Paul, 1894–98), XXIII, pp. 444–45.

11 *State* v. *Heddon*, 1795, Richard S. Coxe, *Reports of Cases Argued and Determined in the Supreme Court of New Jersey, 1790–1795* (Newark, 1901), p. 377.

12 *Commonwealth* v. *Griffith*, 1823, Octavius Pickering, *Reports of Cases Argued and Determined in the Supreme Judicial Court of Massachusetts, 1822–1839*, II, p. 18; *In Re Martin*, 1835, *The Federal Cases, Comprising Cases Argued and Determined in the Circuit and District Courts of the United States from the Earliest Times to the Beginning of the Federal Reporter*, XVI, pp. 881–84; *In Re Sims*, 1851, Luther S. Cushing, *Reports of Cases Argued and Determined in the Supreme Judicial Court of Massachusetts, 1848–1853* (12 vols., Boston, 1850–66), VII, pp. 285–319.

13 *Johnson* v. *Tompkins and Others*, 1833, Henry Baldwin, *Reports of Cases Determined in the Circuit Court of the United States in and for the Third Circuit, 1828–1833* (Philadelphia, 1837), pp. 571–605; *In Re Martin*, Elijah Paine, *Reports of Cases Argued and Determined in the Circuit Court of the United States for the Second Circuit, 1810–1840* (2 vols., New York, 1827–60), II, pp. 348–55.

14 *Worthington* v. *Preston*, 1824, *The Federal Cases, Comprising Cases Argued and Determined in the Circuit and District Courts of the United States from the Earliest Times to the Beginning of the Federal Reporter*, XXX, p. 645. Said Washington: "He [the magistrate] has no authority to issue a warrant to apprehend the fugitive in the first instance, or to commit him after the examination is concluded, and the certificate given. Pending the examination, whilst the fugitive is in *custodia legis*, the judge of the district and myself have always considered ourselves at liberty to commit, from day to day, till the examination is closed, or else the fugitive could not safely be indulged with time to get his witnesses to disprove the claim of the asserted owner, should he have any." *Ibid.*, p. 463.

15 *Jack* v. *Martin*, 1834, John L. Wendell, *Reports of Cases Argued and Determined in the Supreme Court of Judicature and in the Court for the Correction of Errors, of the State of New York, 1828–1841* (26 vols., New York, 1829–52), XII, pp. 311–29.

16 *Jones* v. *Van Zandt*, 1847, John McLean, *Reports Argued and Decided in the Circuit Court of the United States for the Seventh Circuit, 1829–1855*, II, pp. 596–632; Salmon P. Chase, *An Argument for the Defendant, Submitted to the Supreme Court of the United States, in the Case of Wharton Jones* v. *John Van Zandt* (Cincinnati, 1847); *Argument of William H. Seward, on the Law of Congress Concerning the Recapture of Fugitive Slaves. In the Supreme Court of the United States. John Van Zandt ad sectum Wharton Jones* (Albany, 1847).

17 *Driskill* v. *Parrish*, 1847, *The Federal Cases, Comprising Cases Argued and Determined in the Circuit and District Courts of the United States from the Earliest Times to the Beginning of the Federal Reporter*, VII, pp. 1093–1104.

18 *Oliver et al.* v. *Kaufman, ibid.*, XVIII, pp. 657–64.

19 *Norris* v. *Newton, ibid.*, XVIII, p. 322.

20 *Johnson* v. *Tompkins*, Helen T. Catterall, *Judicial Cases Concerning American Slavery and the Negro* (6 vols., Washington, 1926–37), IV, pp. 286–89; *Giltner* v. *Gorham, ibid.*, pp. 81–84.

21 New York State Legislature, in Assembly, April 11, 1840. Document 310. *Message from the Governor Transmitting a Communication from the Governor of Virginia, and Proceedings of the Legislature of That State, in Relation to Certain Alleged Fugitives from Justice* (Albany, 1840). The seamen were Negroes, and Seward's refusal was considered a triumph for Negro civil rights.

22 *Greathouse* v. *Dunlap, ibid.*, V, p. 9.

23 *Ex parte Robinson*, 1855, John McLean, *Reports Argued and Decided in the Circuit Court of the United States for the Seventh Circuit, 1829–1855*, VL, p. 365; *Ex Parte Bushnell*, 1859, *Reports of Cases Argued and*

Determined in the Supreme Court of Ohio, 1852 (Cincinnati, 1874), IX, pp. 62–325.

24 Antislavery conventions said a thousand times over that the main function of government is to secure the natural, inalienable, and equal rights of all persons. See, for example, *Proceedings of the Ohio State Christian Anti-Slavery Convention, Held at Columbus, August 10 and 11, 1859* (Columbus, 1859), p. 10.

25 Charles Sumner, *Speech of Hon. Charles Sumner of Massachusetts on His Motion to Repeal the Fugitive Slave Bill in the Senate of the United States, August 26, 1852*, p. 10.

26 *The [Tenth] Annual Report of the American and Foreign Anti-Slavery Society, Presented at New York, May 7, 1850, with the Addresses and Resolutions* (New York, 1850), p. 129. See also an earlier statement in *Sixth Annual Report of the Executive Committee of the American Anti-Slavery Society, with the Speeches Delivered at the Anniversary Meeting Held in the City of New York, on the 7th of May, 1839* (New York, 1839), p. 99.

27 The law violated prohibition of unreasonable search and seizure. It recognized ex parte testimony; denied cross-examination, public hearings, public judgment, testimony by or for the accused, jury trial; required no records. See Gerrit Smith, *Abstract of the Argument on the Fugitive Slave Law, Made by Gerrit Smith, in Syracuse, June, 1852, on the Trial of Henry W. Allen, U. S. Deputy Marshal, for Kidnapping* (Syracuse, 1852); Salmon P. Chase, *Speech of Salmon P. Chase in the Case of the Colored Woman, Matilda, Who Was Brought Before the Court of Common Pleas of Hamilton County, Ohio, by Writ of Habeas Corpus, March 11, 1837* (Cincinnati, 1837).

28 See *Annual Report Presented to the American Anti-Slavery Society, by the Executive Committee, at the Annual Meeting Held in New York, May 9, 1855* (New York, 1855), p. 41.

29 *In re Booth, 1854, Reports of Cases Argued and Determined in the Supreme Court of the State of Wisconsin, 1839–1860* (Chicago, 1782), III, p. 69.

30 Edwin Channing Larned, "Argument in a Slave Case," *In Memory of Edwin Channing Larned* (Chicago, 1886), p. 97. See also Luther Hamilton (ed.), *Memoirs, Speeches and Writings of Robert Rantoul* (Boston, 1854), pp. 747–51.

31 Gerrit Smith, *Abstract of the Argument on the Fugitive Slave Law, Made by Gerrit Smith, in Syracuse, June, 1852, on the Trial of Henry W. Allen . . .* , p. 26.

32 *Annual Report, Presented to the American Anti-Slavery Society, by the Executive Committee, at the Annual Meeting, Held in New York, May 9, 1855*, p. 48.

33 *Speech of Wendell Phillips at the Franklin Hall* [Philadelphia], *May 12, 1848*, in the *Pennsylvania Freeman*, June 8, 1848. See also his speech at the anniversary of the American Anti-Slavery Society, New York, May 9, 1848, in *ibid.*, June 1, 1848. Said Gerrit Smith, in reply to the arguments of Phillips, Garrison, and others: "You ask me to join you in abandoning the Constitution. My whole heart—my whole sense of duty to God and man forbids my doing so . . . The Constitution has put weapons into the hands of the American people entirely

sufficient for staying the monster within whose bloody and crushing grasp are the three millions of American slaves . . . To give up the Constitution is to give up the slave. His hope of a peaceful deliverance is, under God, in the application of the antislavery principles of the Constitution." Gerrit Smith to Edmund Quincy, November 23, 1846, in *The Pennsylvania Freeman*, January 7, 1847.

34 *Congressional Globe*, 31 Cong., 2 Sess., p. 828.

35 See speech by Joshua Giddings, *Congressional Globe*, 32 Cong., 1 Sess., Appendix, p. 775; William Uhler Hensel, *The Christiana Riot and the Treason Trials of 1851* (Lancaster, 1911).

36 *United States v. Cobb, 1857, The Federal Cases, Comprising Cases Argued and Determined in the Circuit and District Courts of the United States from the Earliest Times to the Beginning of the Federal Reporter*, XXV, p. 481.

37 *Boston Slave Riot, and Trial of Antony Burns* (Boston, 1854).

38 Charles Sumner, *Speech on His Motion to Repeal the Fugitive Slave Bill . . . August 26, 1852* (Washington, 1852), p. 30. See, also, remarks by Giddings, *Congressional Globe*, 32 Cong., 1 Sess., Appendix, p. 740.

*Chapter 39
Negro Leaders*

1 George S. Brookes, *Friend Anthony Benezet* (Philadelphia, 1937); Robert Vaux, *Memoirs of the Life of Anthony Benezet* (New York, 1817); Carter Godwin Woodson, *The Education of the Negro Prior to 1861* (New York, 1915).

2 See Charles Wesley, *Richard Allen, Apostle of Freedom* (Washington, 1935); and his "The Negro in the Organization of Abolition," *Phylon*, II (1941), pp. 223–35; "The Negroes of New York in the Emancipation Movement," *Journal of Negro History*, XXIV, pp. 65–103; "The Negro's Struggle for Freedom in Its Birthplace," *ibid.*, XXX, pp. 62–81. See also *A Statistical Inquiry into the Condition of the People of Colour of the City and Districts of Philadelphia* (Philadelphia, 1849).

3 Henry Baker, "Benjamin Banneker," *Journal of Negro History*, III (1919), pp. 100–112.

4 *Memoir and Poems of Phillis Wheatley* (Boston, 1838).

5 See the report of a meeting of the Western Reserve Anti-Slavery Society in *The Anti-Slavery Record*, I, pp. 110–11.

6 For a biographical sketch of Horton, see Jay Saunders Redding, *To Make a Poet Black* (Chapel Hill, 1939).

7 *Annals of Congress*, 6 Cong., 1 Sess., pp. 229–45.

8 There was opposition among the Negroes, of course, but rather general acceptance by the time of the 1847 convention. *The North Star*, December 3, 1847.

9 See Weld to Lewis Tappan, March 9, 1836, Gilbert H. Barnes and Dwight L. Dumond (eds.), *Letters of Theodore Dwight Weld, Angelina Grimké Weld, and Sarah Grimké, 1822–1844* (2 vols., New York, 1934), I, pp. 270–74, for a full discussion of the subject.

10 *Ibid.*, II, p. 741–44.

11 Said in connection with the call to the first Ohio convention at Putnam.

12 *American and Foreign Anti-Slavery Reporter, June 1842;* and *American and Foreign Anti-Slavery Society, Annual Report, 1847,* p. 31.

13 See Weld to Gerrit Smith, October 23, 1839, Gilbert H. Barnes and Dwight L. Dumond (eds.), *Letters of Theodore Dwight Weld, Angelina Grimké Weld, and Sarah Grimké, 1822–1844,* II, p. 811; *Fifth Annual Report of the Board of Managers of the Massachusetts Anti-Slavery Society with Some Account of the Annual Meeting, January 24, 1837* (Boston, 1837), p. 39.

14 Henry Highland Garnet, *Walker's Appeal, with a Brief Sketch of His Life; and Also Garnet's Address to the Slaves of the United States of America* (New York, 1848).

15 For the evolution of his ideas and his break with Garrison, see Benjamin Quarles, "The Break Between Douglass and Garrison," *Journal of Negro History,* XXIII, pp. 144–54.

16 Douglass' paper was the best of the antislavery papers edited by Negroes. *The Colored American,* edited by Samuel E. Cornish, and Charles B. Ray, 1837–42, had 1,600 subscribers, three-fourths of whom were Negroes. Henry Bibb's *Voice of the Fugitive* was equally important. Any one of the three was more important in the movement while they were being published than Garrison's *Liberator,* which also was supported almost entirely by Negroes.

17 See *The Anti-Slavery Record,* I, pp. 150–51.

18 Jesse Torrey, *A Portraiture of Domestic Slavery in the United States; with Reflections on the Practicability of Restoring the Moral Rights of the Slaves, without Impairing the Legal Privileges of the Possessor; and a Project of a Colonial Asylum for Free Persons of Color; Including Memoirs of Facts on the Interior Traffic in Slaves, and on Kidnapping* (Philadelphia, 1817).

19 William Still, *The Underground Railroad* (Philadelphia, 1872).

20 See the *Emancipator,* August 30, 1838.

21 [Margaret Matilda Odell], *Memoir and Poems of Phillis Wheatley* (third edition; Boston, 1838).

22 Richard Hildreth, *The Slave; or, Memoirs of Archy Moore* (Boston, 1836).

23 See *Anti-Slavery Record,* III, pp. 74–83.

24 Frederick Douglass, *Narrative of the Life of Frederick Douglass, an American Slave; Written by Himself* (Boston, 1845).

25 See also *The Anti-Slavery Harp: A Collection of Songs for Anti-Slavery Meetings* (Boston, 1849); and *The Black Man, His Antecedents, His Genius, and His Achievements* (New York, 1863); *The Pennsylvania Freeman,* August 10, 1848, and January 8, 1849.

26 Jermain Wesley Loguen, *The Rev. J. W. Loguen, as a Slave and as a Freeman; A Narrative of Real Life* (Syracuse, 1859).

27 James W. C. Pennington, *The Fugitive Blacksmith; or, Events in the History of James Pennington, Pastor of the Presbyterian Church, Formerly a Slave in the State of Maryland, United States* (third edition; London, 1850). See also *A Text Book of the Origin and History . . . of the Colored People* (Hartford, 1841); and *Cov-*

enants Involving Moral Wrong Are Not Obligatory upon Man; A Sermon Delivered in the Fifth Congregational Church, Hartford, on Thanksgiving Day, Nov. 17th, 1842 (Hartford, 1842).

Chapter 40
Here the Slave Found Freedom

1 Slavery was not abolished by legislation in Lower Canada until the Parliamentary Act of 1833, which freed all slaves in the British dominions, but judicial decisions in a series of fugitive slave cases effectively terminated it between 1798 and 1800.

2 The rate of payment agreed upon by arbitration was $580 for slaves from Louisiana; $390 for slaves from Alabama, Georgia, and South Carolina; and $280 for slaves from other states.

3 See *Annals of Congress,* 16 Cong., 2 Sess., I, 942; *Niles Weekly Register,* XXX, p. 300; *ibid.,* XXIV, p. 198; *Congressional Globe,* 25 Cong., 3 Sess., VII, pt. 2, pp. 34–39.

4 The chairman of the Philadelphia vigilance committee said that fear of being separated by sale and anger at having been separated were the first causes of flight. William Still, *The Underground Railroad* (Philadelphia, 1872), p. 3.

5 *Proceedings of the Ohio Anti-Slavery Convention, Held at Putnam on the Twenty-Second, Twenty-Third, and Twenty-Fourth of April, 1835* (New York, 1835), pp. 18–19.

6 *The Quarterly Anti-Slavery Magazine,* II, p. 350.

7 Canadian census reports before 1850 are totally unreliable, after 1850 confusing and incomplete. For various estimates, see Fred Landon, "Social Conditions Among the Negroes in Upper Canada before 1865," Ontario Historical Society, *Papers and Records,* XXII (1925), pp. 144–58.

8 *Reminiscences of Levi Coffin* (Cincinnati, 1880), p. 253.

9 *The Liberator,* February 14, 1851.

10 *The Voice of the Fugitive,* May 7, 1851; December 3, 1851; April 22, 1852.

11 *The Liberator,* October 4, 1850.

12 *The Annual Report of the American and Foreign Anti-Slavery Society, Presented at New York, May 6, 1851, with the Addresses and Resolutions* (New York, 1851), p. 31.

13 Fred Landon, "The Negro Migration to Canada After the Passing of the Fugitive Slave Act," *The Journal of Negro History,* V (1920), pp. 22–36.

14 See Samuel Gridley Howe, *The Refugees from Slavery in Canada West* (Boston, 1864).

15 See *Voice of the Fugitive,* July 2, 1851; November 4, 1852.

16 *The Voice of the Fugitive,* March 12, 1851; January 1, 1852; January 29, 1852.

17 Fred Landon, "History of the Wilberforce Refugee Colony," London and Middlesex, Ontario, Historical Society, *Transactions,* IX, pp. 30–34.

18 *Signal of Liberty,* March 4, 1844; Josiah Henson, *The Life of Josiah Henson, Formerly a Slave, Now an Inhabitant of Canada, As Narrated by Himself* (Boston, 1849).

19 Fred Landon, "The Buxton Settlement in Canada,"

Journal of Negro History, III (1918), pp. 360–61; Samuel Gridley Howe, *The Refugees from Slavery in Canada West*, pp. 109–11; *The Voice of the Fugitive*, November 5, 1851; Benjamin Drew, *A North-Side View of Slavery. The Refugee: or the Narratives of Fugitive Slaves in Canada* (Boston, 1856), pp. 291–96.

20 Nathan Stone, A. L. Power of Farmington, and Harvard Hallock were officers and Henry Bibb was a trustee. *Voice of the Fugitive*, June 4, 1851.

21 *Voice of the Fugitive*, March 12, 1851; February 12, 1852.

22 Henry Bibb, *Narrative of the Life and Adventures of Henry Bibb, an American Slave, Written by Himself* (New York, 1849).

23 Fred Coyne Hamil, *The Valley of the Lower Thames, 1640–1850* (Toronto, 1951), p. 123.

24 See *The Voice of the Fugitive*, September 10, 1851.

25 *Congressional Globe*, 36 Cong., 1 Sess., IV, Appendix, p. 250.

26 Charles E. Barnes, "Battle Creek as a Station on the Underground Railway," Michigan Pioneer and Historical Society *Collections*, XXXVIII (1912), p. 280.

27 Benjamin Drew, *A North-Side View of Slavery. The Refugee: or the Narratives of Fugitive Slaves in Canada,* pp. 234–36.

28 See William C. Nell, *The Colored Patriots of the American Revolution, with an Additional Survey of the Condition and Prospects of Colored Americans* (Boston, 1855), p. 359.

29 Peter H. Clark, an active participant in the National Convention movement, said the midwestern state conventions were held solely to improve conditions of Negroes in their respective states. They were not concerned with the interests of the Negroes as a whole nor with slavery. The conventions in the East, on the other hand, were antislavery conventions. See John W. Cromwell, *The Negro in American History* (Washington, 1914), pp. 36–38.

30 Address by Douglass before the National Negro Convention of Rochester, July 6–8, 1853, in Philip S. Foner, *The Life and Writings of Frederick Douglass* (4 vols., New York, 1850), I, p. 41.

31 *Ibid.,* I, pp. 331–36.

32 John W. Cromwell, *The Negro in American History*, pp. 39–40.

33 Samuel Gridley Howe, *The Refugees from Slavery in Canada West*, p. 39.

34 Fred Landon, "Fugitive Slaves in London, Ontario, Before 1860," London and Middlesex Historical Society, *Transactions*, X (1919), p. 30.

35 Benjamin Drew, *A North-Side View of Slavery, The Refugee: or the Narratives of Fugitive Slaves in Canada,* p. 29.

36 *First Annual Report, Presented to the Anti-Slavery Society of Canada, by Its Executive Committee, March 24, 1852* (Toronto, 1852).

Chapter 41
The Churches

1 Speech of Wendell Phillips, May 12, 1848, at the Franklin Hall, Philadelphia, *The Pennsylvania Freeman*, June 8, 1848.

2 Antislavery literature is replete with the most severe condemnation by such men as John Wesley, Jonathan Edwards, Samuel Johnson, Edmund Burke, Montesquieu, William Pitt, Samuel Hopkins, Grotius, Benjamin Rush, Abbe Gregoire, Joseph Addison, Abraham Booth, James Beattie, George Fox, John Locke, Thomas Jefferson, John Jay, Benjamin Franklin, James Oglethorpe, J.J. Rousseau. Race prejudice was less strong before 1800 than afterward. It was magnified out of all proportion to its actual strength by the Colonization Society.

3 Quoted in James G. Birney, *The American Churches the Bulwarks of American Slavery* (London, 1840), p. 14.

4 *Ibid.*

5 The reader will profit at this point by rereading the summary of Elizabeth Heyrich's pamphlet, Chapter 15.

6 *Ibid.,* pp. 15–16; William Goodell, *Slavery and Anti-Slavery; A History of the Great Struggle in Both Hemispheres; with a View of the Slavery Question in the United States* (New York, 1855), pp. 145–46. See also James G. Birney and Orange Scott, *Debate on Modern Abolitionism in the General Conference of the Methodist Episcopal Church, Held in Cincinnati, May, 1836* (Cincinnati, 1836); and Orange Scott, *An Appeal to the Methodist Episcopal Church* (Boston, 1838).

7 James G. Birney, *The American Churches the Bulwarks of American Slavery*, pp. 16–18.

8 George Gordon, *Secession from a Pro-Slavery Church a Christian Duty* (Mercer, 1850), pp. 15–16; Presbyterian Church, *Extracts from the Minutes of the General Assembly of the Presbyterian Church in the United States of America, 1818* (Philadelphia, 1818), pp. 28–29.

9 Quoted in William Goodell, *Slavery and Anti-Slavery; A History of the Great Struggle in Both Hemispheres* . . . , pp. 152–53.

10 Jonathan Edwards, *The Injustice and Impolicy of the Slave Trade, and of the Slavery of the Africans; Illustrated in a Sermon Preached Before the Connecticut Society for the Promotion of Freedom, and for the Relief of Persons Unlawfully Holden in Bondage, at Their Annual Meeting in New Haven, September 15, 1791* (New Haven, 1791), p. 25.

11 Samuel Hopkins, *A Dialogue Concerning the Slavery of the Africans; Shewing It To Be the Duty and Interest of the American States To Emancipate All Their African Slaves* (Norwich, 1776).

12 Congregational Union of Scotland, *Address . . . to Their Fellow Christians in the United States on the Subject of American Slavery* (New York, 1840). See also Churchill Babington, *The Influence of Christianity in Promoting the Abolition of Slavery in Europe* (Cambridge, Deighton, 1846).

13 John Ripon (ed.), *The Baptist Annual Register* (London, 1802), I, p. 97.

14 R. B. Semple, *A History of the Rise and Progress of the Baptists in Virginia* (Richmond, 1810), p. 79.

15 John H. Spencer, *A History of Kentucky Baptists from 1769 to 1833, Including More Than 800 Biographical Sketches* (2 vols., Cincinnati, 1885), p. 184.

16 *Ibid.,* pp. 185–86. See also William W. Sweet, *Religion on the American Frontier* (New York, 1931), I, p. 564.

17 Robert G. Torbet, *A History of the Baptists* (Philadelphia, 1950), p. 301.

18 See James G. Birney, *The American Churches the Bulwarks of American Slavery*, p. 32.

19 *Ibid.*, p. 8.

20 Quoted in William Goodell, *Slavery and Anti-Slavery: A History of the Great Struggle in Both Hemispheres . . .*, p. 185.

21 See William W. Sweet, *The Baptists, 1783–1830* (New York, 1931), p. 324.

22 Marilla Marks (ed.), *Memoirs of the Life of David Marks, Minister of the Gospel* (Dover, N. H., 1846), p. 397. See [Nathaniel Southard], *The Negro Pew; Being an Inquiry Concerning the Propriety of Distinctions in the House of God, on Account of Color* (Boston, 1837).

23 See James Smylie, *A Review of a Letter, from the Presbytery of Chillicothe, to the Presbytery of Mississippi, on the Subject of Slavery* (Woodville, Miss., 1836).

24 See, for example, [Evan Lewis], *An Address to Christians of the [Several] Denominations on the Inconsistency of Admitting Slave-Holders to Communion and Church Membership* (Philadelphia, 1831). Lewis urged every Christian of every church and religious society to refuse communion with slaveholders.

25 Marilla Marks (ed.), *Memoirs of the Life of David Marks, Minister of the Gospel* (Dover, N. H., 1846), p. 339.

26 See Smith Hayne, *Baptist Trail-Makers of Michigan* (Philadelphia, 1936), p. 106.

27 *Address to the Churches of Jesus Christ, by the Evangelical Union Anti-Slavery Society of the City of New York, Auxiliary to the American Anti-Slavery Society, with the Constitution, Names of Officers, Boards of Managers, and Executive Committee* (New York, 1839).

Chapter 42
Labor

1 *The Constitution of the American Anti-Slavery Society, with the Declaration of the National Anti-Slavery Convention at Philadelphia, December, 1833, and the Address to the Public, Issued by the Executive Committee of the Society in September, 1835* (New York, 1838), pp. 7–9.

2 See argument of Enoch Lewis, *The Non-Slaveholder* (Old Series), I (1846), p. 102. See also *An Address to the People of Great Britain, on the Propriety of Abstaining from West India Sugar and Rum* (tenth edition; London, Philadelphia, 1792).

3 *Ibid.*, p. 89.

4 Quakers generally were opposed to violent controversy, particularly Garrisonian invective. See William Bassett, *Letter to a Member of the Society of Friends in Reply to Objections Against Joining Anti-Slavery Societies* (Boston, 1837).

5 Mary S. Locke, *Anti-Slavery in America, from the Introduction of African Slaves to the Prohibition of the Slave Trade* (Boston, 1901), pp. 189–90.

6 *Minutes of the Proceedings of the Third Convention of Delegates from the Abolition Societies Established in Different Parts of the United States, Assembled at Philadelphia on the First Day of January, One Thousand Seven Hundred and Ninety-Six, and Continued by Adjournments, until the Seventh Day of the Same Month* (Philadelphia, 1796), pp. 31–32.

7 Elihu Burritt, *A Plan of Brotherly Copartnership of the North and South, for the Peaceful Extinction of Slavery* (New York, 1856); see also David Irish, *Observations on a Living and Effectual Testimony against Slavery* (New York, 1836).

8 [Samuel Rhoads], *Considerations on the Use of the Productions of Slavery, Especially Addressed to the Religious Society of Friends Within the Limits of Philadelphia Yearly Meeting* (Philadelphia, 1844), pp. 34–35. See also [Lewis Carstairs Gunn], *Address to Abolitionists* (Philadelphia, 1838).

9 Angelina G. Weld to Lewis Tappan, August ——, 1841, in Gilbert H. Barnes and Dwight L. Dumond (eds.), *Letters of Theodore Dwight Weld, Angelina Grimké Weld, and Sarah Grimké, 1822–1844* (2 vols., New York, 1934), II, pp. 872–76.

10 Angelina Grimké to Weld, March 28, 1838, *ibid.*, pp. 607–12.

11 Elizabeth Margaret Chandler, *The Poetical Works of Elizabeth Margaret Chandler with a Memoir of Her Life and Character by Benjamin Lundy* (Philadelphia, 1845), p. 111.

12 See *Quarterly Anti-Slavery Magazine*, I, pp. 394–98.

13 *Minutes of the Adjourned Session of the Twentieth Biennial American Convention for Promoting the Abolition of Slavery, and Improving the Condition of the African Race, Held at Baltimore, Nov. 1828* (Philadelphia, 1828), pp. 31–32.

14 *Third Annual Report of the American Anti-Slavery Society; with the Speeches Delivered at the Anniversary Meeting Held in the City of New York, on the 10th May, 1836, and the Minutes of the Meetings of the Society for Business* (New York, 1836), p. 27.

15 *An Appeal to the Women of the Nominally Free States, Issued by an Anti-Slavery Convention of American Women, Held by Adjournment from the 9th to the 12th of May, 1837* (New York, 1837), pp. 24–28. See also *Proceedings of the Anti-Slavery Convention of American Women Held in Philadelphia, May 15th, 16th, 17th, 18th, 1838* (Philadelphia, 1838), p. 7.

16 American and Foreign Anti-Slavery Society, *An Address to the Anti-Slavery Christians of the United States* (New York, 1852), p. 15.

17 *The Non-Slaveholder*, Old Series, I (1846), p. 78.

18 *Ibid.*, II (1847), p. 276.

19 *The [Tenth] Annual Report of the American and Foreign Anti-Slavery Society, Presented at New York, May 7, 1850, with the Addresses and Resolutions* (New York, 1850), p. 136.

20 *Ibid.*

21 Gilbert H. Barnes and Dwight L. Dumond (eds.), *Letters of Theodore Dwight Weld, Angelina Grimké Weld, and Sarah Grimké, 1822–1844*, II, p. 797; D. L. Miller and B. S. Jones to Weld, Sept. 27, 1842, *ibid.*, 944.

22 *National Anti-Slavery Standard*, May 5, 1842; *The Non-Slaveholder*, Old Series, I (1846), pp. 23, 161.

23 The constitution of the society was published in the *Non-Slaveholder*, Old Series, I (1846), pp. 9–10. The association published only two reports: *Fifth Annual Report of the American Free Produce Association* (Phila-

delphia, 1843); and *Sixth Annual Report of the American Free Produce Association* (Philadelphia, 1844).

24 *The Liberator*, January 1, 1831; see also John R. Commons, *A Documentary History of American Industrial Society* (11 vols., Cleveland, 1910–11), VII, pp. 351–52.

25 *Ibid.*, VII, pp. 348.

26 Henry Fred James, *Abolitionism Unveiled; or, Its Origin, Progress, and Pernicious Tendency Fully Developed* (Cincinnati, 1856), p. 27.

27 *New York Tribune*, July 6, 1844.

28 William Ellery Channing, *Slavery* (Boston, 1835), p. 51. The extremes of Garrison caused Channing to hesitate about espousing the antislavery cause. Channing, in *A Letter to the Hon. Henry Clay, on the Annexation of Texas to the United States* (Boston, 1837), opposed annexation on principles of morality and religion, but disavowed any desire to abolish slavery against the wishes of the slave states.

29 See George Duffield, *A Sermon on American Slavery: Its Nature, and the Duties of Christians in Relation to It* (Detroit, 1840).

30 Salmon Portland Chase and Charles Dexter Cleveland, *Anti-Slavery Addresses of 1844 and 1845* (London and Philadelphia, 1867), p. 116; Richard Hildreth, *Despotism in America; an Inquiry into the Nature, Results, and Legal Basis of the Slaveholding System in the United States* (Boston, 1854), p. 100.

31 This was the argument of Lewis Tappan in his address to the nonslaveholding whites of the South and was to be the argument of Hinton Rowan Helper in his *Impending Crisis*. See also *American and Foreign Anti-Slavery Reporter*, March 1, 1843; and Theodore Parker, *A Letter to the People of the United States Touching the Matter of Slavery* (Boston, 1848), p. 42.

32 Hinton Rowan Helper, *The Impending Crisis of the South: How to Meet It* (New York, 1860), pp. 25–41.

33 Charles Francis Adams, *What Makes Slavery a Question of National Concern? A Lecture, Delivered by Invitation, at New York, January 30, at Syracuse, February 1, 1855* (Boston, 1855).

34 J. B. Ferguson, *An Address on the History, Authority, and Influence of Slavery, Delivered in the First Presbyterian Church, Nashville, Tennessee, 21st of November, 1850* (Nashville, 1850), p. 26.

35 William J. Grayson, *The Hireling and the Slave, Chicora, and Other Poems* (Charleston, 1856).

36 The complete argument may be found in William Harper, James H. Hammond, and others, *The Pro-Slavery Argument as Maintained by the Most Distinguished Writers of the Southern States* (Philadelphia, 1853).

37 *DeBow's Review*, March, 1847, p. 80. In the early years after Ohio became a state probably 2,000 slaves were hired out to work in Ohio by slaveholders of Virginia and Kentucky.

38 C. G. Memminger to Hammond, April 28, 1849. See Chauncey S. Boucher, "The Ante-Bellum Attitude of South Carolina Towards Manufacturing and Agriculture," *Washington University Studies*, No. 3 (1916), pp. 248–65; J. D. B. DeBow, *The Industrial Resources of the Southern and Western States* (New Orleans, 1852), III, pp. 24–37.

39 Hinton Rowan Helper, *The Impending Crisis of the South and How To Meet It* (New York, 1860), p. 281; Frederick Law Olmstead, *A Journey in the Seaboard Slave States, with Remarks on Their Economy* (New York, 1865), p. 84; Charles Nordhoff, *America for the Free Working Man* (New York, 1865).

40 See John R. Commons, *A Documentary History of American Industrial Society*, I, p. 139; II, pp. 365–67.

41 *Ibid.*, VI, p. 523.

42 Evans died in 1854.

43 William Harper, *Pro Slavery Argument* (Charleston, 1852), p. 52.

44 George Fitzhugh, *Sociology for the South, or the Failure of Free Society* (Richmond, 1854), p. 94.

45 As quoted in Frank T. Carlton, *Organized Labor in American History* (New York, 1920), p. 147.

46 Roy P. Basler (ed.), *The Collected Works of Abraham Lincoln* (8 vols., New Brunswick, 1953), II, pp. 461–62.

47 George E. Baker, *Works of William H. Seward* (5 vols., Boston, 1884), IV, p. 291.

Chapter 43
Free Soil

1 Slavery was abolished in Mexico in 1829, but the Texans did about as they pleased until Santa Anna set up his dictatorship in 1835. They declared themselves independent on March 2, 1836, proved their ability to maintain independence at San Jacinto the following month, and asked for recognition by the United States, then for annexation in November 1837. For antislavery arguments see David Lee Child, "Texas," *Quarterly Anti-Slavery Magazine*, I (January, 1836), pp. 193–205; Benjamin Lundy, *The War in Texas* (Philadelphia, 1836); American Anti-Slavery Society, *The Legion of Liberty! and Force of Truth, Containing the Thoughts, Words, and Deeds of Some Prominent Apostles, Champions, and Martyrs* (New York, 1843); William Ellery Channing, *A Letter to the Hon. Henry Clay, on the Annexation of Texas to the United States* (Boston, 1837).

2 William L. G. Smith, *Fifty Years of Public Life. The Life and Times of Lewis Cass* (New York, 1856), pp. 607–16.

3 John W. DuBose, *The Life and Times of William Lowndes Yancey. A History of Political Parties in the United States, from 1834 to 1864; Especially As to the Origin of the Confederate States* (Birmingham, 1892), pp. 212–13.

Chapter 44
The Road to Freedom

1 Quoted from *Journal of the House of Delegates*, in Theodore M. Whitfield, *Slavery Agitation in Virginia, 1829–1832* (Baltimore, 1930), p. 76.

2 See Asa Earl Martin, *The Anti-Slavery Movement in Kentucky, Prior to 1850* (Louisville, 1918), p. 126.

3 Jefferson to William Gordon, July 16, 1788, in Paul L.

Ford, *The Writings of Thomas Jefferson* (10 vols., New York, 1892–99), II, p. 426.

4 *Pennsylvania Freeman*, May 23, 1840.

5 Charles Francis Adams (ed.), *Memoirs of John Quincy Adams, Comprising Portions of His Diary from 1795 to 1848* (12 vols., Philadelphia, 1874–77), IV, pp. 530–31.

6 *Ibid.*, V, p. 210.

7 *Congressional Debates*, 24 Cong., 1 Sess. (1835–36), XII, pt. 4, p. 4047.

8 *Ibid.*, p. 4049.

9 Joshua R. Giddings, "The Florida War," in *Speeches in Congress* (Boston, 1853), pp. 1–20.

10 For a brief statement of the facts, judgment, and law in the case of the "Creole," see James Brown Scott, *Cases on International Law Selected from the Decisions of English and American Courts* (St. Paul, 1906), pp. 252–55; or John Bassett Moore, *A Digest of International Law* (8 vols., Washington, 1906), II, pp. 358–61; "Message from the President of the United States Communicating . . . the Proceedings Adopted by the Executive in Reference to the Case of the Brig Creole," *Senate Documents*, 27 Cong., 2 Sess., III, Doc. No. 137.

11 See New York *American*, February 18, 1842, for Birney's article; and *Congressional Globe*, 27 Cong., 2 Sess., p. 342 for Giddings' Resolutions; Seth M. Gates to Birney, January 24, 1842, in Dwight L. Dumond (ed.), *Letters of James Gillespie Birney, 1831–1857* (2 vols., New York, 1938), II, pp. 667–70; and Seth M. Gates to Birney, April 4, 1842, in *ibid.*, pp. 687–88.

12 Charles Francis Adams (ed.), *Memoirs of John Quincy Adams . . .* , XI, p. 103.

13 *Congressional Globe*, 27 Cong., 2 Sess., p. 429.

14 Frank Moore (ed.), *The Rebellion Record: A Diary of American Events, with Documents, Narratives, Illus-trated Incidents, Poetry, etc.* (12 vols., 1862–68), II, p. 437.

15 *Ibid.*, III, p. 33.

16 New York *Tribune*, September 1, 1861. Among the more important public discussions were William Whiting, *The Power of the President, and the Legislative Powers of Congress in Relation to Rebellion, Treason and Slavery* (Boston, 1862); David Lee Child, *Rights and Duties of the United States Relative to Slavery Under the Laws of War* (Boston, 1861); George B. Cheever, *The Salvation of the Country Secured by Immediate Emancipation* (New York, 1861); Henry Ward Beecher, *War and Emancipation: A Thanksgiving Sermon Preached in the Plymouth Church, Brooklyn, N. Y., on Thursday, November 21, 1861* (Philadelphia, 1861); and Robert Dale Owen, *The Policy of Emancipation in Three Letters to the Secretary of War, the President of the United States, and the Secretary of Treasury* (Philadelphia, 1863).

17 Charles Sumner, *War Powers of Congress. Speech of Hon. Charles Sumner, of Massachusetts, on the House Bills for the Confiscation of Property and the Liberation of Slaves Belonging to Rebels, Delivered in the Senate of the United States, June 27, 1862* (Washington, D. C., 1862). See also *Indemnity for the Past and Security for the Future. Speech of Charles Sumner of Massachusetts on the Bill for the Confiscation of Property and the Liberation of Slaves Belonging to Rebels, in the Senate of the United States, May 19, 1862* (Washington, 1862); and *Emancipation! Its Policy and Necessity as a War Measure for the Suppression of the Rebellion. Speech of Hon. Charles Sumner, at Faneuil Hall, October 6, 1862* [Boston, 1862].

18 *Congressional Globe*, 37 Cong., 2 Sess., Appendix, pp. 412–13.

INDEX

No 5

Negroes	Jerry	1000
	Berry	900
	Ishmael	800
Little Harriet & Son		1050
	Amanda	650
	Georgia Ann	630
Silla	Waity	500
	Oliver	400
	Mose	325
	Betsy	125
Sandy & Matilda		10
Mule	Hager	175
"	Dick	5
"	Pete	100
Hors	Frank	75
Jack	As	25
Ploughs & gear		5
Carpenter Tools		5
Narrow tread Waggon		15
Household & Kitchen fur		50
Stock Hogs		35
Cattle		12
Sheep	45	6,947

No 6

Negroes	Billy	1000
	Albert	900
	Phill	800
Big Harriet & Sandy		1050
	Eliza	800
	Warren	600
Old Anthony		400
	Scipio	600
	Peggy	300
Mules	Sal	150
"	Kit	100
Mare	Dane	135
Ploughs & gear		5
Carpenters Tools		5
Shot gun		15
Houshould & Kitchen furniture		50
Stock Hogs		35
Cattle		12
Sheep		45
		6,990